ANSON F. RAINEY

TEACHING HISTORY & HISTORICAL GEOGRAPHY OF BIBLE LANDS

A Syllabus

carta
Jerusalem

Teaching History and Historical Geography of Bible Lands: A Syllabus
by
Anson F. Rainey, M.Th., Ph.D., Emeritus Professor of
Ancient Near Eastern Cultures and Semitic Linguistics
Tel Aviv University

First edition, cloth
Second edition, paper

ISBN 978-965-220-821-7

On front cover and title page:
El-Amarna Letter (photo from author)

Carta books are available at special discounts for bulk purchases for sales promotions, premiums, fund-raising, or educational use. For details, contact:

Carta, The Israel Map and Publishing Company, Ltd.
18 Ha'uman Street, POB 2500
Jerusalem 91024, Israel
Tel. 972-2-678 3355   Fax: 972-2-678 2373
carta@carta.co.il   www.holyland-jerusalem.com

Please address comments or suggestions to Carta, Jerusalem.

Printed in Israel

TABLE OF CONTENTS

INSTRUCTIONS FOR USE OF THE LESSON SYLLABUS

The ensuing set of documents consists of twenty lesson outlines for teaching *History and Historical Geography of Bible Lands* during the Bronze and Iron Ages. These lesson plans have been developed over the course of the past forty years of teaching the subject, mainly at the Jerusalem University College/American Institute of Holy Land Studies, and also at Tel Aviv and Bar-Ilan Universities. The first syllabus was devised in the spring term of 1963 at the American Institute. Lesson outlines and source translations have been developed over the years since that time.

The fundamental principle was the presentation of historical chapters in chronological order with emphasis on the geographical and social dimension. Relevant archaeological information has been included when directly related but the main emphasis has been on the epigraphic sources, including biblical passages, that contain geographical details. The analysis of the geographical data is done in relation to the actual situation on the ground which then may lead to an understanding not only of the ancient event but also its implications for the people involved.

The pedagogical principle adopted herein is the presentation of each lesson unit in a manner that helps the student to absorb the factual information while also gaining insight unto the deeper implications and nuances involved. The syllabus provided to the class members contains the bibliography of required reference books. The daily (or weekly) schedule lists every passage to be discussed in that particular lesson, the exact page numbers and/or map numbers. Biblical passages are included by chapter and verse. The student can thus read all the material for the lesson beforehand. The dedicated student would read all the assignments for his lesson both before and after the lecture itself.

Since these lesson outlines were developed for teaching in either English or Hebrew, the related passages from the biblical text have been inserted in their proper place. The development of word processing and the creation of programs for searching biblical and other literature opened up a new era in the production of research and teaching documents undreamed of when this syllabus was first conceived. Special credit must be given to the Accordance programs which are now the leading facilitators for the creation of documents built on texts from the Hebrew, Greek and Aramaic sources. Even when lecturing in Hebrew, it was easier for this writer to use outlines composed in English that served as the basis for extemporaneous lecturing, built on sight translation from English to Hebrew. Rather than having to thumb through a copy of the Hebrew or Greek Bible (or Qumran, Targums or Josephus), the actual passages have been inserted into the outlines. In this manner, the lecturer may read the text as part of his verbal discussion without wasting time and without a break in the pace of his narration.

When lecturing to a class in English, sometimes the students know enough of the original language(s) to follow a reading as part of the lecture. But in all cases, the ancient language is followed by a translation into English. Such English passages, by the way, may employ some recognized version as a base but with modifications according to the needs and taste of the lecturer. Unfortunately, in many cases the modern translations do not reflect a first-hand knowledge of the geography so that the proper meaning and nuances are obscured. The texts must be rendered in accordance with the geographical realities and the implications thereof.

When designing a course of this nature, the author is faced with the perennial problem of any historian. History operates not only in a linear progression but also in a simultaneous spacial dimension. As an example, in the chapters on the Israelite and Judean monarchies, one may treat the affairs and events in one kingdom up to a certain point before it becomes necessary to go over to the neighboring kingdom to bring the discussion up to the same chronological stage. Occasions in which the two kingdoms were interacting may be treated in tandem, thus repeating some of the material twice. Matters of this nature are unavoidable and the teacher will do well to adapt his instruction to each situation on its own merits.

Titles Available from Carta and Authorized Dealers

The Carta Bible Atlas. 5th revised & expanded edition
Aharoni, Y., M. Avi-Yonah, A. F. Rainey, Z. Safrai, and R. S. Notley

The Holy Land. A Historical Geography from the Persian to the Arab Conquest (536 B.C. to A.D. 640) by M. Avi-Yonah. With Text Revisions and Toponymic Index by A. F. Rainey

Parallels in the Bible, edited by A. Bendavid (Hebrew only)

The Raging Torrent: Historical Inscriptions from Assyria and Babylonia relating to Ancient Israel by M. Cogan

The Sacred Bridge: Carta's Atlas of the Biblical World
A. F. Rainey and R. S. Notley

MINIMUM REQUIREMENTS FOR THE INDEPENDENT STUDY OF HISTORICAL GEOGRAPHY OF THE BIBLE

1. Bible (modern version)
2. *The Carta Bible Atlas* (5th revised & expanded edition)
3. A map of modern Israel 1:250,000
4. Obtain library access to other books in the bibliography (*infra*).

Using the map assignments in the syllabus, start reading *The Carta Bible Atlas.*

After that you may read through the lesson outline to see how the material untolds.

Every historical event has its associated map.

If you are attending a course of lectures based on this syllabus, it is advisable to read the assigned pages once again.

Students not versed in Hebrew can safely ignore the Hebrew text because the English translations are always based upon it and are relatively independent of the available modern versions of the Bible. You will probably want to keep your own Bible open to follow the lesson at hand.

On occasion suggested variants from the Greek Septuagint or emendations proposed independently in the light of the geographical situation are proposed for the passage at hand.

BIBLIOGRAPHY OF REQUIRED READING*

<u>Reference Work</u>   <u>Abbreviation</u>

Aharoni, Y., M. Avi-Yonah, A. F. Rainey, Z. Safrai, and R. S. Notley
    2011   *The Carta Bible Atlas*. 5th revised & expanded edition. Jerusalem.   MAP(S)

Avi-Yonah, M.
    2002   *The Holy Land. A Historical Geography from the Persian*
            to the Arab Conquest (536 B.C. to A.D. 640). With Text
            Revisions and Toponymic Index by A. F. Rainey.
            Introduction to the 2002 editon by Y. Tsafrir. Jerusalem.   Avi-Yonah

Baly, D.
    1974   *The Geography of the Bible*. Revised edition. New York.   Baly

Bendavid, A., ed.
    1972   *Parallels in the Bible* (Hebrew only). Jerusalem
    2010   Introduction to the 2010 edition by A. F. Rainey.

Bible   All assigned passages should be read in a modem version.

Cogan, M.
    2008   *The Raging Torrent: Historical Inscriptions from Assyria and*
            Babylonia relating to Ancient Israel. Jerusalem   Cogan

Hallo, W. W., ed.
    1997   *The Context of Scripture*. Leiden, Boston, Köln. 3 vols.   COS
    2002   Up-to-date translations of ancient sources.

Lichtheim, M.
    1973   *Ancient Egyptan Literature: A Book of Readings. Vol. I*: The
            Old and Middle Kingdom. Berkeley, Los Angeles, London.   Lichtheim

Lichtheim, M.
    1976   Ancient Egyptan Literature: A Book of Readings. *Vol. II*:
            The New Kingdom. Berkeley, Los Angeles, London.   Lichtheim

Lichtheim, M.
    1980   *Ancient Egyptan Literature: A Book of Readings. Vol. III*:
            The Late Period. Berkeley, Los Angeles, London.   Lichtheim

Pritchard, J. B., ed.
    1955   *Ancient Near Eastern Texts*. Second edition. Princeton.   ANET
            Older translations of ancient sources.

Pritchard, J. B., ed.
    1969   Ancient Near East Supplementary Texts and Pictures.
            Princeton.   ANES

Rainey, A. F. and Notley, R. S.
    2006   *The Sacred Bridge: Carta's Atlas of the Biblical World*. Jerusalem.   BRIDGE

Map of Israel, 1:250,000. English or Hebrew, topographical **with shading**.
Optional: Set of Maps (Hebrew-English), 1:100,000.

* * *

* Check availability of revised and/or updated editions.

LESSON ASSIGNMENTS

I & II. INTRODUCTION
BRIDGE 9–24; Avi-Yonah 127–129; MAPS Nos. 1–2, 16–19.

III. ERETZ-ISRAEL IN ITS NEAR EASTERN SETTING
BRIDGE 25–29; MAPS Nos. 3–8, 104–105; Baly, 15, 115–130. Gn. 10; Ezk. 27:5 ff.

IV. ROADS, CLIMATE, AGRICULTURE AND INDUSTRY
BRIDGE 30–42; ANET, Gezer Calendar, 320a, Baal Epic (g–h), 138a–141b
(*108–116), Aqht C (i), 153; Gen. 15:18–21; Ex. 13:1–10, 23:12–17, 26–33; Nu.
13:27–29; Lv. 23; Dt. 1:1–8, 8:7–10, 11:10–12, 34:1–3; Josh. 1:1–14, 10:40–43, 11:16–17,
22:9; Judg. 1:9, 1 Sam. 13:19; 1 Ki. 4:21, 24–25; 2 Ki. 7:62 Chr. 26:10; Avi-Yonah,
181–211; MAPS Nos. 9–12; Baly, 42–100.

V. EARLY AND MIDDLE BRONZE AGES
BRIDGE 43–60; ANET, 18–23, 227–30, 265–274a, 328–329a, 482–483a, 133–150;
ANES, 553–557a, 623–626a; Lichtheim 1973, 18–23, 103–104, 222–235; COS 1, pp.
77–82; COS 2, pp. 256–261; COS 3, pp. 35–36; MAPS Nos. 13–15, 20–31; Gen. 12–14.

VI. LATE BRONZE AGE I, RISE OF 18ᵗʰ DYNASTY
BRIDGE 61–76; ANET, 230–234, 234–244a, 244–250; ANES, 531–532a, 557–558a;
12–15, 25–28, COS 2, pp. 3–22; MAPS Nos. 32–41; Baly, 144–163.

VII. LATE BRONZE AGE II, EL–ᶜAMARNAH PERIOD
BRIDGE 77–90; ANET, 318–319, 394c–396, 483–490; ANES, 529–530; COS 2, pp.
91–105; COS 3, pp. 237–242; Lichtheim 1976, 48–51; MAPS Nos. 42–46.

VIII. LATE BRONZE AGE III, 19ᵗʰ DYNASTY
BRIDGE 91–103; MAPS Nos. 47–53; ANET 253a–259b, 376–378 (*231), 476–478b;
COS 2, pp. 23–41; COS 3, pp. 9–18; Lichtheim 1976, 57–78; Nu. 34:1–12; Josh. 15:2–4,
22:9; Ezk. 47:15–19, 48:15–28.

IX. CRISIS AND TRANSITION
BRIDGE 104–122; MAPS Nos. 54–59; Baly 101–111; Gen. 12–14, 18–21, 23,
26, 33–35, 37–38, 47; Ex. 13:17–14:8, 15:22–16:1, 17:1, 19:1; Num. 10:33–11:3,
11:34–35, 12:16–13:29, 14:39–45, 20:1, 20:14–29, 21:1–22:1; Num. 33; Dt. 1:3.

X. THE EARLY IRON AGE
BRIDGE 122–130; MAPS Nos. 60–70, 74–76, 79–85; ANET, 260, 274b–275; Josh. 6–12;
Nu. 21:21–35, 22:36–41., 25:1, 31:7–8, 32:1–3, 32:33–42; Dt. 2:26–3:17; Josh. 13;
Judg. 1; Josh. 14–19, 20–21.

XI & XII. THE HEROIC AGE
BRIDGE 131–156; MAPS Nos. 71–73, 77–78, 86–109; Baly, 131–143; Judges and
1 Samuel (geog. info.); ANET, 25b–29, 262–263b bottom; Lichtheim 1976, 224–230.

XIII & XIV. UNITED MONARCHY

BRIDGE 157–168, 171–185; MAPS Nos. 110–129; Baly, 191–209; 2 Sam. 1–6, 8–10, 15–21, 24; 1 Chr. 10–15, 18–20, 27; Josh. 20–21; 1 Chr. 23–25; 1 Ki. 3–5, 9:10–11:43; 2 Chr. 1–2; ANET, 274–275b.

XV. DIVIDED MONARCHY, 10th–9th CENTURIES BCE

BRIDGE 168–171, 185–189; MAPS Nos. 130–137; 1 Ki. 12:1–16:25; 2 Chr. 10–18; ANET, 263–264.

XVI. DIVIDED MONARCHY, 9th CENTURY BCE

BRIDGE 190–213; MAPS Nos. 138–151; Baly, 210–240; ANET 276b–279a, 280a–282b, 320a–321b, 499–504; ANES, 558–560, 653–661; COS 2, pp. 135–138, 145–147; 261–283; Cogan, 12–31.2 Ki. 1–3, 6:1–14, 22; 2 Chr. 19–25.

XVII. DIVIDED MONARCHY, 8th CENTURY BCE

BRIDGE 214–234; MAPS Nos. 152–167; Baly, 164–176; ANET, 282–287a, 50lb–502a; ANES, 532b–533; COS 2, pp. 145, 152–162; pp. 283–292; Cogan, 32–79, 2 Ki. 14:23–18:12; 2 Chr. 26–28; Amos 1–2, 9:7, 8; Isa. 4:1–10:4.

XVIII. JUDAH ALONE, 8th–7th CENTURIES BCE

BRIDGE 234–253; MAPS Nos. 168–172; Baly, 177–190; ANET, 285a–289a, 32lb–322; Lichtheim 1980, 66–84; COS 2, pp. 293–305; Cogan 80–129, LOB, 387–400; 2 Ki. 18:13–20:30; 2 Chr. 29–32; Isa. 20; Micah 1.

XIX. JUDAH ALONE, 7th–6th CENTURIES BCE

BRIDGE 254–277; MAPS Nos. 173–181; ANET, 289a–305b, 32lb–322; ANES, 533b–541, 568–569, 605–607; COS 2, pp. 164, 306–310; Cogan, 130–165; 176–210; 2 Ki. 21–25; 2 Chr. 33–36; Jer. 1: 1–3, 11:1–23, 47:1–7; 22:11–12; 26:1–24, 28 1–38, 36:9–10, 46:1–28, 22:13–19, 36:9–32, 49:28–33, 13:18–19; 22:24–30, 24:1, 27:1, 28:1, 29:1–32, 51:59–64, 21;1–14, 32:1–34:22, 37:1–44:30, 52:1–34, 48:1–49:39; Zeph., Nahum, Habakkuk, Joel, Obadiah.

XX. EXILE AND RETURN, PERSIAN PERIOD

BRIDGE 278–296; MAPS Nos. 182–194; Avi-Yonah, 11–31; Baly, 241–251; 2 Ki. 24–25; 2 Chr. 36; Jer. 42–43, 52; Ezra 1–7,9; Neh–2:9–4:9, 6:1–9, 11; ANET, 315a–316b, 505, 560–565a; ANES, 548–549, 662, 633, 657b; COS 2, pp. 310–315; Cogan 210–233; Lichtheim 1980, 36–41.

LESSONS 1 & 2

INTRODUCTION TO HISTORICAL GEOGRAPHY

Sacred Bridge, Chap. 1.

I. DIMENSIONS of Historical Geography

    A. SPATIAL — topography, interest in small patch in earth's surface. OT requires geography for its understanding.

    B. TEMPORAL — experienc of a real people in its land; history: man's reflections on his past.

    C. CULTURAL — biblical message is couched in human terms; must read OT in terms of the ANE culture.

    D. SPIRITUAL — "Holy Land" & "Holy Places." Religious motivation in writing most ANE literature including OT.

II. DISCIPLINES of Historical Geography

    A. PHYSICAL GEOGRAPHY — study of ecology

        1. Geology and Orography — geomorphology
        2. Ecology — soils and rocks and their potential
        3. Hydrology — water sources
        4. Meteorology — weather pattern
        5. Cartography — recording of data

1. BIBLICAL GEOGRAPHICAL TEXTS

GEN. 14:2 בֶּלַע הִיא־צֹעַר;

עֵין מִשְׁפָּט הִוא קָדֵשׁ 14:7

and the king of Bela (that is, Zoar); En-mishpat (that is, Kadesh),

1 Sam. 17:1-3

1 וַיַּאַסְפוּ פְלִשְׁתִּים אֶת־מַחֲנֵיהֶם לַמִּלְחָמָה וַיֵּאָסְפוּ שֹׂכֹה ·

אֲשֶׁר לִיהוּדָה וַיַּחֲנוּ בֵּין־שׂוֹכֹה וּבֵין־עֲזֵקָה בְּאֶפֶס דַּמִּים

2 וְשָׁאוּל וְאִישׁ־יִשְׂרָאֵל נֶאֶסְפוּ וַיַּחֲנוּ בְּעֵמֶק הָאֵלָה וַיַּעַרְכוּ מִלְחָמָה

לִקְרַאת פְּלִשְׁתִּים

3 וּפְלִשְׁתִּים עֹמְדִים אֶל־הָהָר מִזֶּה וְיִשְׂרָאֵל עֹמְדִים

אֶל־הָהָר מִזֶּה וְהַגַּיְא בֵּינֵיהֶם ,

Now the Philistines gathered their armies for battle; and they were gathered at Socoh which belongs to Judah, and they camped between Socoh and Azekah, in Ephes-dammim. Saul and the men of Israel were gathered and camped in the valley of Elah, and drew up in battle array to encounter the Philistines. The Philistines stood on the mountain on one side while Israel stood on the mountain on the other side, with the valley between them.

2 Ki. 15:29

בִּימֵי פֶּקַח מֶלֶךְ־יִשְׂרָאֵל בָּא תִּגְלַת פִּלְאֶסֶר מֶלֶךְ אַשּׁוּר

אֶת־עִיּוֹן וְאֶת־אָבֵל בֵּית־מַעֲכָה וְאֶת־יָנוֹחַ וְאֶת־קֶדֶשׁ וְאֶת־הָצוֹר

וְאֶת־הַגִּלְעָד וַיִּקַּח וְאֶת־הַגָּלִילָה כֹּל אֶרֶץ נַפְתָּלִי וַיַּגְלֵם אַשּׁוּרָה

In the days of Pekah king of Israel, Tiglath-pileser king of Assyria came and captured **Ijon** and **Abel-beth-maacah** and **Janoah** and **Kedesh** and **Hazor** and **Gilead** and **Galilee**, all the land of Naphtali; and he carried them captive to Assyria.

Isaiah 8:23

כִּי לֹא מוּעָף לַאֲשֶׁר מוּצָק לָהּ כָּעֵת הָרִאשׁוֹן הֵקַל אַרְצָה

זְבֻלוּן וְאַרְצָה נַפְתָּלִי וְהָאַחֲרוֹן הִכְבִּיד דֶּרֶךְ הַיָּם עֵבֶר הַיַּרְדֵּן גְּלִיל הַגּוֹיִם

But there will be no [more] gloom for her who was in anguish; in earlier
times He treated the land of Zebulun and the land of Naphtali with
contempt, but later on He shall make [it] glorious, by the way of the sea,
on the other side of Jordan, Galilee of the Gentiles.

Josh. 15:21 — אֶל־גְּבוּל אֱדוֹם בַּנֶּגְבָּה

toward the border of Edom in the south

Josh. 15:32 — כָּל־עָרִים עֶשְׂרִים וָתֵשַׁע וְחַצְרֵיהֶן

in all, twenty-nine cities with their villages.

Josh. 15:33 — בַּשְּׁפֵלָה

In the lowland

Josh. 15:36 — עָרִים אַרְבַּע־עֶשְׂרֵה וְחַצְרֵיהֶן

fourteen cities with their villages

2. RABBINIC GEOGRAPHICAL TEXTS

Hallakhic rule for living in Eretz Israel

Borders of Eretz Israel — Rehov mosaic

Debates on location of sites

Eshtori Haparḥi — lived in Beth-shean 14th cent. C.E.
Spent seven years studying geography of Eretz
Israel. Many of his ID's still stand.

A. Neubauer, *La géographie du Talmud* (Paris, 1868)

G. Reeg, *Die Ortsnamen Israels nach der rabbinischen
Literatur* (Wiesbaden, 1989)

3. ECCLESIASTICAL GEOGRAPHICAL TEXTS

Eusebius (263-339 C.E.) — Bishop of Caesarea
Onomasticon; used road maps

Jerome (c. 345-420 C.E.) — translated *Onomasticon* to
Latin; Translated OT from Heb. to Latin

Madeba Map — Sixth century C.E.; based on
Onomasticon plus other sources

Peutinger Table — 10th cent. C.E. monastic copy; based

on 2nd cent. sources.

Adriaan Reland, *Palaestina ex monumentis veteribus illustrata*(Utrech, 1714) — compiled massive collection of information from all available sources but never visited the Land.

4. Arabic Geographical Texts

Le Strange, Guy, *Palestine under the Moslems* (London, 1890)

Marmadji, A. S., *Textes géographiques arabes sur la Palestine* (Paris, 1951).

5. Ancient Near Eastern Geographical Texts

Egyptian — Execration texts, Pharaonic lists, school texts.

Mesopotamian — royal annals, correspondence, **Amarna** texts ***

Local Epigraphic — Mesha^c Stone, Tel Dan Stele, Samaria Ostraca, Lachish Ltrs, Hashavyahu Letter, Arad Letters

6. Modern approach to ancient sources:

Text as Artifact — where found, where now, materials, script method (incised, relief, ink, etc.)

Text as Document —

Script: palaeography, orthography.

Language: lexicography, morphology, syntax.

Genre — display, correspondence, administrative,

literary, ritual/cultic (incl. funerary).

Content — events, places, relationships, social
data

C. Toponymy — Study of Place Names

1. 19th century research

Seetzen, U. J., travelled here 1803-1810, *Reisen durch
Syrien, Palästina, Phönicien, etc.* (Berlin 1854-59).

Burckhardt, J. L., traveled here in 1805-1816, *Travels in
Syria and the Holy Land* (London, 1822).

Robinson, Edward, visited in 1838, 1852, *Biblical
Researches in Palestine and the Adjacent Regions*
(London, 1856).

*** Robinson and E. Smith established the base for future studies

[Porter, J. L.] *Handbook for Travellers in Syria and
Palestine*
London: John Murray 1858. 2nd edition, 1875.

Guérin, M. V. *Description de la Palestine*
(Paris 1868-1880).

Conder, C. R. and Kitchener, H. H. *The Survey of
Western Palestine* (London 1881-1883), surveyed
1872-1879.

Palmer. E. H. *Arabic and English Name Lists, Survey of
Western Palestine* (London 1881).

Kampffmeyer, G. 'Alte Namen im heutigen Palästina
und Syrien,' *ZDPV* 15 (1892), 1-33, 65-116; 16
(1893), 1-71.

Smith, G. A. *The Historical Geography of the Holy Land*
(London 1894), rev. 1931.

2. 20th century research

Biblical names — Heb. and LXX forms

ANE sources — Egypt & Akkadian, Moabite, Heb.

Second Temple — Rabbinic and Church sources

Arabic toponyms — phonetic and cultural changes

Rainey, A. F. "The Toponymy of Eretz Israel," *Bulletin of the American Schools of Oriental Research* 231 (Oct., 1978), 1-17; "LXX Toponyms as a Contribution to Linguistic Reasearch." *Lingua Aegyptica* 9 (2001),179-192.

D. ARCHAEOLOGY

1. History:

Archaeology in Bible and Talmud — items of everyday life as discussed in the written sources.

Archaeology of the explorers — surface finds, monuments, Mesopotamian mounds, Egyptian temples & tombs.

Palestinian archaeology — Petrie at Tell el-Ḥesī (1890). Bliss at Tell el-Ḥesī 1891 (first stratified excavation)

2. Study of ancient cultures

a. Pre-historic: man's earliest existence — no written data.

b. Historical Archaeology: study of material culture in periods that have written records
   (1) Philological study of **written data** discovered; not thought of as "archaeology" today
   (2) **Material** culture: concentrates on non-written materials such as pottery, architecture, implements general study of types of settlements.

3. Activities:

Excavation — identification of nature of sites,

uncovering of occupation remains.

(1) How the ancient mound of remains was
     deposited.

(2) Objective: How did people live here and when?

(3) Method of excavation: digging in 3 dimension,
     recording in two dimension

Survey — ecological, occupational, chronological

Types of settlements: fortified towns, villages,
     caves, encampments, tombs.

Distribution of settlements in a certain area and
     which areas are blank and which occupied.

Ecological relationships of the settlements:
     watersoures, agriculturalpotential, security,
     lines of comminication.

Artifactual and organic analysis — pottery, architecture,
     other utensils, traces of botanical and zoological
     data,and also other geological (ecological)
     materials.

III. LINKAGE AND SYNTHESIS —

A. Connection between archaeological finds and historical
   information:

1. Texts found at the site — stratigraphic situation, relation
     to the context.

2. Special kinds of epigraphic materials: seals and other small
     objects bearing inscriptions.

3. Uninscribed finds: structures, artifacts, especially pottery,
     jewelry, weapons, tools.

TYPOLOGY — classification chronologically,
regionally.

4. Major features, both natural, man made and accidental.

  Kind of site, buildings, etc.

  Relation to wadies, hills, valleys, routes

  Destructions and/or abandonments.

B. What to look for in the sources:

  1. Names of sites and features (wadies, cliffs, hills).

  2. Events describing geographical relationships.

  3. Relationships to regions and districts

C. What to look for in the field:

  1. Local Toponymy

  2. Sites of various kinds.

  3. Artifacts large and small

D. Historical interpretation: must find link with written sources.

LESSON 3

THE ANCIENT NEAR EAST

I. WORLD ECONOMY AND SOCIETY — SIXTH CENTURY B.C.E.

EZEKIEL 27

Ezek. 27:1-3

1 וַיְהִי דְבַר־יְהֹוָה אֵלַי לֵאמֹר

2 וְאַתָּה בֶן־אָדָם שָׂא עַל־צֹר קִינָה

3 וְאָמַרְתָּ לְצוֹר הַיֹּשֶׁבֶתי [הַ][יֹּשֶׁבֶת] עַל־מְבוֹאֹת

יָם רֹכֶלֶת הָעַמִּים אֶל־אִיִּים רַבִּים כֹּה אָמַר אֲדֹנָי יְהֹוִה

צוֹר אַתְּ אָמַרְתְּ אֲנִי כְּלִילַת יֹפִי

4 בְּלֵב יַמִּים גְּבוּלָיִךְ בֹּנַיִךְ כָּלְלוּ יָפְיֵךְ

Moreover, the word of Yahweh came to me saying, "And you, son of man, take up a lamentation over **Tyre**; and say to Tyre, who dwells at the entrance to the sea, merchant of the peoples to many coastlands," Thus says the Lord Yahweh, "O Tyre, you have said, 'I am perfect in beauty.'"

LUMBER FOR SHIP BUILDING

Ezek. 27:4-7

4 בְּלֵב יַמִּים גְּבוּלָיִךְ בֹּנַיִךְ כָּלְלוּ יָפְיֵךְ

בְּרוֹשִׁים (fir)   5 בְּרוֹשִׁים מִשְּׂנִיר בָּנוּ לָךְ אֵת כָּל־לֻחֹתָיִם

אֶרֶז (cedar)   אֶרֶז מִלְּבָנוֹן לָקָחוּ לַעֲשׂוֹת תֹּרֶן עָלָיִךְ

אַלּוֹנִים (oaks)   6 אַלּוֹנִים מִבָּשָׁן עָשׂוּ מִשּׁוֹטָיִךְ קַרְשֵׁךְ עָשׂוּ־שֵׁן

בַּתְאֲשֻׁרִים (boxwood) (?)   מֵאִיֵּי כִּתִּים [כִּתִּיִּם]

בַּת־אֲשֻׁרִים

7 שֵׁשׁ־בְּרִקְמָה מִמִּצְרַיִם הָיָה מִפְרָשֵׂךְ לִהְיוֹת (linen) שֵׁשׁ־בְּרִקְמָה

לָךְ לְנֵס תְּכֵלֶת וְאַרְגָּמָן מֵאִיֵּי אֱלִישָׁה הָיָה מְכַסֵּךְ

"Your regions are in the heart of the seas; Your builders have perfected your beauty.
They have made all [your] planks of fir trees from **Senir**;

They have taken a cedar from **Lebanon** to make a mast for you.
Of oaks from **Bashan** they have made your oars;
With ivory they have inlaid your deck of boxwood from the coastlands of the **Kittim** (Kition).
Your sail was of fine embroidered linen from **Egypt** So that it became your distinguishing mark;
Your awning was blue and purple from the coastlands of **Elishah** (Alashia)."

PERSONNEL FOR MARITIME INDUSTRY

Ezek. 27:8-11

8 יֹשְׁבֵי צִידוֹן וְאַרְוַד הָיוּ שָׁטִים לָךְ חֲכָמַיִךְ צוֹר הָיוּ בָךְ
הֵמָּה חֹבְלָיִךְ

9 זִקְנֵי גְבַל וַחֲכָמֶיהָ הָיוּ בָךְ מַחֲזִיקֵי בִּדְקֵךְ
כָּל־אֳנִיּוֹת הַיָּם וּמַלָּחֵיהֶם הָיוּ בָךְ לַעֲרֹב מַעֲרָבֵךְ

10 פָּרַס וְלוּד וּפוּט הָיוּ בְחֵילֵךְ אַנְשֵׁי
מִלְחַמְתֵּךְ מָגֵן וְכוֹבַע תִּלּוּ־בָךְ הֵמָּה נָתְנוּ הֲדָרֵךְ

11 בְּנֵי אַרְוַד וְחֵילֵךְ עַל־חוֹמוֹתַיִךְ סָבִיב
וְגַמָּדִים בְּמִגְדְּלוֹתַיִךְ הָיוּ שִׁלְטֵיהֶם תִּלּוּ עַל־חוֹמוֹתַיִךְ
סָבִיב הֵמָּה כָּלְלוּ יָפְיֵךְ

"The inhabitants of **Sidon** and **Arvad** were your rowers; Your wise men, O **Tyre**, were aboard; they were your pilots. The elders of **Gebal** (Byblos) and her wise men were with you repairing your seams; All the ships of the sea and their sailors were with you in order to deal in your merchandise. **Persia** and **Lud** (Lydia) and **Put** (Libya) were in your army, your men of war. They hung shield and helmet in you; they set forth your splendor. The sons of **Arvad** and your army were on your walls, [all] around, and the **Gammadim** (Kômidim?) were in your towers. They hung their shields on your walls [all] around; they perfected your beauty."

NORTHWEST

Ezek. 27:12

12 תַּרְשִׁישׁ (Tarsus? Tartessos?)

סֹחַרְתֵּךְ מֵרֹב כָּל־הוֹן בְּכֶסֶף בַּרְזֶל בְּדִיל וְעוֹפֶרֶת נָתְנוּ עִזְבוֹנָיִךְ

"Tarshish (Tarsus) was your customer because of the abundance of all [kinds] of wealth; with <u>silver</u>, <u>iron</u>, <u>tin</u> and <u>lead</u> they paid for your wares."

Ezek. 27:13

יָוָן תֻּבַל וָמֶשֶׁךְ הֵמָּה רֹכְלָיִךְ בְּנֶפֶשׁ אָדָם וּכְלֵי נְחֹשֶׁת

נָתְנוּ מַעֲרָבֵךְ(Ionia, Tabal, Muški)

"Javan (Ionia), **Tubal** (Tabal) and **Meshech** (Muški), they were your traders; with the <u>human beings</u> and <u>vessels of bronze</u> they paid for your merchandise."

Ezek. 27:14

(Til-garimmu)

(Til-garimmu)מִבֵּית תּוֹגַרְמָה סוּסִים וּפָרָשִׁים וּפְרָדִים נָתְנוּ עִזְבוֹנָיִךְ

14

"Those from **Beth-togarmah** (Til-garimmu) gave <u>horses</u> and <u>horsemen</u> and <u>mules</u> for your wares."

Ezek. 27:15

Ῥόδιοι = רֹדָן 1Ch 1:7

15 בְּנֵי דְדָן רֹכְלַיִךְ אִיִּים רַבִּים סְחֹרַת יָדֵךְ קַרְנוֹת שֵׁן

וְהוֹבְנִים [וְ][הָבְנִים] הֵשִׁיבוּ אֶשְׁכָּרֵךְ

"The sons of **Rhodes**(!) were your traders. Many coastlands were your market; <u>ivory tusks</u> and <u>ebony</u> they brought as your payment."

LEVANT

Ezek. 27:16

(LXX ἀνθρώπους)

16 אֲרָם (אֱדוֹם) סֹחַרְתֵּךְ מֵרֹב מַעֲשָׂיִךְ בְּנֹפֶךְ אַרְגָּמָן וְרִקְמָה וּבוּץ

וְרָאמֹת וְכַדְכֹּד נָתְנוּ בְּעִזְבוֹנָיִךְ

"**Edom**(!)was your customer because of the abundance of your goods; they paid for your wares with <u>emeralds</u>, <u>purple</u>, <u>embroidered work</u>, <u>fine linen</u>, <u>coral</u> and <u>rubies</u>."

Ezek. 27:17

17 יְהוּדָה וְאֶרֶץ יִשְׂרָאֵל הֵמָּה רֹכְלָיִךְ בְּחִטֵּי מִנִּית וּפַנַּג

וּדְבַשׁ וָשֶׁמֶן וָצֹרִי נָתְנוּ מַעֲרָבֵךְ

"Judah and the land of Israel, they were your traders; with the wheat of export, and cakes (?), and honey, and oil and balm they paid for your merchandise."

Ezek. 27:18-19

18 דַּמֶּשֶׂק סֹחַרְתֵּךְ בְּרֹב מַעֲשַׂיִךְ מֵרֹב כָּל־הוֹן בְּיֵין חֶלְבּוֹן

וְצֶמֶר צָחַר

19 ‹וְדָן› וְיָוָן (וְיַיִן=οἶνον LXX) מְאוּזָל בְּעִזְבוֹנַיִךְ נָתְנוּ בַּרְזֶל

עָשׂוֹת קִדָּה וְקָנֶה בְּמַעֲרָבֵךְ הָיָה

קָנֶה (calamus) קִדָּה (cassia)

"**Damascus** was your customer because of the abundance of your goods, because of the abundance of all [kinds] of wealth, because of the <u>wine</u> of Helbon and <u>white wool</u>, and wine(!) paid for your wares from Uzal; wrought iron, cassia and sweet cane were among your merchandise.

SOUTHEAST

<u>North Arabia</u>

Ezek. 27:20

20 דְּדָן (Δαιδαν) רֹכַלְתֵּךְ בְבִגְדֵי־חֹפֶשׁ לְרִכְבָּה

"**Dedan** (el-ᶜUla) traded with you in saddlecloths for riding."

Ezek. 27:21

21 עֲרַב וְכָל־נְשִׂיאֵי קֵדָר הֵמָּה סֹחֲרֵי יָדֵךְ בְּכָרִים וְאֵילִים

וְעַתּוּדִים בָּם סֹחֲרָיִךְ

עַתּוּדִים = (he-goat) אֵילִים = (rams) כָּרִים = (young ram)

"**Arabia** and all the princes of **Kedar**, they were your customers for lambs, rams and goats; for these they were your customers."

South Arabia

Ezek. 27:22

רֹכְלֵי שְׁבָא וְרַעְמָה (Ραγμα) הֵמָּה רֹכְלָיִךְ בְּרֹאשׁ כָּל־בֹּשֶׂם 22

וּבְכָל־אֶבֶן יְקָרָה וְזָהָב נָתְנוּ עִזְבוֹנָיִךְ

The traders of **Sheba** and **Raamah**, they traded with you; they paid for your wares with the best of all [kinds] of spices, and with all [kinds] of precious stones and gold.

NORTH EAST

Ezek. 27:23-24

חָרָן וְכַנֵּה וָעֶדֶן רֹכְלֵי ‹שְׁבָא› (not LXX) אַשּׁוּר· 23

(Χαρμαν)כִּלְמַד רֹכַלְתֵּךְ

הֵמָּה רֹכְלַיִךְ בְּמַכְלֻלִים בִּגְלוֹמֵי תְּכֵלֶת 24

וְרִקְמָה וּבְגִנְזֵי בְּרֹמִים בַּחֲבָלִים חֲבֻשִׁים וַאֲרֻזִים בְּמַרְכֻלְתֵּךְ

(colored carpets=) בְּרֹמִים גִּנְזֵי (cloaks=) תְּכֵלֶת גְלוֹמֵי (garments =) מַכְלֻלִים

"**Haran, Canneh, Eden**, the traders of (›Sheba‹) **Asshur** [and] **Chilmad**(?) traded with you. They traded with you in <u>choice garments</u>, in <u>clothes of blue</u> and <u>embroidered work</u>, and in <u>carpets</u> of many colors [and] tightly wound <u>cords</u>, [which were] among your merchandise."

THE VIEW OF WORLD SOCIETY

<u>II. Genesis 10</u> — TABLE OF NATIONS

1 וְאֵלֶּה תּוֹלְדֹת בְּנֵי־נֹחַ שֵׁם חָם וָיָפֶת וַיִּוָּלְדוּ לָהֶם בָּנִים

אַחַר הַמַּבּוּל

2 בְּנֵי יֶפֶת גֹּמֶר וּמָגוֹג וּמָדַי וְיָוָן וְתֻבָל וּמֶשֶׁךְ

וְתִירָס

3 וּבְנֵי גֹּמֶר אַשְׁכֲּנַז וְרִיפַת וְתֹגַרְמָה

<u>Gen. 10:4</u> וּבְנֵי יָוָן אֱלִישָׁה וְתַרְשִׁישׁ כִּתִּים וְדֹדָנִים

<u>Gen. 10:5</u> מֵאֵלֶּה נִפְרְדוּ אִיֵּי הַגּוֹיִם בְּאַרְצֹתָם אִישׁ

לִלְשֹׁנוֹ לְמִשְׁפְּחֹתָם בְּגוֹיֵהֶם

<u>Gen. 10:6</u> וּבְנֵי חָם כּוּשׁ וּמִצְרַיִם וּפוּט וּכְנָעַן

<u>Gen. 10:7</u> וּבְנֵי כוּשׁ סְבָא וַחֲוִילָה וְסַבְתָּה וְרַעְמָה

וְסַבְתְּכָא וּבְנֵי רַעְמָה שְׁבָא וּדְדָן

<u>Gen. 10:8</u> וְכוּשׁ יָלַד אֶת־נִמְרֹד הוּא הֵחֵל לִהְיוֹת גִּבֹּר

בָּאָרֶץ

<u>Gen. 10:9</u> הוּא־הָיָה גִבֹּר־צַיִד לִפְנֵי יְהוָה עַל־כֵּן יֵאָמַר

כְּנִמְרֹד גִּבּוֹר צַיִד לִפְנֵי יְהוָה

<u>Gen. 10:10</u> וַתְּהִי רֵאשִׁית מַמְלַכְתּוֹ בָּבֶל וְאֶרֶךְ וְאַכַּד

וְכַלְנֵה בְּאֶרֶץ שִׁנְעָר

<u>Gen. 10:11</u> מִן־הָאָרֶץ הַהִוא יָצָא אַשּׁוּר וַיִּבֶן אֶת־נִינְוֵה

וְאֶת־רְחֹבֹת עִיר וְאֶת־כָּלַח

<u>Gen. 10:12</u> וְאֶת־רֶסֶן בֵּין נִינְוֵה וּבֵין כָּלַח הוּא הָעִיר

הַגְּדֹלָה

<u>Gen. 10:13</u> וּמִצְרַיִם יָלַד אֶת־לוּדִים וְאֶת־עֲנָמִים

וְאֶת־לְהָבִים וְאֶת־נַפְתֻּחִים

Gen. 10:14 וְאֶת־פַּתְרֻסִים וְאֶת־כַּסְלֻחִים אֲשֶׁר יָצְאוּ מִשָּׁם

פְּלִשְׁתִּים וְאֶת־כַּפְתֹּרִים ס

Gen. 10:15 וּכְנַעַן יָלַד אֶת־צִידֹן בְּכֹרוֹ וְאֶת־חֵת

Gen. 10:16 וְאֶת־הַיְבוּסִי וְאֶת־הָאֱמֹרִי וְאֵת הַגִּרְגָּשִׁי

Gen. 10:17 וְאֶת־הַחִוִּי וְאֶת־הַעַרְקִי וְאֶת־הַסִּינִי

Gen. 10:18 וְאֶת־הָאַרְוָדִי וְאֶת־הַצְּמָרִי וְאֶת־הַחֲמָתִי וְאַחַר

נָפֹצוּ מִשְׁפְּחוֹת הַכְּנַעֲנִי

Gen. 10:19 וַיְהִי גְּבוּל הַכְּנַעֲנִי מִצִּידֹן בֹּאֲכָה גְרָרָה

עַד־עַזָּה בֹּאֲכָה סְדֹמָה וַעֲמֹרָה וְאַדְמָה וּצְבֹיִם עַד־לָשַׁע

Gen. 10:20 אֵלֶּה בְנֵי־חָם לְמִשְׁפְּחֹתָם לִלְשֹׁנֹתָם בְּאַרְצֹתָם

בְּגוֹיֵהֶם ס

Gen. 10:21 וּלְשֵׁם יֻלַּד גַּם־הוּא אֲבִי כָּל־בְּנֵי־עֵבֶר אֲחִי

יֶפֶת הַגָּדוֹל

Gen. 10:22 בְּנֵי שֵׁם עֵילָם וְאַשּׁוּר וְאַרְפַּכְשַׁד וְלוּד וַאֲרָם

Gen. 10:23 וּבְנֵי אֲרָם עוּץ וְחוּל וְגֶתֶר וָמַשׁ

Gen. 10:24 וְאַרְפַּכְשַׁד יָלַד אֶת־שָׁלַח וְשֶׁלַח יָלַד

אֶת־עֵבֶר

Gen. 10:25 וּלְעֵבֶר יֻלַּד שְׁנֵי בָנִים שֵׁם הָאֶחָד פֶּלֶג כִּי

בְיָמָיו נִפְלְגָה הָאָרֶץ וְשֵׁם אָחִיו יָקְטָן

Gen. 10:26 וְיָקְטָן יָלַד אֶת־אַלְמוֹדָד וְאֶת־שָׁלֶף

וְאֶת־חֲצַרְמָוֶת וְאֶת־יָרַח

Gen. 10:27 וְאֶת־הֲדוֹרָם וְאֶת־אוּזָל וְאֶת־דִּקְלָה

Gen. 10:28 וְאֶת־עוֹבָל וְאֶת־אֲבִימָאֵל וְאֶת־שְׁבָא

Gen. 10:29 וְאֶת־אוֹפִר וְאֶת־חֲוִילָה וְאֶת־יוֹבָב כָּל־אֵלֶּה

בְּנֵי יָקְטָן

<u>Gen. 10:30</u> וַיְהִי מוֹשָׁבָם מִמֵּשָׁא בֹּאֲכָה סְפָרָה הַר הַקֶּדֶם

<u>Gen. 10:31</u> אֵלֶּה בְנֵי־שֵׁם לְמִשְׁפְּחֹתָם לִלְשֹׁנֹתָם בְּאַרְצֹתָם

לְגוֹיֵהֶם

<u>Gen. 10:32</u> אֵלֶּה מִשְׁפְּחֹת בְּנֵי־נֹחַ לְתוֹלְדֹתָם בְּגוֹיֵהֶם

וּמֵאֵלֶּה נִפְרְדוּ הַגּוֹיִם בָּאָרֶץ אַחַר הַמַּבּוּל

<u>Gen. 10:1</u> Now these are [the records of] the generations of Shem, Ham, and Japheth, the **sons of Noah**; and sons were born to them after the flood.

<u>Gen. 10:2</u> The sons of **Japheth** [were] Gomer and Magog and Madai and
                 Javan and Tubal and Meshech and Tiras.
<u>Gen. 10:3</u> The sons of **Gomer** [were] Ashkenaz and Riphath and Togarmah.

<u>Gen. 10:4</u> The sons of **Javan** [were] Elishah and Tarshish, Kittim and
                 Dodanim = Rodamin (LXX Ῥόδιοι)
<u>Gen. 10:5</u> From these the islands (coastlands) of the nations were separated
into their lands, every one according to his language, according to their
families, into their nations.

<u>Gen. 10:6</u> The sons of **Ham** [were] Cush and Mizraim and Put and Canaan.
<u>Gen. 10:7</u> The sons of **Cush** [were] Seba and Havilah and Sabtah and Raamah
                 and Sabteca; and the sons of Raamah [were] Sheba and Dedan.
<u>Gen. 10:8</u> Now Cush became the father of Nimrod; he became a mighty one
                 on the earth.
<u>Gen. 10:9</u> He was a mighty hunter before the LORD; therefore it is said, "Like
                 Nimrod a mighty hunter before the LORD."
<u>Gen. 10:10</u> The beginning of his kingdom was Babel and Erech and Accad and
Calneh, in the land of **Shinar**.
<u>Gen. 10:11</u> From that land he went forth into Assyria, and built Nineveh and
Rehoboth-ir and Calah,
<u>Gen. 10:12</u> and Resen between Nineveh and Calah; that is the great city.

<u>Gen. 10:13</u> **Mizraim** became the father of Ludim and Anamim and Lehabim
                 and Naphtuhim
<u>Gen. 10:14</u> and Pathrusim and Casluhim (from which came the **Philistines**)
                 and **Caphtorim**.

<u>Gen. 10:15</u> **Canaan** became the father of Sidon, his firstborn, and Heth
<u>Gen. 10:16</u> and the Jebusite and the Amorite and the Girgashite
<u>Gen. 10:17</u> and the Hivite and the Arkite and the Sinite

Gen. 10:18 and the Arvadite and the Zemarite and the Hamathite; and
          afterward the families of the Canaanite were spread abroad.

Gen. 10:19 **The territory of the Canaanite** extended from Sidon as you go
toward Gerar, as far as Gaza; as you go toward Sodom and Gomorrah and
Admah and Zeboiim, as far as Lasha.

Gen. 10:20 These are the sons of **Ham**, according to their families, according
to their languages, by their lands, by their nations.

Gen. 10:21 ¶ Also to **Shem**, the father of all the children of **Eber**, [and] the
older brother of Japheth, children were born.
Gen. 10:22 The sons of Shem [were] Elam and Asshur and Arpachshad and
          Lud and Aram.
Gen. 10:23 The sons of Aram [were] Uz and Hul and Gether and Mash.
Gen. 10:24 Arpachshad became the father of Shelah; and Shelah became the
          father of Eber.
Gen. 10:25 Two sons were born to **Eber**; the name of the one [was] Peleg, for
          in his days the earth was divided; and his brother's name [was]
          Joktan.
Gen. 10:26 **Joktan** became the father of Almodad and Sheleph and
          Hazarmaveth and Jerah
Gen. 10:27 and Hadoram and Uzal and Diklah
Gen. 10:28 and Obal and Abimael and Sheba
Gen. 10:29 and Ophir and Havilah and Jobab;
          all these were the sons of Joktan.
Gen. 10:30 Now their settlement extended from Mesha as you go toward
Sephar, the hill country of the east.
Gen. 10:31 These are the sons of Shem, according to their families, according
to their languages, by their lands, according to their nations.
Gen. 10:32 These are the families of the sons of Noah, according to their
genealogies, by their nations; and out of these the nations were separated on
the earth after the flood.

1 Chron. 1:4-23

נֹחַ שֵׁם חָם וָיָפֶת

1Chr. 1:5 בְּנֵי יֶפֶת גֹּמֶר וּמָגוֹג וּמָדַי וְיָוָן וְתֻבָל וּמֶשֶׁךְ
וְתִירָס ס

1Chr. 1:6 וּבְנֵי גֹּמֶר אַשְׁכְּנַז וְדִיפַת וְתוֹגַרְמָה

1Chr. 1:7 וּבְנֵי יָוָן אֱלִישָׁה וְתַרְשִׁישָׁה כִּתִּים וְרוֹדָנִים ס

בְּנֵי חָם כּוּשׁ וּמִצְרַיִם פּוּט וּכְנָעַן 1Chr. 1:8

וּבְנֵי כוּשׁ סְבָא וַחֲוִילָה וְסַבְתָּא וְרַעְמָא 1Chr. 1:9
וְסַבְתְּכָא וּבְנֵי רַעְמָא שְׁבָא וּדְדָן ס

וְכוּשׁ יָלַד אֶת־נִמְרוֹד הוּא הֵחֵל לִהְיוֹת גִּבּוֹר 1Chr. 1:10
בָּאָרֶץ

וּמִצְרַיִם יָלַד אֶת־לוּדִיִּים [לוּדִים] 1Chr. 1:11
וְאֶת־עֲנָמִים וְאֶת־לְהָבִים וְאֶת־נַפְתֻּחִים

וְאֶת־פַּתְרֻסִים וְאֶת־כַּסְלֻחִים אֲשֶׁר יָצְאוּ מִשָּׁם 1Chr. 1:12
פְלִשְׁתִּים וְאֶת־כַּפְתֹּרִים

וּכְנַעַן יָלַד אֶת־צִידוֹן בְּכֹרוֹ וְאֶת־חֵת 1Chr. 1:13

וְאֶת־הַיְבוּסִי וְאֶת־הָאֱמֹרִי וְאֵת הַגִּרְגָּשִׁי 1Chr. 1:14

וְאֶת־הַחִוִּי וְאֶת־הַעַרְקִי וְאֶת־הַסִּינִי 1Chr. 1:15

וְאֶת־הָאַרְוָדִי וְאֶת־הַצְּמָרִי וְאֶת־הַחֲמָתִי 1Chr. 1:16

בְּנֵי שֵׁם עֵילָם וְאַשּׁוּר וְאַרְפַּכְשַׁד וְלוּד וַאֲרָם 1Chr. 1:17
וְעוּץ וְחוּל וְגֶתֶר וָמֶשֶׁךְ

וְאַרְפַּכְשַׁד יָלַד אֶת־שָׁלַח וְשֶׁלַח יָלַד 1Chr. 1:18
אֶת־עֵבֶר

וּלְעֵבֶר יֻלַּד שְׁנֵי בָנִים שֵׁם הָאֶחָד פֶּלֶג כִּי 1Chr. 1:19
בְיָמָיו נִפְלְגָה הָאָרֶץ וְשֵׁם אָחִיו יָקְטָן

וְיָקְטָן יָלַד אֶת־אַלְמוֹדָד וְאֶת־שָׁלֶף 1Chr. 1:20
וְאֶת־חֲצַרְמָוֶת וְאֶת־יָרַח

וְאֶת־הֲדוֹרָם וְאֶת־אוּזָל וְאֶת־דִּקְלָה 1Chr. 1:21

וְאֶת־עֵיבָל וְאֶת־אֲבִימָאֵל וְאֶת־שְׁבָא 1Chr. 1:22

וְאֶת־אוֹפִיר וְאֶת־חֲוִילָה וְאֶת־יוֹבָב כָּל־אֵלֶּה 1Chr. 1:23
בְּנֵי יָקְטָן

1Chr. 1:4 **Noah**, Shem, Ham and Japheth.

1Chr. 1:5 ¶ The sons of **Japheth** [were] Gomer, Magog, Madai, Javan, Tubal,
Meshech and Tiras.

1Chr. 1:6 The sons of **Gomer** [were] Ashkenaz, Diphath, and Togarmah.

1Chr. 1:7 The sons of **Javan** [were] Elishah, Tarshish, Kittim and Rodanim.

1Chr. 1:8 ¶ The sons of **Ham** [were] Cush, Mizraim, Put, and Canaan.

<u>1Chr. 1:9</u> The sons of **Cush** [were] Seba, Havilah, Sabta, Raama and Sabteca; and the sons of Raamah [were] Sheba and Dedan.

<u>1Chr. 1:10</u> **Cush** became the father of Nimrod; he began to be a mighty one in the earth.

<u>1Chr. 1:11</u> ¶ **Mizraim** became the father of the people of Lud, Anam, Lehab, Naphtuh,

<u>1Chr. 1:12</u> Pathrus, Casluh, from which the **Philistines** came, and **Caphtor**.

<u>1Chr. 1:13</u> ¶ **Canaan** became the father of Sidon, his firstborn, Heth,

<u>1Chr. 1:14</u> and the Jebusites, the Amorites, the Girgashites,

<u>1Chr. 1:15</u> the Hivites, the Arkites, the Sinites,

<u>1Chr. 1:16</u> the Arvadites, the Zemarites and the Hamathites.

<u>1Chr. 1:17</u> ¶ The sons of **Shem** [were] Elam, Asshur, Arpachshad, Lud, Aram, Uz, Hul, Gether and Meshech.

<u>1Chr. 1:18</u> Arpachshad became the father of Shelah and Shelah became the father of **Eber**.

<u>1Chr. 1:19</u> Two sons were born to **Eber**, the name of the one was Peleg, for in his days the earth was divided, and his brother's name was Joktan.

<u>1Chr. 1:20</u> **Joktan** became the father of Almodad, Sheleph, Hazarmaveth, Jerah,

<u>1Chr. 1:21</u> Hadoram, Uzal, Diklah,

<u>1Chr. 1:22</u> Ebal, Abimael, Sheba,

<u>1Chr. 1:23</u> Ophir, Havilah and Jobab; all these [were] the sons of Joktan.

LESSON 4

ʿAVAR NAHᵃRÂ⁾, KᵊNAʿAN, ⁾EREṢ YIŚRĀ⁾ĒL

THE LAND BRIDGE

I.   THE "PROMISED LAND" — Eastern Mediterranean Littoral

Genesis 15:18-21

18 בַּיּוֹם הַהוּא כָּרַת יְהוָה אֶת־אַבְרָם בְּרִית
לֵאמֹר לְזַרְעֲךָ נָתַתִּי אֶת־הָאָרֶץ הַזֹּאת מִנְּהַר מִצְרַיִם
עַד־הַנָּהָר הַגָּדֹל נְהַר־פְּרָת

On that day Yahweh made a covenant with Abram, saying, "To your descendants I have given this land, From the **River of Egypt** as far as the great river, the **River Euphrates**:

19 אֶת־הַקֵּינִי וְאֶת־הַקְּנִזִּי וְאֵת הַקַּדְמֹנִי

20 וְאֶת־הַחִתִּי וְאֶת־הַפְּרִזִּי וְאֶת־הָרְפָאִים

21 וְאֶת־הָאֱמֹרִי וְאֶת־הַכְּנַעֲנִי וְאֶת־הַגִּרְגָּשִׁי

וְאֶת־הַיְבוּסִי

the Kenite and the Kenizzite and the Kadmonite and the Hittite and the Perizzite and the Rephaim and the Amorite and the Canaanite and the Girgashite and the Jebusite."

1 Ki. 5:4 — **Solomon's** sphere of influence

1 Ki. 5:4

4 כִּי־הוּא רֹדֶה בְּכָל־עֵבֶר הַנָּהָר מִתִּפְסַח וְעַד־עַזָּה

בְּכָל־מַלְכֵי עֵבֶר הַנָּהָר וְשָׁלוֹם הָיָה לוֹ מִכָּל־עֲבָרָיו מִסָּבִיב

For he had dominion over everything Beyond the River, from Tiphsah even to Gaza, over all the kings of Beyond the River; and he had peace on all sides around about him.

1 Ki. 5:1 (Heb = 4:21 in Eng.) should be 10:26a ‖ 2 Chron. 9:26

1 Ki. 5:1

וּשְׁלֹמֹה הָיָה מוֹשֵׁל בְּכָל־הַמַּמְלָכוֹת מִן־הַנָּהָר

‹הַגָּדֹל נְהַר־פְּרָת› אֶרֶץ פְּלִשְׁתִּים וְעַד גְּבוּל מִצְרָיִם

מַגִּשִׁים מִנְחָה וְעֹבְדִים אֶת־שְׁלֹמֹה כָּל־יְמֵי חַיָּיו

Now Solomon ruled over all the kingdoms from the ‹Great› River ‹the Euphrates› [to] the land of the Philistines and to the border of Egypt; [they] brought tribute and served Solomon all the days of his life.

Cf. also Ezra 4:20

20 וּמַלְכִין תַּקִּיפִין הֲווֹ עַל־יְרוּשְׁלֶם וְשַׁלִּיטִין בְּכֹל עֲבַר

נַהֲרָה וּמִדָּה בְלוֹ וַהֲלָךְ מִתְיְהֵב לְהוֹן

And mighty kings have ruled over Jerusalem, governing all (the provinces) Beyond the River, and tribute, custom and toll were paid to them.

Cf. also Deut. 1:7 (below)

B. ANCIENT NAMES in non-biblical sources

1. Mesopotamian

Mar.tu = *Amurru*

Ḫatti — Included Philistia and Judah!

eber nāri = עֵבֶר הַנָּהָר = עֲבַר נַהֲרָה

Cedar Mountains

2. Egyptian

ḫryw-šᶜ "Sand dwellers"

nmiw-šᶜ "Those who traverse the sand"

Rtnw = not related to רוֹזְנִים !

Ḏȝhy and *Ḫȝrw* = Canaan

II.   THE LAND OF CANAAN

A. The Canaanite "Sphere" — Genesis 10:15-19

Gen. 10:15 וּכְנַעַן יָלַד אֶת־צִידֹן בְּכֹרוֹ וְאֶת־חֵת

Gen. 10:16 וְאֶת־הַיְבוּסִי וְאֶת־הָאֱמֹרִי וְאֵת הַגִּרְגָּשִׁי

Gen. 10:17 וְאֶת־הַחִוִּי וְאֶת־הַעַרְקִי וְאֶת־הַסִּינִי

Gen. 10:18 וְאֶת־הָאַרְוָדִי וְאֶת־הַצְּמָרִי וְאֶת־הַחֲמָתִי

וְאַחַר נָפֹצוּ מִשְׁפְּחוֹת הַכְּנַעֲנִי

Gen. 10:19 וַיְהִי גְּבוּל הַכְּנַעֲנִי מִצִּידֹן בֹּאֲכָה גְרָרָה

עַד־עַזָּה בֹּאֲכָה סְדֹמָה וַעֲמֹרָה וְאַדְמָה וּצְבֹיִם עַד־לָשַׁע

Canaan became the father of Sidon, his firstborn, and Heth and the Jebusite
and the Amorite and the Girgashite and the Hivite and the Arkite and the
Sinite and the Arvadite and the Zemarite and the Hamathite; and afterward
the families of the Canaanite were spread abroad.

Gen. 10:19 וַיְהִי גְּבוּל הַכְּנַעֲנִי מִצִּידֹן בֹּאֲכָה גְרָרָה

עַד־עַזָּה בֹּאֲכָה סְדֹמָה וַעֲמֹרָה וְאַדְמָה וּצְבֹיִם עַד־לָשַׁע

The territory of the Canaanite extended from Sidon as you go toward Gerar,
as far as Gaza; as you go toward Sodom and Gomorrah and Admah and
Zeboiim, as far as Lasha.

B. The Province of **Canaan**

1. Num. 34:1-12

1 וַיְדַבֵּר יְהוָה אֶל־מֹשֶׁה לֵּאמֹר 2 צַו אֶת־בְּנֵי יִשְׂרָאֵל וְאָמַרְתָּ אֲלֵהֶם

כִּי־אַתֶּם בָּאִים אֶל־הָאָרֶץ כְּנָעַן זֹאת הָאָרֶץ אֲשֶׁר תִּפֹּל לָכֶם

בְּנַחֲלָה אֶרֶץ כְּנַעַן לִגְבֻלֹתֶיהָ 3 וְהָיָה לָכֶם פְּאַת־נֶגֶב מִמִּדְבַּר־צִן עַל־יְדֵי

אֱדוֹם וְהָיָה לָכֶם גְּבוּל נֶגֶב מִקְצֵה יָם־הַמֶּלַח קֵדְמָה

Then Yahweh spoke to Moses, saying, "Command the sons of Israel and say to
them, 'When you enter the land of Canaan, this is the land that shall fall to
you as an inheritance, [even the] land of Canaan according to its borders.'"

גְּבוּל נֶגֶב

4 וְנָסַב לָכֶם הַגְּבוּל מִנֶּגֶב לְמַעֲלֵה עַקְרַבִּים וְעָבַר צִנָה וְהָיָה [וְ][הָיוּ] תּוֹצְאֹתָיו

מִנֶּגֶב לְקָדֵשׁ בַּרְנֵעַ וְיָצָא חֲצַר־אַדָּר וְעָבַר עַצְמֹנָה 5 וְנָסַב הַגְּבוּל מֵעַצְמוֹן

נַחְלָה מִצְרַיִם וְהָיוּ תוֹצְאֹתָיו הַיָּמָּה

Your **southern border** shall extend from the wilderness of Zin along the
side of Edom, and your southern border shall extend from the end of the **Salt
Sea** eastward. Then your border shall turn [direction] from the south to the
ascent of **Akrabbim** and continue to **Zin**, and its termination shall be to the
south of **Kadesh-barnea**; and it shall reach **Hazar-addar** and continue to
Azmon. The border shall turn [direction] from Azmon to the **Brook of
Egypt**, and its termination shall be at the sea.

גְּבוּל יָם

6 וּגְבוּל יָם וְהָיָה לָכֶם הַיָּם הַגָּדוֹל וּגְבוּל זֶה־יִהְיֶה לָכֶם גְּבוּל יָם
As for the **western border**, you shall have the Great Sea, that is, [its]
coastline; this shall be your west border.

גְּבוּל צָפוֹן

7 וְזֶה־יִהְיֶה לָכֶם גְּבוּל צָפוֹן מִן־הַיָּם הַגָּדֹל תְּתָאוּ לָכֶם הֹר הָהָר

8 מֵהֹר הָהָר תְּתָאוּ לְבֹא חֲמָת וְהָיוּ תוֹצְאֹת הַגְּבֻל צְדָדָה

9 וְיָצָא הַגְּבֻל זִפְרֹנָה וְהָיוּ תוֹצְאֹתָיו חֲצַר עֵינָן זֶה־יִהְיֶה לָכֶם גְּבוּל צָפוֹן
And this shall be your **northern border**: you shall draw your [border] line
from the Great Sea to Mount Hor. You shall draw a line from Mount Hor to
the Lebo-hamath, and the termination of the border shall be at Zedad; and the
border shall proceed to Ziphron, and its termination shall be at Hazar-enan.
This shall be your north border.

גְּבוּל קֵדְמָה

10 וְהִתְאַוִּיתֶם לָכֶם לִגְבוּל קֵדְמָה מֵחֲצַר עֵינָן שְׁפָמָה 11 וְיָרַד הַגְּבֻל

מִשְּׁפָם הָרִבְלָה מִקֶּדֶם לָעָיִן וְיָרַד הַגְּבֻל וּמָחָה עַל־כֶּתֶף יָם־כִּנֶּרֶת קֵדְמָה

12 וְיָרַד הַגְּבוּל הַיַּרְדֵּנָה וְהָיוּ תוֹצְאֹתָיו יָם הַמֶּלַח

זֹאת תִּהְיֶה לָכֶם הָאָרֶץ לִגְבֻלֹתֶיהָ סָבִיב

For your **eastern border** you shall also draw a line from Hazar-enan to
Shepham, and the border shall go down from Shepham to Riblah on the east
side of Ain; and the border shall go down and reach to the slope on the east

side of the **Sea of Chinnereth**. And the border shall go down to the **Jordan** and its termination shall be at the **Salt Sea**. This shall be your land according to its borders all around.

2. Ezekiel 47:15-20

פְּאַת צָפוֹנָה

15 וְזֶה גְּבוּל הָאָרֶץ לִפְאַת צָפוֹנָה מִן־הַיָּם הַגָּדוֹל הַדֶּרֶךְ חֶתְלֹן לְבוֹא צְדָדָה

16 חֲמָת בֵּרוֹתָה סִבְרַיִם אֲשֶׁר בֵּין־גְּבוּל דַּמֶּשֶׂק וּבֵין גְּבוּל חֲמָת הָצֵר הַתִּיכוֹן

אֲשֶׁר אֶל־גְּבוּל חַוְרָן 17 וְהָיָה גְבוּל מִן־הַיָּם חֲצַר עֵינוֹן גְּבוּל דַּמֶּשֶׂק

וְצָפוֹן צָפוֹנָה וּגְבוּל חֲמָת וְאֵת פְּאַת צָפוֹן

This [shall be] the **boundary** of the land: on the **north side**, from the **Great Sea** [by] the way of Hethlon, to the entrance of **Zedad**; **Hamath**, Berothah, Sibraim, which is between the border of **Damascus** and the border of **Hamath**; Hazer-hatticon, which is by the border of **Hauran**. The boundary shall extend from the sea [to] Hazar-enan [at] the border of Damascus, and on the north toward the north is the border of Hamath. This is the north side..

פְּאַת קָדִימָה

18 וּפְאַת קָדִים מִבֵּין חַוְרָן וּמִבֵּין־דַּמֶּשֶׂק וּמִבֵּין הַגִּלְעָד וּמִבֵּין אֶרֶץ יִשְׂרָאֵל

הַיַּרְדֵּן מִגְּבוּל עַל־הַיָּם הַקַּדְמוֹנִי תָּמֹדּוּ וְאֵת פְּאַת קָדִימָה

The **east side**, from between **Hauran**, **Damascus**, **Gilead** and the **land of Israel**, [shall be] the **Jordan**; from the [north] border to the **eastern sea** you shall measure. This is the **east side**.

פְּאַת־תֵּימָנָה נֶגְבָּה

19 וּפְאַת נֶגֶב תֵּימָנָה מִתָּמָר עַד־מֵי מְרִיבוֹת קָדֵשׁ נַחֲלָה

אֶל־הַיָּם הַגָּדוֹל וְאֵת פְּאַת־תֵּימָנָה נֶגְבָּה

The **south side** toward the south [shall extend] from Tamar as far as the waters of **Meribath-kadesh**, to the Brook ‹of Egypt› to the Great Sea. This is the south side toward the south.

פְּאַת־יָם

וּפְאַת־יָם הַיָּם הַגָּדוֹל מִגְּבוּל עַד־נֹכַח לְבוֹא חֲמָת זֹאת פְּאַת־יָם

The west side [shall be] the Great Sea, from the [south] border to a point opposite Lebo-hamath. This is the west side.

3. Josh. 22:32 (cf. vv. 9, 21-25)

32 וַיָּשָׁב פִּינְחָס בֶּן־אֶלְעָזָר הַכֹּהֵן וְהַנְּשִׂיאִים מֵאֵת

בְּנֵי־רְאוּבֵן וּמֵאֵת בְּנֵי־גָד מֵאֶרֶץ הַגִּלְעָד אֶל־אֶרֶץ כְּנַעַן

אֶל־בְּנֵי יִשְׂרָאֵל וַיָּשִׁבוּ אוֹתָם דָּבָר

Then Phinehas the son of Eleazar the priest and the leaders returned from the sons of Reuben and from the sons of Gad, from the land of Gilead to the land of Canaan, to the sons of Israel, and brought back word to them.

4. Numbers 13:29

29 עֲמָלֵק יוֹשֵׁב בְּאֶרֶץ הַנֶּגֶב וְהַחִתִּי וְהַיְבוּסִי וְהָאֱמֹרִי יוֹשֵׁב בָּהָר

וְהַכְּנַעֲנִי יֹשֵׁב עַל־הַיָּם וְעַל יַד הַיַּרְדֵּן

Amalek is living in the land of the **Negeb** and the Hittites and the Jebusites and the Amorites are living in the **Hill Country**, and the Canaanites are living by the **Sea** and by the side of the **Jordan**.

III. ʾEreṣ Yiśrāʾēl — THE LAND OF ISRAEL

A. North-south descriptions

1. Deut. 34:1-3

1 וַיַּעַל מֹשֶׁה מֵעַרְבֹת מוֹאָב אֶל־הַר נְבוֹ רֹאשׁ הַפִּסְגָּה אֲשֶׁר עַל־פְּנֵי יְרֵחוֹ

וַיַּרְאֵהוּ יְהוָה אֶת־כָּל־הָאָרֶץ אֶת־הַגִּלְעָד עַד־דָּן 2 וְאֵת כָּל־נַפְתָּלִי

וְאֶת־אֶרֶץ אֶפְרַיִם וּמְנַשֶּׁה וְאֵת כָּל־אֶרֶץ יְהוּדָה עַד הַיָּם הָאַחֲרוֹן

3 וְאֶת־הַנֶּגֶב וְאֶת־הַכִּכָּר בִּקְעַת יְרֵחוֹ עִיר הַתְּמָרִים עַד־צֹעַר

Now Moses went up from the plains of Moab to **Mount Nebo**, to the top of Pisgah, which is opposite Jericho. And Yahweh showed him all the land, **Gilead as far as Dan**, and all **Naphtali** and the land of **Ephraim** and **Manasseh**, and all the land of **Judah** as far as the nether **sea**, and the **Negeb** and the **Plain** in the valley of **Jericho**, the city of palm trees, as far as **Zoar**.

2. Josh. 1:1-4; like ʿevar naharah

1 וַיְהִי אַחֲרֵי מוֹת מֹשֶׁה עֶבֶד יְהוָה וַיֹּאמֶר יְהוָה אֶל־יְהוֹשֻׁעַ בִּן־נוּן מְשָׁרֵת מֹשֶׁה

לֵאמֹר 2 מֹשֶׁה עַבְדִּי מֵת וְעַתָּה קוּם עֲבֹר אֶת־הַיַּרְדֵּן הַזֶּה אַתָּה וְכָל־הָעָם הַזֶּה

אֶל־הָאָרֶץ אֲשֶׁר אָנֹכִי נֹתֵן לָהֶם לִבְנֵי יִשְׂרָאֵל

3 כָּל־מָקוֹם אֲשֶׁר תִּדְרֹךְ כַּף־רַגְלְכֶם בּוֹ לָכֶם נְתַתִּיו כַּאֲשֶׁר דִּבַּרְתִּי אֶל־מֹשֶׁה

4 מֵהַמִּדְבָּר וְהַלְּבָנוֹן הַזֶּה וְעַד־הַנָּהָר הַגָּדוֹל נְהַר־פְּרָת כֹּל אֶרֶץ הַחִתִּים

וְעַד־הַיָּם הַגָּדוֹל מְבוֹא הַשֶּׁמֶשׁ יִהְיֶה גְּבוּלְכֶם

Now it came about after the death of Moses the servant of Yahweh, that Yahweh spoke to Joshua the son of Nun, Moses' servant, saying, "Moses My servant is dead; now therefore arise, cross this Jordan, you and all this people, to the land which I am giving to them, to the sons of Israel. Every place on which the sole of your foot treads, I have given it to you, just as I spoke to Moses:

From the **steppe** and this **Lebanon**, even as far as the **Great River**, the **River Euphrates**, all the **land of the Hittites** (N. Syria), and as far as the **Great Sea** toward the setting of the sun will be your territory.

3. Josh. 11:17

17 מִן־הָהָר הֶחָלָק הָעוֹלֶה שֵׂעִיר וְעַד־בַּעַל גָּד בְּבִקְעַת

הַלְּבָנוֹן תַּחַת הַר־חֶרְמוֹן וְאֵת כָּל־מַלְכֵיהֶם לָכַד וַיַּכֵּם וַיְמִיתֵם

from **Mount Halak**, that rises toward **Seir**, even as far as **Baal-gad** in the **Valley of Lebanon** at the foot of **Mount Hermon**.

4. 2 Sam. 24:2

2 וַיֹּאמֶר הַמֶּלֶךְ אֶל־יוֹאָב שַׂר־הַחַיִל אֲשֶׁר־אִתּוֹ שׁוּט־נָא בְּכָל־שִׁבְטֵי יִשְׂרָאֵל

מִדָּן וְעַד־בְּאֵר שֶׁבַע וּפִקְדוּ אֶת־הָעָם וְיָדַעְתִּי אֵת מִסְפַּר הָעָם

The king said to Joab the commander of the army who was with him, "Go about now through all the tribes of Israel, from **Dan to Beersheba**, and register the people, that I may know the number of the people."

5. 1 Kings 5:5 (Eng. 4:25)

5 וַיֵּשֶׁב יְהוּדָה וְיִשְׂרָאֵל לָבֶטַח אִישׁ תַּחַת גַּפְנוֹ וְתַחַת

תְּאֵנָתוֹ מִדָּן וְעַד־בְּאֵר שָׁבַע כֹּל יְמֵי שְׁלֹמֹה

So **Judah** and **Israel** lived in safety, every man under his vine and his fig tree, from **Dan** even to **Beersheba**, all the days of Solomon.

B. Cross section descriptions
   1. Deut. 1:7

7 פְּנוּ וּסְעוּ לָכֶם וּבֹאוּ הַר הָאֱמֹרִי וְאֶל־כָּל־שְׁכֵנָיו בָּעֲרָבָה

בָהָר וּבַשְּׁפֵלָה וּבַנֶּגֶב וּבְחוֹף הַיָּם אֶרֶץ הַכְּנַעֲנִי וְהַלְּבָנוֹן

עַד־הַנָּהָר הַגָּדֹל נְהַר־פְּרָת

Turn and set out, and go to the hill country of the Amorite, and to all his neighbors in the **Arabah**, in the **Hill country** and in the **Shephelah** and in the **Negeb** and by the seacoast, the land of the **Canaanites**, and **Lebanon**, as far as the **Great River**, the **River Euphrates**.

*****   2. Josh. 10:40

40 וַיַּכֶּה יְהוֹשֻׁעַ אֶת־כָּל־הָאָרֶץ הָהָר וְהַנֶּגֶב וְהַשְּׁפֵלָה וְהָאֲשֵׁדוֹת

Thus Joshua struck all the land: the **Hill Country** and the **Negeb** and the **Shephelah** and the **Slopes**

3. Josh. 11:16-17

16 וַיִּקַּח יְהוֹשֻׁעַ אֶת־כָּל־הָאָרֶץ הַזֹּאת הָהָר וְאֶת־כָּל־הַנֶּגֶב

וְאֵת כָּל־אֶרֶץ הַגֹּשֶׁן וְאֶת־הַשְּׁפֵלָה וְאֶת־הָעֲרָבָה וְאֶת־הַר יִשְׂרָאֵל וּשְׁפֵלָתֹה

17 מִן־הָהָר הֶחָלָק הָעוֹלֶה שֵׂעִיר וְעַד־בַּעַל גָּד

בְּבִקְעַת הַלְּבָנוֹן תַּחַת הַר־חֶרְמוֹן וְאֵת כָּל־מַלְכֵיהֶם לָכַד

וַיַּכֵּם וַיְמִיתֵם

Thus Joshua took all that land: the **Hill Country** and all the **Negeb**, all that land of **Goshen**, the **Shephelah**, the **Arabah**, the **Hill Country** of Israel and its **Shephelah**

4. Judges 1:9

וְאַחַר יָרְדוּ בְּנֵי יְהוּדָה לְהִלָּחֵם בַּכְּנַעֲנִי יוֹשֵׁב הָהָר

וְהַנֶּגֶב וְהַשְּׁפֵלָה

Afterward the sons of Judah went down to fight against the Canaanites living in the **Hill Country** and in the **Negeb** and in the **Shephelah**.

C. Topographical Descriptions

1. Deut. 8:7-8

7 כִּי יְהוָה אֱלֹהֶיךָ מְבִיאֲךָ אֶל־אֶרֶץ טוֹבָה אֶרֶץ נַחֲלֵי מָיִם

עֲיָנֹת וּתְהֹמֹת יֹצְאִים בַּבִּקְעָה וּבָהָר

8 אֶרֶץ חִטָּה וּשְׂעֹרָה וְגֶפֶן וּתְאֵנָה וְרִמּוֹן

אֶרֶץ־זֵית שֶׁמֶן וּדְבָשׁ

For Yahweh your God is bringing you into a good land, a land of brooks of water, of fountains and springs, flowing forth in **valleys** and **hills**;
a land of wheat and barley (valleys), of vines and fig trees and pomegranates, a land of olive oil and honey (hills);

2. Deut. 11:10-12 (climatology)

10 כִּי הָאָרֶץ אֲשֶׁר אַתָּה בָא־שָׁמָּה לְרִשְׁתָּהּ לֹא כְאֶרֶץ

מִצְרַיִם הִוא אֲשֶׁר יְצָאתֶם מִשָּׁם אֲשֶׁר תִּזְרַע אֶת־זַרְעֲךָ

וְהִשְׁקִיתָ בְרַגְלְךָ כְּגַן הַיָּרָק

11 וְהָאָרֶץ אֲשֶׁר אַתֶּם עֹבְרִים שָׁמָּה לְרִשְׁתָּהּ

אֶרֶץ הָרִים וּבְקָעֹת לִמְטַר הַשָּׁמַיִם תִּשְׁתֶּה־מָּיִם

12 אֶרֶץ אֲשֶׁר־יְהֹוָה אֱלֹהֶיךָ דֹּרֵשׁ אֹתָהּ תָּמִיד

עֵינֵי יְהֹוָה אֱלֹהֶיךָ בָּהּ מֵרֵשִׁית הַשָּׁנָה וְעַד אַחֲרִית שָׁנָה

For the land, into which you are entering to possess it, is not like the land of Egypt from which you came, where you used to sow your seed and water it with your foot like a vegetable garden. But the land into which you are about to cross to possess it,

a land of **hills** and **valleys**, drinks water from the rain of heaven,

a land for which Yahweh your God cares; the eyes of Yahweh your God are always on it, from the beginning even to the end of the year.

D. Normal Weather Pattern

    1. Two seasons:
        a. Winter — low pressure in the West
        b. Summer — low pressure in the East — stable
    2. Rainfall Pattern

a. "Rain" (מָטָר, גֶשֶׁם) Oct. to May (75% Dec. to
   Feb.)
   Dt. 11:13-17 (*māṭār*); Jer. 5:24 (*gešem*); Hos. 6:3-4
   (*gešem*); Joel 2:23 (*gešem*); Zech. 9:17(*gešem*)-10:1
   (*māṭār*); Prov. 16:15 (*malqôš*); Job. 29:23
   (*malqôš, māṭār*)

b. Dew — synagogue prayers: all year mentioning dew,
   but "rain" only from Succoth to Pesah.
   Gen. 27:28-29; Hos. 6:4

c. Former and Latter rain: יוֹרֶה וּמַלְקוֹשׁ
   Yōre early (Oct.), to soften the ground.
   Malqôš, late (April, May)

E. Literary references concerning the wearther:

From Th. Jacobsen, *The Treasures of Darkness*

Grant him a pleasant reign to come! Grant him a royal throne, firm in its foundations, Grant him a scepter righting (wrongs) in the land, all shepherd's crooks; Grant him the good crowns, the turban that makes a head distinguished. . . . May he like a farmer till the fields, may he like a good shepherd make the folds teem, may there be vines under him, may there be barley under him, may there be carp folds in the river under him, may there be mottled barley in the fields under him, may fishes and birds sound off in the marshes under him, may old and new reeds grow in the canebrake under him, may deer multiply in the forests under him, may (well) watered gardens bear honey and wine under him, may lettuce and cress grow in the vegetable plots under him, may there be long life in the palace under him. May the high flood rise in the Tigris and Euphrates under him, may grass grow on their banks, may vegetables fill the commons, may the holy Lady of the grains, Nidaba, gather grain piles there!

You half a year, your sister half a year: while you are walking around (alive), she will lie prostrate, while your sister is I walking around (alive), you will lie prostrate.

From Ugaritic Literature

Clouds in the heat of morning, the early rains, Clouds that rain on the summer fruit, Dew that falls on the grapes! Seven years may Baal fail, Eight, the rider of the Clouds. Without dew, without rain, without the surging of the Two Deeps, without the goodness of Baal's voice!

Dead is the Mighty Baal, Perished is the Prince, Lord of .Earth.

Baal is dead! Woe to the people of Dagan's son, Woe to the multitudes of Baal'!

She seizes the god Mot, With a sword she cleaves him, With a pitch fork she winnows him, With fire she burns him, With millstones she grinds him, In the fields she sows him, So that the birds may verily eat his flesh and the fowl may destroy his carcass.

In a vision of the Creator of Creatures, the heavens rain oil, the wadies run with honey, . . . Let me sit and rest, and let my soul repose in my breast, for the Mighty Baal is alive, for the Prince, Lord of the Earth exists!

From days to months, from months to years, lo in the seventh year . . . .

Texts from the Cycle of Baal and Mot

1.   At the death of the hero, Aqht, his father Daniel pronounces a curse on nature:

Thereupon Daniel, the man of Rapha, imprecates, "Clouds in the heat of morning, the early rains, Clouds that rain on the summer fruit; Dew that falls on the grapes! Seven years may Baal fail, Eight, the Rider of the clouds! Without dew, without rain, Without the upsurge of the Two Deeps, Without the goodness of Baal's voice!"

2.   Baal, who has arisen as a young, vigorous deity and has delivered the gods from the threat of Yamm, god of the sea, is intimidated by Mot, god of death. Mot sends messengers to threaten Baal and tells them to deliver the following message:

He warns Baal not to be overconfident just because,

"You did smite Lotan the writhing serpent, did destroy the crooked serpent, the ruler of seven heads . . . ."

In response to the threat that Mot will devour Baal,

Mighty Baal fears him, the Rider of the Clouds dreads him. "Depart! Speak to the god Mot, declare to El's beloved, Mot, 'The Message of Mighty Baal, the word of the Mighty Hero, Be merciful, 0 god Mot! Thy slave am I, yea yours forever!'"

3.   Baal, in the form of a bull, has a torrid encounter with a heifer; he apparently fell asleep and, as reported later, was swallowed by Mot. The divine messengers report finding Baal's fallen body:

"We came upon Baal prostrate on the earth. The Mighty Baal is dead, perished is the Prince, Lord of Earth!" Thereupon, Litpan, god of Mercy, descends from the throne, sits on the footstool, and from the footstool sits on the ground. He pours the ashes of grief on his head, the dust of mourning on his pate. As clothing he is covered with a double garment. He scratches the skin with stones, the side curls he cuts with a razor. He cuts cheeks and chin, he lacerates the forearms, he plows the chest like a garden, the rib cage like a vale. He lifts his voice and shouts, "Baal is dead! Woe to the people of Dagan's son, Woe to the multitudes of Baal'!"

4.   Anat seeks revenge on Mot.

She approaches him. As with the heart of a cow toward her calf, As with the heart of a ewe toward her lamb, So is the heart of Anat toward Baal. She seizes Mot by the hem of his garment, She grabs him, tearing his clothes. She lifts her voice and shouts, "Come, Mot, yield my brother!" And the god Mot replies, "What are you asking, 0 Virgin Anat? I was going and roaming every mountain in the midst of the earth, every hill in the midst of the fields. A soul was missing among men, a soul of the multitudes of the earth . . . . I came upon the Mighty Baal, I made him like a lamb in my mouth, like a kid in my jaws . . . . The Luminary of the gods glows white, the heavens turn pale because of the god, Mot. A day, two days pass, from days to months, then the Maiden Anat meets him. . . . She seizes the god Mot, with a sword she cleaves him, with a pitchfork she winnows him, with fire she burns him, with millstones she grinds him, in the field she sows him so that the birds may eat his flesh.

5. In a dream, El sees that Baal has risen.

In a dream of Litpan, god of mercy, in a vision of the creator of creatures, the heavens rain oil, the wadies run with honey. The god of mercy rejoices, his feet he sets on the footstool, he opens his mouth and laughs, he lifts his voice and shouts; "I will sit me down and rest, and may my soul repose in my breast, For the Mighty Baal lives, for the Prince, Lord of Earth exists!"

6.   The clash between Baal and Mot

Baal seizes the son of Ashera, the Great One he smites on the shoulder, the Lord he smites with a stick. Mot is beaten, he falls to the earth. [Baal returns] to the throne of his kingship, [Dagan's son] to the seat of his sovereignty. From [days] to months, from months to years, [Behold] in the seventh year, then the god Mot [returns to] the Mighty Baal; He lifts his voice and shouts; "Because of you, 0 Baal, I have had humiliation, because of you, I had scattering by the sword, because of you, I had burning in the fire, because of you, I had grinding in the millstones . . . ."

7.   Mot returns again to challenge Baal and blames him for the indignities he suffered at the hands of Anat. They clash in mortal combat.

They shake each other like *gmr*-beasts; Mot is strong, Baal is strong; they gore like buffaloes, Mot is strong, Baal is strong; they bite like serpents, Mot is strong, Baal is strong; they kick like steeds, Mot is down, Baal is down. The sun goddess cries to Mot: "Hear 0 god, Mot, how can you fight with the Mighty Baal? Will not the Bull, El, thy father, hear you? Will he not remove the foundation of thy throne? Will he not overturn the seat of your kingship? Will he not break the scepter of thy rule?" The god Mot is frightened, El's beloved, the Hero, is frightened.

F. Gezer Calendar

The Text

(1)	⌜y⌝⌜r⌝ḥw ᵓsp / yrḥw z	יוזר⌐חו אספ | ירחו ז
(2)	rᶜ / yrḥw lqš	רע | ירחו לקש
(3)	yrḥ ᶜṣd pšt	ירח עצד פשת
(4)	yrḥ qṣr śᶜrm	ירח קצר שערמ
(5)	yrḥ qṣr wkl	ירח קצר וכל
(6)	yrḥw zmr	ירחו זמר
(7)	yrḥ qṣ	ירח קצ
Lo. edge	ᵓby	אבי

TRANSLATION

(1)   His two months: Ingathering;
(2)   His two months: Sowing
(3)   His two months: Late sowing
(4)   His month: Chopping flax (or grass)
(5)   His month: Barley harvest
(6)   His month: Harvest and measuring
(7)   His two months: Vine tending
(8)   His month: Summer fruit

Lower edge   Abiya

EARLY AND MIDDLE BRONZE AGES

I.   **EARLY BRONZE AGE** — Third Millennium BCE

A.   MESOPOTAMIA

The Urban Revolution (Jemdet Nasr) ca.	3100-2900 BCE
The Golden Age EARLY DYNASTIC I	ca. 2900-2700
The Heroic Age EARLY DYNASTIC II	ca. 2700-2500
The Dynastic Age EARLY DYNASTIC III	2500-2300

Kingdom of Akkad

Sargon and the Rise of Akkad   (ca. 2300-2230)
        Sargon was high official in Kiš, who rebelled against his
        master and founded a new dynasty with Agade
(Akkad) as capital.

The **Akkadian** kings: Sargon, Rimuš, Maništušu (sons of
        Sargon), Naram-Sin (grandson of Sargon), Šar-kali-šarrī
        (son of Naram-Sin)

Naram-Sin and the Fall of Akkad (2230-2100) - **Gutian**
        invasion (2200 to nearly 2110) — "Who was king?, Who
        was not king?"
UR III — Neo-Sumerian Renaissance (ca. 2100-2000)

        Utuḫengal, ruler of Uruk expelled the Gutians a. 2120.

        Meanwhile, Lagaš under Gudea was also a strong state
            ca. 2120

Ur III Dynasty

Ur-nammu was governor of Ur under Utuḫengal, but
        he displaced his benefactor and established himself
        as King of Ur (**Law Code of Urnammu**)

Šulgi (2094-2047) — continued to expand militarily and
economically

Šulgi's sons followed him: Amar-Sin (2046-2038)
and Šu-Sin (2037-2029) **Amorites** making inroads

Last ruler, Ibbi-Sin (2038-2004) — Amorite invasions
caused severe economic chaos (rise in prices x 60)!

Invasion by Elamites and other Zagros tribes destroyed
Ur (2004).

B.   **EGYPTIAN CHRONOLOGY**

Dynasty Ø —   ? - 3050

Horus **Narmer** 'Catfish' — last Pharaoh. United Upper and
Lower Egypt. His name is found on Jars in southern Canaan: En
Besor, Arad, Tel ᶜErani, Lod

OLD KINGDOM

Dynasty I		3050-2857
Dynasty II	2857-2705	
Dynasty III		2705-2630

Horus Sekhmet (**Djoser-Teti**) 2667-2660 — pyramid

Dynasty IV	2630-2524 — pyramids
Snefru	2630-2606
(Khnum-)Khufwi ('Khufu')	2606-2583
Menkaureᶜ ('Myrcinus')	2548-2530
Dynasty V	2524-2400
Sahureᶜ	2517-2505
Unis	2430-2400
Dynasty VI	2400-2250?
Teti	2400-2390
* Pepi I(First reign)	2390-
Userkareᶜ	-2382
* Pepi I (again)	2382-2355

*** **Weni's campaigns** against the "<u>sand dwellers</u>"

FIRST INTERMEDIATE PERIOD

Dynasty VII	2250?-2230
Dynasty VIII	2230-2213
Dynasty IX	2213-ca. 2175
Dynasty X	ca. 2175-ca. 2035

Transition to Middle Kingdom

Dynasty XI	2134-1991
Mentuḥotep IV	-1991

Reunited Egypt

C.   **LEVANT**

Chalcolithic	4000-3150 B.C.E.

Early Bronze Age

EB I A-C	3150-2850

Horus **Narmer** 'Catfish' — last Pharaoh. His name is found on

Jars in southern Canaan: Arad, Ein Besor, Tel ᶜErani, Lod

EB II	2850-2650

'Abydos Ware' exported to Egypt

EB IIIA	2650-2350

***   **EBLA** — archive from <u>Tell Mardîkh</u> — overlaps at the end,

the reigns of Sargon and Naram-Sin

EB IV (IIIB)	2350-2200

Campaigns by **Sargon the Great** and **Naram-Sin**

Campaigns by **Weni** under Pepi I

II. "INTERMEDIATE BRONZE AGE" — Pastoralist Interlude (American EB
IV, Albright's MB I)
2200-2000 (or 2050?)

III. MIDDLE BRONZE AGE

A.   **MESOPOTAMIA**

Old Babylonian Period (Amurrite Dynasties)

Small kingdoms arose:

> **Isin** and Larsa. — Išbi-Erra, gov. of Mari under Ur,
> founded independent kingdom at Isin (2017)
> **Ur** was cultural and comercial center, subject first
>   to Isin, then to Larsa.
> **Nippur** was chief religious center

Other dynasties eventually rose: **Babylon** under
> **First Babylonian** dynasty — began in 1894.

> **ᶜAmmurapi** — (1792-1750)
> Defeated Elam, then Rim-Sin of Larsa (1763)
> and Mari (in 1761, destroyed it in 1759).
> His "empire" shrank and finally disappeared
> under ᶜAmmurapi's successors.

Larger "empires" actually kingdoms with vassal states
> **Shamshi-Adad** — (1830-1776) ruler of
>   Ekallatum,
>   subdued <u>Asshur</u> in the east, and *Mari* in West.
>   Split his kingdom between Ishme-Dagan in
>   Ekallatum and Yasmaᶜ-Addu in **Mari**. (

Assyrian Trade expansion — (ca. 1900-1800)
> Merchant colony at **Kārum Kaniš** in Anatolia

North Syrian Amurrite Kingdoms

<u>The ethnic group</u>:

> The **Amurrites** = **Mar.tu** = pastoralists from
>   Jebel Bishri
> Individuals known in Ur III documents
>   (mercenaries?)
> Infiltrated into the territories outside cities

Eventually dominated the cities

Some of the most important <u>city states</u>:

1. **Yamkhad** in Aleppo — senior state

2. **Mari** subject to Yamkhad, later to Shamshi-Adad and later to Babylon

3. Other states: **Carchemish, Qatna,** and others **(Hazor)**

4. Society: <u>urban,</u> <u>agricultural</u> and <u>pastoralist</u> sectors.

5. Language: WS from PN's and GN's

B.   EGYPT

Middle Kingdom

XIIth Dynasty (1991-1803 B.C.E.) — <u>Age of Splendor</u>

Amenemḥat I	1991-1962

Sinuhe 's flight to Retenu

Senwosret I	1971-1928
Amenemḥat II	1929-1895
Senwosret II	1897-1878
Senwosret III	1878-1859

Campaign against *SKMM* (<u>Khu-sebek</u> inscription)

Early Execration Texts (on saucers)

Amenemḥat III	1860-1815

Expedition to Retenu

Amenemḥat IV	1816-1807
Nofrusobek	1807-1803

XIIIth Dynasty   1803-1649 BCE

57 rulers, lost control of NE Delta, famine and plagues.

Later Execration Tests — On statuettes

Second Intermediate Period

XIVth   Dynasty   (1805-1649 BCE)

Semitic rulers in North Eastern Delta. Minimum of 56 Kings. Had seized the NE Delta from the kings of the XIIIth Dynasty. Intermarriage with a king of Kush.

Wide commercial relations in early part of the dynasty.

XVth **Dynasty**   (1649-1540 BCE)

Semitic rulers in N. Eastern Delta. So-called 'Hyksos.'
Came from Levant and conquered NE Delta. Brought
an end to both the XIIIth and XIVth Dynasties.
Capital city at **Auaris** (*Ḥwt-wᶜrt*; Tell Dabaᶜ)
Fought with rulers of Abydos Dynasty and XVIth
        Dynasty (Controlled No-Ammon 1582-1580)
Conflict with XVIIth Dynasty; defeated by Aḥmose I of
the XVIIIth Dynasty.

Abydos **Dynasty**   (1649-1629 BCE)

Obscure rulers, ca. 20 years; conflict with rulers of
XVth Dynasty

XVIth **Dynasty**   (1649-1582 BCE)

Ruled at No-Ammon for about 50 years; constant war
With rulers of the XVth Dynasty that finally conquered
No-Ammon

XVIIth **Dynasty**   (1580-1549 BCE)

Established independence of No-Ammon and fought
Against the rulers of the XVth Dynasty. Inscriptions of
Kamose, the last Pharaoh of this Dynasty

C.   **SOUTHERN LEVANT (Canaan)**

MIDDLE BRONZE I (= MB IIA) c. 2050-1800 BCE || Dyn. XII

1. Renewed sea trade between Byblos and Egypt
    with new fortified cities along the coast, e.g.
    Acco, Tel Poleg, Tel Gerisa, Joppa, Ashkelon
2. Also new cities along main trade route, e.g. Laish,
    Hazor, Megiddo, Aphek.

3. Statue of Egyptian official at Megiddo.

4. **Early Execration Texts**: on bowls in the mid-12th

dyn. Time of Senwosret III. Multiple rulers.

Campaign by **Khu-sebek** against *SKMM*

5. West Semitic population (Amurrite and Canaanite[?])

MIDDLE BRONZE II (= MB IIB) c. 1800-1650 || Dyn. XIII

1. Amurrite kingdoms in Syria and Mesopotamia, e.g.

Yamḥad, Mari, Qatna, Carchemish, Babylon

2. Caravan trade between Hazor and Mari

3. Egyptian contacts also intensive.

4. **Late Execration Texts**: on statuettes; many more

identified towns; usually one ruler in each town.

MIDDLE BRONZE III (= MB IIC) c. 1650-1540 || Dyn. XV

1. Seal of Egyptian officials found in southern part of the

land; usually south of Jezreel Valley.

2. Many towns destroyed by fire.

3. Transition to Late Bronze Age

LESSON 6

THE RISE OF THE EIGHTEENTH DYNASTY

I.   EIGHTEENTH DYNASTY PHARAOHS

Aḥmose I	1550-1525	Expulsion of foreign rulers campaign against Sharḥan

Tomb Inscription of Iᶜaḥmes

Amenḥotep I	1525-1504	son of Aḥmose; campaigns in Nubia
Thutmose I	1504-1492	vizier of Amenḥop I; one documented campaign to N. Syria; other campaigns to Nubia

Tomb Inscription of Iᶜaḥmes

Thutmose II	1492-1457	son of secondary wife; married Ḥatshepsut
Thutmose III	1479-1425	son of secondary wife; married Ḥatshepsut's daughter? At least one campaign to Nubia for Ḥatshepsut.
*** [Ḥatshepsut	1479/1473-1457	ruled as "king"; sent one expedition to Punt.
Thutmose III	"First campaign" in year 22 (1457) 16 campaigns, last in year 42 (1437)	
Amenḥotep II	1427-1400	
	Year 3	Crown Prince: Campaign to Taḫsi, 1425/1424
	Year 7	Campaign to N. Syria 1420
	Year 9	Campaign to Canaan 1418
Thutmose IV	1419-1386	Peace with Mitanni (Hittite

pressure; prisoners from
Gezer)

II.   KINGDOM OF MITANNI

A. Beginnings
    1.   Hurrians from north (S. Russia? Caucasus?)
          Some contact with Indo-Europeans
    2.   On the perphery in Mari Age
***   3.   Formed a kingdom after Mursili I's campaign in N.
          Syria and Babylonia
    4.   Thutmose I invaded N. Syria; caught the ruler by
          surprise
    5.   Thutmose III invaded N. Syria about 15 times!
    6.   Amenhotep II invaded N. Syria one time
    7.   They made peace with Thutmose IV because the
          Hittites were threatening them.

B. Kings:

Sauštatar — (son of Parsatatar) after Thutmose III —
    reunified Mitanni, conquered Asshur, controlled Khalab
    — capital at Waššukani.
    Had controlled Kizzuwatna (in Cilicia)

[Šuttarna son of Kirta — on dynastic seal — where do they fit
    in?]
Parrattarna — (possibly end of 15th cent.?) — was king when Idrimi
    took over Alalakh
Artatama I, sucessor, possibly son of Sauštatar, made treaty
    with Thutmose IV and sent his daughter to him.
    (Diplomatic contats began with Amenhotep II).

Kizzuwatna became independent ca. 1400

Šuttarna II, son of Artatama — sent Gilu-Ḫeba to
    Amenhotep III (ca. 1381-1380?).
    Also sent him Ištar of Nineveh
Artašumara, son of Šuttarna, probably murdered by Utḫi (Pirḫi)

Tušratta, young bro. of Artašumara, made king by Utḫi,
    later killed Utḫi.

    Rivalled for awhile by an Artatama II, who was a
    puppet of the Hittites (did he have a territory?)

    Šuttarna II, son of Artatama II, supported by Assyria

    el ꜥAmârnah texts from Tušratta

    Sent Tadu-Ḫeba to Amenhotep III.

    Suppiluliuma and the Assyrians supported Artatama II
        against Tušratta

    Tušratta murdered, perhaps by a certain Akit-Teššub

Sattiwaza, son of Tušratta, escaped to Suppiluliuma and was placed
    as Mitannian ruler. Later he defected, became independent,
    and his kingdom wiped out by Mursili II (ca. 1320).

[Suppiluliuma died of plague and also his successor Arnuwanda,
    followed by Mursili II.

III.   EGYPTIAN MILITARY CAMPAIGNS

    A.   AḤMOSE (1550-1525)

        1.   Drove the Foreign Rulers (*ḥq3w ḥswt*) out of Egypt and conquered Avaris

        2.   Campaigned three years against Sharḥân

    B.   THUTMOSE I (1504-1462)— One campaign to **Naharina**.

        1.   Arrived there while the ruler there was in the process of calling up his forces.

        2.   Erected a stele on the banks of the Euphrates.

        3.   Must have been able to march across Retenu without opposition.

    C.   THUTMOSE III (1479-1425)

        1.   **First Campaign** — in his 22nd year (1457), after death of Ḥatshepsut. Marched against Canaanite coalition assembled at **Megiddo**.

"Regnal year 22, fourth month of the second season,

[his majesty passed the fortress of] Sillû"

"Regnal year 23, first month of the third season, day ⌜4⌝,

the day of his majesty's coronation festival: arrival

at "The town which the ruler had seized," Gaza

[being its name] . . . ."

240 kilometers in **10** days.

"[Regnal year 23,] first month of the third season, day 5:

Departure from this place . . . ."

"Regnal year 23, first month of the third season, day 16:

to the town of **Yaḥm**. Council of war."

"Regnal year 23, first month of the third season, day 19:

awakening in the royal tent: To the town of

ᶜAruna."

"‹ Regnal year 23, first month of the third season, day

20:› Marched through ᶜAruna pass to **Megiddo**."

"Regnal year 23, first month of the third season, day 21,

exactly on the festival of the New Moon:

Appearance of his majesty at first light of dawn. "

Took **seven** more months to conquer the city.

2.   **Fifth Campaign**, yr. 29 (1450). Into
       N. Lebanon and central Syria, against **Tunip** and
       Ardata.

3.   **Sixth Campaign**, yr. 30 (1449), against **Kedesh** on the
       Orontes (northern end of Lebanese Beqaᶜ Valley);
       west to Ṣumur on the, north of modern Lebanese
       border with Syria; on to **Ardata**.

4.   **Seventh Campaign**, yr. 31 (1448), against **Ullasa**,
       troops from **Tunip** tried to interfere.

5.   **Eighth Campaign**, yr. 33 (1446), major thrust into
       Syria against **Mitanni** in **Naharina**; near **Byblos**
       (Gubla) he built wagons to haul boats from the
       shore of the Mediterranean across Syria to the
       River Euphrates; set up his victory stele beside
       the stele of Thutmose I (his grandfather).
       On his way back, in the Orontes Valley near **Niʾi**,
       he hunted elephants and killed 120 (!?).

6.   **Ninth Campaign**, yr. 34 (1445); emphasizes concern
       for sea ports on the coast of **Djahi**, and for export
       of cedar wood to Egypt from Lebanon.

7.   **Tenth through Fifteenth Campaigns**, mainly lists
       of tribute collected.

8.   **Sixteenth Campaign**, yr. 42 (1437); up the coast of
       Fenḫu; destroyed ᶜ**Irqata**; turned inland to
       attack **Tunip**; back to **Kedesh**.

D.   AMENḤOTEP II (1427-1400)

1.   First Campaign (as co regent), yr. 3 (1425/1424)
             Campaign to Taḥsi, seven rebels slain.

2.   First Campaign as sole ruler, yr. 7 (1420)
             Campaign to N. Syria; side expedition to **Ugarit**;
             captured messanger from Mitanni in plain of
             Siryon.

3.   Second Campaign as sole ruler, yr. 9 (1418)
             Campaign to Canaan: past **Aphek**, to **Yaḥam**,
             plundering villages in Sharon Plain, conflict in
             northern Sharon plain near **Migdal**, in to Jezreel
             Valley, conquered **Anaharath**, back to the
             "**Vicinity of Megiddo**(!); arrested ruler of
             Gebaᶜ-ṭoman ("Hill of Eight").

E.   THUTMOSE IV 1419-1386
             Peace with **Mitanni** (Hittite pressure); prisoners from
             Gezer.

IV.   IDRĪMI, *king of Alalakh.*

A.   History

1.   His father was ruler of **Aleppo**; fell out of favor with
             king of Mitanni
2.   Idrimi with his family fled to his mother's family home
             at **Emar**.
3.   Visited **Sutû** warriors in the Syrian desert. Felt
             uncomfortable and left with his squire.
4.   Continued to **Canaan** and found refuge at **Ammia**.

5.   Recognized as being of noble birth by other political refugees there; stayed seven years among the ʿapîru.

6.   Got ships and weapons and sailed with his men up to the mouth of the Orontes, marched inland and seized Alalakh. Later got recognition my the king of Mitanni.

B.   Lessons

1.   Chronology still disputed
2.   Shows Canaan was in southern Levant (Ammia)
3.   Shows that the were ʿapîru political renegades who sought to get back into the Bronze Age society.

V.   THE TAANACH TEXTS.

A.   Discovery — 1903 season at Tell Tiʿinik.

1.   Find spot disputed. Stratigraphy not clear but seems to be LB I.
2.   Twelve tablets and fragments, including lists of personal names. Four epistles are legible.
3.   Two texts found by Lapp's excavations in the 1960's.
       a. Another list of personal names.
       b. Alphabetic text (ca 13th or 12th century BCE).

B.   Contents

1.   Personal names show West Semitic and also Hurrian elements in the population.
2.   Two Epistles from local rulers to the ruler of Taanach. One mentions Raḥābu. One talks about corvée.

3.   Name of the local ruler probably Talwi-šarruma.

4.   Two letters from an Egyptian official named
     Amenḥatpe. He came to **Gaza** and then to
     Megiddo.

VI.   PAPYRUS PETERSBURG 1116A.

A.   List of *maryannu* who got rations from the Egyptian
     Palace.

B.   Towns who sent emissaries to Egypt:

     Hazor, Shimᶜon, and others

LESSON 7
FOURTEENTH CENTURY BCE

I.   EIGHTEENTH DYNASTY PHARAOHS

Amenḥotep III   1390-1352   son of Thutmose IV; long
                              And prosperous reign of
                              38 years
                  Amara west temple inscription:
                  against groups of Shasu
                  (93) *ta ša-śu Si-ᶜ- r-r*
                  (94) '   '   *La-bá-na*
                  (95) '   '   *Pí-s-pì-ś*
                  (96) '   '   *Śa-ma-ᶜa-ta*
                  (97) '   '   *Ya-h-wa*   ****
                  (98) '   '   *ᵓu-ur-b-il*

Amenḥotep IV   1352-1336   16/17 yrs. Changed name to
                              Akhenaten, moved his
                              Capital to Akhetaten
                              (Amarna); his chief wife
                              was **Nefertiti**; six daughters
                              Aten (sun disc) worship
***
                  Supported by the military against large temple
                  corporations

Semenkhkare   1338-1336   2 yrs. Coregent with his
                              father.

Tutankhamen   1336-1327   9 yrs.; brother of
                              Semenkhkare; married
                              Ankhesenpaaten (daughter
                              of Akhenaten

Ay   1327-1323   4 yrs.; father of Nefertiti;
                              he was grandfather of

Tutankhamen; had high
military rank; was senior
minister for Akhenaten

Horemheb   1323-1295   28 yrs. Army commander;
restored order and opened
temples; erased the heretic
kings' names

II.   el-ᶜAmârnah Letters

A.   Discovery — in 1887A.D. — 381 cuneiform documents
found at Amarnah; diplomatic correspondence and
scribal texts (32 texts)
Texts from the reigns of Amenḥotep III, IV and
Tutankhamen. About 349 letters.

B.   International Correspondence

Babylon — commercial trade and royal marriages;
rulers are **Cassites**.

Mitanni — commercial trade and royal marriages;
Letters of Tušratta (who was murdered later)

Ḥatti (land of the Hittites) — desire for diplomatic
relations; from **Suppululiuma** and from his
brother.

Arzawa (southern Turkey)— diplomatic relations

Alashia (on Cyprus) — diplomatic relations and trade
in copper ore in exchange for grain and silver.

Assyria — two letters; Assyria is now independent of Mitanni rule.

C.   Letters from **Canaan**

Correspondence with the vassals of Egypt about affairs In the land of Canaan. Over 250 letters!!!

III.   CANAANITE AFFAIRS

A.   THE TEXTS

1.   Dialect — hybrid language, Akkadian words with Canaanite verbal prefixes and suffixes.

2.   Dates — from the reigns of Amenhotep III and IV.

***

3.   Diplomacy and Policy — Amenhotep IV's government **did not neglect the empire !!!**

B.   NORTHERN AFFAIRS — POLITICAL BLUNDERS

1.   The ʿ**Abdi-Ashirta** Affair; Rib-Haddi is ruler of Byblos.

a.   Leader of ʿapîru renegades/mercenaries
b.   Seized Ṣumur, the Egyptian base.
c.   Undermined local rulers to have them killed.
d.   Sought to create league of cities (Amurru)
e.   Amenhotep sent small force but failed to capture ʿAbdi-Ashirta.
f.   Finally sent a large force; captured ʿAbdi-Ashirta.

2.   The **Aziru** Affair; Rib-Haddi is still ruler of Byblos

a.   Son of ʿAbdi-Ashirta, worked with his brother(s)

***

    b.   Received (bought?) the ships and weapons of the Egyptian force that captured their father!!!

    c.   Began to do the same things their father had done.

    d.   Received (bought?) the support of high Egyptian officials

    e.   Rib-Haddi complains but Pharaoh and his ministers do not help him.

    f.   Rib-Haddi expelled from Byblos by his younger brother; he flees to Beirut; later he is killed in Sidon

    g.   **Aziru** established dynasty of Amurru; then sent to **Suppililiuma** and became his vassal!!!

C.   <u>SOME</u> <u>MORE</u> <u>CANAANITE</u> <u>AFFAIRS</u>

1.   The **Lab²ayu** Affair — ruler of **Shechem**.

    a.   Made alliance with **Milkilu** ruler of **Gezer**; he was punished but not Milkilu.

    b.   Milkilu was son-in-law of **Tagi**, ruler in plain of Acco, who sent troops to **Beth-shean**.

    c.   Lab²ayu's son arrested for associating with the *ᶜapîrū* renegades in the mountains of Samaria.

    d.   Lab²ayu had another son, **Mut-Baᶜlu**, who was ruler of **Peḥel** across the Jordan River.

    d.   Lab²ayu forced **Baᶜl-Meher**, ruler of **Gath-Padalla** to become his vassal.

    e.   Lab²ayu conquered towns in biblical Valley of Dothan: **ᶜArabu**, and **Burquna** and took **Shunem** and **Gitti-rimuna** in the Plain of Jezreel.

    f.   Lab²ayu then laid siege to Biridiya, ruler of **Megiddo** because the unit of regular Egyptian troops had been sent back to Egypt and was not replaced.

g. Finally, the order went out from Pharaoh to arrest Lab'ayu. He was captured but released by **Surata**, ruler of **Acco** (at Hannathon on the way from Megiddo); on his way home, Lab'ayu was Ambushed and slain.

2. The sons of **Lab'ayu** started to renew their father's program by threatening the ruler of Gath-padalla.

3. The ᶜ**Abdi-Ḥeba** Affair — ruler of **Jerusalem**.

    a. ᶜAbdi-Ḥeba bribed the men of **Qila** to join him.
    b. **Shuwardata**, ruler of (Gath?), got permission to take Qila back by using armed force; he did it.
    c. Shuwardata, Milkilu of Gezer, and Tagi took two cities from ᶜAbdi-Ḥeba

4. **Lachish** — **Zimreddi** is ruler, his brother **Shipti-Baᶜlu**, urges him to rebel. Zimreddi is murdered and Shipti-Baᶜlu becomes ruler. A diplomat slain on the way to Sillu

D. SOME MORE NORTHERN AFFAIRS:

1. **Biryawaza** was governor/ruler at **Komidi** and **Damascus**. He had troubles with neighbors from ᶜ**Ashtartu** (biblical Ashtaroth).

2. **Biryawaza** himself robbed a caravan from Babylon.

3. **Etakkama** of **Qidshi** (Kedesh) serves the Hittites and works with **Aziru** against friends of Egypt.

4. **Statna** of **Acco** and **Shum-Haddi** of **Shimona** (biblical Shimron) robbed a Babylonian caravan at **Hanathon**.

E.   <u>PLANS</u> <u>FOR</u> <u>AN</u> <u>EGYPTIAN</u> <u>CAMPAIGN</u>

    1.   Letters sent to all the rulers of Canaan to get ready for the coming of the Egyptian army.

    2.   The local rulers wrote letters to Pharaoh and promised to have the supplies ready with their own troops.

    3.   Not sure that the Egyptian army ever came forth.

LESSON 8
LATE BRONZE III, 13TH CENTURY BCE

I.   **NINETEENTH DYNASTY PHARAOHS** Chose new northern
capital at Avaris = "House of Ramesses"

Ramesses I   1295-1294 1 yr., army commander;
                          very old, died soon.

Seti I   1294-1279   15 yrs. Young military
                          Commander; goes forth on
                          his first military campaign in
                          his first year.

Ramesses II 1279-1213 66 yrs. Wars against the
                          Hittites; then against towns
                          In Canaan.
                          Peace Treaty with Hittites;
                          marries Hittite princess; has
                          about 100 children.

Merenptah   1212-1203 10 yrs.; war against **Libyans**
                          and **Sea Peoples**
                          campaign in Canaan;
                          mentions **Israel**; reliefs on
                          Karnak outside wall

Amenmesse 1203-1200 3 yrs.; who was he?? Maybe
                          Usurper(?). Put is name on
                          Merenptaḥ's reliefs.

Seti II   1200-1194   6 yrs., son of Merenptah; put
                          His name in place of
                           Amenmesse on Karnak
                          Reliefs.

Siptaḥ   1194-1188 6 yrs., son of Seti II; ruled
                          with his mother.

Tewosert   1194-1186   6 + 2 = 8 yrs. Wife of Seti II;
                          ruled with her son and after
                          him.

II.   THE EARLY WARS OF THE NINETEENTH DYNASTY

A.   Seti I

          1.   First year of his reign —
                   a.   three kinds of sources:
                            (1)   Reliefs at Karnak
                            (2)   Topographical lists
                            (3)   Vistory Stelae at Beth-shean and
                                  Tell Sheikh esh-Shiḥab
                   b.   Course of the campaign:
                            (1)   Across Sinai — against Shosu
                            (2)   Beth-shean valley (stela)
                            (3)   Against Yenoᶜam (relief at Karnak)
                            (4)   Across Bashan & Galilee (topographical lists)
                            (5)   Up the Lebanese coast (topographical lists);
                                  relief at Karnak of trees being cut

          2.   Subsequent campaigns — against the Hittites;
                   Karnak reliefs.

III.   THE LATER WARS OF THE NINETEENTH DYNASTY

A.   Ramesses II

          1.   Year 4 — inscription at Nahr el-Kalb, unreadable text.

          2.   Year 5 — Battle of Qedesh — recorded on five temples!
                   a.   Marched to Lebanese Beqaᶜ Valley
                   b.   Continued northward across watershed; and
                            approached Qedesh with his HQ unit.
                   c.   Hittites attacked the Amon Division on the march;
                            they fled rtowards Ramesses' camp.
                   d.   Ramesses drove the Hittes back with the help of
                            elite unit (*naᶜaruna*) that came by way of

Amurru.

  e. Huge battle next day; Ramesses retreats

  f. Hittite king, Muwatallis, campaigns in **Apa** =

  Upe = Damascus area

2. Year 8 — Against towns in Galilee and northwards —
Luxor Reliefs; and on the pylon of the Ramesseum:

Gib[ʿa], ʿÊn-naʿam, on the mountain of Beth-ʿAnat
- Karpuna(?) Qana, in the land of Amurru - Dapur,
Kawil, ʾAn-mayim, Marom, Šalom.

3, Year 10 — Another victory inscription at Nahr el-Kalb

4. Year 18 — Stele at Beth-shean, no war details.

5. Other conquests in Canaan (no dates available):

  a. Topographical list of coastal road:
Rapiḥ, Shar[ḥan], [Yurza?], Muʾḫazi, Socho,
ʾA[dori]nu, [. . . . , ...], Dor, Rehob.

  b. Punishment of Acco (at Luxor)

6. Transjordan

Reliefs on east side of Luxor temple include:

˹Mu˺-ʾa-bu (Moʾab); *Bu-ta-ár-ta* (Batora?);
Ta-bu-nù (Dibon?)

B. <u>Merenptah</u> — Stele in his 5ᵗʰ year (1207 B.C.E.)

1. Mainly about his war with the Libyans and Sea
Peoples; inside walls of the southern courtyard
bear reliefs of this battle.

2.   Victory Poem about campaign in Canaan:

Ashkelon, Gezer, Yeno‘am, **Israel**

POEM IN THE MERNEPTAH STELE

The great ones are prostrate, saying "Peace" (*ša-la-ma*),

Not one raises his head among the Nine Bows

Plundered is Tjehenu (Libya), Khatti is at peace,

Canaan is plundered with every evil,

Ashkelon ( ) is conquered,

Gezer ( ) is seized,

Yano‘am ( ) is made non-existent,

Israel ( ) is laid waste, his seed is no more,

Kharu has become a widow because of Egypt,

All lands together are at peace,

Any who roamed have been subdued.

3.   Papyrus Anastasi VI

. . . We have completed the transfer of the Shosu tribes past the fortress "Merneptah-ḥotep-ḥer-Maᶜat . . ." which is in **Ṣəku** (= Succo[th]) to the pools(sic!) of **Per-Atum** (= Pithom) of "Merneptah-ḥotep-ḥer-Maᶜat . . . ," which are in **Ṣəku** (= Succo[th]), in order to keep them alive and in order to keep their cattle alive (Lines 51-57; Gardiner 1937:76-77).

THE PATRIARCHS

I.   FATHERS OF THE NATION

A. MESOPOTAMIAN ORIGIN - EGYPTIAN CAPTIVITY

JOSHUA 24:2-4

2 וַיֹּאמֶר יְהוֹשֻׁעַ אֶל־כָּל־הָעָם כֹּה־אָמַר יְהוָה אֱלֹהֵי

יִשְׂרָאֵל בְּעֵבֶר הַנָּהָר יָשְׁבוּ אֲבוֹתֵיכֶם מֵעוֹלָם תֶּרַח אֲבִי

אַבְרָהָם וַאֲבִי נָחוֹר וַיַּעַבְדוּ אֱלֹהִים אֲחֵרִים

3 וָאֶקַּח אֶת־אֲבִיכֶם אֶת־אַבְרָהָם מֵעֵבֶר הַנָּהָר

וָאוֹלֵךְ אוֹתוֹ בְּכָל־אֶרֶץ כְּנָעַן וָאֶרֶב [וָ][אַרְבֶּה] אֶת־זַרְעוֹ

וָאֶתֶּן־לוֹ אֶת־יִצְחָק

4 וָאֶתֵּן לְיִצְחָק אֶת־יַעֲקֹב וְאֶת־עֵשָׂו וָאֶתֵּן לְעֵשָׂו

אֶת־הַר שֵׂעִיר לָרֶשֶׁת אוֹתוֹ וְיַעֲקֹב וּבָנָיו יָרְדוּ מִצְרָיִם

Joshua said to all the people, "Thus says Yahweh, the God of Israel, 'From ancient times your fathers lived beyond the River, [namely], Terah, the father of Abraham and the father of Nahor, and they served other gods. Then I took your father Abraham from beyond the River, and led him through all the land of Canaan, and multiplied his descendants and gave him Isaac. To Isaac I gave Jacob and Esau, and to Esau I gave Mount Seir to possess it; but Jacob and his sons went down to Egypt.'"

GENESIS 11:27-32

Gen. 11:27 וְאֵלֶּה תּוֹלְדֹת תֶּרַח תֶּרַח הוֹלִיד אֶת־אַבְרָם אֶת־נָחוֹר

וְאֶת־הָרָן וְהָרָן הוֹלִיד אֶת־לוֹט

Gen. 11:28 וַיָּמָת הָרָן עַל־פְּנֵי תֶּרַח אָבִיו בְּאֶרֶץ מוֹלַדְתּוֹ

בְּאוּר כַּשְׂדִּים

Gen. 11:29 וַיִּקַּח אַבְרָם וְנָחוֹר לָהֶם נָשִׁים שֵׁם

אֵשֶׁת־אַבְרָם שָׂרָי וְשֵׁם אֵשֶׁת־נָחוֹר מִלְכָּה בַּת־הָרָן

אֲבִי־מִלְכָּה וַאֲבִי יִסְכָּה

<u>Gen. 11:30</u> וַתְּהִי שָׂרַי עֲקָרָה אֵין לָהּ וָלָד

<u>Gen. 11:31</u> וַיִּקַּח תֶּרַח אֶת־אַבְרָם בְּנוֹ וְאֶת־לוֹט בֶּן־הָרָן

בֶּן־בְּנוֹ וְאֵת שָׂרַי כַּלָּתוֹ אֵשֶׁת אַבְרָם בְּנוֹ וַיֵּצְאוּ אִתָּם מֵאוּר

כַּשְׂדִּים לָלֶכֶת אַרְצָה כְּנַעַן וַיָּבֹאוּ עַד־חָרָן וַיֵּשְׁבוּ שָׁם

<u>Gen. 11:32</u> וַיִּהְיוּ יְמֵי־תֶרַח חָמֵשׁ שָׁנִים וּמָאתַיִם שָׁנָה

וַיָּמָת תֶּרַח בְּחָרָן

Now these are [the records of] the generations of Terah. Terah became the father of Abram, Nahor and Haran; and Haran became the father of Lot. Haran died in the presence of his father Terah in the land of his birth, in **Ur of the Chaldeans**. Abram and Nahor took wives for themselves. The name of Abram's wife was Sarai; and the name of Nahor's wife was Milcah, the daughter of Haran, the father of Milcah and Iscah. Sarai was barren; she had no child. Terah took Abram his son, and Lot the son of **Haran**, his grandson, and Sarai his daughter-in-law, his son Abram's wife; and they went out together from Ur of the Chaldeans in order to enter the land of Canaan; and they went as far as Haran, and settled there. The days of Terah were two hundred and five years; and Terah died in **Haran**.

B. LAND OF CANAAN

GENESIS 12:1-5

1 וַיֹּאמֶר יְהוָה אֶל־אַבְרָם לֶךְ־לְךָ מֵאַרְצְךָ וּמִמּוֹלַדְתְּךָ

וּמִבֵּית אָבִיךָ אֶל־הָאָרֶץ אֲשֶׁר אַרְאֶךָּ

2 וְאֶעֶשְׂךָ לְגוֹי גָּדוֹל וַאֲבָרֶכְךָ וַאֲגַדְּלָה שְׁמֶךָ וֶהְיֵה בְּרָכָה

3 וַאֲבָרֲכָה מְבָרְכֶיךָ וּמְקַלֶּלְךָ אָאֹר וְנִבְרְכוּ בְךָ כֹּל מִשְׁפְּחֹת הָאֲדָמָה

4 וַיֵּלֶךְ אַבְרָם כַּאֲשֶׁר דִּבֶּר אֵלָיו יְהוָה וַיֵּלֶךְ אִתּוֹ לוֹט וְאַבְרָם בֶּן־חָמֵשׁ שָׁנִים וְשִׁבְעִים שָׁנָה

בְּצֵאתוֹ מֵחָרָן

5 וַיִּקַּח אַבְרָם אֶת־שָׂרַי אִשְׁתּוֹ וְאֶת־לוֹט בֶּן־אָחִיו וְאֶת־כָּל־רְכוּשָׁם אֲשֶׁר רָכָשׁוּ וְאֶת־הַנֶּפֶשׁ אֲשֶׁר־עָשׂוּ

בְחָרָן וַיֵּצְאוּ לָלֶכֶת אַרְצָה כְּנַעַן וַיָּבֹאוּ אַרְצָה כְּנַעַן

Now Yahweh said to Abram, "Go forth from your country, And from your relatives And from your father's house, To the land which I will show you; And I will make you a great nation, And I will bless you, And make your name great; And so you shall be a blessing; And I will bless those who bless And the one who curses you I will curse. And in you all the families of the earth will be blessed." So Abram went forth as Yahweh had spoken to him; and Lot went with him. Now Abram was seventy-five years old when he departed from **Haran**. Abram took Sarai his wife and Lot his nephew, and all their possessions which they had accumulated, and the persons which they had acquired in Haran, and they set out for the land of Canaan; thus they came to **the land of Canaan**.

II.   CENTRAL HILL COUNTRY — AND SOUTHERN STEPPE LAND

A. ABRAHAM

GENESIS 12:1-5

1 וַיֹּאמֶר יְהוָה אֶל־אַבְרָם לֶךְ־לְךָ מֵאַרְצְךָ וּמִמּוֹלַדְתְּךָ וּמִבֵּית אָבִיךָ אֶל־הָאָרֶץ אֲשֶׁר אַרְאֶךָּ

2 וְאֶעֶשְׂךָ לְגוֹי גָּדוֹל וַאֲבָרֶכְךָ וַאֲגַדְּלָה שְׁמֶךָ וֶהְיֵה בְּרָכָה

3 וַאֲבָרֲכָה מְבָרֲכֶיךָ וּמְקַלֶּלְךָ אָאֹר וְנִבְרְכוּ בְךָ כֹּל מִשְׁפְּחֹת הָאֲדָמָה

4 וַיֵּלֶךְ אַבְרָם כַּאֲשֶׁר דִּבֶּר אֵלָיו יְהוָה וַיֵּלֶךְ אִתּוֹ לוֹט וְאַבְרָם בֶּן־חָמֵשׁ שָׁנִים וְשִׁבְעִים שָׁנָה בְּצֵאתוֹ מֵחָרָן

5 וַיִּקַּח אַבְרָם אֶת־שָׂרַי אִשְׁתּוֹ וְאֶת־לוֹט בֶּן־אָחִיו וְאֶת־כָּל־רְכוּשָׁם אֲשֶׁר רָכָשׁוּ וְאֶת־הַנֶּפֶשׁ אֲשֶׁר־עָשׂוּ בְחָרָן וַיֵּצְאוּ לָלֶכֶת אַרְצָה כְּנַעַן וַיָּבֹאוּ אַרְצָה כְּנַעַן

Abram passed through the land as far as the site of **Shechem**, to the **Oak of Moreh**. Now the Canaanite [was] then in the land. Yahweh appeared to Abram and said, "To your descendants I will give this land." So he built an altar there to Yahweh who had appeared to him. Then he proceeded from there to the mountain on the east of **Bethel**, and pitched his tent, with Bethel on the west and Ai on the east; and there he built an altar to Yahweh and called upon the name of Yahweh. Abram journeyed on, continuing toward the **Negeb**. Now there was a famine in the land; so Abram went down to **Egypt** to sojourn there, for the famine was severe in the land.

GENESIS 13:1-7

1 וַיַּעַל אַבְרָם מִמִּצְרַיִם הוּא וְאִשְׁתּוֹ וְכָל־אֲשֶׁר־לוֹ וְלוֹט עִמּוֹ הַנֶּגְבָּה

2 וְאַבְרָם כָּבֵד מְאֹד בַּמִּקְנֶה בַּכֶּסֶף וּבַזָּהָב

3 וַיֵּלֶךְ לְמַסָּעָיו מִנֶּגֶב וְעַד־בֵּית־אֵל עַד־הַמָּקוֹם אֲשֶׁר־הָיָה שָׁם אָהֳלֹה [אָהֳלוֹ] בַּתְּחִלָּה בֵּין בֵּית־אֵל

וּבֵין הָעָי

4 אֶל־מְקוֹם הַמִּזְבֵּחַ אֲשֶׁר־עָשָׂה שָׁם בָּרִאשֹׁנָה וַיִּקְרָא שָׁם אַבְרָם בְּשֵׁם יְהוָה

5 וְגַם־לְלוֹט הַהֹלֵךְ אֶת־אַבְרָם הָיָה צֹאן־וּבָקָר וְאֹהָלִים

6 וְלֹא־נָשָׂא אֹתָם הָאָרֶץ לָשֶׁבֶת יַחְדָּו כִּי־הָיָה רְכוּשָׁם רָב וְלֹא יָכְלוּ לָשֶׁבֶת יַחְדָּו

7 וַיְהִי־רִיב בֵּין רֹעֵי מִקְנֵה־אַבְרָם וּבֵין רֹעֵי מִקְנֵה־לוֹט וְהַכְּנַעֲנִי וְהַפְּרִזִּי אָז יֹשֵׁב בָּאָרֶץ

So Abram went up from Egypt to the Negev, he and his wife and all that belonged to him, and Lot with him. Now Abram was very rich in livestock, in silver and in gold. He went on his journeys from the Negev as far as Bethel, to the place where his tent had been at the beginning, between Bethel and Ai, to the place of the altar which he had made there formerly; and there Abram called on the name of Yahweh. Now Lot, who went with Abram, also had flocks and herds and tents. And the land could not sustain them while dwelling together, for their possessions were so great that they were not able to remain together. And there was strife between the herdsmen of Abram's livestock and the herdsmen of Lot's livestock. Now the Canaanite and the Perizzite were dwelling then in the land. So Abram said to Lot, "Please let there be no strife between you and me, nor between my herdsmen and your herdsmen, for we are brothers. "Is not the whole land before you? Please separate from me; if [to] the left, then I will go to the right; or if [to] the right, then I will go to the left." Lot lifted up his eyes and saw all the valley of the Jordan, that it was well watered everywhere —[this was] before Yahweh destroyed Sodom and Gomorrah — like the garden of Yahweh, like the land of Egypt as you go to Zoar. So Lot chose for himself all the valley of the Jordan, and Lot journeyed eastward. Thus they separated from each other. Abram settled in the land of Canaan, while Lot settled in the cities of the valley, and moved his tents as far as Sodom.

GENESIS 13:18

וַיֶּאֱהַל אַבְרָם וַיָּבֹא וַיֵּשֶׁב בְּאֵלֹנֵי מַמְרֵא אֲשֶׁר בְּחֶבְרוֹן וַיִּבֶן־שָׁם מִזְבֵּחַ לַיהוָה

Then Abram moved his tent and came and dwelt by the oaks of Mamre, which are in Hebron, and there he built an altar to Yahweh.

GENESIS 14:13

וַיָּבֹא הַפָּלִיט וַיַּגֵּד לְאַבְרָם הָעִבְרִי וְהוּא שֹׁכֵן בְּאֵלֹנֵי מַמְרֵא הָאֱמֹרִי אֲחִי אֶשְׁכֹּל וַאֲחִי עָנֵר וְהֵם בַּעֲלֵי

בְּרִית־אַבְרָם

Then a fugitive came and told Abram the Hebrew. Now he was living by the oaks of Mamre the Amorite, brother of Eshcol and brother of Aner, and these were allies with Abram.

GENESIS 20:1

וַיִּסַּע מִשָּׁם אַבְרָהָם אַרְצָה הַנֶּגֶב וַיֵּשֶׁב בֵּין־קָדֵשׁ וּבֵין שׁוּר וַיָּגָר בִּגְרָר

Now Abraham journeyed from there toward the land of the Negeb, and settled between Kadesh and Shur; then he sojourned in Gerar.

GENESIS 22:2

וַיֹּאמֶר קַח־נָא אֶת־בִּנְךָ אֶת־יְחִידְךָ אֲשֶׁר־אָהַבְתָּ אֶת־יִצְחָק וְלֶךְ־לְךָ אֶל־אֶרֶץ הַמֹּרִיָּה וְהַעֲלֵהוּ

שָׁם לְעֹלָה עַל אַחַד הֶהָרִים אֲשֶׁר אֹמַר אֵלֶיךָ

He said, "Take now your son, your only son, whom you love, Isaac, and go to the land of **Moriah**, and offer him there as a burnt offering on one of the mountains of which I will tell you."

GENESIS 22:19

וַיָּשָׁב אַבְרָהָם אֶל־נְעָרָיו וַיָּקֻמוּ וַיֵּלְכוּ יַחְדָּו אֶל־בְּאֵר

שָׁבַע וַיֵּשֶׁב אַבְרָהָם בִּבְאֵר שָׁבַע

So Abraham returned to his young men, and they arose and went together to Beersheba; and Abraham lived at **Beersheba**.

B.   ISAAC (Gen. 21-27)

GENESIS 26:1-33

<u>1</u> וַיְהִי רָעָב בָּאָרֶץ מִלְּבַד הָרָעָב הָרִאשׁוֹן אֲשֶׁר הָיָה בִּימֵי

אַבְרָהָם וַיֵּלֶךְ יִצְחָק אֶל־אֲבִימֶלֶךְ מֶלֶךְ־פְּלִשְׁתִּים גְּרָרָה

<u>2</u> וַיֵּרָא אֵלָיו יְהוָה וַיֹּאמֶר אַל־תֵּרֵד מִצְרָיְמָה שְׁכֹן בָּאָרֶץ אֲשֶׁר אֹמַר אֵלֶיךָ

<u>3</u> גּוּר בָּאָרֶץ הַזֹּאת וְאֶהְיֶה עִמְּךָ וַאֲבָרְכֶךָּ כִּי־לְךָ וּלְזַרְעֲךָ אֶתֵּן אֶת־כָּל־הָאֲרָצֹת הָאֵל וַהֲקִמֹתִי

אֶת־הַשְּׁבֻעָה אֲשֶׁר נִשְׁבַּעְתִּי לְאַבְרָהָם אָבִיךָ

<u>4</u> וְהִרְבֵּיתִי אֶת־זַרְעֲךָ כְּכוֹכְבֵי הַשָּׁמַיִם וְנָתַתִּי לְזַרְעֲךָ אֵת כָּל־הָאֲרָצֹת הָאֵל וְהִתְבָּרֲכוּ בְזַרְעֲךָ כֹּל גּוֹיֵי הָאָרֶץ

<u>5</u> עֵקֶב אֲשֶׁר־שָׁמַע אַבְרָהָם בְּקֹלִי וַיִּשְׁמֹר מִשְׁמַרְתִּי מִצְוֹתַי חֻקּוֹתַי וְתוֹרֹתָי

<u>6</u> וַיֵּשֶׁב יִצְחָק בִּגְרָר

<u>7</u> וַיִּשְׁאֲלוּ אַנְשֵׁי הַמָּקוֹם לְאִשְׁתּוֹ וַיֹּאמֶר אֲחֹתִי הִוא כִּי יָרֵא לֵאמֹר אִשְׁתִּי פֶּן־יַהַרְגֻנִי אַנְשֵׁי הַמָּקוֹם

עַל־רִבְקָה כִּי־טוֹבַת מַרְאֶה הִיא

<u>8</u> וַיְהִי כִּי אָרְכוּ־לוֹ שָׁם הַיָּמִים וַיַּשְׁקֵף אֲבִימֶלֶךְ מֶלֶךְ פְּלִשְׁתִּים בְּעַד הַחַלּוֹן וַיַּרְא וְהִנֵּה יִצְחָק

מְצַחֵק אֵת רִבְקָה אִשְׁתּוֹ

<u>9</u> וַיִּקְרָא אֲבִימֶלֶךְ לְיִצְחָק וַיֹּאמֶר אַךְ הִנֵּה אִשְׁתְּךָ הִוא וְאֵיךְ אָמַרְתָּ אֲחֹתִי הִוא

וַיֹּאמֶר אֵלָיו יִצְחָק כִּי אָמַרְתִּי פֶּן־אָמוּת עָלֶיהָ

<u>10</u> וַיֹּאמֶר אֲבִימֶלֶךְ מַה־זֹּאת עָשִׂיתָ לָּנוּ כִּמְעַט שָׁכַב אַחַד הָעָם אֶת־אִשְׁתֶּךָ וְהֵבֵאתָ עָלֵינוּ אָשָׁם

<u>Gen. 26:11</u> וַיְצַו אֲבִימֶלֶךְ אֶת־כָּל־הָעָם לֵאמֹר הַנֹּגֵעַ

בָּאִישׁ הַזֶּה וּבְאִשְׁתּוֹ מוֹת יוּמָת

<u>12</u> וַיִּזְרַע יִצְחָק בָּאָרֶץ הַהִוא וַיִּמְצָא בַּשָּׁנָה הַהִוא מֵאָה שְׁעָרִים וַיְבָרֲכֵהוּ יְהוָה

<u>13</u> וַיִּגְדַּל הָאִישׁ וַיֵּלֶךְ הָלוֹךְ וְגָדֵל עַד כִּי־גָדַל מְאֹד

<u>14</u> וַיְהִי־לוֹ מִקְנֵה־צֹאן וּמִקְנֵה בָקָר וַעֲבֻדָּה רַבָּה וַיְקַנְאוּ אֹתוֹ פְּלִשְׁתִּים

<u>15</u> וְכָל־הַבְּאֵרֹת אֲשֶׁר חָפְרוּ עַבְדֵי אָבִיו בִּימֵי אַבְרָהָם אָבִיו סִתְּמוּם פְּלִשְׁתִּים וַיְמַלְאוּם עָפָר

<u>16</u> וַיֹּאמֶר אֲבִימֶלֶךְ אֶל־יִצְחָק לֵךְ מֵעִמָּנוּ כִּי־עָצַמְתָּ מִמֶּנּוּ מְאֹד

<u>17</u> וַיֵּלֶךְ מִשָּׁם יִצְחָק וַיִּחַן בְּנַחַל־גְּרָר וַיֵּשֶׁב שָׁם

<u>18</u> וַיָּשָׁב יִצְחָק וַיַּחְפֹּר אֶת־בְּאֵרֹת הַמַּיִם אֲשֶׁר

חָפְרוּ בִּימֵי אַבְרָהָם אָבִיו וַיְסַתְּמוּם פְּלִשְׁתִּים אַחֲרֵי מוֹת

אַבְרָהָם וַיִּקְרָא לָהֶן שֵׁמוֹת כַּשֵּׁמֹת אֲשֶׁר־קָרָא לָהֶן אָבִיו

<u>19</u> וַיַּחְפְּרוּ עַבְדֵי־יִצְחָק בַּנָּחַל וַיִּמְצְאוּ־שָׁם בְּאֵר מַיִם חַיִּים

<u>20</u> וַיָּרִיבוּ רֹעֵי גְרָר עִם־רֹעֵי יִצְחָק לֵאמֹר לָנוּ

הַמַּיִם וַיִּקְרָא שֵׁם־הַבְּאֵר עֵשֶׂק כִּי הִתְעַשְּׂקוּ עִמּוֹ

<u>21</u> וַיַּחְפְּרוּ בְּאֵר אַחֶרֶת וַיָּרִיבוּ גַּם־עָלֶיהָ וַיִּקְרָא שְׁמָהּ שִׂטְנָה

<u>22</u> וַיַּעְתֵּק מִשָּׁם וַיַּחְפֹּר בְּאֵר אַחֶרֶת וְלֹא רָבוּ

עָלֶיהָ וַיִּקְרָא שְׁמָהּ רְחֹבוֹת וַיֹּאמֶר כִּי־עַתָּה הִרְחִיב יְהוָה לָנוּ וּפָרִינוּ בָאָרֶץ

<u>Gen. 26:23</u> וַיַּעַל מִשָּׁם בְּאֵר שָׁבַע

<u>24</u> וַיֵּרָא אֵלָיו יְהוָה בַּלַּיְלָה הַהוּא וַיֹּאמֶר אָנֹכִי

אֱלֹהֵי אַבְרָהָם אָבִיךָ אַל־תִּירָא כִּי־אִתְּךָ אָנֹכִי וּבֵרַכְתִּיךָ

וְהִרְבֵּיתִי אֶת־זַרְעֲךָ בַּעֲבוּר אַבְרָהָם עַבְדִּי

<u>25</u> וַיִּבֶן שָׁם מִזְבֵּחַ וַיִּקְרָא בְּשֵׁם יְהוָה וַיֶּט־שָׁם

אָהֳלוֹ וַיִּכְרוּ־שָׁם עַבְדֵי־יִצְחָק בְּאֵר

<u>26</u> וַאֲבִימֶלֶךְ הָלַךְ אֵלָיו מִגְּרָר וַאֲחֻזַּת מֵרֵעֵהוּ וּפִיכֹל שַׂר־צְבָאוֹ

<u>27</u> וַיֹּאמֶר אֲלֵהֶם יִצְחָק מַדּוּעַ בָּאתֶם אֵלָי וְאַתֶּם

שְׂנֵאתֶם אֹתִי וַתְּשַׁלְּחוּנִי מֵאִתְּכֶם

<u>28</u> וַיֹּאמְרוּ רָאוֹ רָאִינוּ כִּי־הָיָה יְהוָה עִמָּךְ וַנֹּאמֶר

תְּהִי נָא אָלָה בֵּינוֹתֵינוּ בֵּינֵינוּ וּבֵינֶךָ וְנִכְרְתָה בְרִית עִמָּךְ

<u>29</u> אִם־תַּעֲשֵׂה עִמָּנוּ רָעָה כַּאֲשֶׁר לֹא נְגַעֲנוּךָ

וְכַאֲשֶׁר עָשִׂינוּ עִמְּךָ רַק־טוֹב וַנְּשַׁלֵּחֲךָ בְּשָׁלוֹם אַתָּה עַתָּה בְּרוּךְ יְהוָה

<u>30</u> וַיַּעַשׂ לָהֶם מִשְׁתֶּה וַיֹּאכְלוּ וַיִּשְׁתּוּ

<u>31</u> וַיַּשְׁכִּימוּ בַבֹּקֶר וַיִּשָּׁבְעוּ אִישׁ לְאָחִיו וַיְשַׁלְּחֵם

יִצְחָק וַיֵּלְכוּ מֵאִתּוֹ בְּשָׁלוֹם

32 וַיְהִי בַּיּוֹם הַהוּא וַיָּבֹאוּ עַבְדֵי יִצְחָק וַיַּגִּדוּ לוֹ

עַל־אֹדוֹת הַבְּאֵר אֲשֶׁר חָפָרוּ וַיֹּאמְרוּ לוֹ מָצָאנוּ מָיִם

33 וַיִּקְרָא אֹתָהּ שִׁבְעָה עַל־כֵּן שֵׁם־הָעִיר בְּאֵר שֶׁבַע עַד הַיּוֹם הַזֶּה

Now there was a famine in the land, besides the previous famine that had occurred in the days of Abraham. So Isaac went to Gerar, to Abimelech king of the Philistines.

Yahweh appeared to him and said, "Do not go down to Egypt; stay in the land of which I shall tell you. Sojourn in this land and I will be with you and bless you, for to you and to your descendants I will give all these lands, and I will establish the oath which I swore to your father Abraham. I will multiply your descendants as the stars of heaven, and will give your descendants all these lands; and by your descendants all the nations of the earth shall be blessed; because Abraham obeyed Me and kept My charge, My commandments, My statutes and My laws."

So Isaac lived in **Gerar**.

When the men of the place asked about his wife, he said, "She is my sister," for he was afraid to say, "my wife," [thinking], "the men of the place might kill me on account of Rebekah, for she is beautiful."

It came about, when he had been there a long time, that Abimelech king of the Philistines **looked out through a window**, and saw, and behold, Isaac was caressing his wife Rebekah. Then Abimelech called Isaac and said, "Behold, certainly she is your wife! How then did you say, 'She is my sister'?" And Isaac said to him, "Because I said, 'I might die on account of her.'" Abimelech said, "What is this you have done to us? One of the people might easily have lain with your wife, and you would have brought guilt upon us." So Abimelech charged all the people, saying, "He who touches this man or his wife shall surely be put to death."

Now Isaac sowed in that land and reaped in the same year a hundredfold. And Yahweh blessed him, and the man became rich, and continued to grow richer until he became very wealthy; for he had possessions of flocks and herds and a great household, so that the Philistines envied him.

> Now all the wells which his father's servants had dug in the days of Abraham his father, the Philistines stopped up by filling them with earth.

Then Abimelech said to Isaac, "Go away from us, for you are too powerful for us." And Isaac departed from there and camped in the **valley of Gerar**, and settled there. Then Isaac dug again the wells of water which had been dug in the days of his father Abraham, for the Philistines had stopped them up after the death of Abraham; and he gave them the same names which his father had given them. But when Isaac's servants dug in the valley and found there a well of flowing water, the herdsmen of Gerar quarreled with the herdsmen of Isaac, saying, "The water is ours!" So he named the well **Esek**, because they contended with him. Then they dug another well, and they quarreled over it too, so he named it **Sitnah**. He moved away from there and dug another well, and they did not quarrel over it; so he named it **Rehoboth**, for he said, "At last Yahweh has made room for us, and we will be fruitful in the land."

Then he went up from there to **Beersheba**.

Yahweh appeared to him the same night and said, "I am the God of your father Abraham; Do not fear, for I am with you. I will bless you, and multiply your descendants, For the sake of My servant Abraham." So he built an altar there and called upon the name of Yahweh, and pitched his tent there; and there Isaac's servants dug a well. Then Abimelech came to him from **Gerar** with his adviser Ahuzzath and Phicol the commander of his army. Isaac said to them, "Why have you come to me, since you hate me and have sent me away from you?" They said, "We see plainly that Yahweh has been with you; so we said, ʿLet there now be an oath between us, [even] between you and us, and let us make a covenant with you, that you will do us no harm, just as we have not touched you and have done to you nothing but good and have sent you away in peace. You are now the blessed of Yahweh.'" Then he made them a feast, and they ate and drank. In the morning they arose early and exchanged oaths; then Isaac sent them away and they departed from him in peace. Now it came about on the same day, that Isaac's servants came in and told him about the well which they had dug, and said to him, "We have found water." So he called it Shibʿah; therefore the name of the city is **Beersheba**ᶜ to this day.

C.   JUDAH

GENESIS 38:1, 12-14

1 וַיְהִי בָּעֵת הַהִוא וַיֵּרֶד יְהוּדָה מֵאֵת אֶחָיו וַיֵּט עַד־אִישׁ עֲדֻלָּמִי וּשְׁמוֹ חִירָה

12 וַיִּרְבּוּ הַיָּמִים וַתָּמָת בַּת־שׁוּעַ אֵשֶׁת־יְהוּדָה וַיִּנָּחֶם יְהוּדָה וַיַּעַל עַל־גֹּזְזֵי צֹאנוֹ הוּא וְחִירָה רֵעֵהוּ הָעֲדֻלָּמִי תִּמְנָתָה

13 וַיֻּגַּד לְתָמָר לֵאמֹר הִנֵּה חָמִיךְ עֹלֶה תִמְנָתָה לָגֹז צֹאנוֹ

14 וַתָּסַר בִּגְדֵי אַלְמְנוּתָהּ מֵעָלֶיהָ וַתְּכַס בַּצָּעִיף וַתִּתְעַלָּף וַתֵּשֶׁב בְּפֶתַח עֵינַיִם אֲשֶׁר עַל־דֶּרֶךְ תִּמְנָתָה כִּי רָאֲתָה כִּי־גָדַל שֵׁלָה וְהִוא לֹא־נִתְּנָה לוֹ לְאִשָּׁה

And it came about at that time, that Judah departed from his brothers and visited a certain **Adullamite**, whose name was Hirah . . . .
Now after a considerable time Shua's daughter, the wife of Judah, died; and when the time of mourning was ended, Judah went up to his sheepshearers at **Timnah**, he and his friend Hirah the Adullamite. It was told to Tamar, "Behold, your father-in-law is going up to Timnah to shear his sheep." So she removed her widow's garments and covered [herself] with a veil, and wrapped herself, and sat in the gateway of Enaim, which is on the road to Timnah; for she saw that Shelah had grown up, and she had not been given to him as a wife.

D. JACOB'S SONS

GENESIS 37:1, *et al.*

1 וַיֵּשֶׁב יַעֲקֹב בְּאֶרֶץ מְגוּרֵי אָבִיו בְּאֶרֶץ כְּנָעַן

2 אֵלֶּה תֹּלְדוֹת יַעֲקֹב יוֹסֵף בֶּן־שְׁבַע־עֶשְׂרֵה שָׁנָה הָיָה רֹעֶה אֶת־אֶחָיו בַּצֹּאן וְהוּא נַעַר אֶת־בְּנֵי בִלְהָה

אֶת־אֶחָיו בַּצֹּאן וְהוּא נַעַר אֶת־בְּנֵי בִלְהָה וְאֶת־בְּנֵי זִלְפָּה נְשֵׁי אָבִיו וַיָּבֵא יוֹסֵף אֶת־דִּבָּתָם רָעָה

אֶל־אֲבִיהֶם

Now Jacob lived in the land where his father had sojourned, in the land of
Canaan. These are [the records of] the generations of Jacob. Joseph, when
seventeen years of age, was pasturing the flock with his brothers while he was
[still] a youth, along with the sons of Bilhah and the sons of Zilpah, his father's
wives. And Joseph brought back a bad report about them to their father.

12 וַיֵּלְכוּ אֶחָיו לִרְעוֹת אֶת־צֹאן אֲבִיהֶם בִּשְׁכֶם

13 וַיֹּאמֶר יִשְׂרָאֵל אֶל־יוֹסֵף הֲלוֹא אַחֶיךָ רֹעִים בִּשְׁכֶם לְכָה

וְאֶשְׁלָחֲךָ אֲלֵיהֶם וַיֹּאמֶר לוֹ הִנֵּנִי

14 וַיֹּאמֶר לוֹ לֶךְ־נָא רְאֵה אֶת־שְׁלוֹם אַחֶיךָ

וְאֶת־שְׁלוֹם הַצֹּאן וַהֲשִׁבֵנִי דָּבָר וַיִּשְׁלָחֵהוּ מֵעֵמֶק חֶבְרוֹן

וַיָּבֹא שְׁכֶמָה

15 וַיִּמְצָאֵהוּ אִישׁ וְהִנֵּה תֹעֶה בַּשָּׂדֶה וַיִּשְׁאָלֵהוּ

הָאִישׁ לֵאמֹר מַה־תְּבַקֵּשׁ

16 וַיֹּאמֶר אֶת־אַחַי אָנֹכִי מְבַקֵּשׁ הַגִּידָה־נָּא לִי

אֵיפֹה הֵם רֹעִים

17 וַיֹּאמֶר הָאִישׁ נָסְעוּ מִזֶּה כִּי שָׁמַעְתִּי אֹמְרִים

נֵלְכָה דֹּתָיְנָה וַיֵּלֶךְ יוֹסֵף אַחַר אֶחָיו וַיִּמְצָאֵם בְּדֹתָן

Then his brothers went to pasture their father's flock in **Shechem**. Israel said
to Joseph, "Are not your brothers pasturing [the flock] in Shechem? Come,
and I will send you to them." And he said to him, "I will go." Then he said to
him, "Go now and see about the welfare of your brothers and the welfare of
the flock, and bring word back to me." So he sent him from the valley of

Hebron, and he came to Shechem. A man found him, and behold, he was wandering in the field; and the man asked him, "What are you looking for?" He said, "I am looking for my brothers; please tell me where they are pasturing [the flock]." Then the man said, "They have moved from here; for I heard [them] say, 'Let us go to **Dothan**.'" So Joseph went after his brothers and found them at Dothan.

25 וַיֵּשְׁבוּ לֶאֱכָל־לֶחֶם וַיִּשְׂאוּ עֵינֵיהֶם וַיִּרְאוּ וְהִנֵּה אֹרְחַת

יִשְׁמְעֵאלִים בָּאָה מִגִּלְעָד וּגְמַלֵּיהֶם נֹשְׂאִים נְכֹאת וּצְרִי

וָלֹט הוֹלְכִים לְהוֹרִיד מִצְרָיְמָה

ladanum resin from the cistus rose = נְכֹאת

"balm", mastic, resin of *Pistacia mutica* = צְרִי·

the bark of *Pistacia mutica* = לֹט

And behold, a caravan of Ishmaelites was coming from **Gilead**, with their camels bearing *ladanum* resin (from the cistus rose = נְכֹאת) and balm (resin of *Pistacia mutica* = צְרִי) and the bark of *Pistacia mutica* (=לֹט), on their way to bring [them] down to **Egypt**.

II.   DOWN TO EGYPT — Background

A. Shosu

1. Seti I,

campaign in Canaan (1291 B.C.E.) — texts on the north outer wall of the Hypostyle Hall, Karnak

Year 1 of the renewal, and of the King of Upper and Lower Egypt, Lord of the two lands: Men-maat-Re, given life. One came to bring word to his majesty: "The foe belonging to the Shosu are plotting rebellion. Their chiefs are gathered in one place, on the mountain ridges of Khurru. They have taken to clamoring and quarreling, one of them killing his fellow. They have no regard for the laws of the palace."

Year 1 of the King of Upper and Lower Egypt: Men-maat-Re. The desolation which the mighty arm of Pharaoh —life, prosperity, health!—made among the foe belonging to Shosu from the fortress of Sillû to the Canaan. His majesty [pre]vailed over them like a fierce lion. They were made into corpses throughout their valleys, stretched out in their (own) blood, like that which has never been.

The return [of] his majesty from Upper Retenu, having extended the frontiers of Egypt.

The plunder which his majesty carried off from these Shosu, whom his majesty himself captured in the year 1 of the Renewal.

2. Merneptah

Papyrus Anastasi VI

We have completed the transfer of the Shosu tribes past the fortress of Merneptah-ḥotep-ḥer-Maat . . . which is in Sekû (Succoth) to the pools(sic!) of Per-Atum (Pithom) of Merneptah-ḥotep-ḥer-Maat . . . which are in Sekî, in order to keep them alive and in order to keep their cattle alive.

Poem in the Victory Stele of Merneptah

The princes lie prostrate, saying: "Peace";
NOT ONE RAISES HIS HEAD AMONG THE NINE BOWS;
Desolation is for Tehenu; Hatti is pacified;
Plundered is the Canaan with every evil;
Carried off is **Ashkelon**;
seized upon is **Gezer**;
Yanoam is as that which does not
exist;
Israel is laid waste, his fruit is not;
Ḫurru is become a widow for Egypt!
All lands together, they are pacified;
EVERYONE WHO WAS RESTLESS, HE HAS BEEN BOUND
by the king of Upper and Lower Egypt: Ba-en-Re Meri-Amon; the Son of Re: Merneptah, Ḥotep-ḥer-Maat, given life like Re everyday.

CAPTION ON MERNEPTAH'S RELIEF ON OUTSIDE WALL SOUTH OF KARNAK

The wretched town which his majesty seized when it was rebellious, **Ashkelon**.

B. GEOGRAPHY (cf. Bietak's map)

1. **Goshen** — Gen. 46:28-29, 34; 47:3-6 — = *Faqûs*

28 וְאֶת־יְהוּדָה שָׁלַח לְפָנָיו אֶל־יוֹסֵף לְהוֹרֹת לְפָנָיו גֹּשְׁנָה וַיָּבֹאוּ אַרְצָה גֹּשֶׁן

29 וַיֶּאְסֹר יוֹסֵף מֶרְכַּבְתּוֹ וַיַּעַל לִקְרַאת־יִשְׂרָאֵל אָבִיו גֹּשְׁנָה וַיֵּרָא אֵלָיו וַיִּפֹּל עַל־צַוָּארָיו

וַיֵּבְךְּ עַל־צַוָּארָיו עוֹד:

Now he sent Judah before him to Joseph, to point out [the way] before him to **Goshen**; and they came into the land of Goshen. Joseph prepared his chariot and went up to Goshen to meet his father Israel; as soon as he appeared before him, he fell on his neck and wept on his neck a long time.

34 וַאֲמַרְתֶּם אַנְשֵׁי מִקְנֶה הָיוּ עֲבָדֶיךָ מִנְּעוּרֵינוּ וְעַד־עַתָּה גַּם־אֲנַחְנוּ גַּם־אֲבֹתֵינוּ בַּעֲבוּר תֵּשְׁבוּ

בְּאֶרֶץ גֹּשֶׁן כִּי־תוֹעֲבַת מִצְרַיִם כָּל־רֹעֵה צֹאן

You shall say, "Your servants have been keepers of livestock from our youth even until now, both we and our fathers," that you may live in the land of Goshen; for every shepherd is loathsome to the Egyptians.

Gen. 47:3 וַיֹּאמֶר פַּרְעֹה אֶל־אֶחָיו מַה־מַּעֲשֵׂיכֶם וַיֹּאמְרוּ אֶל־פַּרְעֹה רֹעֵה צֹאן עֲבָדֶיךָ

גַּם־אֲנַחְנוּ גַּם־אֲבוֹתֵינוּ 4 וַיֹּאמְרוּ אֶל־פַּרְעֹה לָגוּר בָּאָרֶץ בָּאנוּ כִּי־אֵין מִרְעֶה לַצֹּאן

אֲשֶׁר לַעֲבָדֶיךָ כִּי־כָבֵד הָרָעָב בְּאֶרֶץ כְּנָעַן וְעַתָּה יֵשְׁבוּ־נָא עֲבָדֶיךָ בְּאֶרֶץ גֹּשֶׁן

5 וַיֹּאמֶר פַּרְעֹה אֶל־יוֹסֵף לֵאמֹר אָבִיךָ וְאַחֶיךָ בָּאוּ אֵלֶיךָ 6 אֶרֶץ מִצְרַיִם לְפָנֶיךָ

הִוא בְּמֵיטַב הָאָרֶץ הוֹשֵׁב אֶת־אָבִיךָ וְאֶת־אַחֶיךָ יֵשְׁבוּ בְּאֶרֶץ גֹּשֶׁן וְאִם־יָדַעְתָּ וְיֶשׁ־בָּם

אַנְשֵׁי־חַיִל וְשַׂמְתָּם שָׂרֵי מִקְנֶה עַל־אֲשֶׁר־לִי

Then Pharaoh said to his brothers, "What is your occupation?" So they said to Pharaoh, "Your servants are **shepherds**, both we and our fathers."

They said to Pharaoh, "We have come to sojourn in the land, for there is no pasture for your servants' flocks, for the famine is severe in the land of Canaan. Now, therefore, please let your servants live in the land of **Goshen**."

Then Pharaoh said to Joseph, "Your father and your brothers have come to you. The land of Egypt is at your disposal; settle your father and your brothers in the best of the land, let them live in the land of **Goshen**; and if

you know any capable men among them, then put them in charge of my
livestock"

2. **Ramses** and **Pithom**

Gen. 47:11

Gen. 47:11 וַיּוֹשֵׁב יוֹסֵף אֶת־אָבִיו וְאֶת־אֶחָיו וַיִּתֵּן לָהֶם אֲחֻזָּה בְּאֶרֶץ מִצְרַיִם בְּמֵיטַב הָאָרֶץ

בְּאֶרֶץ רַעְמְסֵס כַּאֲשֶׁר צִוָּה פַרְעֹה

So Joseph settled his father and his brothers and gave them a possession in
the land of Egypt, in the best of the land, in the land of **Rameses**, as Pharaoh
had ordered.

Exod. 1:11

11 וַיָּשִׂימוּ עָלָיו שָׂרֵי מִסִּים לְמַעַן עַנֹּתוֹ בְּסִבְלֹתָם וַיִּבֶן עָרֵי מִסְכְּנוֹת לְפַרְעֹה אֶת־פִּתֹם וְאֶת־רַעַמְסֵס

So they appointed taskmasters over them to afflict them with hard labor. And
they built for Pharaoh store cities, **Pithom** and **Raamses**.

III.　　ROUTE OF THE EXODUS

A. <u>WAY</u> <u>OF</u> <u>THE</u> <u>LAND</u> <u>OF</u> <u>THE</u> <u>PHILISTINES</u>
NOT TAKEN

Exod. 13:17

<u>Ex. 13:17</u> וַיְהִי בְּשַׁלַּח פַּרְעֹה אֶת־הָעָם וְלֹא־נָחָם אֱלֹהִים דֶּרֶךְ אֶרֶץ פְּלִשְׁתִּים כִּי קָרוֹב הוּא

כִּי אָמַר אֱלֹהִים פֶּן־יִנָּחֵם הָעָם בִּרְאֹתָם מִלְחָמָה וְשָׁבוּ מִצְרָיְמָה

Now when Pharaoh had let the people go, God did not lead them by the **way
of the land of the Philistines**, even though it was near; for God said, "The
people might change their minds when they see war, and return to Egypt."

B. <u>WAY</u> <u>OF</u> <u>THE</u> <u>WILDERNESS</u>

Exod. 13:18

<u>18</u> וַיַּסֵּב אֱלֹהִים אֶת־הָעָם דֶּרֶךְ הַמִּדְבָּר יַם־סוּף וַחֲמֻשִׁים עָלוּ בְנֵי־יִשְׂרָאֵל מֵאֶרֶץ מִצְרָיִם

Hence God led the people around by the **way of the wilderness** to the Reed
Sea; and the sons of Israel went up in martial array from the land of Egypt.

C. <u>THE</u> <u>STATIONS</u> — to Sinai

Exod. 13:19-14:9 — leaving Egypt

<u>13:20</u> וַיִּסְעוּ מִסֻּכֹּת וַיַּחֲנוּ בְאֵתָם בִּקְצֵה הַמִּדְבָּר

Then they set out from **Succoth** and camped in **Etham** on the edge of the
wilderness.

<u>Ex. 14:1</u> וַיְדַבֵּר יְהוָֹה אֶל־מֹשֶׁה לֵּאמֹר <u>2</u> דַּבֵּר אֶל־בְּנֵי יִשְׂרָאֵל וְיָשֻׁבוּ וְיַחֲנוּ לִפְנֵי פִּי

הַחִירֹת בֵּין מִגְדֹּל וּבֵין הַיָּם לִפְנֵי בַּעַל צְפֹן נִכְחוֹ תַחֲנוּ עַל־הַיָּם

Now Yahweh spoke to Moses, saying, "Tell the sons of Israel to turn back and
camp before **Pi-haḥiroth**, between **Migdol** and the sea; you shall camp in
front of **Baal-zephon**, opposite it, by the sea."

<u>Ex. 14:9</u> וַיִּרְדְּפוּ מִצְרַיִם אַחֲרֵיהֶם וַיַּשִּׂיגוּ אוֹתָם חֹנִים עַל־הַיָּם כָּל־סוּס רֶכֶב פַּרְעֹה וּפָרָשָׁיו וְחֵילוֹ

עַל־פִּי הַחִירֹת לִפְנֵי בַּעַל צְפֹן

Then the Egyptians chased after them [with] all the horses [and] chariots of
Pharaoh, his horsemen and his army, and they overtook them camping by
the sea, beside **Pi-haḥiroth**, in front of **Baal-zephon**.

KAI No. 50 — Papyrus from Saqqârah in Phoenician:

. אל ארשת בת אשמני[תנ] / אמר . לאחתי . ארשת
אמר .אחתכ. בשא . ושלמ את . אפ אנכ . שלמ . ברכתכ
. לב/על צפנ ולכל אל . תחפנחס יפעלכ . שלמ

To ʾIrist, daughter of ʾAshmun-ya[tan]; speak to my sister, ʾIrist, the word of
your sister, Basha: So are you well? I am well. I bless you to Baal-Zephon, and
may all the gods of Taḥpanes strive for your welfare . . . .

Exod. 15:22-19:2

<u>Ex. 15:22</u> וַיַּסַּע מֹשֶׁה אֶת־יִשְׂרָאֵל מִיַּם־סוּף וַיֵּצְאוּ אֶל־מִדְבַּר־שׁוּר וַיֵּלְכוּ שְׁלֹשֶׁת־יָמִים בַּמִּדְבָּר
וְלֹא־מָצְאוּ מָיִם

Then Moses led Israel from the **Reed Sea**, and they went out into the
wilderness of Shur; and they went three days in the wilderness and found
no water.

<u>Ex. 15:23</u> וַיָּבֹאוּ מָרָתָה וְלֹא יָכְלוּ לִשְׁתֹּת מַיִם מִמָּרָה כִּי מָרִים הֵם עַל־כֵּן קָרָא־שְׁמָהּ מָרָה
When they came to **Marah**, they could not drink the waters of Marah, for
they were bitter; therefore it was named Marah (Bitter).

<u>Ex. 15:27</u> וַיָּבֹאוּ אֵילִמָה וְשָׁם שְׁתֵּים עֶשְׂרֵה עֵינֹת מַיִם וְשִׁבְעִים תְּמָרִים וַיַּחֲנוּ־שָׁם עַל־הַמָּיִם
Then they came to **Elim** (= Terebinths) where there [were] twelve springs of
water and seventy date palms, and they camped there beside the waters.

<u>Ex. 16:1</u> וַיִּסְעוּ מֵאֵילִם וַיָּבֹאוּ כָּל־עֲדַת בְּנֵי־יִשְׂרָאֵל אֶל־מִדְבַּר־סִין אֲשֶׁר בֵּין־אֵילִם וּבֵין סִינָי
בַּחֲמִשָּׁה עָשָׂר יוֹם לַחֹדֶשׁ הַשֵּׁנִי לְצֵאתָם מֵאֶרֶץ מִצְרָיִם

Then they set out from Elim, and all the congregation of the sons of Israel
came to the **wilderness of Sin**, which is between Elim and Sinai, on the
fifteenth day of the second month after their departure from the land of
Egypt.

<u>Ex. 17:1</u> וַיִּסְעוּ כָּל־עֲדַת בְּנֵי־יִשְׂרָאֵל מִמִּדְבַּר־סִין לְמַסְעֵיהֶם עַל־פִּי יְהוָה וַיַּחֲנוּ בִּרְפִידִים

וְאֵין מַיִם לִשְׁתֹּת הָעָם

Then all the congregation of the sons of Israel journeyed by stages from the wilderness of Sin, according to the command of Yahweh, and camped at **Rephidim**, and there was no water for the people to drink.

Ex. 19:1 בַּחֹדֶשׁ הַשְּׁלִישִׁי לְצֵאת בְּנֵי־יִשְׂרָאֵל מֵאֶרֶץ מִצְרָיִם בַּיּוֹם הַזֶּה בָּאוּ מִדְבַּר סִינָי

In the third month after the sons of Israel had gone out of the land of Egypt, on that very day they came into the **wilderness of Sinai.**

Num. 33:1-15 — **Itinerary** from Ramesses to Sinai

Num. 33:1 אֵלֶּה מַסְעֵי בְנֵי־יִשְׂרָאֵל אֲשֶׁר יָצְאוּ מֵאֶרֶץ מִצְרַיִם לְצִבְאֹתָם בְּיַד־מֹשֶׁה וְאַהֲרֹן

2 וַיִּכְתֹּב מֹשֶׁה אֶת־מוֹצָאֵיהֶם לְמַסְעֵיהֶם עַל־פִּי יְהוָה וְאֵלֶּה מַסְעֵיהֶם לְמוֹצָאֵיהֶם

These are the journeys of the sons of Israel, by which they came out from the land of Egypt by their armies, under the leadership of Moses and Aaron. Moses recorded their starting places according to their journeys by the command of Yahweh, and these are their journeys according to their starting places:

Num. 33:3 וַיִּסְעוּ מֵרַעְמְסֵס בַּחֹדֶשׁ הָרִאשׁוֹן בַּחֲמִשָּׁה עָשָׂר יוֹם לַחֹדֶשׁ הָרִאשׁוֹן מִמָּחֳרַת הַפֶּסַח

רַעְמְסֵס

יָצְאוּ בְנֵי־יִשְׂרָאֵל בְּיָד רָמָה לְעֵינֵי כָּל־מִצְרָיִם 4 וּמִצְרַיִם מְקַבְּרִים אֵת אֲשֶׁר הִכָּה יְהוָה בָּהֶם כָּל־בְּכוֹר וּבֵאלֹהֵיהֶם עָשָׂה יְהוָה שְׁפָטִים

They journeyed from **Rameses** in the first month, on the fifteenth day of the first month; on the next day after the Passover the sons of Israel started out boldly in the sight of all the Egyptians, while the Egyptians were burying all their firstborn whom Yahweh had struck down among them. Yahweh had also executed judgments on their gods.

סֻכֹּת

Num. 33:5 וַיִּסְעוּ בְנֵי־יִשְׂרָאֵל מֵרַעְמְסֵס וַיַּחֲנוּ בְּסֻכֹּת

Then the sons of Israel journeyed from **Rameses** and camped in **Succoth**.

אֵתָם

Num. 33:6 וַיִּסְעוּ מִסֻּכֹּת וַיַּחֲנוּ בְאֵתָם אֲשֶׁר בִּקְצֵה הַמִּדְבָּר

They journeyed from Succoth and camped in **Etham**, which is on the edge of the wilderness.

פִּי הַחִירֹת

Num. 33:7 וַיִּסְעוּ מֵאֵתָם וַיָּשָׁב עַל־פִּי הַחִירֹת אֲשֶׁר

בַּעַל צְפוֹן   מִגְדֹּל   עַל־פְּנֵי בַּעַל צְפוֹן וַיַּחֲנוּ לִפְנֵי מִגְדֹּל

They journeyed from Etham and turned back to **Pi-ḥahiroth**, which faces
Baal-zephon, and they camped before **Migdol**.

Num. 33:8   וַיִּסְעוּ מִפְּנֵי הַחִירֹת וַיַּעַבְרוּ בְתוֹךְ־הַיָּם הַמִּדְבָּרָה וַיֵּלְכוּ דֶּרֶךְ שְׁלֹשֶׁת יָמִים בְּמִדְבַּר

מָרָה   הַחִירֹת   אֵתָם וַיַּחֲנוּ בְּמָרָה

They journeyed from before **Ḥahiroth** and passed through the midst of the
sea into the wilderness; and they went three days' journey in the **wilderness
of Etham** and camped at **Marah**.

Num. 33:9   וַיִּסְעוּ מִמָּרָה וַיָּבֹאוּ אֵילִמָה וּבְאֵילִם שְׁתֵּים עֶשְׂרֵה עֵינֹת מַיִם וְשִׁבְעִים תְּמָרִים

אֵילִם   וַיַּחֲנוּ־שָׁם

They journeyed from **Marah** and came to **Elim**; and in Elim there were
twelve springs of water and seventy palm trees, and they camped there

יַם־סוּף   Num. 33:10   וַיִּסְעוּ מֵאֵילִם וַיַּחֲנוּ עַל־יַם־סוּף

They journeyed from Elim and camped by the Reed Sea.

מִדְבַּר־סִין   Num. 33:11   וַיִּסְעוּ מִיַּם־סוּף וַיַּחֲנוּ בְּמִדְבַּר־סִין

They journeyed from the Red Sea and camped in the **wilderness of Sin**.

דָפְקָה   Num. 33:12   וַיִּסְעוּ מִמִּדְבַּר־סִין וַיַּחֲנוּ בְּדָפְקָה

They journeyed from the wilderness of Sin and camped at **Dophkah**.

אָלוּשׁ   Num. 33:13   וַיִּסְעוּ מִדָּפְקָה וַיַּחֲנוּ בְּאָלוּשׁ

They journeyed from Dophkah and camped at **Alush**.

רְפִידִם   Num. 33:14   וַיִּסְעוּ מֵאָלוּשׁ וַיַּחֲנוּ בִּרְפִידִם וְלֹא־הָיָה שָׁם מַיִם לָעָם לִשְׁתּוֹת

They journeyed from Alush and camped at Rephidim; now it was there that
the people had no water to drink.

מִדְבַּר סִינָי   Num. 33:15   וַיִּסְעוּ מֵרְפִידִם וַיַּחֲנוּ בְּמִדְבַּר סִינָי

They journeyed from Rephidim and camped in the **wilderness of Sinai**.

D. THE STATIONS — to Kadesh

Num. 33:16-36 — Itinerary

Num. 33:16 וַיִּסְעוּ מִמִּדְבַּר סִינָי וַיַּחֲנוּ בְּקִבְרֹת הַתַּאֲוָה

They journeyed from the wilderness of Sinai and camped at **Kibroth-hattaavah**.

Num. 33:17 וַיִּסְעוּ מִקִּבְרֹת הַתַּאֲוָה וַיַּחֲנוּ בַּחֲצֵרֹת

They journeyed from Kibroth-hattaavah and camped at **Hazeroth**.

Num. 33:18 וַיִּסְעוּ מֵחֲצֵרֹת וַיַּחֲנוּ בְּרִתְמָה

They journeyed from Hazeroth and camped at **Rithmah**.

Num. 33:19 וַיִּסְעוּ מֵרִתְמָה וַיַּחֲנוּ בְּרִמֹּן פָּרֶץ

They journeyed from Rithmah and camped at **Rimmon-perez**.

Num. 33:20 וַיִּסְעוּ מֵרִמֹּן פָּרֶץ וַיַּחֲנוּ בְּלִבְנָה

They journeyed from Rimmon-perez and camped at Libnah.

Num. 33:21 וַיִּסְעוּ מִלִּבְנָה וַיַּחֲנוּ בְּרִסָּה

They journeyed from Libnah and camped at **Rissah**.

Num. 33:22 וַיִּסְעוּ מֵרִסָּה וַיַּחֲנוּ בִּקְהֵלָתָה

They journeyed from Rissah and camped in **Kehelathah**.

Num. 33:23 וַיִּסְעוּ מִקְּהֵלָתָה וַיַּחֲנוּ בְּהַר־שָׁפֶר

They journeyed from Kehelathah and camped at **Mount Shepher**.

Num. 33:24 וַיִּסְעוּ מֵהַר־שָׁפֶר וַיַּחֲנוּ בַּחֲרָדָה

They journeyed from Mount Shepher and camped at **Ḥaradah**.

Num. 33:25 וַיִּסְעוּ מֵחֲרָדָה וַיַּחֲנוּ בְּמַקְהֵלֹת

They journeyed from Ḥaradah and camped at **Makheloth**.

Num. 33:26 וַיִּסְעוּ מִמַּקְהֵלֹת וַיַּחֲנוּ בְתָחַת

They journeyed from Makheloth and camped at **Tahath**.

Num. 33:27 וַיִּסְעוּ מִתָּחַת וַיַּחֲנוּ בְּתָרַח

They journeyed from Tahath and camped at **Teraḥ**.

Num. 33:28 וַיִּסְעוּ מִתָּרַח וַיַּחֲנוּ בְּמִתְקָה

They journeyed from Terah and camped at **Mithkah**

Num. 33:29 וַיִּסְעוּ מִמִּתְקָה וַיַּחֲנוּ בְּחַשְׁמֹנָה

They journeyed from Mithkah and camped at **Hashmonah**

Num. 33:30 וַיִּסְעוּ מֵחֲשְׁמֹנָה וַיַּחֲנוּ בְּמֹסֵרוֹת

They journeyed from Hashmonah and camped at **Moseroth.**

Num. 33:31 וַיִּסְעוּ מִמֹּסֵרוֹת וַיַּחֲנוּ בִּבְנֵי יַעֲקָן

They journeyed from Moseroth and camped at **Bene-jaakan.**

Num. 33:32 וַיִּסְעוּ מִבְּנֵי יַעֲקָן וַיַּחֲנוּ בְּחֹר הַגִּדְגָּד

They journeyed from Bene-jaakan and camped at **Hor-haggidgad.**

Num. 33:33 וַיִּסְעוּ מֵחֹר הַגִּדְגָּד וַיַּחֲנוּ בְּיָטְבָתָה

They journeyed from Hor-haggidgad and camped at **Jotbathah.**

Num. 33:34 וַיִּסְעוּ מִיָּטְבָתָה וַיַּחֲנוּ בְּעַבְרֹנָה

They journeyed from Jotbathah and camped at **ᶜAbronah.**

Num. 33:35 וַיִּסְעוּ מֵעַבְרֹנָה וַיַּחֲנוּ בְּעֶצְיוֹן גָּבֶר

They journeyed from Abronah and camped at **Ezion-geber.**

Num. 33:36 וַיִּסְעוּ מֵעֶצְיוֹן גָּבֶר וַיַּחֲנוּ בְמִדְבַּר־צִן הִוא קָדֵשׁ

They journeyed from Ezion-geber and camped in the wilderness of **Zin**, that

is, **Kadesh.**

E. THE STATIONS — to Moab

Num. 33:37-49 — Itinerary

Num. 33:37 וַיִּסְעוּ מִקָּדֵשׁ וַיַּחֲנוּ בְּהֹר הָהָר בִּקְצֵה אֶרֶץ אֱדוֹם

They journeyed from Kadesh and camped at **Mount Hor**, at the edge of the

land of Edom.

Num. 33:38 וַיַּעַל אַהֲרֹן הַכֹּהֵן אֶל־הֹר הָהָר עַל־פִּי יְהוָה וַיָּמָת שָׁם בִּשְׁנַת הָאַרְבָּעִים

לְצֵאת בְּנֵי־יִשְׂרָאֵל מֵאֶרֶץ מִצְרַיִם בַּחֹדֶשׁ הַחֲמִישִׁי בְּאֶחָד לַחֹדֶשׁ

Num. 33:39 וְאַהֲרֹן בֶּן־שָׁלֹשׁ וְעֶשְׂרִים וּמְאַת שָׁנָה בְּמֹתוֹ

בְּהֹר הָהָר

Then Aaron the priest went up to Mount Hor at the command of Yahweh,

and died there in the fortieth year after the sons of Israel had come from the

land of Egypt, on the first [day] in the fifth month. Aaron was one hundred

twenty-three years old when he died on Mount Hor.

Num. 33:40 וַיִּשְׁמַע הַכְּנַעֲנִי מֶלֶךְ עֲרָד וְהוּא־יֹשֵׁב בַּנֶּגֶב בְּאֶרֶץ כְּנָעַן בְּבֹא בְּנֵי יִשְׂרָאֵל

Now the Canaanite, the king of **Arad** who lived in the **Negeb** in the land of

Canaan, heard of the coming of the sons of Israel.

Num. 33:41 וַיִּסְעוּ מֵהֹר הָהָר וַיַּחֲנוּ בְּצַלְמֹנָה

Then they journeyed from Mount Hor and camped at **Zalmonah**.

Num. 33:42 וַיִּסְעוּ מִצַּלְמֹנָה וַיַּחֲנוּ בְּפוּנֹן

They journeyed from Zalmonah and camped at **Punon**.

Num. 33:43 וַיִּסְעוּ מִפּוּנֹן וַיַּחֲנוּ בְּאֹבֹת

They journeyed from Punon and camped at **Oboth**.

Num. 33:44 וַיִּסְעוּ מֵאֹבֹת וַיַּחֲנוּ בְּעִיֵּי הָעֲבָרִים בִּגְבוּל מוֹאָב

They journeyed from Oboth and camped at **Iye-abarim**, at the border of Moab.

Num. 21:12 מִשָּׁם נָסָעוּ וַיַּחֲנוּ בְּנַחַל זָרֶד

***From there they set out and camped in Naḥal Zered.

Num. 21:13 מִשָּׁם נָסָעוּ וַיַּחֲנוּ מֵעֵבֶר אַרְנוֹן אֲשֶׁר בַּמִּדְבָּר הַיֹּצֵא

מִגְּבוּל הָאֱמֹרִי כִּי אַרְנוֹן גְּבוּל מוֹאָב בֵּין מוֹאָב וּבֵין הָאֱמֹרִי

From there they journeyed and camped on the other side of the Arnon, which

is in the wilderness that comes out of the border of the Amorites, for the

Arnon is the border of Moab, between Moab and the Amorites.

Num. 33:45 וַיִּסְעוּ מֵעִיִּים וַיַּחֲנוּ בְּדִיבֹן גָּד

They journeyed from Iyim and camped at **Dibon-gad**.

Num. 33:46 וַיִּסְעוּ מִדִּיבֹן גָּד וַיַּחֲנוּ בְּעַלְמֹן דִּבְלָתָיְמָה

They journeyed from Dibon-gad and camped at **Almon-diblathaim**.

Num. 33:47 וַיִּסְעוּ מֵעַלְמֹן דִּבְלָתָיְמָה וַיַּחֲנוּ בְּהָרֵי הָעֲבָרִים לִפְנֵי נְבוֹ

They journeyed from Almon-diblathaim and camped in the mountains of

Abarim, before **Nebo**.

Num. 33:48 וַיִּסְעוּ מֵהָרֵי הָעֲבָרִים וַיַּחֲנוּ בְּעַרְבֹת מוֹאָב עַל יַרְדֵּן יְרֵחוֹ

They journeyed from the mountains of Abarim and camped in the plains of

Moab by the Jordan [opposite] Jericho.

Num. 33:49 וַיַּחֲנוּ עַל־הַיַּרְדֵּן מִבֵּית הַיְשִׁמֹת עַד אָבֵל הַשִּׁטִּים בְּעַרְבֹת מוֹאָב

They camped by the Jordan, from Beth-jeshimoth as far as Abel-shittim in the

plains of Moab.

LESSON 10
CONQUEST AND SETTLEMENT

I.   **ATTEMPT FROM THE SOUTH** Num. 14

A. From Kadesh-barnea

    1. Num. 14:40-45

40 וַיַּשְׁכִּמוּ בַבֹּקֶר וַיַּעֲלוּ אֶל־רֹאשׁ־הָהָר לֵאמֹר

הִנֶּנּוּ וְעָלִינוּ אֶל־הַמָּקוֹם אֲשֶׁר־אָמַר יְהוָה כִּי חָטָאנוּ

41 וַיֹּאמֶר מֹשֶׁה לָמָּה זֶּה אַתֶּם עֹבְרִים אֶת־פִּי

יְהוָה וְהִוא לֹא תִצְלָח

42 אַל־תַּעֲלוּ כִּי אֵין יְהוָה בְּקִרְבְּכֶם וְלֹא

תִּנָּגְפוּ לִפְנֵי אֹיְבֵיכֶם

43 כִּי הָעֲמָלֵקִי וְהַכְּנַעֲנִי שָׁם לִפְנֵיכֶם וּנְפַלְתֶּם

בֶּחָרֶב כִּי־עַל־כֵּן שַׁבְתֶּם מֵאַחֲרֵי יְהוָה וְלֹא־יִהְיֶה יְהוָה עִמָּכֶם

44 וַיַּעְפִּלוּ לַעֲלוֹת אֶל־רֹאשׁ הָהָר וַאֲרוֹן

בְּרִית־יְהוָה וּמֹשֶׁה לֹא־מָשׁוּ מִקֶּרֶב הַמַּחֲנֶה

45 וַיֵּרֶד הָעֲמָלֵקִי וְהַכְּנַעֲנִי הַיֹּשֵׁב בָּהָר הַהוּא

וַיַּכּוּם וַיַּכְּתוּם עַד־הַחָרְמָה

In the morning, however, they rose up early and went up to the ridge of the hill country, saying, "Here we are; we have indeed sinned, but we will go up to the place which Yahweh has promised." But Moses said, "Why then are you transgressing the commandment of Yahweh, when it will not succeed? Do not go up, or you will be struck down before your enemies, for Yahweh is not among you. For the Amalekites and the Canaanites will be there in front of you, and you will fall by the sword, inasmuch as you have turned back from following Yahweh. And Yahweh will not be with you." But they went up heedlessly to the ridge of the hill country; neither the ark of the covenant of Yahweh nor Moses left the camp. Then the **Amalekites** and the **Canaanites** who lived in that hill country came down, and struck them and beat them down as far as **Ḥormah**.

2. Deut. 1:41-46

41 וַתַּעֲנוּ וַתֹּאמְרוּ אֵלַי חָטָאנוּ לַיהוָה אֲנַחְנוּ

נַעֲלֶה וְנִלְחַמְנוּ כְּכֹל אֲשֶׁר־צִוָּנוּ יְהוָה אֱלֹהֵינוּ וַתַּחְגְּרוּ אִישׁ

אֶת־כְּלֵי מִלְחַמְתּוֹ וַתָּהִינוּ לַעֲלֹת הָהָרָה

42 וַיֹּאמֶר יְהוָה אֵלַי אֱמֹר לָהֶם לֹא תַעֲלוּ

וְלֹא־תִלָּחֲמוּ כִּי אֵינֶנִּי בְּקִרְבְּכֶם וְלֹא תִּנָּגְפוּ לִפְנֵי אֹיְבֵיכֶם

43 וָאֲדַבֵּר אֲלֵיכֶם וְלֹא שְׁמַעְתֶּם וַתַּמְרוּ אֶת־פִּי

יְהוָה וַתָּזִדוּ וַתַּעֲלוּ הָהָרָה

44 וַיֵּצֵא הָאֱמֹרִי הַיֹּשֵׁב בָּהָר הַהוּא לִקְרַאתְכֶם

וַיִּרְדְּפוּ אֶתְכֶם כַּאֲשֶׁר תַּעֲשֶׂינָה הַדְּבֹרִים וַיַּכְּתוּ אֶתְכֶם

בְּשֵׂעִיר עַד־חָרְמָה

45 וַתָּשֻׁבוּ וַתִּבְכּוּ לִפְנֵי יְהוָה וְלֹא־שָׁמַע יְהוָה

בְּקֹלְכֶם וְלֹא הֶאֱזִין אֲלֵיכֶם

46 וַתֵּשְׁבוּ בְקָדֵשׁ יָמִים רַבִּים כַּיָּמִים אֲשֶׁר יְשַׁבְתֶּם

Then you said to me, "We have sinned against Yahweh; we will indeed go up and fight, just as Yahweh our God commanded us." And every man of you girded on his weapons of war, and regarded it as easy to go up into the hill country. And Yahweh said to me, "Say to them, 'Do not go up nor fight, for I am not among you; otherwise you will be defeated before your enemies.'" So I spoke to you, but you would not listen. Instead you rebelled against the command of Yahweh, and acted presumptuously and went up into the hill country. The **Amorites** who lived in that hill country came out against you and chased you as bees do, and crushed you from **Seir** to **Hormah**. Then you returned and wept before Yahweh; but Yahweh did not listen to your voice nor give ear to you. So you remained in **Kadesh** many days, the days that you spent [there].

I.   (Cont.)

B.   Hormah - King of Arad

1. Num. 21:1-3 — Play on וְהַחֲרַמְתִּי

1 וַיִּשְׁמַע הַכְּנַעֲנִי מֶלֶךְ־עֲרָד יֹשֵׁב הַנֶּגֶב כִּי בָּא

יִשְׂרָאֵל דֶּרֶךְ הָאֲתָרִים (= *הַתָּרִים) וַיִּלָּחֶם בְּיִשְׂרָאֵל וַיִּשְׁבְּ מִמֶּנּוּ שֶׁבִי

2 וַיִּדַּר יִשְׂרָאֵל נֶדֶר לַיהוָה וַיֹּאמַר אִם־נָתֹן

תִּתֵּן אֶת־הָעָם הַזֶּה בְּיָדִי וְהַחֲרַמְתִּי אֶת־עָרֵיהֶם

3 וַיִּשְׁמַע יְהוָה בְּקוֹל יִשְׂרָאֵל וַיִּתֵּן אֶת־הַכְּנַעֲנִי

וַיַּחֲרֵם אֶתְהֶם וְאֶת־עָרֵיהֶם וַיִּקְרָא שֵׁם־הַמָּקוֹם חָרְמָה

When the Canaanite, the king of ᶜArad, who lived in the Negeb, heard that Israel was coming by the way of Atharim ("the spies"), then he fought against Israel and took some of them captive. So Israel made a vow to Yahweh and said, "If You will indeed deliver this people into my hand, then I will utterly destroy their cities." Yahweh heard the voice of Israel and delivered up the Canaanites; then they utterly destroyed them and their cities. Thus the name of the place was called Ḥormah.

2. Cf. also Num. 33:40

וַיִּשְׁמַע הַכְּנַעֲנִי מֶלֶךְ עֲרָד וְהוּא־יֹשֵׁב בַּנֶּגֶב

בְּאֶרֶץ כְּנָעַן בְּבֹא בְּנֵי יִשְׂרָאֵל׃

Now the Canaanite, the king of ᶜArad who lived in the Negeb in the land of Canaan, heard of the coming of the sons of Israel.

3. Realization in Judg. 1:17

Judg. 1:17 וַיֵּלֶךְ יְהוּדָה אֶת־שִׁמְעוֹן אָחִיו וַיַּכּוּ

אֶת־הַכְּנַעֲנִי יוֹשֵׁב צְפַת וַיַּחֲרִימוּ אוֹתָהּ וַיִּקְרָא

אֶת־שֵׁם־הָעִיר חָרְמָה

Then Judah went with Simeon his brother, and they struck the **Canaanites** living in **Zephath**, and utterly destroyed it. So the name of the city was called **Ḥormah**.

II.   CAMPAIGN FROM THE EAST

A. Against Sihon, king of Heshbon — Num. 21:21-24

21 וַיִּשְׁלַח יִשְׂרָאֵל מַלְאָכִים אֶל־סִיחֹן מֶלֶךְ־הָאֱמֹרִי לֵאמֹר

22 אֶעְבְּרָה בְאַרְצֶךָ לֹא נִטֶּה בְּשָׂדֶה וּבְכֶרֶם לֹא נִשְׁתֶּה מֵי בְאֵר בְּדֶרֶךְ הַמֶּלֶךְ נֵלֵךְ עַד אֲשֶׁר־נַעֲבֹר גְּבֻלֶךְ

23 וְלֹא־נָתַן סִיחֹן אֶת־יִשְׂרָאֵל עֲבֹר בִּגְבֻלוֹ וַיֶּאֱסֹף סִיחֹן אֶת־כָּל־עַמּוֹ וַיֵּצֵא לִקְרַאת יִשְׂרָאֵל הַמִּדְבָּרָה וַיָּבֹא יָהְצָה וַיִּלָּחֶם בְּיִשְׂרָאֵל

24 וַיַּכֵּהוּ יִשְׂרָאֵל לְפִי־חָרֶב וַיִּירַשׁ אֶת־אַרְצוֹ מֵאַרְנֹן עַד־יַבֹּק עַד־בְּנֵי עַמּוֹן כִּי עַז (**יַעְזֵר** =LXX Ιαζηρ) גְּבוּל בְּנֵי עַמּוֹן

Then Israel sent messengers to Sihon, king of the Amorites, saying, "Let me pass through your land. We will not turn off into field or vineyard; we will not drink water from wells. We will go by the king's highway until we have passed through your border." But Sihon would not permit Israel to pass through his border. So Sihon gathered all his people and went out against Israel in the wilderness, and came to **Jahaz** and fought against Israel. Then Israel struck him with the edge of the sword, and took possession of his land from the **Arnon** to the **Jabbok**, as far as the sons of **Ammon**; for the border of the sons of Ammon was **Jazer** (LXX).

Num. 21:25-31

25 וַיִּקַּח יִשְׂרָאֵל אֵת כָּל־הֶעָרִים הָאֵלֶּה וַיֵּשֶׁב יִשְׂרָאֵל בְּכָל־עָרֵי הָאֱמֹרִי בְּחֶשְׁבּוֹן וּבְכָל־בְּנֹתֶיהָ

26 כִּי חֶשְׁבּוֹן עִיר סִיחֹן מֶלֶךְ הָאֱמֹרִי הִוא וְהוּא נִלְחַם בְּמֶלֶךְ מוֹאָב הָרִאשׁוֹן וַיִּקַּח אֶת־כָּל־אַרְצוֹ מִיָּדוֹ עַד־אַרְנֹן

27 עַל־כֵּן יֹאמְרוּ הַמֹּשְׁלִים בֹּאוּ חֶשְׁבּוֹן תִּבָּנֶה וְתִכּוֹנֵן עִיר סִיחוֹן

28 כִּי־אֵשׁ יָצְאָה מֵחֶשְׁבּוֹן לֶהָבָה מִקִּרְיַת סִיחֹן

אָכְלָה עָר מוֹאָב בַּעֲלֵי בָּמוֹת אַרְנֹן

29 אוֹי־לְךָ מוֹאָב אָבַדְתָּ עַם־כְּמוֹשׁ נָתַן בָּנָיו

פְּלֵיטִם וּבְנֹתָיו בַּשְּׁבִית לְמֶלֶךְ אֱמֹרִי סִיחוֹן

30 וַנִּירָם אָבַד חֶשְׁבּוֹן עַד־דִּיבוֹן וַנַּשִּׁים

עַד־נֹפַח אֲשֶׁר עַד־מֵידְבָא וַיֵּשֶׁב יִשְׂרָאֵל בְּאֶרֶץ הָאֱמֹרִי

Israel took all these cities and Israel lived in all the cities of the **Amorites**, in **Ḥeshbon**, and in all her villages. For Heshbon was the city of Sihon, king of the Amorites, who had fought against the **former king of Moab** and had taken all his land out of his hand, as far as the **Arnon**. Therefore those who use proverbs say,

"Come to **Heshbon**! Let it be built! So let the city of Sihon be established. For a fire went forth from Heshbon, A flame from the town of Sihon; It devoured **Ar** of Moab, The dominant heights of the **Arnon**. Woe to you, O Moab! You are ruined, O people of Chemosh! He has given his sons as fugitives, And his daughters into captivity, To an Amorite king, Sihon. But we have cast them down, Heshbon is ruined as far as **Dibon**, Then we have laid waste even to **Nophah**, Which [reaches] to **Medeba**."

Thus Israel lived in the land of the Amorites.

B. JAZER (יַעְזֵר) — Num. 21:32

וַיִּשְׁלַח מֹשֶׁה לְרַגֵּל אֶת־יַעְזֵר וַיִּלְכְּדוּ בְּנֹתֶיהָ וַיִּירֶשׁ

[ו][יּוֹרֶשׁ] אֶת־הָאֱמֹרִי אֲשֶׁר־שָׁם

Moses sent to spy out Jazer, and they captured its villages and dispossessed the Amorites who [were] there.

C. Og, king of Bashah — Num. 21:33-35

33 וַיִּפְנוּ וַיַּעֲלוּ דֶּרֶךְ הַבָּשָׁן וַיֵּצֵא עוֹג מֶלֶךְ־הַבָּשָׁן לִקְרָאתָם

הוּא וְכָל־עַמּוֹ לַמִּלְחָמָה אֶדְרֶעִי

34 וַיֹּאמֶר יְהוָה אֶל־מֹשֶׁה אַל־תִּירָא אֹתוֹ כִּי

בְיָדְךָ נָתַתִּי אֹתוֹ וְאֶת־כָּל־עַמּוֹ וְאֶת־אַרְצוֹ וְעָשִׂיתָ לּוֹ

כַּאֲשֶׁר עָשִׂיתָ לְסִיחֹן מֶלֶךְ הָאֱמֹרִי אֲשֶׁר יוֹשֵׁב בְּחֶשְׁבּוֹן

35 וַיַּכּוּ אֹתוֹ וְאֶת־בָּנָיו וְאֶת־כָּל־עַמּוֹ עַד־בִּלְתִּי
הִשְׁאִיר־לוֹ שָׂרִיד וַיִּירְשׁוּ אֶת־אַרְצוֹ

Then they turned and went up by the way of Bashan, and Og the king of
Bashan went out with all his people, for battle at **Edrei**. But Yahweh said to
Moses, "Do not fear him, for I have given him into your hand, and all his
people and his land; and you shall do to him as you did to Sihon, king of the
Amorites, who lived at Heshbon." So they killed him and his sons and all his
people, until there was no remnant left him; and they possessed his land.

III.CIS-JORDAN

A. Central Hill Country

1. Jericho (Josh. 1-6)
    a. Waters at Adam near Zarethan Josh. 3:15b-16

15b וְהַיַּרְדֵּן מָלֵא עַל־כָּל־גְּדוֹתָיו כֹּל יְמֵי קָצִיר
16 וַיַּעַמְדוּ הַמַּיִם הַיֹּרְדִים מִלְמַעְלָה קָמוּ
נֵד־אֶחָד הַרְחֵק מְאֹד בְּאָדָם [מֵ][אָדָם] הָעִיר אֲשֶׁר מִצַּד
צָרְתָן וְהַיֹּרְדִים עַל יָם הָעֲרָבָה יָם־הַמֶּלַח תַּמּוּ נִכְרָתוּ
וְהָעָם עָבְרוּ נֶגֶד יְרִיחוֹ

(for the Jordan overflows all its banks all the days of harvest), the waters
which were flowing down from above stood [and] rose up in one heap, a
great distance away at Adam, the city that is beside Zarethan; and those
which were flowing down toward the sea of the Arabah, the Salt Sea, were
completely cut off. So the people crossed opposite Jericho.

b. Encamped at Gilgal Josh. 4:19

Josh. 4:19 וְהָעָם עָלוּ מִן־הַיַּרְדֵּן בֶּעָשׂוֹר לַחֹדֶשׁ הָרִאשׁוֹן
וַיַּחֲנוּ בַּגִּלְגָּל בִּקְצֵה מִזְרַח יְרִיחוֹ
Josh. 4:20 וְאֵת שְׁתֵּים עֶשְׂרֵה הָאֲבָנִים הָאֵלֶּה אֲשֶׁר לָקְחוּ
מִן־הַיַּרְדֵּן הֵקִים יְהוֹשֻׁעַ בַּגִּלְגָּל

Now the people came up from the Jordan on the tenth of the first month and camped at **Gilgal** on the eastern edge of **Jericho**. Those twelve stones which they had taken from the Jordan, Joshua set up at **Gilgal**.

2. Ai (Josh. 7-8) — Locale in relation to Bethel.

a. Josh. 7:2

וַיִּשְׁלַ֣ח יְהוֹשֻׁ֩עַ֩ אֲנָשִׁ֨ים מִירִיח֜וֹ הָעַ֗י אֲשֶׁ֨ר Josh. 7:2

עִם־בֵּ֤ית אָ֙וֶן֙ מִקֶּ֣דֶם לְבֵֽית־אֵ֔ל וַיֹּ֤אמֶר אֲלֵיהֶם֙ לֵאמֹ֔ר עֲל֣וּ

וְרַגְּל֖וּ אֶת־הָאָ֑רֶץ וַֽיַּעֲלוּ֙ הָֽאֲנָשִׁ֔ים וַֽיְרַגְּל֖וּ אֶת־הָעָֽי

Now Joshua sent men from Jericho to **Ai**, which is near **Beth-aven**, east of **Bethel**, and said to them, "Go up and spy out the land." So the men went up and spied out Ai.

b. Gen. 12:8

וַיַּעְתֵּ֨ק מִשָּׁ֜ם הָהָ֗רָה מִקֶּ֛דֶם לְבֵֽית־אֵ֖ל וַיֵּ֣ט 8

אָהֳלֹ֑ה בֵּֽית־אֵ֤ל מִיָּם֙ וְהָעַ֣י מִקֶּ֔דֶם וַיִּֽבֶן־שָׁ֤ם מִזְבֵּ֙חַ֙ לַֽיהוָ֔ה

וַיִּקְרָ֖א בְּשֵׁ֥ם יְהוָֽה

Then he proceeded from there to the mountain on the east of Bethel, and pitched his tent, with Bethel on the west and Ai on the east; and there he built an altar to Yahweh and called upon the name of Yahweh.

c. Onom. 4:27-6:3

Ἀγγαί ʼ(Gen 12, 8). κατὰ δυσμὰς Βαιθήλ. διεστήκασιν ἀλλήλων
οὐ πλεῖστον. κεῖται δὲ ἡ Βαιθήλ ἀπιόντων εἰς Αἰλίαν ἀπὸ Νέας

6

πόλεως ἐν λαιοῖς τῆς ὁδοῦ ἀμφὶ τὸ δωδέκατον Αἰλίας σημεῖον. καὶ
ἡ μὲν Βαιθήλ εἰς ἔτι νῦν μένει, ἡ δὲ Ἀγγαί τόπος ἔρημος αὐτὸ
μόνον δείκνυται. καλεῖ δὲ αὐτὴν καὶ Γαὶ ἡ γραφή.

העי, למערב בית אל. רחוקות זו מזו לא בהרבה. ובית אל נמצאת
מסביב למיל הי״ב מירושלם משמאל הדרך בלכתך מנאפוליס
ירושלימה.ובית אל יושבת עד היום; אבל את העי לבדה מראים
מקום חרב.

(3/4:27) **Ai** (Ἀγγαί | הָעַי: Gen 12:8). West of Bethel. These are not a great distance from each other. Bethel lies on the left side of the road close to the twelfth mile from Jerusalem on the way from Neapolis to Jerusalem. Bethel remains until the present day, while Ai itself is shown only as a deserted place. The scripture also calls it Ai (LXX Josh 7:2: Γαί).

d. Onom. 40:20-24

Βαιθήλ '(γεν 12, 8). καὶ νῦν ἐστι κώμη Αἰλίας ἄποθεν σημείοις ιβd [2ἀπιόντων εἰς Νέαν πόλιν δεξιά· Οὐλαμμα]2οῦς δὲ τὸ πρότερον ἐκα-λεῖτο καὶ Λουζά. ἣ καὶ γέγονε φυλῆς Βενιαμίν, πλησίον Βηθαῦν καὶ τῆς Γαί. καὶ ταύτην δὲ Ἰησοῦς ἐπολιόρκησε, τὸν βασιλέα αὐτῆς ἀνελών.

Onom. 41:17-21

Bethel uicus in duodecimo ab Aelia lapide ad dexteram euntibus Neapolim, quae primum Luza, id est Œmúgdalon, uocabatur et cecidit in sortem tribus Beniamin, iuxta Bethaun et Gai . . . .

בית-אל. — גם היום הוא כפר רחוק מירושלים בי״ב
מילים[לימין ההולך לנאפוליס. ולפנים נקראה אולם
-ל]וזולוזה, והיתה במטה בנימין, אצל בית און והעי.

(192/40:20) **Bethel** (Βαιθήλ | בֵּית־אֵל: Gen 12:8). It is now a village twelve miles from Jerusalem on the right as one travels to Neapolis. Previously it was called Ulam-luz (Gen 28:19) and Luz (Josh 18:13). It was included in the tribe of Benjamin (Josh 18:22), near Beth-aven and Ai (Josh 7:2). Joshua besieged it and killed its king (Josh 12:16).

e. Josh. 8:10-15

10 וַיַּשְׁכֵּם יְהוֹשֻׁעַ בַּבֹּקֶר וַיִּפְקֹד אֶת־הָעָם וַיַּעַל
הוּא וְזִקְנֵי יִשְׂרָאֵל לִפְנֵי הָעָם הָעָי

11 וְכָל־הָעָם הַמִּלְחָמָה אֲשֶׁר אִתּוֹ עָלוּ וַיִּגְּשׁוּ וַיָּבֹאוּ נֶגֶד הָעִיר ·
וַיַּחֲנוּ מִצְּפוֹן לָעַי וְהַגַּי בֵּינוֹ [בֵּינָיו] וּבֵין־הָעָי

12 וַיִּקַּח כַּחֲמֵשֶׁת אֲלָפִים אִישׁ וַיָּשֶׂם אוֹתָם אֹרֵב

בֵּין בֵּית־אֵל וּבֵין הָעַי מִיָּם לָעִיר

13 וַיָּשִׂימוּ הָעָם אֶת־כָּל־הַמַּחֲנֶה אֲשֶׁר מִצְּפוֹן לָעִיר וְאֶת־עֲקֵבוֹ מִיָּם

לָעִיר וַיֵּלֶךְ יְהוֹשֻׁעַ בַּלַּיְלָה הַהוּא בְּתוֹךְ הָעֵמֶק

14 וַיְהִי כִּרְאוֹת מֶלֶךְ־הָעַי וַיְמַהֲרוּ וַיַּשְׁכִּימוּ וַיֵּצְאוּ

אַנְשֵׁי־הָעִיר לִקְרַאת־יִשְׂרָאֵל לַמִּלְחָמָה הוּא וְכָל־עַמּוֹ

לַמּוֹעֵד לִפְנֵי הָעֲרָבָה וְהוּא לֹא יָדַע כִּי־אֹרֵב לוֹ מֵאַחֲרֵי הָעִיר

15 וַיִּנָּגְעוּ יְהוֹשֻׁעַ וְכָל־יִשְׂרָאֵל לִפְנֵיהֶם וַיָּנֻסוּ דֶּרֶךְ הַמִּדְבָּר

Now Joshua rose early in the morning and mustered the people, and he went up with the elders of Israel before the people to **Ai**. Then all the people of war who [were] with him went up and drew near and arrived in front of the city, and camped on the **north side of Ai**. Now [there was] a **valley between him and Ai.** And he took about 5,000 men and set them in ambush **between Bethel and Ai**, on the west side of the city. So they stationed the people, all the army that was on the north side of the city, and its rear guard on the west side of the city, and Joshua spent that night in the midst of the valley. It came about when the king of Ai saw [it], that the men of the city hurried and rose up early and went out to meet Israel in battle, he and all his people at the appointed place before the desert plain. But he did not know that [there was] an ambush against him behind the city. Joshua and all Israel pretended to be beaten before them, and fled by the way of the wilderness.

3. Gibeonites — against Jerusalem and allies:

a. Gibeonite cities: Josh. 9:17

Josh. 9:17 וַיִּסְעוּ בְנֵי־יִשְׂרָאֵל וַיָּבֹאוּ אֶל־עָרֵיהֶם בַּיּוֹם

הַשְּׁלִישִׁי וְעָרֵיהֶם גִּבְעוֹן וְהַכְּפִירָה וּבְאֵרוֹת וְקִרְיַת יְעָרִים

Now their cities [were] **Gibeon** and **Chephirah** and **Beeroth** and **Kiriath-jearim**.

Gibeon = el-Jîb

Chephirah = Kh. el-Kefîrah

Kiriath-jearim = Qiryet el ᶜAnab = Abu Ghosh
Beeroth = Kh. el-Burj? (above Kh. El-Biyyârah)

b. Canaanite allies Josh. 10:3-4:

3 וַיִּשְׁלַח אֲדֹנִי־צֶדֶק מֶלֶךְ יְרוּשָׁלַם אֶל־הוֹהָם

מֶלֶךְ־חֶבְרוֹן וְאֶל־פִּרְאָם מֶלֶךְ־יַרְמוּת וְאֶל־יָפִיעַ

מֶלֶךְ־לָכִישׁ וְאֶל־דְּבִיר מֶלֶךְ־עֶגְלוֹן לֵאמֹר

4 עֲלוּ־אֵלַי וְעִזְרֻנִי וְנַכֶּה אֶת־גִּבְעוֹן כִּי־הִשְׁלִימָה

אֶת־יְהוֹשֻׁעַ וְאֶת־בְּנֵי יִשְׂרָאֵל

Therefore Adoni-zedek king of Jerusalem sent [word] to Hoham king of **Hebron** and to Piram king of **Jarmuth** and to Japhia king of **Lachish** and to Debir king of **Eglon**, saying,

"Come up to me and help me, and let us attack **Gibeon**, for it has made peace with Joshua and with the sons of Israel."

Josh. 10:5 So the five kings of the Amorites, the king of **Jerusalem**, the king of **Hebron**, the king of **Jarmuth**, the king of **Lachish**, [and] the king of **Eglon**, gathered together and went up, they with all their armies, and camped by **Gibeon** and fought against it.

c. Line of retreat Josh. 10:10-11

10 וַיְהֻמֵּם יְהוָה לִפְנֵי יִשְׂרָאֵל וַיַּכֵּם מַכָּה־גְדוֹלָה בְּגִבְעוֹן

וַיִּרְדְּפֵם דֶּרֶךְ מַעֲלֵה בֵית־חוֹרֹן וַיַּכֵּם עַד־עֲזֵקָה וְעַד־מַקֵּדָה

11 וַיְהִי בְּנֻסָם מִפְּנֵי יִשְׂרָאֵל הֵם בְּמוֹרַד

בֵּית־חוֹרֹן וַיהוָה הִשְׁלִיךְ עֲלֵיהֶם אֲבָנִים גְּדֹלוֹת

מִן־הַשָּׁמַיִם עַד־עֲזֵקָה וַיָּמֻתוּ רַבִּים אֲשֶׁר־מֵתוּ בְּאַבְנֵי

הַבָּרָד מֵאֲשֶׁר הָרְגוּ בְּנֵי יִשְׂרָאֵל בֶּחָרֶב

And Yahweh confounded them before Israel, and He slew them with a great slaughter at **Gibeon**, and pursued them by the way of the _ascent_ of **Beth-horon** and struck them as far as **Azekah** and **Makkedah**. As they fled

from before Israel, [while] they were at the *descent* of **Beth-horon**, Yahweh
threw large stones from heaven on them as far as **Azekah**, and they died;
[there were] more who died from the hailstones than those whom the sons of
Israel killed with the sword.

B. The Shephelah

1. Where was the camp?

a. At Gilgal (Josh. 10:15) —editorial note not in LXX!!!

Josh. 10:15 וַיָּשָׁב יְהוֹשֻׁעַ וְכָל־יִשְׂרָאֵל עִמּוֹ אֶל־הַמַּחֲנֶה הַגִּלְגָּלָה

Then Joshua and all Israel with him returned to the camp to Gilgal.

b. At Makkedah (Josh. 10:21)

Josh. 10:21 וַיָּשֻׁבוּ כָל־הָעָם אֶל־הַמַּחֲנֶה אֶל־יְהוֹשֻׁעַ

מַקֵּדָה בְּשָׁלוֹם לֹא־חָרַץ לִבְנֵי יִשְׂרָאֵל לְאִישׁ אֶת־לְשֹׁנוֹ

all the people returned to the camp to Joshua at **Makkedah** in
peace.

2. The sequence of towns: (Josh. 10:28, 29, 31, 33, 34)

Josh. 10:28 וְאֶת־מַקֵּדָה לָכַד יְהוֹשֻׁעַ בַּיּוֹם הַהוּא וַיַּכֶּהָ

לְפִי־חֶרֶב וְאֶת־מַלְכָּהּ הֶחֱרִם אוֹתָם וְאֶת־כָּל־הַנֶּפֶשׁ

אֲשֶׁר־בָּהּ לֹא הִשְׁאִיר שָׂרִיד וַיַּעַשׂ לְמֶלֶךְ מַקֵּדָה כַּאֲשֶׁר

עָשָׂה לְמֶלֶךְ יְרִיחוֹ

Now Joshua captured **Makkedah** on that day, and struck it and its king with
the edge of the sword; he utterly destroyed it and every person who was in it.
He left no survivor. Thus he did to the king of **Makkedah** just as he had done
to the king of Jericho.

Josh. 10:29 וַיַּעֲבֹר יְהוֹשֻׁעַ וְכָל־יִשְׂרָאֵל עִמּוֹ מִמַּקֵּדָה

לִבְנָה וַיִּלָּחֶם עִם־לִבְנָה

Josh. 10:30 וַיִּתֵּן יְהוָה גַּם־אוֹתָהּ בְּיַד יִשְׂרָאֵל וְאֶת־מַלְכָּהּ

וַיַּכֶּהָ לְפִי־חֶרֶב וְאֶת־כָּל־הַנֶּפֶשׁ אֲשֶׁר־בָּהּ לֹא־הִשְׁאִיר בָּהּ

שָׂרִיד וַיַּעַשׂ לְמַלְכָּהּ כַּאֲשֶׁר עָשָׂה לְמֶלֶךְ יְרִיחוֹ

Then Joshua and all Israel with him passed on from Makkedah to **Libnah**, and fought against **Libnah**. Yahweh gave it also with its king into the hands of Israel, and he struck it and every person who [was] in it with the edge of the sword. He left no survivor in it. Thus he did to its king just as he had done to the king of Jericho.

Josh. 10:31 וַיַּעֲבֹר יְהוֹשֻׁעַ וְכָל־יִשְׂרָאֵל עִמּוֹ מִלִּבְנָה

לָכִישָׁה וַיִּחַן עָלֶיהָ וַיִּלָּחֶם בָּהּ

Josh. 10:32 וַיִּתֵּן יְהוָה אֶת־לָכִישׁ בְּיַד יִשְׂרָאֵל וַיִּלְכְּדָהּ

בַּיּוֹם הַשֵּׁנִי וַיַּכֶּהָ לְפִי־חֶרֶב וְאֶת־כָּל־הַנֶּפֶשׁ אֲשֶׁר־בָּהּ

כְּכֹל אֲשֶׁר־עָשָׂה לְלִבְנָה

And Joshua and all Israel with him passed on from Libnah to **Lachish**, and they camped by it and fought against it. Yahweh gave **Lachish** into the hands of Israel; and he captured it on the second day, and struck it and every person who [was] in it with the edge of the sword, according to all that he had done to Libnah.

Josh. 10:33 אָז עָלָה הֹרָם מֶלֶךְ גֶּזֶר לַעְזֹר אֶת־לָכִישׁ

וַיַּכֵּהוּ יְהוֹשֻׁעַ וְאֶת־עַמּוֹ עַד־בִּלְתִּי הִשְׁאִיר־לוֹ שָׂרִיד

Then Horam [LXX Ailam] king of **Gezer** came up to help Lachish, and Joshua defeated him and his people [LXX by the edge of the sword] until he had left him no survivor.

Josh. 10:34 וַיַּעֲבֹר יְהוֹשֻׁעַ וְכָל־יִשְׂרָאֵל עִמּוֹ מִלָּכִישׁ

עֶגְלֹנָה וַיַּחֲנוּ עָלֶיהָ וַיִּלָּחֲמוּ עָלֶיהָ

Josh. 10:35 וַיִּלְכְּדוּהָ בַּיּוֹם הַהוּא וַיַּכּוּהָ לְפִי־חֶרֶב וְאֵת

כָּל־הַנֶּפֶשׁ אֲשֶׁר־בָּהּ בַּיּוֹם הַהוּא הֶחֱרִים כְּכֹל אֲשֶׁר־עָשָׂה לְלָכִישׁ

And Joshua and all Israel with him passed on from Lachish to **Eglon**, and they camped by it and fought against it. They captured it on that day and struck it with the edge of the sword; and he utterly destroyed that day every person who [was] in it, according to all that he had done to Lachish.

C. JUDEAN HILL COUNTRY

1. The Joshua version: (Josh 10:36-39)

Josh. 10:36 וַיַּעַל יְהוֹשֻׁעַ וְכָל־יִשְׂרָאֵל עִמּוֹ מֵעֶגְלוֹנָה

חֶבְרוֹנָה וַיִּלָּחֲמוּ עָלֶיהָ

Josh. 10:37 וַיִּלְכְּדוּהָ וַיַּכּוּהָ לְפִי־חֶרֶב וְאֶת־מַלְכָּהּ

וְאֶת־כָּל־עָרֶיהָ וְאֶת־כָּל־הַנֶּפֶשׁ אֲשֶׁר־בָּהּ לֹא־הִשְׁאִיר

שָׂרִיד כְּכֹל אֲשֶׁר־עָשָׂה לְעֶגְלוֹן וַיַּחֲרֵם אוֹתָהּ

וְאֶת־כָּל־הַנֶּפֶשׁ אֲשֶׁר־בָּהּ

Josh. 10:38 וַיָּשָׁב יְהוֹשֻׁעַ וְכָל־יִשְׂרָאֵל עִמּוֹ דְּבִרָה וַיִּלָּחֶם עָלֶיהָ

Josh. 10:39 וַיִּלְכְּדָהּ וְאֶת־מַלְכָּהּ וְאֶת־כָּל־עָרֶיהָ וַיַּכּוּם

לְפִי־חֶרֶב וַיַּחֲרִימוּ אֶת־כָּל־נֶפֶשׁ אֲשֶׁר־בָּהּ לֹא הִשְׁאִיר

שָׂרִיד כַּאֲשֶׁר עָשָׂה לְחֶבְרוֹן כֵּן־עָשָׂה לִדְבִרָה וּלְמַלְכָּהּ

וְכַאֲשֶׁר עָשָׂה לְלִבְנָה וּלְמַלְכָּהּ

Then Joshua and all Israel with him went up from Eglon to **Hebron**, and they fought against it. They captured it and struck it and its king and all its cities and all the persons who [were] in it with the edge of the sword. He left no survivor, according to all that he had done to Eglon. And he utterly destroyed it and every person who [was] in it.

¶ Then Joshua and all Israel with him returned to **Debir**, and they fought against it. He captured it and its king and all its cities, and they struck them with the edge of the sword, and utterly destroyed every person [who was] in it. He left no survivor. Just as he had done to Hebron, so he did to Debir and its king, as he had also done to Libnah and its king.

2. The Caleb version
Josh. 15:13-19 ‖ Judg. 1:10-15 [Judah]

13 וּלְכָלֵב בֶּן־יְפֻנֶּה נָתַן חֵלֶק בְּתוֹךְ בְּנֵי־יְהוּדָה

אֶל־פִּי יְהוָה לִיהוֹשֻׁעַ אֶת־קִרְיַת אַרְבַּע אֲבִי הָעֲנָק הִיא חֶבְרוֹן

14 וַיֹּרֶשׁ מִשָּׁם כָּלֵב אֶת־שְׁלוֹשָׁה בְּנֵי הָעֲנָק

אֶת־שֵׁשַׁי וְאֶת־אֲחִימַן וְאֶת־תַּלְמַי יְלִידֵי הָעֲנָק

15 וַיַּעַל מִשָּׁם אֶל־יֹשְׁבֵי דְּבִר וְשֵׁם־דְּבִר לְפָנִים קִרְיַת־סֵפֶר

16 וַיֹּאמֶר כָּלֵב אֲשֶׁר־יַכֶּה אֶת־קִרְיַת־סֵפֶר

וּלְכָדָהּ וְנָתַתִּי לוֹ אֶת־עַכְסָה בִתִּי לְאִשָּׁה

17 וַיִּלְכְּדָהּ עָתְנִיאֵל בֶּן־קְנַז אֲחִי כָלֵב וַיִּתֶּן־לוֹ

אֶת־עַכְסָה בִתּוֹ לְאִשָּׁה

18 וַיְהִי בְּבוֹאָהּ וַתְּסִיתֵהוּ לִשְׁאוֹל מֵאֵת־אָבִיהָ

שָׂדֶה וַתִּצְנַח מֵעַל הַחֲמוֹר וַיֹּאמֶר־לָהּ כָּלֵב מַה־לָּךְ

19 וַתֹּאמֶר תְּנָה־לִּי בְרָכָה כִּי אֶרֶץ הַנֶּגֶב נְתַתָּנִי וְנָתַתָּה לִי

גֻּלֹּת מָיִם וַיִּתֶּן־לָהּ אֵת גֻּלֹּת עִלִּיֹּת וְאֵת גֻּלֹּת תַּחְתִּיֹּת

Now he gave to **Caleb the son of Jephunneh** a portion among the sons of Judah, according to the command of Yahweh to Joshua,   [namely], **Kiriath-arba,** [Arba being] the father of Anak (that is, **Hebron**).

Caleb drove out from there the _three sons of Anak: Sheshai and Ahiman and Talmai, the children of Anak_.

Then he went up from there against the inhabitants of **Debir**; now the name of Debir formerly was **Kiriath-sepher**.

And Caleb said, "The one who attacks Kiriath-sepher and captures it, I will give him Achsah my daughter as a wife." Othniel the son of Kenaz, the brother of Caleb, captured it; so he gave him Achsah his daughter as a wife. It came about that when she came [to him], she persuaded him to ask her father for a field. So she alighted from the donkey, and Caleb said to her, "What do you want?" Then she said, "Give me a blessing; since you have given me the land of the **Negeb**, give me also springs of water." So he gave her the **upper springs** and the **lower springs**.

D. GALILEE (Upper Galilee)

1. The Canaanite allies (Josh. 11:1-3)

1 וַיְהִי כִּשְׁמֹעַ יָבִין מֶלֶךְ־חָצוֹר וַיִּשְׁלַח אֶל־יוֹבָב מֶלֶךְ

מָדוֹן (LXX Μαρρων) וְאֶל־מֶלֶךְ שִׁמְרוֹן (LXX Συμοων) וְאֶל־מֶלֶךְ אַכְשָׁף ׃

2 וְאֶל־הַמְּלָכִים אֲשֶׁר מִצְּפוֹן בָּהָר וּבָעֲרָבָה נֶגֶב

כִּנֲרוֹת וּבַשְּׁפֵלָה וּבְנָפוֹת דּוֹר מִיָּם

3 הַכְּנַעֲנִי מִמִּזְרָח וּמִיָּם וְהָאֱמֹרִי וְהַחִתִּי וְהַפְּרִזִּי

וְהַיְבוּסִי בָּהָר וְהַחִוִּי תַּחַת חֶרְמוֹן בְּאֶרֶץ הַמִּצְפָּה

The Hill Country	מִצְּפוֹן בָּהָר
Jordan Valley S. of Chinnereth	וּבָעֲרָבָה נֶגֶב כִּנֲרוֹת
Mediterranean Coast	וּבַשְּׁפֵלָה וּבְנָפוֹת דּוֹר מִיָּם

Then it came about, when Jabin king of **Hazor** heard [of it], that he sent to Jobab king of **Marron** (LXX) and to the king of **Shim°on** (LXX) and to the king of **Achshaph**, and to the kings who were of the north in the hill country, and in the Arabah — south of **Chinneroth** and in the Shephelah and in the district of Dor on the west — to the Canaanite on the east and on the west, and the Amorite and the Hittite and the Perizzite and the Jebusite in the hill country, and the Hivite at the foot of **Hermon** in the land of **Mizpeh**.

2. The venue (Josh. 11:5)

Josh. 11:5 וַיִּוָּעֲדוּ כֹּל הַמְּלָכִים הָאֵלֶּה וַיָּבֹאוּ וַיַּחֲנוּ יַחְדָּו

אֶל־מֵי מֵרוֹם (LXX Μαρρων) לְהִלָּחֵם עִם־יִשְׂרָאֵל

So all of these kings having agreed to meet, came and encamped together at the waters of Marron (LXX), to fight against Israel.

3. The Retreat (Josh. 11:7-8)

Josh. 11:7 וַיָּבֹא יְהוֹשֻׁעַ וְכָל־עַם הַמִּלְחָמָה עִמּוֹ עֲלֵיהֶם

עַל־מֵי מֵרוֹם פִּתְאֹם וַיִּפְּלוּ בָּהֶם

Josh. 11:8 וַיִּתְּנֵם יְהוָה בְּיַד־יִשְׂרָאֵל וַיַּכּוּם וַיִּרְדְּפוּם

עַד־צִידוֹן רַבָּה וְעַד מִשְׂרְפוֹת מַיִם וְעַד־בִּקְעַת מִצְפֶּה

מִזְרָחָה וַיַּכֻּם עַד־בִּלְתִּי הִשְׁאִיר־לָהֶם שָׂרִיד

Yahweh delivered them into the hand of Israel, so that they defeated them, and pursued them as far as **Great Sidon** and **Misrephoth-maim** and the valley of **Mizpeh** to the east; and they struck them until no survivor was left to them.

LESSON 11
THE HEROIC AGE

I. THE PEOPLES OF THE SEA

    A. Eighteenth Dynasty Contacts

        1. The *Kftiw* people are depicted bringing good
            ("tribute") to Egypt in tombs of officials in the
            15th century — they disappear in later scenes.
            Kftiw = *Kap̄tôr.*

        2. EA texts

           a. *Lukki/Lukku* raided the territory of Alashia
              (EA 38:10).
           b. *Šerdāni* appear as mercenary troops that can be
              stationed by the Egyptians in Canaan (EA 88:16;
              122:35;123:15).
           c. Land of *Danuna* mentioned by king of Tyre
              (EA 151:52);
              No need to suppose that it is in Canaan!!!!

    B. Nineteenth Dynasty Contacts
        1. Battle of Kedesh

        2. Anatolian allies of the Hittites: *Rkw* (*Lukku*), *Drdnw,*
             Mʾsw, ʾIrwnw, Pdsw, Krks
        3. On the Egyptian side: *Srdn*

        4. Merneptah (1212-1202 BCE)

           a. Fought them off on the west, attempted invasion
              from west in company with the Lybians:
      ʾkw(ʾ)sw, Trsw, Rkw, Srdnw, skrsw

           b. No mention of them in Canaan!

C. Nineteenth Dynasty—last pharaohs:

    1. [Amenmesse] possibly a usurper ? (1202-1199).

    2. Seti II — wife was Towesret (1199-1193)

    3. Siptah/Merneptah (1193-1187)

    4. Towesret took over after Siptah's death (1193-1185).

    5. (Merenptah II son of Siptah ?)

D. Twentieth Dynasty (1185-1070 BCE)

    1. Sethnakhte (1185-1182).

    2. Rameses III (1182-1151).

        a. Year 5 (1177) — against the Libyans (Libu, Meshwesh, Seped)

        b. Year 8 (1174) — against Sea Peoples

        c. Year 11 (1171) — Libu and Meshwesh again

        d. Minor campaign in Pap. Harris against Shasu of Mt. Seir

E. Invasion from the west

    1. Eighth year of Ramses III (1174 BCE)

The foreign lands were restless in their islands . . . No land could withstand their might, from Hatti, Qode, Carchemish, Arzawa and Alashia on, being defeated one by one. A camp was set up on the border of Amurru. They slaughtered its people, and the land was as if it had never been. They came toward Egypt, fire preceding them. Their league comprised the Philistines, Sicels, Shekelesh, Denyen and Weshesha.

    2. Land and sea battle

    3. Papyrus Harris records their being settled in Egypt

    4. Under what conditions did they settle in Canaan? ****

F. The Pentapolis — Myc III C shows up at these sites with
     destruction of LB cities and new settlement:

1. Gaza
2. Ashkelon
3. Ashdod
4. Gath   Tell eṣ-Ṣâfī
5. Ekron   Tell el-Muqannaᶜ

G. Expansion northward — Eleventh Century:

1. Joppa, Gezer, Aphek, Tel Gerisa, Tel Qasila
2. Myc. III C doesn't show up there, only the bi-chrome
     "Philistine ware" which developed <u>after</u> the Philistines
     had been settled in Canaan for more than a generation.

H. Sicels at Dor according to Wenamon; others may have settled in
     Haifa Bay area I.

II. EXTENT OF ISRAELITE SETTLEMENT (Judges ch. 1)

A. Judah Judges 1:1-3

1 וַיְהִי אַחֲרֵי מוֹת יְהוֹשֻׁעַ וַיִּשְׁאֲלוּ בְּנֵי יִשְׂרָאֵל בַּיהוָה
לֵאמֹר מִי יַעֲלֶה־לָּנוּ אֶל־הַכְּנַעֲנִי בַּתְּחִלָּה לְהִלָּחֶם בּוֹ
2 אִתָּךְ אָחִיו עֲלֵה אִתִּי וַיֹּאמֶר יְהוָה יְהוּדָה יַעֲלֶה הִנֵּה נָתַתִּי אֶת־הָאָרֶץ בְּיָדוֹ
3 וַיֹּאמֶר יְהוּדָה לְשִׁמְעוֹן בְּגוֹרָלִי וְנִלָּחֲמָה בַּכְּנַעֲנִי וְהָלַכְתִּי גַם־אֲנִי
בְּגוֹרָלֶךָ וַיֵּלֶךְ אִתּוֹ שִׁמְעוֹן

Now it came about after the death of Joshua that the sons of Israel inquired of
Yahweh, saying, "Who shall go up first for us against the Canaanites, to fight
against them?" Yahweh said, "Judah shall go up; behold, I have given the
land into his hand." Then Judah said to Simeon his brother, "Come up with
me into the territory allotted me, that we may fight against the Canaanites;

and I in turn will go with you into the territory allotted you." So Simeon went with him.

1. Against Jerusalem Judges 1:4-7

4 וַיַּעַל יְהוּדָה וַיִּתֵּן יְהוָה אֶת־הַכְּנַעֲנִי וְהַפְּרִזִּי

בְּיָדָם וַיַּכּוּם בְּבֶזֶק עֲשֶׂרֶת אֲלָפִים אִישׁ

5 וַיִּמְצְאוּ אֶת־אֲדֹנִי בֶזֶק בְּבֶזֶק וַיִּלָּחֲמוּ בּוֹ וַיַּכּוּ

אֶת־הַכְּנַעֲנִי וְאֶת־הַפְּרִזִּי

6 וַיָּנָס אֲדֹנִי בֶזֶק וַיִּרְדְּפוּ אַחֲרָיו וַיֹּאחֲזוּ אֹתוֹ

וַיְקַצְּצוּ אֶת־בְּהֹנוֹת יָדָיו וְרַגְלָיו

7 וַיֹּאמֶר אֲדֹנִי־בֶזֶק שִׁבְעִים מְלָכִים בְּהֹנוֹת

יְדֵיהֶם וְרַגְלֵיהֶם מְקֻצָּצִים הָיוּ מְלַקְּטִים תַּחַת שֻׁלְחָנִי

כַּאֲשֶׁר עָשִׂיתִי כֵּן שִׁלַּם־לִי אֱלֹהִים וַיְבִיאֻהוּ יְרוּשָׁלַם

וַיָּמָת שָׁם

8 וַיִּלָּחֲמוּ בְנֵי־יְהוּדָה בִּירוּשָׁלַם וַיִּלְכְּדוּ אוֹתָהּ

וַיַּכּוּהָ לְפִי־חָרֶב וְאֶת־הָעִיר שִׁלְּחוּ בָאֵשׁ

Judah went up, and Yahweh gave the Canaanites and the Perizzites into their hands, and they defeated ten thousand men at Bezek. They found Adoni-bezek in Bezek and fought against him, and they defeated the Canaanites and the Perizzites. But Adoni-bezek fled; and they pursued him and caught him and cut off his thumbs and big toes. Adoni-bezek said, "Seventy kings with their thumbs and their big toes cut off used to gather up [scraps] under my table; as I have done, so God has repaid me." So they brought him to Jerusalem and he died there. Then the sons of Judah fought against Jerusalem and captured it and struck it with the edge of the sword and set the city on fire.

2. Conquest of Judea Judges 1:9-15

9 וְאַחַר יָרְדוּ בְּנֵי יְהוּדָה לְהִלָּחֵם בַּכְּנַעֲנִי יוֹשֵׁב

הָהָר וְהַנֶּגֶב וְהַשְּׁפֵלָה

10 וַיֵּ֫לֶךְ יְהוּדָה אֶל־הַכְּנַעֲנִי הַיּוֹשֵׁב בְּחֶבְרוֹן

וְשֵׁם־חֶבְרוֹן לְפָנִים קִרְיַת אַרְבַּע וַיַּכּוּ אֶת־שֵׁשַׁי

וְאֶת־אֲחִימַן וְאֶת־תַּלְמָי

11 וַיֵּ֫לֶךְ מִשָּׁם אֶל־יוֹשְׁבֵי דְּבִיר וְשֵׁם־דְּבִיר

לְפָנִים קִרְיַת־סֵפֶר

12 וַיֹּ֫אמֶר כָּלֵב אֲשֶׁר־יַכֶּה אֶת־קִרְיַת־סֵפֶר

וּלְכָדָהּ וְנָתַתִּי לוֹ אֶת־עַכְסָה בִתִּי לְאִשָּׁה

13 וַיִּלְכְּדָהּ עָתְנִיאֵל בֶּן־קְנַז אֲחִי כָלֵב הַקָּטֹן

מִמֶּ֫נּוּ וַיִּתֶּן־לוֹ אֶת־עַכְסָה בִתּוֹ לְאִשָּׁה

14 וַיְהִי בְּבוֹאָהּ וַתְּסִיתֵ֫הוּ לִשְׁאוֹל מֵאֵת־אָבִיהָ

הַשָּׂדֶה וַתִּצְנַח מֵעַל הַחֲמוֹר וַיֹּ֫אמֶר־לָהּ כָּלֵב מַה־לָּךְ

15 וַתֹּ֫אמֶר לוֹ הָבָה־לִּי בְרָכָה כִּי אֶרֶץ הַנֶּגֶב

נְתַתָּ֫נִי וְנָתַתָּה לִי גֻּלֹּת מָיִם וַיִּתֶּן־לָהּ כָּלֵב אֵת גֻּלֹּת

עִלִּית וְאֵת גֻּלֹּת תַּחְתִּית

Afterward the sons of Judah went down to fight against the Canaanites living in the hill country and in the Negev and in the lowland. So Judah went against the Canaanites who lived in **Hebron** (now the name of Hebron formerly [was] Kiriath-arba); and they struck Sheshai and Ahiman and Talmai. Then from there he went against the inhabitants of **Debir** (now the name of Debir formerly [was] **Kiriath-sepher**). And Caleb said, "The one who attacks Kiriath-sepher and captures it, I will even give him my daughter Achsah for a wife." Othniel the son of Kenaz, Caleb's younger brother, captured it; so he gave him his daughter Achsah for a wife. Then it came about when she came [to him], that she persuaded him to ask her father for a field. Then she alighted from her donkey, and Caleb said to her, "What do you want?" She said to him, "Give me a blessing, since you have given me the land of the Negev, give me also springs of water." So Caleb gave her the upper springs and the lower springs.

B. Kenites — at Arad Judges 1:16

וּבְנֵי <חֹבָב> <הַ>קֵינִי חֹתֵן מֹשֶׁה עָלוּ מֵעִיר הַתְּמָרִים אֶת־בְּנֵי
יְהוּדָה מִדְבַּר יְהוּדָה אֲשֶׁר בְּנֶגֶב עֲרָד וַיֵּלֶךְ וַיֵּשֶׁב
אֶת־הָעָם

The descendants of ‹Hobab the› Kenite, Moses' father-in-law, went up from the **city of palms** **to** the sons of Judah, (to) the wilderness of Judah which is in the Negeb of Arad; and they went and lived with Am‹alek›.

C. Simeon — at Zephat = Hormah Judges 1:17

17 וַיֵּלֶךְ יְהוּדָה אֶת־שִׁמְעוֹן אָחִיו וַיַּכּוּ
אֶת־הַכְּנַעֲנִי יוֹשֵׁב צְפַת וַיַּחֲרִימוּ אוֹתָהּ וַיִּקְרָא

אֶת־שֵׁם־הָעִיר חָרְמָה Then Judah went with Simeon his brother, and they struck the Canaanites living in **Zephath**, and utterly destroyed it. So the name of the city was called **Hormah**.

D. Summary — of Judah and Judea Judges 1:18-20

18 <וְלֹא הוֹרִישׁ> (LXX καὶ οὐκ ἐκληρονόμησεν) יְהוּדָה אֶת־עַזָּה·
וְאֶת־גְּבוּלָהּ וְאֶת־אַשְׁקְלוֹן וְאֶת־גְּבוּלָהּ וְאֶת־עֶקְרוֹן וְאֶת־גְּבוּלָהּ
19 וַיְהִי יְהוָה אֶת־יְהוּדָה וַיֹּרֶשׁ אֶת־הָהָר כִּי לֹא
לְהוֹרִישׁ אֶת־יֹשְׁבֵי הָעֵמֶק כִּי־רֶכֶב בַּרְזֶל לָהֶם
20 וַיִּתְּנוּ לְכָלֵב אֶת־חֶבְרוֹן כַּאֲשֶׁר דִּבֶּר מֹשֶׁה
וַיֹּרֶשׁ מִשָּׁם אֶת־שְׁלֹשָׁה בְּנֵי הָעֲנָק

And Judah ‹did not› (LXX) take **Gaza** with its territory and **Ashkelon** with its territory and **Ekron** with its territory. Now Yahweh was with Judah, and they took possession of the hill country; but they could not drive out the inhabitants of the valley because they had iron chariots. Then they gave **Hebron** to Caleb, as Moses had promised; and he drove out from there the three sons of Anak.

E. The other Tribes:

1. Benjamin Judges 1:21

Judg. 1:21 וְאֶת־הַיְבוּסִי יֹשֵׁב יְרוּשָׁלַם לֹא הוֹרִישׁוּ בְּנֵי בִנְיָמִן

וַיֵּשֶׁב הַיְבוּסִי אֶת־בְּנֵי בִנְיָמִן בִּירוּשָׁלַם עַד הַיּוֹם הַזֶּה

But the sons of Benjamin did not drive out the **Jebusites** who lived in
Jerusalem; so the Jebusites have lived with the sons of Benjamin in Jerusalem
to this day.

2. House of Joseph (Ephraim) Judges 1:22-26

22 וַיַּעֲלוּ בֵית־יוֹסֵף גַּם־הֵם בֵּית־אֵל וַיהוָה עִמָּם

23 וַיָּתִירוּ בֵית־יוֹסֵף בְּבֵית־אֵל וְשֵׁם־הָעִיר לְפָנִים לוּז

24 וַיִּרְאוּ הַשֹּׁמְרִים אִישׁ יוֹצֵא מִן־הָעִיר וַיֹּאמְרוּ

לוֹ הַרְאֵנוּ נָא אֶת־מְבוֹא הָעִיר וְעָשִׂינוּ עִמְּךָ חָסֶד

25 וַיַּרְאֵם אֶת־מְבוֹא הָעִיר וַיַּכּוּ אֶת־הָעִיר

לְפִי־חָרֶב וְאֶת־הָאִישׁ וְאֶת־כָּל־מִשְׁפַּחְתּוֹ שִׁלֵּחוּ

26 וַיֵּלֶךְ הָאִישׁ אֶרֶץ הַחִתִּים וַיִּבֶן עִיר וַיִּקְרָא

שְׁמָהּ לוּז הוּא שְׁמָהּ עַד הַיּוֹם הַזֶּה

Likewise the **House of Joseph** (Ephraim) went up against **Bethel**, and
Yahweh was with them. The house of Joseph spied out Bethel (now the name
of the city was formerly **Luz**). The spies saw a man coming out of the city and
they said to him, "Please show us the entrance to the city and we will treat
you kindly." So he showed them the entrance to the city, and they struck the
city with the edge of the sword, but they let the man and all his family go
free. The man went into the land of the Hittites and built a city and named it
Luz which is its name to this day.

3. Manasseh Judges 1:27-28

27 וְלֹא־הוֹרִישׁ מְנַשֶּׁה אֶת־בֵּית־שְׁאָן

וְאֶת־בְּנוֹתֶיהָ וְאֶת־תַּעְנַךְ וְאֶת־בְּנֹתֶיהָ וְאֶת־יֹשֵׁב [יֹשְׁבֵי]

דּוֹר וְאֶת־בְּנוֹתֶיהָ וְאֶת־יוֹשְׁבֵי יִבְלְעָם וְאֶת־בְּנֹתֶיהָ

וְאֶת־יוֹשְׁבֵי מְגִדּוֹ וְאֶת־בְּנוֹתֶיהָ וַיּוֹאֶל הַכְּנַעֲנִי לָשֶׁבֶת

בָּאָרֶץ הַזֹּאת

28 וַיְהִי כִּי־חָזַק יִשְׂרָאֵל וַיָּשֶׂם אֶת־הַכְּנַעֲנִי לָמַס

וְהוֹרֵישׁ לֹא הוֹרִישׁוֹ

But **Manasseh** did not take possession of **Beth-shean** and its villages, or **Taanach** and its villages, or the inhabitants of **Dor** and its villages, or the inhabitants of **Ibleam** and its villages, or the inhabitants of **Megiddo** and its villages; so the Canaanites persisted in living in that land. It came about when Israel became strong, that they put the Canaanites to forced labor, but they did not drive them out

4. Ephraim Judges 1:29

29 וְאֶפְרַיִם לֹא הוֹרִישׁ אֶת־הַכְּנַעֲנִי הַיּוֹשֵׁב

בְּגָזֶר וַיֵּשֶׁב הַכְּנַעֲנִי בְּקִרְבּוֹ בְּגָזֶר

Ephraim did not drive out the Canaanites who were living in **Gezer**; so the Canaanites lived in Gezer among them.

1 Ch. 7:20-24

20 וּבְנֵי אֶפְרַיִם שׁוּתָלַח וּבֶרֶד בְּנוֹ וְתַחַן(!) בְּנוֹ

וְאֶלְעָדָה בְּנוֹ וְנַעֲמִי (LXX) בְּנוֹ

21 וְזָבָד בְּנוֹ וְשׁוּתֶלַח בְּנוֹ וְעֵזֶר וְאֶלְעָד

וַהֲרָגוּם אַנְשֵׁי־גַת הַנּוֹלָדִים בָּאָרֶץ כִּי יָרְדוּ לָקַחַת

אֶת־מִקְנֵיהֶם

22 וַיִּתְאַבֵּל אֶפְרַיִם אֲבִיהֶם יָמִים רַבִּים וַיָּבֹאוּ

אֶחָיו לְנַחֲמוֹ

23 וַיָּבֹא אֶל־אִשְׁתּוֹ וַתַּהַר וַתֵּלֶד בֵּן וַיִּקְרָא

אֶת־שְׁמוֹ בְּרִיעָה כִּי בְרָעָה הָיְתָה בְּבֵיתוֹ

24 וּבִתּוֹ שֶׁאֱרָה וַתִּבֶן אֶת־בֵּית־חוֹרוֹן הַתַּחְתּוֹן

וְאֶת־הָעֶלְיוֹן וְאֵת אֻזֵּן שֶׁאֱרָה

And the sons of **Ephraim**, Shutelah and Bered his son and Tahan (Num. 26:35) his son and Eleadah his son, Naami (LXX B Νοομε) his son and Zabad his son and Shutelah his son and Ezer and Elead were killed by the autochthonous men of **Gath** because they had come down to rustle their cattle. And their father Ephraim mourned many days and his relatives came to comfort him. Then he went in to his wife and she conceived and gave birth to a son and he called his name Beriah because there had been misfortune in his house. His daughter was Sheerah, who built **Lower and Upper Beth-horon** and **Uzzen Sheerah**.

5. Zebulun Judges 1:30

30 זְבוּלֻן לֹא הוֹרִישׁ אֶת־יוֹשְׁבֵי קִטְרוֹן

וְאֶת־יוֹשְׁבֵי נַהֲלֹל וַיֵּשֶׁב הַכְּנַעֲנִי בְּקִרְבּוֹ וַיִּהְיוּ לָמַס

Zebulun did not drive out the inhabitants of **Kitron**, or the inhabitants of
Nahalol; so the Canaanites lived among them and became subject to forced
labor.

6. Asher Judges 1:31-32

31 אָשֵׁר לֹא הוֹרִישׁ אֶת־יֹשְׁבֵי עַכּוֹ וְאֶת־יוֹשְׁבֵי צִידוֹן

וְאֶת־אַחְלָב וְאֶת־אַכְזִיב וְאֶת־חֶלְבָּה וְאֶת־אֲפִיק וְאֶת־רְחֹב

32 וַיֵּשֶׁב הָאָשֵׁרִי בְּקֶרֶב הַכְּנַעֲנִי יֹשְׁבֵי הָאָרֶץ כִּי לֹא הוֹרִישׁוֹ

Asher did not drive out the inhabitants of **Acco**, or the inhabitants of **Sidon**,
or of **Ahlab**, or of **Achzib**, or of **Helbah**, or of **Aphik**, or of **Rehob**. So the
Asherites lived among the Canaanites, the inhabitants of the land; for they
did not drive them out.

7. Naphtali Judges 1:33

33 נַפְתָּלִי לֹא־הוֹרִישׁ אֶת־יֹשְׁבֵי בֵית־שֶׁמֶשׁ

וְאֶת־יֹשְׁבֵי בֵית־עֲנָת וַיֵּשֶׁב בְּקֶרֶב הַכְּנַעֲנִי יֹשְׁבֵי הָאָרֶץ

וְיֹשְׁבֵי בֵית־שֶׁמֶשׁ וּבֵית עֲנָת הָיוּ לָהֶם לָמַס

Naphtali did not drive out the inhabitants of **Beth-shemesh**, or the
inhabitants of **Beth-anath**, but lived among the Canaanites, the inhabitants of
the land; and the inhabitants of **Beth-shemesh** and **Beth-anath** became forced
labor for them.

8. Danites Judges 1:34-35

34 וַיִּלְחֲצוּ הָאֱמֹרִי אֶת־בְּנֵי־דָן הָהָרָה כִּי־לֹא נְתָנוֹ לָרֶדֶת לָעֵמֶק

35 וַיּוֹאֶל הָאֱמֹרִי לָשֶׁבֶת בְּהַר־חֶרֶס בְּאַיָּלוֹן

וּבְשַׁעַלְבִים וַתִּכְבַּד יַד בֵּית־יוֹסֵף וַיִּהְיוּ לָמַס

Then the **Amorites** forced the sons of **Dan** into the hill country, for they did not allow them to come down to the valley; yet the Amorites persisted in living in **Mount Heres**, in **Aijalon** and in **Shaalbim**; but when the power of the house of Joseph grew strong, they became forced labor.

F. Fragmentary Border Description Judg. 1:36

36 וּגְבוּל הָאֱמֹרִי מִמַּעֲלֵה עַקְרַבִּים מֵהַסֶּלַע וָמָעְלָה

The border of the Amorites ran from the ascent of Akrabbim, from Sela and upward.

III.   THE JUDGES

A. **Othniel** son of Kenaz (Judg. 3:8-11).

B. **Ehud** — against Eglon king of Moab, at Jericho (Judg. 3:12-30).

C. **Deborah and Barak** (Josh. 12:19-23; Judg. 4-5)

1. Israelites gathered at <u>Kedesh</u> overlooking Chinnereth
Judges 4:2

וַיִּמְכְּרֵם יְהוָה בְּיַד יָבִין מֶלֶךְ־כְּנַעַן אֲשֶׁר מָלַךְ בְּחָצוֹר
וְשַׂר־צְבָאוֹ סִיסְרָא וְהוּא יוֹשֵׁב בַּחֲרֹשֶׁת הַגּוֹיִם

And Yahweh sold them into the hand of **Jabin king of Canaan**, who reigned in **Hazor**; and the commander of his army was **Sisera**, who lived in **Harosheth-hagoyim**.

2. Marched to Tabor

Judges 4:9-12

9 וַתֹּאמֶר הָלֹךְ אֵלֵךְ עִמָּךְ אֶפֶס כִּי לֹא תִהְיֶה
תִּפְאַרְתְּךָ עַל־הַדֶּרֶךְ אֲשֶׁר אַתָּה הוֹלֵךְ כִּי בְיַד־אִשָּׁה
יִמְכֹּר יְהוָה אֶת־סִיסְרָא וַתָּקָם דְּבוֹרָה וַתֵּלֶךְ עִם־בָּרָק קֶדְשָׁה

10 וַיַּזְעֵק בָּרָק אֶת־זְבוּלֻן וְאֶת־נַפְתָּלִי קֶדְשָׁה

וַיַּעַל בְּרַגְלָיו עֲשֶׂרֶת אַלְפֵי אִישׁ וַתַּעַל עִמּוֹ דְּבוֹרָה

11 וְחֶבֶר הַקֵּינִי נִפְרָד מִקַּיִן מִבְּנֵי חֹבָב חֹתֵן מֹשֶׁה

וַיֵּט אָהֳלוֹ עַד־אֵלוֹן בַּצְעַנִּים [בְּ][צַעֲנַנִּים] אֲשֶׁר אֶת־קֶדֶשׁ

12 וַיַּגִּדוּ לְסִיסְרָא כִּי עָלָה בָּרָק בֶּן־אֲבִינֹעַם הַר־תָּבוֹר

Then Deborah arose and went with Barak to **Kedesh**. Barak called **Zebulun**
and **Naphtali** together to **Kedesh**, and ten thousand men went up with him;
Deborah also went up with him. Now **Heber the Kenite** had separated
himself from the Kenites, from the sons of Hobab the father-in-law of Moses,
and had pitched his tent as far away as **the oak in Zaanannim**, which is near
Kedesh.

Then they told **Sisera** that Barak the son of Abinoam had gone up to
Mount Tabor.

3. Canaanites gathered at Harosheth Hagoiim

Judg. 4:13

13 וַיַּזְעֵק סִיסְרָא אֶת־כָּל־רִכְבּוֹ תְּשַׁע מֵאוֹת רֶכֶב בַּרְזֶל

וְאֶת־כָּל־הָעָם אֲשֶׁר אִתּוֹ מֵחֲרֹשֶׁת הַגּוֹיִם אֶל־נַחַל קִישׁוֹן

Sisera called together all his chariots, nine hundred iron chariots, and all the
people who [were] with him, from **Harosheth-hagoyim** to the river **Kishon**.

****The form and meaning of חֲרֹשֶׁת הַגּוֹיִם "Harosheth of the gentiles."

Judg. 4:16, the LXX A tradition translated עַד חֲרֹשֶׁת הַגּוֹיִם by ἕως
δρυμοῦ τῶν ἐθνῶν "to the **forest** of the gentiles" חֹרֶשׁ = חֲרֹשֶׁת
"forest"

גְּלִיל הַגּוֹיִם "the district of the gentiles" (Isaiah 8:23; Eng. 9:1)

חֲרֹשֶׁת הַגּוֹיִם in Judges 4 || מְגִדּוֹ עַל־מֵי בְּתַעְנָךְ "By Taanach on the
waters of Megiddo" in Judges 5:19.

חֲרֹשֶׁת feminine noun on the stative pattern, i.e. *ḥᵃrōšeṯ* ‹ **ḥarušt-*.

The LXX Αρισωθ thus points to an original **ḥarišt-* most likely from *ḤRṮ, and **ḥarišt-* is a perfect cognate to Akkadian *erištu* "cultivable ground."

LXX Αρισωθ τῶν ἐθνῶν "*Arisōth* of the gentiles," = *ḥarišôṯ,

The Massoretes were probably influenced by חֲרֹשֶׁת "skilled work" Exod. 31:5; 35:33) from the root *ḤRŠ* גְּלִיל הַגּוֹיִם "the **district** of the gentiles" in Isaiah 8:23

****   Harosheth of the Goiim = "**the good farm land of the gentiles**."

4. Retreated to their assembly grounds:

Judges 5:19-21

19 בָּ֤אוּ מְלָכִים֙ נִלְחָ֔מוּ אָ֤ז נִלְחֲמוּ֙ מַלְכֵ֣י כְנַ֔עַן

בְּתַעְנַ֖ךְ עַל־מֵ֣י מְגִדּ֑וֹ בֶּ֥צַע כֶּ֖סֶף לֹ֥א לָקָֽחוּ׃

20 מִן־שָׁמַ֖יִם נִלְחָ֑מוּ הַכּֽוֹכָבִים֙ מִמְּסִלּוֹתָ֔ם נִלְחֲמ֖וּ עִם־סִיסְרָֽא׃

21 נַ֤חַל קִישׁוֹן֙ גְּרָפָ֔ם נַ֥חַל קְדוּמִ֖ים נַ֣חַל קִישׁ֑וֹן

The kings came, they fought; <u>Then fought the kings of Canaan</u>

At **Taanach** near the waters of **Megiddo**; They took no plunder in silver.

<u>The stars fought from heaven</u>, From their courses they fought against Sisera.

The torrent of **Kishon** swept them away, The ancient torrent, the torrent

   Kishon.

D. Gideon (Judg. 6-8; Psalms 83:10-11)

Judges 7:1

וַיַּשְׁכֵּ֨ם יְרֻבַּ֜עַל ה֣וּא גִדְע֗וֹן וְכָל־הָעָם֙ אֲשֶׁ֣ר

אִתּ֔וֹ וַֽיַּחֲנ֖וּ עַל־עֵ֣ין חֲרֹ֑ד וּמַחֲנֵ֤ה מִדְיָן֙ הָֽיָה־ל֣וֹ מִצָּפ֔וֹן

מִגִּבְעַ֥ת הַמּוֹרֶ֖ה בָּעֵֽמֶק

Then **Jerubbaal** (that is, **Gideon**) and all the people who were with him, rose early and camped beside **the spring of Harod**; and the camp of **Midian** was on the north side of them by **the hill of Moreh** on the plain.

E. Abimelech (Judg. 8:30-9:57)

    1. Arumah = Kh. el-ᶜOrmah

    2. Ophrah = should be in Abiezer clan SW of Mt. Gerizim (near Kh. ᶜAwfar ?).

F. Jephtah Judg 11-12:7

G. Samson (Judg. 13-16)

H. Concluding stories; anti Saul (Benjaminite) and pro Bethlehem

Judges 17:7-8

7 וַיְהִי־נַעַר מִבֵּית לֶחֶם יְהוּדָה מִמִּשְׁפַּחַת יְהוּדָה וְהוּא לֵוִי

וְהוּא גָר־שָׁם 8 וַיֵּלֶךְ הָאִישׁ מֵהָעִיר מִבֵּית לֶחֶם יְהוּדָה לָגוּר בַּאֲשֶׁר

יִמְצָא וַיָּבֹא הַר־אֶפְרַיִם עַד־בֵּית מִיכָה לַעֲשׂוֹת דַּרְכּוֹ

Now there was a young man from **Bethlehem in Judah**, of the family of Judah, who was a Levite; and he was staying there. Then the man departed from the city, from Bethlehem in Judah, to stay wherever he might find [a place]; and as he made his journey, he came to **the hill country of Ephraim** to the house of Micah.

Judges 19:1

וַיְהִי בַּיָּמִים הָהֵם וּמֶלֶךְ אֵין בְּיִשְׂרָאֵל וַיְהִי אִישׁ לֵוִי גָּר בְּיַרְכְּתֵי

הַר־אֶפְרַיִם וַיִּקַּח־לוֹ אִשָּׁה פִילֶגֶשׁ מִבֵּית לֶחֶם יְהוּדָה

Now it came about in those days, when there was no king in Israel, that there was a certain **Levite** staying in the remote part of **the hill country of Ephraim**, who took a concubine for himself from **Bethlehem in Judah**.

Judg. 19:11 הֵם עִם־יְבוּס וְהַיּוֹם רַד מְאֹד וַיֹּאמֶר הַנַּעַר אֶל־אֲדֹנָיו

לְכָה־נָּא וְנָסוּרָה אֶל־עִיר־הַיְבוּסִי הַזֹּאת וְנָלִין בָּהּ

Judg. 19:12 וַיֹּאמֶר אֵלָיו אֲדֹנָיו לֹא נָסוּר אֶל־עִיר נָכְרִי

אֲשֶׁר לֹא־מִבְּנֵי יִשְׂרָאֵל הֵנָּה וְעָבַרְנוּ עַד־גִּבְעָה

Judg. 19:13 וַיֹּאמֶר לְנַעֲרוֹ לֵךְ וְנִקְרְבָה בְּאַחַד

הַמְּקֹמוֹת וְלַנּוּ בַגִּבְעָה אוֹ בָרָמָה

Judg. 19:14 וַיַּעֲבְרוּ וַיֵּלֵכוּ וַתָּבֹא לָהֶם הַשֶּׁמֶשׁ אֵצֶל

הַגִּבְעָה אֲשֶׁר לְבִנְיָמִן

Judg. 19:15 וַיָּסֻרוּ שָׁם לָבוֹא לָלוּן בַּגִּבְעָה וַיָּבֹא וַיֵּשֶׁב

בִּרְחוֹב הָעִיר וְאֵין אִישׁ מְאַסֵּף־אוֹתָם הַבַּיְתָה לָלוּן

Judg. 19:11 When they [were] near Jebus, the day was almost gone; and the servant said to his master, "Please come, and let us turn aside into this city of the Jebusites and spend the night in it."

Judg. 19:12 However, his master said to him, "We will not turn aside into the city of foreigners who are not of the sons of Israel; but we will go on as far as Gibeah."

Judg. 19:13 He said to his servant, "Come and let us approach one of these places; and we will spend the night in Gibeah or Ramah."

Judg. 19:14 So they passed along and went their way, and the sun set on them near Gibeah which belongs to Benjamin.

Judges 20:1

Judg. 20:1 וַיֵּצְאוּ כָּל־בְּנֵי יִשְׂרָאֵל וַתִּקָּהֵל הָעֵדָה כְּאִישׁ

אֶחָד לְמִדָּן וְעַד־בְּאֵר שֶׁבַע וְאֶרֶץ הַגִּלְעָד אֶל־יְהוָה

הַמִּצְפָּה

Judg. 20:1 ¶ Then all the sons of Israel from Dan to Beersheba, including the land of Gilead, came out, and the congregation assembled as one man to Yahweh at Mizpah.

J. Concluding Statement:

Judges 21:25

בַּיָּמִים הָהֵם אֵין מֶלֶךְ בְּיִשְׂרָאֵל אִישׁ הַיָּשָׁר בְּעֵינָיו יַעֲשֶׂה

In those days there was no king in Israel; everyone did what was right in his own eyes.

LESSON 12

SAMUEL AND SAUL

I. SAMUEL

A. Battle of Ebenezer

1. Location: ꜥIzbet Ṣarṭa (?)

1 Sam 4:1

וַיְהִי דְבַר־שְׁמוּאֵל לְכָל־יִשְׂרָאֵל וַיֵּצֵא יִשְׂרָאֵל לִקְרַאת פְּלִשְׁתִּים
לַמִּלְחָמָה וַיַּחֲנוּ עַל־הָאֶבֶן הָעֵזֶר וּפְלִשְׁתִּים חָנוּ בַאֲפֵק

Thus the word of Samuel came to all Israel. Now Israel went out to meet the
Philistines in battle and camped beside Ebenezer while the Philistines
camped in Aphek.

1 Sam 4:12

וַיָּרָץ אִישׁ־בִּנְיָמִן מֵהַמַּעֲרָכָה וַיָּבֹא שִׁלֹה
בַּיּוֹם הַהוּא וּמַדָּיו קְרֻעִים וַאֲדָמָה עַל־רֹאשׁוֹ

Now a man of Benjamin ran from the battle line and came to Shiloh the same
day with his clothes torn and dust on his head.

2. Shilo destroyed Jer. 7:12, 14

כִּי לְכוּ־נָא אֶל־מְקוֹמִי אֲשֶׁר בְּשִׁילוֹ אֲשֶׁר Jer. 7:12

12 שִׁכַּנְתִּי שְׁמִי שָׁם בָּרִאשׁוֹנָה וּרְאוּ אֵת אֲשֶׁר־עָשִׂיתִי לוֹ
מִפְּנֵי רָעַת עַמִּי יִשְׂרָאֵל

14 וְעָשִׂיתִי לַבַּיִת אֲשֶׁר נִקְרָא־שְׁמִי עָלָיו אֲשֶׁר
אַתֶּם בֹּטְחִים בּוֹ וְלַמָּקוֹם אֲשֶׁר־נָתַתִּי לָכֶם וְלַאֲבוֹתֵיכֶם
כַּאֲשֶׁר עָשִׂיתִי לְשִׁלוֹ

"But go now to My place which was in **Shiloh**, where I made My name dwell
at the first, and see what I did to it because of the wickedness of My people
Israel. . . . therefore, I will do to the house which is called by My name, in

which you trust, and to the place which I gave you and your fathers, as I did
to **Shiloh**.

Jer 26:6,9

וְנָתַתִּי אֶת־הַבַּיִת הַזֶּה כְּשִׁלֹה וְאֶת־הָעִיר Jer. 26:6

הַזֹּאתָה [הַ][זֹּאת] אֶתֵּן לִקְלָלָה לְכֹל גּוֹיֵי הָאָרֶץ

מַדּוּעַ נִבֵּיתָ בְשֵׁם־יְהוָה לֵאמֹר כְּשִׁלוֹ יִהְיֶה Jer. 26:9

הַבַּיִת הַזֶּה וְהָעִיר הַזֹּאת תֶּחֱרַב מֵאֵין יוֹשֵׁב וַיִּקָּהֵל

כָּל־הָעָם אֶל־יִרְמְיָהוּ בְּבֵית יְהוָה

then I will make this house like Shiloh, and this city I will make a curse to all
the nations of the earth" . . . "Why have you prophesied in the name of
Yahweh saying, ʿThis house will be like Shiloh and this city will be desolate,
without inhabitantʾ?"

Psalms 78:60

וַיִּטֹּשׁ מִשְׁכַּן שִׁלוֹ אֹהֶל שִׁכֵּן בָּאָדָם

So that He abandoned the dwelling place at **Shiloh**, The tent which He had
pitched among men,

cf. 1 Sam 21:2 ff. Cult center at Nob

3. The Ark in captivity: 1 Sam chaps. 5-6 — **Ashdod,
   Gath, Ekron; to Beth-shemesh, Kiriath-jearim**
   1 Sam. 6:12-13

וַיִּשַּׁרְנָה הַפָּרוֹת בַּדֶּרֶךְ עַל־דֶּרֶךְ בֵּית שֶׁמֶשׁ בִּמְסִלָּה אַחַת

הָלְכוּ הָלֹךְ וְגָעוֹ וְלֹא־סָרוּ יָמִין וּשְׂמֹאול וְסַרְנֵי פְלִשְׁתִּים

הֹלְכִים אַחֲרֵיהֶם עַד־גְּבוּל בֵּית שָׁמֶשׁ וּבֵית שֶׁמֶשׁ קֹצְרִים

קְצִיר־חִטִּים בָּעֵמֶק וַיִּשְׂאוּ אֶת־עֵינֵיהֶם וַיִּרְאוּ אֶת־הָאָרוֹן

וַיִּשְׂמְחוּ לִרְאוֹת

<u>1Sam. 6:12-13</u> And the cows took the straight way in the direction of **Beth-
shemesh**; they went along the highway, lowing as they went, and did not
turn aside to the right or to the left. And the rulers of the Philistines followed

them to the border of **Beth-shemesh**. Now [the people of] **Beth-shemesh** were reaping their wheat harvest in the valley, and they raised their eyes and saw the ark and were glad to see [it].

B. Samuel's victory
1 Sam 7:11

וַיֵּצְאוּ אַנְשֵׁי יִשְׂרָאֵל מִן־הַמִּצְפָּה וַיִּרְדְּפוּ
אֶת־פְּלִשְׁתִּים וַיַּכּוּם עַד־מִתַּחַת לְבֵית כָּר (= בֵּית חֹרוֹן?)

The men of Israel went out of **Mizpah** and pursued the Philistines, and struck them down as far as below **Beth-car**. (Beth-Horon???)

1 Sam 7:14

1Sam. 7:14 וַתָּשֹׁבְנָה הֶעָרִים אֲשֶׁר לָקְחוּ־פְלִשְׁתִּים מֵאֵת
יִשְׂרָאֵל לְיִשְׂרָאֵל מֵעֶקְרוֹן וְעַד־גַּת וְאֶת־גְּבוּלָן הִצִּיל
יִשְׂרָאֵל מִיַּד פְּלִשְׁתִּים וַיְהִי שָׁלוֹם בֵּין יִשְׂרָאֵל וּבֵין הָאֱמֹרִי

The cities which the Philistines had taken from Israel were restored to Israel, from **Ekron** and beside **Gath** (**-rimmon** = **Gittaim** ?); and Israel delivered their territory from the hand of the Philistines. So there was peace between Israel and the Amorites.

C. Samuel's itinerary: 1 Sam 7:15-17

15 וַיִּשְׁפֹּט שְׁמוּאֵל אֶת־יִשְׂרָאֵל כֹּל יְמֵי חַיָּיו
16 וְהָלַךְ מִדֵּי שָׁנָה בְּשָׁנָה וְסָבַב בֵּית־אֵל וְהַגִּלְגָּל וְהַמִּצְפָּה
וְשָׁפַט אֶת־יִשְׂרָאֵל אֵת כָּל־הַמְּקוֹמוֹת הָאֵלֶּה
17 וּתְשֻׁבָתוֹ הָרָמָתָה כִּי־שָׁם בֵּיתוֹ וְשָׁם שָׁפָט
אֶת־יִשְׂרָאֵל וַיִּבֶן שָׁם מִזְבֵּחַ לַיהוָה

Now Samuel judged Israel all the days of his life. He used to go annually on circuit to **Bethel** and **Gilgal** and **Mizpah**, and he judged Israel in all these places. Then his return [was] to **Ramah**, for his house [was] there, and there he judged Israel; and he built there an altar to Yahweh.

hārâmāṯ^{āh} = הָרָמָתַיִם צוֹפִים of 1 Sam 1:1

II. SAUL

    A. Initial rescue operation: Jabesh-gilead delivered from
        Nahashthe Ammonite; attack launched via Bezek
        1 Sam 11:1 ff.

    B. Central Hill Country — Removal of Philistine garrison at
        Michmash —

        1. Israelites assemble: Saul with troops at Michmash
           and Mt. Bethel, Jonathan at Gibeah of
           Benjamin,1 Sam 13:2
        2. Jonathan smites the Philistine *n^eṣîḇ* at Geba^c
           1 Sam 13:3
        3. Philistines encamp at Michmash east of Beth-aven

        1 Sam 13:16-18

1Sam. 13:16 וְשָׁאוּל וְיוֹנָתָן בְּנוֹ וְהָעָם הַנִּמְצָא עִמָּם

יֹשְׁבִים בְּגֶבַע בִּנְיָמִן וּפְלִשְׁתִּים חָנוּ בְמִכְמָשׂ

1Sam. 13:17 וַיֵּצֵא הַמַּשְׁחִית מִמַּחֲנֵה פְלִשְׁתִּים שְׁלֹשָׁה

רָאשִׁים הָרֹאשׁ אֶחָד יִפְנֶה אֶל־דֶּרֶךְ עָפְרָה אֶל־אֶרֶץ שׁוּעָל

1Sam. 13:18 וְהָרֹאשׁ אֶחָד יִפְנֶה דֶּרֶךְ בֵּית חֹרוֹן וְהָרֹאשׁ אֶחָד

יִפְנֶה דֶּרֶךְ הַגְּבוּל הַנִּשְׁקָף עַל־גֵּי הַצְּבֹעִים הַמִּדְבָּרָה

Now Saul and his son Jonathan and the people who were present with them
were staying in **Geba of Benjamin** while the Philistines camped at
Michmash. And the raiders came from the camp of the Philistines in three
companies: one company turned toward **Ophrah**, to the land of **Shual**, and
another company turned toward **Beth-horon**, and another company turned
toward the border which overlooks the **valley of Zeboim** toward the
wilderness.

4. Jonathan attacks their outpost; the Philistines are routed
1 Sam 14:4-5 *Bôṣēṣ* and *Senne^h* the two cliffs

1Sam. 14:4 וּבֵין הַמַּעְבְּרוֹת אֲשֶׁר בִּקֵּשׁ יוֹנָתָן לַעֲבֹר

עַל־מַצַּב פְּלִשְׁתִּים שֵׁן־הַסֶּלַע מֵהָעֵבֶר מִזֶּה וְשֵׁן־הַסֶּלַע

מֵהָעֵבֶר מִזֶּה וְשֵׁם הָאֶחָד בּוֹצֵץ וְשֵׁם הָאֶחָד סֶנֶּה

1Sam. 14:5 הַשֵּׁן הָאֶחָד מָצוּק מִצָּפוֹן מוּל מִכְמָשׂ

וְהָאֶחָד מִנֶּגֶב מוּל גָּבַע

Between the passes by which Jonathan sought to cross over to the Philistines'
garrison, there was a sharp crag on the one side and a sharp crag on the other
side, and the name of the one was **Bozez**, and the name of the other **Seneh**.
The one crag rose on the north opposite **Michmash**, and the other on the
south opposite **Geba**.

1 Sam 14:31

1Sam. 14:13 וַיַּעַל יוֹנָתָן עַל־יָדָיו וְעַל־רַגְלָיו וְנֹשֵׂא

כֵלָיו אַחֲרָיו וַיִּפְּלוּ לִפְנֵי יוֹנָתָן וְנֹשֵׂא כֵלָיו מְמוֹתֵת אַחֲרָיו

They struck among the Philistines that day from **Michmash** to **Aijalon**. And
the people were very weary.

C. The Negeb — against the Amalekites

1 Sam 15:5-7

5 וַיָּבֹא שָׁאוּל עַד־עִיר עֲמָלֵק וַיָּרֶב בַּנָּחַל

6 וַיֹּאמֶר שָׁאוּל אֶל־הַקֵּינִי לְכוּ סֻּרוּ רְדוּ מִתּוֹךְ עֲמָלֵקִי פֶּן־אֹסִפְךָ

עִמּוֹ וְאַתָּה עָשִׂיתָה חֶסֶד עִם־כָּל־בְּנֵי יִשְׂרָאֵל בַּעֲלוֹתָם מִמִּצְרָיִם

וַיָּסַר קֵינִי מִתּוֹךְ עֲמָלֵק

7 וַיַּךְ שָׁאוּל אֶת־עֲמָלֵק מֵחֲוִילָה בּוֹאֲךָ שׁוּר אֲשֶׁר עַל־פְּנֵי מִצְרָיִם

Saul came to the **city of Amalek** and set an ambush in the valley. Saul said to
the **Kenites**, "Go, depart, go down from among the **Amalekites**, so that I do

not destroy you with them; for you showed kindness to all the sons of Israel when they came up from Egypt." So the **Kenites** departed from among the **Amalekites**. So Saul defeated the **Amalekites**, from **Havilah** as you go to **Shur**, which is east of **Egypt**.

D. In the Shephelah — protecting Judah from the Philistines

Vale of Elah 1 Sam 17:1-3

1 וַיַּאַסְפוּ פְלִשְׁתִּים אֶת־מַחֲנֵיהֶם לַמִּלְחָמָה וַיֵּאָסְפוּ שֹׁכֹה אֲשֶׁר לִיהוּדָה וַיַּחֲנוּ בֵּין־שׂוֹכֹה וּבֵין־עֲזֵקָה בְּאֶפֶס דַּמִּים

2 וְשָׁאוּל וְאִישׁ־יִשְׂרָאֵל נֶאֶסְפוּ וַיַּחֲנוּ בְּעֵמֶק הָאֵלָה וַיַּעַרְכוּ מִלְחָמָה לִקְרַאת פְּלִשְׁתִּים

3 וּפְלִשְׁתִּים עֹמְדִים אֶל־הָהָר מִזֶּה וְיִשְׂרָאֵל עֹמְדִים אֶל־הָהָר מִזֶּה וְהַגַּיְא בֵּינֵיהֶם

Now the Philistines gathered their armies for battle; and they were gathered at **Socoh** which belongs to Judah, and they camped between **Socoh** and **Azekah**, without any bloodshed. Saul and the men of Israel were gathered and camped in the **valley of Elah**, and drew up in battle array to encounter the Philistines. The Philistines stood on the mountain on one side while Israel stood on the mountain on the other side, with the valley between them.

Philistine retreat, 1 Sam 17:52

וַיָּקֻמוּ אַנְשֵׁי יִשְׂרָאֵל וִיהוּדָה וַיָּרִעוּ וַיִּרְדְּפוּ אֶת־הַפְּלִשְׁתִּים עַד־בּוֹאֲךָ גַיְא (LXX Γεθ) וְעַד שַׁעֲרֵי עֶקְרוֹן (LXX ᾿Ασκαλῶνος) וַיִּפְּלוּ חַלְלֵי פְלִשְׁתִּים בְּדֶרֶךְ שַׁעֲרַיִם וְעַד־גַּת וְעַד־עֶקְרוֹן

The men of Israel and Judah arose and shouted and pursued the Philistines as far as the valley (LXX **Gath**), and to the gates of **Ekron** (LXX **Ashkelon**). And the slain Philistines fell on the **way to Shaaraim**, even to **Gath** and **Ekron**.

(Concerning Elhanan: 2 Sam. 21:19; 1 Chron. 20:5; 1 Sam 21:10; 22:10; cf. Psalms 151 LXX)

⟨151:1⟩   Οὗτος ὁ ψαλμὸς ἰδιόγραφος εἰς Δαυιδ
            καὶ ἔξωθεν τοῦ ἀριθμοῦ· ὅτε ἐμονομάχησεν
                        τῷ Γολιαδ.
            Μικρὸς ἤμην ἐν τοῖς ἀδελφοῖς μου
            καὶ νεώτερος ἐν τῷ οἴκῳ τοῦ πατρός μου·
            ἐποίμαινον τὰ πρόβατα τοῦ πατρός μου.
⟨2⟩   αἱ χεῖρές μου ἐποίησαν ὄργανον,
            οἱ δάκτυλοί μου ἥρμοσαν ψαλτήριον.
⟨3⟩   καὶ τίς ἀναγγελεῖ τῷ κυρίῳ μου;
            αὐτὸς κύριος, αὐτὸς εἰσακούει.
⟨4⟩   αὐτὸς ἐξαπέστειλεν τὸν ἄγγελον αὐτοῦ
            καὶ ἦρέν με ἐκ τῶν προβάτων τοῦ πατρός μου
            καὶ ἔχρισέν με ἐν τῷ ἐλαίῳ τῆς χρίσεως αὐτοῦ.
⟨5⟩   οἱ ἀδελφοί μου καλοὶ καὶ μεγάλοι,
            καὶ οὐκ εὐδόκησεν ἐν αὐτοῖς κύριος.
⟨6⟩   ἐξῆλθον εἰς συνάντησιν τῷ ἀλλοφύλῳ,
            καὶ ἐπικατηράσατό με ἐν τοῖς εἰδώλοις αὐτοῦ·
⟨7⟩   ἐγὼ δὲ σπασάμενος τὴν παρ᾽ αὐτοῦ μάχαιραν
            ἀπεκεφάλισα αὐτὸν καὶ ἦρα ὄνειδος ἐξ υἱῶν Ισραηλ.

E. In the Jezreel Valley

1. Philistines march north from Aphek
Flashback: 1 Sam 29:1

וַיִּקְבְּצוּ פְלִשְׁתִּים אֶת־כָּל־מַחֲנֵיהֶם אֲפֵקָה

וְיִשְׂרָאֵל חֹנִים בַּעַיִן אֲשֶׁר בְּיִזְרְעֶאל

Now the Philistines gathered together all their armies to **Aphek**, while the
Israelites were camping by the **spring which is in Jezreel**.

1 Sam 28:4

וַיִּקָּבְצוּ פְלִשְׁתִּים וַיָּבֹאוּ וַיַּחֲנוּ בְשׁוּנֵם

וַיִּקְבֹּץ שָׁאוּל אֶת־כָּל־יִשְׂרָאֵל וַיַּחֲנוּ בַּגִּלְבֹּעַ

So the Philistines gathered together and came and camped in **Shunem**; and
Saul gathered all Israel together and they camped in **Gilboa**.

1 Sam 31:1

וּפְלִשְׁתִּים נִלְחָמִים בְּיִשְׂרָאֵל וַיָּנֻסוּ אַנְשֵׁי יִשְׂרָאֵל מִפְּנֵי פְלִשְׁתִּים

וַיִּפְּלוּ חֲלָלִים בְּהַר הַגִּלְבֹּעַ

Now the Philistines were fighting against Israel, and the men of Israel fled from before the Philistines and fell slain on **Mount Gilboa**.

1 Sam 31:8-13

8 וַיְהִי מִמָּחֳרָת וַיָּבֹאוּ פְלִשְׁתִּים לְפַשֵּׁט אֶת־הַחֲלָלִים
וַיִּמְצְאוּ אֶת־שָׁאוּל וְאֶת־שְׁלֹשֶׁת בָּנָיו נֹפְלִים בְּהַר הַגִּלְבֹּעַ

9 וַיִּכְרְתוּ אֶת־רֹאשׁוֹ וַיַּפְשִׁיטוּ אֶת־כֵּלָיו וַיְשַׁלְּחוּ בְאֶרֶץ־פְּלִשְׁתִּים
סָבִיב לְבַשֵּׂר בֵּית עֲצַבֵּיהֶם וְאֶת־הָעָם

10 וַיָּשִׂמוּ אֶת־כֵּלָיו בֵּית עַשְׁתָּרוֹת וְאֶת־גְּוִיָּתוֹ תָּקְעוּ בְּחוֹמַת בֵּית שָׁן

11 וַיִּשְׁמְעוּ אֵלָיו יֹשְׁבֵי יָבֵישׁ גִּלְעָד אֵת אֲשֶׁר־עָשׂוּ פְלִשְׁתִּים לְשָׁאוּל

12 וַיָּקוּמוּ כָּל־אִישׁ חַיִל וַיֵּלְכוּ כָל־הַלַּיְלָה וַיִּקְחוּ אֶת־גְּוִיַּת שָׁאוּל וְאֵת
גְּוִיֹּת בָּנָיו מֵחוֹמַת בֵּית שָׁן וַיָּבֹאוּ יָבֵשָׁה וַיִּשְׂרְפוּ אֹתָם שָׁם

13 וַיִּקְחוּ אֶת־עַצְמֹתֵיהֶם וַיִּקְבְּרוּ תַחַת־הָאֶשֶׁל בְּיָבֵשָׁה וַיָּצֻמוּ שִׁבְעַת יָמִים

It came about on the next day when the Philistines came to strip the slain, that they found Saul and his three sons fallen on **Mount Gilboa**. They cut off his head and stripped off his weapons, and sent [them] throughout the land of the Philistines, to carry the good news to the house of their idols and to the people. They put his weapons in the temple of **Ashtaroth**, and they fastened his body to the wall of **Beth-shan**. Now when the inhabitants of **Jabesh-gilead** heard what the Philistines had done to Saul, all the valiant men rose and walked all night, and took the body of Saul and the bodies of his sons from the wall of **Beth-shan**, and they came to **Jabesh** and burned them there. They took their bones and buried them under the tamarisk tree at **Jabesh**, and fasted seven days.

III. DAVID AT ZIKLAG

A. Vassal of Achish (Ikayaus) 1 Sam 27:5-6

5 וַיֹּאמֶר דָּוִד אֶל־אָכִישׁ אִם־נָא מָצָאתִי חֵן בְּעֵינֶיךָ יִתְּנוּ־לִי מָקוֹם בְּאַחַת
עָרֵי הַשָּׂדֶה וְאֵשְׁבָה שָּׁם וְלָמָּה יֵשֵׁב עַבְדְּךָ בְּעִיר הַמַּמְלָכָה עִמָּךְ

6 וַיִּתֶּן־לוֹ אָכִישׁ בַּיּוֹם הַהוּא אֶת־צִקְלָג לָכֵן הָיְתָה צִקְלַג לְמַלְכֵי יְהוּדָה עַד הַיּוֹם הַזֶּה

Then David said to Achish, "If now I have found favor in your sight, let them give me a place in one of the cities in the country, that I may live there; for why should your servant live in the royal city with you?" So Achish gave him **Ziklag** that day; therefore **Ziklag** has belonged to the kings of Judah to this day.

B. Took offensive against nomadic groups 1 Sam 27:8-11

8 וַיַּעַל דָּוִד וַאֲנָשָׁיו וַיִּפְשְׁטוּ אֶל־הַגְּשׁוּרִי וְהַגִּרְזִי [וְ][הַ][גִּזְרִי] וְהָעֲמָלֵקִי כִּי הֵנָּה יֹשְׁבוֹת הָאָרֶץ אֲשֶׁר מֵעוֹלָם בּוֹאֲךָ שׁוּרָה וְעַד־אֶרֶץ מִצְרָיִם

9 וְהִכָּה דָוִד אֶת־הָאָרֶץ וְלֹא יְחַיֶּה אִישׁ וְאִשָּׁה וְלָקַח צֹאן וּבָקָר וַחֲמֹרִים וּגְמַלִּים וּבְגָדִים וַיָּשָׁב וַיָּבֹא אֶל־אָכִישׁ

10 וַיֹּאמֶר אָכִישׁ אַל־‹מִי› פְּשַׁטְתֶּם הַיּוֹם (LXX ἐπὶ **τίνα** ἐπέθεσθε σήμερον)
וַיֹּאמֶר דָּוִד עַל־נֶגֶב יְהוּדָה וְעַל־נֶגֶב הַיַּרְחְמְאֵלִי וְאֶל־נֶגֶב הַקֵּינִי

11 וְאִישׁ וְאִשָּׁה לֹא־יְחַיֶּה דָוִד לְהָבִיא גַת לֵאמֹר פֶּן־יַגִּדוּ עָלֵינוּ לֵאמֹר כֹּה־עָשָׂה דָוִד וְכֹה מִשְׁפָּטוֹ כָּל־הַיָּמִים אֲשֶׁר יָשַׁב בִּשְׂדֵה פְלִשְׁתִּים

Now David and his men went up and raided the **Geshurites** and the **Girzites** and the **Amalekites**; for they were the inhabitants of the land from ancient times, as you come to **Shur** even as far as the land of Egypt. David attacked the land and did not leave a man or a woman alive, and he took away the sheep, the cattle, the donkeys, the camels, and the clothing. Then he returned and came to Achish. Now Achish said, "Against whom (LXX) have you made a raid today?" And David said, "Against the **Negeb of Judah** and against the **Negeb of the Jerahmeelites** and against the **Negeb of the Kenites**." David did not leave a man or a woman alive to bring to **Gath**, saying, "Otherwise they will tell about us, saying, ʿSo has David done and so [has been] his practice all the time he has lived in the country of the Philistines.ʾ"

1 Sam 30:13-14

<u>13</u> וַיֹּאמֶר לוֹ דָוִד לְמִי־אַתָּה וְאֵי מִזֶּה אָתָּה וַיֹּאמֶר נַעַר מִצְרִי אָנֹכִי עֶבֶד
לְאִישׁ עֲמָלֵקִי וַיַּעַזְבֵנִי אֲדֹנִי כִּי חָלִיתִי הַיּוֹם שְׁלֹשָׁה

<u>14</u> אֲנַחְנוּ פָּשַׁטְנוּ נֶגֶב הַכְּרֵתִי וְעַל־אֲשֶׁר לִיהוּדָה וְעַל־נֶגֶב כָּלֵב
וְאֶת־צִקְלַג שָׂרַפְנוּ בָאֵשׁ

14 καὶ ἡμεῖς ἐπεθέμεθα ἐπὶ νότον τοῦ Χολθι καὶ ἐπὶ τὰ τῆς Ιουδαίας
μέρη καὶ ἐπὶ νότον Χελουβ καὶ τὴν Σεκελακ ἐνεπυρίσαμεν ἐν πυρί

"We made a raid on the **Negeb of the Cherethites**, and on **that which
belongs to Judah**, and on the **Negeb of Caleb**, and we burned **Ziklag** with
fire."

C. Won favor of southern settlements:

1 Sam 30:26-31

<u>26</u> וַיָּבֹא דָוִד אֶל־צִקְלַג וַיְשַׁלַּח מֵהַשָּׁלָל לְזִקְנֵי יְהוּדָה לְרֵעֵהוּ לֵאמֹר
הִנֵּה לָכֶם בְּרָכָה מִשְּׁלַל אֹיְבֵי יְהוָה

29 וְלַאֲשֶׁר בְּרָכָל וְלַאֲשֶׁר בְּעָרֵי הַיְּרַחְמְאֵלִי
וְלַאֲשֶׁר בְּעָרֵי הַקֵּינִי

30 וְלַאֲשֶׁר בְּחָרְמָה וְלַאֲשֶׁר בְּבוֹר־עָשָׁן
וְלַאֲשֶׁר בַּעֲתָךְ

31 וְלַאֲשֶׁר בְּחֶבְרוֹן וּלְכָל־הַמְּקֹמוֹת
אֲשֶׁר־הִתְהַלֶּךְ־שָׁם דָּוִד הוּא וַאֲנָשָׁיו

27 לַאֲשֶׁר בְּבֵית־אֵל		וְלַאֲשֶׁר בְּרָמוֹת־נֶגֶב	
וְלַאֲשֶׁר בְּיַתִּר	28	וְלַאֲשֶׁר בַּעֲרֹעֵר	
וְלַאֲשֶׁר בִּשְׂפָמוֹת		וְלַאֲשֶׁר בְּאֶשְׁתְּמֹעַ	
29 וְלַאֲשֶׁר בְּרָכָל		וְלַאֲשֶׁר בְּעָרֵי הַיְּרַחְמְאֵלִי	
וְלַאֲשֶׁר בְּעָרֵי הַקֵּינִי	30	וְלַאֲשֶׁר בְּחָרְמָה	
וְלַאֲשֶׁר בְּבוֹר־עָשָׁן		וְלַאֲשֶׁר בַּעֲתָךְ	
31 וְלַאֲשֶׁר בְּחֶבְרוֹן			

וּלְכָל־הַמְּקֹמוֹת אֲשֶׁר־הִתְהַלֶּךְ־שָׁם דָּוִד הוּא וַאֲנָשָׁיו

καὶ ἦλθεν Δαυιδ εἰς Σεκελακ καὶ ἀπέστειλεν τοῖς πρεσβυτέροις Ιουδα
τῶν σκύλων καὶ τοῖς πλησίον αὐτοῦ λέγων ἰδοὺ ἀπὸ τῶν σκύλων τῶν
ἐχθρῶν κυρίου

τοῖς ἐν Βαιθσουρ	καὶ τοῖς ἐν Ραμα νότου
καὶ τοῖς ἐν Ιεθθορ	καὶ τοῖς ἐν Αροηρ
καὶ τοῖς Αμμαδι	καὶ τοῖς ἐν Σαφι
καὶ τοῖς ἐν Εσθιε [28α]	καὶ τοῖς ἐν Γεθ
καὶ τοῖς ἐν Κιναν	καὶ τοῖς ἐν Σαφεκ
καὶ τοῖς ἐν Θιμαθ	καὶ τοῖς ἐν Καρμήλῳ
καὶ τοῖς ἐν ταῖς πόλεσιν τοῦ Ιεραμηλι	καὶ τοῖς ἐν ταῖς πόλεσιν τοῦ Κενεζι
καὶ τοῖς ἐν Ιεριμουθ	καὶ τοῖς ἐν Βηρσαβεε
καὶ τοῖς ἐν Νοο	καὶ τοῖς ἐν Χεβρων

καὶ εἰς πάντας τοὺς τόπους οὓς διῆλθεν Δαυιδ ἐκεῖ αὐτὸς καὶ οἱ ἄνδρες
αὐτοῦ

Now when David came to Ziklag, he sent [some] of the spoil to the elders of Judah, to his friends, saying, "Behold, a gift for you from the spoil of the enemies of Yahweh":

to those who were in **Bethel**, and to those who were in **Ramoth of the Negev**, and to those who were in **Jattir**, and to those who were in **Aroer**, and to those who were in **Siphmoth**, and to those who were in **Eshtemoa**, and to those who were in **Racal**, and to those who were in **the cities of the Jerahmeelites**, and to those who were in t**he cities of the Kenites**, and to those who were in **Hormah**, and to those who were in **Bor-ashan**, and to those who were in **Athach**, and to those who were in **Hebron**, and to all the places where David himself and his men were accustomed to go."

LESSON 13

THE UNITED MONARCHY, Part 1

I. DAVID -- RISE TO POWER

  A. ZIKLAG (See Lesson XII)

    1. Location

    2. Activities

    3. The Negeb's (1 Sam 27:5- ; 30:11-14, 26-3l)

  B. HEBRON

    1. United Judah and the other tribes: Caleb, Kenaz,

       Kenite,Jerahmeelite, Cherethites (?),

    2. Simeon -- 1 Chron 4:24, 28-33

24 בְּנֵי שִׁמְעוֹן . . . 28 וַיֵּשְׁבוּ בִּבְאֵר־שֶׁבַע וּמוֹלָדָה

וַחֲצַר שׁוּעָל 29 וּבְבִלְהָה וּבְעֶצֶם וּבְתוֹלָד 30 וּבִבְתוּאֵל

וּבְחָרְמָה וּבְצִיקְלַג 31 וּבְבֵית מַרְכָּבוֹת וּבַחֲצַר סוּסִים

וּבְבֵית בִּרְאִי וּבְשַׁעֲרָיִם

אֵלֶּה עָרֵיהֶם עַד־מְלֹךְ דָּוִיד

32 וְחַצְרֵיהֶם

עֵיטָם וָעַיִן רִמּוֹן וְתֹכֶן וְעָשָׁן עָרִים חָמֵשׁ

33 וְכָל־חַצְרֵיהֶם אֲשֶׁר סְבִיבוֹת הֶעָרִים הָאֵלֶּה

עַד־בָּעַל‹ת באר› זֹאת מוֹשְׁבֹתָם וְהִתְיַחְשָׂם לָהֶם

The sons of Simeon . . . and they lived at Beersheba, Moladah and Hazar-shual, at Bilhah, Ezem, Tolad, Bethuel, Hormah, Ziklag, Beth-marcaboth, Hazar-susim, Beth-biri and Shaaraim.

These [were] their cities <u>until</u> the <u>reign</u> of <u>David</u> and their villages:

Etam, Ain, Rimmon, Tochen and Ashan, five cities;

and all their villages that [were] around the same cities as far as Baal‹ath Be'er›. These [were] their settlements, and they have their registration.

    NOTE: v. 32 lists towns **prior** to David's reign; vv. 28-31a list towns **after** David began to reign.

Cf. Josh. 19:1-8

1 וַיֵּצֵא הַגּוֹרָל הַשֵּׁנִי לְשִׁמְעוֹן לְמַטֵּה בְנֵי־שִׁמְעוֹן

לְמִשְׁפְּחוֹתָם וַיְהִי נַחֲלָתָם בְּתוֹךְ נַחֲלַת בְּנֵי־יְהוּדָה:

2 וַיְהִי לָהֶם בְּנַחֲלָתָם בְּאֵר־שֶׁבַע וְשֶׁבַע וּמוֹלָדָה:

3 וַחֲצַר שׁוּעָל וּבָלָה וָעָצֶם: 4 וְאֶלְתּוֹלַד וּבְתוּל

וְחָרְמָה: 5 וְצִקְלַג וּבֵית־הַמַּרְכָּבוֹת

וַחֲצַר סוּסָה: 6 וּבֵית לְבָאוֹת וְשָׁרוּחֶן

עָרִים שְׁלֹשׁ־עֶשְׂרֵה וְחַצְרֵיהֶן:

7 עַיִן רִמּוֹן וָעֶתֶר וְעָשָׁן עָרִים אַרְבַּע וְחַצְרֵיהֶן:

8 וְכָל־הַחֲצֵרִים אֲשֶׁר סְבִיבוֹת הֶעָרִים הָאֵלֶּה

עַד־בַּעֲלַת בְּאֵר רָאמַת נֶגֶב זֹאת נַחֲלַת מַטֵּה בְנֵי־שִׁמְעוֹן

לְמִשְׁפְּחֹתָם:

Then the second lot fell to Simeon, to the tribe of the sons of Simeon according to their families, and their inheritance was in the midst of the inheritance of the sons of Judah. So they had as their inheritance Beersheba or Sheba and Moladah, and Hazar-shual and Balah and Ezem, and Eltolad and Bethul and Hormah, and Ziklag and Beth-marcaboth and Hazar-susah, and Beth-lebaoth and Sharuhen; thirteen cities with their villages; Ain, Rimmon and Ether and Ashan; four cities with their villages; and all the villages which [were] around these cities as far as **Baalath-beer, Ramah of the Negev.** This [was] the inheritance of the tribe of the sons of Simeon according to their families.

9 מֵחֶבֶל בְּנֵי יְהוּדָה נַחֲלַת בְּנֵי שִׁמְעוֹן כִּי־הָיָה חֵלֶק

בְּנֵי־יְהוּדָה רַב מֵהֶם וַיִּנְחֲלוּ בְנֵי־שִׁמְעוֹן בְּתוֹךְ נַחֲלָתָם:

The inheritance of the sons of Simeon was from the portion of the sons of Judah, for the share of the sons of Judah was too large for them; so the sons of Simeon settled in the midst of Judah's inheritance.

Further expansion in 8th century 1 Chron. 4:38-42

1Chr. 4:38 אֵלֶּה הַבָּאִים בְּשֵׁמוֹת נְשִׂיאִים

בְּמִשְׁפְּחוֹתָם וּבֵית אֲבוֹתֵיהֶם פָּרְצוּ לָרוֹב

1Chr. 4:39 וַיֵּלְכוּ לִמְבוֹא גְדֹר (LXX Γεραρα) עַד לְמִזְרַח

הַגַּיְא לְבַקֵּשׁ מִרְעֶה לְצֹאנָם

1Chr. 4:40 וַיִּמְצְאוּ מִרְעֶה שָׁמֵן וָטוֹב

וְהָאָרֶץ רַחֲבַת יָדַיִם וְשֹׁקֶטֶת וּשְׁלֵוָה כִּי

מִן־חָם הַיֹּשְׁבִים שָׁם לְפָנִים

1Chr. 4:41 וַיָּבֹאוּ אֵלֶּה הַכְּתוּבִים בְּשֵׁמוֹת

בִּימֵי יְחִזְקִיָּהוּ מֶלֶךְ־יְהוּדָה וַיַּכּוּ

אֶת־אָהֳלֵיהֶם וְאֶת־הַמְּעִינִים [הַ][מְּעוּנִים]

אֲשֶׁר נִמְצְאוּ־שָׁמָּה וַיַּחֲרִימֻם עַד־הַיּוֹם הַזֶּה

וַיֵּשְׁבוּ תַחְתֵּיהֶם כִּי־מִרְעֶה לְצֹאנָם שָׁם

1Chr. 4:42 וּמֵהֶם מִן־בְּנֵי שִׁמְעוֹן הָלְכוּ

לְהַר שֵׂעִיר (!west of the Arabah) אֲנָשִׁים חֲמֵשׁ מֵאוֹת וּפְלַטְיָה

וּנְעַרְיָה וּרְפָיָה וְעֻזִּיאֵל בְּנֵי יִשְׁעִי בְּרֹאשָׁם

These mentioned by name [were] leaders in their families; and their fathers' houses increased greatly. They went to the entrance of **Gerar** (! LXX), even to the east side of the valley, to seek pasture for their flocks. They found rich and good pasture, and the land was broad and quiet and peaceful; for those who lived there formerly [were] Hamites. These, recorded by name, came in the days of Hezekiah king of Judah, and attacked their tents and the Meunites who were found there, and destroyed them utterly to this day, and lived in their place, because there was pasture there for their flocks. From them, from the sons of Simeon, five hundred men went to Mount Seir, with Pelatiah, Neariah, Rephaiah and Uzziel, the sons of Ishi, as their leaders.

3. War with Ish-baal (2 Sam 2:8-9; 4:2,7) men of Gittaim

8 וְאַבְנֵר בֶּן־נֵר שַׂר־צָבָא אֲשֶׁר לְשָׁאוּל לָקַח אֶת־אִישׁ בֹּשֶׁת
בֶּן־שָׁאוּל וַיַּעֲבִרֵהוּ מַחֲנָיִם

9 וַיַּמְלִכֵהוּ אֶל־הַגִּלְעָד וְאֶל־הָאֲשׁוּרִי וְאֶל־יִזְרְעֶאל
וְעַל־אֶפְרַיִם וְעַל־בִּנְיָמִן וְעַל־יִשְׂרָאֵל כֻּלֹּה

But Abner the son of Ner, commander of Sauls's army, had taken Ish-bosheth
the son of Saul and brought him over to **Mahanaim**. And he made him king
over **Gilead**, over the **Ashurites** (Geshurites?), over **Jezreel**, over **Ephraim**,
and over **Benjamin**, even over all Israel.

2 Sam. 4:1 וַיִּשְׁמַע בֶּן־שָׁאוּל כִּי מֵת אַבְנֵר בְּחֶבְרוֹן וַיִּרְפּוּ יָדָיו

4:2 וְכָל־יִשְׂרָאֵל נִבְהָלוּ וּשְׁנֵי אֲנָשִׁים שָׂרֵי־גְדוּדִים הָיוּ
‹לְ›בֶן־שָׁאוּל שֵׁם הָאֶחָד בַּעֲנָה וְשֵׁם הַשֵּׁנִי רֵכָב בְּנֵי רִמּוֹן הַבְּאֵרֹתִי
מִבְּנֵי בִנְיָמִן כִּי גַּם־בְּאֵרוֹת תֵּחָשֵׁב עַל־בִּנְיָמִן

4:3 וַיִּבְרְחוּ הַבְּאֵרֹתִים גִּתָּיְמָה וַיִּהְיוּ־שָׁם גָּרִים עַד הַיּוֹם הַזֶּה

. . . .

4:5 וַיֵּלְכוּ בְּנֵי־רִמּוֹן הַבְּאֵרֹתִי רֵכָב וּבַעֲנָה וַיָּבֹאוּ כְּחֹם הַיּוֹם אֶל־בֵּית אִישׁ
בֹּשֶׁת וְהוּא שֹׁכֵב אֵת מִשְׁכַּב הַצָּהֳרָיִם 6 וְהִנֵּה בָּאוּ עַד־תּוֹךְ הַבַּיִת לֹקְחֵי
חִטִּים וַיַּכֻּהוּ אֶל־הַחֹמֶשׁ וְרֵכָב וּבַעֲנָה אָחִיו
לֹקְחֵי חִטִּים   נִמְלָטוּ

staff bearers(?)   7 וַיָּבֹאוּ הַבַּיִת וְהוּא־שֹׁכֵב

עַל־מִטָּתוֹ בַּחֲדַר מִשְׁכָּבוֹ וַיַּכֻּהוּ וַיְמִתֻהוּ וַיָּסִירוּ אֶת־רֹאשׁוֹ
וַיִּקְחוּ אֶת־רֹאשׁוֹ וַיֵּלְכוּ דֶּרֶךְ הָעֲרָבָה כָּל־הַלָּיְלָה 8 וַיָּבִאוּ אֶת־רֹאשׁ
אִישׁ־בֹּשֶׁת אֶל־דָּוִד חֶבְרוֹן וַיֹּאמְרוּ אֶל־הַמֶּלֶךְ הִנֵּה־רֹאשׁ אִישׁ־בֹּשֶׁת
בֶּן־שָׁאוּל אֹיִבְךָ אֲשֶׁר בִּקֵּשׁ אֶת־נַפְשֶׁךָ וַיִּתֵּן יְהוָה לַאדֹנִי
הַמֶּלֶךְ נְקָמוֹת הַיּוֹם הַזֶּה מִשָּׁאוּל וּמִזַּרְעוֹ

Now when ‹Ish-bosheth›, Sauls's son, heard that Abner had died in Hebron,
he lost courage, and all Israel was disturbed. Saul's son ‹had› two men who

were commanders of bands: the name of the one was Baanah and the name of

the other Rechab, sons of **Rimmon** the **Beerothite**, of the sons of Benjamin

(for Beeroth is also reckoned to Benjamin, and the Beerothites fled to **Gittaim**

and have been sojourners there until this day).

2 Sam. 4:1 καὶ ἤκουσεν **Μεμφιβοσθε** υἱὸς Σαουλ ὅτι τέθνηκεν Αβεννηρ ἐν Χεβρων καὶ ἐξελύθησαν αἱ χεῖρες αὐτοῦ καὶ πάντες οἱ ἄνδρες Ισραηλ παρείθησαν

2 Sam. 4:2 καὶ δύο ἄνδρες ἡγούμενοι συστρεμμάτων **τῷ Μεμφιβοσθε** υἱῷ Σαουλ ὄνομα τῷ ἑνὶ Βαανα καὶ ὄνομα τῷ δευτέρῳ Ρηχαβ υἱοὶ Ρεμμων τοῦ Βηρωθαίου ἐκ τῶν υἱῶν Βενιαμιν ὅτι Βηρωθ ἐλογίζετο τοῖς υἱοῖς Βενιαμιν

2 Sam. 4:3 καὶ ἀπέδρασαν οἱ Βηρωθαῖοι εἰς Γεθθαιμ καὶ ἦσαν ἐκεῖ παροικοῦντες ἕως τῆς ἡμέρας ταύτης

2Sam. 4:5 ¶ So the sons of Rimmon the Beerothite, Rechab and Baanah, departed and came to the house of Ish-bosheth in the heat of the day while he was taking his midday rest.

2Sam. 4:6 They came into the palace, **staff bearers**, and they struck him in the belly; and Rechab and Baanah his brother escaped.

2Sam. 4:7 Now when they came into the house, as he was lying on his bed in his bedroom, they struck him and killed him and beheaded him. And they took his head and traveled by way of the Arabah all night.

2Sam. 4:8 Then they brought the head of Ish-bosheth to David at Hebron and

said to the king, "Behold, the head of Ish-bosheth the son of Saul, your

enemy, who sought your life; thus Yahweh has given my lord the king

vengeance this day on Saul and his descendants."

II.   DAVID — THE KINGDOM UNITED

A. JERUSALEM

1. Made the new capital
2. Philistine attacks warded off

a. **Valley of Rephaim** (2x)
2 Sam 5:17-25 ‖ 1 Chron 14:8-17

2Sam. 5:17 וַיִּשְׁמְעוּ פְלִשְׁתִּים כִּי־מָשְׁחוּ   אֶת־דָּוִד לְמֶלֶךְ עַל־יִשְׂרָאֵל וַיַּעֲלוּ
כָל־פְּלִשְׁתִּים לְבַקֵּשׁ אֶת־דָּוִד וַיִּשְׁמַע דָּוִד   וַיֵּרֶד אֶל־הַמְּצוּדָה

2Sam. 5:18 וּפְלִשְׁתִּים בָּאוּ וַיִּנָּטְשׁוּ בְּעֵמֶק   רְפָאִים

2Sam. 5:19 וַיִּשְׁאַל דָּוִד בַּיהוָה לֵאמֹר הַאֶעֱלֶה אֶל־פְּלִשְׁתִּים הֲתִתְּנֵם בְּיָדִי
וַיֹּאמֶר יְהוָה אֶל־דָּוִד עֲלֵה כִּי־נָתֹן אֶתֵּן אֶת־הַפְּלִשְׁתִּים בְּיָדֶךְ

2Sam. 5:20 וַיָּבֹא דָוִד בְּבַעַל־פְּרָצִים וַיַּכֵּם
שָׁם דָּוִד וַיֹּאמֶר פָּרַץ יְהוָה אֶת־אֹיְבַי לְפָנַי* כְּפֶרֶץ מָיִם
עַל־כֵּן קָרָא שֵׁם־הַמָּקוֹם הַהוּא בַּעַל פְּרָצִים

2Sam. 5:21 וַיַּעַזְבוּ־שָׁם אֶת־עֲצַבֵּיהֶם   וַיִּשָּׂאֵם דָּוִד וַאֲנָשָׁיו

2Sam. 5:22 וַיֹּסִפוּ עוֹד פְּלִשְׁתִּים לַעֲלוֹת   וַיִּנָּטְשׁוּ בְּעֵמֶק רְפָאִים

2Sam. 5:23 וַיִּשְׁאַל דָּוִד בַּיהוָה וַיֹּאמֶר לֹא תַעֲלֶה הָסֵב אֶל־אַחֲרֵיהֶם
וּבָאתָ לָהֶם מִמּוּל בְּכָאִים

2Sam. 5:24 וִיהִי בְּשָׁמְעֲךָ [כְּ][שָׁמְעֲךָ] אֶת־קוֹל צְעָדָה בְּרָאשֵׁי הַבְּכָאִים
אָז תֶּחֱרָץ כִּי אָז יָצָא יְהוָה לְפָנֶיךָ לְהַכּוֹת   בְּמַחֲנֵה פְלִשְׁתִּים

2Sam. 5:25 וַיַּעַשׂ דָּוִד כֵּן כַּאֲשֶׁר צִוָּהוּ יְהוָה וַיַּךְ אֶת־פְּלִשְׁתִּים
מִגֶּבַע עַד־בֹּאֲךָ גָזֶר

When the Philistines heard that they had anointed David king over Israel, all the Philistines went up to seek out David; and when David heard [of it], he went down to the stronghold. Now the Philistines came and spread themselves out in the **Valley of Rephaim**. Then David inquired of Yahweh, saying, "Shall I go up against the Philistines? Will You give them into my hand?" And Yahweh said to David, "Go up, for I will certainly give the Philistines into your hand." So David came to **Baal-perazim** and defeated them there; and he said, "Yahweh has broken through my enemies before me like the breakthrough of waters." Therefore *he named that place* **Baal-perazim**. They abandoned their idols there, so David and his men carried them away.

Now the Philistines came up once again and spread themselves out in the **Valley of Rephaim**. When David inquired of Yahweh, He said, "You shall not go [directly] up; circle around behind them and come at them in front of the balsam trees. It shall be, when you hear the sound of marching in the tops of the balsam trees, then you shall act promptly, for then Yahweh will have gone out before you to strike the army of the Philistines." Then David did so, just as Yahweh had commanded him, and struck down the Philistines from **Geba** as far as **Gezer**.

1 Chron. 14:8-16

1Chr. 14:8 וַיִּשְׁמְעוּ פְלִשְׁתִּים כִּי־נִמְשַׁח דָּוִיד לְמֶלֶךְ עַל־כָּל־יִשְׂרָאֵל וַיַּעֲלוּ

כָל־פְּלִשְׁתִּים לְבַקֵּשׁ אֶת־דָּוִיד וַיִּשְׁמַע דָּוִיד וַיֵּצֵא לִפְנֵיהֶם

1Chr. 14:9 וּפְלִשְׁתִּים בָּאוּ וַיִּפְשְׁטוּ בְּעֵמֶק רְפָאִים

1Chr. 14:10 וַיִּשְׁאַל דָּוִיד בֵּאלֹהִים לֵאמֹר הַאֶעֱלֶה עַל־פְּלִשְׁתִּיים [פְּלִשְׁתִּים]

וּנְתַתָּם בְּיָדִי וַיֹּאמֶר לוֹ יְהוָה עֲלֵה וּנְתַתִּים בְּיָדֶךָ

1Chr. 14:11 וַיַּעֲלוּ בְּבַעַל־פְּרָצִים וַיַּכֵּם שָׁם

דָּוִיד וַיֹּאמֶר דָּוִיד פָּרַץ הָאֱלֹהִים אֶת־אוֹיְבַי* בְּיָדִי כְּפֶרֶץ מָיִם עַל־כֵּן

קָרְאוּ שֵׁם־הַמָּקוֹם הַהוּא בַּעַל פְּרָצִים

1Chr. 14:12 וַיַּעַזְבוּ־שָׁם אֶת־אֱלֹהֵיהֶם וַיֹּאמֶר דָּוִיד וַיִּשָּׂרְפוּ בָּאֵשׁ

1Chr. 14:13 וַיֹּסִיפוּ עוֹד פְּלִשְׁתִּים וַיִּפְשְׁטוּ בָּעֵמֶק

1Chr. 14:14 וַיִּשְׁאַל עוֹד דָּוִיד בֵּאלֹהִים וַיֹּאמֶר לוֹ הָאֱלֹהִים לֹא תַעֲלֶה

אַחֲרֵיהֶם הָסֵב מֵעֲלֵיהֶם וּבָאתָ לָהֶם מִמּוּל הַבְּכָאִים

1Chr. 14:15 וִיהִי כְּשָׁמְעֲךָ אֶת־קוֹל הַצְּעָדָה בְּרָאשֵׁי הַבְּכָאִים

אָז תֵּצֵא בַמִּלְחָמָה כִּי־יָצָא הָאֱלֹהִים לְפָנֶיךָ לְהַכּוֹת אֶת־מַחֲנֵה

פְּלִשְׁתִּים

1Chr. 14:16 וַיַּעַשׂ דָּוִיד כַּאֲשֶׁר צִוָּהוּ הָאֱלֹהִים וַיַּכּוּ אֶת־מַחֲנֵה פְלִשְׁתִּים

מִגִּבְעוֹן וְעַד־גָּזְרָה

When the Philistines heard that David had been anointed king over all Israel,
all the Philistines went up in search of David; and David heard of it and went
out against them. Now the Philistines had come and made a raid in the
Valley of Rephaim. David inquired of God, saying,"Shall I go up against the
Philistines? And will You give them into my hand?" Then Yahweh said to
him, "Go up, for I will give them into your hand." So they came up to **Baal-
perazim**, and David defeated them there; and David said, "God has broken
through my enemies by my hand, like the breakthrough of waters." Therefore
they named that place **Baal-perazim**. They abandoned their gods there; so
David gave the order and they were burned with fire.

The Philistines made yet another raid in the **Valley**. David inquired again
of God, and God said to him, "You shall not go up after them; circle around
behind them and come at them in front of the balsam trees. It shall be when
you hear the sound of marching in the tops of the balsam trees, then you shall
go out to battle, for God will have gone out before you to strike the army of
the Philistines. David did just as God had commanded him, and they struck
down the army of the Philistines from **Gibeon** even as far as **Gezer**.

b. **Gath** 2 Sam 8:1; 1 Chron 18:1 (superior text)

2 Sam. 8:1 וַיְהִי אַחֲרֵי־כֵן וַיַּךְ דָּוִד אֶת־פְּלִשְׁתִּים וַיַּכְנִיעֵם

וַיִּקַּח דָּוִד אֶת־מֶתֶג הָאַמָּה מִיַּד פְּלִשְׁתִּים

Now after this it came about that David defeated the Philistines
and subdued them; and David took the **divider** (τὴν
ἀφωρισμένην) from the hand of the Philistines.

1 Chr. 18:1 וַיְהִי אַחֲרֵי־כֵן וַיַּךְ דָּוִיד אֶת־פְּלִשְׁתִּים וַיַּכְנִיעֵם

וַיִּקַּח אֶת־גַּת וּבְנֹתֶיהָ מִיַּד פְּלִשְׁתִּים

Now after this it came about that David defeated the Philistines
and subdued them and took **Gath and its towns** from the hand
of the Philistines.

Probably **Gath-Gittaim / Gath-rimmon!**

B. TRANSJORDANIAN WARS AND THE ARAMAEAN CONFLICT

1. Moab — 2 Sam 8:2 ‖ 1 Ch. 18:2

2 Sam. 8:2 וַיַּךְ אֶת־מוֹאָב וַיְמַדְּדֵם בַּחֶבֶל הַשְׁכֵּב אוֹתָם אַרְצָה
וַיְמַדֵּד שְׁנֵי־חֲבָלִים לְהָמִית וּמְלֹא הַחֶבֶל לְהַחֲיוֹת וַתְּהִי
מוֹאָב לְדָוִד לַעֲבָדִים נֹשְׂאֵי מִנְחָה

And he defeated Moab,

(and he measured them with the line, making them lie down on the ground;

and he measured two lines to put to death and one full line to keep alive).

And the Moabites became servants to David, bringing tribute.

1 Chron. 18:2

1 Chr. 18:2 וַיַּךְ אֶת־מוֹאָב וַיִּהְיוּ מוֹאָב עֲבָדִים לְדָוִיד נֹשְׂאֵי מִנְחָה

He defeated Moab, and the Moabites became servants to David, bringing tribute.

INSERT SUGGESTED BY B. MAZAR:

2 Sam. 10:1-11:1; 12:26-31‖ 1 Chron. 19:1-20:3)

2. The sons of Ammon — Ḥanun ben Naḥash

a. Diplomatic insult: 2 Sam 10:1-5 ‖ 1 Chron. 19:1-5

2 Sam. 10:1 וַיְהִי אַחֲרֵי־כֵן וַיָּמָת מֶלֶךְ בְּנֵי עַמּוֹן וַיִּמְלֹךְ חָנוּן
בְּנוֹ תַּחְתָּיו

2 וַיֹּאמֶר דָּוִד אֶעֱשֶׂה־חֶסֶד עִם־חָנוּן בֶּן־נָחָשׁ
כַּאֲשֶׁר עָשָׂה אָבִיו עִמָּדִי חֶסֶד וַיִּשְׁלַח דָּוִד לְנַחֲמוֹ
בְּיַד־עֲבָדָיו אֶל־אָבִיו וַיָּבֹאוּ עַבְדֵי דָוִד אֶרֶץ בְּנֵי עַמּוֹן

3 וַיֹּאמְרוּ שָׂרֵי בְנֵי־עַמּוֹן אֶל־חָנוּן אֲדֹנֵיהֶם
הַמְכַבֵּד דָּוִד אֶת־אָבִיךָ בְּעֵינֶיךָ כִּי־שָׁלַח לְךָ מְנַחֲמִים הֲלוֹא

בַּעֲבוּר חֲקֹר אֶת־הָעִיר וּלְרַגְּלָהּ וּלְהָפְכָהּ שָׁלַח דָּוִד
אֶת־עֲבָדָיו אֵלֶיךָ

4 וַיִּקַּח חָנוּן אֶת־עַבְדֵי דָוִד וַיְגַלַּח אֶת־חֲצִי זְקָנָם
וַיִּכְרֹת אֶת־מַדְוֵיהֶם בַּחֵצִי עַד שְׁתוֹתֵיהֶם וַיְשַׁלְּחֵם

5 וַיַּגִּדוּ לְדָוִד וַיִּשְׁלַח לִקְרָאתָם כִּי־הָיוּ הָאֲנָשִׁים נִכְלָמִים מְאֹד
וַיֹּאמֶר הַמֶּלֶךְ שְׁבוּ בִירֵחוֹ עַד־יְצַמַּח זְקַנְכֶם וְשַׁבְתֶּם

Now it happened afterwards that the king of the Ammonites died, and
Hanun his son became king in his place. Then David said, "I will show
kindness to Hanun the son of Nahash, just as his father showed kindness to
me." So David sent some of his servants to console him concerning his father.
But when David's servants came to the land of the Ammonites, the princes of
the Ammonites said to Hanun their lord, "Do you think that David is
honoring your father because he has sent consolers to you? Has David not
sent his servants to you in order to search the city, to spy it out and
overthrow it?"

So Hanun took David's servants and shaved off half of their beards, and
cut off their garments in the middle as far as their buttocks, and sent them
away. When they told [it] to David, he sent to meet them, for the men were
greatly humiliated. And the king said, "Stay at Jericho until your beards
grow, and [then] return."

1 Chron. 19:1-5

1 וַיְהִי אַחֲרֵי־כֵן וַיָּמָת נָחָשׁ מֶלֶךְ בְּנֵי־עַמּוֹן וַיִּמְלֹךְ בְּנוֹ תַּחְתָּיו

2 וַיֹּאמֶר דָּוִיד אֶעֱשֶׂה־חֶסֶד עִם־חָנוּן בֶּן־נָחָשׁ כִּי־עָשָׂה אָבִיו עִמִּי
חֶסֶד וַיִּשְׁלַח דָּוִיד מַלְאָכִים לְנַחֲמוֹ עַל־אָבִיו וַיָּבֹאוּ עַבְדֵי דָוִיד
אֶל־אֶרֶץ בְּנֵי־עַמּוֹן אֶל־חָנוּן לְנַחֲמוֹ

3 וַיֹּאמְרוּ שָׂרֵי בְנֵי־עַמּוֹן לְחָנוּן הַמְכַבֵּד דָּוִיד
אֶת־אָבִיךָ בְּעֵינֶיךָ כִּי־שָׁלַח לְךָ מְנַחֲמִים הֲלֹא בַּעֲבוּר
לַחְקֹר וְלַהֲפֹךְ וּלְרַגֵּל הָאָרֶץ בָּאוּ עֲבָדָיו אֵלֶיךָ

4 וַיִּקַּח חָנוּן אֶת־עַבְדֵי דָוִיד וַיְגַלְּחֵם וַיִּכְרֹת
אֶת־מַדְוֵיהֶם בַּחֵצִי עַד־הַמִּפְשָׂעָה וַיְשַׁלְּחֵם

5 וַיֵּלְכוּ וַיַּגִּדוּ לְדָוִד עַל־הָאֲנָשִׁים וַיִּשְׁלַח

לִקְרָאתָם כִּי־הָיוּ הָאֲנָשִׁים נִכְלָמִים מְאֹד וַיֹּאמֶר הַמֶּלֶךְ שְׁבוּ

בִירֵחוֹ עַד אֲשֶׁר־יְצַמַּח זְקַנְכֶם וְשַׁבְתֶּם

Now it came about after this, that Nahash the king of the sons of Ammon died, and his son ‹Hanun› became king in his place. Then David said, "I will show kindness to Hanun the son of Nahash, because his father showed kindness to me." So David sent messengers to console him concerning his father. And David's servants came into the land of the sons of Ammon to Hanun to console him.

But the princes of the sons of Ammon said to Hanun, "Do you think that David is honoring your father, in that he has sent comforters to you? Have not his servants come to you to search and to overthrow and to spy out the land?"

So Hanun took David's servants and shaved them and cut off their garments in the middle as far as their crotch, and sent them away. Then they went and told David about the men. And he sent to meet them, for the men were greatly humiliated. And the king said, "Stay at Jericho until your beards grow, and then you shall return."

b. **Medeba** battle — Aramaeans came to help
Ammonites

2 Sam 10:6-14 ‖ 1 Chron. 19:6-15

6 וַיִּרְאוּ בְּנֵי עַמּוֹן כִּי נִבְאֲשׁוּ בְּדָוִד וַיִּשְׁלְחוּ בְנֵי־עַמּוֹן וַיִּשְׂכְּרוּ אֶת־אֲרַם

בֵּית־רְחוֹב וְאֶת־אֲרַם צוֹבָא עֶשְׂרִים אֶלֶף רַגְלִי וְאֶת־מֶלֶךְ מַעֲכָה

אֶלֶף אִישׁ וְאִישׁ טוֹב שְׁנֵים־עָשָׂר אֶלֶף אִישׁ

7 וַיִּשְׁמַע דָּוִד וַיִּשְׁלַח אֶת־יוֹאָב וְאֵת כָּל־הַצָּבָא הַגִּבֹּרִים

8 וַיֵּצְאוּ בְּנֵי עַמּוֹן וַיַּעַרְכוּ מִלְחָמָה פֶּתַח הַשָּׁעַר

וַאֲרַם צוֹבָא וּרְחוֹב וְאִישׁ־טוֹב וּמַעֲכָה לְבַדָּם בַּשָּׂדֶה

9 וַיַּרְא יוֹאָב כִּי־הָיְתָה אֵלָיו פְּנֵי הַמִּלְחָמָה מִפָּנִים וּמֵאָחוֹר

וַיִּבְחַר מִכֹּל בְּחוּרֵי בְיִשְׂרָאֵל [וְיִשְׂרָאֵל] וַיַּעֲרֹךְ לִקְרַאת אֲרָם

10 וְאֵת יֶתֶר הָעָם נָתַן בְּיַד אַבְשַׁי אָחִיו וַיַּעֲרֹךְ לִקְרַאת בְּנֵי עַמּוֹן

11 וַיֹּאמֶר אִם־תֶּחֱזַק אֲרָם מִמֶּנִּי וְהָיְתָה לִּי לִישׁוּעָה וְאִם־בְּנֵי עַמּוֹן

יֶחֱזְקוּ מִמְּךָ וְהָלַכְתִּי לְהוֹשִׁיעַ לָךְ

12 חֲזַק וְנִתְחַזַּק בְּעַד־עַמֵּנוּ וּבְעַד עָרֵי אֱלֹהֵינוּ

וַיהוָה יַעֲשֶׂה הַטּוֹב בְּעֵינָיו

13 וַיִּגַּשׁ יוֹאָב וְהָעָם אֲשֶׁר עִמּוֹ לַמִּלְחָמָה בַּאֲרָם וַיָּנֻסוּ מִפָּנָיו

14 וּבְנֵי עַמּוֹן רָאוּ כִּי־נָס אֲרָם וַיָּנֻסוּ מִפְּנֵי אֲבִישַׁי

וַיָּבֹאוּ הָעִיר וַיָּשָׁב יוֹאָב מֵעַל בְּנֵי עַמּוֹן וַיָּבֹא יְרוּשָׁלָם

Now when the sons of Ammon saw that they had become odious to David, the sons of Ammon sent and hired the **Arameans of Beth-rehob** and the **Arameans of Zobah**, 20,000 foot soldiers, and the **king of Maacah** with 1,000 men, and the **men of Tob** with 12,000 men. And David heard so then he sent Joab and all the army, the mighty men. And the sons of Ammon came out and drew up in battle array at the entrance of the city, while the Arameans of Zobah and of Rehob and the men of Tob and Maacah [were] by themselves in the field.

Now when Joab saw that the battle was set against him in front and in the rear, he selected from all the choice men of Israel, and arrayed [them] against the Arameans. But the remainder of the people he placed in the hand of Abishai his brother, and he arrayed [them] against the sons of Ammon. And he said, "If the Arameans are too strong for me, then you shall help me, but if the sons of Ammon are too strong for you, then I will come to help you. Be strong, and let us strengthen ourselves courageous for the sake of our people and for the cities of our God; and may Yahweh do what is good in His sight."

So Joab and the people who were with him drew near to the battle against the Arameans, and they fled before him. When the sons of Ammon saw that the Arameans fled, they fled before Abishai and entered the city. Then Joab returned from fighting against the sons of Ammon and came to Jerusalem.

1 Chron. 19:6-15

6 וַיִּרְאוּ בְּנֵי עַמּוֹן כִּי הִתְבָּאֲשׁוּ עִם־דָּוִיד וַיִּשְׁלַח

חָנוּן וּבְנֵי עַמּוֹן אֶלֶף כִּכַּר־כֶּסֶף לִשְׂכֹּר לָהֶם מִן־אֲרַם

נַהֲרַיִם וּמִן־אֲרַם מַעֲכָה וּמִצּוֹבָה רֶכֶב וּפָרָשִׁים

7 וַיִּשְׂכְּרוּ לָהֶם שְׁנַיִם וּשְׁלֹשִׁים אֶלֶף רֶכֶב וְאֶת־מֶלֶךְ

מַעֲכָה וְאֶת־עַמּוֹ וַיָּבֹאוּ וַיַּחֲנוּ לִפְנֵי מֵידְבָא וּבְנֵי עַמּוֹן

נֶאֶסְפוּ מֵעָרֵיהֶם וַיָּבֹאוּ לַמִּלְחָמָה

8 וַיִּשְׁמַע דָּוִיד וַיִּשְׁלַח אֶת־יוֹאָב וְאֵת כָּל־צָבָא הַגִּבּוֹרִים

9 וַיֵּצְאוּ בְּנֵי עַמּוֹן וַיַּעַרְכוּ מִלְחָמָה פֶּתַח הָעִיר

וְהַמְּלָכִים אֲשֶׁר־בָּאוּ לְבַדָּם בַּשָּׂדֶה

10 וַיַּרְא יוֹאָב כִּי־הָיְתָה פְנֵי־הַמִּלְחָמָה אֵלָיו פָּנִים

וְאָחוֹר וַיִּבְחַר מִכָּל־בָּחוּר בְּיִשְׂרָאֵל וַיַּעֲרֹךְ לִקְרַאת אֲרָם

11 וְאֵת יֶתֶר הָעָם נָתַן בְּיַד אַבְשַׁי אָחִיו וַיַּעַרְכוּ לִקְרַאת בְּנֵי עַמּוֹן

12 וַיֹּאמֶר אִם־תֶּחֱזַק מִמֶּנִּי אֲרָם וְהָיִיתָ לִּי לִתְשׁוּעָה

וְאִם־בְּנֵי עַמּוֹן יֶחֶזְקוּ מִמְּךָ וְהוֹשַׁעְתִּיךָ

13 חֲזַק וְנִתְחַזְּקָה בְּעַד־עַמֵּנוּ וּבְעַד עָרֵי אֱלֹהֵינוּ

וַיהוָה הַטּוֹב בְּעֵינָיו יַעֲשֶׂה

14 וַיִּגַּשׁ יוֹאָב וְהָעָם אֲשֶׁר־עִמּוֹ לִפְנֵי אֲרָם

לַמִּלְחָמָה וַיָּנוּסוּ מִפָּנָיו

15 וּבְנֵי עַמּוֹן רָאוּ כִּי־נָס אֲרָם וַיָּנוּסוּ גַם־הֵם

מִפְּנֵי אַבְשַׁי אָחִיו וַיָּבֹאוּ הָעִירָה וַיָּבֹא יוֹאָב יְרוּשָׁלָ͏ִם

When the sons of Ammon saw that they had made themselves odious to David, Hanun and the sons of Ammon sent 1,000 talents of silver to hire for themselves chariots and horsemen from **ARAM-NAHARAIM**, from **Aram-maacah** and from **Zobah**. So they hired for themselves 32,000 chariots, and the **king of Maacah** and his people, who came and camped before <u>Medeba</u>. And the sons of Ammon gathered together from their cities and came to battle. When David heard, then he sent Joab and all the army, the mighty men. And the sons of Ammon came out and drew up in battle array at the entrance of the city, and the kings who had come were by themselves in the field.

Now when Joab saw that the battle was set against him in front and in the rear, he selected from all the choice men of Israel and they arrayed themselves against the Arameans. But the remainder of the people he placed in the hand of Abshai his brother; and they arrayed themselves against the sons of Ammon. And he said, "If the Arameans are too strong for me, then you shall help me; but if the sons of Ammon are too strong for you, then I will help you. Be strong, and let us strengthen ourselves for the sake of our people and for the cities of our God; and may Yahweh do what is good in His sight."

So Joab and the people who were with him drew near to the battle against the Arameans, and they fled before him. When the sons of Ammon saw that the Arameans fled, they also fled before Abshai his brother and entered the city. Then Joab came to Jerusalem.

3. Ḥêlām — defeat of allied Aramaean armies

2 Sam 10:15-19 ‖ 1 Chron. 19:16-19

15 וַיַּרְא אֲרָם כִּי נִגַּף לִפְנֵי יִשְׂרָאֵל וַיֵּאָסְפוּ יָחַד

16 וַיִּשְׁלַח הֲדַדְעֶזֶר וַיֹּצֵא אֶת־אֲרָם אֲשֶׁר מֵעֵבֶר
הַנָּהָר וַיָּבֹאוּ חֵילָם וְשׁוֹבַךְ שַׂר־צְבָא הֲדַדְעֶזֶר לִפְנֵיהֶם

17 וַיֻּגַּד לְדָוִד וַיֶּאֱסֹף אֶת־כָּל־יִשְׂרָאֵל וַיַּעֲבֹר
אֶת־הַיַּרְדֵּן וַיָּבֹא חֵלָאמָה וַיַּעַרְכוּ אֲרָם לִקְרַאת דָּוִד   וַיִּלָּחֲמוּ עִמּוֹ

18 וַיָּנָס אֲרָם מִפְּנֵי יִשְׂרָאֵל וַיַּהֲרֹג דָּוִד מֵאֲרָם
שְׁבַע מֵאוֹת רֶכֶב וְאַרְבָּעִים אֶלֶף פָּרָשִׁים וְאֵת שׁוֹבַךְ
שַׂר־צְבָאוֹ הִכָּה וַיָּמָת שָׁם

19 וַיִּרְאוּ כָל־הַמְּלָכִים עַבְדֵי הֲדַדְעֶזֶר כִּי נִגְּפוּ
לִפְנֵי יִשְׂרָאֵל וַיַּשְׁלִמוּ אֶת־יִשְׂרָאֵל וַיַּעַבְדוּם וַיִּרְאוּ אֲרָם
לְהוֹשִׁיעַ עוֹד אֶת־בְּנֵי עַמּוֹן

And the Arameans saw that they had been defeated by Israel, they gathered themselves together. And **Hadadezer** sent and brought out the Arameans who were **beyond the River**, and they came to **Helam**; and Shobach the commander of the army of Hadadezer led them.

And it was told David, so he gathered all Israel together and crossed the Jordan, and came to **Helam**. And the Arameans arrayed themselves to meet David and fought against him. But the Arameans fled before Israel, and David killed 700 charioteers of the Arameans and 40,000 horsemen and struck down Shobach the commander of their army, and he died there.

And all **the kings, servants of Hadadezer**, saw that they were defeated by Israel, so they made peace with Israel and served them. So the Arameans feared to help the sons of Ammon anymore.

1 Chron. 19:16-19

16 וַיַּרְא אֲרָם כִּי נִגְּפוּ לִפְנֵי יִשְׂרָאֵל וַיִּשְׁלְחוּ
מַלְאָכִים וַיּוֹצִיאוּ אֶת־אֲרָם אֲשֶׁר מֵעֵבֶר הַנָּהָר וְשׁוֹפַךְ
שַׂר־צְבָא הֲדַדְעֶזֶר לִפְנֵיהֶם

17 וַיֻּגַּד לְדָוִיד וַיֶּאֱסֹף אֶת־כָּל־יִשְׂרָאֵל וַיַּעֲבֹר הַיַּרְדֵּן וַיָּבֹא אֲלֵהֶם
וַיַּעֲרֹךְ אֲלֵהֶם וַיַּעֲרֹךְ דָּוִיד לִקְרַאת אֲרָם מִלְחָמָה וַיִּלָּחֲמוּ עִמּוֹ

18 וַיָּנָס אֲרָם מִלִּפְנֵי יִשְׂרָאֵל וַיַּהֲרֹג דָּוִיד מֵאֲרָם שִׁבְעַת אֲלָפִים רֶכֶב
וְאַרְבָּעִים אֶלֶף אִישׁ רַגְלִי וְאֵת שׁוֹפַךְ שַׂר־הַצָּבָא הֵמִית

19 וַיִּרְאוּ עַבְדֵי הֲדַדְעֶזֶר כִּי נִגְּפוּ לִפְנֵי יִשְׂרָאֵל וַיַּשְׁלִימוּ עִם־דָּוִיד
וַיַּעַבְדֻהוּ וְלֹא־אָבָה אֲרָם לְהוֹשִׁיעַ אֶת־בְּנֵי־עַמּוֹן עוֹד

And the Arameans saw that they had been defeated by Israel, so they sent messengers and brought out the Arameans who were **beyond the River**, with Shophach the commander of the army of Hadadezer leading them.

And it was told David, so he gathered all Israel together and crossed the Jordan, and came upon them and drew up in formation against them. And when David drew up in battle array against the Arameans, they fought against him. But the Arameans fled before Israel, and David killed of the Arameans 7,000 charioteers and 40,000 foot soldiers, and put to death Shophach the commander of the army.

So when the **servants of Hadadezer** saw that they were defeated by
Israel, they made peace with David and served him. Thus the Arameans were
not willing to help the sons of Ammon anymore.

4. Conquest of Rabbath-ammon
2 Sam. 11:1; 12:26-11 || 1 Chron. 20:1-3 (!)

1 וַיְהִי לִתְשׁוּבַת הַשָּׁנָה לְעֵת צֵאת הַמַּלְאָכִים (LXX τῶν βασιλέων)

וַיִּשְׁלַח דָּוִד אֶת־יוֹאָב וְאֶת־עֲבָדָיו עִמּוֹ וְאֶת־כָּל־יִשְׂרָאֵל

וַיַּשְׁחִתוּ אֶת־בְּנֵי עַמּוֹן וַיָּצֻרוּ עַל־רַבָּה וְדָוִד יוֹשֵׁב בִּירוּשָׁלָ͏ִם

Then it happened in the spring, at the time when kings (LXX) go out [to
battle], that David sent Joab and his servants with him and all Israel, and they
destroyed the sons of Ammon and besieged Rabbah. But David stayed at
Jerusalem. . . .

2 Sam. 12:26-31

26 וַיִּלָּחֶם יוֹאָב בְּרַבַּת בְּנֵי עַמּוֹן וַיִּלְכֹּד אֶת־עִיר הַמְּלוּכָה

27 וַיִּשְׁלַח יוֹאָב מַלְאָכִים אֶל־דָּוִד וַיֹּאמֶר נִלְחַמְתִּי

בְרַבָּה גַּם־לָכַדְתִּי אֶת־עִיר הַמָּיִם

28 וְעַתָּה אֱסֹף אֶת־יֶתֶר הָעָם וַחֲנֵה עַל־הָעִיר

וְלָכְדָהּ פֶּן־אֶלְכֹּד אֲנִי אֶת־הָעִיר וְנִקְרָא שְׁמִי עָלֶיהָ

29 וַיֶּאֱסֹף דָּוִד אֶת־כָּל־הָעָם וַיֵּלֶךְ רַבָּתָה וַיִּלָּחֶם בָּהּ וַיִּלְכְּדָהּ

30 וַיִּקַּח אֶת־עֲטֶרֶת־מַלְכָּם מֵעַל רֹאשׁוֹ וּמִשְׁקָלָהּ כִּכַּר זָהָב

וְאֶבֶן יְקָרָה וַתְּהִי עַל־רֹאשׁ דָּוִד וּשְׁלַל הָעִיר הוֹצִיא הַרְבֵּה מְאֹד

31 וְאֶת־הָעָם אֲשֶׁר־בָּהּ הוֹצִיא וַיָּשֶׂם בַּמְּגֵרָה וּבַחֲרִצֵי הַבַּרְזֶל וּבְמַגְזְרֹת

הַבַּרְזֶל וְהֶעֱבִיר אוֹתָם בַּמַּלְכֵּן [בַּ]וּמַלְבֵּן] וְכֵן יַעֲשֶׂה לְכֹל עָרֵי בְנֵי־עַמּוֹן

וַיָּשָׁב דָּוִד   וְכָל־הָעָם יְרוּשָׁלָ͏ִם

Now Joab fought against Rabbah of the sons of Ammon and captured the
royal city. So Joab sent messengers to David and said, "I have fought against
Rabbah, I have even captured the city of waters. Now therefore, gather the
rest of the people together and camp against the city and capture it, or I will
capture the city myself and it will be named after me."

So David gathered all the people and went to Rabbah, fought against it and captured it. Then he took the crown of their king from his head; and its weight [was] a talent of gold, and [in it] [was] a precious stone; and it was [placed] on David's head. And he brought out the spoil of the city in great amounts. He also brought out the people who were in it, and set [them] under saws, sharp iron instruments, and iron axes, and made them pass through the brickkiln. And thus he did to all the cities of the sons of Ammon. Then David and all the people returned [to] Jerusalem.

1 Chron. 20:1-3

1 וַיְהִי לְעֵת תְּשׁוּבַת הַשָּׁנָה לְעֵת צֵאת הַמְּלָכִים וַיִּנְהַג יוֹאָב אֶת־חֵיל

הַצָּבָא וַיַּשְׁחֵת אֶת־אֶרֶץ בְּנֵי־עַמּוֹן וַיָּבֹא וַיָּצַר אֶת־רַבָּה וְדָוִיד

יֹשֵׁב בִּירוּשָׁלָם וַיַּךְ יוֹאָב אֶת־רַבָּה וַיֶּהֶרְסֶהָ

2 וַיִּקַּח דָּוִיד אֶת־עֲטֶרֶת־מַלְכָּם מֵעַל רֹאשׁוֹ וַיִּמְצָאָהּ מִשְׁקָל כִּכַּר־זָהָב

וּבָהּ אֶבֶן יְקָרָה וַתְּהִי עַל־רֹאשׁ דָּוִיד וּשְׁלַל הָעִיר הוֹצִיא הַרְבֵּה מְאֹד

3 וְאֶת־הָעָם אֲשֶׁר־בָּהּ הוֹצִיא וַיָּשַׂר בַּמְּגֵרָה וּבַחֲרִיצֵי הַבַּרְזֶל וּבַמְּגֵרוֹת וְכֵן

יַעֲשֶׂה דָוִיד לְכֹל עָרֵי בְנֵי־עַמּוֹן וַיָּשָׁב דָּוִיד וְכָל־הָעָם יְרוּשָׁלָם

Then it happened in the spring, at the time when kings (τῶν βασιλέων) go out [to battle], that Joab led out the army and ravaged the land of the sons of Ammon, and came and besieged Rabbah. But David stayed at Jerusalem. And Joab struck Rabbah and overthrew it. Then David took the crown of their king from his head, and he found it to weigh a talent of gold, and there was a precious stone in it; and it was placed on David's head. And he brought out the spoil of the city, a very great amount. Thjen he brought out the people who [were] in it, and cut [them] with saws and with sharp instruments and with axes. And thus David did to all the cities of the sons of Ammon. Then David and all the people returned [to] Jerusalem.

5. David attacks **Hadadezer** while the latter is engaged in trying to reassert his authority over his disillusioned vassals along the **Euphrates**

2 S 8:3-8 ‖ 1 Chron. 18:3-8.

3 וַיַּךְ דָּוִד אֶת־הֲדַדְעֶזֶר בֶּן־רְחֹב מֶלֶךְ צוֹבָה בְּלֶכְתּוֹ

לְהָשִׁיב יָדוֹ בִּנְהַר־ (LXX ἐπὶ τὸν ποταμὸν Εὐφράτην) [פְּרָת]

4 וַיִּלְכֹּד דָּוִד מִמֶּנּוּ אֶלֶף וּשְׁבַע־מֵאוֹת פָּרָשִׁים וְעֶשְׂרִים אֶלֶף אִישׁ

רַגְלִי וַיְעַקֵּר דָּוִד אֶת־כָּל־הָרֶכֶב וַיּוֹתֵר מִמֶּנּוּ מֵאָה רָכֶב

5 וַתָּבֹא אֲרַם דַּמֶּשֶׂק לַעְזֹר לַהֲדַדְעֶזֶר מֶלֶךְ צוֹבָה וַיַּךְ

דָּוִד בַּאֲרָם עֶשְׂרִים־וּשְׁנַיִם אֶלֶף אִישׁ

6 וַיָּשֶׂם דָּוִד נְצִבִים בַּאֲרַם דַּמֶּשֶׂק וַתְּהִי אֲרָם לְדָוִד

לַעֲבָדִים נוֹשְׂאֵי מִנְחָה וַיֹּשַׁע יְהוָה אֶת־דָּוִד בְּכֹל אֲשֶׁר הָלָךְ

7 וַיִּקַּח דָּוִד אֵת שִׁלְטֵי הַזָּהָב אֲשֶׁר הָיוּ אֶל עַבְדֵי

הֲדַדְעֶזֶר וַיְבִיאֵם יְרוּשָׁלָם

8 וּמִבֶּטַח וּמִבֵּרֹתַי עָרֵי הֲדַדְעֶזֶר לָקַח הַמֶּלֶךְ דָּוִד

נְחֹשֶׁת הַרְבֵּה מְאֹד

Then David defeated Hadadezer, the son of Rehob king of Zobah, <u>as he went to restore his rule at the River</u>. And David captured from him 1,700 horsemen and 20,000 foot soldiers; and David hamstrung the chariot horses, but reserved [enough] of them for 100 chariots. When the Arameans of Damascus came to help Hadadezer, king of Zobah, David killed 22,000 Arameans. Then David put garrisons among the **Arameans of Damascus,** and the Arameans became servants to David, bringing tribute. And Yahweh helped David wherever he went. And David took the shields of gold which were carried by the servants of Hadadezer and brought them to Jerusalem. From **Betah and from Berothai,** cities of Hadadezer, King David took a very large amount of bronze.

1 Chron. 18:3-8

3 וַיַּךְ דָּוִיד אֶת־הֲדַדְעֶזֶר מֶלֶךְ־צוֹבָה חֲמָתָה בְּלֶכְתּוֹ

לְהַצִּיב יָדוֹ בִּנְהַר־פְּרָת

4 וַיִּלְכֹּד דָּוִיד מִמֶּנּוּ אֶלֶף רֶכֶב וְשִׁבְעַת אֲלָפִים

פָּרָשִׁים וְעֶשְׂרִים אֶלֶף אִישׁ רַגְלִי וַיְעַקֵּר דָּוִיד

אֶת־כָּל־הָרֶכֶב וַיּוֹתֵר מִמֶּנּוּ מֵאָה רָכֶב

5 וַיָּבֹא אֲרַם דַּרְמֶשֶׂק לַעְזוֹר לַהֲדַדְעֶזֶר מֶלֶךְ צוֹבָה

וַיַּךְ דָּוִיד בַּאֲרָם עֶשְׂרִים־וּשְׁנַיִם אֶלֶף אִישׁ

6 וַיָּשֶׂם דָּוִיד בַּאֲרַם דַּרְמֶשֶׂק וַיְהִי אֲרָם לְדָוִיד

עֲבָדִים נֹשְׂאֵי מִנְחָה וַיּוֹשַׁע יְהוָה לְדָוִיד בְּכֹל אֲשֶׁר הָלָךְ

7 וַיִּקַּח דָּוִיד אֵת שִׁלְטֵי הַזָּהָב אֲשֶׁר הָיוּ עַל עַבְדֵי

הֲדַדְעֶזֶר וַיְבִיאֵם יְרוּשָׁלָם

8 וּמִטִּבְחַת וּמִכּוּן עָרֵי הֲדַדְעֶזֶר לָקַח דָּוִיד נְחֹשֶׁת רַבָּה מְאֹד בָּהּ עָשָׂה

שְׁלֹמֹה אֶת־יָם הַנְּחֹשֶׁת וְאֶת־הָעַמּוּדִים וְאֵת כְּלֵי הַנְּחֹשֶׁת

And David smote Hadadezer king of Zobah as far as Hamath, <u>as he went to establish his rule</u> to the **Euphrates River**. And David took from him 1,000 chariots and 7,000 horsemen and 20,000 foot soldiers, and David hamstrung all the chariot horses, but reserved [enough] of them for 100 chariots. When the Arameans of Damascus came to help Hadadezer king of Zobah, David killed 22,000 men of the Arameans. Then David put [garrisons] among the **Arameans of Damascus**; and the Arameans became servants to David, bringing tribute. And Yahweh helped David wherever he went. And David took the shields of gold which were carried by the servants of Hadadezer and brought them to Jerusalem. Also from **Tibhath and from Cun**, cities of Hadadezer, David took a very large amount of bronze, with which Solomon made the bronze sea and the pillars and the bronze utensils.

6. Hamath — becomes David's ally —
2 Sam. 8:9-10 ‖ 1 Chron. 18:9-10

9 וַיִּשְׁמַע תֹּעִי מֶלֶךְ חֲמָת כִּי הִכָּה דָוִד אֵת כָּל־חֵיל הֲדַדְעֶזֶר

10 וַיִּשְׁלַח תֹּעִי אֶת־יוֹרָם־בְּנוֹ אֶל־הַמֶּלֶךְ־דָּוִד לִשְׁאָל־לוֹ לְשָׁלוֹם וּלְבָרְכוֹ

עַל אֲשֶׁר נִלְחַם בַּהֲדַדְעֶזֶר וַיַּכֵּהוּ כִּי־אִישׁ מִלְחֲמוֹת תֹּעִי הָיָה הֲדַדְעֶזֶר

וּבְיָדוֹ הָיוּ כְּלֵי־כֶסֶף וּכְלֵי־זָהָב וּכְלֵי נְחֹשֶׁת

Now **Toi king of Hamath** heard that David had defeated all the army of Hadadezer, So Toi sent **Joram** his son to King David to greet him and bless him, because he had fought against Hadadezer and defeated him; for Hadadezer had been at war with Toi. And [Joram] brought with him articles of silver, of gold and of bronze.

1 Chron. 18:9-10

9 וַיִּשְׁמַע תֹּעוּ מֶלֶךְ חֲמָת כִּי הִכָּה דָוִיד אֶת־כָּל־חֵיל הֲדַדְעֶזֶר מֶלֶךְ־צוֹבָה

10 וַיִּשְׁלַח אֶת־הֲדוֹרָם־בְּנוֹ אֶל־הַמֶּלֶךְ־דָּוִיד לִשְׁאוֹל־[וְלוֹ][שָׁאַל]־לוֹ לְשָׁלוֹם וּלְבָרֲכוֹ עַל אֲשֶׁר נִלְחַם בַּהֲדַדְעֶזֶר וַיַּכֵּהוּ כִּי־אִישׁ מִלְחֲמוֹת תֹּעוּ הָיָה הֲדַדְעֶזֶר וְכֹל כְּלֵי זָהָב וָכֶסֶף וּנְחֹשֶׁת

Corrected = 2 Sam

Now Tou king of Hamath heard that David had defeated all the army of Hadadezer king of Zobah. So he sent **Hadoram** his son to King David to greet him and to bless him, because he had fought against Hadadezer and had defeated him; for Hadadezer had been at war with Tou. And [Hadoram brought] all kinds of articles of gold and silver and bronze.

7. **Edom** — 2 Sam. 8:13b-14 ‖ 1 Chron. 18:12-13.

2 Sam. 8:13-14

13 וַיַּעַשׂ דָּוִד שֵׁם בְּשֻׁבוֹ מֵהַכּוֹתוֹ אֶת־אֲרָם (Ἰδουμαίαν) בְּגֵיא־מֶלַח שְׁמוֹנָה עָשָׂר אָלֶף

14 וַיָּשֶׂם בֶּאֱדוֹם נְצִבִים בְּכָל־אֱדוֹם שָׂם נְצִבִים וַיְהִי כָל־אֱדוֹם עֲבָדִים לְדָוִד וַיּוֹשַׁע יְהוָה אֶת־דָּוִד בְּכֹל אֲשֶׁר הָלָךְ

So David made a name [for himself] when he returned from killing 18,000 Edomites (LXX) in the Valley of Salt. And he put garrisons in Edom, and all the Edomites became servants to David. And Yahweh helped David wherever he went.

1 Chron. 18:12-13

12 וְאַבְשַׁי בֶּן־צְרוּיָה הִכָּה אֶת־אֱדוֹם בְּגֵיא הַמֶּלַח שְׁמוֹנָה עָשָׂר אָלֶף

13 וַיָּשֶׂם בֶּאֱדוֹם נְצִיבִים וַיִּהְיוּ כָל־אֱדוֹם עֲבָדִים

לְדָוִד וַיּוֹשַׁע יְהוָה אֶת־דָּוִד בְּכֹל אֲשֶׁר הָלָךְ

Moreover Abishai the son of Zeruiah defeated 18,000 Edomites in the Valley of Salt. Then he put commissioners in Edom, and all the Edomites became servants to David. And Yahweh helped David wherever he went.

C. POLITICAL UNREST.

1. Absalom's revolt — 2 Sam. 13-19.

2 Sam. 13:23

וַיְהִי לִשְׁנָתַיִם יָמִים וַיִּהְיוּ גֹזְזִים לְאַבְשָׁלוֹם בְּבַעַל חָצוֹר

אֲשֶׁר עִם־אֶפְרָיִם וַיִּקְרָא אַבְשָׁלוֹם לְכָל־בְּנֵי הַמֶּלֶךְ

¶ Now it came about after two full years that Absalom had sheepshearers in **Baal-hazor**, which is near Ephraim, and Absalom invited all the king's sons.

2 Sam. 13:37

וְאַבְשָׁלוֹם בָּרַח וַיֵּלֶךְ אֶל־תַּלְמַי בֶּן־עַמִּיחוּר [עַמִּיהוּד]

מֶלֶךְ גְּשׁוּר וַיִּתְאַבֵּל עַל־בְּנוֹ כָּל־הַיָּמִים

Now Absalom fled and went to Talmai the son of Ammihud, the king of **Geshur**. And [David] mourned for his son every day.

2 Sam. 15:10   וַיִּשְׁלַח אַבְשָׁלוֹם מְרַגְּלִים בְּכָל־שִׁבְטֵי

יִשְׂרָאֵל לֵאמֹר כְּשָׁמְעֲכֶם אֶת־קוֹל הַשֹּׁפָר וַאֲמַרְתֶּם מָלַךְ

אַבְשָׁלוֹם בְּחֶבְרוֹן

But Absalom sent spies throughout all the tribes of Israel, saying, "As soon as you hear the sound of the trumpet, then you shall say, 'Absalom is king in Hebron.'"

2 Sam. 17:24   וְדָוִד בָּא מַחֲנָיְמָה וְאַבְשָׁלֹם עָבַר אֶת־הַיַּרְדֵּן הוּא

וְכָל־אִישׁ יִשְׂרָאֵל עִמּוֹ

¶ Then David came to Mahanaim. And Absalom crossed the Jordan, he and all the men of Israel with him.

2 Sam. 18:6   וַיֵּצֵא הָעָם הַשָּׂדֶה לִקְרַאת יִשְׂרָאֵל וַתְּהִי

הַמִּלְחָמָה בְּיַעַר אֶפְרָיִם

¶ Then the people went out into the field against Israel, and the battle took place in the forest of Ephraim.

2. Shiba ben Bichri's revolt 2 Sam. 20:1-22.

וַיָּבֹאוּ וַיָּצֻרוּ עָלָיו בְּאָבֵלָה בֵּית הַמַּעֲכָה וַיִּשְׁפְּכוּ סֹלְלָה   Sam. 20:15
אֶל־הָעִיר וַתַּעֲמֹד בַּחֵל וְכָל־הָעָם אֲשֶׁר אֶת־יוֹאָב
מַשְׁחִיתִם לְהַפִּיל הַחוֹמָה

They came and besieged him in **Abel Beth-maacah**, and they cast up a siege ramp against the city, and it stood by the rampart; and all the people who were with Joab were wreaking destruction in order to topple the wall.

D. THE CENSUS 2 Sam. 24:4-7

4 וַיֶּחֱזַק דְּבַר־הַמֶּלֶךְ אֶל־יוֹאָב וְעַל שָׂרֵי הֶחָיִל
וַיֵּצֵא יוֹאָב וְשָׂרֵי הַחַיִל לִפְנֵי הַמֶּלֶךְ לִפְקֹד אֶת־הָעָם אֶת־יִשְׂרָאֵל
5 וַיַּעַבְרוּ אֶת־הַיַּרְדֵּן וַיַּחֲנוּ בַעֲרוֹעֵר יְמִין הָעִיר
אֲשֶׁר בְּתוֹךְ־הַנַּחַל הַגָּד וְאֶל־יַעְזֵר
6 וַיָּבֹאוּ הַגִּלְעָדָה וְאֶל־אֶרֶץ *תַּחְתִּים חָדְשִׁי וַיָּבֹאוּ
דָּנָה יַּעַן (עִיּוֹן!) וְסָבִיב אֶל־צִידוֹן
7 וַיָּבֹאוּ מִבְצַר־צֹר וְכָל־עָרֵי הַחִוִּי וְהַכְּנַעֲנִי וַיֵּצְאוּ
אֶל־נֶגֶב יְהוּדָה בְּאֵר שָׁבַע

*LXX Luc. γῆν Χεττιειμ Καδης

LXX B   καὶ εἰς γῆν Θαβασων (בָּשָׁן?) ἥ ἐστιν Αδασαι,

But the king's word prevailed against Joab and against the commanders of the army. So Joab and the commanders of the army went out from the presence of the king to register the people of Israel. And they crossed the Jordan and camped in **Aroer**, on the right side of the city that is in the middle of the valley; Gad and toward **Jazer**. Then they came to **Gilead** and to the land of **Tahtim-hodshi** (? = LXX B **Bashan which is Hadasha?**), and they came to **Dan**, **Iyon**(!) and around to **Sidon**, and came to the **fortress of Tyre**

and to **all** **the** **cities** **of** **the** **Hivites** **and** **of** **the** **Canaanites**, and they went out
to the **Negeb of Judah,** [to] **Beersheba**.

   E. LEVITICAL CITIES

   1. Functions of the Levites (1 Chron 23-26)

      a. Assisting in temple management, both conduct
         of rituals and management of storehouses
         (23:4a, 28-29; 26:20, 22-23, 25)
      b. Officers and judges (23:4b; 26:29-32)
      c. Guarding the gates of the temple compound
         (23:5a)
      d. Temple music (23:5b, 30-31)
      e. Border garrisons:

   1 Chron. 26:29-32

29 לַיִּצְהָרִי כְּנַנְיָהוּ וּבָנָיו לַמְּלָאכָה הַחִיצוֹנָה
עַל־יִשְׂרָאֵל לְשֹׁטְרִים וּלְשֹׁפְטִים

As for the Izharites, Chenaniah and his sons were [assigned] to outside duties
for Israel, as officers and judges.

30 לַחֶבְרוֹנִי חֲשַׁבְיָהוּ וְאֶחָיו בְּנֵי־חַיִל אֶלֶף
וּשְׁבַע־מֵאוֹת עַל פְּקֻדַּת יִשְׂרָאֵל מֵעֵבֶר לַיַּרְדֵּן מַעְרָבָה
לְכֹל מְלֶאכֶת יְהוָה וְלַעֲבֹדַת הַמֶּלֶךְ

As for the Hebronites, Hashabiah and his relatives, 1,700 capable men, had
charge of the affairs of Israel west of the Jordan, for all the work of the LORD
and the service of the king.

31 לַחֶבְרוֹנִי יְרִיָּה הָרֹאשׁ לַחֶבְרוֹנִי לְתֹלְדֹתָיו
לְאָבוֹת בִּשְׁנַת הָאַרְבָּעִים לְמַלְכוּת דָּוִיד נִדְרָשׁוּ וַיִּמָּצֵא בָהֶם
גִּבּוֹרֵי חַיִל בְּיַעְזֵיר גִּלְעָד

32וְאֶחָיו בְּנֵי־חַיִל אַלְפַּיִם וּשְׁבַע מֵאוֹת רָאשֵׁי
הָאָבוֹת וַיַּפְקִידֵם דָּוִיד הַמֶּלֶךְ עַל־הָראוּבֵנִי וְהַגָּדִי וַחֲצִי שֵׁבֶט

הַמְנַשִּׁי לְכָל־דְּבַר הָאֱלֹהִים וּדְבַר הַמֶּלֶךְ

As for the Hebronites, Jerijah the chief (these Hebronites were investigated according to their genealogies and fathers' [households], in the fortieth year of David's reign, and men of outstanding capability were found among them at **Jazer** of Gilead) and his relatives, capable men, [were] 2,700 in number, heads of fathers' [households]. And King David made them overseers of the Reubenites, the Gadites and the half-tribe of the Manassites concerning all the affairs of God and of the king.

> 2. Distribution of settlements (Josh. 21; 1 Chron 6:54-81)
>   See *Carta Bible Atlas,* MAP 108
>   a. S. Judah, Hill Country: among the non-Judean
>   areas
>   b. Transjordan: on the frontier (compare Simeon,
>   his brother, settled in the Negeb)
>   c. Throughout Cisjordan, mainly in the formerly
>   Canaanite territories on the plains — Jezreel
>   Valley, border with Philistia along corridor
>   from Joppa to Jerusalem

LESSON 14
THE UNITED MONARCHY, Part 2

I. "EMPIRE" & FOREIGN POLICY

    A. Extent of his so-called "Empire" and of Israel proper

        1. 1 Ki. 5:4-5 (Eng. 4:24-25)

            a. <u>The</u> <u>Levant</u> = עֵבֶר נַעֲרָא

1 Kings 5:4 כִּי־הוּא רֹדֶה בְּכָל־עֵבֶר הַנָּהָר מִתִּפְסַח וְעַד־עַזָּה

Eng. 4:24 בְּכָל־מַלְכֵי עֵבֶר הַנָּהָר וְשָׁלוֹם הָיָה לוֹ מִכָּל־עֲבָרָיו מִסָּבִיב

For he had dominion over everything **west of the River**, (from **Tiphsah** even to **Gaza**, over all the kings **west of the River**; not in LXX) and he had peace on all sides around about him.

            b. <u>Israel</u> <u>proper</u> — Dan to Beer-sheba

1Kings 5:5 וַיֵּשֶׁב יְהוּדָה וְיִשְׂרָאֵל לָבֶטַח אִישׁ תַּחַת גַּפְנוֹ וְתַחַת תְּאֵנָתוֹ

(Eng. 4:25) מִדָּן וְעַד־בְּאֵר שָׁבַע כֹּל יְמֵי שְׁלֹמֹה

So **Judah and Israel** lived in safety, every man under his vine and his fig tree, from **Dan** even to **Beersheba**, all the days of Solomon.

        2. 1 Ki 4:20-5:1 (Eng 4:20-21) <u>LXX</u> <u>does</u> <u>not</u> <u>have</u> <u>it</u>!
           It belongs after 1 Ki. 10:26a parallel to 2 Chron.
           9:26.

            a. <u>Nation</u> <u>of</u> <u>Israel</u>

1Kings 4:20 יְהוּדָה וְיִשְׂרָאֵל רַבִּים כַּחוֹל אֲשֶׁר־עַל־הַיָּם

לָרֹב אֹכְלִים וְשֹׁתִים וּשְׂמֵחִים

Judah and Israel were as numerous as the sand that is on the seashore in abundance, eating and drinking and rejoicing.

            b. <u>The</u> <u>Levant</u> = עֵבֶר נַעֲרָא

1Kings 5:1 וּשְׁלֹמֹה הָיָה מוֹשֵׁל בְּכָל־הַמַּמְלָכוֹת מִן־הַנָּהָר

אֶרֶץ פְּלִשְׁתִּים וְעַד (2 Chr. 9:26)‹וְעַד› »הַגָּדוֹל נְהַר־פְּרָת«

גְּבוּל מִצְרָיִם מַגִּשִׁים מִנְחָה וְעֹבְדִים אֶת־שְׁלֹמֹה כָּל־יְמֵי חַיָּיו (Eng 4:21)

Now Solomon ruled over all the kingdoms from the ‹‹Great›› **River** ‹‹the

River Euphrates›› ‹to› the **land of the Philistines** and to the **border of**

Egypt; [they] brought tribute and served Solomon all the days of his life.

2.Chron.9:26

2Chr. 9:26 וַיְהִי מוֹשֵׁל בְּכָל־הַמְּלָכִים מִן־הַנָּהָר »הַגָּדוֹל נְהַר־פְּרָת«

וְעַד־אֶרֶץ פְּלִשְׁתִּים וְעַד גְּבוּל מִצְרָיִם

B. Building activities
1. In Jerusalem: Temple — 1 Kings 6:37-38

37 בַּשָּׁנָה הָרְבִיעִית יֻסַּד בֵּית יְהוָה בְּיֶרַח זִו

38 וּבַשָּׁנָה הָאַחַת עֶשְׂרֵה בְּיֶרַח בּוּל הוּא הַחֹדֶשׁ

הַשְּׁמִינִי כָּלָה הַבַּיִת לְכָל־דְּבָרָיו וּלְכָל־מִשְׁפָּטוֹ [מִשְׁפָּטָיו]

וַיִּבְנֵהוּ שֶׁבַע שָׁנִים

In the fourth year the foundation of the house of Yahweh was laid, in the
month of Ziv. In the eleventh year, in the month of Bul, which is the eighth
month, the house was finished throughout all its parts and according to all its
plans. So he was seven years in building it.

2. His palace — 1 Kings 7:1

וְאֶת־בֵּיתוֹ בָּנָה שְׁלֹמֹה שְׁלֹשׁ עֶשְׂרֵה שָׁנָה וַיְכַל אֶת־כָּל־בֵּיתוֹ

Now Solomon was building his own house thirteen years, and he finished all
his house.

3. Key fortified centers 1 Kings 9:15-19

15 וְזֶה דְבַר־הַמַּס אֲשֶׁר־הֶעֱלָה הַמֶּלֶךְ שְׁלֹמֹה לִבְנוֹת

אֶת־בֵּית יְהוָה וְאֶת־בֵּיתוֹ וְאֶת־הַמִּלּוֹא וְאֵת חוֹמַת יְרוּשָׁלָ͏ִם

וְאֶת־חָצֹר וְאֶת־מְגִדּוֹ וְאֶת־גָּזֶר

16 פַּרְעֹה מֶלֶךְ־מִצְרַיִם עָלָה וַיִּלְכֹּד אֶת־גֶּזֶר וַיִּשְׂרְפָהּ בָּאֵשׁ

וְאֶת־הַכְּנַעֲנִי הַיֹּשֵׁב בָּעִיר הָרָג וַיִּתְּנָהּ שִׁלֻּחִים לְבִתּוֹ אֵשֶׁת שְׁלֹמֹה

17 וַיִּבֶן שְׁלֹמֹה אֶת־גֶּזֶר וְאֶת־בֵּית חֹרֹן תַּחְתּוֹן

18וְאֶת־בַּעֲלָת וְאֶת־תָּמָר [תַּדְמֹר] בַּמִּדְבָּר בָּאָרֶץ

19וְאֵת כָּל־עָרֵי הַמִּסְכְּנוֹת אֲשֶׁר הָיוּ לִשְׁלֹמֹה וְאֵת

עָרֵי הָרֶכֶב וְאֵת עָרֵי הַפָּרָשִׁים וְאֵת חֵשֶׁק שְׁלֹמֹה אֲשֶׁר חָשַׁק

לִבְנוֹת בִּירוּשָׁלַם וּבַלְּבָנוֹן וּבְכֹל אֶרֶץ מֶמְשַׁלְתּוֹ

¶ Now this is the account of the forced labor which King Solomon levied to
build the house of Yahweh, his own house, the Millo, the wall of Jerusalem,
Hazor, Megiddo, and **Gezer**. [For] Pharaoh king of Egypt had gone up and
captured Gezer and burned it with fire, and killed the Canaanites who lived
in the city, and had given it [as] a dowry to his daughter, Solomon's wife. So
Solomon rebuilt Gezer and **the lower Beth-horon** and **Baalath** and **Tamar**
[Tadmor] in the wilderness, in the land [of Judah], and all the storage cities
which Solomon had, even the cities for his chariots and the cities for his
horsemen, and all that it pleased Solomon to build in Jerusalem, in Lebanon,
and in all the land under his rule.

C. <u>Strong military establishment</u> 2 Chron. 1:14 ‖ 1 Ki. 10:26
also ‖ 1 Ki. 5:6 and 2 Chron. 9:25

<u>2Chr. 1:14</u> וַיֶּאֱסֹף שְׁלֹמֹה רֶכֶב וּפָרָשִׁים וַיְהִי־לוֹ אֶלֶף

וְאַרְבַּע־מֵאוֹת רֶכֶב וּשְׁנֵים־עָשָׂר אֶלֶף פָּרָשִׁים וַיַּנִּיחֵם בְּעָרֵי

הָרֶכֶב וְעִם־הַמֶּלֶךְ בִּירוּשָׁלָם

(2 Chron. 9:25a) ‹אֻרְיוֹת סוּסִים וּמַרְכָּבוֹת› (‖ 1 Ki. 5:6)

<u>2Chr. 9:25</u> וַיְהִי לִשְׁלֹמֹה אַרְבַּעַת אֲלָפִים אֻרְיוֹת סוּסִים

וּמַרְכָּבוֹת וּשְׁנֵים־עָשָׂר אֶלֶף פָּרָשִׁים וַיַּנִּיחֵם בְּעָרֵי הָרֶכֶב

וְעִם־הַמֶּלֶךְ בִּירוּשָׁלָם

And Solomon amassed chariots and horsemen; he had 1,400 chariots ‹**stalls**
for horses and chariots›(2 Chron. 9:25a) and 12,000 horsemen, and he
stationed them in the chariot cities and with the king at Jerusalem.

1 Ki. 9:17-19

17 וַיִּבֶן שְׁלֹמֹה אֶת־גֶּזֶר וְאֶת־בֵּית חֹרֹן תַּחְתּוֹן

18 וְאֶת־בַּעֲלָת וְאֶת־תָּמָר [תַּדְמֹר] בַּמִּדְבָּר בָּאָרֶץ

19 וְאֵת כָּל־עָרֵי הַמִּסְכְּנוֹת אֲשֶׁר הָיוּ לִשְׁלֹמֹה וְאֵת

עָרֵי הָרֶכֶב וְאֵת עָרֵי הַפָּרָשִׁים וְאֵת חֵשֶׁק שְׁלֹמֹה אֲשֶׁר חָשַׁק

לִבְנוֹת בִּירוּשָׁלַם וּבַלְּבָנוֹן וּבְכֹל אֶרֶץ מֶמְשַׁלְתּוֹ

17 וַיִּבֶן שְׁלֹמֹה . . . 19. . . עָרֵי הָרֶכֶב וְאֵת עָרֵי הַפָּרָשִׁים . . . .

So Solomon built . . . **the cities for his chariots and the cities for his
horsemen**, and all that it pleased Solomon to build in Jerusalem, in Lebanon,
and in all the land under his rule.

D. Diplomacy
    1. Marriage (treaty) with Siamon (979-960 BCE)
       1 Ki. 3:1; 9:16
    2. Marriage alliances with neighboring states —
       1 Ki. 11:1

וְהַמֶּלֶךְ שְׁלֹמֹה אָהַב נָשִׁים נָכְרִיּוֹת רַבּוֹת

וְאֶת־בַּת־פַּרְעֹה מוֹאֲבִיּוֹת עַמֳּנִיּוֹת אֲדֹמִית צֵדְנִית חִתִּיֹּת

Now King Solomon loved many foreign women along with the daughter of
Pharaoh: **Moabite, Ammonite, Edomite, Sidonian, and Hittite women**,

    3. Some power plays? Note 2 Chron. 8:3

וַיֵּלֶךְ שְׁלֹמֹה חֲמָת צוֹבָה וַיֶּחֱזַק עָלֶיהָ

Then Solomon went to **Hamath-zobah** and overpowered it.

E. Commercial and Economic Policy —

    1. "Vast income"
       a. 2 Chron. 1:15 || 1 Ki. 10:27; 2 Chron. 9:27

2 Chr. 1:15 וַיִּתֵּן הַמֶּלֶךְ אֶת־הַכֶּסֶף וְאֶת־הַזָּהָב בִּירוּשָׁלַם

כָּאֲבָנִים וְאֵת הָאֲרָזִים נָתַן כַּשִּׁקְמִים אֲשֶׁר־בַּשְּׁפֵלָה לָרֹב

The king made silver and gold as plentiful in Jerusalem as stones, and cedars
he made as plentiful as sycamores in the lowland.

b. 1 Ki. 10:14 ‖ 2 Chron. 9:14

1 Kings 10:14 וַיְהִי מִשְׁקַל הַזָּהָב אֲשֶׁר־בָּא לִשְׁלֹמֹה בְּשָׁנָה

אֶחָת שֵׁשׁ מֵאוֹת שִׁשִּׁים וָשֵׁשׁ כִּכַּר זָהָב

Now the weight of gold which came in to Solomon in one year was 666
talents of gold.

2. Conducted overseas trade, 1 Ki. 10:15a

15a לְבַד מֵאַנְשֵׁי הַתָּרִים וּמִסְחַר הָרֹכְלִים

וְכָל־מַלְכֵי הָעֶרֶב (עֶרֶב 2 Chron. 9:14 ‖) וּפַחוֹת הָאָרֶץ

besides from the entrepreneurs and the merchandice of the merchants and all
the kings of Arabia and the governors of the country.

1 Ki. 10:28-29 — munitions trade

28 וּמוֹצָא הַסּוּסִים אֲשֶׁר לִשְׁלֹמֹה מִמִּצְרָיִם וּמִקְוֵה

סֹחֲרֵי הַמֶּלֶךְ יִקְחוּ מִקְוֵה בִּמְחִיר

29 וַתַּעֲלֶה וַתֵּצֵא מֶרְכָּבָה מִמִּצְרַיִם בְּשֵׁשׁ מֵאוֹת

כֶּסֶף וְסוּס בַּחֲמִשִּׁים וּמֵאָה וְכֵן לְכָל־מַלְכֵי הַחִתִּים וּלְמַלְכֵי

אֲרָם בְּיָדָם יֹצִא

Also Solomon's import of horses was from **Egypt and Que**, [and] the king's
merchants procured [them] from **Que** for a price.
A chariot was imported from **Egypt** for 600 [shekels] of silver, and a horse for
150; and by the same means they exported them to all the kings of the
Hittites and to the kings of the **Arameans**.

II. INTERNAL ADMINISTRATION

A. The Roster of Commissioners' Districts

1 Kings 4:7-19

1 Kings 4:7 וְלִשְׁלֹמֹה שְׁנֵים־עָשָׂר נִצָּבִים עַל־כָּל־יִשְׂרָאֵל

וְכִלְכְּלוּ אֶת־הַמֶּלֶךְ וְאֶת־בֵּיתוֹ חֹדֶשׁ בַּשָּׁנָה יִהְיֶה עַל־אֶחָד

[הָ][אֶחָד] לְכַלְכֵּל

1Kings 4:8 וְאֵלֶּה שְׁמוֹתָם בֶּן־חוּר בְּהַר אֶפְרָיִם

Solomon had twelve deputies over all Israel, who provided for the king and

his household; each man had to provide for a month in the year.

These are their names:

First District -- Mt. Ephraim

בֶּן־חוּר בְּהַר אֶפְרָיִם

Ben-hur, in the hill country of Ephraim

Second District — "Danite Territory"

9 בֶּן־דֶּקֶר בְּמָקַץ וּבְשַׁעַלְבִים וּבֵית שָׁמֶשׁ וְאֵילוֹן בֵּית חָנָן

(9) Ben-deker in **Makaz** and **Shaalbim** and **Beth-shemesh** and **Elonbeth-hanan**;

Third District — N. Sharon Plain

10 בֶּן־חֶסֶד בָּאֲרֻבּוֹת לוֹ שֹׂכֹה וְכָל־אֶרֶץ חֵפֶר

(10) Ben-hesed, in **Arubboth** (**Socoh** was his and all the land of **Hepher**);

Fourth District — Naphoth Dor

11 בֶּן־אֲבִינָדָב כָּל־נָפַת דֹּאר טָפַת בַּת־שְׁלֹמֹה הָיְתָה לּוֹ לְאִשָּׁה

(11) Ben-abinadab, [in] all the district of Dor (Taphath the daughter of Solomon was his wife)

Fifth District — Jezreel and Beth-shean Valleys

12 בַּעֲנָא בֶּן־אֲחִילוּד תַּעְנַךְ וּמְגִדּוֹ וְכָל־בֵּית שְׁאָן אֲשֶׁר אֵצֶל
צָרְתַנָה מִתַּחַת לְיִזְרְעֶאל מִבֵּית שְׁאָן עַד אָבֵל מְחוֹלָה עַד
מֵעֵבֶר לְיָקְמְעָם

(12) Baana the son of Ahilud: **Taanach** and **Megiddo**, and all **Beth-shean** which is beside **Zarethan** below Jezreel, from **Beth-shean** to **Abel-meholah** as far as the other side of **Jokmeam**;

Sixth District — N. Gilead and Bashan

13 בֶּן־גֶּבֶר בְּרָמֹת גִּלְעָד לוֹ חַוֹּת יָאִיר בֶּן־מְנַשֶּׁה אֲשֶׁר בַּגִּלְעָד
לוֹ חֶבֶל אַרְגֹּב אֲשֶׁר בַּבָּשָׁן שִׁשִּׁים עָרִים גְּדֹלוֹת חוֹמָה וּבְרִיחַ נְחֹשֶׁת

(13) Ben-geber, in **Ramoth-gilead** (the towns of Jair, the son of Manasseh, which are in Gilead were his: the region of **Argob**, which is in **Bashan**, sixty great cities with walls and bronze bars [were] his)

Seventh District — E. Jordan Valley

14 אֲחִינָדָב בֶּן־עִדֹּא מַחֲנָיְמָה

(14) Ahinadab the son of Iddo: Mahanaim;

Eighth District — Naphtali

15 אֲחִימַעַץ בְּנַפְתָּלִי גַּם־הוּא לָקַח אֶת־בָּשְׂמַת בַּת־שְׁלֹמֹה לְאִשָּׁה

(15) Ahimaaz, in **Naphtali** (he also married Basemath the daughter of Solomon);

Ninth District — Asher and Zebulun(?)

16 בַּעֲנָא בֶּן־חוּשָׁי בְּאָשֵׁר וּבְעָלוֹת (= זבולון?):

(16) Baana the son of Hushai, in **Asher** and **Bealoth** (= Zebulun?)

Tenth District — Issachar

17   יְהוֹשָׁפָט בֶּן־פָּרוּחַ בְּיִשָּׂשכָר

(17) Jehoshaphat the son of Paruah, in **Issachar**

Eleventh District — Benjamin

18   שִׁמְעִי בֶן־אֵלָא בְּבִנְיָמִן

(18) Shimei the son of Ela, in **Benjamin**

Twelfth District — Gilead (LXX GAD)

19a   גֶּבֶר בֶּן־אֻרִי בְּאֶרֶץ גִּלְעָד אֶרֶץ סִיחוֹן מֶלֶךְ הָאֱמֹרִי
וְעֹג מֶלֶךְ הַבָּשָׁן . . . .

(19a) Geber the son of Uri, in the land of **Gilead**, the country of Sihon king of
the Amorites and of Og king of Bashan;

Thirteenth District

19b   וּנְצִיב אֶחָד אֲשֶׁר בָּאָרֶץ 20a יְהוּדָה

(19b-20a) And one commissioner was in the land of **Judah**

The Second district= "Danite Inheritance"
HYPOTHETICAL RECONSTRUCTION

Heading: בֶּן־דֶּקֶר (לְמַטֵּה בְנֵי־דָן).

SUB-DISTRICT I — Approaches to the Hills

Sorek Valley   צָרְעָה וְאֶשְׁתָּאוֹל וְעִיר (= בֵּית)־שֶׁמֶשׁ

Aijalon Valley   וּמָקַץ וְגֶזֶר וְשַׁעֲלַבִּין וְאַיָּלוֹן וְיִתְלָה וְאֵילוֹן בֵּית חָנָן

SUB-DISTRICT II — Border with Philistia

Sorek Valley to   וְתִמְנָתָה ‹וְ‹עֶקְרוֹן וְאֶלְתְּקֵה וְגִבְּתוֹן וּבַעֲלָת
the Sea

SUB-DISTRICT III — Valley of Ono

Valley of the Craftsmen   וְאָזוֹר וּבֵית דָּגוֹן וִיהֻד וּבְנֵי־בְרַק וְאוֹנוֹ
(Cultivators?)

SUB-DISTRICT IV — Lod and Environs

Shephelah of Lod   וְלֹד וּצְבֹעִים וְחָדִיד וְגַת־רִמּוֹן (= גִּתַּיִם)

WESTERN BORDER

Facing the Joppa   וּמְיָם הַיַּרְקוֹן ‹וְהָרַקּוֹן› עִם־הַגְּבוּל מוּל יָפוֹ:
Port District   καὶ ἀπὸ θαλάσσης Ιερακων ὅριον πλησίον Ιόππης

TRANSLATION

Ben-deker (and from the tribe of Dan):

Zorah and Eshtaol and Ir(= Beth)-shemesh and Makaz and Gezer and Shaalbin and Aijalon and Ithlah and Elon (Beth-hanan);

and Timnatha (of) Ekron and Eltekeh and Gibbethon and Baalath;

and Azor and Beth-dagon and Jehud and Bene-barak and Ono;

and Lod and Zeboim and Hadid and Gath-rimmon (= Gittaim);

and from the sea (= "on the western side"), the Jarkon, with the boundary over against Joppa.

DOCUMENTATION

Ben-deker — and Makaz — Beth-hanan	1 Kings 4:9
and Gezer	Josh. 21:21
and Azor — and from the sea	LXX B Josh. 19:45
and Beth-dagon	Sennacherib's Annals
Ono; and Lod and Zeboim and Hadid and . . . (= Gittaim)	Neh. 11:33b-35

B. The forced Labor

> 1. *Mas ʿōḇēḏ* Corveé imposed on **former**
> **Canaanites**, under directorship of Adoniram;
> worked in Lebanon, one month out of three —
> 30,000 people obviously came from the districts
> on the plains.

1 Kings 5:27-28 (not ‖ in 2 Chron.!)

27 וַיַּעַל הַמֶּלֶךְ שְׁלֹמֹה מַס מִכָּל־יִשְׂרָאֵל וַיְהִי הַמַּס
שְׁלֹשִׁים אֶלֶף אִישׁ

28 וַיִּשְׁלָחֵם לְבָנוֹנָה עֲשֶׂרֶת אֲלָפִים בַּחֹדֶשׁ חֲלִיפוֹת
חֹדֶשׁ יִהְיוּ בַלְּבָנוֹן שְׁנַיִם חֳדָשִׁים בְּבֵיתוֹ וַאֲדֹנִירָם עַל־הַמַּס

Now King Solomon levied forced laborers from all Israel; and the forced
laborers numbered 30,000 men. And he sent them to Lebanon, 10,000 a month
in relays; they were in Lebanon a month [and] two months at home. And
Adoniram [was] over the forced laborers.

> 2. *Sēḇel* — imposed on **Israelites** though Chron.
> tries to deny this; worked in quarries, in the
> hills — 70,000 burden bearers, 80,000 quarry
> workers; obviously came from the districts in
> the hills!

1 Ki. 5:29-32 (Eng. 1 Ki. 5:15-16) ‖ 2 Chron. 2:16-17, 2:1

29 וַיְהִי לִשְׁלֹמֹה שִׁבְעִים אֶלֶף נֹשֵׂא סַבָּל וּשְׁמֹנִים
אֶלֶף חֹצֵב בָּהָר

30 לְבַד מִשָּׂרֵי הַנִּצָּבִים לִשְׁלֹמֹה אֲשֶׁר
עַל־הַמְּלָאכָה שְׁלֹשֶׁת אֲלָפִים וּשְׁלֹשׁ מֵאוֹת הָרֹדִים בָּעָם
הָעֹשִׂים בַּמְּלָאכָה

5:31 וַיְצַו הַמֶּלֶךְ וַיַּסִּעוּ אֲבָנִים גְּדֹלוֹת אֲבָנִים יְקָרוֹת
לְיַסֵּד הַבָּיִת אַבְנֵי גָזִית

32 וַיִּפְסְלוּ בֹּנֵי שְׁלֹמֹה וּבֹנֵי חִירוֹם וְהַגִּבְלִים וַיָּכִינוּ
הָעֵצִים וְהָאֲבָנִים לִבְנוֹת הַבָּיִת

Now Solomon had 70,000 transporters, and 80,000 hewers of stone **in the
mountains**, besides Solomon's 3,300 chief deputies who [were] over the
project [and] who ruled over the people who were doing the work.

Then the king commanded, and they quarried great stones, costly stones, to
lay the foundation of the house with cut stones.

So Solomon's builders and Hiram's builders and the Gebalites cut them, and
prepared the timbers and the stones to build the house.

> *śārê hanniṣṣāḇîm* = officers working under the district
> commissioners!
>
> 2 Kings: *rôḏîm* || 2 Chron. *mənaṣṣəḥîm*
>
> 2 Kings: 3,300 cadre || 2 Chron. 3,600 cadre

THE TWO KINDS OF DISTRICTS IN 1 Ki. 4 REFLECT A SOCIOLOGICAL
FACT:

THERE WERE TWO CLASSES OF ISRAELITES, the old tribesmen and the
newly conquered Canaanites, Hivites, etc.

III. OPPOSITION TO SOLOMON

A. Tyre

1. At first Solomon traded wheat for technical assistance in building and shipping. 1 Ki. 9:11 (not in 2 Chron.!)

11 חִירָם מֶלֶךְ־צֹר נִשָּׂא אֶת־שְׁלֹמֹה בַּעֲצֵי אֲרָזִים
וּבַעֲצֵי בְרוֹשִׁים וּבַזָּהָב לְכָל־חֶפְצוֹ אָז יִתֵּן הַמֶּלֶךְ שְׁלֹמֹה
לְחִירָם עֶשְׂרִים עִיר בְּאֶרֶץ הַגָּלִיל

Hiram king of Tyre had supplied Solomon with cedar and cypress timber and gold according to all his desire. Then King Solomon gave Hiram twenty cities in the land of Galilee.

2. Chronicler could not admit loss of towns 2 Chron. 8:2

2וְהֶעָרִים אֲשֶׁר נָתַן חוּרָם לִשְׁלֹמֹה בָּנָה שְׁלֹמֹה
אֹתָם וַיּוֹשֶׁב שָׁם אֶת־בְּנֵי יִשְׂרָאֵל

that he built the cities which Huram had given to him, and settled the sons of Israel there.

3. After 20 years, Solomon had to give Hiram some cities 1 Ki. 9:10-13 — **balance of payments problem!**

10 וַיְהִי מִקְצֵה עֶשְׂרִים שָׁנָה אֲשֶׁר־בָּנָה שְׁלֹמֹה
אֶת־שְׁנֵי הַבָּתִּים אֶת־בֵּית יְהוָה וְאֶת־בֵּית הַמֶּלֶךְ
11 חִירָם מֶלֶךְ־צֹר נִשָּׂא אֶת־שְׁלֹמֹה בַּעֲצֵי אֲרָזִים
וּבַעֲצֵי בְרוֹשִׁים וּבַזָּהָב לְכָל־חֶפְצוֹ אָז יִתֵּן הַמֶּלֶךְ שְׁלֹמֹה
לְחִירָם עֶשְׂרִים עִיר בְּאֶרֶץ הַגָּלִיל
12 וַיֵּצֵא חִירָם מִצֹּר לִרְאוֹת אֶת־הֶעָרִים אֲשֶׁר
נָתַן־לוֹ שְׁלֹמֹה וְלֹא יָשְׁרוּ בְּעֵינָיו
13 וַיֹּאמֶר מָה הֶעָרִים הָאֵלֶּה אֲשֶׁר־נָתַתָּה לִּי אָחִי
וַיִּקְרָא לָהֶם אֶרֶץ כָּבוּל עַד הַיּוֹם הַזֶּה

It came about at the end of twenty years in which Solomon had built the two houses, the house of Yahweh and the king's house

Hiram king of Tyre had supplied Solomon with cedar and cypress timber
and gold according to all his desire, then King Solomon gave Hiram twenty
cities in the land of Galilee.

So Hiram came out from Tyre to see the cities which Solomon had given him,
and they did not please him. He said, "What are these cities which you have
given me, my brother?" So they were called the land of **Cabu**l to this day.

B. Egypt

1. 21st Dynasty (1070-946) — Siamon (979-960) perhaps his
   campaign to Gezer related to Philistine revolt against
   the house of David

2. 22nd Dynasty (946-712) — Shishak (946-913)

C. Edom — 1 Ki. 11:14-22 — Hadad escapes across Sinai (v. 8)

14 וַיָּקֶם יְהוָה שָׂטָן לִשְׁלֹמֹה אֵת הֲדַד הָאֲדֹמִי
מִזֶּרַע הַמֶּלֶךְ הוּא בֶּאֱדוֹם

15 וַיְהִי בִּהְיוֹת דָּוִד אֶת־אֱדוֹם בַּעֲלוֹת יוֹאָב שַׂר
הַצָּבָא לְקַבֵּר אֶת־הַחֲלָלִים וַיַּךְ כָּל־זָכָר בֶּאֱדוֹם

16 כִּי שֵׁשֶׁת חֳדָשִׁים יָשַׁב־שָׁם יוֹאָב וְכָל־יִשְׂרָאֵל
עַד־הִכְרִית כָּל־זָכָר בֶּאֱדוֹם

17 וַיִּבְרַח אֲדַד הוּא וַאֲנָשִׁים אֲדֹמִיִּים מֵעַבְדֵי אָבִיו
אִתּוֹ לָבוֹא מִצְרָיִם וַהֲדַד נַעַר קָטָן

18 וַיָּקֻמוּ מִמִּדְיָן וַיָּבֹאוּ פָּארָן וַיִּקְחוּ אֲנָשִׁים
עִמָּם מִפָּארָן וַיָּבֹאוּ מִצְרַיִם אֶל־פַּרְעֹה מֶלֶךְ־מִצְרַיִם וַיִּתֶּן־לוֹ
בַיִת וְלֶחֶם אָמַר לוֹ וְאֶרֶץ נָתַן לוֹ

19 וַיִּמְצָא הֲדַד חֵן בְּעֵינֵי פַרְעֹה מְאֹד וַיִּתֶּן־לוֹ
אִשָּׁה אֶת־אֲחוֹת אִשְׁתּוֹ אֲחוֹת תַּחְפְּנֵיס הַגְּבִירָה

20 וַתֵּלֶד לוֹ אֲחוֹת תַּחְפְּנֵיס אֵת גְּנֻבַת בְּנוֹ

וַתִּגְמְלֵהוּ תַחְפְּנֵס בְּתוֹךְ בֵּית פַּרְעֹה וַיְהִי גְנֻבַת בֵּית פַּרְעֹה בְּתוֹךְ
בְּנֵי פַרְעֹה

21 וַהֲדַד שָׁמַע בְּמִצְרַיִם כִּי־שָׁכַב דָּוִד עִם־אֲבֹתָיו
וְכִי־מֵת יוֹאָב שַׂר־הַצָּבָא וַיֹּאמֶר הֲדַד אֶל־פַּרְעֹה שַׁלְּחֵנִי וְאֵלֵךְ
אֶל־אַרְצִי

22 וַיֹּאמֶר לוֹ פַרְעֹה כִּי מָה־אַתָּה חָסֵר עִמִּי וְהִנְּךָ
מְבַקֵּשׁ לָלֶכֶת אֶל־אַרְצֶךָ וַיֹּאמֶר לֹא כִּי שַׁלֵּחַ תְּשַׁלְּחֵנִי

Then Yahweh raised up an adversary to Solomon, **Hadad the Edomite**; he was of the royal line in **Edom**. For it came about, when David was in Edom, and Joab the commander of the army had gone up to bury the slain, and had struck down every male in Edom (for Joab and all Israel stayed there six months, until he had cut off every male in Edom), that Hadad fled to **Egypt**, he and certain Edomites of his father's servants with him, while Hadad was a young boy. So they arose from **Midian** and came to **Paran**; and they took men with them from Paran and came to Egypt, to Pharaoh king of Egypt, who gave him a house and assigned him food and gave him land. Now Hadad found great favor before Pharaoh, so that he gave him in marriage the sister of his own wife, the sister of Tahpenes the queen. The sister of Tahpenes bore his son Genubath, whom Tahpenes weaned in Pharaoh's house; and Genubath was in Pharaoh's house among the sons of Pharaoh. But when Hadad heard in Egypt that David slept with his fathers and that Joab the commander of the army was dead, Hadad said to Pharaoh, "Send me away, that I may go to my own country." Then Pharaoh said to him, "But what have you lacked with me, that behold, you are seeking to go to your own country?" And he answered, "Nothing; nevertheless you must surely let me go."

D. Damascus — Rezon (1 Ki. 11:23-25)

23 וַיָּקֶם אֱלֹהִים לוֹ שָׂטָן אֶת־רְזוֹן בֶּן־אֶלְיָדָע
אֲשֶׁר בָּרַח מֵאֵת הֲדַדְעֶזֶר מֶלֶךְ־צוֹבָה אֲדֹנָיו
24 וַיִּקְבֹּץ עָלָיו אֲנָשִׁים וַיְהִי שַׂר־גְּדוּד בַּהֲרֹג דָּוִד

אֹתָם וַיֵּלְכוּ דַמֶּשֶׂק וַיֵּשְׁבוּ בָהּ וַיִּמְלְכוּ בְּדַמָּשֶׂק

25 וַיְהִי שָׂטָן לְיִשְׂרָאֵל כָּל־יְמֵי שְׁלֹמֹה

וְאֶת־הָרָעָה אֲשֶׁר הֲדָד וַיָּקָץ בְּיִשְׂרָאֵל וַיִּמְלֹךְ עַל־אֲרָם

And God also raised up an adversary to him, **Rezon** the son of Eliada, who

had fled from his lord **Hadadezer king of Zobah**. And he gathered men to

himself and became leader of a marauding band, after David slew them of

[Zobah]; and they went to **Damascus** and stayed there, and reigned in

Damascus. So he was an adversary to Israel all the days of Solomon, along

with the evil that Hadad did; and he abhorred Israel and reigned over **Aram**.

E. Israel — Jeroboam son of Nebat (1 Ki. 11:26-40) found refuge in Egypt with Shishak

26 וְיָרָבְעָם בֶּן־נְבָט אֶפְרָתִי מִן־הַצְּרֵדָה וְשֵׁם

אִמּוֹ צְרוּעָה אִשָּׁה אַלְמָנָה עֶבֶד לִשְׁלֹמֹה וַיָּרֶם יָד בַּמֶּלֶךְ

27 וְזֶה הַדָּבָר אֲשֶׁר־הֵרִים יָד בַּמֶּלֶךְ שְׁלֹמֹה בָּנָה

אֶת־הַמִּלּוֹא סָגַר אֶת־פֶּרֶץ עִיר דָּוִד אָבִיו

28 וְהָאִישׁ יָרָבְעָם גִּבּוֹר חָיִל וַיַּרְא שְׁלֹמֹה

אֶת־הַנַּעַר כִּי־עֹשֵׂה מְלָאכָה הוּא וַיַּפְקֵד אֹתוֹ לְכָל־סֵבֶל בֵּית יוֹסֵף

29 וַיְהִי בָּעֵת הַהִיא וְיָרָבְעָם יָצָא מִירוּשָׁלָםִ

וַיִּמְצָא אֹתוֹ אֲחִיָּה הַשִּׁילֹנִי הַנָּבִיא בַּדֶּרֶךְ וְהוּא מִתְכַּסֶּה בְּשַׂלְמָה חֲדָשָׁה וּשְׁנֵיהֶם לְבַדָּם בַּשָּׂדֶה

30 וַיִּתְפֹּשׂ אֲחִיָּה בַּשַּׂלְמָה הַחֲדָשָׁה אֲשֶׁר עָלָיו

וַיִּקְרָעֶהָ שְׁנֵים עָשָׂר קְרָעִים

31 וַיֹּאמֶר לְיָרָבְעָם קַח־לְךָ עֲשָׂרָה קְרָעִים כִּי

כֹה אָמַר יְהוָה אֱלֹהֵי יִשְׂרָאֵל הִנְנִי קֹרֵעַ אֶת־הַמַּמְלָכָה מִיַּד שְׁלֹמֹה וְנָתַתִּי לְךָ אֵת עֲשָׂרָה הַשְּׁבָטִים

32 וְהַשֵּׁבֶט הָאֶחָד יִהְיֶה־לּוֹ לְמַעַן עֲבָדִּי דָוִד

וּלְמַעַן יְרוּשָׁלַ͏ִם הָעִיר אֲשֶׁר בָּחַרְתִּי בָהּ מִכֹּל שִׁבְטֵי יִשְׂרָאֵל

33 יַעַן אֲשֶׁר עֲזָבוּנִי וַיִּשְׁתַּחֲווּ לְעַשְׁתֹּרֶת אֱלֹהֵי

צִדֹנִין לִכְמוֹשׁ אֱלֹהֵי מוֹאָב וּלְמִלְכֹּם אֱלֹהֵי בְנֵי־עַמּוֹן

וְלֹא־הָלְכוּ בִדְרָכַי* לַעֲשׂוֹת הַיָּשָׁר בְּעֵינַי* וְחֻקֹּתַי* וּמִשְׁפָּטַי*

כְּדָוִד אָבִיו

34 וְלֹא־אֶקַּח אֶת־כָּל־הַמַּמְלָכָה מִיָּדוֹ כִּי נָשִׂיא

אֲשִׁתֶנּוּ כֹּל יְמֵי חַיָּיו לְמַעַן דָּוִד עַבְדִּי אֲשֶׁר בָּחַרְתִּי אֹתוֹ

אֲשֶׁר שָׁמַר מִצְוֺתַי* וְחֻקֹּתָי

35 וְלָקַחְתִּי הַמְּלוּכָה מִיַּד בְּנוֹ וּנְתַתִּיהָ לְךָ אֵת

עֲשֶׂרֶת הַשְּׁבָטִים

36 וְלִבְנוֹ אֶתֵּן שֵׁבֶט־אֶחָד לְמַעַן הֱיוֹת־נִיר

לְדָוִיד־עַבְדִּי כָּל־הַיָּמִים לְפָנַי* בִּירוּשָׁלַ͏ִם הָעִיר אֲשֶׁר בָּחַרְתִּי

לִי לָשׂוּם שְׁמִי שָׁם

37 וְאֹתְךָ אֶקַּח וּמָלַכְתָּ בְּכֹל אֲשֶׁר־תְּאַוֶּה־נַפְשֶׁךָ

וְהָיִיתָ מֶּלֶךְ עַל־יִשְׂרָאֵל

38 וְהָיָה אִם־תִּשְׁמַע אֶת־כָּל־אֲשֶׁר אֲצַוֶּךָ וְהָלַכְתָּ

בִדְרָכַי* וְעָשִׂיתָ הַיָּשָׁר בְּעֵינַי* לִשְׁמוֹר חֻקּוֹתַי וּמִצְוֺתַי* כַּאֲשֶׁר

עָשָׂה דָּוִד עַבְדִּי וְהָיִיתִי עִמָּךְ וּבָנִיתִי לְךָ בַיִת־נֶאֱמָן כַּאֲשֶׁר

בָּנִיתִי לְדָוִד וְנָתַתִּי לְךָ אֶת־יִשְׂרָאֵל

39 וַאֲעַנֶּה אֶת־זֶרַע דָּוִד לְמַעַן זֹאת אַךְ לֹא

כָל־הַיָּמִים

40 וַיְבַקֵּשׁ שְׁלֹמֹה לְהָמִית אֶת־יָרָבְעָם וַיָּקָם

יָרָבְעָם וַיִּבְרַח מִצְרַיִם אֶל־שִׁישַׁק מֶלֶךְ־מִצְרַיִם וַיְהִי בְמִצְרַיִם

עַד־מוֹת שְׁלֹמֹה

Then Jeroboam the son of Nebat, an Ephraimite of Zeredah, Solomon's servant, whose mother's name was Zeruah, a widow, also rebelled against the king. Now this was the reason why he rebelled against the king:

Solomon built the Millo, [and] closed up the breach of the city of his father David. Now the man Jeroboam was a valiant warrior, and when Solomon saw that the young man was industrious, he appointed him over all the **corvée** of **the house of Joseph**.

It came about at that time, when Jeroboam went out of Jerusalem, that the prophet Ahijah the Shilonite found him on the road. Now Ahijah had clothed himself with a new cloak; and both of them were alone in the field. Then Ahijah took hold of the new cloak which was on him and tore it into twelve pieces. He said to Jeroboam, "Take for yourself ten pieces; for thus says the LORD, the God of Israel, ᶜBehold, I will tear the kingdom out of the hand of Solomon and give you ten tribes(but he will have one tribe, for the sake of My servant David and for the sake of Jerusalem, the city which I have chosen from all the tribes of Israel), ...

Solomon sought therefore to put Jeroboam to death; but Jeroboam arose and fled to Egypt to Shishak king of Egypt, and he was in Egypt until the death of Solomon.

IV. SOURCES FOR 2 Sam

1 Chron 29:29-30 — relating life of David || 2 Sam.

29 וְדִבְרֵי דָּוִיד הַמֶּלֶךְ הָרִאשֹׁנִים וְהָאַחֲרֹנִים הִנָּם

כְּתוּבִים עַל־דִּבְרֵי שְׁמוּאֵל הָרֹאֶה וְעַל־דִּבְרֵי נָתָן הַנָּבִיא

וְעַל־דִּבְרֵי גָּד הַחֹזֶה

30 עִם כָּל־מַלְכוּתוֹ וּגְבוּרָתוֹ וְהָעִתִּים אֲשֶׁר עָבְרוּ

עָלָיו וְעַל־יִשְׂרָאֵל וְעַל כָּל־מַמְלְכוֹת הָאֲרָצוֹת

דִּבְרֵי דָּוִיד הַמֶּלֶךְ הָרִאשֹׁנִים וְהָאַחֲרֹנִים = "Chronicles of David"
|| 2 Sam.

1. דִּבְרֵי שְׁמוּאֵל הָרֹאֶה = "Chronicles of Samuel the seer"

2. דִּבְרֵי נָתָן הַנָּבִיא = "Chronicles of Nathan the prophet"

3. דִּבְרֵי גָּד הַחֹזֶה "Chronicles of Gad the seer"

V. BOOK OF KINGS — all one book in Hebrew Bible (MT)

A. Authorship — unk. Tradition is Jeremiah but impossible;
   recent theory says Baruch the scribe. Has Deuteronomistic
   editorial comments throughout.

B. Date — 2 Ki. 25:27 = 2 April, 561 BCE — after this date the final
   edition of the book must have been made.

27 וַיְהִי בִשְׁלֹשִׁים וָשֶׁבַע שָׁנָה לְגָלוּת יְהוֹיָכִין

מֶלֶךְ־יְהוּדָה בִּשְׁנֵים עָשָׂר חֹדֶשׁ בְּעֶשְׂרִים וְשִׁבְעָה לַחֹדֶשׁ נָשָׂא

אֱוִיל מְרֹדַךְ מֶלֶךְ בָּבֶל בִּשְׁנַת מָלְכוֹ אֶת־רֹאשׁ יְהוֹיָכִין

מֶלֶךְ־יְהוּדָה מִבֵּית כֶּלֶא

And it happened in the thirty-seventh year of the exile of Jehoiachin, king of Judah, in the twelfth month on the twenty seventh day of the month, that Evil-merodach, king of Babylon, in his accession year, granted an amnesty to Jehoiachin, king of Judah from the house of detention (2 Kings 25:27 = Jer. 52:31-34).

C. Sources cited:

1. סֵפֶר דִּבְרֵי שְׁלֹמֹה = "Chronicles of Solomon" 1 Ki. 11:41

2. סֵפֶר דִּבְרֵי הַיָּמִים לְמַלְכֵי יְהוּדָה "Chronicles of the kings of Judah" (15x): 1 Ki. 14:29; 15:7; 15:23; 22:45; 2 Ki. 8:23;12:19; 14:18; 15:36; 16:19; 20:20; 21:17; 21:25; 23:28; 24:5.

3. סֵפֶר דִּבְרֵי הַיָּמִים לְמַלְכֵי יִשְׂרָאֵל "Chronicles of the kings of Israel" (14x): 1 Ki. 14:19; 15:31; 16:27; 22:39; 2 Ki. 1:18; 10:34; 13:8; 13:12; 14:28; 15:11; 15:15; 15:26; 15:31.

D. Comparison of sources in Kings and Chronicles.
   See BRIDGE 172–173; *Parallels in the Bible*

E. EVIDENCE FOR COMBINED DOCUMENTS — Chronicles cites "chronicles of the kings of Judah and Israel" or "Israel and Judah"

1 Ki. 22:46 of Judah	2 Chr. 20:34 of Israel
2 Ki. 14:18 of Judah	2 Chr. 25:26 of Israel and Judah
2 Ki. 15:36 of Judah	2 Chr. 27:7 of Israel and Judah
2 Ki. 16:19 of Judah	2 Chr. 28:26 of Judah and Israel
2 Ki. 21:17 of Judah	2 Chr. 33:18 of Israel
2 Ki. 23:28 of Judah	2 Chr. 35:27 of Israel and Judah
2 Ki. 24:5 of Judah	2 Chr. 36:8 of Israel and Judah

DIVISION OF THE MONARCHY

I. THE SPLIT — 1 Ki. 12:1 at Shechem.

    A. **Northern Kingdom**. Jeroboam I, 22 yrs, 1Ki 14:20;

           931/930-910/909.

        1. Political Centers: 1 Ki. 12:25

וַיִּבֶן יָרָבְעָם אֶת־שְׁכֶם בְּהַר אֶפְרַיִם וַיֵּשֶׁב

בָּהּ וַיֵּצֵא מִשָּׁם וַיִּבֶן אֶת־פְּנוּאֵל

Then Jeroboam built **Shechem** in the hill country of Ephraim, and dwelled
there. And he went out from there and built **Penuel**.

           a. Shechem

           b. Penuel (cf. Shishak below)

        2. Religious centers: a. **Dan** (Laish); b. **Bethel**

           1 Ki. 12:29-30

29 וַיָּשֶׂם אֶת־הָאֶחָד בְּבֵית־אֵל וְאֶת־הָאֶחָד נָתַן בְּדָן

30 וַיְהִי הַדָּבָר הַזֶּה לְחַטָּאת וַיֵּלְכוּ הָעָם

לִפְנֵי הָאֶחָד עַד־דָּן

So the king held consultations, and made two golden calves, and he said to
them, "It is too much for you to go up to Jerusalem; behold your gods, O
Israel, that brought you up from the land of Egypt!" He set one in **Bethel**, and
the other he put in **Dan**. Now this thing became a sin, for the people went
before the one as far as Dan.

    Note: בֵּית בָּמוֹת, "House of high places"

        1 Ki. 12:31

וַיַּעַשׂ אֶת־בֵּית בָּמוֹת וַיַּעַשׂ כֹּהֲנִים מִקְצוֹת

הָעָם אֲשֶׁר לֹא־הָיוּ מִבְּנֵי לֵוִי׃

And he made houses of high places, and made priests from a
sector of the people who were not of the sons of Levi.

3. <u>Other</u> <u>centers</u>:

    a. **Shiloh**, home of prophets

1 Ki. 14:1-2 (verses 1-20 not in LXX!)

1 בָּעֵת הַהִיא חָלָה אֲבִיָּה בֶן־יָרָבְעָם 2 וַיֹּאמֶר יָרָבְעָם לְאִשְׁתּוֹ

קוּמִי נָא וְהִשְׁתַּנִּית וְלֹא יֵדְעוּ כִּי־אַתְּ [אַתְּ] אֵשֶׁת יָרָבְעָם

וְהָלַכְתְּ שִׁלֹה הִנֵּה־שָׁם אֲחִיָּה הַנָּבִיא הוּא־דִבֶּר עָלַי לְמֶלֶךְ עַל־הָעָם

הַזֶּה

At that time Abijah the son of Jeroboam became sick. So Jeroboam said to his
wife, "Arise now, and disguise yourself so that they will not know that you
are the wife of Jeroboam, and go to **Shiloh**; behold, Ahijah the prophet is
there, who spoke concerning me [that I would be] king over this people."

    b. **Tirzah**, political capital

    1 Ki. 14:17

וַתָּקָם אֵשֶׁת יָרָבְעָם וַתֵּלֶךְ וַתָּבֹא תִרְצָתָה הִיא בָּאָה בְסַף־הַבַּיִת

וְהַנַּעַר מֵת׃

Then Jeroboam's wife arose and departed and came to **Tirzah**. As she was
entering the threshold of the house, the child died.

    Cf. 1 Ki. 15:21

וַיְהִי כִּשְׁמֹעַ בַּעְשָׁא וַיֶּחְדַּל מִבְּנוֹת אֶת־הָרָמָה וַיֵּשֶׁב בְּתִרְצָה

When Baasha heard of it, then he ceased fortifying Ramah and
remained in **Tirzah**.

B. **Southern kingdom**. Rehoboam 17 yrs, 1 Ki 14:21; 2 Ch
12:13, 931/930—913.

1. <u>Rehoboam's</u> <u>list</u> <u>of</u> <u>forts</u>,

2 Chron. 11:5-12

5 וַיֵּשֶׁב רְחַבְעָם בִּירוּשָׁלָ͏ִם וַיִּבֶן עָרִים לְמָצוֹר בִּיהוּדָה

6 וַיִּבֶן אֶת־בֵּית־לֶחֶם וְאֶת־עֵיטָם וְאֶת־תְּקוֹעַ

7 וְאֶת־בֵּית־צוּר וְאֶת־שׂוֹכוֹ וְאֶת־עֲדֻלָּם

8 וְאֶת־גַּת וְאֶת־מָרֵשָׁה וְאֶת־זִיף

9 וְאֶת־אֲדוֹרַיִם וְאֶת־לָכִישׁ וְאֶת־עֲזֵקָה

10 וְאֶת־צָרְעָה וְאֶת־אַיָּלוֹן וְאֶת־חֶבְרוֹן אֲשֶׁר
בִּיהוּדָה וּבְבִנְיָמִן עָרֵי מְצֻרוֹת

11 וַיְחַזֵּק אֶת־הַמְּצֻרוֹת וַיִּתֵּן בָּהֶם נְגִידִים
וְאֹצְרוֹת מַאֲכָל וְשֶׁמֶן וָיָיִן

12 וּבְכָל־עִיר וָעִיר צִנּוֹת וּרְמָחִים וַיְחַזְּקֵם
לְהַרְבֵּה מְאֹד וַיְהִי־לוֹ יְהוּדָה וּבִנְיָמִן

Rehoboam lived in Jerusalem and built cities for defense in Judah: Thus he
built **Bethlehem, Etam, Tekoa, Beth-zur, Soco, Adullam, Gath, Mareshah
Ziph, Adoraim, Lachish, Azekah, Zorah, Aijalon** and **Hebron**, which are
fortified cities in Judah and in Benjamin.

He also strengthened the fortresses and put officers in them and stores of
food, oil and wine, and in every town, shields and spears and he
strengthened them greatly. So he had Judah and Benjamin.

<u>Groupings</u>:   a. **Bethlehem, Etam, Tekoa, Beth-zur**

N - S watershed route, Eastern frontier

b. **Sochoh, Adullam**

W - E lateral connecting route to Beth-Zur

c. (**Moresheth**?)-**Gath, Mareshah**

W - E lateral route to Adoraim and Hebron

   d. **Ziph, Adoraim**

      E and W flanks of Hebron

   e. **Lachish, Azekah, Zorah, Aijalon**

      Western frontier guarding approaches

   f. **Hebron**

      Central control center

2. <u>Priests</u> <u>and</u> <u>Levites</u> from up north leave their cities and
   come to Jerusalem and Judah,
   2 Chron. 11:13-17

3 וְהַכֹּהֲנִים וְהַלְוִיִּם אֲשֶׁר בְּכָל־יִשְׂרָאֵל הִתְיַצְּבוּ עָלָיו מִכָּל־גְּבוּלָם

14 כִּי־עָזְבוּ הַלְוִיִּם אֶת־מִגְרְשֵׁיהֶם וַאֲחֻזָּתָם וַיֵּלְכוּ לִיהוּדָה וְלִירוּשָׁלָ͏ִם

כִּי־הִזְנִיחָם יָרָבְעָם וּבָנָיו מִכַּהֵן לַיהוָה 15 וַיַּעֲמֶד־לוֹ כֹּהֲנִים לַבָּמוֹת

וְלַשְּׂעִירִים = שְׂעִירִם = "satyrs") (LXX τοῖς ματαίοις "empty, vain"

וְלָעֲגָלִים אֲשֶׁר עָשָׂה 16 וְאַחֲרֵיהֶם מִכֹּל שִׁבְטֵי יִשְׂרָאֵל הַנֹּתְנִים

אֶת־לְבָבָם לְבַקֵּשׁ אֶת־יְהוָה אֱלֹהֵי יִשְׂרָאֵל בָּאוּ יְרוּשָׁלַ͏ִם לִזְבּוֹחַ לַיהוָה

אֱלֹהֵי אֲבוֹתֵיהֶם 17 וַיְחַזְּקוּ אֶת־מַלְכוּת יְהוּדָה וַיְאַמְּצוּ אֶת־רְחַבְעָם

בֶּן־שְׁלֹמֹה לְשָׁנִים שָׁלוֹשׁ כִּי הָלְכוּ בְּדֶרֶךְ דָּוִיד וּשְׁלֹמֹה לְשָׁנִים שָׁלוֹשׁ

(3 yrs 930-927 BCE)

And the priests and the Levites who were in **all Israel** presented themselves
to him from all their districts.

(For the Levites left their lands and their estates and came to Judah
and Jerusalem, for Jeroboam and his sons had excluded them from
serving as priests to Yahweh. And He set up priests of his own for
the high places, for the satyrs and for the calves which he had made).

Those from **all the tribes of Israel** who set their hearts to seek Yahweh God
of Israel followed them to Jerusalem, to sacrifice to Yahweh God of their
fathers. They strengthened the kingdom of Judah and supported Rehoboam
the son of Solomon for three years, for they walked in the way of David and
Solomon for **three years**.

3. 926 BCE, **fourth year**: credited with "high places and
   stelae and pillars in every high hill and under every
   green tree" and the male prostitutes were in the land,
   2 Chron. 12:1.

וַיְהִי כְּהָכִין מַלְכוּת רְחַבְעָם וּכְחֶזְקָתוֹ עָזַב

אֶת־תּוֹרַת יְהוָה וְכָל־יִשְׂרָאֵל עִמּוֹ

But when the kingdom of Rehoboam was established and strong, he forsook
the law of Yahweh and all Israel with him.

1 Ki. 14:22-24

22 וַיַּעַשׂ יְהוּדָה הָרַע בְּעֵינֵי יְהוָה וַיְקַנְאוּ

אֹתוֹ מִכֹּל אֲשֶׁר עָשׂוּ אֲבֹתָם בְּחַטֹּאתָם אֲשֶׁר חָטָאוּ

23 וַיִּבְנוּ גַם־הֵמָּה לָהֶם בָּמוֹת וּמַצֵּבוֹת

וַאֲשֵׁרִים עַל כָּל־גִּבְעָה גְבֹהָה וְתַחַת כָּל־עֵץ רַעֲנָן

24 וְגַם־קָדֵשׁ הָיָה בָאָרֶץ עָשׂוּ כְּכֹל

הַתּוֹעֲבֹת הַגּוֹיִם אֲשֶׁר הוֹרִישׁ יְהוָה מִפְּנֵי בְּנֵי יִשְׂרָאֵל

Judah did evil in the sight of Yahweh, and they provoked Him to jealousy
more than all that their fathers had done, with the sins which they
committed. And they also built for themselves high places and stelae and
Asherim on every high hill and beneath every luxuriant tree. There were also
male cult prostitutes (LXX σύνδεσμος "conspiracy" = קשר)in the land.
They did according to all the foreign abominations which Yahweh
dispossessed before the sons of Israel.

II. SHISHAK'S CAMPAIGN (Shishak = Šošenq I, 946-913 BCE;
Libyan ruler, founder of XXII Dynasty)

A. Fifth yr of Rehoboam **925 BCE**

2 Chron 12:2-12 ‖ 1 Ki. 14:25-26.

2 וַיְהִי בַּשָּׁנָה הַחֲמִישִׁית לַמֶּלֶךְ רְחַבְעָם עָלָה שִׁישַׁק מֶלֶךְ־מִצְרַיִם עַל־יְרוּשָׁלִָם

כִּי מָעֲלוּ בַּיהוָה 3 בְּאֶלֶף וּמָאתַיִם רֶכֶב וּבְשִׁשִּׁים אֶלֶף פָּרָשִׁים וְאֵין מִסְפָּר לָעָם

אֲשֶׁר־בָּאוּ עִמּוֹ מִמִּצְרַיִם לוּבִים סֻכִּיִּים וְכוּשִׁים 4 וַיִּלְכֹּד אֶת־עָרֵי הַמְּצֻרוֹת

אֲשֶׁר לִיהוּדָה וַיָּבֹא עַד־יְרוּשָׁלִָם 5 וּשְׁמַעְיָה הַנָּבִיא בָּא אֶל־רְחַבְעָם וְשָׂרֵי

יְהוּדָה אֲשֶׁר־נֶאֶסְפוּ אֶל־יְרוּשָׁלַם מִפְּנֵי שִׁישַׁק וַיֹּאמֶר לָהֶם כֹּה־אָמַר יְהוָה

אַתֶּם עֲזַבְתֶּם אֹתִי וְאַף־אֲנִי עָזַבְתִּי אֶתְכֶם בְּיַד־שִׁישָׁק 6 וַיִּכָּנְעוּ שָׂרֵי־יִשְׂרָאֵל

וְהַמֶּלֶךְ וַיֹּאמְרוּ צַדִּיק יְהוָה 7 וּבִרְאוֹת יְהוָה כִּי נִכְנְעוּ הָיָה דְבַר־יְהוָה

אֶל־שְׁמַעְיָה לֵאמֹר נִכְנְעוּ לֹא אַשְׁחִיתֵם וְנָתַתִּי לָהֶם כִּמְעַט לִפְלֵיטָה

וְלֹא־תִתַּךְ חֲמָתִי בִּירוּשָׁלַם בְּיַד־שִׁישָׁק 8 כִּי יִהְיוּ־לוֹ לַעֲבָדִים וְיֵדְעוּ

עֲבוֹדָתִי וַעֲבוֹדַת מַמְלְכוֹת הָאֲרָצוֹת 9 וַיַּעַל שִׁישַׁק מֶלֶךְ־מִצְרַיִם

עַל־יְרוּשָׁלַ͏ִם וַיִּקַּח אֶת־אֹצְרוֹת בֵּית־יְהוָה וְאֶת־אֹצְרוֹת בֵּית הַמֶּלֶךְ

אֶת־הַכֹּל לָקָח וַיִּקַּח אֶת־מָגִנֵּי הַזָּהָב אֲשֶׁר עָשָׂה שְׁלֹמֹה 10 וַיַּעַשׂ הַמֶּלֶךְ רְחַבְעָם

תַּחְתֵּיהֶם מָגִנֵּי נְחֹשֶׁת וְהִפְקִיד עַל־יַד שָׂרֵי הָרָצִים הַשֹּׁמְרִים פֶּתַח בֵּית הַמֶּלֶךְ

11 וַיְהִי מִדֵּי־בֹא הַמֶּלֶךְ בֵּית יְהוָה בָּאוּ הָרָצִים וּנְשָׂאוּם וֶהֱשִׁבוּם אֶל־תָּא

הָרָצִים 12 וּבְהִכָּנְעוֹ שָׁב מִמֶּנּוּ אַף־יְהוָה וְלֹא לְהַשְׁחִית לְכָלָה וְגַם בִּיהוּדָה

הָיָה דְּבָרִים טוֹבִים

And it came about in King Rehoboam's **fifth year**, because they had been unfaithful to Yahweh, that Shishak king of Egypt came up against Jerusalem with 1,200 chariots and 60,000 horsemen. And the people who came with him from Egypt were without number: the **Lubim**, the **Sukkiim** and the Cushites. He captured the **fortified cities** of Judah and came as far as **Jerusalem**.

> Then Shemaiah the prophet came to Rehoboam and the princes of Judah who had gathered at Jerusalem because of Shishak, and he said to them, "Thus says Yahweh, "You have forsaken Me, so I also have forsaken you to Shishak."" So the princes of Israel and the king humbled themselves and said, "Yahweh is righteous." When Yahweh saw that they humbled themselves, the word of Yahweh came to Shemaiah, saying, "They have humbled themselves [so] I will not destroy them, but I will grant them some [measure] of deliverance, and My wrath shall not be poured out on Jerusalem by means of Shishak. But they will become his slaves so that they may learn [the difference between] My service and the service of the kingdoms of the countries."

So Shishak king of Egypt came up against **Jerusalem**, and took the treasures of the house of Yahweh and the treasures of the king's palace. He took everything; he even took the golden shields which Solomon had made.

1 Ki. 14:25-26

25 וַיְהִי בַּשָּׁנָה הַחֲמִישִׁית לַמֶּלֶךְ רְחַבְעָם עָלָה שׁוּשַׁק [שִׁישַׁק] מֶלֶךְ־מִצְרַיִם

עַל־יְרוּשָׁלָ͏ִם 26 וַיִּקַּח אֶת־אֹצְרוֹת בֵּית־יְהוָה וְאֶת־אֹצְרוֹת בֵּית הַמֶּלֶךְ

וְאֶת־הַכֹּל לָקָח וַיִּקַּח אֶת־כָּל־מָגִנֵּי הַזָּהָב אֲשֶׁר עָשָׂה שְׁלֹמֹה ·

Now it happened in the **fifth year** of King Rehoboam, that Shishak the king of Egypt came up against Jerusalem. He took away the treasures of the house of Yahweh and the treasures of the king's house, and he took everything, even taking all the shields of gold which Solomon had made.

    B. His allies 2 Chron. 12:3 — לוּבִים = *Rbw* "Libyans";

               סֻכִּיִּם = *Tjk* (*tn*), from Kharga oasis and Dakhla

               כוּשִׁים = *Kš* , "Cusites," Nubians

    C. **Note only Egyptian date:** "Year 21, second month of the third season . . . " on a stele of Haremsaf, at Silsileh, who was sent to quarry the stones for the Bubasite Portal (Breasted, *ARE* IV, §706, p. 347) — 946 - 21 = 925.

    D **Northern** phase of campaign (note problem of reading):

1 (11) Gaza	24 (18) Hapharaim
2 (12) Gezer (?)	25 (65) The Valley (*p.ʿmq*)
3 (13) Rubuti	26 (17) Rehob
4. (26) Aijalon	27 (16) Beth-shean
5 (25) Kir(!)iathaim	28 (15) Shunem
6 (24) Beth-horon	29 (14) Taanach
7 (23) Gibeon	30 (27) Megiddo
8 (57) Zemaraim	31 (28) Adar
9 (64) [Go]phnah?	32 (29) Yad-hammelech
10 - 13 (60-63) Missing	33 (30) Missing
14 (59) [Ti]rzah?	34 (31) Honim
15 (58) Migdal	35 (32) ʿAruna
16 (56) Adam	36 (33) Borim
17 (55) Succoth	37 (34) Gath-padalla
18 (54) Kedesh	38 (35) Yaḥam
19 (53) Penuel	39 (36) Beth-olam ?
20 (22) Mahanaim	40 (37) *k-q-r-w*
21 (21) *š-w-t*	41 (38) Socoh
22 (20) Zaphon	42 (39) Beth-tappuah
23 (19) Adoraim	

E. **Southern** phase

  1. Forts

      68-69 *p₃ ḥ[q]ruya* / *f-ti-ša-ya*

      71-72   *p₃ ḥqruya* / *ʾbrm*

      77-78   *p₃ ḥqruya* / *n ᶜ-ḏ-y-t*

      87-88   *p₃ ḥqru* / *ša-ni-ya*

      99-95   *p₃ ḥqruya* / *ḥ-₃-ni-ni-y*

      101-102 *p₃ ḥqru* / *t-r-wa-n*

      107-109 *ḥqrum* / *ᶜ-r-d-ya* / *r-b-t*

      110-112 *ᶜ-r-d-ya* / *n b-t* / *y-r-ḥ-m*

  2. The Negebs

      84-85   *p₃ ngbu* / *ᶜ-ḏ-n-t* Eznites עֶצְנִ"ֹֹה

                  2 Sam. 23:8 Qri

      90-91   *p₃ ngbu* / *wa-h-t-wa-ru-k-ya*

      92-93   *p₃ ngbu* / *ʾ-ša-ḥ-ta* Shuhah שׁוּחָה

                  1 Chron. 4:11

  3. Some towns:

      133   Yurza

      125   Sharḥôn! (*ša-r-ḥa-na!*)

      69   Photis (Φωτις), *Paṭîš (Kh. Fuṭeis is later)

      108, 110 Arad (2x)

               ḥá-q-rú-ma / *ᶜá-rú-d-ʾe* / *rú-bí-tá* /

               ᶜá-rú-di-ʾe / *n bá-tí* / *yu-ra-ḥá-ma*

               š-b-l-t / *n gbr* "fountain(s) of Geber"?

               Rapiḥ (*R-p-ḥ*)

               Laban (*L-b-n*)

  4. Some clans

      70   Jahallel (₃-l-h-r-r) 1 Chr. 4:16

      82   Tappuah 1 Chr. 2:43

      94   Hanan and 101 Tilon 1 Chr. 4:20

      112   Yuraḥem = Jerahmeel 1 Chr. 2:9

      121   Peleth 1 Chr. 2:33

      140   Onan (Onam) 1 Chr. 2:26

      145   Maachah, wife of Caleb 1 Chr. 2:48

III. WAR BETWEEN NORTH AND SOUTH

A. Between Jeroboam and **Abija/Abijam** (913-911/10 BCE;
ruled 3 yrs, 1 Ki 15:1,2; 2 Ch 13:1,2; 931-18 = 913, 18th yr
of Jeroboam I).

1. Clash at **Mt. Zemaraim** 2 Chron. 13:2-4

וּמִלְחָמָה הָיְתָה בֵּין אֲבִיָּה וּבֵין יָרָבְעָם׃

וַיֶּאְסֹר אֲבִיָּה אֶת־הַמִּלְחָמָה בְּחַיִל גִּבּוֹרֵי מִלְחָמָה . . .

וְיָרָבְעָם עָרַךְ עִמּוֹ מִלְחָמָה . . . וַיָּקָם אֲבִיָּה מֵעַל ׀ לְהַר צְמָרַיִם

אֲשֶׁר בְּהַר אֶפְרָיִם וַיֹּאמֶר שְׁמָעוּנִי יָרָבְעָם וְכָל־יִשְׂרָאֵל׃

Now there was war between Abijah and Jeroboam. Abijah began the battle
with an army of valiant warriors,. . . while Jeroboam drew up in battle
formation against him . . . Then Abijah stood on **Mount Zemaraim**, which is
in the **Hill Country of Ephraim**, and said, "Listen to me, Jeroboam and all
Israel: . . .

2. Towns taken from Israel 2 Chr 13:15-20 (vs 19)

וַיָּרִיעוּ אִישׁ יְהוּדָה וַיְהִי בְּהָרִיעַ אִישׁ יְהוּדָה וְהָאֱלֹהִים

נָגַף אֶת־יָרָבְעָם וְכָל־יִשְׂרָאֵל לִפְנֵי אֲבִיָּה וִיהוּדָה׃

וַיָּנוּסוּ בְנֵי־יִשְׂרָאֵל מִפְּנֵי יְהוּדָה וַיִּתְּנֵם אֱלֹהִים בְּיָדָם׃

וַיַּכּוּ בָהֶם אֲבִיָּה וְעַמּוֹ מַכָּה רַבָּה . . . וַיִּכָּנְעוּ בְנֵי־יִשְׂרָאֵל בָּעֵת

הַהִיא וַיֶּאֶמְצוּ בְּנֵי יְהוּדָה כִּי נִשְׁעֲנוּ עַל־יְהוָה אֱלֹהֵי אֲבוֹתֵיהֶם׃

וַיִּרְדֹּף אֲבִיָּה אַחֲרֵי יָרָבְעָם וַיִּלְכֹּד מִמֶּנּוּ עָרִים

אֶת־בֵּית־אֵל ׀ וְאֶת־בְּנוֹתֶיהָ וְאֶת־יְשָׁנָה וְאֶת־בְּנוֹתֶיהָ וְאֶת־עֶפְרוֹן

[עֶפְרַיִן] וּבְנֹתֶיהָ׃

וְלֹא־עָצַר כֹּחַ־יָרָבְעָם עוֹד בִּימֵי אֲבִיָּהוּ וַיִּגְּפֵהוּ יְהוָה וַיָּמֹת׃

Then the men of Judah raised a war cry, and when the men of Judah raised
the war cry, then it was that God routed Jeroboam and all Israel before Abijah
and Judah. So the sons of Israel fled before Judah, and God gave them into
their hand. Abijah and his people defeated them with a great slaughter, . . .
Thus the sons of Israel were subdued at that time, and the sons of Judah

conquered because they trusted in Yahweh, the God of their fathers. Abijah
pursued Jeroboam and captured from him [several] cities:
Bethel with its villages, **Jeshanah** with its villages and **Ephron** with its
villages.

Jeroboam did not again recover strength in the days of Abijah; and
Yahweh struck him and he died.

B. Asa 911/10—870/69 BCE; 41 yrs 1 Ki 15:9, 10; 2 Ch 16:13);

931-20 (of Jeroboam) = 911.

1. Cleansed the high places

2 Chron. 14:1-4; cf. 15:8

1 וַיַּעַשׂ אָסָא הַטּוֹב וְהַיָּשָׁר בְּעֵינֵי יְהוָה אֱלֹהָיו׃

2 וַיָּסַר אֶת־מִזְבְּחוֹת הַנֵּכָר וְהַבָּמוֹת וַיְשַׁבֵּר אֶת־הַמַּצֵּבוֹת

וַיְגַדַּע אֶת־הָאֲשֵׁרִים׃ 3 וַיֹּאמֶר לִיהוּדָה לִדְרוֹשׁ אֶת־יְהוָה

אֱלֹהֵי אֲבוֹתֵיהֶם וְלַעֲשׂוֹת הַתּוֹרָה וְהַמִּצְוָה׃

4 וַיָּסַר מִכָּל־עָרֵי יְהוּדָה אֶת־הַבָּמוֹת וְאֶת־הַחַמָּנִים

וַתִּשְׁקֹט הַמַּמְלָכָה לְפָנָיו׃

Asa did good and right in the sight of Yahweh his God, for he removed the
foreign altars and high places, tore down the stelae, cut down the Asherim,
and commanded Judah to seek Yahweh God of their fathers and to observe
the law and the commandment. And he also removed the high places and the
incense altars from all the cities of Judah. And the kingdom was undisturbed
under him.

2. Built more towns

2 Chron. 14:5-6

5 וַיִּבֶן עָרֵי מְצוּרָה בִּיהוּדָה כִּי־שָׁקְטָה הָאָרֶץ וְאֵין־עִמּוֹ מִלְחָמָה

בַּשָּׁנִים הָאֵלֶּה כִּי־הֵנִיחַ יְהוָה לוֹ׃ 6 וַיֹּאמֶר לִיהוּדָה נִבְנֶה | אֶת־הֶעָרִים

הָאֵלֶּה וְנָסֵב חוֹמָה וּמִגְדָּלִים דְּלָתַיִם וּבְרִיחִים עוֹדֶנּוּ הָאָרֶץ לְפָנֵינוּ

כִּי דָרַשְׁנוּ אֶת־יְהוָה אֱלֹהֵינוּ דָּרַשְׁנוּ וַיָּנַח לָנוּ מִסָּבִיב וַיִּבְנוּ וַיַּצְלִיחוּ׃

He built fortified cities in Judah, since the land was undisturbed, and there
was no one at war with him during those years, because Yahweh had given

him rest. For he said to Judah, "Let us build these cities and encompass [them] with walls and towers, gates and bars. The land is still ours because we have sought Yahweh our God; we have sought Him, and He has given us rest on every side." So they built and prospered.

3. Repels invasion by Zerah the Cushite <u>897 BCE</u>
2 Chron. 14:8-9,

8 וַיֵּצֵא אֲלֵיהֶם זֶרַח הַכּוּשִׁי בְּחַיִל אֶלֶף אֲלָפִים וּמַרְכָּבוֹת שְׁלֹשׁ מֵאוֹת

וַיָּבֹא עַד־מָרֵשָׁה 9 וַיֵּצֵא אָסָא לְפָנָיו וַיַּעַרְכוּ מִלְחָמָה בְּגֵיא

צְפַתָה לְמָרֵשָׁה

Now Zerah the Ethiopian came out against them . . . and he came to Mareshah.

So Asa went out to meet him, and they drew up in battle formation in the valley of **Zephathah at Mareshah**. (LXX **to the north of Mareshah**).

<u>Note</u>: LXX κατὰ βορρᾶν Μαρισης צָפֹנָה לְמָרֵשָׁה
2 Chron. 14:11-14

11 וַיִּגֹּף יְהוָה אֶת־הַכּוּשִׁים לִפְנֵי אָסָא וְלִפְנֵי יְהוּדָה וַיָּנֻסוּ הַכּוּשִׁים

12 וַיִּרְדְּפֵם אָסָא וְהָעָם אֲשֶׁר־עִמּוֹ עַד־לִגְרָר וַיִּפֹּל מִכּוּשִׁים לְאֵין לָהֶם

מִחְיָה כִּי־נִשְׁבְּרוּ לִפְנֵי־יְהוָה וְלִפְנֵי מַחֲנֵהוּ וַיִּשְׂאוּ שָׁלָל הַרְבֵּה מְאֹד

13 וַיַּכּוּ אֶת כָּל־הֶעָרִים סְבִיבוֹת גְּרָר כִּי־הָיָה פַחַד־יְהוָה עֲלֵיהֶם

וַיָּבֹזּוּ אֶת־כָּל־הֶעָרִים כִּי־בִזָּה רַבָּה הָיְתָה בָהֶם 14 וְגַם־אָהֳלֵי מִקְנֶה

הִכּוּ וַיִּשְׁבּוּ צֹאן לָרֹב וּגְמַלִּים וַיָּשֻׁבוּ יְרוּשָׁלָם

So Yahweh routed the Cushites before Asa and before Judah, and the Cushites fled. And Asa and the people with him pursued them as far as **Gerar**. And they destroyed all the cities around **Gerar**, for the dread of Yahweh had fallen on them; and they despoiled all the cities, for there was much plunder in them. And the tents of those who owned livestock, they also smote, and they carried away large numbers of sheep and camels. Then they returned to Jerusalem.

cf. 2 Ch 21:16

וַיָּעַר יְהוָה עַל־יְהוֹרָם אֵת רוּחַ הַפְּלִשְׁתִּים

וְהָעַרְבִים אֲשֶׁר עַל־יַד כּוּשִׁים

Then Yahweh stirred up against Jehoram the spirit of the Philistines and the
Arabs who bordered the Cushites;

cf. 1 Chron. 4:39-40 כִּי מִן־חָם הַיֹּשְׁבִים שָׁם לְפָנִים

for those who lived there formerly [were] Hamites.

4. Cultic reform, even supported by people from Israel

2 Chron. 15:8-9

8 וְכִשְׁמֹעַ אָסָא הַדְּבָרִים הָאֵלֶּה וְהַנְּבוּאָה עֹדֵד הַנָּבִיא הִתְחַזַּק וַיַּעֲבֵר
הַשִּׁקּוּצִים מִכָּל־אֶרֶץ יְהוּדָה וּבִנְיָמִן וּמִן־הֶעָרִים אֲשֶׁר לָכַד מֵהַר אֶפְרָיִם
וַיְחַדֵּשׁ אֶת־מִזְבַּח יְהוָה אֲשֶׁר לִפְנֵי אוּלָם יְהוָה 9 וַיִּקְבֹּץ אֶת־כָּל־יְהוּדָה
וּבִנְיָמִן וְהַגָּרִים עִמָּהֶם מֵאֶפְרַיִם וּמְנַשֶּׁה וּמִשִּׁמְעוֹן כִּי־נָפְלוּ עָלָיו
מִיִּשְׂרָאֵל לָרֹב בִּרְאֹתָם כִּי־יְהוָה אֱלֹהָיו עִמּוֹ

Now when Asa heard these words and the prophecy which Azariah the son
of Oded the prophet spoke, he took courage and removed the abominable
idols from all the land of **Judah** and **Benjamin** and from the cities which he
had captured in the **Hill Country of Ephraim**. He then restored the altar of
Yahweh which was in front of the porch of Yahweh.

He gathered all **Judah** and **Benjamin** and those from **Ephraim**, **Manasseh**
and **Simeon** who resided with them, for many defected to him from Israel
when they saw that Yahweh his God was with him.

NOTE: שִׁמְעוֹן (LXX Συμεων) = שִׁמְרוֹן (LXX Συμοων)

Shimron from Josh. 11:1; 12:20 in Jezreel Valley

5. Convened a great assembly in Jerusalem 15th yr. of Asa **896 BCE**

2 Chron. 15:10-19

10 וַיִּקָּבְצוּ יְרוּשָׁלַם בַּחֹדֶשׁ הַשְּׁלִישִׁי לִשְׁנַת חֲמֵשׁ־עֶשְׂרֵה לְמַלְכוּת אָסָא

11 וַיִּזְבְּחוּ לַיהוָה בַּיּוֹם הַהוּא מִן־הַשָּׁלָל הֵבִיאוּ בָּקָר שְׁבַע מֵאוֹת

וְצֹאן שִׁבְעַת אֲלָפִים 12 וַיָּבֹאוּ בַבְּרִית לִדְרוֹשׁ אֶת־יְהוָה אֱלֹהֵי

אֲבוֹתֵיהֶם בְּכָל־לְבָבָם וּבְכָל־נַפְשָׁם 15:13 וְכֹל אֲשֶׁר לֹא־יִדְרֹשׁ לַיהוָה

אֱלֹהֵי־יִשְׂרָאֵל יוּמָת לְמִן־קָטֹן וְעַד־גָּדוֹל לְמֵאִישׁ וְעַד־אִשָּׁה

14 וַיִּשָּׁבְעוּ לַיהוָה בְּקוֹל גָּדוֹל וּבִתְרוּעָה וּבַחֲצֹצְרוֹת וּבְשׁוֹפָרוֹת

15 וַיִּשְׂמְחוּ כָל־יְהוּדָה עַל־הַשְּׁבוּעָה כִּי בְכָל־לְבָבָם נִשְׁבָּעוּ וּבְכָל־רְצוֹנָם

בִּקְשֻׁהוּ וַיִּמָּצֵא לָהֶם וַיָּנַח יְהוָה לָהֶם מִסָּבִיב

16 וְגַם־מַעֲכָה אֵם אָסָא הַמֶּלֶךְ הֱסִירָהּ מִגְּבִירָה אֲשֶׁר־עָשְׂתָה לַאֲשֵׁרָה

מִפְלָצֶת וַיִּכְרֹת אָסָא אֶת־מִפְלַצְתָּהּ וַיָּדֶק וַיִּשְׂרֹף בְּנַחַל קִדְרוֹן

17 וְהַבָּמוֹת לֹא־סָרוּ מִיִּשְׂרָאֵל רַק לְבַב־אָסָא הָיָה שָׁלֵם כָּל־יָמָיו

18 וַיָּבֵא אֶת־קָדְשֵׁי אָבִיו וְקָדָשָׁיו בֵּית הָאֱלֹהִים כֶּסֶף וְזָהָב וְכֵלִים

19 וּמִלְחָמָה לֹא הָיָתָה עַד שְׁנַת־שְׁלֹשִׁים וְחָמֵשׁ לְמַלְכוּת אָסָא

So they assembled at Jerusalem in the third month of the **fifteenth year** of Asa's reign. They sacrificed to Yahweh that day 700 oxen and 7,000 sheep from the spoil they had brought. And they entered into the covenant to seek Yahweh, God of their fathers, with all their heart and soul; and whoever would not seek Yahweh, God of Israel, should be put to death, whether small or great, man or woman. And, they made an oath to Yahweh with a loud voice, with shouting, with trumpets and with horns. And all Judah rejoiced concerning the oath, for they had sworn with their whole heart and had sought Him earnestly, and He was found by them. So Yahweh gave them rest on every side.

And Maacah, the mother of King Asa, he also removed from the status of queen mother, because she had made an abominable image for Asherah, and Asa cut down her abominable image, crushed [it] and burned [it] at the Brook Kidron.

But the high places were not removed from Israel; nevertheless Asa's heart was blameless all his days.

He brought into the house of God the dedicated things of his father and his own dedicated things: silver and gold and utensils.

And there was no more war until the thirty-fifth year of Asa's reign.

Note: 35th and 36th years of 2 Chron. 15:19 and 16:1 =
            15th and 16th yrs. of Asa, i.e. 896-895 BCE

19 וּמִלְחָמָה לֹא הָיָתָה עַד שְׁנַת־שְׁלֹשִׁים וְחָמֵשׁ לְמַלְכוּת אָסָא

2Chr. 16:1 בִּשְׁנַת שְׁלֹשִׁים וָשֵׁשׁ לְמַלְכוּת אָסָא עָלָה בַּעְשָׁא מֶלֶךְ־יִשְׂרָאֵל

עַל־יְהוּדָה וַיִּבֶן אֶת־הָרָמָה לְבִלְתִּי תֵּת יוֹצֵא וָבָא לְאָסָא מֶלֶךְ יְהוּדָה

And there was no more war until the thirty-fifth (= 15th) year of Asa's reign. In the thirty-sixth year of Asa's reign Baasha king of Israel came up against Judah and fortified Ramah in order to prevent anyone from going out or coming in to Asa king of Judah.

C. Baasha's usurpation in Israel —
1. Nadab (910/909 -909/908); 2nd of Asa, 2 yrs
   1 Ki 15:25; non-accession 912 - 2! = 910; murdered
   by Baasha at **Gibbethon**
   1 Ki. 15:25-33

25 וְנָדָב בֶּן־יָרָבְעָם מָלַךְ עַל־יִשְׂרָאֵל בִּשְׁנַת שְׁתַּיִם לְאָסָא מֶלֶךְ יְהוּדָה

וַיִּמְלֹךְ עַל־יִשְׂרָאֵל שְׁנָתָיִם 26 וַיַּעַשׂ הָרַע בְּעֵינֵי יְהוָה וַיֵּלֶךְ בְּדֶרֶךְ אָבִיו

וּבְחַטָּאתוֹ אֲשֶׁר הֶחֱטִיא אֶת־יִשְׂרָאֵל 27 וַיִּקְשֹׁר עָלָיו בַּעְשָׁא בֶן־אֲחִיָּה

לְבֵית יִשָּׂשׂכָר וַיַּכֵּהוּ בַעְשָׁא בְּגִבְּתוֹן אֲשֶׁר לַפְּלִשְׁתִּים וְנָדָב

וְכָל־יִשְׂרָאֵל צָרִים עַל־גִּבְּתוֹן 28 וַיְמִתֵהוּ בַעְשָׁא בִּשְׁנַת שָׁלֹשׁ לְאָסָא מֶלֶךְ

יְהוּדָה (909 BCE) וַיִּמְלֹךְ תַּחְתָּיו 29 וַיְהִי כְמָלְכוֹ הִכָּה אֶת־כָּל־בֵּית יָרָבְעָם

לֹא־הִשְׁאִיר כָּל־נְשָׁמָה לְיָרָבְעָם עַד־הִשְׁמִדוֹ כִּדְבַר יְהוָה אֲשֶׁר דִּבֶּר בְּיַד־עַבְדּוֹ

אֲחִיָּה הַשִּׁילֹנִי 30 עַל־חַטֹּאות יָרָבְעָם אֲשֶׁר חָטָא וַאֲשֶׁר הֶחֱטִיא אֶת־יִשְׂרָאֵל

בְּכַעְסוֹ אֲשֶׁר הִכְעִיס אֶת־יְהוָה אֱלֹהֵי יִשְׂרָאֵל   31 וְיֶתֶר דִּבְרֵי נָדָב

וְכָל־אֲשֶׁר עָשָׂה הֲלֹא־הֵם כְּתוּבִים עַל־סֵפֶר דִּבְרֵי הַיָּמִים

לְמַלְכֵי יִשְׂרָאֵל   32 וּמִלְחָמָה הָיְתָה בֵין אָסָא וּבֵין בַּעְשָׁא מֶלֶךְ־יִשְׂרָאֵל

כָּל־יְמֵיהֶם   33 בִּשְׁנַת שָׁלֹשׁ לְאָסָא מֶלֶךְ יְהוּדָה מָלַךְ בַּעְשָׁא בֶן־אֲחִיָּה

עַל־כָּל־יִשְׂרָאֵל בְּתִרְצָה עֶשְׂרִים וְאַרְבַּע שָׁנָה

Now **Nadab** the son of Jeroboam became king over Israel in the second year of Asa (910 BCE) king of Judah, and he reigned over Israel two years. And he did evil in the sight of Yahweh, and walked in the way of his father and in his sin which he made Israel sin.

Then **Baasha** the son of Ahijah of the house of Issachar conspired against him, and Baasha struck him down at **Gibbethon**, which belonged to the **Philistines**, while Nadab and all Israel were laying siege to **Gibbethon**. So Baasha killed him in the third year of Asa king of Judah (909 BCE) and reigned in his place.

It came about as soon as he was king, he struck down all the household of Jeroboam. He did not leave to Jeroboam any persons alive, until he had destroyed them, according to the word of Yahweh, which He spoke by His servant Ahijah the Shilonite, because of the sins of Jeroboam which he sinned, and which he made Israel sin, because of his provocation with which he provoked Yahweh God of Israel to anger.

Now the rest of the acts of Nadab and all that he did, are they not written in the Book of the Chronicles of the Kings of Israel?

D. War between Asa and **Baasha** (909/8-886-5; non-acc., 3rd
     of Asa 1 Ki 15:28, 33; 913 - 3! = 909).

1 Ki. 15:16-22 ‖ 2 Chron. 16:1-6   **895 BCE**

16 וּמִלְחָמָה הָיְתָה בֵּין אָסָא וּבֵין בַּעְשָׁא מֶלֶךְ־יִשְׂרָאֵל כָּל־יְמֵיהֶם

17 וַיַּעַל בַּעְשָׁא מֶלֶךְ־יִשְׂרָאֵל עַל־יְהוּדָה וַיִּבֶן אֶת־הָרָמָה לְבִלְתִּי תֵּת

יֹצֵא וָבָא לְאָסָא מֶלֶךְ יְהוּדָה   18 וַיִּקַּח אָסָא אֶת־כָּל־הַכֶּסֶף וְהַזָּהָב

הַנּוֹתָרִים בְּאוֹצְרוֹת בֵּית־יְהוָה וְאֶת־אוֹצְרוֹת בֵּית מֶלֶךְ [הַ][מֶּלֶךְ]

וַיִּתְּנֵם בְּיַד־עֲבָדָיו וַיִּשְׁלָחֵם אָסָא הַמֶּלֶךְ אֶל־בֶּן־הֲדַד בֶּן־טַבְרִמֹּן

בֶּן־חֶזְיוֹן מֶלֶךְ אֲרָם הַיֹּשֵׁב בְּדַמֶּשֶׂק לֵאמֹר 19 בְּרִית בֵּינִי וּבֵינֶךָ

בֵּין אָבִי וּבֵין אָבִיךָ הִנֵּה שָׁלַחְתִּי לְךָ שֹׁחַד כֶּסֶף וְזָהָב לֵךְ הָפֵרָה

אֶת־בְּרִיתְךָ אֶת־בַּעְשָׁא מֶלֶךְ־יִשְׂרָאֵל וְיַעֲלֶה מֵעָלָי

20 וַיִּשְׁמַע בֶּן־הֲדַד אֶל־הַמֶּלֶךְ אָסָא וַיִּשְׁלַח אֶת־שָׂרֵי הַחֲיָלִים אֲשֶׁר־לוֹ

עַל־עָרֵי יִשְׂרָאֵל וַיַּךְ אֶת־עִיּוֹן וְאֶת־דָּן וְאֵת אָבֵל בֵּית־מַעֲכָה

וְאֵת כָּל־כִּנְרוֹת עַל כָּל־אֶרֶץ נַפְתָּלִי 21 וַיְהִי כִּשְׁמֹעַ בַּעְשָׁא וַיֶּחְדַּל מִבְּנוֹת

אֶת־הָרָמָה וַיֵּשֶׁב בְּתִרְצָה 22 וְהַמֶּלֶךְ אָסָא הִשְׁמִיעַ אֶת־כָּל־יְהוּדָה אֵין

נָקִי וַיִּשְׂאוּ אֶת־אַבְנֵי הָרָמָה וְאֶת־עֵצֶיהָ אֲשֶׁר בָּנָה בַּעְשָׁא

וַיִּבֶן בָּם הַמֶּלֶךְ אָסָא אֶת־גֶּבַע בִּנְיָמִן וְאֶת־הַמִּצְפָּה

(895/4 BCE).

There was war between Asa and Baasha king of Israel all their days.

In the third year of Asa king of Judah (909 BCE), Baasha the son of Ahijah became king over all Israel at **Tirzah**, twenty-four years.

Baasha king of Israel went up against Judah and fortified Ramah in order to prevent [anyone] from going out or coming in to Asa king of Judah

Then Asa took all the silver and the gold which were left in the treasuries of the house of Yahweh and the treasuries of the king's house, and delivered them into the hand of his servants. And King Asa sent them to **Ben-hadad** the son of Tabrimmon, the son of Hezion, **king of Aram**, who lived in **Damascu**s, saying,

"[Let there be] a treaty between you and me, [as] between my father and your father. Behold, I have sent you a present of silver and gold; go, break your treaty with Baasha king of Israel so that he will withdraw from me." So Ben-hadad listened to King Asa and sent the commanders of his armies against the cities of Israel, and conquered **Ijon, Dan, Abel-beth-maacah** and all **Chinneroth**, besides all the land of **Naphtali**.

When Baasha heard [of it], he ceased fortifying Ramah and remained in **Tirzah**.

Then King Asa made a proclamation to all Judah — none was exempt — and they carried away the stones of **Ramah** and its timber with which Baasha had built. And King Asa built with them **Geba** of Benjamin and **Mizpah**.

2 Chron. 16:1-6

1 בִּשְׁנַת שְׁלֹשִׁים וָשֵׁשׁ לְמַלְכוּת אָסָא עָלָה בַּעְשָׁא

מֶלֶךְ־יִשְׂרָאֵל עַל־יְהוּדָה וַיִּבֶן אֶת־הָרָמָה לְבִלְתִּי תֵּת יוֹצֵא

וָבָא לְאָסָא מֶלֶךְ יְהוּדָה

2 וַיֹּצֵא אָסָא כֶּסֶף וְזָהָב מֵאֹצְרוֹת בֵּית יְהוָה

וּבֵית הַמֶּלֶךְ וַיִּשְׁלַח אֶל־בֶּן־הֲדַד מֶלֶךְ אֲרָם הַיּוֹשֵׁב

בְּדַרְמֶשֶׂק לֵאמֹר

3 בְּרִית בֵּינִי וּבֵינֶךָ וּבֵין אָבִי וּבֵין אָבִיךָ הִנֵּה

שָׁלַחְתִּי לְךָ כֶּסֶף וְזָהָב לֵךְ הָפֵר בְּרִיתְךָ אֶת־בַּעְשָׁא מֶלֶךְ

יִשְׂרָאֵל וְיַעֲלֶה מֵעָלָי

4 וַיִּשְׁמַע בֶּן הֲדַד אֶל־הַמֶּלֶךְ אָסָא וַיִּשְׁלַח

אֶת־שָׂרֵי הַחֲיָלִים אֲשֶׁר־לוֹ אֶל־עָרֵי יִשְׂרָאֵל וַיַּכּוּ אֶת־עִיּוֹן

וְאֶת־דָּן וְאֶת אָבֵל מַיִם וְאֵת כָּל־מִסְכְּנוֹת עָרֵי נַפְתָּלִי

5 וַיְהִי כִּשְׁמֹעַ בַּעְשָׁא וַיֶּחְדַּל מִבְּנוֹת אֶת־הָרָמָה

וַיַּשְׁבֵּת אֶת־מְלַאכְתּוֹ

6 וְאָסָא הַמֶּלֶךְ לָקַח אֶת־כָּל־יְהוּדָה וַיִּשְׂאוּ

אֶת־אַבְנֵי הָרָמָה וְאֶת־עֵצֶיהָ אֲשֶׁר בָּנָה בַּעְשָׁא וַיִּבֶן בָּהֶם

אֶת־גֶּבַע וְאֶת־הַמִּצְפָּה

In the thirty-sixth year of Asa's reign (16th year, 895/4) Baasha king of Israel came up against Judah and fortified Ramah in order to prevent [anyone] from going out or coming in to Asa king of Judah.

Then Asa brought out silver and gold from the treasuries of the house of Yahweh and the king's house, and sent them to **Ben-hadad king of Aram**, who lived in **Damascus**, saying,

"[Let there be] a treaty between you and me, [as] between my father and your father. Behold, I have sent you silver and gold; go, break your treaty with Baasha king of Israel so that he will withdraw from me." So Ben-hadad listened to King Asa and sent the commanders of his armies against the cities of Israel, and they conquered **Ijon, Dan, Abel-maim** and all the <u>store cities</u> of **Naphtali**.

1. Baasha built Ramah 1 Ki 15:17 ‖ 2 Chron. 16:1
2. Asa bribed Ben-hadad to invade Galilee; the latter took **Iyon, Dan, Abel-beth-maacah = (Abel-maim**)and all **Chinneroth** (= store cities) and all Naphtali (**895/4 BCE**)
3. Baasha returned to **Tirzah** — 1 Ki. 15:21

וַיְהִי כִּשְׁמֹעַ בַּעְשָׁא וַיֶּחְדַּל מִבְּנוֹת אֶת־הָרָמָה וַיֵּשֶׁב בְּתִרְצָה

When Baasha heard [of it], he ceased fortifying **Ramah** and dwelt in **Tirzah**.

‖ 2 Chron. 16:5

וַיְהִי כִּשְׁמֹעַ בַּעְשָׁא וַיֶּחְדַּל מִבְּנוֹת אֶת־הָרָמָה וַיַּשְׁבֵּת אֶת־מְלַאכְתּוֹ

When Baasha heard [of it], he ceased fortifying **Ramah** and stopped his work.

4. Asa fortified Geba (of Benjamin) and Mizpah 2 Chron. 16:6 ‖ 1 Ki. 15:22

6 וְאָסָא הַמֶּלֶךְ לָקַח אֶת־כָּל־יְהוּדָה וַיִּשְׂאוּ

אֶת־אַבְנֵי הָרָמָה וְאֶת־עֵצֶיהָ אֲשֶׁר בָּנָה בַעְשָׁא וַיִּבֶן בָּהֶם

אֶת־גֶּבַע וְאֶת־הַמִּצְפָּה

Then King Asa brought all Judah, and they carried away the stones of **Ramah** and its timber with which Baasha had been building, and with them he fortified **Geba** and **Mizpah**.

THUS WAS ACHIEVED A RECOGNIZED BORDER BETWEEN ISRAEL AND JUDAH — between Mizpah and Bethel, i.e. about on the ridge of Ramallah—el-Bîrā.

LESSON 16

HOUSE OF OMRI AND REBELLION OF JEHU

I. **ISRAEL**

A. Series of Usurpations

1. Elah, son of Baasha 886/5-885/4 1 Ki. 16:8-14; n.a. 26 of
   Asa 1 Ki. 16:8 (912 minus 26 = 886 B.C.E.)

16:8 בִּשְׁנַת עֶשְׂרִים וָשֵׁשׁ שָׁנָה לְאָסָא מֶלֶךְ יְהוּדָה מָלַךְ אֵלָה

Tirzah (886/5-885/4) בֶּן־בַּעְשָׁא עַל־יִשְׂרָאֵל בְּתִרְצָה שְׁנָתָיִם

Zimri 16:9 וַיִּקְשֹׁר עָלָיו עַבְדּוֹ זִמְרִי שַׂר מַחֲצִית הָרֶכֶב וְהוּא

16:10 וַיָּבֹא זִמְרִי וַיַּכֵּהוּ וַיְמִיתֵהוּ בִּשְׁנַת עֶשְׂרִים וָשֶׁבַע לְאָסָא

מֶלֶךְ יְהוּדָה וַיִּמְלֹךְ תַּחְתָּיו

16:11 וַיְהִי בְמָלְכוֹ כְּשִׁבְתּוֹ עַל־כִּסְאוֹ הִכָּה

אֶת־כָּל־בֵּית בַּעְשָׁא לֹא־הִשְׁאִיר לוֹ מַשְׁתִּין בְּקִיר וְגֹאֲלָיו

וְרֵעֵהוּ

16:12 וַיַּשְׁמֵד זִמְרִי אֵת כָּל־בֵּית בַּעְשָׁא כִּדְבַר

יְהוָה אֲשֶׁר דִּבֶּר אֶל־בַּעְשָׁא בְּיַד יֵהוּא הַנָּבִיא

16:13 אֶל כָּל־חַטֹּאות בַּעְשָׁא וְחַטֹּאות אֵלָה בְנוֹ

אֲשֶׁר חָטְאוּ וַאֲשֶׁר הֶחֱטִיאוּ אֶת־יִשְׂרָאֵל לְהַכְעִיס אֶת־יְהוָה

אֱלֹהֵי יִשְׂרָאֵל בְּהַבְלֵיהֶם

16:14 וְיֶתֶר דִּבְרֵי אֵלָה וְכָל־אֲשֶׁר עָשָׂה

הֲלוֹא־הֵם כְּתוּבִים עַל־סֵפֶר דִּבְרֵי הַיָּמִים לְמַלְכֵי יִשְׂרָאֵל

In the twenty-sixth year of Asa king of Judah, Elah the son of Baasha became king over Israel at Tirzah, [and reigned] two years. His servant Zimri, commander of half his chariots, conspired against him. Now he [was] at Tirzah drinking himself drunk in the house of Arza, who [was] over the household at Tirzah. Then Zimri went in and struck him and put him to death in the twenty-seventh year of Asa king of Judah, and became king in his place. It came about when he became king, as soon as he sat on his throne, that he killed all the household of Baasha; he did not leave a single male, neither of his relatives nor of his friends. Thus Zimri destroyed all the household of Baasha, according to the word of Yahweh, which He spoke against Baasha through Jehu the prophet, for all the sins of Baasha and the sins of Elah his son, which they sinned and which they made Israel sin, provoking Yahweh God of Israel to anger with their idols.

Now the rest of the acts of Elah and all that he did, are they not written in the Book of the Chronicles of the Kings of Israel?

> 2. <u>Zimri</u> 885/4 (seven days) — 1 Ki. 16:15-20; n.a. 27 of Asa
> 1 Ki. 16:10,15 (912 minus 27 = 885 B.C.E.).

16:15 בִּשְׁנַת עֶשְׂרִים וָשֶׁבַע שָׁנָה לְאָסָא מֶלֶךְ יְהוּדָה מָלַךְ זִמְרִי

שִׁבְעַת יָמִים בְּתִרְצָה וְהָעָם חֹנִים עַל־גִּבְּתוֹן אֲשֶׁר(885/4)

Gibbethon of the Philistines לַפְּלִשְׁתִּים

16 וַיִּשְׁמַע הָעָם הַחֹנִים לֵאמֹר קָשַׁר זִמְרִי וְגַם הִכָּה אֶת־הַמֶּלֶךְ

Omri ּ וַיַּמְלִכוּ כָל־יִשְׂרָאֵל אֶת־עָמְרִי שַׂר־צָבָא עַל־יִשְׂרָאֵל בַּיּוֹם הַהוּא

17 וַיַּעֲלֶה עָמְרִי וְכָל־יִשְׂרָאֵל עִמּוֹ מִגִּבְּתוֹן וַיָּצֻרוּ עַל־תִּרְצָה

18 וַיְהִי כִּרְאוֹת זִמְרִי כִּי־נִלְכְּדָה הָעִיר וַיָּבֹא אֶל־אַרְמוֹן בֵּית־הַמֶּלֶךְ

ּ וַיִּשְׂרֹף עָלָיו אֶת־בֵּית־מֶלֶךְ בָּאֵשׁ וַיָּמֹת

In the twenty-seventh year of Asa king of Judah, Zimri reigned seven days at Tirzah. Now the people were camped against Gibbethon, which belonged to the Philistines. The people who were camped heard it said, "Zimri has conspired and has also struck down the king." Therefore all Israel made Omri, the commander of the army, king over Israel that day in the camp. Then Omri and all Israel with him went up from Gibbethon and besieged Tirzah. When Zimri saw that the city was taken, he went into the citadel of the king's house and burned the king's house over him with fire, and died,

3. Tibni and Omri rivals 885/4 - 880

a. People divided between Omri and Tibni 1 Ki. 16:21-22

21 אָז יֵחָלֵק הָעָם יִשְׂרָאֵל לַחֵצִי חֲצִי הָעָם הָיָה אַחֲרֵי תִבְנִי

בֶּן־גִּינַת לְהַמְלִיכוֹ וְהַחֲצִי אַחֲרֵי עָמְרִי

22 וַיֶּחֱזַק הָעָם אֲשֶׁר אַחֲרֵי עָמְרִי אֶת־הָעָם

אֲשֶׁר אַחֲרֵי תִבְנִי בֶן־גִּינַת וַיָּמָת תִּבְנִי וַיִּמְלֹךְ עָמְרִ

¶ Then the people of Israel were divided into two parts: half of the people followed Tibni the son of Ginath, to make him king; the [other] half followed Omri. But the people who followed Omri prevailed over the people who followed Tibni the son of Ginath. And Tibni died and Omri became king.

b. Six year civil war (1 Ki. 16:23), Omri "reigned **six years** in Tirzah" בְּתִרְצָה מָלַךְ שֵׁשׁ־שָׁנִים (885/4-880)

בִּשְׁנַת שְׁלֹשִׁים וְאַחַת שָׁנָה לְאָסָא מֶלֶךְ יְהוּדָה

מָלַךְ עָמְרִי עַל־יִשְׂרָאֵל שְׁתֵּים עֶשְׂרֵה שָׁנָה

בְּתִרְצָה מָלַךְ שֵׁשׁ־שָׁנִים

In the thirty-first year of Asa king of Judah, Omri became king over Israel [and reigned] twelve years; he reigned six years at Tirzah.

*****

c. Damascus may have taken advantage of this situation

to seize towns in Trans-jordan (cf. 1 Ki. 20:34).

וַיֹּאמֶר אֵלָיו הֶעָרִים אֲשֶׁר־לָקַח־אָבִי מֵאֵת אָבִיךָ אָשִׁיב

וְחוּצוֹת תָּשִׂים לְךָ בְדַמֶּשֶׂק כַּאֲשֶׁר־שָׂם אָבִי בְּשֹׁמְרוֹן וַאֲנִי

בַבְּרִית אֲשַׁלְּחֶךָ וַיִּכְרָת־לוֹ בְרִית וַיְשַׁלְּחֵהוּ

[Ben-hadad] said to him, "The cities which my father took from your father I will restore, and you shall make streets for yourself in Damascus, as my father made in Samaria." [Ahab said], "And I will let you go with this covenant." So he made a covenant with him and let him go.

B. Rise of the House of Omri — internal and external policies,
geared to face challenge of Damascus

1. Omri begins his sole reign 880 BCE — 1 Ki. 16:23
n.a. 31 Asa (911 minus 31 = 880 B.C.E.) Sole reign begins:

בִּשְׁנַת שְׁלֹשִׁים וְאַחַת שָׁנָה לְאָסָא מֶלֶךְ יְהוּדָה

מָלַךְ עָמְרִי עַל־יִשְׂרָאֵל שְׁתֵּים עֶשְׂרֵה שָׁנָה

בְּתִרְצָה מָלַךְ שֵׁשׁ־שָׁנִים

In the thirty-first year of Asa king of Judah, Omri became king over
Israel [and reigned] twelve years; he reigned six years at Tirzah.

Sole reign 880 to 874 BCE — 12 yrs. is total of whole reign.

2. New capital purchased 1 Ki. 16:24 (880 B.C.E.)

24 וַיִּקֶן אֶת־הָהָר שֹׁמְרוֹן מֵאֵת שֶׁמֶר בְּכִכְּרַיִם כָּסֶף

וַיִּבֶן אֶת־הָהָר וַיִּקְרָא אֶת־שֵׁם הָעִיר אֲשֶׁר בָּנָה עַל

שֶׁם־שֶׁמֶר אֲדֹנֵי הָהָר שֹׁמְרוֹן

He bought the hill Samaria from Shemer for two talents of silver; and he built
on the hill, and named the city which he built Samaria, after the name of
Shemer, the owner of the hill.

Was Shemer a clan or a person? In any case, there must
have been a settlement there. Omri may have been the
gôʾēl (Mazar, EI 20 [1989]:215-219)

3. Alliance with Tyre — His son Ahab married to Jezebel
אִיזֶבֶל בַּת־אֶתְבַּעַל מֶלֶךְ צִידֹנִים "daughter of
Eth‹ô›-Baal, king of the Sidonians (= Phoenicians)."
4. Seizure of Table Land (of Moab); about 880 B.C.E. or after.
a. Established a base at Medeba, for "forty years"

(4)- עמר

(5) י . מלכ . ישראל . ויענו . את . מאב . ימנ . רבנ . כי . יאנפ . כמש . באר

(6) צה [ויחלפה . בנה . ויאמר . גמ . הא . אענו . את . מאב [בימי . אמר . וכדבר]

(7) וארא . בה . ובבתה] וישראל . אבד . אבד . עלמ . וירש . עמרי . אר

(8) צ . מהדבא | וישב . בה . ימה . וחצי . ימי בנה . ארבענ . שת . וינ]ש[

(9) בה . כמש . בימי] -

Omr[5]i was king of Israel and he oppressed Moab many days because Chemosh was angry with his la[6]nd. And his son replaced him and he also said, "I will oppress Moab." In my days he spoke ⌜thus⌝ [7]but I was victorious over him and his house and Israel suffered everlasting destruction.

But Omri had conquered the lan[8]d of Madeba and he dwelt there during his reign and half the reign of his son, forty years but Chemosh [9]returned it in my days.

Mesha Stone, lines 4b-5—"40 yrs" round number, between **880-853= 27 yrs.**

b. Built Ataroth for the Gadites and Yahaz:
Mesha Stele, lines 10-11

(10) - - - אש . גד . ישב . בארצ . עטרת . מעלמ . ויבנ . לה . מלכ . י.

(11) שראל . את . עטרת

The man of Gad had dwelt in ᶜAṭarot (Ataroth) from of old and the king of Israel [11]built ᶜAṭarot (Ataroth) for him.

Meshaᶜ Stele, lines 18-19

(18) - - - - - - - - - - - - ומלכ . ישראל . בנה]. את [.

(19) יהצ . וישב . בה . בהלתחמה . בי -

And the king of Israel had built [19]Yahaz and he dwelt in it while he was fighting with me,

5. Alliance with Judah — Athaliah married to Jehoram son of Jehoshaphat
2 Ki. 8:18 || 2 Chr. 21:6 called "dau. of Ahab"
2 Ki. 8:26 || 2 Chr. 22:2 called "dau. of Omri"

I.   ISRAEL (cont.)

C. Ahab — 874/3 - 853 BCE — n.a. 38 Asa

(22 yrs.; 911 minus 38) 1Kings 16:29

וְאַחְאָב בֶּן־עָמְרִי מָלַךְ עַל־יִשְׂרָאֵל בִּשְׁנַת

שְׁלֹשִׁים וּשְׁמֹנֶה שָׁנָה לְאָסָא מֶלֶךְ יְהוּדָה וַיִּמְלֹךְ אַחְאָב

בֶּן־עָמְרִי עַל־יִשְׂרָאֵל בְּשֹׁמְרוֹן עֶשְׂרִים וּשְׁתַּיִם שָׁנָה

Now Ahab the son of Omri became king over Israel in the thirty-
eighth year of Asa king of Judah, and Ahab the son of Omri reigned
over Israel in Samaria twenty-two years.

1. Internal policies:
   a. Introduction of Baal worship 1 Ki. 16:30-34.in
      addition to continuing Jeroboam I's cult centers
   b. Three year drought: 1 Ki. 17:1-19:21 Contest on
      Mt. Carmel
   c Social injustice — illustrated by case of Naboth's
      vineyard 1 Ki. 21

D. Wars with Aram
   1. Arameans beseige Samaria 1 Ki. 20:1-22 — ca. 857 BCE;
      Ahab repels them. בַּסֻּכּוֹת not GN!, "pavilions"
   2. Encounter at Aphek in Golan 1 Ki. 20:23-43 — 3 years
      before battle of Qarqar, i.e. 856 BCE
      a. Aramaean reorganization: הַמְּלָכִים replaced by פַּחוֹת
         1 Kings 20:24
      b. Israelite victory vv. 29-31
      c. Ahab receives favorable terms as victor:
         (1) return of towns formerly lost to Aram
             (1 Ki. 15:20 ‖ 2 Chr. 16:4; during Omri's
             reign? Probably between 885 and 880 B.C.E.)
         (2) Ahab can establish חוּצוֹת in Damascus
         (3) treaty will be established between the two
             states; 1 Ki. 22:1 — 3 yrs. no war (c. 855-853)

22:1 וַיֵּשְׁבוּ שָׁלֹשׁ שָׁנִים אֵין מִלְחָמָה בֵּין אֲרָם וּבֵין יִשְׂרָאֵל

And they sat three years while there was no war between Aram and Israel.

3. BATTLE OF QARQAR 853 BCE— Shalmaneser III (859-824) crosses Euphrates and encountered coalition of western states: <u>According to the Kurkh stelae</u>

Leader & Country	Chariots	Infantry
Hadad-ezer of Damascus	1,200	20,000
Irḫuleni of Ḥamath	700	10,000
Ahab the Israelite	2,000	10,000
Byblos(?)		500
Egypt		1,000
Irqanata	10	10,000
Matinu-baᶜlu of Arvad		200
Ushnata		200
Adunu-baᶜlu of Sianu	30	10,000
Gindibu of Arabia		1,000 Camels
Baasha son of Rehob of Ammon		(?),000

NOTE: The figures are unreliable, especially regarding Ahab's forces; but note that arch rivals like Irḫuleni and Hadad-ezer worked together — so why not Ahab and Hadad-ezer?

The battle was a victory for the western allies; Shalmaneser III claimed victory but had to withdraw to Mesopotamia. Did not return to the west until 849 BCE.

4. Renewal of war between Israel and Damascus 853 BCE
1 Ki. 22:1-40 | | 2 Chr. 18:2-34
a. at Ramoth-gilead
b. Jehoshaphat goes to war as ally of Ahab
c. Ahab lost his life 853 BCE

II.   MESHA, KING OF MOAB (CONT.)

A. His capital at Dibon

(1) אנכ . משע . בן . כמש[ית] . מאב . הד

(2) יבני | אבי . מלכ . על . סאב . שלשנ . שת . ואנכ . סלכ

(3) תי . אחר . אבי | ואעש . הבמת . זאת . לכמש . בקרחה | במ[ת . י]

(4) שע . כי . השעני . מכל . המלכנ . וכי . הראני . בכל . שנאי | - - -

[1]I am Mesha^c the son of Chemosh[-yat?] king of Moab, the Da[2]ibonite.
My father reigned over Moab thirty years and I reign[3]ed after my father and
I built this altar platform for Chemosh in the citadel, an altar platform of
[sal][4]vation because he saved me from all the kings and because he gave me
the victory over all my adversaries.

B. Liberation of the Mishor 853 BCE when Ahab died
      2 Ki. 1:1; 3:4-5;

1:1   וַיִּפְשַׁע מוֹאָב בְּיִשְׂרָאֵל אַחֲרֵי מוֹת אַחְאָב

Cf. Mesha Stele, lines 8-21:

1. Conquest of Israelite base at Madeba (lines 7b-9a)

(7)- . וירש . עמרי . את . אר

(8) צ . מהדבא | וישב . בה . ימה . וחצי . ימי . בנה . ארבענ . שת . וי[ש]

(9) בה . כמש . בימי - - -

But Omri had conquered the lan[8]d of Madeba and he dwelt there during his
reign and half the reign of his son, forty years but Chemosh [9]returned it in
my days.

2. Fortified Baal-meon and Qiriaten (lines 9b-10a)

(9) - - - | ואבנ . את . בעלמענ . ואעש . בה . האשוח . ואבנ . [.]

(10) את . קריתנ - - -

So I (re)built Baal-maon and I made the reservoir in it and I bu[ilt] [10]Kiriaten.

3. Conquest of Ataroth (lines 10-14a) — ouster of Gad;
     resettlement by people of Sharon and Maḥrat(?) —
     the cult implements taken to Kirioth

(10) ‏- - - - - אש . גד . ישב . בארץ . עטרת . מעלמ . ויבנ . לה . מלכ . י.

(11) ‏שראל . את . עטרת [ואלתחמ . בקר . ואחזה] ואהרג . את . כל . העמ [ו ן]

(12) ‏הקר . הית . לכמש . ולמאב [ואשב . משמ . את . אראל . דודה . ואנ]ס[

(13) ‏חבה . לפני . כמש . בקרית [ואשב . בה. את . אש . שרנ . ואת . א]ש[

(14) ‏מחרת ‏- -

The man of Gad had dwelt in ʿAṭarot (Ataroth) from of old and the king of
Israel [11]built ʿAṭarot (Ataroth) for him. But I fought against the city and I
took it and I slew all the people, [but] [12]the city became the property of
Chemosh and of Moab and I confiscated from there its Davidic altar hearth
and I [13]dragged it before Chemosh in Kerioth, and I settled in it men of
Sharon and m[en] [14]of Maḥaroth.

4. Conquest of Nebo (lines 14-18); cult implements of YHWH also taken as trophies

(14) ‏- - - - ויאמר . לי . כמש . לכ אחז . את . נבה . על . ישראל [וא

(15) ‏הלכ . בללה . ואלתחמ . בה . מבקע . השחרת . עד . הצהרמ [ואח

(16) ‏זה . ואהרג . כלה . שבעת . אלפנ . גברנ . וגרנ [וגברת . וגר]

(17) ‏ת . ורחמת [כי . לעשתר . כמש . החרמתה] ואקח . משמ . אר]א[

(18) ‏לי . יהוה . ואסחב . המ . לפני . כמש] - - - - -

And Chemosh said to me, "Go! Seize Nebo against Israel," so I [15]proceeded
by night and I fought with it from the crack of dawn to midday and I to[16]ok
it and I slew all of it, seven thousand men and youths and women and
maid[17]ens and slave girls because I had dedicated it to ʿAshtar-Chemosh.
And I took [the al][18]tar hearths of Yahweh and I dragged them before
Chemosh.

5. Conquest of Yahaz (lines 18b-21a)

(18) ‏- - - - - - - - - - - - - - - ומלכ . ישראל . בנה [. בנה .] את [.

(19) ‏יהצ . וישב . בה . בהלתחמה . בי [ויגרשה . כמש . מפני [.] ו

(20) ‏אקח . ממאב . מאתנ . אש . כל . רשה] ואשאה . ביהצ . ואחזה .

(21) ‏לספת . על . דיבנ ‏- - - - - - - - - - - - - - - - -

And the king of Israel had built [19]Yahaz and he dwelt in it while he was fighting with me, but Chemosh drove him out from before me, so [20]I took from Moab two hundred men, all of his best, and I brought them to Yahaz and I seized it [21]in order to add (it) to Daibon.

[2 Chron. 20:1-30 — Attempted invasion of Judah]

C. Moabite attempted invasion of Judah 2 Chron 20:1-30 — 853 BCE
    prior to Jehoshaphat's partnership with Ahaziah of Israel
    who only ruled 853-852 (two yrs. in non-accession system)
    1. The allies: (Edom still allied to Judah!; cf. vs. 2, Aram!)
       West of Arabah, 1 Ch. 4:42

2Chr. 20:1 וַיְהִי אַחֲרֵיכֵן בָּאוּ בְנֵי־מוֹאָב וּבְנֵי עַמּוֹן וְעִמָּהֶם

מֵהָעַמּוֹנִים (*הַמְּעוּנִים = ἐκ τῶν Μιναίων LXX) עַל־יְהוֹשָׁפָט לַמִּלְחָמָה

2Chr. 20:2 וַיָּבֹאוּ וַיַּגִּידוּ לִיהוֹשָׁפָט לֵאמֹר בָּא עָלֶיךָ

הָמוֹן רָב מֵעֵבֶר לַיָּם מֵאֲרָם וְהִנָּם בְּחַצְצוֹן תָּמָר הִיא עֵין גֶּדִי

Now it came about after this that the sons of Moab and the sons of Ammon, together with some of the **Meunites**, came to make war against Jehoshaphat. 2Chr. 20:2 Then some came and reported to Jehoshaphat, saying, "A great multitude is coming against you from beyond the sea, out of Aram and behold, they are in Hazazon-tamar (that is Engedi)."

2Chr. 20:10 וְעַתָּה הִנֵּה בְנֵי־עַמּוֹן וּמוֹאָב וְהַר־שֵׂעִיר

אֲשֶׁר לֹא־נָתַתָּה לְיִשְׂרָאֵל לָבוֹא בָהֶם בְּבֹאָם מֵאֶרֶץ

מִצְרָיִם כִּי סָרוּ מֵעֲלֵיהֶם וְלֹא הִשְׁמִידוּם

"Now behold, the sons of Ammon and Moab and Mount Seir, whom You did not let Israel invade when they came out of the land of Egypt (they turned aside from them and did not destroy them),"

a. (בְּנֵי)·מוֹאָב
b. בְּנֵי־עַמּוֹן
c. (*הַמְּעוּנִים = ἐκ τῶν Μιναίων LXX) מֵהָעַמּוֹנִים
   cf. 20:10, 22 — בְּנֵי־עַמּוֹן וּמוֹאָב וְהַר־שֵׂעִיר ;
   Mt. Seir = Negeb highlands & NE. Sinai!

(1 Ch. 4:42)

****

d. הָמוֹן רָב מֵעֵבֶר לַיָּם מֵאֲרָם (vs. 2) ἀπὸ Συρίας;

sent by **Aram** to punish Jehoshaphat for

helping Ahab!***

2. The attempt — to En-gedi, allies fall on one another; note

בְּמַעֲלֵה הַצִּיץ וּמְצָאתֶם אֹתָם בְּסוֹף הַנַּחַל פְּנֵי מִדְבַּר

יְרוּאֵל, מִדְבַּר תְּקוֹעַ.

The ascent of Hazziz, the wady before the steppe of Yeru'el, the steppe of

Tekoa.

D. Invasion of Moab by Israel and Judah — 852 BCE after Joram

comes to throne of Israel — 2 Ki. 3:4-27

1. Joined by Jehoshaphat (vs. 7) and the Edomites who were

subject to Judah — the "king" was a *niṣṣāḇ* (1 Ki. 22:48).

2. Took "way of the wilderness of Edom" — route southwards

from Judah, around S. end of Dead Sea.

3. Moab ravaged but Kir-hareseth was delivered. Son of king

of Edom offered up (according to Radak).

2 Kings 3:25-27

25 וְהֶעָרִים יַהֲרֹסוּ וְכָל־חֶלְקָה טוֹבָה יַשְׁלִיכוּ אִישׁ־אַבְנוֹ וּמִלְאוּהָ

וְכָל־מַעְיַן־מַיִם יִסְתֹּמוּ וְכָל־עֵץ־טוֹב יַפִּילוּ עַד־הִשְׁאִיר אֲבָנֶיהָ

בַּקִּיר חֲרָשֶׂת וַיָּסֹבּוּ הַקַּלָּעִים וַיַּכּוּהָ

26 וַיַּרְא מֶלֶךְ מוֹאָב כִּי־חָזַק מִמֶּנּוּ הַמִּלְחָמָה וַיִּקַּח אוֹתוֹ שְׁבַע־מֵאוֹת

אִישׁ שֹׁלֵף חֶרֶב לְהַבְקִיעַ אֶל־מֶלֶךְ אֱדוֹם וְלֹא יָכֹלוּ

27 וַיִּקַּח אֶת־בְּנוֹ הַבְּכוֹר אֲשֶׁר־יִמְלֹךְ תַּחְתָּיו וַיַּעֲלֵהוּ עֹלָה

עַל־הַחֹמָה וַיְהִי קֶצֶף־גָּדוֹל עַל־יִשְׂרָאֵל וַיִּסְעוּ מֵעָלָיו וַיָּשֻׁבוּ לָאָרֶץ

25 Thus they destroyed the cities; and each one threw a stone on every piece

of good land and filled it. So they stopped all the springs of water and felled

all the good trees, until in Kir-hareseth [only] they left its stones; however,

the slingers went about [it] and struck it.

26 When the king of Moab saw that the battle was too fierce for him, he took
with him 700 men who drew swords, to break through to the king of Edom;
but they could not.

27 Then he took his oldest son who was to reign in his place, and offered him
as a burnt offering on the wall. And there came great wrath against Israel,
and they departed from him and returned to their own land.

4. Mesha's version: fighting at Ḥawronen (Horonaim)
Lines 31, 32

(31) . . . וחורננ.ישב.בה.בה.ב'ית'[ד]וד [כ]א[שר]

(32) [הלתחמ.בי . וי]אמר . לי . כמש . רד . הלתחמ . בחורננ | וארד . [ואל]

(33) [תחמ . בקר . ואחזה . ויש] בה . כמש . בימי . ועלתי . משמ . עש[ת]

(34) [................................ עש[ת . צדק | וֹאנ]כ[

(35) [....]

And (as for) **Hawronen**, Beth David dwelt there [w]hi[le] / [he fought with
me and] Chemosh [s]aid to me: "Go down, fight at Ḥawronen." So I went
down [and I fo] / [ught at the city and I took it and] Chemosh [re]turned it in
my days. And I went up from there to make .... / ....……...... to do
] justice and I .... "

Jer. 48:3,5, 34; = Ορωναιμα in Ant. XIII, 15, 1,
Ὠρωναῖν in XIV 1, 4; 2 Ki 3:21?,

III.   Successors of Ahab (853-841 BCE)

  A. Ahaziah, son of Ahab 853-852 1 Ki. 22:52-54; 2 Ki. 1:

     1. Partnership with Jehoshaphat to send ships from
          Ezion-geber (1 Ki. 49-50 | | 2 Chr. 21:35-37) 852 BCE
     2. Died as aftermath of a fall

  B. Jehoram (Joram) 852-841, also son of Ahab

     1. Went with Jehoshaphat against Moab (cf. above) 852 BCE
     2. Wounded in Ramoth-gilead 841 BCE,
     3. Assassinated by Jehu 841 BCE

IV. IN JUDAH

A. Jehoshaphat — co. regent 873/2, sole ruler 870/9, died 848 BCE

1. Revitalized administration 2 Chr. 17:2-6.
2. Levites sent to teach the law 2 Chr 17:7-9 in his third yr.
    i.e. 870 BCE when he became sole ruler
3. <u>Neighbors subjugated</u> 2 Chr. 17:10-11

10 וַיְהִי פַּחַד יְהוָה עַל כָּל־מַמְלְכוֹת הָאֲרָצוֹת אֲשֶׁר סְבִיבוֹת יְהוּדָה

וְלֹא נִלְחֲמוּ עִם־יְהוֹשָׁפָט 11 וּמִן־פְּלִשְׁתִּים מְבִיאִים לִיהוֹשָׁפָט מִנְחָה Philistines

וְכֶסֶף מַשָּׂא גַּם הָעַרְבִיאִים מְבִיאִים לוֹ צֹאן אֵילִים שִׁבְעַת אֲלָפִים וּשְׁבַע

מֵאוֹת וּתְיָשִׁים שִׁבְעַת אֲלָפִים וּשְׁבַע מֵאוֹת   Arabs

Now the dread of Yahweh was on all the kingdoms of the lands which [were] around Judah, so that they did not make war against Jehoshaphat.

2Chr. 17:11 Some of the Philistines brought gifts and silver as tribute to Jehoshaphat; the Arabians also brought him flocks, 7,700 rams and 7,700 male goats

1 Ki. 22:48 — וּמֶלֶךְ אֵין בֶּאֱדוֹם נִצָּב מֶלֶךְ Now there was no king
in Edom; a deputy was king.

4. Built בִּירָנִיּוֹת וְעָרֵי מִסְכְּנוֹת fortresses and store cities
    2 Chron. 17:12-13;

5. Gave fortified towns to his sons to rule 2 Chr. 21:2-3 ! ****

6. Reformed the judiciary 2 Chr. 19:4-11;

B.   853 BCE — Went with Ahab to Ramoth-gilead
        1 Ki 22:1-40 | | 2 Chr. 18:2-34
C. Invasion from Moab 853 BCE 2 Chr. 20:1-30 (cf. above); reprisal
    for helping Ahab, instigated by Aram (2 Chr. 20:2)
D. Ships to Ophir after way open to Ezion-geber because of defeat
    of Meunites (?) 2 Chr. 20:35-37 | | 1 Ki. 22:49-50;

in partnership with Ahaziah who only reigned in 853-852!

E. Invasion of Moab by Israel and Judah — 852 BCE after Joram
    comes to throne of Israel — 2 Ki. 3:4-27

    1. Joram joined by Jehoshaphat (vs. 7) and by the Edomites
    who were subject to Judah — the "king" was a *niṣṣāḇ*
    (1 Ki. 22:48). 2 Kings 3:1-7

1 וִיהוֹרָם בֶּן־אַחְאָב מָלַךְ עַל־יִשְׂרָאֵל בְּשֹׁמְרוֹן בִּשְׁנַת שְׁמֹנֶה עֶשְׂרֵה

לִיהוֹשָׁפָט מֶלֶךְ יְהוּדָה וַיִּמְלֹךְ שְׁתֵּים־עֶשְׂרֵה שָׁנָה 2 וַיַּעֲשֶׂה הָרַע בְּעֵינֵי

יְהוָה רַק לֹא כְאָבִיו וּכְאִמּוֹ וַיָּסַר אֶת־מַצְּבַת הַבַּעַל אֲשֶׁר עָשָׂה אָבִיו

3 רַק בְּחַטֹּאות יָרָבְעָם בֶּן־נְבָט אֲשֶׁר־הֶחֱטִיא אֶת־יִשְׂרָאֵל דָּבֵק

לֹא־סָר מִמֶּנָּה 4 וּמֵישַׁע מֶלֶךְ־מוֹאָב הָיָה נֹקֵד וְהֵשִׁיב לְמֶלֶךְ־יִשְׂרָאֵל

מֵאָה־אֶלֶף כָּרִים וּמֵאָה אֶלֶף אֵילִים צָמֶר 5 וַיְהִי כְּמוֹת אַחְאָב וַיִּפְשַׁע

מֶלֶךְ־מוֹאָב בְּמֶלֶךְ יִשְׂרָאֵל 6 וַיֵּצֵא הַמֶּלֶךְ יְהוֹרָם בַּיּוֹם הַהוּא מִשֹּׁמְרוֹן

וַיִּפְקֹד אֶת־כָּל־יִשְׂרָאֵל 7 וַיֵּלֶךְ וַיִּשְׁלַח אֶל־יְהוֹשָׁפָט מֶלֶךְ־יְהוּדָה לֵאמֹר

מֶלֶךְ מוֹאָב פָּשַׁע בִּי הֲתֵלֵךְ אִתִּי אֶל־מוֹאָב לַמִּלְחָמָה וַיֹּאמֶר אֶעֱלֶה כָּמוֹנִי

כָמוֹךָ כְּעַמִּי כְעַמֶּךָ כְּסוּסַי׃ כְּסוּסֶיךָ

Now Jehoram the son of Ahab became king over Israel at Samaria in the
eighteenth year of Jehoshaphat king of Judah, and reigned twelve years. He
did evil in the sight of Yahweh, though not like his father and his mother; for
he put away the [sacred] pillar of Baal which his father had made.
Nevertheless, he clung to the sins of Jeroboam the son of Nebat, which he
made Israel sin; he did not depart from them. Now Mesha king of Moab was
a sheep breeder, and used to pay the king of Israel 100,000 lambs and the
wool of 100,000 rams. But when Ahab died, the king of Moab rebelled against
the king of Israel. And King Jehoram went out of Samaria at that time and
mustered all Israel. Then he went and sent [word] to Jehoshaphat the king of
Judah, saying, "The king of Moab has rebelled against me. Will you go with
me to fight against Moab?" And he said, "I will go up; I am as you are, my
people as your people, my horses as your horses."

2. Took "way of the wilderness of Edom" — route
   southwards from Judah, around S. end of Dead Sea.
   2 Kings 3:8-20

8 וַיֹּאמֶר אֵי־זֶה הַדֶּרֶךְ נַעֲלֶה וַיֹּאמֶר דֶּרֶךְ מִדְבַּר אֱדוֹם

9 וַיֵּלֶךְ מֶלֶךְ יִשְׂרָאֵל וּמֶלֶךְ־יְהוּדָה וּמֶלֶךְ אֱדוֹם וַיָּסֹבּוּ דֶּרֶךְ שִׁבְעַת יָמִים

וְלֹא־הָיָה מַיִם לַמַּחֲנֶה וְלַבְּהֵמָה אֲשֶׁר בְּרַגְלֵיהֶם 10 וַיֹּאמֶר מֶלֶךְ יִשְׂרָאֵל

אֲהָהּ כִּי־קָרָא יְהוָה לִשְׁלֹשֶׁת הַמְּלָכִים הָאֵלֶּה לָתֵת אוֹתָם בְּיַד־מוֹאָב

11 וַיֹּאמֶר יְהוֹשָׁפָט הַאֵין פֹּה נָבִיא לַיהוָה וְנִדְרְשָׁה אֶת־יְהוָה מֵאוֹתוֹ

וַיַּעַן אֶחָד מֵעַבְדֵי מֶלֶךְ־יִשְׂרָאֵל וַיֹּאמֶר פֹּה אֱלִישָׁע בֶּן־שָׁפָט אֲשֶׁר־יָצַק

מַיִם עַל־יְדֵי אֵלִיָּהוּ 12 וַיֹּאמֶר יְהוֹשָׁפָט יֵשׁ אוֹתוֹ דְּבַר־יְהוָה וַיֵּרְדוּ אֵלָיו

מֶלֶךְ יִשְׂרָאֵל וִיהוֹשָׁפָט וּמֶלֶךְ אֱדוֹם 13 וַיֹּאמֶר אֱלִישָׁע אֶל־מֶלֶךְ יִשְׂרָאֵל מַה־לִּי

וָלָךְ לֵךְ אֶל־נְבִיאֵי אָבִיךָ וְאֶל־נְבִיאֵי אִמֶּךָ וַיֹּאמֶר לוֹ מֶלֶךְ יִשְׂרָאֵל אַל כִּי־קָרָא

יְהוָה לִשְׁלֹשֶׁת הַמְּלָכִים הָאֵלֶּה לָתֵת אוֹתָם בְּיַד־מוֹאָב 14 וַיֹּאמֶר אֱלִישָׁע

חַי־יְהוָה צְבָאוֹת אֲשֶׁר עָמַדְתִּי לְפָנָיו כִּי לוּלֵי פְּנֵי יְהוֹשָׁפָט מֶלֶךְ־יְהוּדָה

אֲנִי נֹשֵׂא אִם־אַבִּיט אֵלֶיךָ וְאִם־אֶרְאֶךָּ 15 וְעַתָּה קְחוּ־לִי מְנַגֵּן וְהָיָה כְּנַגֵּן הַמְנַגֵּן

וַתְּהִי עָלָיו יַד־יְהוָה 16 וַיֹּאמֶר כֹּה אָמַר יְהוָה עָשֹׂה הַנַּחַל הַזֶּה גֵּבִים גֵּבִים

17 כִּי־כֹה אָמַר יְהוָה לֹא־תִרְאוּ רוּחַ וְלֹא־תִרְאוּ גֶשֶׁם וְהַנַּחַל הַהוּא יִמָּלֵא

מַיִם וּשְׁתִיתֶם אַתֶּם וּמִקְנֵיכֶם וּבְהֶמְתְּכֶם 18 וְנָקַל זֹאת בְּעֵינֵי יְהוָה וְנָתַן

אֶת־מוֹאָב בְּיֶדְכֶם 19 וְהִכִּיתֶם כָּל־עִיר מִבְצָר וְכָל־עִיר מִבְחוֹר וְכָל־עֵץ

טוֹב תַּפִּילוּ וְכָל־מַעְיְנֵי־מַיִם תִּסְתֹּמוּ וְכֹל הַחֶלְקָה הַטּוֹבָה תַּכְאִבוּ בָּאֲבָנִים

20 וַיְהִי בַבֹּקֶר כַּעֲלוֹת הַמִּנְחָה וְהִנֵּה־מַיִם בָּאִים מִדֶּרֶךְ אֱדוֹם וַתִּמָּלֵא הָאָרֶץ

אֶת־הַמָּיִם

He said, "Which way shall we go up?" And he answered, "The way of the
wilderness of Edom." So the king of Israel went with the king of Judah and
the king of Edom; and they made a circuit of seven days' journey, and there
was no water for the army or for the cattle that followed them. Then the king
of Israel said, "Alas! For Yahweh has called these three kings to give them
into the hand of Moab." But Jehoshaphat said, "Is there not a prophet of

Yahweh here, that we may inquire of Yahweh by him?" And one of the king
of Israel's servants answered and said, "Elisha the son of Shaphat is here,
who used to pour water on the hands of Elijah." Jehoshaphat said, "The word
of Yahweh is with him." So the king of Israel and Jehoshaphat and the king of
Edom went down to him. Now Elisha said to the king of Israel, "What do I
have to do with you? Go to the prophets of your father and to the prophets of
your mother." And the king of Israel said to him, "No, for Yahweh has called
these three kings [together] to give them into the hand of Moab." Elisha said,
"As Yahweh of hosts lives, before whom I stand, were it not that I regard the
presence of Jehoshaphat the king of Judah, I would not look at you nor see
you. "But now bring me a minstrel." And it came about, when the minstrel
played, that the hand of Yahweh came upon him. He said, "Thus says
Yahweh, 'Make this valley full of trenches.' For thus says Yahweh, 'You shall
not see wind nor shall you see rain; yet that valley shall be filled with water,
so that you shall drink, both you and your cattle and your beasts.'" 'This is
but a slight thing in the sight of Yahweh; He will also give the Moabites into
your hand. 'Then you shall strike every fortified city and every choice city,
and fell every good tree and stop all springs of water, and mar every good
piece of land with stones.'" It happened in the morning about the time of
offering the sacrifice, that behold, water came by the way of Edom, and the
country was filled with water.

3. Invaded by way of Horonaim (in S. Moab; Jer. 48:3,5, 34; =
Ορωναιμα in Ant. XIII, 15, 1, Ὠρωναῖν in XIV 1, 4; 2 Ki 3:21?,

(31) . . . וחורננ.ישב.בה.ב'ת.[ד]וד [כ]א[שר]
(32) [הלתחם.בי . וי]אמר . לי . כמש . רד . הלתחם . בחורננ | וארד . [ואל]
(33) [תחם . בקר . ואחזה . ויש] בה . כמש . בימי . ועלתי . משמ . עש[ת]
(34)] . . . . עש[ת . צדק | ואנ]כ]
(35)] . . . . [

"And (as for) Hawronen, Beth David dwelt there [w]hi[le] / [he fought with
me and] Chemosh [s]aid to me: 'Go down, fight at Ḥawronen.' So I went
down [and I fo] / [ught at the city and I took it and] Chemosh [re]turned it in

my days. And I went up from there to make . . . . / . . . . to[do]
justice and I . . . . "

2 Kings 3:21-24

21 וְכָל־מוֹאָב שָׁמְעוּ כִּי־עָלוּ הַמְּלָכִים לְהִלָּחֶם בָּם וַיִּצָּעֲקוּ מִכֹּל חֹגֵר חֲגֹרָה
וָמַעְלָה וַיַּעַמְדוּ עַל־הַגְּבוּל 22 וַיַּשְׁכִּימוּ בַבֹּקֶר וְהַשֶּׁמֶשׁ זָרְחָה עַל־הַמָּיִם
23 וַיֹּאמְרוּ דָם זֶה הָחָרֵב נֶחֶרְבוּ הַמְּלָכִים וַיַּכּוּ אִישׁ אֶת־רֵעֵהוּ וְעַתָּה לַשָּׁלָל מוֹאָב 24 וַיָּבֹאוּ אֶל־מַחֲנֵה
יִשְׂרָאֵל וַיָּקֻמוּ יִשְׂרָאֵל וַיַּכּוּ אֶת־מוֹאָב וַיָּנֻסוּ מִפְּנֵיהֶם וַיָּבוֹ־[וֹ][וַיַּכּוּ־]בָהּ
וְהַכּוֹת אֶת־מוֹאָב 26 וַיַּרְא מֶלֶךְ מוֹאָב כִּי־חָזַק מִמֶּנּוּ הַמִּלְחָמָה וַיִּקַּח אוֹתוֹ
שְׁבַע־מֵאוֹת אִישׁ שֹׁלֵף חֶרֶב לְהַבְקִיעַ אֶל־מֶלֶךְ אֱדוֹם וְלֹא יָכֹלוּ
27 וַיִּקַּח אֶת־בְּנוֹ הַבְּכוֹר אֲשֶׁר־יִמְלֹךְ תַּחְתָּיו וַיַּעֲלֵהוּ עֹלָה עַל־הַחֹמָה
וַיְהִי קֶצֶף־גָּדוֹל עַל־יִשְׂרָאֵל וַיִּסְעוּ מֵעָלָיו וַיָּשֻׁבוּ לָאָרֶץ

3. Moab ravaged but Kir-haresheth was delivered.

וְהֶעָרִים יַהֲרֹסוּ וְכָל־חֶלְקָה טוֹבָה יַשְׁלִיכוּ אִישׁ־אַבְנוֹ וּמִלְאוּהָ וְכָל־מַעְיַן־מַיִם
25
וְכָל־עֵץ־טוֹב יַפִּילוּ עַד־הִשְׁאִיר אֲבָנֶיהָ בַּקִּיר חֲרָשֶׂת וַיָּסֹבּוּ הַקַּלָּעִים
יַסְתֹּמּוּ
בַּקִּיר חֲרָשֶׂת וַיָּסֹבּוּ הַקַּלָּעִים וַיַּכּוּהָ בַּקִּיר חֲרָשֶׂת וַיָּסֹבּוּ הַקַּלָּעִים וַיַּכּוּהָ

Thus they destroyed the cities; and each one threw a stone on every piece of
good land and filled it. So they stopped all the springs of water and felled all
the good trees, until in Kir-haresheth [only] they left its stones; however, the
slingers went about [it] and struck it.

Son of king of Edom offered up (according to Radak)

26 וַיַּרְא מֶלֶךְ מוֹאָב כִּי־חָזַק מִמֶּנּוּ הַמִּלְחָמָה וַיִּקַּח אוֹתוֹ שְׁבַע־מֵאוֹת אִישׁ שֹׁלֵף
חֶרֶב לְהַבְקִיעַ אֶל־מֶלֶךְ אֱדוֹם וְלֹא יָכֹלוּ 27 וַיִּקַּח אֶת־בְּנוֹ הַבְּכוֹר אֲשֶׁר־יִמְלֹךְ
תַּחְתָּיו וַיַּעֲלֵהוּ עֹלָה עַל־הַחֹמָה וַיְהִי קֶצֶף־גָּדוֹל עַל־יִשְׂרָאֵל
וַיִּסְעוּ מֵעָלָיו וַיָּשֻׁבוּ לָאָרֶץ

When the king of Moab saw that the battle was too fierce for him, he took with him 700 men who drew swords, to break through to the king of Edom; but they could not.

2Kings 3:27 Then he took his oldest son who was to reign in his place, and offered him as a burnt offering on the wall. And there came great wrath against Israel, and they departed from him and returned to their own land.

Comments by Rav David Kimḥi:

[כז] ויקח את בנו הבכור - פי' אדוני אבי ז"ל כי בן מלך אדום הראוי למלוך תחתיו היה ברשות מלך מואב ומפני זה בא עם שני המלכים כי חשב להוציא בעזרתם בנו מתחת יד מלך מואב וכשחשב מלך מואב להבקיע אל מלך אדום ולא יכול לקח בקצפו את בן מלך אדום והעלהו על החומה ושרפו לעיני אביו זהו ויעלהו עולה ששרפו כמו ששורפין העולה:
ויהי קצף גדול על ישראל - ממלך אדום כי חשב כי בעזרתם יוציא בנו מתחת יד מלך מואב וזהו שאמר הכתוב על שרפו את עצמות מלך אדום לשיד ורבי אחי ר' משה ז"ל פי' כי כאשר חשב להבקיע מלך מואב אל מלך אדום אז לקח בנו באותה המלחמה חטפו מהם והעלהו על החומה ושרפו לעיני אביו ויהי' קצף גדול על ישראל ממלך אדום שלא עזרהו להצילו מידם,

"So he took his firstborn son" — the interpretation of my father of blessed memory, that the son of the king of Edom who was qualified to reign in his stead was under the control of the king of Moab and for that reason he had come with the two kings because he thought to rescue, with their help, his son from the hand of the king of Moab and when the king of Moab thought to make a breakthrough against the king of Edom and was not able to do so, he took in his anger the son of the king of Edom and offered him up on the wall and burned him before the eyes of his father, that is "and he offered him up as an offering and burned him just as they burn the burnt offering.

"and there was great wrath on Israel" — from the king of Edom because he thought that with their help he would deliver his son from the hand of the king of Moab, and that is what is written "concerning his burning the bones of the king of Edom to lime" [Amos 2:1]. And Rabbi, my brother, Rav Moshe, of blessed memory, interpreted: that when the king of Moab thought to make a breakthrough against the king of Edom, then he took his son in the same fighting, he snatched him from them and offered him up on the wall and burned him within sight of his father "and there was great wrath on Israel" from the king of Edom because they did not help him to deliver him from their hand."

V.   DECLINE OF JUDAH

A. Jehoram of Judah, son of Jehoshaphat; cf. 2 Ki 8:16

  1. Co-regent 853 (when Jehoshaphat went to war in Ramoth-gilead), sole ruler 848
  2. Killed all his brothers 2 Chr. 21:2-4 <u>848 BCE as sole ruler</u>

  3. <u>Lost control</u>:

of EDOM 2 Ki. 8:20-22; <u>2 Chron. 21:8-10</u>

8 בְּיָמָיו פָּשַׁע אֱדוֹם מִתַּחַת יַד־יְהוּדָה וַיַּמְלִיכוּ עֲלֵיהֶם מֶלֶךְ

9 וַיַּעֲבֹר יְהוֹרָם עִם־שָׂרָיו וְכָל־הָרֶכֶב עִמּוֹ וַיְהִי קָם לַיְלָה וַיַּךְ אֶת־אֱדוֹם

הַסּוֹבֵב אֵלָיו וְאֵת שָׂרֵי הָרָכֶב 10 וַיִּפְשַׁע אֱדוֹם מִתַּחַת יַד־יְהוּדָה עַד הַיּוֹם הַזֶּה

אָז תִּפְשַׁע לִבְנָה בָּעֵת הַהִיא מִתַּחַת יָדוֹ

In his days Edom revolted against the rule of Judah and set up a king over themselves. Then Jehoram crossed over with his commanders and all his chariots with him. And he arose by night and struck down the Edomites who were surrounding him and the commanders of the chariots. So Edom revolted against Judah to this day.

of LIBNAH 2 Chr. 21:10-11 — because he built *bâmôt* in Hill country of Judah

אָז תִּפְשַׁע לִבְנָה בָּעֵת הַהִיא מִתַּחַת יָדוֹ כִּי עָזַב אֶת־יְהוָה אֱלֹהֵי אֲבֹתָיו

כִּי עָזַב אֶת־יְהוָה אֱלֹהֵי אֲבֹתָיו 11 גַּם־הוּא עָשָׂה־בָמוֹת

בְּהָרֵי יְהוּדָה וַיֶּזֶן אֶת־יֹשְׁבֵי יְרוּשָׁלַם וַיַּדַּח אֶת־יְהוּדָה

Then Libnah revolted at the same time against his rule, because he had forsaken Yahweh God of his fathers. Moreover, he made high places in the mountains of Judah, and caused the inhabitants of Jerusalem to play the harlot and led Judah astray.

4. Judah suffered invasion by <u>Philistines</u> and <u>Arabs</u>

2 Chron. 21:16-17

16 וַיָּעַר יְהוָה עַל־יְהוֹרָם אֵת רוּחַ הַפְּלִשְׁתִּים וְהָעַרְבִים אֲשֶׁר עַל־יַד כּוּשִׁים

17 וַיַּעֲלוּ בִיהוּדָה וַיִּבְקָעוּהָ וַיִּשְׁבּוּ אֵת כָּל־הָרְכוּשׁ הַנִּמְצָא לְבֵית־הַמֶּלֶךְ

וְגַם־בָּנָיו וְנָשָׁיו וְלֹא נִשְׁאַר־לוֹ בֵּן כִּי אִם־יְהוֹאָחָז קְטֹן בָּנָיו ׃

Then Yahweh stirred up against Jehoram the spirit of the **Philistines** and the **Arabs** who bordered the Cushites; and they came against Judah and invaded it, and carried away all the possessions found in the king's house together with his sons and his wives, so that no son was left to him except Jehoahaz, the youngest of his sons.

5. Died of stomach disease 2 Chr. 21:18-20

B. Ahaziah, son of Jehoram of Judah — 841 BCE Son of Athaliah
2 Ki 8:25-29; 2 Chr. 22:2-6

1. Went to war alongside <u>Joram of Israel at Ramoth-gilead</u>
2. Went to visit Joram at Jezreel -- <u>mortally wounded there.</u>

VI. SHALMENESER III

A. His tenth year, 849 B.C.E. — (Michel *WO* 1 (1947), 67 ff.;
ANET, 279b)

Conflict at Carchemish, mentions Hadad-Idri,
Assyrians claimed to have <u>defeated</u> them.

B. His eleventh year, 848 B.C.E. — (Bull Inscription, 90-96,
Luckenbill, *AR*, I, §653; *ANET*, 279b; Black Obelisk,
Face A (base), 87-89; *ANET*, 280a). (**Jehoshaphat's death**)

Conquered many towns in N. Syria, to Mt. Amanus,
against Hamath, Ashtamaku and 90 smaller towns;

faced Hadad-Iḏri and Irḫuleni plus "12 kings from the seacoast"; claims victory.

C. His fourteenth year, **845** B.C.E. (Bull Inscription (Bull B), Luckenbill *AR*, I, §§658-659; also Black Obelisk face A, Base, 91-93; Luckenbill *AR*, I, §571; *ANET*, 280a).

Crossed Euphrates to face Ḥazael and Irḫuleni and the 12 kings of the shore of the Upper and the Lower Sea.

D. 841 B.C.E.
  1. Defeated Haza'el at Mt. Senir
  2. Besieged Damascus, afterwards ravaged Hauran
  3. Marched to Baˤli-rāsi (Mt. Carmel) with sea on one side and land of Tyre on the other.— **probably received tribute from Jehu here**
  4. Continued on into Lebanon

VII. THE HOUSE OF JEHU

A. Jehu — 841-814/13 (n.a 28 yrs = 27 actual) 841 - 27 = 814

  1. Coup d'etat 2 Ki. 9 & 10 841 BCE —
    a. from Ramoth-gilead to Jezreel
    b. Ahaziah wounded at ascent of Gur

9:27 וַאֲחַזְיָה מֶלֶךְ־יְהוּדָה רָאָה וַיָּנָס דֶּרֶךְ בֵּית הַגָּן וַיִּרְדֹּף אַחֲרָיו יֵהוּא

וַיֹּאמֶר גַּם־אֹתוֹ הַכֻּהוּ אֶל־הַמֶּרְכָּבָה בְּמַעֲלֵה־גוּר אֲשֶׁר אֶת־יִבְלְעָם

וַיָּנָס מְגִדּוֹ וַיָּמָת שָׁם

When Ahaziah the king of Judah saw [this], he fled by the way of the garden house. And Jehu pursued him and said, "Shoot him too, in the chariot." [So they shot him] at the ascent of Gur, which is at Ibleam. But he fled to Megiddo and died there.

Cf.2 Chron.22:8-9

8 וַיְהִי כְּהִשָּׁפֵט יֵהוּא עִם־בֵּית אַחְאָב וַיִּמְצָא אֶת־שָׂרֵי יְהוּדָה וּבְנֵי אֲחֵי

אֲחַזְיָהוּ מְשָׁרְתִים לַאֲחַזְיָהוּ וַיַּהַרְגֵם 9 וַיְבַקֵּשׁ אֶת־אֲחַזְיָהוּ וַיִּלְכְּדֻהוּ וְהוּא

מִתְחַבֵּא בְשֹׁמְרוֹן וַיְבִאֻהוּ אֶל־יֵהוּא וַיְמִתֻהוּ וַיִּקְבְּרֻהוּ כִּי אָמְרוּ בֶּן־יְהוֹשָׁפָט

הוּא אֲשֶׁר־דָּרַשׁ אֶת־יְהוָה בְּכָל־לְבָבוֹ וְאֵין לְבֵית אֲחַזְיָהוּ לַעְצֹר כֹּחַ לְמַמְלָכָה

It came about when Jehu was executing judgment on the house of Ahab, he
found the princes of Judah and the sons of Ahaziah's brothers ministering to
Ahaziah, and slew them. He also sought Ahaziah, and they caught him while
he was hiding in Samaria; they brought him to Jehu, put him to death and
buried him. For they said, "He is the son of Jehoshaphat, who sought
Yahweh with all his heart." So there was no one of the house of Ahaziah to
retain the power of the kingdom.

Caught at ascent of Gur and mortally wounded; died at **Megiddo**.

c. Slew the priests of Baal at the "House of Baal"
2 Ki. 10:21

2. Losses to Aram-Damascus — bet. 852 and 814/13 BCE
2 Ki. 10:32-33 — In league with Mesha!!!
Hazael in power at least since 841 B.C.E. with Mesha!

32 בַּיָּמִים הָהֵם הֵחֵל יְהוָה לְקַצּוֹת בְּיִשְׂרָאֵל וַיַּכֵּם חֲזָאֵל בְּכָל־גְּבוּל יִשְׂרָאֵל

33 מִן־הַיַּרְדֵּן מִזְרַח הַשֶּׁמֶשׁ אֵת כָּל־אֶרֶץ הַגִּלְעָד הַגָּדִי וְהָרֶאוּבֵנִי וְהַמְנַשִּׁי

מֵעֲרֹעֵר אֲשֶׁר עַל־נַחַל אַרְנֹן וְהַגִּלְעָד וְהַבָּשָׁן

In those days Yahweh began to cut off [portions] from Israel; and Hazael
defeated them throughout the territory of Israel: from the Jordan eastward,
all the land of Gilead, the Gadites and the Reubenites and the Manassites,
from Aroer, which is by the valley of the Arnon, even Gilead and Bashan.

THE TEL DAN INSCRIPTION:

1. [. . .]MR ᶜ[. . .]and made (a treaty) ? [. . .]

2. [. . .]-el my father, went up [against him when] he was fighting in A[bel?

3. and my father passed away; he went to [his ancestors.] Now the king of Israel entered

4. formerly into the land of my father; [but] Hadad made me myself king,

5. and Hadad went before me; [and] I departed from [the] seven [. . .]

6. of my kingdom; and I slew seve[nty ki]ngs, who harnessed thou[sands of cha]

7. riots and thousands of horsemen. [And then was killed Jo]ram, son of [Ahab,]

8. king of Israel, and [was] killed [Ahazi]yahu, son of [Joram, kin]

9. g of the house of David; and I set [their towns to ruins?? . . . the ci]

10. ties of their land into de[solation ? . . .]

11. [. . .] other and to over[turn . . . and Jehu ru]

12. led over Is[rael . . .]

13. siege upon [. . .]

   B. Jehoahaz, son of Jehu — 814/13-798 BCE   2 Ki. 13:1-9
      (n.a. 23rd of Joash, 17 = 16 actual)
      1. Further losses to Hazael and
         also to his son, Ben-hadad II (after 798 B.C.E.)

2 Ki. 13:3-5.

3 וַיִּחַר־אַף יְהוָה בְּיִשְׂרָאֵל וַיִּתְּנֵם בְּיַד חֲזָאֵל מֶלֶךְ־אֲרָם וּבְיַד בֶּן־הֲדַד

בֶּן־חֲזָאֵל כָּל־הַיָּמִים 4 וַיְחַל יְהוֹאָחָז אֶת־פְּנֵי יְהוָה וַיִּשְׁמַע אֵלָיו יְהוָה

כִּי רָאָה אֶת־לַחַץ יִשְׂרָאֵל כִּי־לָחַץ אֹתָם מֶלֶךְ אֲרָם 5 וַיִּתֵּן יְהוָה לְיִשְׂרָאֵל

מוֹשִׁיעַ וַיֵּצְאוּ מִתַּחַת יַד־אֲרָם וַיֵּשְׁבוּ בְנֵי־יִשְׂרָאֵל בְּאָהֳלֵיהֶם כִּתְמוֹל שִׁלְשׁוֹם

So the anger of Yahweh was kindled against Israel, and He gave them continually into the hand of Hazael king of Aram, and into the hand of Ben-hadad the son of Hazael. Then Jehoahaz entreated the favor of Yahweh, and Yahweh listened to him; for He saw the oppression of Israel, how the king of Aram oppressed them. So Yahweh gave Israel a deliverer, so that they escaped from under the hand of the Arameans; and the sons of Israel lived in their tents as formerly.

2. The deliverer in vv. 4-6 was Jehoash, the next king or Adad-nirari III

LESSON 17

DIVIDED MONARCHY, 9ᵀᴴ–8ᵀᴴ CENTURIES BCE

I.   **JUDAH**

    A. Athaliah 841-835 BCE 2 Ki. 11:1-20; 2 Chr. 22:10-12; 23:1-21

        Chron. stresses participation of the Levites in the coup

    B. Joash 835-796 BCE — 2 Ki. 12:1-22; 2 Chr. 24:1-27 — 7th of

        Jehu, n.a. reckoning = <u>6th actual yr; 40 yrs n.a. = 39</u>

        <u>actual</u>

        1. Ordered repairs to the temple

        2. His 23rd yr. repairs not yet done 814/813

        3. After death of Jehoiada, <u>probably c. 800-799 BCE</u>

            permitted the princes of Judah to return to worship

            of Asherim and idols: 2 Chron. 24:17-24

וְאַחֲרֵי מוֹת יְהוֹיָדָע בָּאוּ שָׂרֵי יְהוּדָה וַיִּשְׁתַּחֲווּ לַמֶּלֶךְ אָז שָׁמַע הַמֶּלֶךְ אֲלֵיהֶם:
וַיַּעַזְבוּ אֶת־בֵּית יְהוָה אֱלֹהֵי אֲבוֹתֵיהֶם וַיַּעַבְדוּ אֶת־הָאֲשֵׁרִים וְאֶת־הָעֲצַבִּים
וַיְהִי־קֶצֶף עַל־יְהוּדָה וִירוּשָׁלִַם בְּאַשְׁמָתָם זֹאת:

But after the death of Jehoiada the **officials** of Judah came and bowed down
to the king, and the king listened to them. They abandoned the house of
Yahweh, the God of their fathers, and served the Asherim and the idols; so
wrath came upon Judah and Jerusalem for this their guilt.

    As a result, prophets denounced him and the HP, (2 Chr. 24:20)

    Zechariah, also denounced him, so he had him slain (2 Chr. 24:21).

        3. The next year, **Hazael** came against **Gath** (798 BCE;

            before Jehoahaz in Israel died)

            2 Ki. 12:18-20 ‖ 2 Chr. 24:23-24

אָז יַעֲלֶה חֲזָאֵל מֶלֶךְ אֲרָם וַיִּלָּחֶם עַל־גַּת וַיִּלְכְּדָהּ וַיָּשֶׂם חֲזָאֵל פָּנָיו
לַעֲלוֹת עַל־יְרוּשָׁלִָם: וַיִּקַּח יְהוֹאָשׁ מֶלֶךְ־יְהוּדָה אֵת כָּל־הַקֳּדָשִׁים
אֲשֶׁר־הִקְדִּישׁוּ יְהוֹשָׁפָט וִיהוֹרָם וַאֲחַזְיָהוּ אֲבֹתָיו מַלְכֵי יְהוּדָה
וְאֶת־קֳדָשָׁיו וְאֵת כָּל־הַזָּהָב הַנִּמְצָא בְּאֹצְרוֹת בֵּית־יְהוָה וּבֵית הַמֶּלֶךְ
וַיִּשְׁלַח לַחֲזָאֵל מֶלֶךְ אֲרָם וַיַּעַל מֵעַל יְרוּשָׁלָם:

Then Hazael king of Aram went up and fought against **Gath** and captured it,
and Hazael set his face to go up to **Jerusalem**. Jehoash king of Judah took all
the sacred things that Jehoshaphat and Jehoram and Ahaziah, his fathers,
kings of Judah, had dedicated, and his own sacred things and all the gold
that was found among the treasuries of the house of Yahweh and of the

king's house, and sent [them] to Hazael king of Aram. Then he went away from Jerusalem.

2 Chr. 24:23-24

וַיְהִי ׀ לִתְקוּפַת הַשָּׁנָה עָלָה עָלָיו חֵיל אֲרָם וַיָּבֹאוּ אֶל־יְהוּדָה וִירוּשָׁלַ͏ִם

וַיַּשְׁחִיתוּ אֶת־כָּל־שָׂרֵי הָעָם מֵעָם וְכָל־שְׁלָלָם שִׁלְּחוּ לְמֶלֶךְ דַּרְמָשֶׂק׃

כִּי בְמִצְעַר אֲנָשִׁים בָּאוּ ׀ חֵיל אֲרָם וַיהוָה נָתַן בְּיָדָם חַיִל ׀ לָרֹב מְאֹד

כִּי עָזְבוּ אֶת־יְהוָה אֱלֹהֵי אֲבוֹתֵיהֶם וְאֶת־יוֹאָשׁ עָשׂוּ שְׁפָטִים׃

Now it happened at the turn of the year that the army of the **Arameans** came up against him; and they came to **Judah** and **Jerusalem**, destroyed all the officials of the people from among the people, and sent all their spoil to the king of Damascus. Indeed the army of the Arameans came with a small number of men; yet Yahweh delivered a very great army into their hands, because they had forsaken Yahweh, the God of their fathers. <u>Thus they executed judgment on Joash.</u>

> Temple treasury and royal treasury emptied to pay Hazael not to conquer Jerusalem.

4. As a result, Joash was forced to pay ransom; his servants conspired against him and slew him on his sick bed — 796 BCE

2 Chron. 24:25-26

25 וּבְלֶכְתָּם מִמֶּנּוּ כִּי־עָזְבוּ אֹתוֹ בְּמַחֲלֻיִים

[בְּ][מַחֲלוּיִם] רַבִּים הִתְקַשְּׁרוּ עָלָיו עֲבָדָיו בִּדְמֵי בְּנֵי

יְהוֹיָדָע הַכֹּהֵן וַיַּהַרְגֻהוּ עַל־מִטָּתוֹ וַיָּמֹת וַיִּקְבְּרֻהוּ בְּעִיר

דָּוִיד וְלֹא קְבָרֻהוּ בְּקִבְרוֹת הַמְּלָכִים

26 וְאֵלֶּה הַמִּתְקַשְּׁרִים עָלָיו זָבָד בֶּן־שִׁמְעָת

הָעַמּוֹנִית וִיהוֹזָבָד בֶּן־שִׁמְרִית הַמּוֹאָבִית

25 When they had departed from him (for they left him very sick), his own servants conspired against him because of the blood of the son of Jehoiada the priest, and murdered him on his bed. So he died, and they buried him in the city of David, but they did not bury him in the tombs of the kings.

26 Now these are those who conspired against him: Zabad the son of Shimeath the Ammonitess, and Jehozabad the son of Shimrith the Moabitess.

2 Kings 12:20-22 (Eng. 19-21)

וְיֶתֶר דִּבְרֵי יוֹאָשׁ וְכָל־אֲשֶׁר עָשָׂה הֲלוֹא־הֵם כְּתוּבִים עַל־סֵפֶר דִּבְרֵי

הַיָּמִים לְמַלְכֵי יְהוּדָה׃ וַיָּקֻמוּ עֲבָדָיו וַיִּקְשְׁרוּ־קָשֶׁר וַיַּכּוּ אֶת־יוֹאָשׁ
בֵּית מִלּוֹא הַיּוֹרֵד סִלָּא׃ וְיוֹזָבָד בֶּן־שִׁמְעָת וִיהוֹזָבָד בֶּן־שֹׁמֵר | עֲבָדָיו
הִכֻּהוּ וַיָּמֹת וַיִּקְבְּרוּ אֹתוֹ עִם־אֲבֹתָיו בְּעִיר דָּוִד וַיִּמְלֹךְ אֲמַצְיָה בְנוֹ
תַּחְתָּיו׃

Now the rest of the acts of Joash and all that he did, are they not written in
the Book of the Chronicles of the Kings of Judah? His servants arose and
made a conspiracy and struck down Joash at the house of Millo as one goes
down to Silla. For Jozacar the son of Shimeath and Jehozabad the son of
Shomer, his servants, struck [him] and he died; and they buried him with his
fathers in the city of David, and **Amaziah** his son became king in his place.

II.   Adad-Nirari III 811-783 BCE

Campaigns to the west (by Eponym chronicle)
805 — against Arpad
804 — against Ḥazazi
803 — against Ba'ali — Most likely Baʿli-Ṣapāni,
N. Syrian coast.
802 — "to the Sea" — most likely Persian Gulf area

**(early 798 — Hazael campaigned against Gath &
Judah)**

796 — against **Manṣuate** in central Syria
according to Eponym List
*** Jehoash of Israel paid tribute during this
campaign.

III.   NORTHERN KINGDOM

A. **Jehoash**, son of Jehoahaz — 798-782/81 — 2 Ki. 13:10-25
(37 of Joash; accession yr. system, 16 = 16 actual yrs;
37 of Joash 835 - 37 = 798 BCE)
1. Pays tribute to Adad-nirari III in **796** BCE (see below)
2. **Treaty with Amaziah** (796 or a bit later)
2 Ki. 14:9 ‖ 2 Chr. 25:13 in a retrospective allusion:

וַיִּשְׁלַח יְהוֹאָשׁ מֶלֶךְ־יִשְׂרָאֵל אֶל־אֲמַצְיָהוּ מֶלֶךְ־יְהוּדָה לֵאמֹר

הַחוֹחַ אֲשֶׁר בַּלְּבָנוֹן שָׁלַח אֶל־הָאֶרֶז אֲשֶׁר בַּלְּבָנוֹן לֵאמֹר

תְּנָה־אֶת־בִּתְּךָ לִבְנִי לְאִשָּׁה וַתַּעֲבֹר חַיַּת הַשָּׂדֶה אֲשֶׁר בַּלְּבָנוֹן

וַתִּרְמֹס אֶת־הַחוֹחַ:

Jehoash king of Israel sent to **Amaziah** king of Judah, saying, "The thorn
bush which was in Lebanon sent to the cedar which was in Lebanon, saying,
'Give your daughter to my son in marriage.' But there passed by a wild beast
that was in Lebanon, and trampled the thorn bush."

Jehoash sent troops to help Amaziah invade Edom but
they were sent back. They ravaged towns in Judah:
2 Chron. 25:13

וּבְנֵי הַגְּדוּד אֲשֶׁר הֵשִׁיב אֲמַצְיָהוּ מִלֶּכֶת עִמּוֹ לַמִּלְחָמָה וַיִּפְשְׁטוּ בְּעָרֵי

יְהוּדָה וְעַד־בֵּית חוֹרוֹן וַיַּכּוּ מֵהֶם שְׁלֹשֶׁת אֲלָפִים וַיָּבֹזּוּ בִּזָּה רַבָּה:

But as for the troops whom Amaziah sent back from going with him to battle,
they raided the cities of Judah from **Samaria** and from around **Beth-horon**,
and struck down 3,000 of them and plundered much spoil.

Towns of Judah taken **from** Samaria = עָרֵי יְהוּדָה מִשֹּׁמְרוֹן

"and **from around** Beth-horon" = וְעַד־בֵּית חוֹרוֹן; i.e. from
those towns on the border which had formerly belonged
to Samaria.

   3. **Jehoash defeats Damascus three times** 2 Ki. 13:19 —
     between 796 and 793; because Damascus had been
     weakened by Adad-nirari's attack in 796 BCE
   4. **Defeats Amaziah at Beth-shemesh** — 793 BCE
****   2 Ki. 14:11-14 ‖ 2 Chr. 25:21-24 — must have
     made Jeroboam co-regent on eve of this battle.

  B. Jeraboam II — 41 yrs, 40 actual due to co-regency;
    2 Ki. 14:23-29   793-753
   1. Co-regent 793/2 during war with Amaziah
    2 Ki 14:8-14 ‖ 2 Chr. 25:17-24
   2. Independent 782/1 to 753 (15 of Amaziah,
    796 - 15 = 781)

3. Expanded the kingdom (based on Jehoash's 3 victories
over Aram 2 Ki. 13:19): 2 Ki. 14:25, 28

25 הוּא הֵשִׁיב אֶת־גְּבוּל יִשְׂרָאֵל מִלְּבוֹא חֲמָת עַד־יָם הָעֲרָבָה כִּדְבַר יְהוָה

אֱלֹהֵי יִשְׂרָאֵל אֲשֶׁר דִּבֶּר בְּיַד־עַבְדּוֹ יוֹנָה בֶן־אֲמִתַּי הַנָּבִיא

אֲשֶׁר מִגַּת הַחֵפֶר׃ ...

28 וְיֶתֶר דִּבְרֵי יָרָבְעָם וְכָל־אֲשֶׁר עָשָׂה וּגְבוּרָתוֹ אֲשֶׁר־נִלְחָם וַאֲשֶׁר הֵשִׁיב

אֶת־דַּמֶּשֶׂק וְאֶת־חֲמָת לִיהוּדָה בְּיִשְׂרָאֵל הֲלֹא־הֵם כְּתוּבִים עַל־סֵפֶר

דִּבְרֵי הַיָּמִים לְמַלְכֵי יִשְׂרָאֵל׃

He restored the border of Israel from **Lebo Hamath** as far as the **Sea of the
Arabah**, according to the word of Yahweh, the God of Israel, which He spoke
through His servant <u>Jonah the son of Amittai</u>, the prophet, who was of **Gath-
hepher**. ...

Now the rest of the acts of Jeroboam and all that he did and his might, how
he fought and how he recovered for Israel, **Damascus and Hamath**, to (its
alliance with) Judah, are they not written in the Book of the Chronicles of the
Kings of Israel?

1 Chr. 5:17 — Census in Transjordan

כֻּלָּם הִתְיַחְשׂוּ בִּימֵי יוֹתָם מֶלֶךְ־יְהוּדָה וּבִימֵי יָרָבְעָם מֶלֶךְ־יִשְׂרָאֵל׃

All of these were registered in the days of **Jotham king of Judah** and in the
days of **Jeroboam king of Israel**.

4. <u>Political relationships</u> — **Amos chs. 1-2** — denounces
neighboring states:

<u>Damascus</u> — for invading Gilead **Amos 1:3-5**

3 כֹּה אָמַר יְהוָה עַל־שְׁלֹשָׁה פִּשְׁעֵי דַמֶּשֶׂק וְעַל־אַרְבָּעָה

לֹא אֲשִׁיבֶנּוּ עַל־דּוּשָׁם בַּחֲרֻצוֹת הַבַּרְזֶל אֶת־הַגִּלְעָד׃

4 וְשִׁלַּחְתִּי אֵשׁ בְּבֵית חֲזָאֵל וְאָכְלָה אַרְמְנוֹת בֶּן־הֲדָד׃

5 וְשָׁבַרְתִּי בְּרִיחַ דַּמֶּשֶׂק וְהִכְרַתִּי יוֹשֵׁב מִבִּקְעַת־אָוֶן

וְתוֹמֵךְ שֵׁבֶט מִבֵּית עֶדֶן וְגָלוּ עַם־אֲרָם קִירָה אָמַר יְהוָה׃

Thus says Yahweh, "For three transgressions of **Damascus** and for four I will
not revoke its [punishment], Because they threshed **Gilead** with sledges of
sharp iron. "So I will send fire upon the **house of Hazael** And it will consume

the citadels of **Ben-hadad**. "I will also break the [gate] bar of **Damascus**, And cut off the inhabitant from the **valley of Aven**, And him who holds the scepter, from **Beth-eden**; So the people of **Aram** will go exiled to **Kir**," Says Yahweh.

<u>Gaza</u> — exiling people to Edom **Amos 1:6-8**

6 כֹּה אָמַר יְהוָה עַל־שְׁלֹשָׁה פִּשְׁעֵי עַזָּה

וְעַל־אַרְבָּעָה לֹא אֲשִׁיבֶנּוּ עַל־הַגְלוֹתָם

גָּלוּת שְׁלֵמָה לְהַסְגִּיר לֶאֱדוֹם:

7 וְשִׁלַּחְתִּי אֵשׁ בְּחוֹמַת עַזָּה וְאָכְלָה אַרְמְנֹתֶיהָ:

8 וְהִכְרַתִּי יוֹשֵׁב מֵאַשְׁדּוֹד וְתוֹמֵךְ שֵׁבֶט מֵאַשְׁקְלוֹן

וַהֲשִׁיבוֹתִי יָדִי עַל־עֶקְרוֹן וְאָבְדוּ שְׁאֵרִית פְּלִשְׁתִּים

אָמַר אֲדֹנָי יְהוִה:

Thus says Yahweh, "For three transgressions of **Gaza** and for four I will not revoke its [punishment], Because they deported an entire population to deliver [it] up to **Edom**.

"So I will send fire upon the wall of **Gaza** And it will consume her citadels.

"I will also cut off the inhabitant from **Ashdod**, And him who holds the scepter, from **Ashkelon**; I will even unleash My power upon **Ekron**, And the remnant of the Philistines will perish," Says my Lord Yahweh.

<u>Tyre</u> — gave exiles to Edom, broke treaty **Amos 1:9-10**

9 כֹּה אָמַר יְהוָה עַל־שְׁלֹשָׁה פִּשְׁעֵי־צֹר וְעַל־אַרְבָּעָה לֹא אֲשִׁיבֶנּוּ

עַל־הַסְגִּירָם גָּלוּת שְׁלֵמָה לֶאֱדוֹם וְלֹא זָכְרוּ בְּרִית אַחִים:

10 וְשִׁלַּחְתִּי אֵשׁ בְּחוֹמַת צֹר וְאָכְלָה אַרְמְנֹתֶיהָ:

Thus says Yahweh, "For three transgressions of **Tyre** and for four I will not revoke its [punishment], Because <u>they delivered up an entire population to Edom</u> And did not remember [the] covenant of brotherhood.

"So I will send fire upon the wall of **Tyre** And it will consume her citadels."

<u>Edom</u> — Attacked their brothers **Amos 1:11-12**

11 כֹּה אָמַר יְהוָה עַל־שְׁלֹשָׁה פִּשְׁעֵי אֱדוֹם וְעַל־אַרְבָּעָה לֹא אֲשִׁיבֶנּוּ

עַל־רָדְפוֹ בַחֶרֶב אָחִיו וְשִׁחֵת רַחֲמָיו וַיִּטְרֹף לָעַד אַפּוֹ וְעֶבְרָתוֹ

שְׁמָרָה נֶצַח:

12 וְשִׁלַּחְתִּי אֵשׁ בְּתֵימָן וְאָכְלָה אַרְמְנוֹת בָּצְרָה:

Thus says Yahweh, ""For three transgressions of **Edom** and for four I will not revoke its [punishment], Because he pursued his brother with the sword, while he stifled his compassion; and his anger also tore continually; and as for his fury, he kept it forever. So I will send fire upon **Teman** And it will consume the citadels of **Bozrah**."

Ammonites — ripping up women with child in
Gilead to enlarge their borders **Amos 1:13-15**

13 כֹּה אָמַר יְהוָה עַל־שְׁלֹשָׁה פִּשְׁעֵי בְנֵי־עַמּוֹן וְעַל־אַרְבָּעָה לֹא אֲשִׁיבֶנּוּ

עַל־בִּקְעָם הָרוֹת הַגִּלְעָד לְמַעַן הַרְחִיב אֶת־גְּבוּלָם:

14 וְהִצַּתִּי אֵשׁ בְּחוֹמַת רַבָּה וְאָכְלָה אַרְמְנוֹתֶיהָ בִּתְרוּעָה בְּיוֹם מִלְחָמָה

בְּסַעַר בְּיוֹם סוּפָה:

15 וְהָלַךְ מַלְכָּם בַּגּוֹלָה הוּא וְשָׂרָיו יַחְדָּו אָמַר יְהוָה:

Thus says Yahweh, "For three transgressions of the sons of **Ammon** and for four I will not revoke its [punishment], because they ripped open the pregnant women of **Gilead** in order to enlarge their borders. So I will kindle a fire on the wall of **Rabbah** and it will consume her citadels; amid war cries on the day of battle, and a storm on the day of tempest, their king will go into exile, he and his princes together," says Yahweh.

Moabites — burned bones of king of Edom
Amos 2:1-3

1 כֹּה אָמַר יְהוָה עַל־שְׁלֹשָׁה פִּשְׁעֵי מוֹאָב וְעַל־אַרְבָּעָה לֹא אֲשִׁיבֶנּוּ

עַל־שָׂרְפוֹ עַצְמוֹת מֶלֶךְ־אֱדוֹם לַשִּׂיד:

2 וְשִׁלַּחְתִּי־אֵשׁ בְּמוֹאָב וְאָכְלָה אַרְמְנוֹת הַקְּרִיּוֹת וּמֵת בְּשָׁאוֹן מוֹאָב

בִּתְרוּעָה בְּקוֹל שׁוֹפָר:

3 וְהִכְרַתִּי שׁוֹפֵט מִקִּרְבָּהּ וְכָל־שָׂרֶיהָ אֶהֱרוֹג עִמּוֹ אָמַר יְהוָה:

Thus says Yahweh, "For three transgressions of Moab and for four I will not revoke its [punishment], Because he burned the bones of the king of Edom to lime. So I will send fire upon **Moab** and it will consume the citadels of **Kerioth**; and **Moab** will die amid tumult, with war cries and the sound of a trumpet and I will also cut off the ruler from her midst and slay all her princes with him," says Yahweh.

JUDAH — rejected the Law **Amos 2:4-5**

4 כֹּה אָמַר יְהוָה עַל־שְׁלֹשָׁה פִּשְׁעֵי יְהוּדָה וְעַל־אַרְבָּעָה לֹא אֲשִׁיבֶנּוּ

עַל־מָאֳסָם אֶת־תּוֹרַת יְהוָה וְחֻקָּיו לֹא שָׁמָרוּ וַיַּתְעוּם כִּזְבֵיהֶם אֲשֶׁר־

הָלְכוּ אֲבוֹתָם אַחֲרֵיהֶם:

5 וְשִׁלַּחְתִּי אֵשׁ בִּיהוּדָה וְאָכְלָה

אַרְמְנוֹת יְרוּשָׁלָם:

Thus says Yahweh, "For three transgressions of **Judah** and for four I will not revoke its [punishment], because they <u>rejected the law of Yahweh</u> and have not kept His statutes; their lies also have led them astray, those after which their fathers walked. So I will send fire upon **Judah** and it will consume the citadels of **Jerusalem**."

<u>ISRAEL</u> — social injustice Amos 2:6-16

6 כֹּה אָמַר יְהוָה עַל־שְׁלֹשָׁה פִּשְׁעֵי יִשְׂרָאֵל וְעַל־אַרְבָּעָה לֹא אֲשִׁיבֶנּוּ

עַל־מִכְרָם בַּכֶּסֶף צַדִּיק וְאֶבְיוֹן בַּעֲבוּר נַעֲלָיִם:

7 הַשֹּׁאֲפִים עַל־עֲפַר־אֶרֶץ בְּרֹאשׁ דַּלִּים וְדֶרֶךְ עֲנָוִים יַטּוּ

וְאִישׁ וְאָבִיו יֵלְכוּ אֶל־הַנַּעֲרָה לְמַעַן חַלֵּל אֶת־שֵׁם קָדְשִׁי:

8 וְעַל־בְּגָדִים חֲבֻלִים יַטּוּ אֵצֶל כָּל־מִזְבֵּחַ וְיֵין עֲנוּשִׁים

יִשְׁתּוּ בֵּית אֱלֹהֵיהֶם:

9 וְאָנֹכִי הִשְׁמַדְתִּי אֶת־הָאֱמֹרִי מִפְּנֵיהֶם אֲשֶׁר כְּגֹבַהּ אֲרָזִים גָּבְהוֹ

וְחָסֹן הוּא כָּאַלּוֹנִים וָאַשְׁמִיד פִּרְיוֹ מִמַּעַל וְשָׁרָשָׁיו מִתָּחַת:

10 וְאָנֹכִי הֶעֱלֵיתִי אֶתְכֶם מֵאֶרֶץ מִצְרָיִם וָאוֹלֵךְ אֶתְכֶם

בַּמִּדְבָּר אַרְבָּעִים שָׁנָה לָרֶשֶׁת אֶת־אֶרֶץ הָאֱמֹרִי:

11 וָאָקִים מִבְּנֵיכֶם לִנְבִיאִים וּמִבַּחוּרֵיכֶם לִנְזִרִים הַאַף אֵין־זֹאת

בְּנֵי יִשְׂרָאֵל נְאֻם־יְהוָה:

12 וַתַּשְׁקוּ אֶת־הַנְּזִרִים יָיִן וְעַל־הַנְּבִיאִים צִוִּיתֶם לֵאמֹר לֹא תִּנָּבְאוּ:

13 הִנֵּה אָנֹכִי מֵעִיק תַּחְתֵּיכֶם כַּאֲשֶׁר תָּעִיק הָעֲגָלָה הַמְלֵאָה לָהּ עָמִיר:

14 וְאָבַד מָנוֹס מִקָּל וְחָזָק לֹא־יְאַמֵּץ כֹּחוֹ וְגִבּוֹר לֹא־יְמַלֵּט נַפְשׁוֹ:

15 וְתֹפֵשׂ הַקֶּשֶׁת לֹא יַעֲמֹד וְקַל בְּרַגְלָיו לֹא יְמַלֵּט וְרֹכֵב הַסּוּס

לֹא יְמַלֵּט נַפְשׁוֹ:

16 וְאַמִּיץ לִבּוֹ בַּגִּבּוֹרִים עָרוֹם יָנוּס בַּיּוֹם־הַהוּא נְאֻם־יְהוָה:

Thus says Yahweh, "For three transgressions of **Israel** and for four I will not revoke its [punishment], Because they <u>sell the righteous for money</u> and the needy for a pair of sandals. These who pant after the dust of the earth on the head of the helpless, also turn aside the way of the humble; and <u>a man and his father resort to the same girl</u> in order to profane My holy name. <u>On garments taken as pledges</u> they stretch out beside every altar, and in the house of their God <u>they drink the wine of those who have been fined</u>.

Yet it was I who destroyed the Amorite before them, Though his height [was] like the height of cedars And he was strong as the oaks; I even destroyed **his fruit above and his root below**. It was I who brought you up from the land of Egypt, And I led you in the wilderness forty years that you might take possession of the land of the Amorite. Then I raised up some of your sons to be prophets and some of your young men to be Nazirites. Is this not so, O sons of Israel?" declares Yahwweh. "But <u>you made the Nazirites drink wine</u>, and you commanded the prophets saying, '<u>You shall not prophesy</u>!' Behold, I am weighted down beneath you as a wagon is weighted down when filled with sheaves. Flight will perish from the swift, And the stalwart will not strengthen his power, nor the mighty man save his life. He who grasps the bow will not stand; the swift of foot will not escape, nor will he who rides the horse save his life. <u>Even the bravest among the warriors will flee naked in that day</u>," declares Yahweh.

5. **Samaria Ostraca** — some 100 sherds with 63 legible
inscriptions found by Reisner in 1910;

> two groups according to the formulae; but both
> groups mixed up together in find spots
> a. <u>Dates</u> — yrs. 9 & 10; yr. 10 + 5 hieratic
> b. <u>Shipments</u>: יין ישן "aged wine" or שמן רחצ
> "purified oil"
> c. <u>Recipients</u> from estates in towns in hills of
> Samaria;yr. 15 group indicates the sender,
> superintendent of the estate, <u>list the</u>
> <u>districts of the towns</u>:

THE MANASSEH TERRITORY

THE GENEALOGY OF MANASSAH

Num. 26:28-34; 27:1-4 (5-11); 36:10-12 (cf. 1-8); Josh. 17:1-6; 1 Chron. 7:14-19!!

Manasseh
|
Machir
|
Gilead
|

<u>Abiezer</u>	<u>Helek</u>	<u>(A)sriel</u>	<u>Shechem</u>	[Hepher]	<u>Shemida^c</u>
		|			
Twl	*Hazeroth*	*Yashub*	|	*Sepher*	
El-mattan	*Baal-maon*	*^cAṣereth*		Zelophehad	

|
_____
| | | | |
Mahlah   <u>Noah</u>   <u>Hoglah</u>   Milcah   [Tirzah]
Yaṣith

<u>Double Underline</u>: Clans appearing on Samaria Ostraca
Italics: Reconstructed place names appearing on Samaria Ostraca

Year 15 of Jehoash — 783 BCE   Years 9 & 10 of Jeroboam II 784 & 783

IV.   JUDAH (Cont.)

A. Amaziah 796-767 BCE — 2nd yr of Joash (Isr.), 29 access.

yrs; <u>captive</u> in <u>Samaria</u> 792-782/1 BCE

2 KI. 14:1-14, 17-21 ‖ 2 Chr. 25:1-28

1. Alliance with Jehoash of Israel 2 Ki. 14:9; 2 Chr. 25:18

2. Conquered Edom 2 Ki. 14:7; <u>2 Chr. 25:5-13</u> **793** BCE

3. Challenged Jehoash 2 Ki. 14:8-14 ‖ 2 Chr. 17-24
   792 BCE

4. <u>Taken</u> <u>captive</u> 2 Ki 14:13 ‖ 2 Chr. 25:23
   792 until death of Jehoash **782/781** BCE;
   cf. 2 Ki. 14:17 ‖ 2 Chr. 25:25

5. Lived until **767** BCE.; was "retired" in Jerusalem until his
   assassination at Lachish (2 Ki. 14:17, 19-21; 2 Chr. 25:25,
   27-28; 26:1)

2 Kings 14:17-22

17 וַיְחִ֨י אֲמַצְיָ֤הוּ בֶן־יוֹאָשׁ֙ מֶ֣לֶךְ יְהוּדָ֔ה אַחֲרֵ֣י מ֗וֹת יְהוֹאָ֥שׁ בֶּן־יְהֽוֹאָחָ֖ז
מֶ֣לֶךְ יִשְׂרָאֵ֑ל חֲמֵ֥שׁ עֶשְׂרֵ֖ה שָׁנָֽה׃

18 וְיֶ֛תֶר דִּבְרֵ֥י אֲמַצְיָ֖הוּ הֲלֹא־הֵ֣ם כְּתוּבִ֗ים עַל־סֵ֛פֶר דִּבְרֵ֥י הַיָּמִ֖ים
לְמַלְכֵ֥י יְהוּדָֽה׃

19 וַיִּקְשְׁר֨וּ עָלָ֤יו קֶ֙שֶׁר֙ בִּירֽוּשָׁלִַ֔ם וַיָּ֖נָס לָכִ֑ישָׁה וַיִּשְׁלְח֤וּ אַחֲרָיו֙ לָכִ֔ישָׁה
וַיְמִתֻ֖הוּ שָֽׁם׃

20 וַיִּשְׂא֥וּ אֹת֖וֹ עַל־הַסּוּסִ֑ים וַיִּקָּבֵ֧ר בִּירֽוּשָׁלַ֛ם עִם־אֲבֹתָ֖יו בְּעִ֥יר דָּוִֽד׃

21 וַיִּקְח֞וּ כָּל־עַ֤ם יְהוּדָה֙ אֶת־עֲזַרְיָ֔ה וְה֕וּא בֶּן־שֵׁ֥שׁ עֶשְׂרֵ֖ה שָׁנָ֑ה
וַיַּמְלִ֣כוּ אֹת֔וֹ תַּ֖חַת אָבִ֥יו אֲמַצְיָֽהוּ׃

22 ה֚וּא בָּנָ֣ה אֶת־אֵילַ֔ת וַיְשִׁבֶ֖הָ לִֽיהוּדָ֑ה אַחֲרֵ֥י שְׁכַֽב־הַמֶּ֖לֶךְ עִם־אֲבֹתָֽיו׃

Amaziah the son of Joash king of Judah lived fifteen years after the death of
Jehoash son of Jehoahaz king of Israel. **(782-767 BCE)** Now the rest of the acts

of Amaziah, are they not written in the Book of the Chronicles of the Kings of Judah?

They conspired against him in Jerusalem, and he fled to **Lachish**; but they sent after him to **Lachish** and killed him there. Then they brought him on horses and he was buried at Jerusalem with his fathers in the city of David. (**767 BCE**)

[And all the people of Judah <u>had taken</u> Azariah, he being sixteen years old, and made him <u>king in place of his father</u> Amaziah (**792 BCE**).]

He built **Elath** and restored it to Judah after the king slept with his fathers (**767**).

2 Chr. 25:25-28

25 וַיְחִי אֲמַצְיָהוּ בֶן־יוֹאָשׁ מֶלֶךְ יְהוּדָה אַחֲרֵי מוֹת יוֹאָשׁ בֶּן־יְהוֹאָחָז מֶלֶךְ יִשְׂרָאֵל חֲמֵשׁ עֶשְׂרֵה שָׁנָה:

And Amaziah, the son of Joash king of Judah, lived fifteen years after the death of Joash, son of Jehoahaz, king of Israel.

26 וְיֶתֶר דִּבְרֵי אֲמַצְיָהוּ הָרִאשֹׁנִים וְהָאַחֲרֹנִים הֲלֹא הִנָּם כְּתוּבִים עַל־סֵפֶר מַלְכֵי־יְהוּדָה וְיִשְׂרָאֵל:

27 וּמֵעֵת אֲשֶׁר־סָר אֲמַצְיָהוּ מֵאַחֲרֵי יְהוָה וַיִּקְשְׁרוּ עָלָיו קֶשֶׁר בִּירוּשָׁלַם וַיָּנָס לָכִישָׁה וַיִּשְׁלְחוּ אַחֲרָיו לָכִישָׁה וַיְמִיתֻהוּ שָׁם:

28 וַיִּשָּׂאֻהוּ עַל־הַסוּסִים וַיִּקְבְּרוּ אֹתוֹ עִם־אֲבֹתָיו בְּעִיר יְהוּדָה:

Now the rest of the acts of **Amaziah**, from first to last, behold, are they not written in the Book of the Kings of Judah and Israel? <u>From the time that Amaziah turned away from following Yahweh they conspired against him in Jerusalem, and he fled to</u> **Lachish**; but they sent after him to **Lachish** and killed him there. Then they brought him on horses and buried him with his fathers in the **city of Judah**.

B. Uzziah/Azariah 792/1 to 740/39 (co-regent 792/1 to 767 BCE)

1. Made king at age **16** when his father, Amaziah was captured by Jehoash (2 Ki. 14:21 || 2 Chr. 26:1) THIELE

2 Kings 14:21

21 וַיִּקְחוּ כָּל־עַם יְהוּדָה אֶת־עֲזַרְיָה וְהוּא בֶּן־שֵׁשׁ עֶשְׂרֵה שָׁנָה

וַיַּמְלִכוּ אֹתוֹ תַּחַת אָבִיו אֲמַצְיָהוּ :

All the people of Judah took **Azariah**, he being sixteen years old, and made
him king in the place of his father Amaziah.

2 Chron. 26:1

1 וַיִּקְחוּ כָּל־עַם יְהוּדָה אֶת־עֻזִּיָּהוּ וְהוּא בֶּן־שֵׁשׁ עֶשְׂרֵה שָׁנָה

וַיַּמְלִיכוּ אֹתוֹ תַּחַת אָבִיו אֲמַצְיָהוּ :

And all the people of Judah took **Uzziah**, he being sixteen years old, and
made him king in the place of his father Amaziah.

2. Attacked **Philistia** and received tribute from
Philistines, Arabs and Meuniites 2 Chr. 26:5-8
***** between 782 and 767 BCE ???
2 Chron. 26:5-8

5 וַיְהִי לִדְרֹשׁ אֱלֹהִים בִּימֵי זְכַרְיָהוּ הַמֵּבִין

בִּרְאֹת הָאֱלֹהִים וּבִימֵי דָּרְשׁוֹ אֶת־יְהוָה הִצְלִיחוֹ

הָאֱלֹהִים

6 וַיֵּצֵא וַיִּלָּחֶם בַּפְּלִשְׁתִּים וַיִּפְרֹץ אֶת־חוֹמַת

גַּת וְאֵת חוֹמַת יַבְנֵה וְאֵת חוֹמַת אַשְׁדּוֹד וַיִּבְנֶה עָרִים

בְּאַשְׁדּוֹד וּבַפְּלִשְׁתִּים

7 וַיַּעְזְרֵהוּ הָאֱלֹהִים עַל־פְּלִשְׁתִּים

וְעַל־הָעַרְבִים [הָ][עַרְבִים] הַיֹּשְׁבִים בְּגוּר־בָּעַל

וְהַמְּעוּנִים (LXX καὶ ἐπὶ τοὺς Μιναίους)

8 וַיִּתְּנוּ הָעַמּוֹנִים (הַמְּעוּנִים = LXX οἱ Μιναῖοι) מִנְחָה לְעֻזִּיָּהוּ וַיֵּלֶךְ שְׁמוֹ

עַד־לְבוֹא מִצְרַיִם כִּי הֶחֱזִיק עַד־לְמָעְלָה

He continued to seek God in the days of **Zechariah**, who had understanding
through the vision of God; and as long as he sought Yahweh, God prospered
him.

And he went out and warred against the **Philistines**, and broke down the wall of **Gath** and the wall of **Jabneh** and the wall of **Ashdod**; and he built cities in [the territory of] **Ashdod** and among the **Philistines**.

And God helped him against the **Philistines**, and against the **Arabians** who lived in Gur-baal, and the **Meunites**.

And the **Meunites**(! LXX) also gave tribute to Uzziah, and his fame extended to **the border of Egypt**, for he became very strong.

3. Restored **Elath** 767 BCE after death of Amaziah

2 Ki. 14:22 ‖ 2 Chr. 26:2

22 הוּא בָּנָה אֶת־אֵילַת וַיְשִׁבֶהָ לִיהוּדָה

אַחֲרֵי שְׁכַב־הַמֶּלֶךְ עִם־אֲבֹתָיו

He built Elath and restored it to Judah after the king slept with his fathers. (**767 BCE**)

2 Chr. 26:2

2 הוּא בָּנָה אֶת־אֵילוֹת וַיְשִׁיבֶהָ לִיהוּדָה אַחֲרֵי

שְׁכַב־הַמֶּלֶךְ עִם־אֲבֹתָיו

He built Elath and restored it to Judah after the king slept with his fathers. (**767 BCE**)

4. **His royal projects** 2 Chr. 26:9-10 —

a. In Jerusalem: 2Chr. 26:9

וַיִּבֶן עֻזִּיָּהוּ מִגְדָּלִים בִּירוּשָׁלַ͏ִם עַל־שַׁעַר הַפִּנָּה וְעַל־שַׁעַר הַגַּיְא

וְעַל־הַמִּקְצוֹעַ וַיְחַזְּקֵם:

Moreover, Uzziah built towers in Jerusalem at the Corner Gate and at the Valley Gate and at the corner buttress and fortified them.

b. Royal agricultural industries:

Cattle in Steppe land
2Chr. 26:10a

וַיִּבֶן מִגְדָּלִים בַּמִּדְבָּר וַיַּחְצֹב בֹּרוֹת רַבִּים כִּי מִקְנֶה־רַּב הָיָה לֹו

He built <u>towers</u> in the **wilderness** and hewed many cisterns, for he had much livestock,

Cultivators in Shephelah and on Coastal Plain
2Chr. 26:10b

וּבַשְּׁפֵלָה וּבַמִּישׁוֹר אִכָּרִים

And in the **Shephelah** and on the **Plain**, <u>cultivators</u>,

<u>Husbandmen in the Hill Country and in Carmel (S. Judah)</u>
2Chr. 26:10c

וְכֹרְמִים בֶּהָרִים וּבַכַּרְמֶל כִּי־אֹהֵב אֲדָמָה הָיָה:

and <u>husbandmen</u> (vinedressers) in the **Hills** and in **Carmel**, because he loved the soil

5. Became a **leper** — 750 BCE — Jotham becomes
co-regent 2 Ki. 15:5-7 ‖ 2 Chr. 26:16-23

6. Mentioned by **Tiglath-piliser III**
ANET pp. 282-283;—Once <u>*Az-ri-a-[u]*</u> occurs
isolated in a broken line. Further on, there is a
reference to

19 *nagê ša* ᵁᴿᵁ*Ḥammatti adi ālānī ša siḫirtišunu ša aḫi tamti ša šulmu* ᵈ*šamši ša ina ḫiṭṭi u gullulti ana* **Az-ri-ia-a-u** *ekimū ana miṣir māt Aššūr utirra,*

nineteen districts of Hamath with the towns around them, which are on the coast of the sea of the setting of the sun, which they had taken away sinfully and wrongfully for **Azriyau**, I restored to the territory of Assyria (Tadmor 1994:62-63).

Cf. 2 Kings 14:28 — Perhaps related to this!

28 וְיֶתֶר דִּבְרֵי יָרָבְעָם וְכָל־אֲשֶׁר עָשָׂה וּגְבוּרָתוֹ אֲשֶׁר־נִלְחָם וַאֲשֶׁר הֵשִׁיב
אֶת־דַּמֶּשֶׂק וְאֶת־חֲמָת לִיהוּדָה בְּיִשְׂרָאֵל הֲלֹא־הֵם כְּתוּבִים עַל־סֵפֶר
דִּבְרֵי הַיָּמִים לְמַלְכֵי יִשְׂרָאֵל:

Now the rest of the acts of **Jeroboam** and all that he did and his might, how he fought and how he recovered for Israel, <u>Damascus and Hamath</u>, **to (its alliance with) Judah**, are they not written in the Book of the Chronicles of the Kings of Israel?

C. Jotham co-regent with Uzziah 750-740 BCE; (cf. Below!)
sole ruler 740/739-735; shared with Ahaz 735-732/1

2 Ki. 15:32-38 ‖ 2 Chr. 27:1-9

<u>NOTE</u>: 2 Chr. 27:5 against Ammon:

וְהוּא נִלְחַם עִם־מֶלֶךְ בְּנֵי־עַמּוֹן וַיֶּחֱזַק עֲלֵיהֶם וַיִּתְּנוּ־לוֹ בְנֵי־עַמּוֹן

בַּשָּׁנָה הַהִיא מֵאָה כִּכַּר־כֶּסֶף וַעֲשֶׂרֶת אֲלָפִים כֹּרִים חִטִּים וּשְׂעוֹרִים

עֲשֶׂרֶת אֲלָפִים זֹאת הֵשִׁיבוּ לוֹ בְּנֵי עַמּוֹן וּבַשָּׁנָה הַשֵּׁנִית וְהַשְּׁלִשִׁית:

He fought also with the king of the **Ammonites** and prevailed over them so
that the Ammonites gave him during that year one hundred talents of silver,
ten thousand kors of wheat and ten thousand of barley; the **Ammonites**
repeated this [amount] in the second and in the third year.

V.   ISRAEL (Cont.)

A. Series of Usurpations:

1. **Zecharia** זְכַרְיָהוּ 2 Ki. 15:8-12 753 BCE—acc.yr. (791 -
        38 = 753)   2 Ki. 15:8

בִּשְׁנַת שְׁלֹשִׁים וּשְׁמֹנֶה שָׁנָה לַעֲזַרְיָהוּ מֶלֶךְ יְהוּדָה

מָלַךְ זְכַרְיָהוּ בֶן־יָרָבְעָם עַל־יִשְׂרָאֵל בְּשֹׁמְרוֹן שִׁשָּׁה חֳדָשִׁים

In the <u>thirty-eighth year of Azariah</u> king of Judah, **Zechariah** the son of

Jeroboam became king over Israel in Samaria [for] six months.

son of Jeroboam II; 6 mo. reign 2 Ki. 15:10

(Luc. ἐν Ιεβλααμ= בְּיִבְלְעָם)וַיִּקְשֹׁר עָלָיו שַׁלֻּם בֶּן־יָבֵשׁ וַיַּכֵּהוּ קָבָלְעָם

וַיְמִיתֵהוּ וַיִּמְלֹךְ תַּחְתָּיו

Then **Shallum** the son of Jabesh conspired against him and struck him <u>before</u>
<u>the people</u> (LXX in Ibleam) and killed him, and reigned in his place.

2. **Shallum** 2 Ki. 15:13; 752 BCE; 1 mo. reign vs. 13

13 שַׁלּוּם בֶּן־יָבֵישׁ מָלַךְ בִּשְׁנַת שְׁלֹשִׁים וָתֵשַׁע

שָׁנָה לְעֻזִּיָּה מֶלֶךְ יְהוּדָה וַיִּמְלֹךְ יֶרַח־יָמִים בְּשֹׁמְרוֹן

14 וַיַּעַל מְנַחֵם בֶּן־גָּדִי מִתִּרְצָה וַיָּבֹא שֹׁמְרוֹן

וַיַּךְ אֶת־שַׁלּוּם בֶּן־יָבֵישׁ בְּשֹׁמְרוֹן וַיְמִיתֵהוּ וַיִּמְלֹךְ תַּחְתָּיו

Shallum son of Jabesh became king in the <u>thirty-ninth year of Uzziah</u> king of Judah, and he reigned <u>one</u> <u>month</u> in Samaria. Then **Menahem** son of Gadi went up from **Tirzah** and came to **Samaria**, and struck Shallum son of Jabesh in Samaria, and killed him and became king in his place.

B. Parallel reigns in Samaria and Gilead:

1. Menahem 2 Ki. 15:17-22 — 752-742/1; vs. 16

usurpation: 2 Kings 15:16

אָז יַכֶּה־מְנַחֵם אֶת־תִּפְסַח [LXX (old Gk) τὴν Θερσα] וְאֶת־כָּל־אֲשֶׁר־בָּהּ

וְאֶת־גְּבוּלֶיהָ מִתִּרְצָה כִּי לֹא פָתַח וַיַּךְ אֵת כָּל־הֶהָרוֹתֶיהָ בִּקֵּעַ

Then Menahem struck **Tiphsah** (LXX Tirzah) and all who were in it and its borders from **Tirzah**, because they did not open [to him]; therefore he struck [it] and ripped up all its women who were with child.

ruled in Samaria, vs. 17 — acc.yr. 791 - 39 = 752

2 Kings 15:17

בִּשְׁנַת שְׁלֹשִׁים וָתֵשַׁע שָׁנָה לַעֲזַרְיָה מֶלֶךְ יְהוּדָה(752 BCE)

מָלַךְ מְנַחֵם בֶּן־גָּדִי עַל־יִשְׂרָאֵל עֶשֶׂר שָׁנִים בְּשֹׁמְרוֹן

In the <u>thirty-ninth year of Azariah</u> king of Judah (752 BCE.), **Menahem** son of Gadi became king over Israel, ten years in Samaria (to 742 BCE).

Battle in 743 BCE — Assyrian victory over Urartu

[*Tukulti-apil-ešarra*] ⌜*šar*⌝*māt Aššūr: ina āl Arpadda*

[- - - - - - - - - - - - - - - *d*]*īktu ša* ⌜*māt Uarṭi : dīkat*

(*Eponym Chronicles*, A-1, IV 26; B-1, 79'-80')

Tiglathpileser (III), king of Assyria: in the city of Arpad

[- - - - - - - - - - - - - - - - - - de]feat of the land of Urarṭu accomplished

Millard 1994:43, 59; cf. Thiele, 3rd ed. pp. 139-162.

vs. 19 Menahem paid tribute to Pul = Tiglath-pileser 743

2 Kings 15:19

בָּא פוּל מֶלֶךְ־אַשּׁוּר עַל־הָאָרֶץ וַיִּתֵּן מְנַחֵם לְפוּל אֶלֶף

כִּכַּר־כָּסֶף לִהְיוֹת יָדָיו אִתּוֹ לְהַחֲזִיק הַמַּמְלָכָה בְּיָדוֹ

Pul, king of Assyria, came against the land, and Menahem gave Pul a thousand talents of silver so that his hand might be with him to strengthen the kingdom under his rule.

As result, Menahem gained Assyrian support for his rule against Pekah, his rival in Gilead. Thus Pekahiah was able to follow his father while Pekah became the "adjutant" of Pekahiah.

2. **Pekahiah**, son of Menahem 2 Ki. 15:23-26742/1-740/39 acc. yr. sys. 791-50 = 741 BCE

2 Kings 15:23

בִּשְׁנַת חֲמִשִּׁים שָׁנָה לַעֲזַרְיָה מֶלֶךְ יְהוּדָה(742/1)

מָלַךְ פְּקַחְיָה בֶן־מְנַחֵם עַל־יִשְׂרָאֵל בְּשֹׁמְרוֹן שְׁנָתָיִם (742/1-740/39)

In the fiftieth year of Azariah king of Judah (742/1), **Pekahiah** son of Menahem became king over Israel in Samaria, two years (742/1-740/39).

3. **Pekah** 2 Ki. 15:25-29

a. Staged a *coup d'etat* **740 BCE**:

2 Kings 15:25

וַיִּקְשֹׁר עָלָיו פֶּקַח בֶּן־רְמַלְיָהוּ שָׁלִישׁוֹ

וַיַּכֵּהוּ בְשֹׁמְרוֹן בְּאַרְמוֹן בֵּית־מֶלֶךְ [הַ][מֶּלֶךְ] אֶת־אַרְגֹּב

וְאֶת־הָאַרְיֵה וְעִמּוֹ חֲמִשִּׁים אִישׁ מִבְּנֵי גִלְעָדִים וַיְמִיתֵהוּ

וַיִּמְלֹךְ תַּחְתָּיו

Then **Pekah** son of Remaliah, his officer, conspired against him and struck him in Samaria, in the palace of the king's house with Argob and Arieh; and with him were fifty men of the **Gileadites**, and he killed him and became king in his place.

b. Length of total reign: 20 years 752-732/1 vs. 27

2 Kings 15:27

בִּשְׁנַת חֲמִשִּׁים וּשְׁתַּיִם שָׁנָה לַעֲזַרְיָה מֶלֶךְ יְהוּדָה (740) מָלַךְ פֶּקַח בֶּן־רְמַלְיָהוּ

עַל־יִשְׂרָאֵל בְּשֹׁמְרוֹן עֶשְׂרִים שָׁנָה(752 to 732/731)

In the fifty-second year of Azariah king of Judah (740), Pekah son of Remaliah became king over Israel in Samaria, (he reigned twenty years, 12 in Gilead, 8 in Samaria; 752 to 732).

20 years prior to his assassination by Hoshea
during the 20th (actual 19th) year of Jotham,
2 Ki. 15:30 — **732/1 BCE**

וַיִּקְשָׁר־קֶשֶׁר הוֹשֵׁעַ בֶּן־אֵלָה עַל־פֶּקַח בֶּן־רְמַלְיָהוּ

· וַיַּכֵּהוּ וַיְמִיתֵהוּ וַיִּמְלֹךְ תַּחְתָּיו בִּשְׁנַת עֶשְׂרִים

לְיוֹתָם בֶּן־עֻזִּיָּה (732 BCE)

And **Hoshea** the son of Elah made a conspiracy against **Pekah** the son of
Remaliah, and struck him and put him to death and became king in his place,
in the twentieth year of Jotham the son of Uzziah (732 BCE).

Note: Jotham begin in Pekah's 2nd year 2 Ki. 15:32

בִּשְׁנַת שְׁתַּיִם לְפֶקַח בֶּן־רְמַלְיָהוּ מֶלֶךְ יִשְׂרָאֵל

מָלַךְ יוֹתָם בֶּן־עֻזִּיָּהוּ מֶלֶךְ יְהוּדָה (751/750)

In the second year of Pekah the son of Remaliah king of Israel, Jotham the son
of Uzziah king of Judah became king. (Jotham as co-regent)

Transjordan 752-740/39 12 years cf. **three** states

Hosea 5:5b

וְיִשְׂרָאֵל וְאֶפְרַיִם יִכָּשְׁלוּ בַּעֲוֺנָם כָּשַׁל גַּם־יְהוּדָה עִמָּם׃

And **Israel** and **Ephraim** stumble in their iniquity; **Judah** also has stumbled
with them.

c. Joined **Rezin** of Damascus in war against Ahaz; they
wanted to form an anti Assyrian coalition and
Ahaz refused, so they intended to depose Ahaz
and install an anti Assyrian named Ṭâb-ʾal
(=Ṭâb-ʾel) in his place 734 BCE
(Atlas Map 144) Isaiah 7:1-2

וַיְהִי בִּימֵי אָחָז בֶּן־יוֹתָם בֶּן־עֻזִּיָּהוּ מֶלֶךְ יְהוּדָה עָלָה רְצִין

מֶלֶךְ־אֲרָם וּפֶקַח בֶּן־רְמַלְיָהוּ מֶלֶךְ־יִשְׂרָאֵל יְרוּשָׁלַם

לַמִּלְחָמָה עָלֶיהָ וְלֹא יָכֹל לְהִלָּחֶם עָלֶיהָ

Is. 7:2 וַיֻּגַּד לְבֵית דָּוִד לֵאמֹר נָחָה אֲרָם עַל־אֶפְרָיִם וַיָּנַע

לְבָבוֹ וּלְבַב עַמּוֹ כְּנוֹעַ עֲצֵי־יַעַר מִפְּנֵי־רוּחַ

Now it came about in the days of **Ahaz**, the son of Jotham, the son of Uzziah, king of Judah, that **Rezin** the king of Aram and **Pekah** the son of Remaliah, king of Israel, went up to Jerusalem to [wage] war against it, but could not conquer it. When it was reported to the house of David, saying, "The Arameans have camped in Ephraim," his heart and the hearts of his people shook as the trees of the forest shake with the wind.

****

d. ATTACKED BY TIGLATH-PILESER III
733 BCE—2 Ki. 15:29

בִּימֵי פֶּקַח מֶלֶךְ־יִשְׂרָאֵל בָּא תִּגְלַת פִּלְאֶסֶר מֶלֶךְ אַשּׁוּר

וַיִּקַּח אֶת־עִיּוֹן וְאֶת־אָבֵל בֵּית־מַעֲכָה

וְאֶת־יָנוֹחַ וְאֶת־קֶדֶשׁ וְאֶת־חָצוֹר וְאֶת־הַגִּלְעָד

וְאֶת־הַגָּלִילָה כֹּל אֶרֶץ נַפְתָּלִי וַיַּגְלֵם אַשּׁוּרָה

In the days of **Pekah** king of Israel, **Tiglath-pileser** king of Assyria came and captured **Ijon** and **Abel-beth-maacah** and **Janoah** and **Kedesh** and **Hazor** and **Gilead** and **Galilee**, all the land of Naphtali; and he carried them captive to Assyria.

NOTE 1 Ch. 5:6, 25-26 (**733 BCE**) — people captured in

Transjordan

1 Chron. 5:6 — Leader of tribe of Reuben

בְּאֵרָה בְנוֹ אֲשֶׁר הֶגְלָה תִּלְגַת פִּלְנְאֶסֶר מֶלֶךְ אַשּׁר

הוּא נָשִׂיא לָראוּבֵנִי

Beerah his son, whom **Tilgath-pilneser** king of Assyria carried away into exile; he was leader of the Reubenites.

1 Chron. 5:25-26 — Half-tribe of Manasseh

25 וַיִּמְעֲלוּ בֵּאלֹהֵי אֲבוֹתֵיהֶם וַיִּזְנוּ אַחֲרֵי אֱלֹהֵי

עַמֵּי־הָאָרֶץ אֲשֶׁר־הִשְׁמִיד אֱלֹהִים מִפְּנֵיהֶם

26 וַיָּעַר אֱלֹהֵי יִשְׂרָאֵל אֶת־רוּחַ פּוּל

מֶלֶךְ־אַשּׁוּר וְאֶת־רוּחַ תִּלְּגַת פִּלְנֶסֶר מֶלֶךְ אַשּׁוּר וַיַּגְלֵם

לָראוּבֵנִי וְלַגָּדִי וְלַחֲצִי שֵׁבֶט מְנַשֶּׁה וַיְבִיאֵם לַחְלַח וְחָבוֹר

וְהָרָא וּנְהַר גּוֹזָן עַד הַיּוֹם הַזֶּה

But they acted treacherously against the God of their fathers and played the harlot after the gods of the peoples of the land, whom God had destroyed before them. So the God of Israel stirred up the spirit of **Pul, king of Assyria**, even the spirit of Tilgath-pilneser king of Assyria, and he carried them away into exile, namely the **Reubenites**, the **Gadites** and the **half-tribe of Manasseh**, and brought them to Halah, Habor, Hara and to the river of Gozan, to this day.

e. **Assassinated by Hoshea** (732/731 to 723/722)

in the 20th year of Jotham, 732/1 BCE

2 Ki. 15:30 — 732/1 BCE

וַיִּקְשָׁר־קֶשֶׁר הוֹשֵׁעַ בֶּן־אֵלָה עַל־פֶּקַח בֶּן־רְמַלְיָהוּ

וַיַּכֵּהוּ וַיְמִיתֵהוּ וַיִּמְלֹךְ תַּחְתָּיו בִּשְׁנַת עֶשְׂרִים לְיוֹתָם בֶּן־עֻזִּיָּה

And **Hoshea** the son of Elah made a conspiracy against **Pekah** the son of Remaliah, and struck him and put him to death and became king in his place, in the twentieth year of Jotham the son of Uzziah.

VI.   JUDAH (Cont.)

A.   Azariah — Uzziah

1. Co-regent 792/1 to 767 BCE
2. Sole ruler 767-750
3. With Jotham 750 to 740
4. 52 years from 792/1 to 740/39

B.   Jotham

1   Co-regent **750** (2nd of Pekah) to 740/39

2 Ki. 15:5, 32

5 וַיְנַגַּע יְהֹוָה אֶת־הַמֶּלֶךְ וַיְהִי מְצֹרָע עַד־יוֹם

מֹתוֹ וַיֵּשֶׁב בְּבֵית הַחָפְשִׁית וְיוֹתָם בֶּן־הַמֶּלֶךְ עַל־הַבַּיִת

שֹׁפֵט אֶת־עַם הָאָרֶץ

So Yahweh struck the king, so that he was a leper to the day of his death.
And he lived in a separate house, while **Jotham** the king's son was over the
household, judging the people of the land.

2 Chr. 26:21

וַיְהִי עֻזִּיָּהוּ הַמֶּלֶךְ מְצֹרָע עַד־יוֹם מוֹתוֹ

וַיֵּשֶׁב בֵּית הַחָפְשׁוּת [הַ][הָפְשִׁית] מְצֹרָע כִּי נִגְזַר מִבֵּית

יְהֹוָה וְיוֹתָם בְּנוֹ עַל־בֵּית הַמֶּלֶךְ שׁוֹפֵט אֶת־עַם הָאָרֶץ

King **Uzziah** was a leper to the day of his death; and he lived in a separate
house, being a leper, for he was cut off from the house of Yahweh. And
Jotham his son was over the king's house judging the people of the land.

2.   Reigned 16 years (750-735 BCE

inclusive) 2 Kings 15:32-33

בִּשְׁנַת שְׁתַּיִם לְפֶקַח בֶּן־רְמַלְיָהוּ מֶלֶךְ יִשְׂרָאֵל מָלַךְ יוֹתָם בֶּן־עֻזִּיָּהוּ מֶלֶךְ

יְהוּדָה׃ בֶּן־עֶשְׂרִים וְחָמֵשׁ שָׁנָה הָיָה בְמָלְכוֹ וְשֵׁשׁ־עֶשְׂרֵה שָׁנָה מָלַךְ בִּירוּשָׁלַ͏ִם

In the second year of Pekah the son of Remaliah king of Israel (750 BCE),
Jotham the son of Uzziah king of Judah became king. He was twenty-five
years old when he became king, and he reigned sixteen years in Jerusalem
(750 to 734 BCE).

3.   Built in Judah and Jerusalem 2 Ki. 15:35; and
2 Chr. 27:3-4

3 הוּא בָּנָה אֶת־שַׁעַר בֵּית־יְהוָה הָעֶלְיוֹן וּבְחוֹמַת הָעֹפֶל בָּנָה לָרֹב

4 וְעָרִים בָּנָה בְּהַר־יְהוּדָה וּבֶחֳרָשִׁים בָּנָה בִּירָנִיּוֹת וּמִגְדָּלִים

He built the upper gate of the house of Yahweh, and he built extensively the
wall of Ophel and he built cities in the **hill country of Judah**, and he built
fortresses and towers on the wooded areas.

4.   Defeated the Ammonites <u>after</u> Pekah seized power
in Samaria in **740 BCE**, therefore in **739 BCE**?
2 Chr. 27:5

וְהוּא נִלְחַם עִם־מֶלֶךְ בְּנֵי־עַמּוֹן וַיֶּחֱזַק עֲלֵיהֶם

וַיִּתְּנוּ־לוֹ בְנֵי־עַמּוֹן בַּשָּׁנָה הַהִיא מֵאָה כִּכַּר־כֶּסֶף

וַעֲשֶׂרֶת אֲלָפִים כֹּרִים חִטִּים וּשְׂעוֹרִים עֲשֶׂרֶת אֲלָפִים זֹאת

הֵשִׁיבוּ לוֹ בְּנֵי עַמּוֹן וּבַשָּׁנָה הַשֵּׁנִית וְהַשְּׁלִשִׁית

He fought also with the king of the **Ammonites** and prevailed over them
so that the Ammonites gave him during that year one hundred talents of
silver, ten thousand kors of wheat and ten thousand of barley. The
Ammonites also paid him this [amount] in the second and in the third year.
recieved tribute 3 years (739, 738, 737)

5.   Deposed in favor of Ahaz **735 BCE** —
Isaiah 7:1 ff. Cf. Ahaz below.

6.   **War with Rezin and Pekah**

2 Ki. 15:37   **734 BCE**

בַּיָּמִים הָהֵם הֵחֵל יְהוָה לְהַשְׁלִיחַ בִּיהוּדָה

רְצִין מֶלֶךְ אֲרָם וְאֵת פֶּקַח בֶּן־רְמַלְיָהוּ

In those days Yahweh began to send Rezin king of Aram and Pekah the son
of Remaliah against Judah.

7.   Lived to 20th yr. **732/31**

2 Ki. 15:30

וַיִּקְשָׁר־קֶשֶׁר הוֹשֵׁעַ בֶּן־אֵלָה עַל־פֶּקַח

בֶּן־רְמַלְיָהוּ וַיַּכֵּהוּ וַיְמִיתֵהוּ וַיִּמְלֹךְ תַּחְתָּיו בִּשְׁנַת עֶשְׂרִים

לְיוֹתָם בֶּן־עֻזִּיָּה

in the twentieth year of Jotham the son of Uzziah.

C.   **Ahaz** 735-715 BCE

1. Began as co-regent 17th of Pekah 735 BCE
2 Ki. 16:1-4; 2 Chr. 28:1-4; Isaiah 7:1-3.
2 Kings 16:1-2

1 בִּשְׁנַת שְׁבַע־עֶשְׂרֵה שָׁנָה לְפֶקַח

בֶּן־רְמַלְיָהוּ מָלַךְ אָחָז בֶּן־יוֹתָם מֶלֶךְ יְהוּדָה

2 בֶּן־עֶשְׂרִים שָׁנָה אָחָז בְּמָלְכוֹ וְשֵׁשׁ־עֶשְׂרֵה

שָׁנָה מָלַךְ בִּירוּשָׁלָם וְלֹא־עָשָׂה הַיָּשָׁר בְּעֵינֵי יְהוָה

אֱלֹהָיו כְּדָוִד אָבִיו

In the seventeenth year of **Pekah** (752 - 17 = 735 BCE) the son of Remaliah,
Ahaz the son of Jotham, king of Judah, became king. Ahaz [was] twenty
years old when he became king, and he reigned sixteen years (sole reign, 732-
716 BCE) in Jerusalem;

Official reign reckoned from death of Jotham 732 BCE
2 Ki. 15:38 (|| 2 Chr. 27:9)

38 וַיִּשְׁכַּב יוֹתָם עִם־אֲבֹתָיו וַיִּקָּבֵר עִם־אֲבֹתָיו בְּעִיר דָּוִד אָבִיו

וַיִּמְלֹךְ אָחָז בְּנוֹ תַּחְתָּיו

And Jotham slept with his fathers, and he was buried with his fathers in the
city of David his father; and Ahaz his son became king in his place.

2. **War with Rezin and Pekah** 735 BCE
Isaiah 7:1-2

1 וַיְהִי בִּימֵי אָחָז בֶּן־יוֹתָם בֶּן־עֻזִּיָּהוּ מֶלֶךְ יְהוּדָה

עָלָה רְצִין מֶלֶךְ־אֲרָם וּפֶקַח בֶּן־רְמַלְיָהוּ מֶלֶךְ־יִשְׂרָאֵל

יְרוּשָׁלַם לַמִּלְחָמָה עָלֶיהָ וְלֹא יָכֹל לְהִלָּחֵם עָלֶיהָ

2 וַיֻּגַּד לְבֵית דָּוִד לֵאמֹר נָחָה אֲרָם עַל־אֶפְרָיִם

וַיָּנַע לְבָבוֹ וּלְבַב עַמּוֹ כְּנוֹעַ עֲצֵי־יַעַר מִפְּנֵי־רוּחַ

Now it came about in the days of Ahaz, the son of Jotham, the son of Uzziah, king of Judah, that Rezin the king of Aram and Pekah the son of Remaliah, king of Israel, went up to Jerusalem to [wage] war against it, but could not conquer it. When it was reported to the house of David, saying, "The Arameans have camped in Ephraim," his heart and the hearts of his people shook as the trees of the forest shake with the wind.

2 Ki. 16:5 — **seige** not in 2 Chr. or in Isaiah

אָז יַעֲלֶה רְצִין מֶלֶךְ־אֲרָם וּפֶקַח בֶּן־רְמַלְיָהוּ מֶלֶךְ־יִשְׂרָאֵל

יְרוּשָׁלַם לַמִּלְחָמָה וַיָּצֻרוּ עַל־אָחָז וְלֹא יָכְלוּ לְהִלָּחֵם

Then Rezin king of Aram and Pekah son of Remaliah, king of Israel, came up to Jerusalem for war; **and they besieged Ahaz**, but could not make war.

Isaiah 7:1-6 — **they wanted to appoint a new ruler**

(Ṭâbʾēl = Ταβεηλ LXX) over Judah; Isaiah was

instructed to tell Ahaz:

Isaiah 7:4-6

4 וְאָמַרְתָּ אֵלָיו הִשָּׁמֵר וְהַשְׁקֵט אַל־תִּירָא וּלְבָבְךָ אַל־יֵרַךְ

· מִשְּׁנֵי זַנְבוֹת הָאוּדִים הָעֲשֵׁנִים הָאֵלֶּה

בָּחֳרִי־אַף רְצִין וַאֲרָם וּבֶן־רְמַלְיָהוּ

5 יַעַן כִּי־יָעַץ עָלֶיךָ אֲרָם רָעָה אֶפְרַיִם וּבֶן־רְמַלְיָהוּ

לֵאמֹר

6 נַעֲלֶה בִיהוּדָה וּנְקִיצֶנָּה וְנַבְקִעֶנָּה אֵלֵינוּ

וְנַמְלִיךְ מֶלֶךְ בְּתוֹכָהּ אֵת בֶּן־טָבְאַל (= Ταβεηλ)

And say to him, "Take care and be calm, have no fear and do not be fainthearted because of these two stubs of smoldering firebrands, on account of the fierce anger of **Rezin** and **Aram** and the **son of Remaliah**. Because Aram, has planned evil against you, [with] Ephraim and the son of Remaliah saying, 'Let us go up against Judah and terrorize it, and make for ourselves a breach in its walls and set up the son of **Tabeel** as king in the midst of it,'"

2 Chr. 28:5-15 — captives returned from Israel:

. . . וַיְבִיאוּם יְרֵחוֹ עִיר־הַתְּמָרִים אֵצֶל אֲחֵיהֶם וַיָּשׁוּבוּ שֹׁמְרוֹן

... and brought them to **Jericho**, the city of palm trees, to their brothers;

2 Ki. 16:6 — lost <u>Elath</u> to Edom helped by Rezin:

16:6 סמ"ב 2 בָּעֵת הַהִיא הֵשִׁיב רְצִין מֶלֶךְ־אֲרָם (LXX Συρια) אֶת־אֵילַת

לַאֲרָם (LXX τῇ Συρίᾳ) אֱדוֹם!; וַיְנַשֵּׁל אֶת־הַיְהוּדִים מֵאֵילוֹת וַאֲרַמִּים

[וַ][אֲדֹומִים] (LXX Ιδουμαῖοι) בָּאוּ אֵילַת וַיֵּשְׁבוּ שָׁם עַד הַיּוֹם הַזֶּה

At that time **Rezin** king of **Aram** recovered Elath for Edom!, and cleared the
Judeans out of Elath entirely; and the **Edomites** (Q°rî, LXX) came to Elath
and have lived there to this day.

Cf. also 2 Chron. 28:17

וְעוֹד אֲדוֹמִים בָּאוּ וַיַּכּוּ בִיהוּדָה וַיִּשְׁבוּ־שֶׁבִי

And still the **Edomites** had come and <u>attacked Judah and carried away
captives</u>.

2 Chr. 28:18 — losses in <u>Shephelah (735 BCE)</u>

וּפְלִשְׁתִּים פָּשְׁטוּ בְּעָרֵי הַשְּׁפֵלָה וְהַנֶּגֶב לִיהוּדָה

וַיִּלְכְּדוּ אֶת־בֵּית־שֶׁמֶשׁ וְאֶת־אַיָּלוֹן

וְאֶת־הַגְּדֵרוֹת וְאֶת־שֹׂוכוֹ וּבְנוֹתֶיהָ וְאֶת־תִּמְנָה וּבְנוֹתֶיהָ

וְאֶת־גִּמְזוֹ וְאֶת־בְּנֹתֶיהָ וַיֵּשְׁבוּ שָׁם

The **Philistines** had invaded the towns of the **Shephelah** and of the **Negeb of
Judah**, and had taken **Beth-shemesh**, **Aijalon**, **Gederoth**, and **Socho** with its
villages, **Timnah** with its villages, and **Gimzo** with its villages, and they
settled there.

3. Appealed to Tiglath-pileser III; 2 Ki. 16:7-18;
2 Chr. 28:16, 20-21

VII. Tiglath-pileser III (745-727 BCE), disgrace crime

1. War with Urartu 743 B.C.E; also note:

19 nagê ša URUḤammatti adi ālānī ša siḫirtišunu ša aḫi tamti ša
šulmu dšamši ša ina ḫiṭṭi u gullulti ana Azriyau ekimū ana miṣir māt
Aššūr utirra,

nineteen districts of Hamath with the towns around them, which are on the coast of the sea of the setting of the sun, **which they had criminally and disgracefully transferred to Azriyau**, I restored to the territory of Assyria (Rost 1893 II, 22, line 131; Tadmor 1994: 62-63).

— received tribute from Menahem 2 Ki. 15:19-20

19 בָּא פוּל מֶלֶךְ־אַשּׁוּר עַל־הָאָרֶץ וַיִּתֵּן מְנַחֵם לְפוּל אֶלֶף כִּכַּר־כָּסֶף

לִהְיוֹת יָדָיו אִתּוֹ לְהַחֲזִיק הַמַּמְלָכָה בְּיָדוֹ

20 וַיֹּצֵא מְנַחֵם אֶת־הַכֶּסֶף עַל־יִשְׂרָאֵל עַל כָּל־גִּבּוֹרֵי הַחַיִל

לָתֵת לְמֶלֶךְ אַשּׁוּר חֲמִשִּׁים שְׁקָלִים כֶּסֶף לְאִישׁ אֶחָד

וַיָּשָׁב מֶלֶךְ אַשּׁוּר וְלֹא־עָמַד שָׁם בָּאָרֶץ

Pul, king of Assyria, came against the land, and Menahem gave Pul a thousand talents of silver so that his hand might be with him to strengthen the kingdom under his rule.

Then Menahem exacted the money from Israel, even from all the mighty men of wealth, from each man fifty shekels of silver to pay the king of Assyria. So the king of Assyria returned and did not remain there in the land.

2. War with **N. Syrian states** and Urartu 742-738, 735 BCE

3. War against **Philistia** 734 BCE (Tadmor 1994:176-179)

14' [… ¹Ḥann]ūnu āl Ǧazzataya lapān kakkē⟨ia⟩ dannúti
       iplaḫma a[na māt Muṣri innabit]

15' [māt Ǧazzutu … akšud/ērub x bilat] ḫurāṣu 800 bilat kaspu nišē u-li
       maršītišunu aššatsu mārē[šu mārātēšu …]

16' [… bušâšu ilānišú ašlul / ēkim] ṣalām ilāni rabûti bēlēya ⟨ù⟩
       ṣalām šarrūtiya ša ḫurāṣī [ēpuš]

17' [ina qirib ekalli ša Ḥazzutu ulziz ana ilāni mātišunu amnūma
       … -šu]nu ukīn u šū ultu māt Muṣri kīma iṣṣu[ri ipparšamma]

18' [… ana ašrišu ūtiršuma … x-šu ana bīt kāri ša māt] ⌈Aš⌉šur amnu
       ṣalām šarrūtiya ina āl Naḥal Muṣur ⌈nāru⌉ [ša … ulziz]

19' [… x + 100 bilat] kaspu assuḫaamma ana māt Aššur [ūrâ]

14' [… Ḥan]nūnu of Gaza feared my powerful weapons and [escaped to Egypt.]

15'   [The city of Gaza ... I conquered/entered. X talents] of gold, 800 talents of silver, people together with their posessions, his wife, [his] sons, [his daughters ...]

16'   [... his property (and) his gods I despoiled/seized.] A (statue) bearing the image of the greatgods, my lords and my (own) royal image out of gold [I fashioned.]

17'   [In the palace of Gaza I set it up (and) counted (it) among the gods of their land. The]ir [ś] I established. As for him, like a bird [he flew (back)] from Egypt.

18'   [... I returned him to his position. His ...] I turned (into an) Assyrian [emporium]. My royal stele [I set up] in the City of the Brook of Egypt, a river[-bed ...]

19'   [... from $x + 100$ talents] of silver I carried off and [brought] to Assyria.

4. War against **Israel** 733 B.C.E

2 Ki. 15:29

בִּימֵי פֶּקַח מֶלֶךְ־יִשְׂרָאֵל בָּא תִּגְלַת פִּלְאֶסֶר מֶלֶךְ אַשּׁוּר

וַיִּקַּח אֶת־עִיּוֹן וְאֶת־אָבֵל בֵּית־מַעֲכָה וְאֶת־יָנוֹחַ וְאֶת־קֶדֶשׁ

וְאֶת־חָצוֹר וְאֶת־הַגִּלְעָד וְאֶת־הַגָּלִילָה כֹּל אֶרֶץ נַפְתָּלִי

וַיַּגְלֵם אַשּׁוּרָה

In the days of Pekah king of Israel, Tiglath-pileser king of Assyria came and captured **Ijon** and **Abel-beth-maacah** and **Janoah** and **Kedesh** and **Hazor** and **Gilead** and **Galilee**, all the land of Naphtali; and he carried them captive to Assyria.

Isaiah 8:23 (Eng. 9:1)

כִּי לֹא מוּעָף לַאֲשֶׁר מוּצָק לָהּ כָּעֵת הָרִאשׁוֹן

הֵקַל אַרְצָה זְבֻלוּן וְאַרְצָה נַפְתָּלִי וְהָאַחֲרוֹן הִכְבִּיד

דֶּרֶךְ הַיָּם עֵבֶר הַיַּרְדֵּן גְּלִיל הַגּוֹיִם

But there will be no [more] gloom for her who was in anguish; in earlier times He treated the land of <u>Zebulun</u> and the land of <u>Naphtali</u> with contempt, but later on He shall make [it] glorious, by the **Way of the Sea**, **Beyond the Jordan**, **Galilee of the Foreigners**.

Towns listed by Tiglath-pileser: **Hannathon, Qanah, [Yo]ṭbath, Yiron, Arumah, Merom.** <u>All</u> in <u>Galilee</u>.

5. War against Damascus 732 B.C.E

2 Ki. 16:8-9

וַיִּקַּח אָחָז אֶת־הַכֶּסֶף וְאֶת־הַזָּהָב הַנִּמְצָא בֵּית יְהוָה וּבְאֹצְרוֹת בֵּית

הַמֶּלֶךְ וַיִּשְׁלַח לְמֶלֶךְ־אַשּׁוּר שֹׁחַד : וַיִּשְׁמַע אֵלָיו מֶלֶךְ אַשּׁוּר וַיַּעַל

מֶלֶךְ אַשּׁוּר אֶל־דַּמֶּשֶׂק וַיִּתְפְּשֶׂהָ וַיַּגְלֶהָ קִירָה וְאֶת־רְצִין הֵמִית :

Ahaz took the silver and gold that was found in the house of Yahweh and in
the treasuries of the king's house, and sent a present to the **king of Assyria**.
So the **king of Assyria** listened to him; and the king of Assyria went up
against **Damascus** and captured it, and carried it away into exile to **Kir**, and
put **Rezin** to death.

6. Claims to have "appointed" Hoshea over Israel
732/31

[*māt bīt ᶜOmriya ša i*]*na gerēteya maḫrāte gimir ālāni*[*šu qaqqariš*] *amnû;* [*nīšēšu u*]
būlišu ašluluma āl Šāmerīna edēnuššu umašši[*ru* ¹*Paqa*]*ḫa šarrašunu ‹idūku›*

[As for the house of Omri, of which i]n foremewer campaigns I razed all [its]
cities [to the ground; [ita people and] its cattle I had despoiled; the city of
Samaria alone did I leave; ‹they slew› Peqah their king (Summ. 13:17'-18';
Tadmor 199:202-203).

māt ᶜOmriya[*. . . ti*]*llat* [*ṣābēšu . . .*]*uḫur nišēšu* [*. . . ana*] *māt Aššur ūrā.* ¹*Paqaḫa
šarrašunu* [*i*]*dū*[*kūšu*]*ma* ¹*Ausiᶜa* [*ana šarrūti i*]*na muḫḫišunu aškun. 10 bilat* X
bilat kaspu [*adi marši*]*tišunu amḫuršunuma*

As for the land of (the house of) Omri [. . .] its [aux]iliary [troops . . .] the
totality of its people [. . . to] the land of Assyria I transported. As for Peqah,
their king, [they] sl[ew him;] Hosea I appointed [to the kingship o]ver them.
AS for ten talents of gold, X talents of silver [with their possess]ions, I
accepted them. (Summ. 14'-15'; Tadmor 1994:140-141).

[*māt Bīt ᶜOmriya*] *ana gimir*[*tišu akšud . . . adi mar*]*šītišunu a*[*na māt Aššur īrâ . . .
Ausiᶜa ana*] *šarruti ina muḫḫišunu* [*aškun. u šu ana āl Sarrabāni adi maḫrišu . . .*

[The land of the House of Omri], in [its] entirety I conquered . . . with] their
[pro]perty t[o the land of Assyria I transported . . . Hoshea, to] the kingship
over them [I appointed. He himself to the city of]Sarrabāni to my presence . .
. (Summ. 9:9-11; Tadmor 1994:188-189).

VIII. LAST DAYS OF ISRAEL

A. **Hoshe**a 732/31 - 723/22 — 9 yr. reign

1. 20th year of Jotham 2 Ki. 15:30-31 — Assassinated
Pekah 2 Ki. 15:30 — 732 BCE

וַיִּקְשָׁר־קֶשֶׁר הוֹשֵׁעַ בֶּן־אֵלָה עַל־פֶּקַח בֶּן־רְמַלְיָהוּ וַיַּכֵּהוּ וַיְמִיתֵהוּ

וַיִּמְלֹךְ תַּחְתָּיו בִּשְׁנַת עֶשְׂרִים לְיוֹתָם בֶּן־עֻזִּיָּה

And **Hoshea** the son of Elah made a conspiracy against **Pekah** the son of
Remaliah, and struck him and put him to death and became king in his place,
in the twentieth year of Jotham the son of Uzziah.

2. Paid tribute to Shalmaneser V (727-722)
2 Ki. 17:3

עָלָיו עָלָה שַׁלְמַנְאֶסֶר מֶלֶךְ אַשּׁוּר וַיְהִי־לוֹ הוֹשֵׁעַ עֶבֶד וַיָּשֶׁב לוֹ מִנְחָה

Shalmaneser king of Assyria came up against him, and **Hoshea** became his
servant and paid him tribute.

3. Sent ambassage to : **So**, ‹to› the king of Egypt
(Osorkon IV 735-712 according to Kitchen) ???
2 Ki. 17:4 סוֹא = Sais — most likely

וַיִּמְצָא מֶלֶךְ־אַשּׁוּר בְּהוֹשֵׁעַ קֶשֶׁר אֲשֶׁר שָׁלַח מַלְאָכִים אֶל־סוֹא

‹אֶל› מֶלֶךְ־מִצְרַיִם וְלֹא־הֶעֱלָה מִנְחָה לְמֶלֶךְ אַשּׁוּר כְּשָׁנָה בְשָׁנָה

וַיַּעַצְרֵהוּ מֶלֶךְ אַשּׁוּר וַיַּאַסְרֵהוּ בֵּית כֶּלֶא

But the king of Assyria found conspiracy in Hoshea, who had sent
messengers to **So** ‹to› **the king of Egypt** and had offered no tribute to the
king of Assyria, as [he had done] year by year; so the king of Assyria shut
him up and bound him in prison.

5. Piye occupied Memphis by 727 BCE

B. **Fall of Samaria**

1. Siege under Shalmaneser V, begins

2 Ki. 17:5

וַיַּעַל מֶלֶךְ־אַשּׁוּר בְּכָל־הָאָרֶץ וַיַּעַל שֹׁמְרוֹן וַיָּצַר עָלֶיהָ שָׁלֹשׁ שָׁנִים

Then the king of Assyria invaded the whole land and went up to **Samaria**
and <u>besieged it three years</u>.

Begins 7th yr. of Hoshea — 725/24 B.C.E

ends 9th yr. of Hoshea — 723/22

2 Kings 17:6

בִּשְׁנַת הַתְּשִׁיעִית לְהוֹשֵׁעַ לָכַד מֶלֶךְ־אַשּׁוּר אֶת־שֹׁמְרוֹן וַיֶּגֶל

אֶת־יִשְׂרָאֵל אַשּׁוּרָה וַיֹּשֶׁב אֹתָם בַּחְלַח וּבְחָבוֹר נְהַר גּוֹזָן וְעָרֵי מָדָי

In the ninth year of Hoshea, the king of Assyria captured Samaria and carried
Israel away into exile to Assyria, and settled them in Halah and Habor, [on]
the river of Gozan, and in the cities of the Medes.

       2. Subsequent attempt to revolt, suppressed by Sargon II
       720 BCE

LESSON 18

JUDEAN MONARCHY ALONE, 8ᵀᴴ–7ᵀᴴ CENTURIES BCE

. I.   **Late Eighth Century**

A. Sargon II (722-705 B.C.E.)

<u>720</u> — against Aramaeans--Palestinian coalition lead by
Hamath. Deported more people from Samaria
ANET 285 2 Ki. 17:6

> In the second year of my reign, . . .Ia'ubidi from **Ḥamath**, a plebe with no claim to the throne, a miserable Hittite, plotted to become king of **Ḥamath**, persuaded the cities of **Arvad, Ṣimirra, Damascus** and **Samaria** to desert me, caused them to work together and equipped an army. I called up the hordes of the soldiers of Asshur and laid seige to him in his warriors in Qarqar, his beloved city. I conquered it and burned it. Himself I flayed. The rebels I slew in their cities and restored peace and quiet.

** **Gibbethon & Ekron** on his reliefs (*contra* Tadmor *JCS* 12
[1958] 83 n. 243)

Shabako, new king of **Cush**, <u>conquered the delta of Egypt</u> and killed
<u>Bocchoris</u>, king of **Sais. Ḥanunu**, king of **Gaza**, must have
heard about this and asked Shabako for help in his rebellion
against **Sargon II**. Shabako sent his commander (*turtan*), **Re'u**,
to help **Ḥanunu**.

> [Ḥanunu, king of **Gaza**] made an agreement, and **Re'u** mus[ter]ed his t[roops] to help him, and in order to do battle [and] onslaught, he advanced against me. In the name of Asshur, my lord, I inflicted a defeat on them. [Re']u, like a shepherd whose flock has been captured, ran fled and took off. I caught [Ha]nunu and brought him as a prisoner to my city, Asshur. [The city of **Raphi**]ḫ I overthrew and razed., and I burned it with fire.

ANET 285, Sargon defeated him at **Raphiaḥ**

<u>716</u> — War with Arabian tribes

> ... I crushed the tribes of **Tamud, Ibadidi, Marsimanu,** and **Ḥaiapa**, the **Arabs** who live, far away, in the desert, who know neither commissioners nor administrators and who had never brought tribute to any king. I deported their survivors and settled them in **Samaria**.

** Campaign to Egyptian border at Naḥal Muṣri

> ... in the region of *Naḥal-M[uṣur* ...] the prince of the town of **Laban** ... **Shilkanni**, king of **Muṣri**, ... sent a "present" of twelve large horses from Muṣri, which have no equal in this country.

ANET 286a-b

Tribute from **Shilkanni** (Osorkon IV), ruler of Bubastis in the
delta; opening of "<u>sealed Harbor of Egypt</u>."

715 — Arabs brought to settle in Samaria (<u>Hezekiah</u> becomes
            <u>king in Judah</u>) —

713 — <u>Azuri</u> replaced at **Ashdod** by <u>Ahimiti</u>

Azuri, king of **Ashdod**, schemed not to deliver any more tribute and he sent
messages of enmity to Assyria to <u>the kings in his region</u>. Because of these
deeds which he committed, I abolished his rule over the people of his country
and appointed <u>Ahimiti</u>, his younger brother, king over them.

712 — Revolt at **Ashdod** under <u>Iamani</u>, appealed to Pharaoh,

But the Hittites (people of the Levant), always devising evil deeds, hated his
(Ahiliti's) rule and raised <u>Iamani</u> , who had no claim to the throne, to rule
over them and who had no respect for authority, just like them. In a wild
rage, I did not wait to muster the full force of my army or to prepare the
camp, but went forth towards **Ashdod** with my warriors (cavalry) who never
leave my side, even in friendly areas. And this <u>Iamani</u> heard about the
progress of my expeditionary force, from afar, and fled into the land of
Muṣru — which now belongs to Cush — and his hiding place was not found.

I besieged and conquered the cities of **Ashdod, Gath, Ashdudimmu** ... I
reorganized these cities and settled there people from the [territories] of the
East which I had conquered myself. I appointed an officer of mine over them
and declared them to be Assyrian citizens and they pulled the straps (on my
yoke).

then he went to Egypt (Aswan) but "king of Cush"

Shabitko, sent him back to Sargon in 706 BCE.

Eponym chronicle "in the land" — Tartan sent (Isa. 20:1)

**   **Ashdod, Gath, Ashdod-yam**

710 — defeated Marduk-apil-idinna (Merodachbaladan)

707 —Shabitko returns Iamani to Sargon II.

As for he king of **Cush** who [lives] in [a far away country] in an

unapproachable region, the road [to which is ...], whose fathers never, from

far off days until now, had sent envoys to inquire about the health of my

royal ancestors, he did hear , from afar, of the might of <u>Asshur, Nebo</u> and

<u>Marduk.</u> The awe-inspiring splendor of my kingship blinded him and terror

overpowered him. He threw him **(Iamani)** into fetters, shackles and iron

bands, and they brought him to **Assyria**, a long journey.

705 — killed fighting the Cimmerians

B. Hezekiah (716/715 — 687/686) 2 Ki17:20-18:3; 2 Chr.28:27-29:2

    1. First year 715 BCE

        a. restoration of the temple 2 Chr. 29:3-36

        b. Passover 2 Chr. 30:1 ff.

c. Reform in Judah

2 Chr. 31:1 || 2 Ki 18:4

1 וּכְכַלּוֹת כָּל־זֹאת יָצְאוּ כָל־יִשְׂרָאֵל

הַנִּמְצְאִים לְעָרֵי יְהוּדָה וַיְשַׁבְּרוּ הַמַּצֵּבוֹת וַיְגַדְּעוּ

הָאֲשֵׁרִים וַיְנַתְּצוּ אֶת־הַבָּמוֹת וְאֶת־הַמִּזְבְּחֹת מִכָּל־יְהוּדָה

וּבִנְיָמִן וּבְאֶפְרַיִם וּמְנַשֶּׁה עַד־לְכַלֵּה וַיָּשׁוּבוּ כָּל־בְּנֵי

יִשְׂרָאֵל אִישׁ לַאֲחֻזָּתוֹ לְעָרֵיהֶם

Now when all this was finished, all Israel who were present went out to the cities of **Judah**, broke the pillars in pieces, cut down the Asherim and pulled down the high places and the altars throughout all **Judah** and **Benjamin**, as well as in **Ephraim** and **Manasseh**, until they had destroyed them all. Then all the sons of Israel returned to their cities, each to his possession.

2 Ki 18:4

4 הוּא הֵסִיר אֶת־הַבָּמוֹת וְשִׁבַּר אֶת־הַמַּצֵּבֹת

וְכָרַת אֶת־הָאֲשֵׁרָה וְכִתַּת נְחַשׁ הַנְּחֹשֶׁת אֲשֶׁר־עָשָׂה מֹשֶׁה

כִּי עַד־הַיָּמִים הָהֵמָּה הָיוּ בְנֵי־יִשְׂרָאֵל מְקַטְּרִים לוֹ

וַיִּקְרָא־לוֹ נְחֻשְׁתָּן

He removed the high places and broke down the [sacred] pillars and cut down the Asherah. He also broke in pieces the bronze serpent that Moses had made, for until those days the sons of Israel burned incense to it; and it was called Nehushtan.

2. <u>712</u> — did not get involved in Ashdod -- paid tribute to
Sargon *ANET* 287a

Isa 20:1-6

1 בִּשְׁנַת בֹּא תַרְתָּן אַשְׁדּוֹדָה בִּשְׁלֹחַ אֹתוֹ סַרְגוֹן
מֶלֶךְ אַשּׁוּר וַיִּלָּחֶם בְּאַשְׁדּוֹד וַיִּלְכְּדָהּ

2 בָּעֵת הַהִיא דִּבֶּר יְהוָה בְּיַד יְשַׁעְיָהוּ בֶן־אָמוֹץ
לֵאמֹר לֵךְ וּפִתַּחְתָּ הַשַּׂק מֵעַל מָתְנֶיךָ וְנַעַלְךָ תַחֲלֹץ
מֵעַל רַגְלֶיךָ וַיַּעַשׂ כֵּן הָלֹךְ עָרוֹם וְיָחֵף

3 וַיֹּאמֶר יְהוָה כַּאֲשֶׁר הָלַךְ עַבְדִּי יְשַׁעְיָהוּ עָרוֹם
וְיָחֵף שָׁלֹשׁ שָׁנִים אוֹת וּמוֹפֵת עַל־מִצְרַיִם וְעַל־כּוּשׁ

4 כֵּן יִנְהַג מֶלֶךְ־אַשּׁוּר אֶת־שְׁבִי מִצְרַיִם וְאֶת־גָּלוּת
כּוּשׁ נְעָרִים וּזְקֵנִים עָרוֹם וְיָחֵף וַחֲשׂוּפַי שֵׁת עֶרְוַת מִצְרָיִם

5 וְחַתּוּ וָבֹשׁוּ מִכּוּשׁ מַבָּטָם וּמִן־מִצְרַיִם תִּפְאַרְתָּם

6 וְאָמַר יֹשֵׁב הָאִי הַזֶּה בַּיּוֹם הַהוּא הִנֵּה־כֹה מַבָּטֵנוּ אֲשֶׁר־נַסְנוּ
שָׁם לְעֶזְרָה לְהִנָּצֵל מִפְּנֵי מֶלֶךְ אַשּׁוּר וְאֵיךְ נִמָּלֵט אֲנָחְנוּ

In the year that the commander came to **Ashdod**, when <u>Sargon the king of Assyria</u> sent him and he fought against **Ashdod** and captured it, at that time Yahweh spoke through Isaiah the son of Amoz, saying, "Go and loosen the sackcloth from your hips and take your shoes off your feet." And he did so, going naked and barefoot. And Yahweh said, "Even as My servant Isaiah has gone naked and barefoot three years as a sign and token against **Egypt** and **Cush**, so the king of **Assyria** will lead away the captives of Egypt and the exiles of Cush, young and old, naked and barefoot with buttocks uncovered, to the shame of Egypt. "Then they will be dismayed and ashamed because of Cush their hope and Egypt their boast. "So **this island inhabitant** (Iamani?) will say in that day, 'Behold, such is our hope, where we fled for help to be delivered from the king of Assyria; and we, how shall we escape?'"

3.   705— begin rebellion against Assyria

> 2 Kings 18:7-8

7 וְהָיָה יְהוָה עִמּוֹ בְּכֹל אֲשֶׁר־יֵצֵא יַשְׂכִּיל

וַיִּמְרֹד בְּמֶלֶךְ־אַשּׁוּר וְלֹא עֲבָדוֹ

8 הוּא־הִכָּה אֶת־פְּלִשְׁתִּים עַד־עַזָּה

וְאֶת־גְּבוּלֶיהָ מִמִּגְדַּל נוֹצְרִים עַד־עִיר מִבְצָר

And Yahweh was with him; wherever he went he prospered. <u>And he rebelled against the king of Assyria</u> and did not serve him. He defeated the **Philistines** as far as **Gaza** and its territory, from watchtower to fortified city.

> 2 Chr. 32:2-18;

2 וַיַּרְא יְחִזְקִיָּהוּ כִּי־בָא סַנְחֵרִיב וּפָנָיו

לַמִּלְחָמָה עַל־יְרוּשָׁלָם

3 וַיִּוָּעַץ עִם־שָׂרָיו וְגִבֹּרָיו לִסְתּוֹם אֶת־מֵימֵי

הָעֲיָנוֹת אֲשֶׁר מִחוּץ לָעִיר וַיַּעְזְרוּהוּ

4 וַיִּקָּבְצוּ עַם־רָב וַיִּסְתְּמוּ אֶת־כָּל־הַמַּעְיָנוֹת

וְאֶת־הַנַּחַל הַשּׁוֹטֵף בְּתוֹךְ־הָאָרֶץ לֵאמֹר לָמָה יָבוֹאוּ

מַלְכֵי אַשּׁוּר וּמָצְאוּ מַיִם רַבִּים

5 וַיִּתְחַזַּק וַיִּבֶן אֶת־כָּל־הַחוֹמָה הַפְּרוּצָה וַיַּעַל

עַל־הַמִּגְדָּלוֹת וְלַחוּצָה הַחוֹמָה אַחֶרֶת וַיְחַזֵּק

אֶת־הַמִּלּוֹא עִיר דָּוִיד וַיַּעַשׂ שֶׁלַח לָרֹב וּמָגִנִּים

6 וַיִּתֵּן שָׂרֵי מִלְחָמוֹת עַל־הָעָם וַיִּקְבְּצֵם אֵלָיו

אֶל־רְחוֹב שַׁעַר הָעִיר וַיְדַבֵּר עַל־לְבָבָם לֵאמֹר

7 חִזְקוּ וְאִמְצוּ אַל־תִּירְאוּ וְאַל־תֵּחַתּוּ מִפְּנֵי

מֶלֶךְ אַשּׁוּר וּמִלִּפְנֵי כָּל־הֶהָמוֹן אֲשֶׁר־עִמּוֹ כִּי־עִמָּנוּ רַב

מֵעִמּוֹ

8 עִמּוֹ זְרוֹעַ בָּשָׂר וְעִמָּנוּ יְהוָה אֱלֹהֵינוּ

לְעָזְרֵנוּ וּלְהִלָּחֵם מִלְחֲמֹתֵנוּ וַיִּסָּמְכוּ הָעָם עַל־דִּבְרֵי

יְחִזְקִיָּהוּ מֶלֶךְ־יְהוּדָה

9 אַחַר זֶה שָׁלַח סַנְחֵרִיב מֶלֶךְ־אַשּׁוּר עֲבָדָיו
יְרוּשָׁלַיְמָה וְהוּא עַל־לָכִישׁ וְכָל־מֶמְשַׁלְתּוֹ עִמּוֹ
עַל־יְחִזְקִיָּהוּ מֶלֶךְ יְהוּדָה וְעַל־כָּל־יְהוּדָה אֲשֶׁר
בִּירוּשָׁלַם לֵאמֹר

10 כֹּה אָמַר סַנְחֵרִיב מֶלֶךְ אַשּׁוּר עַל־מָה
אַתֶּם בֹּטְחִים וְיֹשְׁבִים בְּמָצוֹר בִּירוּשָׁלָם

11 הֲלֹא יְחִזְקִיָּהוּ מַסִּית אֶתְכֶם לָתֵת אֶתְכֶם
לָמוּת בְּרָעָב וּבְצָמָא לֵאמֹר יְהוָה אֱלֹהֵינוּ יַצִּילֵנוּ מִכַּף מֶלֶךְ אַשּׁוּר

12 הֲלֹא־הוּא יְחִזְקִיָּהוּ הֵסִיר אֶת־בָּמֹתָיו
וְאֶת־מִזְבְּחֹתָיו וַיֹּאמֶר לִיהוּדָה וְלִירוּשָׁלַם לֵאמֹר לִפְנֵי
מִזְבֵּחַ אֶחָד תִּשְׁתַּחֲווּ וְעָלָיו תַּקְטִירוּ

13 הֲלֹא תֵדְעוּ מֶה עָשִׂיתִי אֲנִי וַאֲבוֹתַי֪ לְכֹל
עַמֵּי הָאֲרָצוֹת הֲיָכוֹל יָכְלוּ אֱלֹהֵי גּוֹיֵ הָאֲרָצוֹת לְהַצִּיל
אֶת־אַרְצָם מִיָּדִי

14 מִי בְּכָל־אֱלֹהֵי הַגּוֹיִם הָאֵלֶּה אֲשֶׁר הֶחֱרִימוּ
אֲבוֹתַי֪ אֲשֶׁר יָכוֹל לְהַצִּיל אֶת־עַמּוֹ מִיָּדִי כִּי יוּכַל
אֱלֹהֵיכֶם לְהַצִּיל אֶתְכֶם מִיָּדִי

15 וְעַתָּה אַל־יַשִּׁיא אֶתְכֶם חִזְקִיָּהוּ וְאַל־יַסִּית
אֶתְכֶם כָּזֹאת וְאַל־תַּאֲמִינוּ לוֹ כִּי־לֹא יוּכַל כָּל־אֱלוֹהַּ
כָּל־גּוֹי וּמַמְלָכָה לְהַצִּיל עַמּוֹ מִיָּדִי וּמִיַּד אֲבוֹתָי֪ אַף
כִּי אֱלֹהֵיכֶם לֹא־יַצִּילוּ אֶתְכֶם מִיָּדִי

16 וְעוֹד דִּבְּרוּ עֲבָדָיו עַל־יְהוָה הָאֱלֹהִים וְעַל יְחִזְקִיָּהוּ עַבְדּוֹ

17 וּסְפָרִים כָּתַב לְחָרֵף לַיהוָה אֱלֹהֵי
יִשְׂרָאֵל וְלֵאמֹר עָלָיו לֵאמֹר כֵּאלֹהֵי גּוֹיֵ הָאֲרָצוֹת אֲשֶׁר
לֹא־הִצִּילוּ עַמָּם מִיָּדִי כֵּן לֹא־יַצִּיל אֱלֹהֵי יְחִזְקִיָּהוּ עַמּוֹ מִיָּדִי

18 וַיִּקְרְאוּ בְקוֹל־גָּדוֹל יְהוּדִית עַל־עַם

יְרוּשָׁלַם אֲשֶׁר עַל־הַחוֹמָה לְיָרְאָם וּלְבַהֲלָם לְמַעַן יִלְכְּדוּ אֶת־הָעִיר

Now when Hezekiah saw that **Sennacherib** had come and that he intended
to make war on Jerusalem, he decided with his officers and his warriors to
cut off the [supply of] water from the springs which [were] outside the city,
and they helped him. So many people assembled and stopped up all the
springs and the stream which flowed through the region, saying, "Why
should the kings of Assyria come and find abundant water?"

And he took courage and rebuilt all the wall that had been broken down
and erected towers on it, and [built] another outside wall and strengthened
the Millo [in] the city of David, and made weapons and shields in great
number. He appointed military officers over the people and gathered them to
him in the square at the city gate, and spoke encouragingly to them, saying,
"Be strong and courageous, do not fear or be dismayed because of the king of
Assyria nor because of all the horde that is with him; for the one with us is
greater than the one with him. With him is [only] an arm of flesh, but with us
is Yahweh our God to help us and to fight our battles." And the people relied
on the words of Hezekiah king of Judah.

2 Chr. 32:27-29;

27 וַיְהִי לִיחִזְקִיָּהוּ עֹשֶׁר וְכָבוֹד הַרְבֵּה מְאֹד

וְאֹצָרוֹת עָשָׂה־לוֹ לְכֶסֶף וּלְזָהָב וּלְאֶבֶן יְקָרָה

וְלִבְשָׂמִים וּלְמָגִנִּים וּלְכֹל כְּלֵי חֶמְדָּה

28 וּמִסְכְּנוֹת לִתְבוּאַת דָּגָן וְתִירוֹשׁ וְיִצְהָר

וְאֻרָוֹת לְכָל־בְּהֵמָה וּבְהֵמָה וַעֲדָרִים לָאֲוֵרוֹת

29 וְעָרִים עָשָׂה לוֹ וּמִקְנֵה־צֹאן וּבָקָר לָרֹב

כִּי נָתַן־לוֹ אֱלֹהִים רְכוּשׁ רַב מְאֹד

Now **Hezekiah** had immense riches and honor; and he made for himself
treasuries for silver, gold, precious stones, spices, shields and all kinds of
valuable articles, storehouses also for the produce of grain, wine and oil, pens
for all kinds of cattle and sheepfolds for the flocks. He made cities for himself
and acquired flocks and herds in abundance, for God had given him very
great wealth.

2 Chr. 32:30-31

27 וַיְהִי לִיחִזְקִיָּהוּ עֹשֶׁר וְכָבוֹד הַרְבֵּה מְאֹד

וְאֹצָרוֹת עָשָׂה־לוֹ לְכֶסֶף וּלְזָהָב וּלְאֶבֶן יְקָרָה

וְלִבְשָׂמִים וּלְמָגִנִּים וּלְכֹל כְּלֵי חֶמְדָּה

28 וּמִסְכְּנוֹת לִתְבוּאַת דָּגָן וְתִירוֹשׁ וְיִצְהָר

וְאֻרָוֹת לְכָל־בְּהֵמָה וּבְהֵמָה וַעֲדָרִים לָאֲוֵרוֹת

29 וְעָרִים עָשָׂה לוֹ וּמִקְנֵה־צֹאן וּבָקָר לָרֹב

כִּי נָתַן־לוֹ אֱלֹהִים רְכוּשׁ רַב מְאֹד

It was Hezekiah <u>who stopped the upper outlet of the waters of Gihon and directed them to the west side of the city of David.</u>
And Hezekiah prospered in all that he did. And thus with **the envoys of the rulers of Babylon**, who sent to him to inquire of the wonder that had happened in the land, God left him to test him, that He might know all that was in his heart.

also put **Padi** in chains (II 73[69]-77[72]);

šakkanakkī rubê u nišī ^cAmqarōna ša Pādî šarra-šunu bēl adê u mamīti ša māt Aššūr birêtu parzilli iddûma and Ḫazaqiya Ia'ūdāya iddinūšu nakriš ana anzilli īpušu . . .

The officials, the nobles and the people of ^c**Aqqarōna** (= Ekron), who had thrown into iron fetters Pādî, their king, a sworn vassal of Asshur, and <u>handed him over to Hezekiah the Judean; he kept him in prison illegally as an enemy</u> . . . .

Philistines, Edom, Moab & Ammon involved, Luli king of Ṣidon leader in Phoenicia

למלך **stamps** — stamped wine (or oil) jar jandles, "to the king," with one of two symbols, scarab beetle or winged sun disc, and one of four places: **Hebron**, **Ziph**, **Socoh** or *MMŠT*. Same jars had a personal seal of some official on another handle. These jars were probably for wine from royal vineyards, one place from each district in the hills, plus *MMŠT* (= *memše[l]et?*) for **Jerusalem**. Cf. 2 Chronicles 26:10c.

***   4. <u>701</u>— his 14th year

              a. Illness — 2 Ki 20:1-6;

1 בַּיָּמִים הָהֵם חָלָה חִזְקִיָּהוּ לָמוּת וַיָּבֹא

אֵלָיו יְשַׁעְיָהוּ בֶן־אָמוֹץ הַנָּבִיא וַיֹּאמֶר אֵלָיו כֹּה־אָמַר

יְהוָה צַו לְבֵיתֶךָ כִּי מֵת אַתָּה וְלֹא תִחְיֶה

2 וַיַּסֵּב אֶת־פָּנָיו אֶל־הַקִּיר וַיִּתְפַּלֵּל

אֶל־יְהוָה לֵאמֹר

3 אָנָּה יְהוָה זְכָר־נָא אֵת אֲשֶׁר הִתְהַלַּכְתִּי

לְפָנֶיךָ בֶּאֱמֶת וּבְלֵבָב שָׁלֵם וְהַטּוֹב בְּעֵינֶיךָ עָשִׂיתִי

וַיֵּבְךְּ חִזְקִיָּהוּ בְּכִי גָדוֹל

4 וַיְהִי יְשַׁעְיָהוּ לֹא יָצָא הָעִיר [הָצֵר]

הַתִּיכֹנָה וּדְבַר־יְהוָה הָיָה אֵלָיו לֵאמֹר

5 שׁוּב וְאָמַרְתָּ אֶל־חִזְקִיָּהוּ נְגִיד־עַמִּי

כֹּה־אָמַר יְהוָה אֱלֹהֵי דָוִד אָבִיךָ שָׁמַעְתִּי אֶת־תְּפִלָּתֶךָ

רָאִיתִי אֶת־דִּמְעָתֶךָ הִנְנִי רֹפֵא לָךְ בַּיּוֹם הַשְּׁלִישִׁי

תַּעֲלֶה בֵּית יְהוָה

6 וְהֹסַפְתִּי עַל־יָמֶיךָ חֲמֵשׁ עֶשְׂרֵה שָׁנָה וּמִכַּף

מֶלֶךְ־אַשּׁוּר אַצִּילְךָ וְאֵת הָעִיר הַזֹּאת וְגַנּוֹתִי עַל־הָעִיר

הַזֹּאת לְמַעֲנִי וּלְמַעַן דָּוִד עַבְדִּי

In those days **Hezekiah** became mortally ill. And **Isaiah** the prophet the son of Amoz came to him and said to him, "Thus says Yahweh, 'Set your house in order, for you shall die and not live.'" Then he turned his face to the wall and prayed to Yahweh, saying, "Remember now, O Yahweh, I beseech You, how I have walked before You in truth and with a whole heart and have done what is good in Your sight." And Hezekiah wept bitterly. Before Isaiah had gone out of the middle court, the word of Yahweh came to him, saying, "Return and say to Hezekiah the leader of My people, 'Thus says Yahweh, the God of your father David, "I have heard your prayer, I have seen your tears; behold, I will heal you. On the third day you shall go up to the house of Yahweh. I will add fifteen years to your life, and I will deliver you and this city from the hand of the king of Assyria; and I will defend this city for My own sake and for My servant David's sake."

Isa 38:1-6;

1 בַּיָּמִים הָהֵם חָלָה חִזְקִיָּהוּ לָמוּת וַיָּבוֹא אֵלָיו

יְשַׁעְיָהוּ בֶן־אָמוֹץ הַנָּבִיא וַיֹּאמֶר אֵלָיו כֹּה־אָמַר יְהוָה

צַו לְבֵיתֶךָ כִּי מֵת אַתָּה וְלֹא תִחְיֶה

2 וַיַּסֵּב חִזְקִיָּהוּ פָּנָיו אֶל־הַקִּיר וַיִּתְפַּלֵּל אֶל־יְהוָה

3 וַיֹּאמַר אָנָּה יְהוָה זְכָר־נָא אֵת אֲשֶׁר הִתְהַלַּכְתִּי

לְפָנֶיךָ בֶּאֱמֶת וּבְלֵב שָׁלֵם וְהַטּוֹב בְּעֵינֶיךָ עָשִׂיתִי וַיֵּבְךְּ

חִזְקִיָּהוּ בְּכִי גָדוֹל

4 וַיְהִי דְּבַר־יְהוָה אֶל־יְשַׁעְיָהוּ לֵאמֹר

5 הָלוֹךְ וְאָמַרְתָּ אֶל־חִזְקִיָּהוּ כֹּה־אָמַר יְהוָה אֱלֹהֵי דָּוִד אָבִיךָ שָׁמַעְתִּי

(LXX 1st sg. προστίθημι) אֶת־תְּפִלָּתֶךָ רָאִיתִי אֶת־דִּמְעָתֶךָ הִנְנִי יֹסִף

עַל־יָמֶיךָ חֲמֵשׁ עֶשְׂרֵה שָׁנָה

6 וּמִכַּף מֶלֶךְ־אַשּׁוּר אַצִּילְךָ וְאֵת הָעִיר הַזֹּאת

וְגַנּוֹתִי עַל־הָעִיר הַזֹּאת

In those days **Hezekiah** became mortally ill. And **Isaiah** the prophet the son of Amoz came to him and said to him, "Thus says Yahweh, 'Set your house in order, for you shall die and not live.'" Then Hezekiah turned his face to the wall and prayed to Yahweh, and said, "Remember now, O Yahweh, I beseech You, how I have walked before You in truth and with a whole heart, and have done what is good in Your sight." And Hezekiah wept bitterly. Then the word of Yahweh came to Isaiah, saying, "Go and say to Hezekiah, 'Thus says Yahweh, the God of your father David, "I have heard your prayer, I have seen your tears; behold, <u>I</u> (LXX) will <u>add</u> <u>fifteen</u> <u>years</u> <u>to</u> <u>your</u> <u>life</u>. <u>I will</u> <u>deliver</u> <u>you</u> <u>and</u> <u>this</u> <u>city</u> <u>from</u> <u>the</u> <u>hand</u> <u>of</u> <u>the</u> <u>king</u> <u>of</u> <u>Assyria;</u> <u>and I will</u> <u>defend</u> <u>this</u> <u>city</u>.'"

***   **Added 15 years — 701 to 686 BCE**

delegation from **Merodachbaladan,** <u>who</u> <u>was</u> <u>in</u> <u>exile</u> <u>in</u> <u>Elam</u>

2 Kings 20:12-13

12 בָּעֵת הַהִיא שָׁלַח בְּראדַךְ בַּלְאֲדָן בֶּן־בַּלְאֲדָן מֶלֶךְ־בָּבֶל

סְפָרִים וּמִנְחָה אֶל־חִזְקִיָּהוּ כִּי שָׁמַע כִּי חָלָה חִזְקִיָּהוּ

13 וַיִּשְׁמַע עֲלֵיהֶם חִזְקִיָּהוּ וַיַּרְאֵם אֶת־כָּל־בֵּית נְכֹתֹה

אֶת־הַכֶּסֶף וְאֶת־הַזָּהָב וְאֶת־הַבְּשָׂמִים וְאֵת שֶׁמֶן הַטּוֹב וְאֵת בֵּית כֵּלָיו

וְאֵת כָּל־אֲשֶׁר נִמְצָא בְּאוֹצְרֹתָיו לֹא־הָיָה דָבָר אֲשֶׁר

לֹא־הֶרְאָם חִזְקִיָּהוּ בְּבֵיתוֹ וּבְכָל־מֶמְשַׁלְתּוֹ

At that time **Berodach-baladan** a son of Baladan, **king of Babylon**, sent letters and a present to Hezekiah, for he heard that Hezekiah had been sick. Hezekiah listened to them, and showed them all his treasure house, the silver

and the gold and the spices and the precious oil and the house of his armor
and all that was found in his treasures. There was nothing in his house nor in
all his dominion that Hezekiah did not show them.

Isaiah 39:1-2

1 בָּעֵת הַהִוא שָׁלַח מְרֹדַךְ בַּלְאֲדָן בֶּן־בַּלְאֲדָן

מֶלֶךְ־בָּבֶל סְפָרִים וּמִנְחָה אֶל־חִזְקִיָּהוּ וַיִּשְׁמַע כִּי חָלָה וַיֶּחֱזָק

2 וַיִּשְׂמַח עֲלֵיהֶם חִזְקִיָּהוּ וַיַּרְאֵם אֶת־בֵּית נְכֹתָה

[נְכֹתוֹ] אֶת־הַכֶּסֶף וְאֶת־הַזָּהָב וְאֶת־הַבְּשָׂמִים וְאֵת הַשֶּׁמֶן הַטּוֹב

וְאֵת כָּל־בֵּית כֵּלָיו וְאֵת כָּל־אֲשֶׁר נִמְצָא בְּאֹצְרֹתָיו לֹא־הָיָה דָבָר

אֲשֶׁר לֹא־הֶרְאָם חִזְקִיָּהוּ בְּבֵיתוֹ וּבְכָל־מֶמְשַׁלְתּוֹ

At that time **Merodach-baladan** son of Baladan, **king of Babylon**, sent letters
and a present to **Hezekiah**, for he heard that he had been sick and had
recovered. Hezekiah was pleased, and showed them his treasure house, the
silver and the gold and the spices and the precious oil and his whole armory
and all that was found in his treasures. There was nothing in his house nor in
all his dominion that Hezekiah did not show them.

***   b. **Sennacherib** comes,

(1) the Phoenician leader flees and meets his death overseas (II 37[34]-40[37])):

ina šalši girriya ana māt Ḥatti lū allik. Lūli šar Ṣīdōna pulḫī melammē bēlūtīya isḫupušuma ana rūqī qabal tamtim innabit-ma šadda-šu ēmid.
In my third campaign I marched to **the land of Ḥatti**. (E)luli, king of **Sidon**, whom the terror inspiring splendor of my lordship had overwhelmed, fled far away in the midst of the sea; there he met his fate.

(2) The **Phoenician cities** surrender (II 41[38]-49[46]):

Ṣīdōnu rabû, Ṣīdōnu ṣeḫru, Bīt-zitti, Ṣariptu, Maḥalliba, Usû, Akzibi, Akkô, ālānīšu dannūti bīt dūrānī ašar rîti u mašqīti bīt tuklāte-šu rašubbāt kakki Aššūr bēliya isḫupūšunūtima iknušū šēpū'a. Tubaᶜalu ina kussi šarrūtišu elīšun ušēšibma biltu mandattu bēlūtiya šattīšam lābaṭlu ukīn ṣēruššu
The terror of the weapon of Asshur, my lord, overwhelmed **Great Sidon, Little Sidon, Beth-zait, Ṣariptu, Maḥalliba, Usû, Achzib, Acco**, his mighty fortified cities, where there was feed and water supply for his fortresses; they bowed in submission at my feet. I installed (E)thō-baᶜl on the throne of their kingship over them; I imposed on him the tribute of my lordship, annually without cessation.

(3) Most of the allies desert Hezekiah and rush to pay their tribute to Sennacherib (II 50[47]-59[58])

ša Miniḫimu Samsimurōnāya, Tūbaᶜlu Ṣīdōnāya, ᶜAbdi-li'ti Arudāya, Urumilki Gublāya, Mittinti Asdōdāya, Bōdu-'ilu Bīt ᶜAmmanāya Kamōšunadbi Ma'abāya Ayarāmu Udōmāya šarrānī māt Amurri kalīšun igisê šadlūti tāmartašunu kabittu adi 4-šu ana maḫriya iššûnimma iššiqū šēpīya
The sumptuous gifts and heavy trribute, four fold, of **Menaḥem the Šamši-Merōnite, (E)thō-baᶜal the Sidonian, ᶜAbdi-līti the Arvadite, Urumilki the Gublite, Mittinti the Ashdodite, Bol-'ilu the Ammonite, Kemosh-nadbi the Moabite, Ayarâmu the Edomite**, all the kings of the land of Amurru, the brought before me and they kissed my feet.

King of Ashkelon deposed [**out of chronological order here**] (II 60[58]-68[65]):

u Ṣidqâ šar Isqalōna ša lā iknušu ana nīrīya ilānī bīt abīšu šâšu aššassu

mārīšu mārātīšu aḫḫīšu zēr bīt abīšu assuḫamma ana māt Aššūr

ūrâššu Šarru-lū-dāri mār Rukibti šarrašunu maḫrû eli nišī Isqalōna

aškunma nadān bilti kadrê bēlūtiya ēmissuma išâṭ abšānī

And as for Ṣidqâ the king of **Ashkelon** who had not submitted to my yoke, the gods of his house, himself, his wife, his sons, his daughters, his brothers, ther seed of his house, I deported and I had him led off to Assyria. Šarru-lū-dāri, son of Rukibti their former king, I placed over the people of Ashkelon, the payment of tribute, the gifts of my lordship, I imposed on him. He pulled my yoke.

Joppa & hinterland (II 68[65]-;

ina mētiq girriya Bīt-Dagāna, Iāpō, Banay-Barqa, Azōru, ālānī ša

Ṣidqā ša ana šēpīya arḫiš lā iknušu, alme, akšud ašlula šallassun.

In the course of my campaign, Beth-Dagan, Yafo, Benei-Baraq, Azor, cities of Ṣidqā who did not bow quicklet at my feet, I surrounded, I conquered, the spoil I took away.

Egyptian intervention (II 73[69]-III 6[82]);

šakkanakkī rubê u nišī ᶜAmqarōna ša Pādî šarra-šunu bēl adê u mamīti

ša māt Aššūr birêtu parzilli iddûma and Ḫazaqiya Ya'ūdāya iddinūšu

nakriš ana anzilli īpušu, iplaḫ libbašun, šarrānī māt Muṣri ṣābī qašti,

narkabāti, sīsî ša šar māt MeluḫḫI emuqī lā nibi ikterûnimma illikū

rēṣussun, ina tāmirti Altaqô ellamū'a sidru šitkunu, uša''alū

kakkīšun, ina tukulti Sššūr bēlīya ittišun amdaḫišma, aštakan

dabdâšun, bēl narkabāti u mārī šarri Muṣrāya adi bēl narkabāti ša šar

māt MeluḫḫI balṭūssun ina qabal tamḫari ikudā qātāya.

As for the officials, the nobles and the people of ᶜ**Aqqarōna** (= Ekron), who had thrown into iron fetters **Pādî**, their king, a sworn vassal of Asshur, and handed him over to Hezekiah the Judean; he kept him in prison illegally as an enemy, their heart feared, they called out for the **kings of the land of Egypt**, an army of bowmen, charioteers, and horses of the **king of the land of Cush**, a host without number; they came to their aid. In the vicinity of **Altaqô** (Eltekeh) they were arraigned in battle order against me and they were sharpening their weapons. Trusting in Asshur, my lord, I engaged them in combat and I accomplished their defeat. The charioteers and the sons of the king of Egypt with the charioteers of the king of Cush, my own hands captured alive.

Elteke, & Timnah (III 6[II 82-83])

Altaqô Tamnâ alme akšud ašlula šallassun.

Altaqô (Eltekeh), **Tamnâ** (Timnah), I surrounded, I captured, their spoil I took away.

Ekron (III 7[III 1]-III 17 [III 11]),

ana ꜥAmqarôna aqribma, šakkanakkī, rubê ša ḫīṭu ušabšû, adūkma, ina dīmāti siḫirti āli ālul pagrīšun, mārī āli ēpiš annî u gillāti ana šallati amnu. Sittūtešunu lā bābil u gullulti ša arānšunu lā ibšû uššuršun aqbi. Pādi šarrašunu ultu qereb Ursalimmu ušēṣâmma, ina kussi bēlūti elīšun ušēšibma, mandattu bēlūtīya ukīn ṣēruššu.

To **ꜥAmqarôna** (Ekron) I drew near; the officials and nobles who had committed a sin, I slew; on stakes around the city I impaled their bodies. The citizens of the city, who committed misdeeds and transgressions, I counted as spoil. As for the remainder, who did not carry any guilt or misdemeanors, who had no guilt, I commanded their release.

Pādi, their king, I brought out from **Jerusalem** and I seated him on the throne over them. The tribute of my lordship I imposed upon him.

⟨**Azekah** and [**Gath**]⟩;

The city of Azekah . . . located on a mountain ridge . . . I captured, I carried off its spoil, I devastated . . . .(Letter to the god Asshur)

A fragmentary "Letter to the god (Asshur)" reporting the king's victory supplements the account in Sennacherib's Annals. Its reference to the capture of Azekah, a lofty Judean fortress, is followed by a Philistine town taken over by Hezekiah, most likely Gath. The seizure of Azekah would leave Gath unprotected. The two main approaches to Judah from the west were now blocked.

Against Judah (III 18[III 12]-III 30 [III 23]),

u Ḥazaqiyahu Iahudāya ša lā iknušu ana nīrīya 46 ālānīšu dannūti bīt dūrānī u ālānī ṣeḫrūti ša limêtišunu ša nība lā īšû ina šukbus arāmm u qitrub šupî mithuṣ zūk šēpī pilši niksi u kalbannāte alme akšud. 200150 nišī ṣeher rabi zikar u sinniš sīsî parî imērī gammalī alpī u ṣēnī ša lā nībi ultu qerbišun ušēṣâmma šallatiš amnu.

As for Hezekiah the Judean, who did not submit to my yoke, I surrounded forty six of his strong walled cities and the numberless small towns in their surroundings, by laying down ramps and applying battering rams, onslaughts by foot troops, tunnels, breeches and siege ladders, I conquered them. Two hundred thousand one hundred and fifty people, small and great, male and female, horses, mules, donkeys, camels, oxen and small cattle without number I brought out of them and I counted them as spoil. Himself like a caged bird in Jerusalem, his royal city, I confined him; I linked together siege forts against him; whoever came forth from the gate I turned back in humiliation.

Micah 1:8-16 — some conquered cities??

8 עַל־זֹאת אֶסְפְּדָה וְאֵילִילָה אֵילְכָה שֵׁילָל

[שׁוֹלָל] וְעָרוֹם אֶעֱשֶׂה מִסְפֵּד כַּתַּנִּים וְאֵבֶל כִּבְנוֹת יַעֲנָה

9 כִּי אֲנוּשָׁה מַכּוֹתֶיהָ כִּי־בָאָה עַד־יְהוּדָה נָגַע

עַד־שַׁעַר עַמִּי עַד־יְרוּשָׁלָם

Because of this I must lament and wail, I must go barefoot and naked; I must make a lament like the jackals And a mourning like the ostriches.
For her wound is incurable, For it has come to Judah; It has reached the gate of my people, [Even] to Jerusalem.

10a בְּגַת אַל־תַּגִּידוּ בָּכוֹ אַל־תִּבְכּוּ ·

Tell it not in Gath, Weep not at all.

10b בְּבֵית לְעַפְרָה עָפָר הִתְפַּלָּשְׁתִּי [הִתְפַּלָּשִׁי]

At Beth-le-aphrah roll yourself in the dust.

11a עִבְרִי לָכֶם יוֹשֶׁבֶת שָׁפִיר עֶרְיָה־בֹשֶׁת

Go on your way, inhabitant of Shaphir, in shameful nakedness.

11b לֹא יָצְאָה יוֹשֶׁבֶת צַאֲנָן ·

The inhabitant of Zaanan does not escape.

11c מִסְפַּד בֵּית הָאֵצֶל יִקַּח מִכֶּם עֶמְדָּתוֹ

The lamentation of Beth-ezel: "He will take from you its support."

12 כִּי־חָלָה לְטוֹב יוֹשֶׁבֶת מָרוֹת כִּי־יָרַד רָע מֵאֵת יְהוָה לְשַׁעַר יְרוּשָׁלָם
For the inhabitant of Maroth becomes weak waiting for good, Because a calamity has come down from Yahweh to the gate of Jerusalem.

13 רְתֹם הַמֶּרְכָּבָה לָרֶכֶשׁ יוֹשֶׁבֶת לָכִישׁ רֵאשִׁית ·

חַטָּאת הִיא לְבַת־צִיּוֹן כִּי־בָךְ נִמְצְאוּ פִּשְׁעֵי יִשְׂרָאֵל

Harness the chariot to the team of horses, O inhabitant of Lachish — She was the beginning of sin to the daughter of Zion — Because in you were found The rebellious acts of Israel.

14a לָכֵן תִּתְּנִי שִׁלּוּחִים עַל מוֹרֶשֶׁת גַּת

Therefore you will give parting gifts On behalf of Moresheth-gath

14b בָּתֵּי אַכְזִיב לְאַכְזָב לְמַלְכֵי יִשְׂרָאֵל:

The houses of Achzib [will] become a deception To the kings of Israel.

15a עֹד הַיֹּרֵשׁ אָבִי לָךְ יוֹשֶׁבֶת מָרֵשָׁה

Moreover, I will bring on you The one who takes possession, O inhabitant of Mareshah.

15b עַד־עֲדֻלָּם יָבוֹא כְּבוֹד יִשְׂרָאֵל:

The glory of Israel will enter Adullam.

16 גָּלִּי וָגֹזִּי עַל־בְּנֵי תַּעֲנוּגָיִךְ הַרְחִבִי קָרְחָתֵךְ כַּנֶּשֶׁר כִּי גָלוּ מִמֵּךְ קָרְחִי

Make yourself bald and cut off your hair, Because of the children of your

delight; Extend your baldness like the eagle, For they will go from you into

exile.

Jerusalem besieged (III 27[III 20]-III 30[23])

šâšu kīma iṣṣūr quppi qereb Ursalimmu āl šarrūtišu ēsiršu, bīrāti elīšu

urakkisma āṣê abul ālīšu utirra ikkibuš

Himself like a caged bird in **Jerusalem**, his royal city, I confined him; I linked together siege forts against him; whoever came forth from the gate I turned back in humiliation.

Lachish besieged:

Inscription on the relief of Sennacherib's conquest of Lachish:

Sîn-aḫḫī-irība šar kiššati šar māt Aššūr ina kussi nēmedi ūšibma šallat

Lakisu maḫaršu ētiq

Sennacherib, king of the world, king of the land of Assyria, sat on a throne; the booty of **Lachish** passed before him.

2 Kings 18:17-20

17 וַיִּשְׁלַח מֶלֶךְ־אַשּׁוּר אֶת־תַּרְתָּן

וְאֶת־רַב־סָרִיס וְאֶת־רַב־שָׁקֵה מִן־לָכִישׁ אֶל־הַמֶּלֶךְ

חִזְקִיָּהוּ בְּחֵיל כָּבֵד יְרוּשָׁלָ͏ִם וַיַּעֲלוּ וַיָּבֹאוּ יְרוּשָׁלַ͏ִם

וַיַּעֲלוּ וַיָּבֹאוּ וַיַּעַמְדוּ בִּתְעָלַת הַבְּרֵכָה הָעֶלְיוֹנָה אֲשֶׁר

בְּמְסִלַּת שְׂדֵה כוֹבֵס

18 וַיִּקְרְאוּ אֶל־הַמֶּלֶךְ וַיֵּצֵא אֲלֵהֶם אֶלְיָקִים

בֶּן־חִלְקִיָּהוּ אֲשֶׁר עַל־הַבַּיִת וְשֶׁבְנָה הַסֹּפֵר וְיוֹאָח

בֶּן־אָסָף הַמַּזְכִּיר

19 וַיֹּאמֶר אֲלֵהֶם רַב־שָׁקֵה אִמְרוּ־נָא

אֶל־חִזְקִיָּהוּ כֹּה־אָמַר הַמֶּלֶךְ הַגָּדוֹל מֶלֶךְ אַשּׁוּר מָה

הַבִּטָּחוֹן הַזֶּה אֲשֶׁר בָּטָחְתָּ

20 אָמַרְתָּ אַךְ־דְּבַר־שְׂפָתַיִם עֵצָה וּגְבוּרָה

לַמִּלְחָמָה עַתָּה עַל־מִי בָטַחְתָּ כִּי מָרַדְתָּ בִּי

Then the king of Assyria sent Tartan and Rab-saris and Rabshakeh from **Lachish** to King Hezekiah <u>with a large army to Jerusalem</u>. So they went up and came to Jerusalem. And when they went up, they came and stood by the conduit of the upper pool, which is on the highway of the fuller's field.

When they called to the king, <u>Eliakim</u> the son of Hilkiah, who was over the household, and <u>Shebnah</u> the scribe and <u>Joah</u> the son of Asaph the recorder, came out to them. Then Rabshakeh said to them, "Say now to Hezekiah, 'Thus says the great king, the king of Assyria, "What is this confidence that you have? You speak only empty words, 'I have counsel and strength for the war.' Now on whom do you rely, that you have rebelled against me?"

Libnah beseiged, rumor about threat from Tirhaka

(= Taharqa; crown prince and probably co-regent)

2 Kings 19:8-9

8 וַיָּשָׁב רַב־שָׁקֵה וַיִּמְצָא אֶת־מֶלֶךְ־אַשּׁוּר

נִלְחָם עַל־לִבְנָה כִּי שָׁמַע כִּי נָסַע מִלָּכִישׁ

9 וַיִּשְׁמַע אֶל־תִּרְהָקָה מֶלֶךְ־כּוּשׁ לֵאמֹר הִנֵּה יָצָא לְהִלָּחֵם

אִתָּךְ וַיָּשָׁב וַיִּשְׁלַח מַלְאָכִים אֶל־חִזְקִיָּהוּ לֵאמֹר

Then Rabshakeh returned and found the king of Assyria fighting against Libnah, for he had heard that the king had left Lachish. When he heard [them] say concerning Tirhakah king of Cush, "Behold, he has come out to fight against you,"

Hezekiah's territory diminished:

Chicago Prism III, 30(23)-37(29)

ālānīšu ša ašlula ultu qereb mātišu abtuqma ana Mitinti šar Asdōdi,
Pādi šar Amqarōna u Ṣil-Bēl šar Ġaziti addinma uṣaḫḫir māssu eli
bilti maḫrīti nadān šattišun mandattu kadrē bēlūtiya uraddīma ukīn
ṣeruššu.

His (Hezekiah's) towns which I plundered, I detached from his country and
gave them to Mitinti, king of Ashdod, to Padi, king of Ekron, and to Ṣil-Baal,
king of Gaza. Thus I diminished his territory. On top of his annual tax, I
added tribute and gifts of my royalty

את עריו אשר בזזתי קרעתי מארצו ונתתי למתנתי (*Mintinti*) מלך אשדוד,
לפדי (*Padi*) מלך עקרון ולצלבעל (*Ṣil-Bēl*) מלך עזה והקטנתי את ארצו.
על המס הקודם, מתן ארצם, הוספתי עליהם מנחה ומתנות ריבונותי.

c. **Manasseh** made co-regent at 12 yrs of age (697/696);

642+55=697

2 Ki. 21:1

1 בֶּן־שְׁתֵּים עֶשְׂרֵה שָׁנָה מְנַשֶּׁה בְמָלְכוֹ וַחֲמִשִּׁים וְחָמֵשׁ שָׁנָה
מָלַךְ בִּירוּשָׁלָם וְשֵׁם אִמּוֹ חֶפְצִי־בָהּ

Manasseh was twelve years old when he became king, and he reigned <u>fifty-
five years</u> in Jerusalem; and his mother's name was Hephzibah.

C. XXV Dynasty —

Kashta (767-753) fa of Piye/Pi'ankhi and Shabako

Piye/Pi'ankhi (753-721), fa. of Shebitku and Taharka

Shabako (721-706) bro of Piye/Pi'ankhi

Shibitku (706-690) son of Piye/Pi'ankhi, fa. of Tanwetamanı

Taharqa (biblical Tirhaka; 690-664) son of Piye/Pi'ankhi — brought
   north with an army by his bro in 701--led in war with
   Sennacherib — <u>possibly already co-regent</u> (Yurco)!!!

Tanwetamani (664-656)

II.   SEVENTH CENTURY

A.   **Manasseh** co-regent 697/696-686; sole 687/686-643/642

2 Ki 21:1-18 2 Chr. 33:1-20

1. Ten years as co-regent —

2. Taharka's active policy in Asia — 690-680 (with Spalinger)

**   3. Brought foreign influences like Ahab (after 686)

2 Ki 21:2-7

2 וַיַּעַשׂ הָרַע בְּעֵינֵי יְהוָה כְּתוֹעֲבֹת הַגּוֹיִם

אֲשֶׁר הוֹרִישׁ יְהוָה מִפְּנֵי בְּנֵי יִשְׂרָאֵל

3 וַיָּשָׁב וַיִּבֶן אֶת־הַבָּמוֹת אֲשֶׁר אִבַּד חִזְקִיָּהוּ

אָבִיו וַיָּקֶם מִזְבְּחֹת לַבַּעַל וַיַּעַשׂ אֲשֵׁרָה כַּאֲשֶׁר עָשָׂה

אַחְאָב מֶלֶךְ יִשְׂרָאֵל וַיִּשְׁתַּחוּ לְכָל־צְבָא הַשָּׁמַיִם וַיַּעֲבֹד אֹתָם

4 וּבָנָה מִזְבְּחֹת בְּבֵית יְהוָה אֲשֶׁר אָמַר יְהוָה

בִּירוּשָׁלַםִ אָשִׂים אֶת־שְׁמִי

5 וַיִּבֶן מִזְבְּחוֹת לְכָל־צְבָא הַשָּׁמָיִם בִּשְׁתֵּי חַצְרוֹת בֵּית־יְהוָה

6 וְהֶעֱבִיר אֶת־בְּנוֹ בָּאֵשׁ וְעוֹנֵן וְנִחֵשׁ וְעָשָׂה

אוֹב וְיִדְּעֹנִים הִרְבָּה לַעֲשׂוֹת הָרַע בְּעֵינֵי יְהוָה לְהַכְעִיס

7 וַיָּשֶׂם אֶת־פֶּסֶל הָאֲשֵׁרָה אֲשֶׁר עָשָׂה בַּבַּיִת אֲשֶׁר אָמַר יְהוָה

אֶל־דָּוִד וְאֶל־שְׁלֹמֹה בְנוֹ בַּבַּיִת הַזֶּה וּבִירוּשָׁלַםִ אֲשֶׁר בָּחַרְתִּי

מִכֹּל שִׁבְטֵי יִשְׂרָאֵל אָשִׂים אֶת־שְׁמִי לְעוֹלָם

He did evil in the sight of Yahweh, according to the abominations of the nations whom Yahweh dispossessed before the sons of Israel. For he rebuilt the high places which Hezekiah his father had destroyed; and he erected altars for Baal and made an Asherah, as Ahab king of Israel had done, and worshiped all the host of heaven and served them. He built altars in the house of Yahweh, of which Yahweh had said, "In Jerusalem I will put My name." For he built altars for all the host of heaven in the two courts of the house of Yahweh. He made his son pass through the fire, practiced witchcraft and used divination, and dealt with mediums and spiritists. He did much evil in the sight of Yahweh provoking [Him to anger]. Then he set the carved image of Asherah that he had made, in the house of which Yahweh said to David and to his son Solomon, "In this house and in Jerusalem, which I have chosen from all the tribes of Israel, I will put My name forever.

4. Took part in **corvée** *ANET* 291 (677 after defeat of Sidon?)

5. Sent **troops to Egypt** with Asshurbanipal 667/666

** 6. Called to Babylon 648 — after the civil war
2 Chr 33:11-17

11 וַיָּבֵא יְהוָה עֲלֵיהֶם אֶת־שָׂרֵי הַצָּבָא אֲשֶׁר

לְמֶלֶךְ אַשּׁוּר וַיִּלְכְּדוּ אֶת־מְנַשֶּׁה בַּחֹחִים וַיַּאַסְרֻהוּ

בַּנְחֻשְׁתַּיִם וַיּוֹלִיכֻהוּ בָּבֶלָה

12 וּכְהָצֵר לוֹ חִלָּה אֶת־פְּנֵי יְהוָה אֱלֹהָיו

וַיִּכָּנַע מְאֹד מִלִּפְנֵי אֱלֹהֵי אֲבֹתָיו

13 וַיִּתְפַּלֵּל אֵלָיו וַיֵּעָתֶר לוֹ וַיִּשְׁמַע תְּחִנָּתוֹ

וַיְשִׁיבֵהוּ יְרוּשָׁלַם לְמַלְכוּתוֹ וַיֵּדַע מְנַשֶּׁה כִּי יְהוָה הוּא הָאֱלֹהִים

14 וְאַחֲרֵי־כֵן בָּנָה חוֹמָה חִיצוֹנָה לְעִיר־דָּוִיד

מַעְרָבָה לְגִיחוֹן בַּנַּחַל וְלָבוֹא בְשַׁעַר הַדָּגִים וְסָבַב

לָעֹפֶל וַיַּגְבִּיהֶהָ מְאֹד וַיָּשֶׂם שָׂרֵי־חַיִל בְּכָל־הֶעָרִים הַבְּצֻרוֹת בִּיהוּדָה

15 וַיָּסַר אֶת־אֱלֹהֵי הַנֵּכָר וְאֶת־הַסֶּמֶל מִבֵּית

יְהוָה וְכָל־הַמִּזְבְּחוֹת אֲשֶׁר בָּנָה בְּהַר בֵּית־יְהוָה

וּבִירוּשָׁלָם וַיַּשְׁלֵךְ חוּצָה לָעִיר

16 וַיִּכֶן [וַ][יִּבֶן] אֶת־מִזְבַּח יְהוָה וַיִּזְבַּח עָלָיו

זִבְחֵי שְׁלָמִים וְתוֹדָה וַיֹּאמֶר לִיהוּדָה לַעֲבוֹד אֶת־יְהוָה אֱלֹהֵי יִשְׂרָאֵל

17 אֲבָל עוֹד הָעָם זֹבְחִים בַּבָּמוֹת רַק לַיהוָה אֱלֹהֵיהֶם

Therefore Yahweh brought the commanders of the army of the **king of Assyria** against them, and they captured **Manasseh** with hooks, bound him with bronze [chains] and took him to __Babylon__. When he was in distress, he entreated Yahweh his God and humbled himself greatly before the God of his fathers. When he prayed to Him, He was moved by his entreaty and heard his supplication, and brought him again to Jerusalem to his kingdom. Then Manasseh knew that Yahweh [was] God. Now after this he built the outer wall of the city of David on the west side of Gihon, in the valley, even to the entrance of the Fish Gate; and he encircled the Ophel [with it] and made it very high. Then he put army commanders in all the fortified cities of Judah. He also removed the foreign gods and the idol from the house of Yahweh, as

well as all the altars which he had built on the mountain of the house of
Yahweh and in Jerusalem, and he threw [them] outside the city. He set up the
altar of Yahweh and sacrificed peace offerings and thank offerings on it; and
he ordered Judah to serve Yahweh God of Israel. Nevertheless the people still
sacrificed in the high places, [although] only to Yahweh their God.

B.   **Assyrian and Egyptian history to mid-century**

1. Esarhaddon 681-669

   a. <u>679</u> — Revolt in Tyre and Sidon

   b. <u>679</u> — occupied Arṣa at el-'Arîsh
      Cylinder B, III, 39-42.

*Arṣâ ša pāṭi naḫal Muṣuri ašlulamma Asuḫili šarrašu birētu addīma
ana māt Aššur urâ . . .*

Arṣa on the border of the **Brook of Egypt** I plundered; Asḫuli its king I cast in
fetters, and brought to the land of Asshur . . . .

(*Na-ḫal māt Mu-ṣur-*[*ri*]) שבגבול נחל מצרים (*Ar-ṣa-a*) את העיר ארצה

   c. <u>677</u> — took **Sidon**; *ANET* 290b-291a
      Cylinder B, II, 65 ff.

*ᶜAbdi-milkutti šar Ṣīdōni lā pāliḫ bēlūtiya lā šēmû zikir šaptiya ša eli
tāmtim gallatim ittakluma islû nīr Aššur, Ṣīdōnu āl tuklātišu ša qereb
tāmtim nadû abūbiš aspun dūršu u šubassu assuḫma qereb tāmtim
addīma ašar maškanišu uḫalliq*

(As for) ᶜAbdi-mulkutti king of Sidon, who revered not my lordship, who
heeded not the proclamations of my lips, who trusted in the raging sea, and
threw off the yoke of Asshur, I swamped like a flood over Sidon, the city of
his trust situated in the midst of the sea. Its wall and its citadel I removed and
cast into the sea and I destroyed his dwelling place.

עבדמלכות מלך צידון לא ירא את שלטוני ולא שמע למוצא שפתי ופרק
את עולו של האל אשור, בבטחו בים הסוער. את צידון עיר מבטחו,
השוכנת בתוך הים, שטפתי כסערת מבול.

   d. <u>677</u> — kings of Ḫatti did corvée; treaty with Baal of Tyre
      ANET 291
         Cylinder B, V, 45 ff.

*adkēma šarrānī māt Ḫatti u eber nāri Ba'lu šar Ṣurri, Menaššî šar
Yahūdi, Qaušgabri šar Udumi, Muṣuri šar Ma'ab, Ṣil-Bēl šar Ġazīti,
Metinti šar Isqalōna, Ikausu šar Amqarōna . . . 22 šarrānī māt Ḫatti*

ahi tāmtim u qabal tāmtim kališunu uma''iršunūtima gušūrē rabûti timmē ṣīrūti adappi šuhūti ša erēni šurmēni tarbīt šad Sirara u Labnāna ša ultu ūmē pāni magal ikbirūma isīhū lānu aladlammē ša ašnan lamassāti apsasāti askuppāti agurri ša gišnugallî ašnan ku.mi.na ku.mi.na.bàn.da alallum girinhliba ultu qereb hurṣānī ašar nabnītušunu ana hešehti ekalliya marṣiš pašqiš ana Ninua āl bēlūtiya ušaldidūni

I called up the kings of the land of Ḫatti and of Beyond the River: Baal king of Tyre, Manasseh king of Judah, Qausgabri king of Edom, Muṣuri king of Moab, Ṣil-Baal king of Gaza, Mitinti king of Ashkelon, Ikausu king of Ekron . . . 22 kings of the land of Ḫatti, the seashore and the islands; all these I sent out and made them transport under terrible difficulties, to Nineveh, the city of my lordship, as material for my palace: big logs, long beams (and) thin boards from cedar and pine trees, products of the Sirara and Lebanon mountains, which had grown for a long time into tall and strong timber, (and) from their quarries in the mountains, statues of protective deities made of *ašnan* stone, statues of female *apsastu*, thresholds, slabs of limestone, of *ašnan* stone, of large and small grained breccia, of *alallu* stone (and) of *girinhliba* stone.

כינסתי את מלכי ארץ חת (*māt Ḥatti*) ועבר הנהר (*eber nāri*): בעל מלך צור, מנשה מלך יהודה, קוסגבר מלך אדום, מוצורו מלך מואב, צלבעל מלך עזה, מתנתי מלך אשקלון, איכאוסו מלך עקרון . . . . ביחד 22 מלכי ארץ חת, חוף הים ולב הים; את כל אלה שלחתי והכרחתים לשאת, תוך קשיים וסבל, אל נינוה עיר ממשלתי, בשביל בניית ארמוני, קורות גדולות, ענפים ארוכים וקרשים(?) דקים של ארזים ואורנים, גידולי הר *Sirara* והר הלבנון (*Lab-na-na*) . . . .

e. 674 – first invasion of **Egypt**, FAILED

ANET 302b Babylonian Chron., 1, 16

šanat 7 Addaru ūm 5 ummāni Aššur ina Miṣir dîkū

Seventh year: On the fifth day of the month Adar, the army of Assyria was defeated in Egypt.

בשנה השביעית ביום ה׳ באדר, הובס צבא אשור במצרים.

f. 676-674 (?) — conflicts with **Arabs**--reinstated loyal leader there; .Prism B, IV, 6-31.

Ḫaza-ilu šar Aribi itti tāmartišu kabittu ana Ninua āl bēlūtiya illikamma unaššiq šēpēya aššu nadān ilānīšu uṣallannima rēmu aršīšuma . . . . Ḫaza-ilu šimtu ūbilšuma Yata' mārušu ina kussîšu ušēšibma . . . . arka Wābu ana epēš šarrūti Arubu kālišu eli Yata' ušbalkitma anāku Aššur-aḫu-iddina šar māt Aššur . . . ṣābē tāḫåziya ana nārarūtu Yata' ašpurma Arubu kālišu ikbusūma.

Hazael, the king of the Arabs, came with heavy gifts to Nineveh. the city of my lordship, and kissed my feet; he implored me to return the images of his gods and I had mercy on him . . . . <u>When fate carried Hazael away, I set Yata^c</u>, <u>his son, upon his throne</u> . . . . Afterwards, Wahb induced all the Arabs to revolt against Yata^c in order to establish (his own) kingship, but I, Esarhaddon, king of Assyria, . . . sent my combat troops to the aid of Yata^c and they subdued all the Arabs;

חזאל מלך הערבים בא עם מנחתו הכבדה, אל נינוה, עיר מכלותי, ונשק
את רגליי. הוא התחנן בפני שאתן את (פסלי) אלוהיו . . . . חזאל הלך
לגורלו ואת ית"ע בנו הושבתי על כסאו . . . . אחר-כך, והב המריד, למען
יתמלך, את כל הערבים נגד ית"ע, ואנוכי אסרהדון מלך אשור . . . שלחתי
את צבא מלחמתי לעזרת ית"ע, ואת הערבים כולם הכניעו . . . .

Letter of Asshurbanipal to the god Asshur, VAT 5600:3-12

kī Wate' mār Ḫaza'ili šar māt Aribi ina tarṣi Aššūr-aḫu-idinna šar māt Aššūr rēšu binût qātēka ikkiruma iṣlû nīr bēlūtišu ina tukultika rabīt emūqīka ṣīrāti Aššur-aḫu-idinna šar māt Aššur abi bānûya ummānātišu idkēma uma''er ṣēruššu ina tāḫāz ṣēri abiktašu iškun išlulū ilānīšu. Wate' ana šūzub napištišu karāssu umaššerma ēdiš ipparšidma innabit ana rūqēti.

When (Y)autha son of Hazael, king of Arabia, in the reign of Esarhaddon, king of Assyria, the slave, the creature of your hands, became hostile and cast off the yoke of his sovereignty, by trust in you, in the greatness of your exalted might, Esarhaddon, king of Assyria, my father my begetter, called up his armies and sent them against him. In an open battle he accomplished his defeat and they carried away his gods. (Y)autha, to save his life, abandoned his camp, fled alone and escaped to distant parts.

g.   <u>671</u> — **conquest of delta**

ANET 292-293

Tablet K 3082 + S 2027 + K 3086 from the British
Museum,

Obv. 6-Rev. 18

ina ešre gerriya Aššur [. . .] ušaṣbita pānū'a ana māt Magan [u
Meluḫḫa] ša ina pî nišē māt Kūsi u māt Muṣur inambu . . .] adkēma
ummānāt Aššur gapšāti ša qer[eb . . .] ina Nisanni arḫi rēštû ultu
āliya Aššur attumuš nār Idiqlat nār Purattu ina mīlišina eber šadānī
marṣūti rīmāniš aštamdiḫ ina mētiq girriya eli Ba'lu šar māt Ṣurri ša
ana Tarqû šar māt Kūsi ibriši ittakluma nīr Aššur bēliya islû ētappalu
mēreḫtu ḫalṣē elišu urakkisma akālu u mû balāṭ napištišun akla ultu
māt Muṣur karāši adkēma ana māt Meluḫḫa uštēšera ḫarrānu 30 bēru
qaqqar ultu Apqu ša pāṭi māt Sāme‹ri›n[a] adi Rapīḫi ana itê naḫal
māt Muṣur ašar nāru lā išû ina ib[lē] ḫarḫarrē kalkaltu mê būri ina
dilûti ummānī ušašqi kî qibīt Aššur bēliya ina uznēya ibšīma [uštābila
k]abattī gammallē ša šarrānī māt Aribi kilišun a[dkēma nādāti
ēmi]ssunūti

In my tenth campaign, Asshur strengthened me and directed my face
towards the land of Magan [and Meluḫḫa] which are called Cush and Egypt
in the common tongue. I called up the numerous troops of Asshur which are
stationed in [. . .]. In the month of Nisan, the first month, I departed from my
city Asshur. I crossed the Tigris and the Euphrates in the time of their flood; I
strode across difficult mountains like a wild ox. In the course of my campaign
<u>I threw up an earthwork against Ba'lu king of Tyre who had trusted his</u>
<u>friend Taharqa, king of Cush</u> and threw off the yoke of Asshur and answered
me with insolence, food and water, sustenance for their lives, I withheld.
From(!) the land of Egypt I called up the camp, to the land of Nubia I set my
course. Thirty double hours distance from **Aphek**, which is in the region of
Sama‹ri›a(?) to **Raphiah**, towards the <u>Brook of Egypt</u>, a place having no
river, by ropes, by chains (and) buckets, I caused the troops to drink well
water. When the command of Asshur, my lord, came to my ear, my heart
rejoiced. <u>I cal[led up] the camels of all the kings of Arabia;</u> [water bottles I]
placed on them; 20 (or 30?) double hours distance, a marching distance of 15
days, I went . . . .

במסעי העשירי, [חיזק אותי] אשור וכיוון אותי אל הארצות של מגן
[ומלוחיה] אשר [נקראות] בפי העם ארץ כוש וארץ מצרים. גייסתי את
גייסות אשור המרובים .... בחודש ניסן, החודש הראשון, יצאתי מעירי
אשור .... עברתי את החידקל ואת הפרת בעת גאותם; התקדמתי

בשטחים קשים כמו ראם. במשך מסעי הרמתי סוללה נגד בעל מלך צור
אשר בטח בחברו תרהקה מלך כוש ופרק את העול של אשור אדוני והשיב
לי בחוצפה. מנעתי מהם (אנשי צור) מזון ומיים טריים . . . . התקדמתי
ישר אל ארץ מלוחיה. שלושים שעות כפולות מאפק אשר בתחום
שומרו\ן עד העיר רפיח, אל הגבול של נחל מצרים, מקום שאין נהר. בחבל,
בשרשרת ובדלי השקיתי את צבאי מיים על ידי דליה מבארות. כשהיתה
פקודת אשור, אדוני, באזניי שמחתי. את כל הגמלים של כל מלכי ערב
[גיי]סתי; העמסתי עליהם [נודות מיים] . . . .

The Babylonian Chronicle 1, 23-28

šanat 10 *Nisannu ummānī Aššur ana Miṣir ittalkū, Du'ūzu ūm 3 ūm 16, ūm 18, 3-šu dīktum ina Miṣir dīkat, ūm 22 Mempi āl šarrūtu* [ṣ]*abit*

In the tenth year, in the month of Nisan, the army of Asshur marched to Egypt; in the month of Tammuz, on the third, sixteenth and eighteenth days — three times — there was a massacre in Egypt. On the twenty second day, Memphis, the royal city, was taken.

בשנה העשירית, בחודש ניסן, עלה צבא אשור על מצרים. בימי ג',
ט"ז, י"ח בתמוז נלחם במצרים בשלושה קרבות דמים. ביום כ"ב
בחודש נלכדה מוף , עיר הבירה.

h. 669 — died on way to Egypt;
Bab.Chron. 1, 30-32.

šanat 12 *šar Aššur ana Miṣir ittalak, ina ḫarrāni imraṣma ina Araḫsamni ūm 10 šīmāti*

In the twelfth year, the king of Assyria marched to Egypt; on the way he became ill and on the tenth day **he died**.

בשנה השתים עשרה עלה מלך אשור על מצרים. בדרך חלה ומת ביום י'
בחודש מרחשוון. 12 שנה מלך אסרחדון באשור.

2.   **Asshurbanipal** 669-627

a. 667 / 666 — First Campaign to Egypt

ANET 294 Judean troops went along

Rassam Cyl., I, 52-89. with supplement in [ ] from Cyl. C I, 23-50.

ina maḫrê gerriya ana māt Magan u māt Meluḫḫa lū allik. Tarqû šar
māt Muṣur u māt Kūsi ša Aššur-aḫ-iddina šar māt Aššur abu bānû'a
abiktašu iškunuma ibēlu māssu u šū Tarqû danān Aššur Ištar u ilānī
rabûti bēlēya imšīma ittakil ana emūq ramāništu eli šarrānī qēpānī ša
qirib māt Muṣur upaqqidu abu bānû'a ana dâki ḫabāte u ekēm māt
Muṣur illika ṣēruššun ērumma ūšib qereb Mempi āli ša abu bānû'a
ikšuduma ana miṣir māt Aššur ūtiru. allāku ḫanṭu ina qereb Ninua
ilikma usannâ yâti eli epšēti annâti libbī ēgugma iṣṣaruḫ kabittī ašši
qātēia uṣalli Aššur u Ištar aššurītu adkē emūqēia ṣerāte ša Aššur u
Ištar umallû qātū'a. ana māt Muṣur u māt Kūsi uštešṣera ḫarrānu .
ina mētik gerriya [Ba'lu šar māt Ṣurri, Minaššê šar māt Ya'ūdi,
Qaušgabri šar māt Udūme, Muṣuri šar māt Mā'aba, Ṣil-Ba'l šar māt
Ġazīti, Mitinti šar Isqalūna, Ikausu šar 'Amqarūna . . .] 22 sarrānī ša
aḫi tāmtim qabal tāmtim u nābali ardānī dāgil pānīya tāmartašunu
kabittu ina maḫriya iššûnimma unaššiqū šēpēya . šarrānī šâtunu adi
emūqišunu eleppātišunu ina tāmtim u nābali itti ummānāteya urḫu
padānu ušaṣbissunūti . . . .

In my first campaign, I marched against Magan and Meluḫḫa. Tirhakah, king
of Egypt and Cush, whom Esarhaddon, king of Assyria, my own father, had
defeated and whose country he had taken over—Tirhakah forgot the might of
Asshur, Ishtar and the great gods, my lords, and put his trust in his own
power. He attacked the kings (and) regents whom my own father had
appointed in Egypt in order to kill, to rob and to take over the land of Egypt;
he entered and took residence in Memphis, the city which my own father had
conquered and incorporated into Assyrian territory. A swift messenger came
to Nineveh to report to me. Because of these deeds my heart raged and my
soul was aflame. I lifted my hands and I prayed to Asshur and the Assyrian
Ishtar. I called up my great forces which Asshur and Ishtar have entrusted to
me and set a straight course for Egypt. During the course of my campaign
[Ba'lu king of Tyre, Manasseh king of Judah, Qausgabri king of Edom,
Muṣuru king of Moab, Ṣil-Ba'al king of Gaza, Mitinti king of Ashkelon,
Ikausu king of Ekron . . .] 22 kings from the sea coast, from the midst of the
sea and from the mainland, servants who are my subjects, brought their
heavy tribute to me and kissed my feet. I made those kings with their forces
(and) their ships accompany me by sea and by land.

במסעי הראשון, עליתי על מגן (mât Magan) ומלוחיה (mât Meluḫḫa).
תרהקה (Tar-qu-u) מלך מצרים (mât Muṣur) וכוש (Kūsu), אשר אסרהדון
מלך אשור, אבי מולידי, הביסו ומשל בארצו — הוא, תרהקה, שכח את
עצמת אשור, אשתר והאלים הגדולים, האדונים שלי, ובטח בכוח עצמו.

הוא עלה על המלכים והממונים, אשר הפקיד אבי מולידי במצרים, כדי
להרוג, לבוז ולתפוס לעצמו את מצרים. הוא נכנס והתיישב ב<u>מוף</u>
(Me-em-pi), העיר אשר אבי מולידי לכדה וספחה לתחום אשור. רץ מהיר
בא לנינוה והודיעני. בגלל המעשים הללו זעם לבי ונזעקו קרבי (=כבדי).
נשאתי ידי ; התפללתי לאשור ואשתר האשורית. קבצתי את צבאותיי
החזקים אשר הפקידו בידי אשור ואשתר והישרתי דרכי אל מצרים וכוש.

בהמשך מסעי [בעל מלך צור, מנשה (Mi-in-se-e) מלך יהודה (māt Ia-u-di),
קוסגבר מלך אדום, מוצור מלך מואב, צלבעל מלך עזה, מתינתי מלך
אשקלון, איכאוס מלך עקרון, מלכיסף מלך גבל, יכינלו מלך ארוד,
אביבעל מלך שמשמרון, עמינדב מלך בית-עמון, אחימלך מלך אשדוד,
. . . (בהמשך הרשימה נמנו 10 שמות של מלכי מדינות הים) — בסך הכל)]
22 מלכי חוף הים, איי הים והיבשה, עבדים הכפופים לי, הביאו לפני את
מנחתם הכבדה ונשקו את רגליי. את המלכים הללו עם צבאותיהם
(ו)ספינותיהם הולכתי בים וביבשה, יחד עם צבאותי. התקדמתי
במהירות כדי להחיש עזרה למלכים ולממונים שבמצרים, עבדים כפופים לי. . . .

b <u>664/663</u> — campaign to No-Amon

  ANET 295

  appointed Psammiticus as ruler of Sais

c. Against Tyre

d. <u>655</u> — Psammiticus sent his daughter to No-Amon
   to be "god's wife" (H.P); thus uniting Egypt.

e. <u>653</u> — Medes attacked but their leader slain.

f. <u>652</u> — rebellion of Shamash-shum-ukin in Babylon.
   Rassam Cylinder, III, 96-106.

u šū Samaš-šum-ukīn, aḫu lā kēnu ša lā iṣṣuru adêya nišê Akkadê, Kaldu, Aramu . . . ardānī dāgil pānīya ušbalkit ina qātēya . . . u šarrānī Gutê, Amurrê, Meluḫḫê . . . napḫaršunu ittiya ušamkirma, ittišu iškunū pīšun . . . .

And he, Shamash-shum-ukin, the unfaithful brother who did not keep my treaty, caused to revolt the people of Akkad, Chaldea, Aram . . . servants subject to me . . . and he caused to revolt the kings of Guti, Amurru and Meluḫḫu . . . all together; they made accord with him.

g. <u>650</u> — first war with Arabs who came to aid Babylon
   Rassam Cyl, VIII, 30-42.

ina qibīt Aššur, Ištar u ilānī rabûti bēlēya, ša Abiyate' Aymu mār Te'ri ša anu rēṣūtu Šamaš-šum-ukīn aḫi nakri ana erēb Bāb-ili illiku rēšēšu adūk, abiktašu aškun, sittūti ša qereb Bāb-ili ērubū ina sunqi ḫušaḫḫi ēkulū šēra aḫamiš ana šūzub napištišunu ultu qereb Bāb-ili ūṣûnimma emūēya ša eli Šamaš-šum-ukīn šaknū šaniyānu abiktašu iškunūma . . .

At the command of Asshur, Ishtar and the great gods, my lords, <u>I overcame and defeated Abiyate' and Aymu</u>, son(s) of Te'ri, who has come to the aid of Shamash-šum-ukīn, my hostile brother; the survivors entered Babylon but because of because of the distress and hunger, they ate each other's flesh. To save their lives, they came forth from Babylon, and my forces that had been positioned against Shamash-shum-ukin, <u>defeated them a second time</u> . . . .

בפקודת אשור, אישתר והאלים הגדולים, האדונים שלי, התקפתי את

הכוחות של אביטע (ושל) איימו בנ(י) תארי, שבאו על מנת להכנס לבבל
לעזור לשמש-שום-אוכן, אחי העוין ואת מפלתם השגתי. השאר שנכנסו
לבבל, אכלו את הבשר זה של זה בגלל עוצמת הרעב. אז הם יצאו מבבל
וכוחותי שחנו במצור על שמש-שום-אוכן, ניצחו אותם שנית.

h. <u>648</u> — conquered Babylon

**   2 Chr. 33:11-17

i. <u>644/643</u> — War against Arabs, also attack on Usû and
ᶜAccô *ANET* 297b-300a

Rassam Cylinder, IX, 115-128

*ina tayārtiya Ušû ša ina aḫi tāmtim nadâta šubassu akšud nišē Ušû ša
ana pāḫātišunu lā sanqū lā inamdinū mandattu nadān mātišun adūk
ina libbi nišē lā kanšūti šipṭu aškun, ilānīšunu nišēšunu ašlula ana
māt Aššur nišē Akkû lā kanšūti anīr, pagrēšunu ina gašīši ālul siḫirti
āli ušalmi sittūtišunu alqâ ana māt Aššur*

On my return, I conquered **Usû** whose site is on the shore of the sea; the
people of Usû who did not obey their governor (and) were not paying their
tribute, the quota of their land, I attacked. I condemned the insubordinate
people; their gods and their people I carried off to Asshur. The insubordinate
people of **Acco**, I slew. Their corpses I impaled on stakes, around the city I
placed them; the remainder I took to the land of Asshur.

בשובי (מן המלחמה בערבים) לכדתי את אוסו (URU *Ú-šu-ú*) היושבת על
חוף הים. את אנשי אוסו אשר לא נכנעו לפחותיהם, לא העלו מס, מתן
ארצם, הרגתי. בקרב האנשים, אשר לא נכנעו, עשיתי שפטים. את
אלהיהם והתושבים (שנותרו) נשאתי לאשור. את אנשי עכו (URU *A-ku-u*)
אשר לא נכנעו, טבחתי. את בויותיהם תליתי על עמודים מסביב לעיר.
את שאריתם לקחתי לארץ אשור. ארגנתי אותם בגדוד וספחתי (אותם)
על צבאותי המרובים, אשר נתן (לי) האל אשור.

END OF JUDEAN MONARCHY, 7TH–6TH CENTURIES BCE

I. **JUDEAN HISTORY**: Second half of 7th century BCE

   A.   **Amon** of Judah 642-640 (2 yrs)

2 Ki 21:19-26; 2 Chr 33:21-25

His mother from **Jotbah**. <u>Assassinated</u>

2 Kings 21:19-24

19 בֶּן־עֶשְׂרִים וּשְׁתַּיִם שָׁנָה אָמוֹן בְּמָלְכוֹ וּשְׁתַּיִם שָׁנִים מָלַךְ בִּירוּשָׁלָ͏ִם

וְשֵׁם אִמּוֹ מְשֻׁלֶּמֶת בַּת־חָרוּץ מִן־יָטְבָה

20 וַיַּעַשׂ הָרַע בְּעֵינֵי יְהוָה כַּאֲשֶׁר עָשָׂה מְנַשֶּׁה אָבִיו

21 וַיֵּלֶךְ בְּכָל־הַדֶּרֶךְ אֲשֶׁר־הָלַךְ אָבִיו וַיַּעֲבֹד אֶת־הַגִּלֻּלִים אֲשֶׁר עָבַד אָבִיו

וַיִּשְׁתַּחוּ לָהֶם

22 וַיַּעֲזֹב אֶת־יְהוָה אֱלֹהֵי אֲבֹתָיו וְלֹא הָלַךְ בְּדֶרֶךְ יְהוָה

23 וַיִּקְשְׁרוּ עַבְדֵי־אָמוֹן עָלָיו וַיָּמִיתוּ אֶת־הַמֶּלֶךְ בְּבֵיתוֹ

24 וַיַּךְ עַם־הָאָרֶץ אֵת כָּל־הַקֹּשְׁרִים

עַל־הַמֶּלֶךְ אָמוֹן וַיַּמְלִיכוּ עַם־הָאָרֶץ אֶת־יֹאשִׁיָּהוּ בְנוֹ תַּחְתָּיו

Amon was twenty-two years old when he became king, and he reigned two years in Jerusalem; and his mother's name [was] Meshullemeth the daughter of Haruz of **Jotbah**. He did evil in the sight of Yahweh, as Manasseh his father had done. For he walked in all the way that his father had walked, and served the idols that his father had served and worshiped them. So he forsook Yahweh, the God of his fathers, and did not walk in the way of Yahweh. <u>The servants of Amon conspired against him and killed the king in his own house.</u> Then **the people of the land** <u>killed all those who had conspired against King Amon</u>, and the people of the land made **Josiah** his son king in his place.

   B.   **Josiah** 641 / 640-609 31 yrs. 2 Ki 22:1-30 2 Chr 34-35

(8 yrs. old, born 649)

<u>633</u> — Jehoiakim born to wife (זבידה = Zebidah) (16 yrs old)from **Rumah** 2 Ki. 23:36 ‖ 2 Chr. 36:5; <u>25 yrs. in 609</u>;

<u>633/632</u> — **8th year** "sought the God of David his faher"

2 Chr. 34:3a

וּבִשְׁמוֹנֶה שָׁנִים לְמָלְכוֹ וְהוּא עוֹדֶנּוּ נַעַר

הֵחֵל לִדְרוֹשׁ לֵאלֹהֵי דָּוִיד אָבִיו

For in the **eighth year** of his reign while he was still a youth, <u>he began to seek the God</u> <u>of his father David</u>

<u>632</u> — Jehoahaz born to wife (חמוטל = Hamutal) from **Libnah** (17 yrs. old) 2 Ki. 23:31 ‖ 2 Chr. 36:2; <u>23 in</u> <u>609</u>

<u>629/628</u> — **12th year** 2 Chr 34:3b-6 — 20 years old one year after Asshurbanipal stepped down as king of Assyria! He **purified Judah** — sent to **Manasseh, Ephraim,** and **Shimᶜôn, Naphtali** 2 Chron. 34:3b-6

3b וּבִשְׁתֵּים עֶשְׂרֵה שָׁנָה הֵחֵל לְטַהֵר אֶת־יְהוּדָה וִירוּשָׁלַם מִן־הַבָּמוֹת וְהָאֲשֵׁרִים וְהַפְּסִלִים וְהַמַּסֵּכוֹת 4 וַיְנַתְּצוּ לְפָנָיו אֵת מִזְבְּחוֹת הַבְּעָלִים וְהַחַמָּנִים אֲשֶׁר־לְמַעְלָה מֵעֲלֵיהֶם גִּדֵּעַ וְהָאֲשֵׁרִים וְהַפְּסִלִים וְהַמַּסֵּכוֹת שִׁבַּר וְהֵדַק וַיִּזְרֹק עַל־פְּנֵי הַקְּבָרִים הַזֹּבְחִים לָהֶם כֹּהֲנִים שָׂרַף עַל־מִזְבְּחוֹתָים [מִזְבְּחוֹתָם] וַיְטַהֵר אֶת־יְהוּדָה וְאֶת־יְרוּשָׁלָם 5 וְעַצְמוֹת

[(2 Ki. 23:20) וַיִּזְבַּח אֶת־כָּל־כֹּהֲנֵי הַבָּמוֹת אֲשֶׁר־שָׁם עַל־הַמִּזְבְּחוֹת]

6 וּבְעָרֵי מְנַשֶּׁה וְאֶפְרַיִם וְשִׁמְעוֹן וְעַד־נַפְתָּלִי בָּהַר בָּתֵּיהֶם [בְּ][חַרְבֹתֵיהֶם] סָבִיב

καὶ τοῖς τόποις αὐτῶν κύκλῳ LXX

... and in the **twelfth year** he began to purge **Judah** and **Jerusalem** of the high places, the Asherim, the carved images and the molten images. And they tore down the altars of the Baals in his presence, and the incense altars that were high above them he chopped down; also the Asherim, the carved images and the molten images he broke in pieces and ground to powder and scattered [it] on the graves of those who had sacrificed to them. And the bones of the priests he burned on their altars and he purified **Judah** and **Jerusalem**. And in the cities of **Manasseh, Ephraim, Simeon,** even as far as **Naphtali,** in their surrounding ruins, he also tore down the altars and beat the Asherim and the carved images into powder, and chopped down all the incense altars throughout the land of Israel. [All the priests of the high places who

[were] there he slaughtered on the altars and burned human bones on them (2 Kings 23:20)]. Then he returned to Jerusalem.

627 — Ashurbanipal dies

Jeremiah begins 23 yrs. of prophecy

Jer 1:2

אֲשֶׁר הָיָה דְבַר־יְהוָה אֵלָיו בִּימֵי יֹאשִׁיָּהוּ

בֶן־אָמוֹן מֶלֶךְ יְהוּדָה בִּשְׁלֹשׁ־עֶשְׂרֵה שָׁנָה לְמָלְכוֹ

to whom the word of Yahweh came in the days of Josiah the son of Amon, king of Judah, **in the thirteenth year of his reign**.

Jer 25:3

מִן־שְׁלֹשׁ עֶשְׂרֵה שָׁנָה לְיֹאשִׁיָּהוּ בֶן־אָמוֹן מֶלֶךְ יְהוּדָה

וְעַד הַיּוֹם הַזֶּה זֶה שָׁלֹשׁ וְעֶשְׂרִים שָׁנָה הָיָה

דְבַר־יְהוָה אֵלָי וָאֲדַבֵּר אֲלֵיכֶם אַשְׁכֵּים וְדַבֵּר וְלֹא שְׁמַעְתֶּם

From the **thirteenth year** of Josiah the son of Amon, king of Judah, even to this day, these **twenty-three years** the word of Yahweh has come to me, and I have spoken to you again and again, but you have not listened.

626-605 — Nabopolasser king of Babylon, firmly entrenched by 623; in his 5th yr. eclipse of moon 22 April, 621.

623/622 — 18th year Josiah renews covenant (26 yrs. old) 2 Ki 22:3-24:28; 2 Chr 34:8-35:39 (Ezek. born Ezk.1:1-3)
Meṣad Ḥªšaḇyāhû — between 629 and 616
2 Ki. 22:3; 23:1-2

3 וַיְהִי בִּשְׁמֹנֶה עֶשְׂרֵה שָׁנָה לַמֶּלֶךְ יֹאשִׁיָּהוּ שָׁלַח הַמֶּלֶךְ אֶת־שָׁפָן

בֶּן־אֲצַלְיָהוּ בֶן־מְשֻׁלָּם הַסֹּפֵר בֵּית יְהוָה לֵאמֹר

1 וַיִּשְׁלַח הַמֶּלֶךְ וַיַּאַסְפוּ אֵלָיו כָּל־זִקְנֵי יְהוּדָה וִירוּשָׁלָם

2 וַיַּעַל הַמֶּלֶךְ בֵּית־יְהוָה וְכָל־אִישׁ יְהוּדָה וְכָל־יֹשְׁבֵי יְרוּשָׁלַם אִתּוֹ

וְהַכֹּהֲנִים וְהַנְּבִיאִים וְכָל־הָעָם לְמִקָּטֹן וְעַד־גָּדוֹל

וַיִּקְרָא בְאָזְנֵיהֶם אֶת־כָּל־דִּבְרֵי סֵפֶר הַבְּרִית הַנִּמְצָא בְּבֵית יְהוָה

Now in the eighteenth year of King Josiah, the king sent Shaphan, the son of Azaliah the son of Meshullam the scribe, to the house of Yahweh saying,

Then the king sent, and they gathered to him all the elders of Judah and of Jerusalem. The king went up to the house of Yahweh and all the men of Judah and all the inhabitants of Jerusalem with him, and the priests and the prophets and all the people, both small and great; and he read in their hearing all the words of the book of the covenant which was found in the house of Yahweh.

2 Chron. 34:8

וּבִשְׁנַת שְׁמוֹנֶה עֶשְׂרֵה לְמָלְכוֹ לְטַהֵר הָאָרֶץ

וְהַבָּיִת שָׁלַח אֶת־שָׁפָן בֶּן־אֲצַלְיָהוּ וְאֶת־מַעֲשֵׂיָהוּ

שַׂר־הָעִיר וְאֵת יוֹאָח בֶּן־יוֹאָחָז הַמַּזְכִּיר לְחַזֵּק אֶת־בֵּית

יְהוָה אֱלֹהָיו

Now in the **eighteenth year** of his reign, <u>when he had purged the land and the house,</u> he sent Shaphan the son of Azaliah, and Maaseiah an official of the city, and Joah the son of Joahaz the recorder, to repair the house of Yahweh his God.

2 Chron. 34:29-30

29 וַיִּשְׁלַח הַמֶּלֶךְ וַיֶּאֱסֹף אֶת־כָּל־זִקְנֵי יְהוּדָה וִירוּשָׁלָם

30 וַיַּעַל הַמֶּלֶךְ בֵּית־יְהוָה וְכָל־אִישׁ יְהוּדָה וְיֹשְׁבֵי יְרוּשָׁלַם וְהַכֹּהֲנִים

וְכָל־הָעָם מִגָּדוֹל וְעַד־קָטָן וַיִּקְרָא בְאָזְנֵיהֶם אֶת־כָּל־דִּבְרֵי סֵפֶר הַבְּרִית

וְהַלְוִיִּם

הַנִּמְצָא בֵּית יְהוָה

Then the king sent and gathered all the elders of Judah and Jerusalem.

The king went up to the house of Yahweh and all the men of Judah, the inhabitants of Jerusalem, the priests, the Levites and all the people, from the greatest to the least; and he read in their hearing all the words of the book of the covenant which was found in the house of Yahweh.

<u>618</u> — Zedekiah born to Hamutal (2 Ki. 24:18; Jer. 52:1;
2 Chr. 36:11); Josiah 31 yrs old

<u>616</u> — Tishre — <u>Egyptian army in Mesopotamia</u> *ANET* 304a

<u>615</u> — Jehoiachin born 2 Ki. 24:8 to Neḥushta of Jerusalem.

<u>614</u> — Fall of **Ashur** to Medes

<u>612</u> — Fall of **Nineveh** to Medes and Babylonians

<u>610</u> — Fall of **Haran** — Necho II comes to power (610-595)

<u>609</u> — Necho marches northward — fights at **Magdolo** in
Sinai and then went on to **Gaza (Kadytes)**

Herodotus II, 159 — Μαγδωλο

καὶ Συρίοισι πεζῇ ὁ Νεκῶς συμβαλὼν ἐν Μαγδώλῳ ἐνίκησε, μετὰ δὲ τὴν μάχην Κάδυτιν πόλιν τῆς Συρίης ἐοῦσαν μεγάλην εἷλε.

and Necho, encountering the Syrians with the land army, defeated them at Magdolo; after the battle he took the great Syrian city of Kadytes (Gaza).

Jer. 47:1-7 confirms Herodtos' account about Gaza:

אֲשֶׁר הָיָה דְבַר־יְהֹוָה אֶל־יִרְמְיָהוּ הַנָּבִיא אֶל־פְּלִשְׁתִּים 1

בְּטֶרֶם יַכֶּה פַרְעֹה אֶת־עַזָּה

That which came as the word of Yahweh to Jeremiah the prophet concerning the Philistines, **before Pharaoh conquered Gaza**.

Death of Josaiah at **Megiddo**

2 Ki. 23:29;

בְּיָמָיו עָלָה פַרְעֹה נְכֹה מֶלֶךְ־מִצְרַיִם

עַל־מֶלֶךְ אַשּׁוּר עַל־נְהַר־פְּרָת וַיֵּלֶךְ הַמֶּלֶךְ יֹאשִׁיָּהוּ

לִקְרָאתוֹ וַיְמִיתֵהוּ בִּמְגִדּוֹ כִּרְאֹתוֹ אֹתוֹ

In his days Pharaoh Neco king of Egypt went up to the king of Assyria to the river Euphrates. And King Josiah went to meet him, and when [Pharaoh Neco] saw him he killed him at Megiddo.

2 Chr 35:20-27

20 אַחֲרֵי כָל־זֹאת אֲשֶׁר הֵכִין יֹאשִׁיָּהוּ

אֶת־הַבַּיִת עָלָה נְכוֹ מֶלֶךְ־מִצְרַיִם לְהִלָּחֵם בְּכַרְכְּמִישׁ

עַל־פְּרָת וַיֵּצֵא לִקְרָאתוֹ יֹאשִׁיָּהוּ

21 וַיִּשְׁלַח אֵלָיו מַלְאָכִים לֵאמֹר מַה־לִּי וָלָךְ

מֶלֶךְ יְהוּדָה לֹא־עָלֶיךָ אַתָּה הַיּוֹם כִּי אֶל־בֵּית

מִלְחַמְתִּי וֵאלֹהִים אָמַר לְבַהֲלֵנִי חֲדַל־לְךָ מֵאֱלֹהִים

אֲשֶׁר־עִמִּי וְאַל־יַשְׁחִיתֶךָ

22 וְלֹא־הֵסֵב יֹאשִׁיָּהוּ פָנָיו מִמֶּנּוּ כִּי

לְהִלָּחֶם־בּוֹ הִתְחַפֵּשׂ וְלֹא שָׁמַע אֶל־דִּבְרֵי נְכוֹ מִפִּי

אֱלֹהִים וַיָּבֹא לְהִלָּחֵם בְּבִקְעַת מְגִדּוֹ

23 וַיֹּרוּ הַיֹּרִים לַמֶּלֶךְ יֹאשִׁיָּהוּ וַיֹּאמֶר הַמֶּלֶךְ

לַעֲבָדָיו הַעֲבִירוּנִי כִּי הָחֳלֵיתִי מְאֹד

24 וַיַּעֲבִירֻהוּ עֲבָדָיו מִן־הַמֶּרְכָּבָה וַיַּרְכִּיבֻהוּ

עַל רֶכֶב הַמִּשְׁנֶה אֲשֶׁר־לוֹ וַיּוֹלִיכֻהוּ יְרוּשָׁלַ͏ִם וַיָּמָת

וַיִּקָּבֵר בְּקִבְרוֹת אֲבֹתָיו וְכָל־יְהוּדָה וִירוּשָׁלַ͏ִם

מִתְאַבְּלִים עַל־יֹאשִׁיָּהוּ פ

25 וַיְקוֹנֵן יִרְמְיָהוּ עַל־יֹאשִׁיָּהוּ וַיֹּאמְרוּ

כָל־הַשָּׁרִים וְהַשָּׁרוֹת בְּקִינוֹתֵיהֶם עַל־יֹאשִׁיָּהוּ עַד־הַיּוֹם

וַיִּתְּנוּם לְחֹק עַל־יִשְׂרָאֵל וְהִנָּם כְּתוּבִים עַל־הַקִּינוֹת

26 וְיֶתֶר דִּבְרֵי יֹאשִׁיָּהוּ וַחֲסָדָיו כַּכָּתוּב

בְּתוֹרַת יְהוָה

27 וּדְבָרָיו הָרִאשֹׁנִים וְהָאַחֲרֹנִים הִנָּם

כְּתוּבִים עַל־סֵפֶר מַלְכֵי־יִשְׂרָאֵל וִיהוּדָה

After all this, when Josiah had set the temple in order, Neco king of Egypt came up to make war at Carchemish on the Euphrates, and Josiah went out to engage him.

But Neco sent messengers to him, saying, "What have we to do with each other, O King of Judah? [I am] not [coming] against you today but against the house with which I am at war, and God has ordered me to hurry. Stop for your own sake from [interfering with] God who is with me, so that He will not destroy you."

However, Josiah would not turn away from him, but disguised himself in order to make war with him; nor did he listen to the words of Neco from the mouth of God, but came to make war on the plain of Megiddo.

The archers shot King Josiah, and the king said to his servants, "Take me away, for I am badly wounded."

So his servants took him out of the chariot and carried him in the second chariot which he had, and brought him to Jerusalem where he died and was buried in the tombs of his fathers. All Judah and Jerusalem mourned for Josiah.

Attempt by Assyrians and Egyptians to retake Haran
ended in failure

II.   LAST DAYS OF JUDAH

A. Jehoahaz 3 mo. in 609 (23 yrs. old)

2 Ki. 23:30-34; 2 Chr 36:1-3a

2 Kings 23:30b-33

וַיִּקַּח עַם־הָאָרֶץ אֶת־יְהוֹאָחָז בֶּן־יֹאשִׁיָּהוּ וַיִּמְשְׁחוּ אֹתוֹ וַיַּמְלִיכוּ

אֹתוֹ תַּחַת אָבִיו: בֶּן־עֶשְׂרִים וְשָׁלֹשׁ שָׁנָה יְהוֹאָחָז בְּמָלְכוֹ וּשְׁלֹשָׁה חֳדָשִׁים

מָלַךְ בִּירוּשָׁלָ‍ִם וְשֵׁם אִמּוֹ חֲמוּטַל בַּת־יִרְמְיָהוּ מִלִּבְנָה: וַיַּעַשׂ הָרַע בְּעֵינֵי

יְהוָה כְּכֹל אֲשֶׁר־עָשׂוּ אֲבֹתָיו: וַיַּאַסְרֵהוּ פַרְעֹה נְכֹה בְרִבְלָה בְּאֶרֶץ חֲמָת

בִּמְלֹךְ [מִמְּלֹךְ] בִּירוּשָׁלָ‍ִם וַיִּתֶּן־עֹנֶשׁ עַל־הָאָרֶץ מֵאָה כִכַּר־כֶּסֶף וְכִכַּר

זָהָב :

Then the people of the land took Jehoahaz the son of Josiah and anointed him and made him king in place of his father. Jehoahaz was twenty-three years old when he became king, and he reigned three months in Jerusalem; and his mother's name was Hamutal the daughter of Jeremiah of **Libnah**. He did evil in the sight of Yahweh, according to all that his fathers had done. Pharaoh Neco imprisoned him at **Riblah in the land of Hamath**, that he might not reign in Jerusalem; and he imposed on the land a fine of one hundred talents of silver and a talent of gold.

                     2 Chron. 36:1-3a

וַיִּקְחוּ עַם־הָאָרֶץ אֶת־יְהוֹאָחָז בֶּן־יֹאשִׁיָּהוּ וַיַּמְלִיכֻהוּ תַחַת־אָבִיו

בִּירוּשָׁלָ‍ִם: בֶּן־שָׁלוֹשׁ וְעֶשְׂרִים שָׁנָה יוֹאָחָז בְּמָלְכוֹ וּשְׁלֹשָׁה חֳדָשִׁים

מָלַךְ בִּירוּשָׁלָ‍ִם: וַיְסִירֵהוּ מֶלֶךְ־מִצְרַיִם בִּירוּשָׁלַ‍ִם וַיַּעֲנֹשׁ אֶת־הָאָרֶץ

מֵאָה כִכַּר־כֶּסֶף וְכִכַּר זָהָב :

Then the people of the land took Joahaz the son of Josiah, and made him king in place of his father in Jerusalem. Joahaz was twenty-three years old when he became king, and he reigned three months in Jerusalem. Then the king of Egypt deposed him at **Jerusalem**, and imposed on the land a fine of one hundred talents of silver and one talent of gold.

       B.   **Jehoiakim** 609-598 (25 yrs. old)

             2 Ki 23:36-24:7 2 Chr 36

             <u>Note:</u> In **2 Chr. 36:5-10** —transfer of vv. 6b-7 ***

             LXX includes here || from 2 Ki. 24:1b-4

             2 Chron. 36:5-6b ‹2 Kings 24:1b-4›, 2 Chron. 36:8

2Chr. 36:5   בֶּן־עֶשְׂרִים וְחָמֵשׁ שָׁנָה יְהוֹיָקִים בְּמָלְכוֹ

וְאַחַת עֶשְׂרֵה שָׁנָה מָלַךְ בִּירוּשָׁלָ‍ִם וַיַּעַשׂ הָרַע בְּעֵינֵי

יְהוָה אֱלֹהָיו

2Chr. 36:6   עָלָיו עָלָה נְבוּכַדְנֶאצַּר מֶלֶךְ בָּבֶל ·

                     (LXX 2 Ki. 24:1b-4)

〉 1b וַיְהִי־לוֹ יְהוֹיָקִים עֶבֶד שָׁלֹשׁ שָׁנִים וַיָּשָׁב וַיִּמְרָד־בּוֹ

2 וַיְשַׁלַּח יְהוָה בּוֹ אֶת־גְּדוּדֵי כַשְׂדִּים וְאֶת־גְּדוּדֵי אֲרָם

וְאֵת גְּדוּדֵי מוֹאָב וְאֵת גְּדוּדֵי בְנֵי־עַמּוֹן וַיְשַׁלְּחֵם בִּיהוּדָה לְהַאֲבִידוֹ

כִּדְבַר יְהוָה אֲשֶׁר דִּבֶּר בְּיַד עֲבָדָיו הַנְּבִיאִים

[3 אַךְ עַל־פִּי יְהוָה הָיְתָה בִּיהוּדָה לְהָסִיר מֵעַל פָּנָיו בְּחַטֹּאת מְנַשֶּׁה

כְּכֹל אֲשֶׁר עָשָׂה 4 וְגַם דַּם־הַנָּקִי אֲשֶׁר שָׁפָךְ 《יְהוֹיָקִים》 = LXX Ιωακιμ《

〉[וַיְמַלֵּא אֶת־יְרוּשָׁלַם דָּם נָקִי וְלֹא־אָבָה יְהוָה לִסְלֹחַ

[ἦν αὐτῷ δουλεύων τρία ἔτη καὶ ἀπέστη ἀπ᾽ αὐτοῦ [5β] καὶ ἀπέστειλεν κύριος ἐπ᾽ αὐτοὺς τοὺς Χαλδαίους καὶ ληστήρια Σύρων καὶ ληστήρια Μωαβιτῶν καὶ υἱῶν Αμμων καὶ τῆς Σαμαρείας καὶ ἀπέστησαν μετὰ τὸν λόγον τοῦτον κατὰ τὸν λόγον κυρίου ἐν χειρὶ τῶν παίδων αὐτοῦ τῶν προφητῶν [5χ] πλὴν θυμὸς κυρίου ἦν ἐπὶ Ιουδαν τοῦ ἀποστῆσαι αὐτὸν ἀπὸ προσώπου αὐτοῦ διὰ τὰς ἁμαρτίας Μανασση ἐν πᾶσιν οἷς ἐποίησεν [5δ] καὶ ἐν αἵματι ἀθῴῳ ᾧ ἐξέχεεν 《Ιωακιμ》 καὶ ἔπλησεν τὴν Ιερουσαλημ αἵματος ἀθῴου καὶ οὐκ ἠθέλησεν κύριος ἐξολεθρεῦσαι αὐτούς

2Chr. 36:8 וְיֶתֶר דִּבְרֵי יְהוֹיָקִים וְתֹעֲבֹתָיו אֲשֶׁר עָשָׂה

וְהַנִּמְצָא עָלָיו הִנָּם כְּתוּבִים עַל־סֵפֶר מַלְכֵי יִשְׂרָאֵל

וִיהוּדָה וַיִּמְלֹךְ יְהוֹיָכִין בְּנוֹ תַּחְתָּיו

Jehoiakim was twenty-five years old when he became king, and he reigned eleven years in Jerusalem; and he did evil in the sight of Yahweh his God. Nebuchadnezzar king of Babylon came up against him ‹*In his days Nebuchadnezzar king of Babylon came up, and Jehoiakim became his servant [for] three years; then he turned and rebelled against him. So Yahweh sent against him bands of Chaldeans, bands of Arameans, bands of Moabites, and bands of Ammonites. So He sent them against Judah to destroy it, according to the word of Yahweh which He had spoken through His servants the prophets. Surely at the command of Yahweh it came upon Judah, to remove [them] from His sight because of the sins of Manasseh, according to all that he had done, and also for the innocent blood which ‹Jehoiakim› shed, for he filled Jerusalem with innocent blood; and Yahweh would not forgive.*› Now the rest of the acts of Jehoiakim and the abominations which he did, and what was found against him, behold, they are written in the Book of the Kings of Israel and Judah. And Jehoiachin his son became king in his place.

***   <u>605</u> — Fall of Carchemish to Nebuchadrezzar, land of

Hamath taken Jer 46:2, 10, 26 (4th yr of Jehoiakim)

Jeremiah 46:1-2

Jer. 46:1 אֲשֶׁר הָיָה דְבַר־יְהוָה אֶל־יִרְמְיָהוּ הַנָּבִיא עַל־הַגּוֹיִם

Jer. 46:2 לְמִצְרַיִם עַל־חֵיל פַּרְעֹה נְכוֹ מֶלֶךְ מִצְרַיִם אֲשֶׁר־הָיָה עַל־נְהַר־פְּרָת

בְּכַרְכְּמִשׁ אֲשֶׁר הִכָּה נְבוּכַדְרֶאצַּר מֶלֶךְ בָּבֶל בִּשְׁנַת הָרְבִיעִית לִיהוֹיָקִים

בֶּן־יֹאשִׁיָּהוּ מֶלֶךְ יְהוּדָה

That which came as the word of Yahweh to Jeremiah the prophet concerning the nations. To Egypt, concerning the army of Pharaoh Neco king of Egypt, which was **by the Euphrates River at Carchemish**, which Nebuchadnezzar king of Babylon defeated in the fourth year of Jehoiakim the son of Josiah, king of Judah:

604 — **Ashkelon** fell Fifth year of Jehoiakim; **Fast in Jerusalem**

Jeremiah 36:9

וַיְהִי בַשָּׁנָה הַחֲמִשִׁית לִיהוֹיָקִים בֶּן־יֹאשִׁיָּהוּ מֶלֶךְ־יְהוּדָה בַּחֹדֶשׁ הַתְּשִׁעִי

קָרְאוּ צוֹם לִפְנֵי יְהוָה כָּל־הָעָם בִּירוּשָׁלָם וְכָל־הָעָם הַבָּאִים מֵעָרֵי יְהוּדָה

בִּירוּשָׁלָם

Now in the fifth year of Jehoiakim the son of Josiah, king of Judah, in the ninth month, all the people in Jerusalem and all the people who came from the cities of Judah to Jerusalem proclaimed a fast before Yahweh.

2 Ki. 24:1a (also 2 Ch. 36:6 LXX)

בְּיָמָיו עָלָה נְבֻכַדְנֶאצַּר מֶלֶךְ בָּבֶל וַיְהִי־לוֹ

יְהוֹיָקִים עֶבֶד שָׁלשׁ שָׁנִים

In his days Nebuchadnezzar king of Babylon came up, and Jehoiakim became his servant [for] three years;

Nebuchadnezzer's campaigns:

603 — against [Gaza? Ekron?] | **Jehoiakim**

602 — campaigned in Hatti land | **paid**

601 — fight to the draw with the Egyptians | **tribute**

Probably Jehoiakim stopped his tribute

2 Ki 24:1b

וַיָּשָׁב וַיִּמְרָד־בּוֹ : — then he turned and rebelled against him.

600 — Nebuchadrezzar stayed in Babylon!

<u>599</u> — Local troops sent against Arabs; against Judah

2 Kings 24:2

2 וַיְשַׁלַּח יְהוָה בּוֹ אֶת־גְּדוּדֵי כַשְׂדִּים וְאֶת־גְּדוּדֵי אֲרָם

וְאֵת גְּדוּדֵי מוֹאָב וְאֵת גְּדוּדֵי בְנֵי־עַמּוֹן וַיְשַׁלְּחֵם בִּיהוּדָה לְהַאֲבִידוֹ

כִּדְבַר יְהוָה אֲשֶׁר דִּבֶּר בְּיַד עֲבָדָיו הַנְּבִיאִים

So Yahweh sent against him companies of **Chaldeans**, companies of **Arameans**, companies of **Moabites**, and companies of **Ammonites**. So He sent them against **Judah** to destroy it, according to the word of Yahweh which He had spoken through His servants the prophets.

2 Chr. 36:5a-5d LXX ‖ MT 2 Ki. 24:1-4 !!!

3] אַךְ עַל־פִּי יְהוָה הָיְתָה בִּיהוּדָה לְהָסִיר מֵעַל פָּנָיו בְּחַטֹּאת מְנַשֶּׁה

《LXX Ιωακιμ = יְהוֹיָקִים》 שָׁפָךְ אֲשֶׁר הַנָּקִי דַם־ וְגַם 4 עָשָׂה אֲשֶׁר כְּכֹל

וַיְמַלֵּא אֶת־יְרוּשָׁלִַם דָּם נָקִי וְלֹא־אָבָה יְהוָה לִסְלֹחַ[〉

3] אַךְ עַל־פִּי יְהוָה הָיְתָה בִּיהוּדָה לְהָסִיר מֵעַל פָּנָיו בְּחַטֹּאת מְנַשֶּׁה

《LXX Ιωακιμ = יְהוֹיָקִים》 שָׁפָךְ אֲשֶׁר הַנָּקִי דַם־ וְגַם 4 עָשָׂה אֲשֶׁר כְּכֹל

וַיְמַלֵּא אֶת־יְרוּשָׁלִַם דָּם נָקִי וְלֹא־אָבָה יְהוָה לִסְלֹחַ[〉

καὶ ἀπέστησαν μετὰ τὸν λόγον τοῦτον κατὰ τὸν λόγον κυρίου ἐν χειρὶ τῶν παίδων αὐτοῦ τῶν προφητῶν [5χ] πλὴν θυμὸς κυρίου ἦν ἐπὶ Ιουδαν τοῦ ἀποστῆσαι αὐτὸν ἀπὸ προσώπου αὐτοῦ διὰ τὰς ἁμαρτίαις Μανασση ἐν πᾶσιν οἷς ἐποίησεν [5δ] καὶ ἐν αἵματι ἀθῴῳ ᾧ ἐξέχεεν «Ιωακιμ» καὶ ἔπλησεν τὴν Ιερουσαλημ αἵματος ἀθῴου καὶ οὐκ ἠθέλησεν κύριος ἐξολεθρεῦσαι αὐτούς

So He sent them against Judah to destroy it, according to the word of Yahweh which He had spoken through His servants the prophets. Surely at the command of Yahweh it came upon Judah, to remove [them] from His sight because of the sins of Manasseh, according to all that he had done, and also for the innocent blood which ‹Jehoiakim› shed, for he filled Jerusalem with innocent blood; and Yahweh would not forgive.›

C.   **Jehoiachin** <u>598/597</u> — 3 months— Capture of Jerusalem

2 Ki 24:8-17; 25:27-30; 2 Ch 36:9-10 ‹6b-7›!

(תְּשׁוּבַת הַשָּׁנָה =10th Nissan, 597)

2 Kings 24:8-13

בֶּן־שְׁמֹנֶה עֶשְׂרֵה שָׁנָה יְהוֹיָכִין בְּמָלְכוֹ וּשְׁלֹשָׁה חֳדָשִׁים מָלַךְ בִּירוּשָׁלָ͏ִם

וְשֵׁם אִמּוֹ נְחֻשְׁתָּא בַת־אֶלְנָתָן מִירוּשָׁלָ͏ִם: וַיַּעַשׂ הָרַע בְּעֵינֵי יְהוָה כְּכֹל

אֲשֶׁר־עָשָׂה אָבִיו: בָּעֵת הַהִיא עָלָה [עָלוּ] עַבְדֵי נְבֻכַדְנֶאצַּר מֶלֶךְ־בָּבֶל

יְרוּשָׁלַ͏ִם וַתָּבֹא הָעִיר בַּמָּצוֹר: וַיָּבֹא נְבוּכַדְנֶאצַּר מֶלֶךְ־בָּבֶל עַל־הָעִיר

וַעֲבָדָיו צָרִים עָלֶיהָ: וַיֵּצֵא יְהוֹיָכִין מֶלֶךְ־יְהוּדָה עַל־מֶלֶךְ בָּבֶל הוּא

וְאִמּוֹ וַעֲבָדָיו וְשָׂרָיו וְסָרִיסָיו וַיִּקַּח אֹתוֹ מֶלֶךְ בָּבֶל בִּשְׁנַת שְׁמֹנֶה לְמָלְכוֹ:

וַיּוֹצֵא מִשָּׁם אֶת־כָּל־אוֹצְרוֹת בֵּית יְהוָה וְאוֹצְרוֹת בֵּית הַמֶּלֶךְ וַיְקַצֵּץ

אֶת־כָּל־כְּלֵי הַזָּהָב אֲשֶׁר עָשָׂה שְׁלֹמֹה מֶלֶךְ־יִשְׂרָאֵל בְּהֵיכַל יְהוָה

כַּאֲשֶׁר דִּבֶּר יְהוָה:

Jehoiachin was eighteen years old when he became king, and he reigned three months in Jerusalem; and his mother's name [was] Nehushta the daughter of Elnathan of Jerusalem. He did evil in the sight of Yahweh, according to all that his father had done. At that time the <u>servants of Nebuchadnezzar king of Babylon went up to Jerusalem, and the city came under siege</u>. And Nebuchadnezzar the king of Babylon came to the city, while his servants were besieging it. <u>Jehoiachin the king of Judah went out to the king of Babylon</u>, he and his mother and his servants and his captains and his officials. So the king of Babylon took him captive in the eighth year of his reign. He carried out from there all the treasures of the house of Yahweh, and the treasures of the king's house, and cut in pieces all the vessels of gold which Solomon king of Israel had made in the temple of Yahweh, just as Yahweh had said.

2 Chron. 36:9-10 + 36:6b-7!

<u>2Chr. 36:9</u> בֶּן־שְׁמוֹנֶה ‹עֶשְׂרֵה› שָׁנִים יְהוֹיָכִין בְּמָלְכוֹ וּשְׁלֹשָׁה

חֳדָשִׁים וַעֲשֶׂרֶת יָמִים מָלַךְ בִּירוּשָׁלָ͏ִם וַיַּעַשׂ הָרַע בְּעֵינֵי יְהוָה

<u>2Chr. 36:10</u> וְלִתְשׁוּבַת הַשָּׁנָה שָׁלַח הַמֶּלֶךְ נְבוּכַדְנֶאצַּר

‹<u>2Chr. 36:6b</u> נְבוּכַדְנֶאצַּר מֶלֶךְ בָּבֶל וַיַּאַסְרֵהוּ בַּנְחֻשְׁתַּיִם לְהֹלִיכוֹ בָּבֶלָה

<u>2Chr. 36:7</u> וּמִכְּלֵי בֵּית יְהוָה הֵבִיא נְבוּכַדְנֶאצַּר לְבָבֶל

וַיִּתְּנֵם בְּהֵיכָלוֹ בְּבָבֶל›

וַיְבִאֵהוּ בָבֶלָה עִם־כְּלֵי חֶמְדַּת בֵּית־יְהוָה וַיַּמְלֵךְ

אֶת־צִדְקִיָּהוּ אָחִיו עַל־יְהוּדָה וִירוּשָׁלָ͏ִם

Jehoiachin was eight years old when he became king, and he reigned three months and ten days in Jerusalem, and he did evil in the sight of Yahweh.

At the turn of the year King Nebuchadnezzar ❮*king of Babylon came up against him and bound him with bronze chains to take him to Babylon. Nebuchadnezzar also brought some of the articles of the house of Yahweh to Babylon and put them in his temple at Babylon. And he brought him to Babylon with the valuable articles of the house of Yahweh, and he made his kinsman Zedekiah king over Judah and Jerusalem.* ❯

Ezekiel 33:21 8 January, 585 — 12 years after 597 BCE

Ezek. 33:21 וַיְהִי בִּשְׁתֵּי עֶשְׂרֵה שָׁנָה בָּעֲשִׂרִי בַּחֲמִשָּׁה לַחֹדֶשׁ

לְגָלוּתֵנוּ בָּא־אֵלַי הַפָּלִיט מִירוּשָׁלַם לֵאמֹר הֻכְּתָה הָעִיר

Now in the **twelfth year of our exile**, on the fifth (day) of the tenth month, the refugees from Jerusalem came to me, saying, "The city has been taken."

Ezekiel 40:1 — 28 April, 573 (10th Nissan)

בְּעֶשְׂרִים וְחָמֵשׁ שָׁנָה לְגָלוּתֵנוּ בְּרֹאשׁ הַשָּׁנָה

בֶּעָשׂוֹר לַחֹדֶשׁ בְּאַרְבַּע עֶשְׂרֵה שָׁנָה אַחַר אֲשֶׁר הֻכְּתָה

הָעִיר בְּעֶצֶם הַיּוֹם הַזֶּה הָיְתָה עָלַי יַד־יְהוָה וַיָּבֵא אֹתִי שָׁמָּה

In the **twenty-fifth year of our exile**, at the beginning of the year, on the tenth of the month, in the **fourteenth year after the city was taken**, on that same day the hand of Yahweh was upon me and He brought me there.

25th year (from 597 BCE); 14th year (from 586 BCE)

Jehoiachin's reign:

21 Marḥešwān	to	10 Nisan
9 Dec, 598		22 April, 597

Cities of Negeb closed up, Jer. 13:18-19

אֱמֹר לַמֶּלֶךְ וְלַגְּבִירָה הַשְׁפִּילוּ שֵׁבוּ כִּי יָרַד מַרְאֲשׁוֹתֵיכֶם עֲטֶרֶת תִּפְאַרְתְּכֶם

18

19 עָרֵי הַנֶּגֶב סֻגְּרוּ וְאֵין פֹּתֵחַ הָגְלָת יְהוּדָה כֻּלָּהּ הָגְלָת שְׁלוֹמִים

Say to the king and the queen mother, "Take a lowly seat, For your beautiful crown has come down from your head." The cities of the Negev have been locked up, And there is no one to open; All Judah is carried into exile, wholly carried into exile.

Jerusalem surrenders 2 Adar = Sat., 16 March, 597

2 Ki. 24:8-17 (8th year Tishre reckoning) & Babylonian Chronicle (7th year, Nisan reckoning)

8 בֶּן־שְׁמֹנֶה עֶשְׂרֵה שָׁנָה יְהוֹיָכִין בְּמָלְכוֹ וּשְׁלֹשָׁה חֳדָשִׁים מָלַךְ בִּירוּשָׁלָ͏ִם

וְשֵׁם אִמּוֹ נְחֻשְׁתָּא בַת־אֶלְנָתָן מִירוּשָׁלָ͏ִם 9 וַיַּעַשׂ הָרַע בְּעֵינֵי יְהוָה

כְּכֹל אֲשֶׁר־עָשָׂה אָבִיו

10 בָּעֵת הַהִיא עָלָה [עָלוּ] עַבְדֵי נְבֻכַדְנֶאצַּר מֶלֶךְ־בָּבֶל יְרוּשָׁלָ͏ִם וַתָּבֹא הָעִיר

בַּמָּצוֹר 11 וַיָּבֹא נְבוּכַדְנֶאצַּר מֶלֶךְ־בָּבֶל עַל־הָעִיר וַעֲבָדָיו צָרִים עָלֶיהָ

12 וַיֵּצֵא יְהוֹיָכִין מֶלֶךְ־יְהוּדָה עַל־מֶלֶךְ בָּבֶל הוּא וְאִמּוֹ וַעֲבָדָיו וְשָׂרָיו וְסָרִיסָיו

וַיִּקַּח אֹתוֹ מֶלֶךְ בָּבֶל בִּשְׁנַת שְׁמֹנֶה לְמָלְכוֹ

13 וַיּוֹצֵא מִשָּׁם אֶת־כָּל־אוֹצְרוֹת בֵּית יְהוָה וְאוֹצְרוֹת בֵּית הַמֶּלֶךְ וַיְקַצֵּץ

אֶת־כָּל־כְּלֵי הַזָּהָב אֲשֶׁר עָשָׂה שְׁלֹמֹה מֶלֶךְ־יִשְׂרָאֵל בְּהֵיכַל יְהוָה

כַּאֲשֶׁר דִּבֶּר יְהוָה 14 וְהִגְלָה אֶת־כָּל־יְרוּשָׁלַ͏ִם וְאֶת־כָּל־הַשָּׂרִים

וְאֵת כָּל־גִּבּוֹרֵי הַחַיִל עֲשָׂרָה [עֲשֶׂרֶת] אֲלָפִים גּוֹלֶה

וְכָל־הֶחָרָשׁ וְהַמַּסְגֵּר לֹא נִשְׁאַר זוּלַת דַּלַּת עַם־הָאָרֶץ

15 וַיֶּגֶל אֶת־יְהוֹיָכִין בָּבֶלָה וְאֶת־אֵם הַמֶּלֶךְ וְאֶת־נְשֵׁי הַמֶּלֶךְ וְאֶת־סָרִיסָיו

וְאֵת אֱוֵלֵי [אֵילֵי] הָאָרֶץ הוֹלִיךְ גּוֹלָה מִירוּשָׁלַ͏ִם בָּבֶלָה 16 וְאֵת כָּל־אַנְשֵׁי

הַחַיִל שִׁבְעַת אֲלָפִים וְהֶחָרָשׁ וְהַמַּסְגֵּר אֶלֶף הַכֹּל גִּבּוֹרִים עֹשֵׂי מִלְחָמָה

וַיְבִיאֵם מֶלֶךְ־בָּבֶל גּוֹלָה בָּבֶלָה

17 וַיַּמְלֵךְ מֶלֶךְ־בָּבֶל אֶת־מַתַּנְיָה דֹדוֹ תַּחְתָּיו

וַיַּסֵּב אֶת־שְׁמוֹ צִדְקִיָּהוּ

Jehoiachin was eighteen years old when he became king, and he reigned three months in Jerusalem; and his mother's name was Nehushta the daughter of Elnathan of Jerusalem. He did evil in the sight of Yahweh, according to all that his father had done. At that time the servants of Nebuchadnezzar king of Babylon went up to Jerusalem, and the city came under siege. And Nebuchadnezzar the king of Babylon came to the city, while his servants were besieging it. Jehoiachin the king of Judah went out to the king of Babylon, he and his mother and his servants and his captains and his officials. **So the king of Babylon took him captive in the eighth year of his reign**. He carried out from there all the treasures of the house of Yahweh, and the treasures of the king's house, and cut in pieces all the vessels of gold which Solomon king of Israel had made in the temple of Yahweh, just as Yahweh had said.

Then he led away into exile all Jerusalem and all the captains and all the mighty men of valor, ten thousand captives, and all the craftsmen and the smiths. None remained except the poorest people of the land.

¶ So he led Jehoiachin away into exile to Babylon; also the king's mother and the king's wives and his officials and the leading men of the land, he led away into exile from Jerusalem to Babylon. All the men of valor, seven thousand, and the craftsmen and the smiths, one thousand, all strong and fit for war, and these the king of Babylon brought into exile to Babylon. Then the king of Babylon made his uncle Mattaniah king in his place, and changed his name to Zedekiah.

Jehoiachin sent for 10th Nissan, 597 (22nd April)

Passage about Jehoiachin misplaced and reinserted for Jehoiakim:

2 Chr. 36:9-10a, 6b-7, 10b ‖ 2 Ki. 24:12-17

9 בֶּן־שְׁמוֹנֶה‹עֶשְׂרֵה› שָׁנִים יְהוֹיָכִין בְּמָלְכוֹ וּשְׁלֹשָׁה חֳדָשִׁים וַעֲשֶׂרֶת יָמִים

מָלַךְ בִּירוּשָׁלָ‍ם וַיַּעַשׂ הָרַע בְּעֵינֵי יְהוָה 10a וְלִתְשׁוּבַת הַשָּׁנָה

6 עָלָיו עָלָה נְבוּכַדְנֶאצַּר מֶלֶךְ בָּבֶל וַיַּאַסְרֵהוּ בַּנְחֻשְׁתַּיִם לְהֹלִיכוֹ בָּבֶלָה

7 וּמִכְּלֵי בֵּית יְהוָה הֵבִיא נְבוּכַדְנֶאצַּר לְבָבֶל וַיִּתְּנֵם בְּהֵיכָלוֹ בְּבָבֶל

10b וַיְבִאֵהוּ בָבֶלָה עִם־כְּלֵי חֶמְדַּת בֵּית־יְהוָה וַיַּמְלֵךְ

אֶת־צִדְקִיָּהוּ אָחִיו עַל־יְהוּדָה וִירוּשָׁלָ‍ם

Jehoiachin was eight years old when he became king, and he reigned three months and ten days in Jerusalem, and he did evil in the sight of Yahweh.

At the turn of the year King Nebuchadnezzar ‹*king of Babylon came up against him and bound him with bronze chains to take him to Babylon. Nebuchadnezzar also brought some of the articles of the house of Yahweh to Babylon and put them in his temple at Babylon.*› And he brought him to Babylon with the valuable articles of the house of Yahweh, and he made his kinsman Zedekiah king over Judah and Jerusalem.

List of captives taken (by Nisan years = Babylonian reckoning)

Jeremiah 52:28

28 זֶה הָעָם אֲשֶׁר הֶגְלָה נְבוּכַדְרֶאצַּר בִּשְׁנַת־שֶׁבַע יְהוּדִים שְׁלֹשֶׁת אֲלָפִים

וְעֶשְׂרִים וּשְׁלֹשָׁה

These are the people whom Nebuchadnezzar carried away into exile: in the **seventh year** 3,023 Jews;

Using Babylonian Nisan reckoning! By Tishre reckoning it was eighth year of Nebuchadcnezzar

    D.   **Zedekiah** 597-586 eleven years (21 yrs. old; born 607 BCE)

        2 Ki 24:18-25:26; 2 Chr 36:11-21

        596 — Nebuchadrezzar marched to **Hatti**

**   595 — **Rebellion in Babylon** crushed

        594 — Nebuchadrezzar returns to **Hatti**

***   593 — **Psammeticus II** (595-589) — made expedition to Phoenicia in this year;

        Rebellion planned by states in the west:

Ambassadors from **Edom, Moab, Ammon, Tyre and Sidon**
were in Jerusalem Jer 27:1-3, 12-18 (cf. 28:1)

Jer. 27:1 בְּרֵאשִׁית מַמְלֶכֶת ›יְהוֹיָקִם‹ ‹צִדְקִיָּה› בֶּן־יֹאשִׁיָהוּ מֶלֶךְ

יְהוּדָה הָיָה הַדָּבָר הַזֶּה אֶל־יִרְמְיָה מֵאֵת יְהוָה לֵאמֹר

Jer. 27:2 כֹּה־אָמַר יְהוָה אֵלַי עֲשֵׂה לְךָ מוֹסֵרוֹת וּמֹטוֹת

וּנְתַתָּם עַל־צַוָּארֶךָ

Jer. 27:3 וְשִׁלַּחְתָּם אֶל־מֶלֶךְ אֱדוֹם וְאֶל־מֶלֶךְ מוֹאָב

וְאֶל־מֶלֶךְ בְּנֵי עַמּוֹן וְאֶל־מֶלֶךְ צֹר וְאֶל־מֶלֶךְ צִידוֹן

בְּיַד מַלְאָכִים הַבָּאִים יְרוּשָׁלַ͏ִם אֶל־צִדְקִיָּהוּ מֶלֶךְ יְהוּדָה

In the beginning of the reign of ›Jehoiakim‹ ‹Zedekiah›!!! the son of Josiah, king of Judah, this word came to Jeremiah from Yahweh, saying — Thus Yahweh said to me: "Make yourself thongs and yoke-bars, and put them on your neck. Send word to the king of **Edom**, the king of **Moab**, the king of the sons of **Ammon**, the king of **Tyre**, and the king of **Sidon** by the hand of the envoys who have come to Jerusalem to Zedekiah king of Judah.

Give them this charge for their masters: 'Thus says Yahweh of hosts, the God of Israel: This is what you shall say to your masters: "It is I who by my great power and my outstretched arm have made the earth, with the men and animals that are on the earth, and I give it to whomever it seems right to me. Now I have given all these lands into the hand of Nebuchadnezzar, the king of Babylon, my servant, and I have given him also the beasts of the field to serve him.

Jer. 27:12 וְאֶל־צִדְקִיָּה מֶלֶךְ־יְהוּדָה דִּבַּרְתִּי כְּכָל־הַדְּבָרִים הָאֵלֶּה

לֵאמֹר הָבִיאוּ אֶת־צַוְּארֵיכֶם בְּעֹל מֶלֶךְ־בָּבֶל וְעִבְדוּ אֹתוֹ וְעַמּוֹ וִחְיוּ

13 לָמָּה תָמוּתוּ אַתָּה וְעַמֶּךָ בַּחֶרֶב בָּרָעָב וּבַדָּבֶר כַּאֲשֶׁר דִּבֶּר יְהוָה אֶל־הַגּוֹי

אֲשֶׁר לֹא־יַעֲבֹד אֶת־מֶלֶךְ בָּבֶל 14 וְאַל־תִּשְׁמְעוּ אֶל־דִּבְרֵי הַנְּבִאִים הָאֹמְרִים

אֲלֵיכֶם לֵאמֹר לֹא תַעַבְדוּ אֶת־מֶלֶךְ בָּבֶל כִּי שֶׁקֶר הֵם נִבְּאִים לָכֶם

15 כִּי לֹא שְׁלַחְתִּים נְאֻם־יְהוָה וְהֵם נִבְּאִים בִּשְׁמִי לַשָּׁקֶר לְמַעַן הַדִּיחִי

וַאֲבַדְתֶּם אַתֶּם וְהַנְּבִאִים הַנִּבְּאִים לָכֶם 16 וְאֶל־הַכֹּהֲנִים וְאֶל־כָּל־הָעָם הַזֶּה

אֶתְכֶם

דִּבַּרְתִּי לֵאמֹר כֹּה אָמַר יְהוָה אַל־תִּשְׁמְעוּ אֶל־דִּבְרֵי נְבִיאֵיכֶם

הַנִּבְּאִים לָכֶם לֵאמֹר הִנֵּה כְלֵי בֵית־יְהוָה מוּשָׁבִים מִבָּבֶלָה עַתָּה מְהֵרָה

כִּי שֶׁקֶר הֵמָּה נִבְּאִים לָכֶם 17 אַל־תִּשְׁמְעוּ אֲלֵיהֶם עִבְדוּ אֶת־מֶלֶךְ־בָּבֶל

לָמָּה תִהְיֶה הָעִיר הַזֹּאת חָרְבָּה 18 וְאִם־נְבִאִים הֵם וְאִם־יֶשׁ דְּבַר־יְהוָה אִתָּם

וְחִיוּ

יִפְגְּעוּ־נָא בַּיהוָה צְבָאוֹת לְבִלְתִּי־בֹאוּ הַכֵּלִים הַנּוֹתָרִים בְּבֵית־יְהוָה וּבֵית

מֶלֶךְ יְהוּדָה וּבִירוּשָׁלַם בָּבֶלָה

Jer. 28:1

Jer. 28:1 וַיְהִי בַּשָּׁנָה הַהִיא בְּרֵאשִׁית מַמְלֶכֶת צִדְקִיָּה מֶלֶךְ־יְהוּדָה בִּשְׁנַת

[בַּ][שָּׁנָה] הָרְבִעִית בַּחֹדֶשׁ הַחֲמִישִׁי אָמַר אֵלַי חֲנַנְיָה בֶן־עַזּוּר הַנָּבִיא אֲשֶׁר

מִגִּבְעוֹן בְּבֵית יְהוָה לְעֵינֵי הַכֹּהֲנִים וְכָל־הָעָם לֵאמֹר

... to **Zedekiah** king of Judah I spoke in like manner: "Bring your necks under the yoke of the king of Babylon, and serve him and his people, and live. Why will you and your people die by the sword, by famine, and by pestilence, as Yahweh has spoken concerning any nation which will not serve the king of Babylon? Do not listen to the words of the prophets who are saying to you, 'You shall not serve the king of Babylon,' for it is a lie which they are prophesying to you. I have not sent them, says Yahweh, but they are prophesying falsely in my name, with the result that I will drive you out and you will perish, you and the prophets who are prophesying to you."

Then I spoke **to the priests** and to all this people, saying, "Thus says Yahweh: Do not listen to the words of your prophets who are prophesying to you, saying, 'Behold, the vessels of Yahweh's house will now shortly be brought back from

Babylon,' for it is a lie which they are prophesying to you. Do not listen to them; <u>serve the king of Babylon and live</u>. Why should this city become a desolation?

If they are prophets, and if the word of Yahweh is with them, then let them intercede with Yahweh of hosts, that the vessels which are left in the house of Yahweh, in the house of the king of Judah, and in Jerusalem may not go to Babylon. ......

<u>Jer. 28:1</u> In that same year, ›at the beginning of the reign of Zedekiah king of Judah,‹ **in the fifth month of the fourth year**, Hananiah the son of Azzur, the prophet from **Gibeon**, spoke to me in the house of Yahweh, in the presence of the priests and all the people, saying, "Thus says Yahweh of hosts, the God of Israel: I have broken the yoke of the king of Babylon. Within two years I will bring back to this place all the vessels of Yahweh's house, which Nebuchadnezzar king of Babylon took away from this place and carried to Babylon. I will also bring back to this place **Jeconiah the son of Jehoiakim**, king of Judah, and all the exiles from Judah who went to Babylon, says Yahweh, for I will break the yoke of the king of Babylon."

Nebuchadrezzar returns to Hatti (Babylonian Chronicle) — squelches the planned rebellion

Zedekiah went to Babylon Jer 51:59-64

59 הַדָּבָר אֲשֶׁר־צִוָּה יִרְמְיָהוּ הַנָּבִיא אֶת־שְׂרָיָה

בֶן־נֵרִיָּה בֶּן־מַחְסֵיָה בְּלֶכְתּוֹ אֶת־צִדְקִיָּהוּ מֶלֶךְ־יְהוּדָה

בָּבֶל בִּשְׁנַת הָרְבִעִית לְמָלְכוֹ וּשְׂרָיָה שַׂר מְנוּחָה

60 וַיִּכְתֹּב יִרְמְיָהוּ אֵת כָּל־הָרָעָה אֲשֶׁר־תָּבוֹא

אֶל־בָּבֶל אֶל־סֵפֶר אֶחָד אֵת כָּל־הַדְּבָרִים הָאֵלֶּה

הַכְּתֻבִים אֶל־בָּבֶל

61 וַיֹּאמֶר יִרְמְיָהוּ אֶל־שְׂרָיָה כְּבֹאֲךָ בָבֶל וְרָאִיתָ

וְקָרָאתָ אֵת כָּל־הַדְּבָרִים הָאֵלֶּה

62 וְאָמַרְתָּ יְהוָה אַתָּה דִבַּרְתָּ אֶל־הַמָּקוֹם הַזֶּה

לְהַכְרִיתוֹ לְבִלְתִּי הֱיוֹת־בּוֹ יוֹשֵׁב לְמֵאָדָם וְעַד־בְּהֵמָה

כִּי־שִׁמְמוֹת עוֹלָם תִּהְיֶה

63 וְהָיָה כְּכַלֹּתְךָ לִקְרֹא אֶת־הַסֵּפֶר הַזֶּה תִּקְשֹׁר

עָלָיו אֶבֶן וְהִשְׁלַכְתּוֹ אֶל־תּוֹךְ פְּרָת

64 וְאָמַרְתָּ כָּכָה תִּשְׁקַע בָּבֶל וְלֹא־תָקוּם מִפְּנֵי הָרָעָה אֲשֶׁר

אָנֹכִי מֵבִיא עָלֶיהָ וְיָעֵפוּ עַד־הֵנָּה דִּבְרֵי יִרְמְיָהוּ

Theword which Jeremiah the prophet commanded Seraiah the son of Neriah, son of Mahseiah, **when he went with Zedekiah king of Judah to Babylon, in the fourth year of his reign**. Seraia was the chief chamberlain.

Jeremiah wrote in a book all the evil that should come upon Babylon, all these words that are written concerning Babylon. And Jeremiah said to Seraiah: "When you come to Babylon, see that you read all these words, and say, ʿO LORD, thou hast said concerning this place that thou wilt cut it off, so that nothing shall dwell in it, neither man nor beast, and it shall be desolate for ever.' When you finish reading this book, bind a stone to it, and cast it into the midst of the Euphrates, and say, ʿThus shall Babylon sink, to rise no more, because of the evil that I am bringing upon her.'"

Fourth year of Zedekiah = 593 BCE (accession year system)
Apparently sent back to Judah; allowed to stay in office.

Ezekiel gets his first vision — 5th day, 4th mo. 5th yr. of exile, no accession year involved = **31 July, 593**
Ezek. 1:1-3

וַיְהִי ׀ בִּשְׁלֹשִׁים שָׁנָה בָּרְבִיעִי בַּחֲמִשָּׁה לַחֹדֶשׁ וַאֲנִי בְתוֹךְ־הַגּוֹלָה

עַל־נְהַר־כְּבָר נִפְתְּחוּ הַשָּׁמַיִם וָאֶרְאֶה מַרְאוֹת אֱלֹהִים:

בַּחֲמִשָּׁה לַחֹדֶשׁ הִיא הַשָּׁנָה הַחֲמִישִׁית לְגָלוּת הַמֶּלֶךְ יוֹיָכִין:

הָיֹה הָיָה דְבַר־יְהוָה אֶל־יְחֶזְקֵאל בֶּן־בּוּזִי הַכֹּהֵן בְּאֶרֶץ כַּשְׂדִּים

עַל־נְהַר־כְּבָר וַתְּהִי עָלָיו שָׁם יַד־יְהוָה:

In the thirtieth year, on the **fifth day of the fourth month**, when I was in the community of exiles by the Chebar Canal, the heavens opened and I saw visions of God. On **the fifth day of the month**, it was **the fifth year of the exile of King Jehoiachin**, the word of Yahweh came to the priest Ezekiel son of Buzi, by the Chebar Canal, in the land of the Chaldeans. And the hand of Yahweh came upon him there.

592 — Ezekiel has a vision of Judah's iniquities:
Ezek. 8:1 — 17 Sept. 592 (Nisan years)

וַיְהִי ׀ בַּשָּׁנָה הַשִּׁשִּׁית בַּשִּׁשִּׁי בַּחֲמִשָּׁה לַחֹדֶשׁ אֲנִי יוֹשֵׁב בְּבֵיתִי וְזִקְנֵי

יְהוּדָה יוֹשְׁבִים לְפָנָי וַתִּפֹּל עָלַי שָׁם יַד אֲדֹנָי יְהוִה:

It came about **in the sixth year, on the fifth of the sixth month**, as I was sitting in my house with the elders of Judah sitting before me, that the hand of thye lord Yahweh fell on me there.

<u>591</u> — Oracle refused to the elders in exile

Ezek. 20:1-3 — 14th August 591

וַיְהִי ׀ בַּשָּׁנָה הַשְּׁבִיעִית בַּחֲמִשִׁי בֶּעָשׂוֹר לַחֹדֶשׁ בָּאוּ אֲנָשִׁים מִזִּקְנֵי

יִשְׂרָאֵל לִדְרֹשׁ אֶת־יְהוָה וַיֵּשְׁבוּ לְפָנָי : וַיְהִי דְבַר־יְהוָה אֵלַי לֵאמֹר :

בֶּן־אָדָם דַּבֵּר אֶת־זִקְנֵי יִשְׂרָאֵל וְאָמַרְתָּ אֲלֵהֶם כֹּה אָמַר אֲדֹנָי יְהוִה

הֲלִדְרֹשׁ אֹתִי אַתֶּם בָּאִים חַי־אָנִי אִם־אִדָּרֵשׁ לָכֶם נְאֻם אֲדֹנָי יְהוִה :

Now in the **seventh year, in the fifth (month), on the tenth of the month**, certain of the elders of Israel came to inquire of Yahweh, and sat before me. And the word of Yahweh came to me saying, "Son of man, speak to the elders of Israel and say to them, ᶜThus says Yahweh GOD, "Do you come to inquire of Me? As I live," declares Yahweh GOD, "I will not be inquired of by you.'"

<u>589</u> — Ḥophraᶜ (W3ḥ-ĭb-Rēᶜ; 589-570) succeeds Psammeticus

2 Kings 24:20b — : וַיִּמְרֹד צִדְקִיָּהוּ בְּמֶלֶךְ בָּבֶל

And Zedekiah rebelled against the king of Babylon

<u>588</u> — 9th year of Zedekiah, siege began 2 Ki 25:1

10.10.9[th] year of captivity = 15 Jan 588 — **Tishre** years

2 Kings 25:1-3

וַיְהִי בִשְׁנַת הַתְּשִׁיעִית לְמָלְכוֹ בַּחֹדֶשׁ הָעֲשִׂירִי בֶּעָשׂוֹר לַחֹדֶשׁ

בָּא נְבֻכַדְנֶאצַּר מֶלֶךְ־בָּבֶל הוּא וְכָל־חֵילוֹ עַל־יְרוּשָׁלַם

וַיִּחַן עָלֶיהָ וַיִּבְנוּ עָלֶיהָ דָּיֵק סָבִיב : וַתָּבֹא הָעִיר בַּמָּצוֹר

עַד עַשְׁתֵּי עֶשְׂרֵה שָׁנָה לַמֶּלֶךְ צִדְקִיָּהוּ :

Now in the **ninth year of his reign, on the tenth day of the tenth month**, Nebuchadnezzar king of Babylon came, he and all his army, against Jerusalem, camped against it and built a siege wall all around it. So the city was under siege until **the eleventh year of King Zedekiah**.

Oracle to Ezekiel about the siege against Jerusalem —

Nisan Years

Ezek. 24:1-2

וַיְהִי דְבַר־יְהוָה אֵלַי בַּשָּׁנָה הַתְּשִׁיעִית בַּחֹדֶשׁ הָעֲשִׂירִי בֶּעָשׂוֹר לַחֹדֶשׁ

לֵאמֹר : בֶּן־אָדָם כְּתוֹב [כְּתָב] לְךָ אֶת־שֵׁם הַיּוֹם אֶת־עֶצֶם הַיּוֹם הַזֶּה

סָמַךְ מֶלֶךְ־בָּבֶל ` אֶל־יְרוּשָׁלִַם בְּעֶצֶם הַיּוֹם הַזֶּה׃

And the word of Yahweh came to me in the **ninth year, in the tenth month, on the tenth of the month**, saying, "Son of man, write the name of the day, this very day. The king of Babylon has laid siege to Jerusalem this very day.

587 — Ḥophraᶜ came out, but was routed before Nissan 586; 10th Zedekiah = 18th Nebuchadrezzar — **Nisan**

years

Jeremiah now in jail

Jer 32:1-3

1 הַדָּבָר אֲשֶׁר־הָיָה אֶל־יִרְמְיָהוּ מֵאֵת יְהוָה בִּשְׁנַת [בַּ][שָּׁנָה] הָעֲשִׂרִית

לְצִדְקִיָּהוּ מֶלֶךְ יְהוּדָה הִיא הַשָּׁנָה שְׁמֹנֶה־עֶשְׂרֵה שָׁנָה לִנְבוּכַדְרֶאצַּר

2 וְאָז חֵיל מֶלֶךְ בָּבֶל צָרִים עַל־יְרוּשָׁלָ֑ם וְיִרְמְיָהוּ הַנָּבִיא הָיָה כָלוּא בַּחֲצַר

הַמַּטָּרָה אֲשֶׁר בֵּית־מֶלֶךְ יְהוּדָה 3 אֲשֶׁר כְּלָאוֹ צִדְקִיָּהוּ מֶלֶךְ־יְהוּדָה

לֵאמֹר מַדּוּעַ אַתָּה נִבָּא לֵאמֹר כֹּה אָמַר יְהוָה הִנְנִי נֹתֵן אֶת־הָעִיר

הַזֹּאת בְּיַד מֶלֶךְ־בָּבֶל וּלְכָדָהּ

The word which came to Jeremiah from Yahweh **in the tenth year of King Zedekiah** of Judah, which was **the eighteenth year of Nebuchadrezzar.**

At that time the army of the king of Babylon was besieging Jerusalem, and the prophet Jeremiah was confined in the prison compound attached to the palace of the king of Judah.

Ezek. 17:15

15 וַיִּמְרָד־בּוֹ לִשְׁלֹחַ מַלְאָכָיו מִצְרַיִם לָתֶת־לוֹ סוּסִים וְעַם־רָב

הֲיִצְלָח הֲיִמָּלֵט הָעֹשֵׂה אֵלֶּה וְהֵפֵר בְּרִית וְנִמְלָט

But he rebelled against him and sent his envoys to **Egypt** to get horses and a large army. Will he succeed? Will he who does such things escape? Shall he break a covenant and escape?

Jer. 37:5-8

וְחֵיל פַּרְעֹה יָצָא מִמִּצְרָיִם וַיִּשְׁמְעוּ הַכַּשְׂדִּים הַצָּרִים עַל־יְרוּשָׁלַ֙ם

אֶת־שִׁמְעָם וַיֵּעָלוּ מֵעַל יְרוּשָׁלָ֑ם׃

וַיְהִי דְּבַר־יְהוָה אֶל־יִרְמְיָהוּ הַנָּבִיא לֵאמֹר׃

כֹּה־אָמַר יְהוָה אֱלֹהֵי יִשְׂרָאֵל כֹּה תֹאמְרוּ אֶל־מֶלֶךְ יְהוּדָה

הַשֹּׁלֵחַ אֶתְכֶם אֵלַי לְדָרְשֵׁנִי

הִנֵּה ׀ חֵיל פַּרְעֹה הַיֹּצֵא לָכֶם לְעֶזְרָה שָׁב לְאַרְצוֹ מִצְרָיִם׃

וְשָׁבוּ הַכַּשְׂדִּים וְנִלְחֲמוּ עַל־הָעִיר הַזֹּאת וּלְכָדֻהָ וּשְׂרָפֻהָ בָאֵשׁ׃

Pharaoh's army had set out from Egypt; and when the Chaldeans who had been besieging Jerusalem heard the report about them, they lifted the [siege] from Jerusalem.

Then the word of Yahweh came to Jeremiah the prophet, saying, Thus says Yahweh God of Israel, "Thus you are to say to the king of Judah, who sent you to Me to inquire of Me: Behold, **Pharaoh's army which has come out for your assistance is going to return to its own land of Egypt**. The Chaldeans will also return and fight against this city, and they will capture it and burn it with fire."

<u>586</u> — Edomites attached Judah from the south:

Arad Letter 24 Reverse

(12) מערד 50 ומקין

(13) ה . ושלחתמ . אתמ . רמת נג[ב בי]

(14) ד . מלכיהו בנ קרבאור . והב

(15) קידמ . על . יד אלישע בנ ירמי

(16) הו . ברמת נגב . פנ . יקרה . את ה

(17) עיר . דבר . ודבר המלכ אתכמ

(18) בנבשכמ . הנה שלחתי להעיד

(19) בכמ . הימ . האנשמ . את אליש

(20) ע . פנ . תבא . אדמ . שמה

... from Arad fifty and from Qinah, and you will send them to Ramath-negeb [under the char]ge of Malkiyahu son of Qerab-'ur, and he will hand them over to the charge of Elishaᶜ son of Jeremiah in Ramath-negeb, lest anything happen to the city. And the word of the king to you is incumbent on your very lives! Behold I have written to warn you today: (Get those) men to Elishaᶜ! Lest Edom should come there.

Cf also the following:

Psalms 137:7

זְכֹר יְהֹוָה ׀ לִבְנֵי אֱדוֹם אֵת יוֹם יְרוּשָׁלָ͏ִם הָאֹמְרִים עָרוּ ׀ עָרוּ

עַד הַיְסוֹד בָּהּ׃

Remember, Yahweh, against the Edomites the day of Jerusalem's fall; how they cried, "Strip her, strip her to her very foundations!"

Obadiah 1:8-14

הֲלֹוא בַּיֹּום הַהוּא נְאֻם יְהוָה וְהַאֲבַדְתִּי חֲכָמִים מֵאֱדֹום

וּתְבוּנָה מֵהַר עֵשָׂו: וְחַתּוּ גִבֹּורֶיךָ תֵּימָן לְמַעַן יִכָּרֶת־אִישׁ

מֵהַר עֵשָׂו מִקָּטֶל:

מֵחֲמַס אָחִיךָ יַעֲקֹב תְּכַסְּךָ בוּשָׁה וְנִכְרַתָּ לְעֹולָם: בְּיֹום עֲמָדְךָ

מִנֶּגֶד בְּיֹום שְׁבֹות זָרִים חֵילֹו וְנָכְרִים בָּאוּ שַׁעֲרֹו [שְׁעָרָיו]

וְעַל־יְרוּשָׁלַם יַדּוּ גֹורָל גַּם־אַתָּה כְּאַחַד מֵהֶם:

וְאַל־תֵּרֶא בְיֹום־אָחִיךָ בְּיֹום נָכְרֹו וְאַל־תִּשְׂמַח לִבְנֵי־יְהוּדָה

בְּיֹום אָבְדָם וְאַל־תַּגְדֵּל פִּיךָ בְּיֹום צָרָה: אַל־תָּבֹוא בְשַׁעַר־עַמִּי

בְּיֹום אֵידָם אַל־תֵּרֶא גַם־אַתָּה בְּרָעָתֹו בְּיֹום אֵידֹו וְאַל־תִּשְׁלַחְנָה

בְחֵילֹו בְּיֹום אֵידֹו: וְאַל־תַּעֲמֹד עַל־הַפֶּרֶק לְהַכְרִית אֶת־פְּלִיטָיו

וְאַל־תַּסְגֵּר שְׂרִידָיו בְּיֹום צָרָה:

In that day — declares Yahweh —I will make the wise vanish from **Edom**, understanding from Esau's mount. Your warriors shall lose heart, O **Teman**, and not a man on **Esau's mount** will survive the slaughter. For the outrage to your brother Jacob, disgrace shall engulf you, and you shall perish forever.

On that day when you stood aloof, when aliens carried off his goods, when foreigners entered his gates and cast lots for **Jerusalem**, you were as one of them. Do not gaze with glee on your brother that day, on his day of calamity! Do not gloat over the people of Judah on that day of ruin! Do not jeer loudly on a day of anguish! Do not enter the gate of My people on its day of disaster, Don't you gaze in glee with the others on its misfortune,on its day of disaster, and don not lay hands on its wealth,on its day of disaster! Do not stand **at the passes** to cut down its fugitives! Do not betray those who fled on that day of anguish!

Jer. 34:7

Jer. 34:7 וְחֵיל מֶלֶךְ־בָּבֶל נִלְחָמִים עַל־יְרוּשָׁלַם וְעַל

כָּל־עָרֵי יְהוּדָה הַנֹּותָרֹות אֶל־לָכִישׁ וְאֶל־עֲזֵקָה כִּי

הֵנָּה נִשְׁאֲרוּ בְּעָרֵי יְהוּדָה עָרֵי מִבְצָר

and the army of **the king of Babylon** was fighting against **Jerusalem** and against all the remaining cities of Judah, against Lachish and against Azekah, because they (only) remained as fortified cities among the cities of Judah.

Lachish Letter 4

Reverse	Obverse

09) כי אמ.בתסבת הבקר
אשלחנו(?)].

01) ישמע.יהו[ה את אד[ני עתכימ

10) וידע <אדני> כי.אל.משאת
לכש.נח

02) שמעת טב.ועת ככל אשר שלח
אדני

11) נו.שמרמ.ככל.האתת
אשר נת[.]

03) כנ.עשה.עבדכ כתבתי על הדלת
ככל.

12) אדני.כי לא.נראה את עז

04) אשר שלה[ח][אדני א[לי.וכי.שלח
א

13) קה

05) דני.על.דבר בית הרפד.אינ.שמ א

06) דמ וסמכיהו לקחה.שמעיהו ו

07) יעלהו העירה ועבדכ אינ

08) י שלח.שמה.אתה ע[[ו][ד היומ(?)]

May Yahwe[h] cause my [lord] to hear, this very day, tidings of good. And now,
according to everything which my lord has sent, this has your servant done. I wrote
on the sheet/door according to everything which [you] sent [t]o me. And inasmuch
as my lord sent to me concerning the matter of **Beth Harapid**, there is no one there.
And as for Səmakyāhû, Shəmaʿyāhû took him and brought him up to the city. And
your servant is not sending him there any[more], although when morning comes
round [*I may send there* (?)]. And may (my lord) be apprised that we are watching out
for the fire signals of **Lachish** according to all the signs which my lord has given,
because we cannot see **Azekeh**.

****** **Jerusalem city** taken 11th year of Zedekiah 2 Ki 25:2-4

18 July, 586; **Tishre** years

2 Kings 25:3-7

בְּתִשְׁעָה לַחֹדֶשׁ וַיֶּחֱזַק הָרָעָב בָּעִיר וְלֹא־הָיָה לֶחֶם לְעַם הָאָרֶץ:

וַתִּבָּקַע הָעִיר וְכָל־אַנְשֵׁי הַמִּלְחָמָה | הַלַּיְלָה דֶּרֶךְ שַׁעַר | בֵּין

הַחֹמֹתַיִם אֲשֶׁר עַל־גַּן הַמֶּלֶךְ וְכַשְׂדִּים עַל־הָעִיר סָבִיב וַיֵּלֶךְ דֶּרֶךְ

הָעֲרָבָה: וַיִּרְדְּפוּ חֵיל־כַּשְׂדִּים אַחַר הַמֶּלֶךְ וַיַּשִּׂגוּ אֹתוֹ בְּעַרְבוֹת יְרֵחוֹ

וְכָל־חֵילוֹ נָפֹצוּ מֵעָלָיו: וַיִּתְפְּשׂוּ אֶת־הַמֶּלֶךְ וַיַּעֲלוּ אֹתוֹ אֶל־מֶלֶךְ בָּבֶל

רִבְלָתָה וַיְדַבְּרוּ אִתּוֹ מִשְׁפָּט: וְאֶת־בְּנֵי צִדְקִיָּהוּ שָׁחֲטוּ לְעֵינָיו

וְאֶת־עֵינֵי צִדְקִיָּהוּ עִוֵּר וַיַּאַסְרֵהוּ בַנְחֻשְׁתַּיִם וַיְבִאֵהוּ בָּבֶל :

On the **ninth day** of the (fourth) month the famine was so severe in the city that there was no food for the people of the land. Then the city was broken into, and all the men of war [fled] by night by way of the gate between the two walls beside the king's garden, though the Chaldeans were all around the city. And they went by **way of the Arabah**. But the army of the Chaldeans pursued the king and overtook him in the **plains of Jericho** and all his army was scattered from him.

Then they captured the king and brought him to the king of Babylon at **Riblah**, and he passed sentence on him. They slaughtered the sons of Zedekiah before his eyes, then put out the eyes of Zedekiah and bound him with bronze fetters and brought him to **Babylon**.

Jeremiah 39:2 — **Nisan** year

בְּעַשְׁתֵּי־עֶשְׂרֵה שָׁנָה לְצִדְקִיָּהוּ בַּחֹדֶשׁ הָרְבִיעִי בְּתִשְׁעָה לַחֹדֶשׁ

הָבְקְעָה הָעִיר :

in the **eleventh year** of Zedekiah, in the **fourth month**, on the **ninth** of the month, the city was breached.

Captives taken from Judah

Jer. 52:29 — 18th yr. of Nebuchadnezzar;

Nisan year

בִּשְׁנַת שְׁמוֹנֶה עֶשְׂרֵה לִנְבוּכַדְרֶאצַּר

מִירוּשָׁלַיִם נֶפֶשׁ שְׁמֹנֶה מֵאוֹת שְׁלֹשִׁים וּשְׁנָיִם

in **the eighteenth year** of Nebuchadnezzar 832 persons from Jerusalem;

Temple and palaces all burned

19th yr. Nebuchadrezzar **Tishre** year

2 Ki 25:8-10; 10th day 5th mo. = 14 Aug. 586 B.C.E.

8 וּבַחֹדֶשׁ הַחֲמִישִׁי בְּשִׁבְעָה לַחֹדֶשׁ הִיא שְׁנַת

תְּשַׁע־עֶשְׂרֵה שָׁנָה לַמֶּלֶךְ נְבֻכַדְנֶאצַּר מֶלֶךְ־בָּבֶל בָּא

נְבוּזַרְאֲדָן רַב־טַבָּחִים עֶבֶד מֶלֶךְ־בָּבֶל יְרוּשָׁלָם

9 וַיִּשְׂרֹף אֶת־בֵּית־יְהוָה וְאֶת־בֵּית הַמֶּלֶךְ

וְאֵת כָּל־בָּתֵּי יְרוּשָׁלַם וְאֶת־כָּל־בֵּית גָּדוֹל שָׂרַף בָּאֵשׁ

10 וְאֶת־חוֹמֹת יְרוּשָׁלַם סָבִיב נָתְצוּ כָּל־חֵיל

כַּשְׂדִּים אֲשֶׁר רַב־טַבָּחִים

Now on **the seventh day** of the **fifth month**, which was the **nineteenth year** of King Nebuchadnezzar, king of Babylon, Nebuzaradan the captain of the guard, a servant of the king of Babylon, came to Jerusalem.He burned the house of Yahweh, the king's house, and all the houses of Jerusalem; even every great house he burned with fire.So all the army of the Chaldeans who (were with) the captain of the guard broke down the walls around Jerusalem.

Jer. 52:12-14, also 19th year, **Nisan** year

12 וּבַחֹדֶשׁ הַחֲמִישִׁי בֶּעָשׂוֹר לַחֹדֶשׁ הִיא שְׁנַת

תְּשַׁע־עֶשְׂרֵה שָׁנָה לַמֶּלֶךְ נְבוּכַדְרֶאצַּר מֶלֶךְ־בָּבֶל בָּא

נְבוּזַרְאֲדָן רַב־טַבָּחִים עָמַד לִפְנֵי מֶלֶךְ־בָּבֶל בִּירוּשָׁלָם

13 וַיִּשְׂרֹף אֶת־בֵּית־יְהוָה וְאֶת־בֵּית הַמֶּלֶךְ וְאֵת

כָּל־בָּתֵּי יְרוּשָׁלַם וְאֶת־כָּל־בֵּית הַגָּדוֹל שָׂרַף בָּאֵשׁ

14 וְאֶת־כָּל־חֹמוֹת יְרוּשָׁלַם סָבִיב נָתְצוּ כָּל־חֵיל ·

כַשְׂדִּים אֲשֶׁר אֶת־רַב־טַבָּחִים

And on the **tenth** of the **fifth month**, which was the **nineteenth year** of King Nebuchadnezzar, king of Babylon, Nebuzaradan the captain of the bodyguard, who was in the service of the king of Babylon, came to Jerusalem. He burned the house of Yahweh, the king's house and all the houses of Jerusalem; even every large house he burned with fire. So all the army of the Chaldeans who [were] with the captain of the guard broke down all the walls around Jerusalem.

<u>585</u> — Messenger reached Ezekiel about fall of Jerusalem

January 8th = 5th day, 10th mo., 12th yr. of exile

(= of Zedekiah's reign) — 12 years after 597 BCE

Ezekiel 33:21

<u>Ezek. 33:21</u> וַיְהִי בִּשְׁתֵּי עֶשְׂרֵה שָׁנָה בָּעֲשִׂרִי בַּחֲמִשָּׁה לַחֹדֶשׁ לְגָלוּתֵנוּ בָּא־אֵלַי

5th day, 10th month, 12th yr.   הַפָּלִיט מִירוּשָׁלַם לֵאמֹר הֻכְּתָה הָעִיר

Now in the **twelfth year of our exile**, on the **fifth** of the **tenth month**, the refugees from Jerusalem came to me, saying, "The city has been taken."

Nebuchadnezzar's siege of Tyre begins (Jos. *Contra Apion* I, 143, 156-159).

<u>582</u> — 23rd yr. of Nebuchadnezzar — campaign against Coele Syria, Moab and Ammon (Jos. *Antiq.* X, ix,7 [181-182]).

Jer. 52:30 — more captives taken from Judah

30 בִּשְׁנַת שָׁלֹשׁ וְעֶשְׂרִים לִנְבוּכַדְרֶאצַּר הֶגְלָה

נְבוּזַרְאֲדָן רַב־טַבָּחִים יְהוּדִים נֶפֶשׁ שְׁבַע מֵאוֹת

אַרְבָּעִים וַחֲמִשָּׁה כָּל־נֶפֶשׁ אַרְבַּעַת אֲלָפִים וְשֵׁשׁ מֵאוֹת

in the **twenty-third year** of Nebuchadnezzar, Nebuzaradan the captain of the guard carried into exile 745 Judeans;

> <u>572</u> — Seige of Tyre ends
> <u>571</u> — Ezk. 29:17-19 — 1 1st mo. (Nissan) 27th yr. of exile
> Egypt promised to Nebuchadnezzar as reward for
> punishment of Tyre

Ezek. 29:17-19

וַיְהִי בְּעֶשְׂרִים וָשֶׁבַע שָׁנָה בָּרִאשׁוֹן בְּאֶחָד לַחֹדֶשׁ הָיָה דְבַר־יְהוָה אֵלַי

לֵאמֹר : בֶּן־אָדָם נְבוּכַדְרֶאצַּר מֶלֶךְ־בָּבֶל הֶעֱבִיד אֶת־חֵילוֹ עֲבֹדָה

גְדֹלָה אֶל־צֹר כָּל־רֹאשׁ מֻקְרָח וְכָל־כָּתֵף מְרוּטָה וְשָׂכָר לֹא־הָיָה

לוֹ וּלְחֵילוֹ מִצֹּר עַל־הָעֲבֹדָה אֲשֶׁר־עָבַד עָלֶיהָ :

לָכֵן כֹּה אָמַר אֲדֹנָי יְהוִה הִנְנִי נֹתֵן לִנְבוּכַדְרֶאצַּר מֶלֶךְ־בָּבֶל

אֶת־אֶרֶץ מִצְרָיִם וְנָשָׂא הֲמֹנָהּ וְשָׁלַל שְׁלָלָהּ וּבָזַז בִּזָּהּ וְהָיְתָה

שָׂכָר לְחֵילוֹ :

Now in the **twenty-seventh** year, in the **first** [month], on the **first** of the month, the word of Yahweh came to me saying, "Son of man, Nebuchadnezzar king of Babylon made his army labor hard against **Tyre**; every head was made bald and every shoulder was rubbed bare. But he and his army had no wages from Tyre for the labor that he had performed against it." Therefore thus says The Lord Yahweh, "Behold, I will give the land of **Egypt** to Nebuchadnezzar king of Babylon. And he will carry off her wealth and capture her spoil and seize her plunder; and it will be wages for his army.

> <u>570</u> — Amasis seizes power from Hophra in Egypt.
> <u>568</u> — Nebuchadnezzar's invasion of Egypt (*ANET*: 308)

> <u>561</u> — 2nd April — 27th day, 12th mo., 37th yr. of
> Jehoiachin's captivity (Tishre reckoning),
> Evil-merodach (Amēl-Marduk) released Jehoiachin
> from prison — just in time for the upcoming New

Year celebration to mark the Babylonian king's
first full year of reign!

2 Kings 25:27 = Jer. 52:31-34

2Kings 25:27 וַיְהִי בִשְׁלֹשִׁים וָשֶׁבַע שָׁנָה לְגָלוּת יְהוֹיָכִין

מֶלֶךְ־יְהוּדָה בִּשְׁנֵים עָשָׂר חֹדֶשׁ בְּעֶשְׂרִים וְשִׁבְעָה

לַחֹדֶשׁ נָשָׂא אֱוִיל מְרֹדַךְ מֶלֶךְ בָּבֶל בִּשְׁנַת מָלְכוֹ

אֶת־רֹאשׁ יְהוֹיָכִין מֶלֶךְ־יְהוּדָה מִבֵּית כֶּלֶא

Jeremiah 52:31

וַיְהִי בִשְׁלֹשִׁים וָשֶׁבַע שָׁנָה לְגָלוּת יְהוֹיָכִן מֶלֶךְ־יְהוּדָה בִּשְׁנֵים

עָשָׂר חֹדֶשׁ בְּעֶשְׂרִים וַחֲמִשָּׁה לַחֹדֶשׁ נָשָׂא אֱוִיל מְרֹדַךְ מֶלֶךְ

בָּבֶל בִּשְׁנַת מַלְכֻתוֹ אֶת־רֹאשׁ יְהוֹיָכִין מֶלֶךְ־יְהוּדָה וַיֹּצֵא אוֹתוֹ

מִבֵּית הַכְּלִיא] הַכְּלוּא [

Now it came about in the thirty-seventh year of the exile of Jehoiachin king of Judah,
in the twelfth month, on the twenty-fifth of the month, that Evil-merodach king of
Babylon, in the [first] year of his reign, showed favor to Jehoiachin king of Judah and
brought him out of prison.

PERSIAN PERIOD: EXILE AND RETURN

I. GEOGRAPHICAL SITUATION — "Beyond the River"

The Levant = עֲבַר נַהֲרָא

A. Biblical Descriptions:

1. In Solomon's reign:

a. 1 Ki. 5:4-5 (Eng. 4:24-25)

4 כִּי־הוּא רֹדֶה בְּכָל־עֵבֶר הַנָּהָר מִתִּפְסַח וְעַד־עַזָּה בְּכָל־מַלְכֵי
עֵבֶר הַנָּהָר וְשָׁלוֹם הָיָה לוֹ מִכָּל־עֲבָרָיו מִסָּבִיב
5 וַיֵּשֶׁב יְהוּדָה וְיִשְׂרָאֵל לָבֶטַח אִישׁ תַּחַת גַּפְנוֹ
וְתַחַת תְּאֵנָתוֹ מִדָּן וְעַד־בְּאֵר שָׁבַע כֹּל יְמֵי שְׁלֹמֹה

1 Kings 4:24 For he had dominion over everything west of the
River, from Tiphsah even to Gaza, over all the kings west of the
River; and he had peace on all sides around about him.
1Kings 4:25 So Judah and Israel lived in safety, every man under
his vine and his fig tree, from Dan even to Beersheba, all the days
of Solomon.

b. 1 Ki 4:20-5:1 (Eng 4:20-21) belongs after 1 Ki.
10:26a parallel to 2 Chron. 9:26;

4:20 יְהוּדָה וְיִשְׂרָאֵל רַבִּים כַּחוֹל אֲשֶׁר־עַל־הַיָּם
לָרֹב אֹכְלִים וְשֹׁתִים וּשְׂמֵחִים
5:1 וּשְׁלֹמֹה הָיָה מוֹשֵׁל בְּכָל־הַמַּמְלָכוֹת מִן־הַנָּהָר ‹הַגָּדוֹל› ‹וְעַד› (1 Chr. 9:26)
אֶרֶץ פְּלִשְׁתִּים וְעַד גְּבוּל מִצְרָיִם
מַגִּשִׁים מִנְחָה וְעֹבְדִים אֶת־שְׁלֹמֹה כָּל־יְמֵי חַיָּיו

1 Kings 4:20 ¶ Judah and Israel [were] as numerous as the sand
that is on the seashore in abundance; [they] were eating and
drinking and rejoicing.

1 Kings 5:1 ¶ Now Solomon was ruling over all the kingdoms from the ‹Great› River ‹to› (1 Chr. 9:26) the land of the Philistines and to the border of Egypt; [they] brought tribute and served Solomon all the days of his life.

2. The "Promised Land" (Gen. 15:18)

18 בַּיּוֹם הַהוּא כָּרַת יְהוָה אֶת־אַבְרָם בְּרִית

לֵאמֹר לְזַרְעֲךָ נָתַתִּי אֶת־הָאָרֶץ הַזֹּאת מִנְּהַר מִצְרַיִם

עַד־הַנָּהָר הַגָּדֹל נְהַר־פְּרָת

On that day Yahweh made a covenant with Abram, saying, "To your descendants I have given this land, From the river of Egypt as far as the great river, the river Euphrates:

Cf. Gen 10:19

Gen. 10:19 וַיְהִי גְּבוּל הַכְּנַעֲנִי מִצִּידֹן בֹּאֲכָה גְרָרָה

עַד־עַזָּה בֹּאֲכָה סְדֹמָה וַעֲמֹרָה וְאַדְמָה וּצְבֹיִם עַד־לָשַׁע

The territory of the Canaanite extended from Sidon as you go toward Gerar, as far as Gaza; as you go toward Sodom and Gomorrah and Admah and Zeboiim, as far as Lasha.

B. Herodotus:

ἀπὸ δὲ Ποσιδηίου πόλιος, τὴν Ἀμφίλοχος ὁ Ἀμφιάρεω
οἴκισε ἐπ᾿ οὔροισι τοῖσι Κιλίκων τε καὶ Συρίων, ἀρξάμενον
ἀπὸ ταύτης μέχρι Αἰγύπτου, πλὴν μοίρης τῆς Ἀραβίων
(ταῦτα γὰρ ἦν ἀτελέα), πεντήκοντα καὶ τριηκόσια τάλαντα
φόρος ἦν· ἔστι δὲ ἐν τῷ νομῷ τούτῳ Φοινίκη τε πᾶσα καὶ
Συρίη ἡ Παλαιστίνη καλεομένη καὶ Κύπρος· νομὸς πέμπτος
οὗτος.

From the town of Posideion, which was founded by
Amphilochus son of Amphiaraus, on the border between Cilicia
and Syria, beginning from this as far as Egypt — omitting
Arabian territory (which was free of tax), came 350 talents. In
this province is the whole of Phoenicia and that part of Syria
which is called Palestine, and Cyprus. This is the fifth
province.(Bk. III, 91).

91. מהעיר פוסידיאון, אשר אמפילוכוס בן אמפיארוס על הגבול שבין
קיליקיה וסוריה, מחעיר הזאת, עד מצרים, — מלבד חבל הערבים כי
זה היה חפשי ממס — היה המס שלוש מאות וחמשים ככר. במחוז הזה
נכללו כל פניקיה וסוריה הנקראת פליסטינא וקירוס. זה המחוז
החמישי.

ὁμουρέει γὰρ ἡ Συρίη Αἰγύπτῳ, οἱ δὲ Φοίνικες, τῶν ἐστι ἡ
Σιδών, ἐν τῇ Συρίῃ οἰκέουσι.

For Syria borders on Egypt, and the Phoenicians, to whom
belongs Sidon, dwell in Syria (Herodotus II, 116).

μούνη δὲ ταύτῃ εἰσὶ φανεραὶ ἐσβολαὶ ἐς Αἴγυπτον· ἀπὸ γὰρ
Φοινίκης μέχρι οὔρων τῶν Καδύτιος πόλιός [ἥ] ἐστι Συρίων
τῶν Παλαιστίνων καλεομένων· ἀπὸ δὲ Καδύτιος πόλιος
ἐούσης, ὡς ἐμοὶ δοκέει, Σαρδίων οὐ πολλῷ ἐλάσσονος, ἀπὸ
ταύτης τὰ ἐμπόρια τὰ ἐπὶ θαλάσσης μέχρι Ἰηνύσου πόλιός

ἐστι τοῦ Ἀραβίου, ἀπὸ δὲ Ἰηνύσου αὖτις Συρίων μέχρι
Σερβωνίδος λίμνης, παρ' ἣν δὴ τὸ Κάσιον ὄρος τείνει ἐς
θάλασσαν· ἀπὸ Σερβωνίδος λίμνης, ἐν τῇ δὴ λόγος τὸν Τυφῶ
κεκρύφθαι, ἀπὸ ταύτης ἤδη Αἴγυπτος. τὸ δὴ μεταξὺ
Ἰηνύσου πόλιος καὶ Κασίου τε ὄρεος καὶ τῆς Σερβωνίδος
λίμνης, ἐὸν τοῦτο οὐκ ὀλίγον χωρίον ἀλλὰ ὅσον τε ἐπὶ τρεῖς
ἡμέρας ὁδοῦ, ἄνυδρόν ἐστι δεινῶς.

Only through this (Arabian desert) is there entry into Egypt. For
from Phoenicia to the boundaries of Kadytis it belongs to the
Syrians known as "Palestinian": from Kadytis, a town, I should
say, not much smaller than Sardis, the seaports as far as Ienysus
belong to the Arabian; from Ienysus as far as Lake Serbonis it is
again Syrian, near which Mt. Casius runs down to the sea; and
after Lake Serbonis (where Typhon is supposed to be buried),
from there it is already Egypt. The whole area between Ienysus
on the one side, and Mt. Casius and the Lake on the other—and
it is of considerable extent, not less than three day's journey—is
desert and completely without water (Bk. III, 5).

כי רק דרך המדבר (הערבי) הזה פתוחים המבואות למצרים כי מפניקיה עד
גבולות העיר קדיטיס (Kadythw) הארץ היא לסורים הנקראים פלשתינאים;
מקדיטיס, עיר אשר אינה נופלת הרבה מסרדיס, כאשר נראה לי, עד העיר יאניסוס,
ערי המסחר על חוף הים הן למלך הערבים; לסורים היא הארץ שוב מיאניסוס עד
האגם הסרבוני, אשר לארכו נמשכים הרי קסיון עד הים. מאגם הסרבוני, אשר בו
נחבא לפי האגדה טיפון, מתחילה כבר מצרים. כברת הארץ בין העיר יאניסוס ובין
הרי קסיון והאגם הסרבוני הוא שטח לא קטן, כי אם מהלך קרוב לשלושה ימים
והוא ציה מאד.

C. Xenophon

The land which Xenophon called Syria included Phoenicia and the
northern coast as far as Myriandos. It extended eastward to the Euphrates.
That Abrokomas was supposedly waiting behind the Cilician Gates does not
mean that the border of his satrapy was there. The boundary between Cilicia
and Syria is not given by Xenophon. In the east, when Cyrus and his troops
were marching from Thapsakos (Tiphsah) to the mouth of the Khabur, he is

said to have been in Syria; from there to Pylae he is in a region called Arabia. Whether this latter belonged to Syria or to Babylonia is not made clear. From Pylae onwards, he is in Babylonia.

II. HISTORICAL REVIEW (Down to end of Fourth Century BCE)

A. SIXTH CENTURY

539 BCE — Decree of Cyrus (Ezra 1:1-11)

1 וּבִשְׁנַת אַחַת לְכוֹרֶשׁ מֶלֶךְ פָּרַס לִכְלוֹת

דְּבַר־יְהוָה מִפִּי יִרְמְיָה הֵעִיר יְהוָה אֶת־רוּחַ כֹּרֶשׁ

מֶלֶךְ־פָּרַס וַיַּעֲבֶר־קוֹל בְּכָל־מַלְכוּתוֹ וְגַם־בְּמִכְתָּב

לֵאמֹר

2 כֹּה אָמַר כֹּרֶשׁ מֶלֶךְ פָּרַס כֹּל מַמְלְכוֹת הָאָרֶץ

נָתַן לִי יְהוָה אֱלֹהֵי הַשָּׁמָיִם וְהוּא־פָקַד עָלַי לִבְנוֹת־לוֹ

בַיִת בִּירוּשָׁלַם אֲשֶׁר בִּיהוּדָה

3 מִי־בָכֶם מִכָּל־עַמּוֹ יְהִי אֱלֹהָיו עִמּוֹ וְיַעַל

לִירוּשָׁלַם אֲשֶׁר בִּיהוּדָה וְיִבֶן אֶת־בֵּית יְהוָה אֱלֹהֵי

יִשְׂרָאֵל הוּא הָאֱלֹהִים אֲשֶׁר בִּירוּשָׁלָם

4 וְכָל־הַנִּשְׁאָר מִכָּל־הַמְּקֹמוֹת אֲשֶׁר הוּא גָר־שָׁם

יְנַשְּׂאוּהוּ אַנְשֵׁי מְקֹמוֹ בְּכֶסֶף וּבְזָהָב וּבִרְכוּשׁ וּבִבְהֵמָה

עִם־הַנְּדָבָה לְבֵית הָאֱלֹהִים אֲשֶׁר בִּירוּשָׁלָם

5 וַיָּקוּמוּ רָאשֵׁי הָאָבוֹת לִיהוּדָה וּבִנְיָמִן וְהַכֹּהֲנִים

וְהַלְוִיִּם לְכֹל הֵעִיר הָאֱלֹהִים אֶת־רוּחוֹ לַעֲלוֹת לִבְנוֹת

אֶת־בֵּית יְהוָה אֲשֶׁר בִּירוּשָׁלָם

6 וְכָל־סְבִיבֹתֵיהֶם חִזְּקוּ בִידֵיהֶם בִּכְלֵי־כֶסֶף

בַּזָּהָב בָּרְכוּשׁ וּבַבְּהֵמָה וּבַמִּגְדָּנוֹת לְבַד עַל־כָּל־הִתְנַדֵּב

7 וְהַמֶּלֶךְ כּוֹרֶשׁ הוֹצִיא אֶת־כְּלֵי בֵית־יְהוָה אֲשֶׁר

הוֹצִיא נְבוּכַדְנֶצַּר מִירוּשָׁלַם וַיִּתְּנֵם בְּבֵית אֱלֹהָיו

8 וַיּוֹצִיאֵם כּוֹרֶשׁ מֶלֶךְ פָּרַס עַל־יַד מִתְרְדָת

הַגִּזְבָּר וַיִּסְפְּרֵם לְשֵׁשְׁבַּצַּר הַנָּשִׂיא לִיהוּדָה

9 וְאֵלֶּה מִסְפָּרָם אֲגַרְטְלֵי זָהָב שְׁלֹשִׁים

אֲגַרְטְלֵי־כֶסֶף אָלֶף מַחֲלָפִים תִּשְׁעָה וְעֶשְׂרִים

10 כְּפוֹרֵי זָהָב שְׁלֹשִׁים כְּפוֹרֵי כֶסֶף מִשְׁנִים

אַרְבַּע מֵאוֹת וַעֲשָׂרָה כֵּלִים אֲחֵרִים אָלֶף ס

11 כָּל־כֵּלִים לַזָּהָב וְלַכֶּסֶף חֲמֵשֶׁת אֲלָפִים

וְאַרְבַּע מֵאוֹת הַכֹּל הֶעֱלָה שֵׁשְׁבַּצַּר עִם הֵעָלוֹת הַגּוֹלָה

מִבָּבֶל לִירוּשָׁלָם

Ezra 1:1 ¶ Now in the first year of Cyrus king of Persia, in order to fulfill the word of Yahweh by the mouth of Jeremiah, Yahweh stirred up the spirit of Cyrus king of Persia, so that he sent a proclamation throughout all his kingdom, and also [put it] in writing, saying:

Ezra 1:2 ¶ "Thus says Cyrus king of Persia, 'Yahweh, the God of heaven, has given me all the kingdoms of the earth and He has appointed me to build Him a house in Jerusalem, which is in Judah.

Ezra 1:3 'Whoever there is among you of all His people, may his God be with him! Let him go up to Jerusalem which is in Judah and rebuild the house of Yahweh, the God of Israel; He is the God who is in Jerusalem.

Ezra 1:4 'Every survivor, at whatever place he may live, let the men of that place support him with silver and gold, with goods and cattle, together with a freewill offering for the house of God which is in Jerusalem.'"

Ezra 1:5 ¶ Then the heads of fathers' [households] of Judah and Benjamin and the priests and the Levites arose, even everyone whose spirit God had stirred to go up and rebuild the house of Yahweh which is in Jerusalem.

Ezra 1:6 All those about them encouraged them with articles of silver, with gold, with goods, with cattle and with valuables, aside from all that was given as a freewill offering.

Ezra 1:7 Also King Cyrus brought out the articles of the house of Yahweh, which Nebuchadnezzar had carried away from Jerusalem and put in the house of his gods;

Ezra 1:8 and Cyrus, king of Persia, had them brought out by the hand of Mithredath the treasurer, and he counted them out to Sheshbazzar, the prince of Judah.

Ezra 1:9 Now this [was] their number: 30 gold dishes, 1,000 silver dishes, 29 duplicates;

Ezra 1:10 30 gold bowls, 410 silver bowls of a second [kind and] 1,000 other articles.

Ezra 1:11 All the articles of gold and silver [numbered] 5,400. Sheshbazzar brought them all up with the exiles who went up from Babylon to Jerusalem.

Restoration of ritual on temple mount (Ezra 2:68-70).

68 וּמֵרָאשֵׁי הָאָבוֹת בְּבוֹאָם לְבֵית יְהוָה אֲשֶׁר
בִּירוּשָׁלָ͏ִם הִתְנַדְּבוּ לְבֵית הָאֱלֹהִים לְהַעֲמִידוֹ עַל־מְכוֹנוֹ
69 כְּכֹחָם נָתְנוּ לְאוֹצַר הַמְּלָאכָה זָהָב דַּרְכְּמוֹנִים
שֵׁשׁ־רִבֹּאות וָאֶלֶף וְכֶסֶף מָנִים חֲמֵשֶׁת אֲלָפִים וְכָתְנֹת
כֹּהֲנִים מֵאָה
70 וַיֵּשְׁבוּ הַכֹּהֲנִים וְהַלְוִיִּם וּמִן־הָעָם וְהַמְשֹׁרְרִים
וְהַשּׁוֹעֲרִים וְהַנְּתִינִים בְּעָרֵיהֶם וְכָל־יִשְׂרָאֵל בְּעָרֵיהֶם

Ezra 2:68 ¶ Some of the heads of fathers' [households], when they arrived at the house of Yahweh which is in Jerusalem, offered willingly for the house of God to restore it on its foundation.

Ezra 2:69 According to their ability they gave to the treasury for the work 61,000 gold drachmas and 5,000 silver minas and 100 priestly garments.

Ezra 2:70 ¶ Now the priests and the Levites, some of the people, the singers, the gatekeepers and the temple servants lived in their cities, and all Israel in their cities.

Ezra 3:1-13

Ezra 3:1 וַיִּגַּע הַחֹדֶשׁ הַשְּׁבִיעִי וּבְנֵי יִשְׂרָאֵל בֶּעָרִים

וַיֵּאָסְפוּ הָעָם כְּאִישׁ אֶחָד אֶל־יְרוּשָׁלָ͏ִם

Ezra 3:2 וַיָּקָם יֵשׁוּעַ בֶּן־יוֹצָדָק וְאֶחָיו הַכֹּהֲנִים וּזְרֻבָּבֶל

בֶּן־שְׁאַלְתִּיאֵל וְאֶחָיו וַיִּבְנוּ אֶת־מִזְבַּח אֱלֹהֵי יִשְׂרָאֵל

לְהַעֲלוֹת עָלָיו עֹלוֹת כַּכָּתוּב בְּתוֹרַת מֹשֶׁה אִישׁ־הָאֱלֹהִים

Ezra 3:3 וַיָּכִינוּ הַמִּזְבֵּחַ עַל־מְכוֹנֹתָיו כִּי בְּאֵימָה עֲלֵיהֶם

מֵעַמֵּי הָאֲרָצוֹת וַיַּעַל [וַ][יַּעֲלוּ] עָלָיו עֹלוֹת לַיהוָה עֹלוֹת לַבֹּקֶר וְלָעָרֶב

Ezra 3:4 וַיַּעֲשׂוּ אֶת־חַג הַסֻּכּוֹת כַּכָּתוּב וְעֹלַת יוֹם בְּיוֹם

בְּמִסְפָּר כְּמִשְׁפַּט דְּבַר־יוֹם בְּיוֹמוֹ

Ezra 3:5 וְאַחֲרֵיכֵן עֹלַת תָּמִיד וְלֶחֳדָשִׁים וּלְכָל־מוֹעֲדֵי

יְהוָה הַמְקֻדָּשִׁים וּלְכֹל מִתְנַדֵּב נְדָבָה לַיהוָה

Ezra 3:6 מִיּוֹם אֶחָד לַחֹדֶשׁ הַשְּׁבִיעִי הֵחֵלּוּ לְהַעֲלוֹת

עֹלוֹת לַיהוָה וְהֵיכַל יְהוָה לֹא יֻסָּד

Ezra 3:7 וַיִּתְּנוּ־כֶסֶף לַחֹצְבִים וְלֶחָרָשִׁים וּמַאֲכָל

וּמִשְׁתֶּה וָשֶׁמֶן לַצִּדֹנִים וְלַצֹּרִים לְהָבִיא עֲצֵי אֲרָזִים

מִן־הַלְּבָנוֹן אֶל־יָם יָפוֹא כְּרִשְׁיוֹן כּוֹרֶשׁ מֶלֶךְ־פָּרַס עֲלֵיהֶם

Ezra 3:8 וּבַשָּׁנָה הַשֵּׁנִית לְבוֹאָם אֶל־בֵּית הָאֱלֹהִים

לִירוּשָׁלַ͏ִם בַּחֹדֶשׁ הַשֵּׁנִי הֵחֵלּוּ זְרֻבָּבֶל בֶּן־שְׁאַלְתִּיאֵל

וְיֵשׁוּעַ בֶּן־יוֹצָדָק וּשְׁאָר אֲחֵיהֶם הַכֹּהֲנִים וְהַלְוִיִּם

וְכָל־הַבָּאִים מֵהַשְּׁבִי יְרוּשָׁלַ͏ִם וַיַּעֲמִידוּ אֶת־הַלְוִיִּם מִבֶּן

עֶשְׂרִים שָׁנָה וָמַעְלָה לְנַצֵּחַ עַל־מְלֶאכֶת בֵּית־יְהוָה

Ezra 3:9 וַיַּעֲמֹד יֵשׁוּעַ בָּנָיו וְאֶחָיו קַדְמִיאֵל וּבָנָיו

בְּנֵי־יְהוּדָה כְּאֶחָד לְנַצֵּחַ עַל־עֹשֵׂה הַמְּלָאכָה בְּבֵית

הָאֱלֹהִים בְּנֵי חֵנָדָד בְּנֵיהֶם וַאֲחֵיהֶם הַלְוִיִּם

Ezra 3:10 וְיִסְּדוּ הַבֹּנִים אֶת־הֵיכַל יְהוָה וַיַּעֲמִידוּ הַכֹּהֲנִים

מְלֻבָּשִׁים בַּחֲצֹצְרוֹת וְהַלְוִיִּם בְּנֵי־אָסָף בַּמְצִלְתַּיִם

לְהַלֵּל אֶת־יְהוָה עַל־יְדֵי דָוִיד מֶלֶךְ־יִשְׂרָאֵל

Ezra 3:11 וַיַּעֲנוּ בְּהַלֵּל וּבְהוֹדֹת לַיהוָה כִּי טוֹב

כִּי־לְעוֹלָם חַסְדּוֹ עַל־יִשְׂרָאֵל וְכָל־הָעָם הֵרִיעוּ תְרוּעָה

גְדוֹלָה בְהַלֵּל לַיהוָה עַל הוּסַד בֵּית־יְהוָה

Ezra 3:12 וְרַבִּים מֵהַכֹּהֲנִים וְהַלְוִיִּם וְרָאשֵׁי הָאָבוֹת

הַזְּקֵנִים אֲשֶׁר רָאוּ אֶת־הַבַּיִת הָרִאשׁוֹן בְּיָסְדוֹ זֶה הַבַּיִת

בְּעֵינֵיהֶם בֹּכִים בְּקוֹל גָּדוֹל וְרַבִּים בִּתְרוּעָה בְשִׂמְחָה לְהָרִים קוֹל

Ezra 3:13 וְאֵין הָעָם מַכִּירִים קוֹל תְּרוּעַת הַשִּׂמְחָה לְקוֹל

בְּכִי הָעָם כִּי הָעָם מְרִיעִים תְּרוּעָה גְדוֹלָה וְהַקּוֹל נִשְׁמַע עַד־לְמֵרָחוֹק

Ezra 3:1 ¶ Now when the seventh month came, and the sons of Israel [were] in the cities, the people gathered together as one man to Jerusalem.

Ezra 3:2 Then Jeshua the son of Jozadak and his brothers the priests, and Zerubbabel the son of Shealtiel and his brothers arose and built the altar of the God of Israel to offer burnt offerings on it, as it is written in the law of Moses, the man of God.

Ezra 3:3 So they set up the altar on its foundation, for they were terrified because of the peoples of the lands; and they offered burnt offerings on it to Yahweh, burnt offerings morning and evening.

Ezra 3:4 They celebrated the Feast of Booths, as it is written, and [offered] the fixed number of burnt offerings daily, according to the ordinance, as each day required;

Ezra 3:5 and afterward [there was] a continual burnt offering, also for the new moons and for all the fixed festivals of Yahweh that were consecrated, and from everyone who offered a freewill offering to Yahweh.

Ezra 3:6 From the first day of the seventh month they began to offer burnt offerings to Yahweh, but the foundation of the temple of Yahweh had not been laid.

Ezra 3:7 Then they gave money to the masons and carpenters, and food, drink and oil to the Sidonians and to the Tyrians, to bring cedar wood from Lebanon to the sea at Joppa, according to the permission they had from Cyrus king of Persia.

Ezra 3:8 ¶ Now in the second year of their coming to the house of God at Jerusalem in the second month, Zerubbabel the son of Shealtiel and Jeshua the son of Jozadak and the rest of their brothers the priests and the Levites, and all who came from the captivity to Jerusalem, began [the work] and appointed the Levites from twenty years and older to oversee the work of the house of Yahweh.

Ezra 3:9 Then Jeshua [with] his sons and brothers stood united [with] Kadmiel and his sons, the sons of Judah [and] the sons of Henadad [with] their sons and brothers the Levites, to oversee the workmen in the temple of God.

Ezra 3:10 ¶ Now when the builders had laid the foundation of the temple of Yahweh, the priests stood in their apparel with trumpets, and the Levites, the sons of Asaph, with cymbals, to praise Yahweh according to the directions of King David of Israel.

Ezra 3:11 They sang, praising and giving thanks to Yahweh, [saying], "For He is good, for His lovingkindness is upon Israel forever." And all the people shouted with a great shout when they praised Yahweh because the foundation of the house of Yahweh was laid.

Ezra 3:12 Yet many of the priests and Levites and heads of fathers' [households], the old men who had seen the first temple, wept with a loud voice when the foundation of this house was laid before their eyes, while many shouted aloud for joy,

Ezra 3:13 so that the people could not distinguish the sound of the shout of joy from the sound of the weeping of the people, for the people shouted with a loud shout, and the sound was heard far away.

Ezra 4:1-5

1 וַיִּשְׁמְעוּ צָרֵי יְהוּדָה וּבִנְיָמִן כִּי־בְנֵי הַגּוֹלָה
בּוֹנִים הֵיכָל לַיהוָה אֱלֹהֵי יִשְׂרָאֵל

2 וַיִּגְּשׁוּ אֶל־זְרֻבָּבֶל וְאֶל־רָאשֵׁי הָאָבוֹת וַיֹּאמְרוּ

לָהֶם נִבְנֶה עִמָּכֶם כִּי כָכֶם נִדְרוֹשׁ לֵאלֹהֵיכֶם וְלֹא

[וְ][לוֹ] אֲנַחְנוּ זֹבְחִים מִימֵי אֵסַר חַדֹּן מֶלֶךְ אַשּׁוּר הַמַּעֲלֶה אֹתָנוּ פֹּה

3 וַיֹּאמֶר לָהֶם זְרֻבָּבֶל וְיֵשׁוּעַ וּשְׁאָר רָאשֵׁי הָאָבוֹת

לְיִשְׂרָאֵל לֹא־לָכֶם וָלָנוּ לִבְנוֹת בַּיִת לֵאלֹהֵינוּ כִּי אֲנַחְנוּ

יַחַד נִבְנֶה לַיהוָה אֱלֹהֵי יִשְׂרָאֵל כַּאֲשֶׁר צִוָּנוּ הַמֶּלֶךְ כּוֹרֶשׁ מֶלֶךְ־פָּרָס

4 וַיְהִי עַם־הָאָרֶץ מְרַפִּים יְדֵי עַם־יְהוּדָה

וּמְבַלַּהִים [וּ][מְבַהֲלִים] אוֹתָם לִבְנוֹת

5 וְסֹכְרִים עֲלֵיהֶם יוֹעֲצִים לְהָפֵר עֲצָתָם

כָּל־יְמֵי כּוֹרֶשׁ מֶלֶךְ פָּרַס וְעַד־מַלְכוּת דָּרְיָוֶשׁ מֶלֶךְ־פָּרָס

Ezra 4:1 ¶ Now when the enemies of Judah and Benjamin heard that the people of the exile were building a temple to Yahweh God of Israel,

Ezra 4:2 they approached Zerubbabel and the heads of fathers' [households], and said to them, "Let us build with you, for we, like you, seek your God; and we have been sacrificing to Him since the days of Esarhaddon king of Assyria, who brought us up here."

Ezra 4:3 But Zerubbabel and Jeshua and the rest of the heads of fathers' [households] of Israel said to them, "You have nothing in common with us in building a house to our God; but we ourselves will together build to Yahweh God of Israel, as King Cyrus, the king of Persia has commanded us."

Ezra 4:4 ¶ Then the people of the land discouraged the people of Judah, and frightened them from building,

Ezra 4:5 and hired counselors against them to frustrate their counsel all the days of Cyrus king of Persia, even until the reign of Darius king of Persia.

525 BCE — Cambyses' campaign to Egypt
        Aided by the Arabians who controlled Gaza

522 BCE — Darius I comes to power — revolt in Babylon,
        Nebuchadnzzar III

521 BCE — Another revolt in Babylon, Nechadnezzar IV

520 BCE — Delegation arrives in Jerusalem from Babylon
        (Zech. 1:1; 6:9-14)

Zech. 1:1 בַּחֹדֶשׁ הַשְּׁמִינִי בִּשְׁנַת שְׁתַּיִם לְדָרְיָוֶשׁ הָיָה

דְבַר־יְהוָה אֶל־זְכַרְיָה בֶּן־בֶּרֶכְיָה בֶּן־עִדּוֹ הַנָּבִיא לֵאמֹר

Zech. 1:1 ¶ In the eighth month of the second year of Darius, the
word of Yahwseh came to Zechariah the prophet, the son of
Berechiah, the son of Iddo saying, Nov. 520 = (mo. began 27 Oct.,
520)

Zech. 6:9-14

Zech. 6:9 וַיְהִי דְבַר־יְהוָה אֵלַי לֵאמֹר

Zech. 6:10 לָקוֹחַ מֵאֵת הַגּוֹלָה מֵחֶלְדַּי וּמֵאֵת טוֹבִיָּה

וּמֵאֵת יְדַעְיָה וּבָאתָ אַתָּה בַּיּוֹם הַהוּא וּבָאתָ בֵּית

יֹאשִׁיָּה בֶן־צְפַנְיָה אֲשֶׁר־בָּאוּ מִבָּבֶל

Zech. 6:11 וְלָקַחְתָּ כֶסֶף־וְזָהָב וְעָשִׂיתָ עֲטָרוֹת וְשַׂמְתָּ

בְּרֹאשׁ יְהוֹשֻׁעַ בֶּן־יְהוֹצָדָק הַכֹּהֵן הַגָּדוֹל

Zech. 6:12 וְאָמַרְתָּ אֵלָיו לֵאמֹר כֹּה אָמַר יְהוָה צְבָאוֹת

לֵאמֹר הִנֵּה־אִישׁ צֶמַח שְׁמוֹ וּמִתַּחְתָּיו יִצְמָח וּבָנָה אֶת־הֵיכַל יְהוָה

Zech. 6:13 וְהוּא יִבְנֶה אֶת־הֵיכַל יְהוָה וְהוּא־יִשָּׂא הוֹד

וְיָשַׁב וּמָשַׁל עַל־כִּסְאוֹ וְהָיָה כֹהֵן עַל־כִּסְאוֹ וַעֲצַת

שָׁלוֹם תִּהְיֶה בֵּין שְׁנֵיהֶם

Zech. 6:14 וְהָעֲטָרֹת תִּהְיֶה לְחֵלֶם וּלְטוֹבִיָּה וְלִידַעְיָה

וּלְחֵן בֶּן־צְפַנְיָה לְזִכָּרוֹן בְּהֵיכַל יְהוָה

Zech. 6:9 ¶ The word of Yahweh also came to me, saying,

Zech. 6:10 "Take [an offering] from the exiles, from Heldai, Tobijah and Jedaiah; and you go the same day and enter the house of Josiah the son of Zephaniah, where they have arrived from Babylon.

Zech. 6:11 "Take silver and gold, make an [ornate] crown and set [it] on the head of Joshua the son of Jehozadak, the high priest.

Zech. 6:12 "Then say to him, 'Thus says Yahweh of hosts, "Behold, a man whose name is Branch, for He will branch out from where He is; and He will build the temple of Yahweh.

Zech. 6:13 "Yes, it is He who will build the temple of Yahweh, and He who will bear the honor and sit and rule on His throne. Thus, He will be a priest on His throne, and the counsel of peace will be between the two offices.'"

Zech. 6:14 "Now the crown will become a reminder in the temple of Yahweh to Helem, Tobijah, Jedaiah and Hen the son of Zephaniah.

****   Accusation against the Jews (Ezra 4:24-6:13), but
            work renewed:

                        Ezra 4:24

בֵּאדַיִן בְּטֵלַת עֲבִידַת בֵּית־אֱלָהָא דִּי בִּירוּשְׁלֶם וַהֲוָת
בָּטְלָא עַד שְׁנַת תַּרְתֵּין לְמַלְכוּת דָּרְיָוֶשׁ מֶלֶךְ־פָּרָס

ואז בטלה מלאכת בית האלהים אשר בירושלים והיתה בטלה
עד שנת שתים למלכות דריוש מלך פרס

Then work on the house of God in Jerusalem ceased, and it was stopped until the second year of the reign of Darius king of Persia.

                        Ezra 5:1-5

Ezra 5:1 וְהִתְנַבִּי חַגַּי נְבִיאָה [נְבִי][א] וּזְכַרְיָה בַר־עִדּוֹא
נְבִיאַיָּא [נְבִיִּי][א] עַל־יְהוּדָיֵא דִּי בִיהוּד וּבִירוּשְׁלֶם
בְּשֻׁם אֱלָהּ יִשְׂרָאֵל עֲלֵיהוֹן

<u>Ezra 5:2</u> בֵּאדַיִן קָמוּ זְרֻבָּבֶל בַּר־שְׁאַלְתִּיאֵל וְיֵשׁוּעַ

בַּר־יוֹצָדָק וְשָׁרִיו לְמִבְנֵא בֵּית אֱלָהָא דִּי בִירוּשְׁלֶם

וְעִמְּהוֹן נְבִיאַיָּא [נְבִיַּ־][א] דִּי־אֱלָהָא מְסָעֲדִין לְהוֹן

<u>Ezra 5:3</u> בֵּהּ־זִמְנָא אֲתָא עֲלֵיהוֹן תַּתְּנַי פַּחַת עֲבַר־נַהֲרָה

וּשְׁתַר בּוֹזְנַי וּכְנָוָתְהוֹן וְכֵן אָמְרִין לְהֹם מַן־שָׂם לְכֹם

טְעֵם בַּיְתָא דְנָה לִבְּנֵא וְאֻשַּׁרְנָא דְנָה לְשַׁכְלָלָה

<u>Ezra 5:4</u> אֱדַיִן כְּנֵמָא אֲמַרְנָא לְהֹם מַן־אִנּוּן שְׁמָהָת גֻּבְרַיָּא

דִּי־דְנָה בִנְיָנָא בָּנַיִן

<u>Ezra 5:5</u> וְעֵין אֱלָהֲהֹם הֲוָת עַל־שָׂבֵי יְהוּדָיֵא

וְלָא־בַטִּלוּ הִמּוֹ עַד־טַעְמָא לְדָרְיָוֶשׁ יְהָךְ וֶאֱדַיִן יְתִיבוּן

נִשְׁתְּוָנָא עַל־דְּנָה

והתנבאו חגי הנביא וזכריה בן עדוא הנביאים אל היהודים
אשר ביהודה ובירושלים בשם אלהי ישראל עליהם. (2) אז
קמו זרבבל בן שאלתיאל וישוע בן יוצדק והחלו לבנות בית
האלהים אשר בירושלים ועמהם נביאי האלהים עוזרים להם.
(3) באותו זמן בא אליהם תתני פחת עבר הנהר ושתר בוזני
ועמיתיהם וכך אמרו להם: מי נתן לכם צו לבנות את הבית
הזה ולהשלים את המבנה? (4) אז אמרנו להם לאמר: מי הם
שמות האנשים אשר בונים את הבנין הזה. (5) ועין אלהיהם
היתה על זקני היהידים ולא בטלו אותם עד שהענין ילך
לדריוש ואז ישיבו מכתב על זה.

<u>Ezra 5:1</u> ¶ When the prophets, Haggai the prophet and Zechariah the son of
Iddo, prophesied to the Jews who were in Judah and Jerusalem in the name
of the God of Israel, who was over them,

<u>Ezra 5:2</u> then Zerubbabel the son of Shealtiel and Jeshua the son of Jozadak
arose and began to rebuild the house of God which is in Jerusalem; and the
prophets of God were with them supporting them.

<u>Ezra 5:3</u> ¶ At that time Tattenai, the governor of [the province] beyond the
River, and Shethar-bozenai and their colleagues came to them and spoke to

them thus, "Who issued you a decree to rebuild this temple and to finish this structure?"

Ezra 5:4 Then we told them accordingly what the names of the men were who were reconstructing this building.

Ezra 5:5 But the eye of their God was on the elders of the Jews, and they did not stop them until a report could come to Darius, and then a written reply be returned concerning it.

Ezra 5:6 פַּרְשֶׁגֶן אִגַּרְתָּא דִּי־שְׁלַח תַּתְּנַי פַּחַת

עֲבַר־נַהֲרָה וּשְׁתַר בּוֹזְנַי וּכְנָוָתֵהּ אֲפַרְסְכָיֵא דִּי בַּעֲבַר

נַהֲרָה עַל־דָּרְיָוֶשׁ מַלְכָּא

Ezra 5:7 פִּתְגָמָא שְׁלַחוּ עֲלוֹהִי וְכִדְנָה כְּתִיב בְּגַוֵּהּ

לְדָרְיָוֶשׁ מַלְכָּא שְׁלָמָא כֹלָּא

(6) עותק האגרת אשר שלח תתני פחת עבר הנהר ושתר בוזני

ועמיתיו הפרסים אשר בעבר הנהר אל דריוש המלך,

(7) דבר שלחו אליו וכזאת כתוב בתוכו:

Ezra 5:6 ¶ [This is] the copy of the letter which Tattenai, the governor of [the province] beyond the River, and Shethar-bozenai and his colleagues the officials, who were beyond the River, sent to Darius the king.

Ezra 5:7 They sent a report to him in which it was written thus: "To Darius the king, all peace.

Ezra 5:7 לְדָרְיָוֶשׁ מַלְכָּא שְׁלָמָא כֹלָּא . . .

Ezra 5:8 יְדִיעַ לֶהֱוֵא לְמַלְכָּא דִּי־אֲזַלְנָא לִיהוּד

מְדִינְתָּא לְבֵית אֱלָהָא רַבָּא וְהוּא מִתְבְּנֵא אֶבֶן גְּלָל

וְאָע מִתְּשָׂם בְּכֻתְלַיָּא וַעֲבִידְתָּא דָךְ אָסְפַּרְנָא מִתְעַבְדָא וּמַצְלַח בְּיֶדְהֹם

Ezra 5:9 אֱדַיִן שְׁאֵלְנָא לְשָׂבַיָּא אִלֵּךְ כְּנֵמָא אֲמַרְנָא לְהֹם

מַן־שָׂם לְכֹם טְעֵם בַּיְתָא דְנָה לְמִבְנְיָה וְאֻשַּׁרְנָא דְנָה לְשַׁכְלָלָה

Ezra 5:10 וְאַף שְׁמָהָתְהֹם שְׁאֵלְנָא לְהֹם לְהוֹדָעוּתָךְ דִּי

נִכְתֻּב שֻׁם־גֻּבְרַיָּא דִּי בְרָאשֵׁיהֹם

Ezra 5:11 וּכְנֵמָא פִתְגָמָא הֲתִיבוּנָא לְמֵמַר אֲנַחְנָא הִמּוֹ

עַבְדוֹהִי דִי־אֱלָהּ שְׁמַיָּא וְאַרְעָא וּבָנַיִן בַּיְתָא דִּי־הֲוָא

בְנֵה מִקַּדְמַת דְּנָה שְׁנִין שַׂגִּיאָן וּמֶלֶךְ לְיִשְׂרָאֵל רַב בְּנָהִי וְשַׁכְלְלֵהּ

Ezra 5:12 לָהֵן מִן־דִּי הַרְגִּזוּ אֲבָהֳתַנָא לֶאֱלָהּ שְׁמַיָּא יְהַב

הִמּוֹ בְּיַד נְבוּכַדְנֶצַּר מֶלֶךְ־בָּבֶל כַּסְדָּיָא [כַּסְדָּא][ה]

וּבַיְתָה דְנָה סַתְרֵהּ וְעַמָּה הַגְלִי לְבָבֶל

Ezra 5:13 בְּרַם בִּשְׁנַת חֲדָה לְכוֹרֶשׁ מַלְכָּא דִּי בָבֶל

כּוֹרֶשׁ מַלְכָּא שָׂם טְעֵם בֵּית־אֱלָהָא דְנָה לִבְּנֵא

Ezra 5:14 וְאַף מָאנַיָּא דִי־בֵית־אֱלָהָא דִּי דַהֲבָה

וְכַסְפָּא דִּי נְבוּכַדְנֶצַּר הַנְפֵּק מִן־הֵיכְלָא דִּי בִירוּשְׁלֶם

וְהֵיבֵל הִמּוֹ לְהֵיכְלָא דִּי בָבֶל הַנְפֵּק הִמּוֹ כּוֹרֶשׁ מַלְכָּא

מִן־הֵיכְלָא דִּי בָבֶל וִיהִיבוּ לְשֵׁשְׁבַּצַּר שְׁמֵהּ דִּי פֶחָה שָׂמֵהּ

Ezra 5:15 וַאֲמַר־לֵהּ אֵלֶּה [אֵל] מָאנַיָּא שֵׂא אֵזֶל־אֲחֵת

הִמּוֹ בְּהֵיכְלָא דִּי בִירוּשְׁלֶם וּבֵית אֱלָהָא יִתְבְּנֵא עַל־אַתְרֵהּ

Ezra 5:16 אֱדַיִן שֵׁשְׁבַּצַּר דֵּךְ אֲתָא יְהַב אֻשַּׁיָּא דִי־בֵית־

אֱלָהָא דִּי בִירוּשְׁלֶם וּמִן־אֱדַיִן וְעַד־כְּעַן מִתְבְּנֵא וְלָא שְׁלִם

Ezra 5:17 וּכְעַן הֵן עַל־מַלְכָּא טָב יִתְבַּקַּר בְּבֵית גִּנְזַיָּא

דִּי־מַלְכָּא תַמָּה דִּי בְּבָבֶל הֵן אִיתַי דִּי־מִן־כּוֹרֶשׁ מַלְכָּא

שִׂים טְעֵם לְמִבְנֵא בֵּית־אֱלָהָא דֵךְ בִּירוּשְׁלֶם וּרְעוּת

מַלְכָּא עַל־דְּנָה יִשְׁלַח עֲלֶינָא

Ezra 6:1 בֵּאדַיִן דָּרְיָוֶשׁ מַלְכָּא שָׂם טְעֵם וּבַקַּרוּ בְּבֵית

סִפְרַיָּא דִּי גִנְזַיָּא מְהַחֲתִין תַּמָּה בְּבָבֶל

לדריוש המלך השלום כולו! (8) ידוע יהיה למלך שהלכנו

למדינת יהודה, לבית האלהים הגדול, והוא נבנה אבן גלל

ועץ מושם בכתלים ומלאכהזו נעשית מהר ומצליחה בידם.

(9) אז שאלנו לזקנים ההם, ככה אמרנו להם: מי נתן לכם צו

לבנות הבית הזה ולהשלים את הבנין? (10) ואף שמותיהם שאלנו להם להודיעך, שנכתוב שם האנשים אשר בראשיהם. (11) וככה השיבונו דבר לאמר: אנחנו הם עבדיו של אלהי השמים והארץ ובונים את הבית אשר היה בנוי מלפני זה שנים רבות, ומלך ישראל גדול בנהו ושכלל אותו. (12) אלא מאחר שהרגיזו אבותינו את אלהי השמים נתן אותם ביד נבוכדנאצר מלך בבל הכשדי, ואת הבית הזה החריב והעם הגלה לבבל. (13) אולם בשנת אחת לכורש מלך בבל, כורש המלך נתן צו חבנות את בית האלהים הזה. (14) ואף הכלים של בית האלהים של זהב ושל כסף, אשר נבוכדנצר הוציא מן ההיכל אשר בירושלים והוביל אותם להיכל של בבל, הוציא אותם כורש המלך מן ההיכל שבבל ונתנם לששבצר שמו, אשר מינה אותם לפחה. (15) ואמר לו: את הכלים האלה שא, לך והנח אותם בהיכל אשר בירושלים וייבנה בית האלהים על מקומו. (16) אז בא ששבצר זה, הניח יסודות של בית האלהים אשר בירושלים, ומאז ועד עתה נבנה ולא נשלם. (17) ועתה אם על המלך טוב, יבוקש בבית גנזי המלך שם בבבל, אם יש אשר מאת כורש המלך ניתן צו את בית האלהים ההוא בירושלים, ורצון המלך על זה ישלח לנו. לבנות

Ezra 5:7 . . . "To Darius the king, all peace.

Ezra 5:8 "Let it be known to the king that we have gone to the province of Judah, to the house of the great God, which is being built with huge stones, and beams are being laid in the walls; and this work is going on with great care and is succeeding in their hands.

Ezra 5:9 "Then we asked those elders and said to them thus, 'Who issued you a decree to rebuild this temple and to finish this structure?'

Ezra 5:10 "We also asked them their names so as to inform you, and that we might write down the names of the men who were at their head.

Ezra 5:11 "Thus they answered us, saying, 'We are the servants of the God of heaven and earth and are rebuilding the temple that was built many years ago, which a great king of Israel built and finished.

Ezra 5:12 'But because our fathers had provoked the God of heaven to wrath, He gave them into the hand of Nebuchadnezzar king of Babylon, the Chaldean, [who] destroyed this temple and deported the people to Babylon.

Ezra 5:13 'However, in the first year of Cyrus king of Babylon, King Cyrus issued a decree to rebuild this house of God.

Ezra 5:14 'Also the gold and silver utensils of the house of God which Nebuchadnezzar had taken from the temple in Jerusalem, and brought them to the temple of Babylon, these King Cyrus took from the temple of Babylon and they were given to one whose name was Sheshbazzar, whom he had appointed governor.

Ezra 5:15 'He said to him, "Take these utensils, go [and] deposit them in the temple in Jerusalem and let the house of God be rebuilt in its place."

Ezra 5:16 'Then that Sheshbazzar came [and] laid the foundations of the house of God in Jerusalem; and from then until now it has been under construction and it is not [yet] completed.'

Ezra 5:17 "Now if it pleases the king, let a search be conducted in the king's treasure house, which is there in Babylon, if it be that a decree was issued by King Cyrus to rebuild this house of God at Jerusalem; and let the king send to us his decision concerning this [matter]."

Ezra 6:1 בֵּאדַיִן דָּרְיָוֶשׁ מַלְכָּא שָׂם טְעֵם וּבַקַּרוּ בְּבֵית

סָפְרַיָּא דִּי גִנְזַיָּא מְהַחֲתִין תַּמָּה בְּבָבֶל

Ezra 6:2 וְהִשְׁתְּכַח בְּאַחְמְתָא בְּבִירְתָא דִּי בְּמָדַי

מְדִינְתָּה מְגִלָּה חֲדָה וְכֵן־כְּתִיב בְּגַוַּהּ דִּכְרוֹנָה

‏(1) אז דריוש המלך נתן צו ובקשו בבית הספרים אשר שם מונחים הגנזים בבבל. (2) ונמצא באחמתא בבירה אשר במדי המדינה מגילה אחת וכך כתוב בתוכה זכרון (הדברים):

Ezra 6:1 ¶ Then King Darius issued a decree, and search was made in the archives, where the treasures were stored in Babylon.

בִּשְׁנַת חֲדָה לְכוֹרֶשׁ מַלְכָּא כּוֹרֶשׁ מַלְכָּא שָׂם טְעֵם Ezra 6:3

בֵּית־אֱלָהָא בִירוּשְׁלֶם בַּיְתָא יִתְבְּנֵא אֲתַר דִּי־דָבְחִין

דִּבְחִין וְאֻשּׁוֹהִי מְסוֹבְלִין רוּמֵהּ אַמִּין שִׁתִּין פְּתָיֵהּ אַמִּין

שִׁתִּין

נִדְבָּכִין דִּי־אֶבֶן גְּלָל תְּלָתָא וְנִדְבָּךְ דִּי־אָע Ezra 6:4

חֲדַת וְנִפְקְתָא מִן־בֵּית מַלְכָּא תִּתְיְהִב

וְאַף מָאנֵי בֵית־אֱלָהָא דִּי דַהֲבָה וְכַסְפָּא דִּי Ezra 6:5

נְבוּכַדְנֶצַּר הַנְפֵּק מִן־הֵיכְלָא דִּי־בִירוּשְׁלֶם וְהֵיבֵל

לְבָבֶל יַהֲתִיבוּן וִיהָךְ לְהֵיכְלָא דִּי־בִירוּשְׁלֶם לְאַתְרֵהּ

וְתַחֵת בְּבֵית אֱלָהָא

(3) בשנת אחת לכורש המלך כורש המלך נתן צו: בית

האלהים אשר בירושלים—הבית ייבנה, מקום אשר זובחים

זבחים ויסודותיו מנושאים, גבהו אמות ששים, רחבו אמות

ששים, (4) נדבכים של אבן גלל שלושה ונדבך של עץ אחד

וההוצאה מבית המלך תינתן.   (5) ואף כלי בית האלהים של

זהב וכסף אשר נבוכדנצר הוציא מן ההיכל שבירושלים

והוביל לבבל—ישיבו וילך להיכל שבירושלים למקומו ויונח

בבית האלהים.

Ezra 6:3 "In the first year of King Cyrus, Cyrus the king issued a decree: '[Concerning] the house of God at Jerusalem, let the temple, the place where sacrifices are offered, be rebuilt and let its foundations be retained, its height being 60 cubits and its width 60 cubits;

Ezra 6:4 with three layers of huge stones and one layer of timbers. And let the cost be paid from the royal treasury.

Ezra 6:5 Also let the gold and silver utensils of the house of God, which Nebuchadnezzar took from the temple in Jerusalem and brought to Babylon, be returned and brought to their places in the temple in Jerusalem; and you shall put [them] in the house of God.'

כְּעַן תַּתְּנַי פַּחַת עֲבַר־נַהֲרָה שְׁתַר בּוֹזְנַי וּכְנָוָתְהוֹן

אֲפַרְסְכָיֵא דִּי בַּעֲבַר נַהֲרָה רַחִיקִין הֲוֹו מִן־תַּמָּה

<u>Ezra 6:7</u> שְׁבֻקוּ לַעֲבִידַת בֵּית־אֱלָהָא דֵךְ פַּחַת יְהוּדָיֵא

וּלְשָׂבֵי יְהוּדָיֵא בֵּית־אֱלָהָא דֵךְ יִבְנוֹן עַל־אַתְרֵהּ

<u>Ezra 6:8</u> וּמִנִּי שִׂים טְעֵם לְמָא דִי־תַעַבְדוּן עִם־שָׂבֵי

יְהוּדָיֵא אִלֵּךְ לְמִבְנֵא בֵּית־אֱלָהָא דֵךְ וּמִנִּכְסֵי מַלְכָּא דִּי

מִדַּת עֲבַר נַהֲרָה אָסְפַּרְנָא נִפְקְתָא תֶּהֱוֵא מִתְיַהֲבָא

לִגֻבְרַיָּא אִלֵּךְ דִּי־לָא לְבַטָּלָא

<u>Ezra 6:9</u> וּמָה חַשְׁחָן וּבְנֵי תוֹרִין וְדִכְרִין וְאִמְּרִין לַעֲלָוָן

לֶאֱלָהּ שְׁמַיָּא חִנְטִין מְלַח חֲמַר וּמְשַׁח כְּמֵאמַר כָּהֲנַיָּא

דִי־בִירוּשְׁלֶם לֶהֱוֵא מִתְיְהֵב לְהֹם יוֹם בְּיוֹם דִּי־לָא שָׁלוּ

<u>Ezra 6:10</u> דִּי־לֶהֱוֹן מְהַקְרְבִין נִיחוֹחִין לֶאֱלָהּ שְׁמַיָּא

וּמְצַלַּיִן לְחַיֵּי מַלְכָּא וּבְנוֹהִי

<u>Ezra 6:11</u> וּמִנִּי שִׂים טְעֵם דִּי כָל־אֱנָשׁ דִּי יְהַשְׁנֵא

פִּתְגָמָא דְנָה יִתְנְסַח אָע מִן־בַּיְתֵהּ וּזְקִיף יִתְמְחֵא עֲלֹהִי

וּבַיְתֵהּ נְוָלוּ יִתְעֲבֵד עַל־דְּנָה

<u>Ezra 6:12</u> וֵאלָהָא דִּי שַׁכִּן שְׁמֵהּ תַּמָּה יְמַגַּר כָּל־מֶלֶךְ

וְעַם דִּי יִשְׁלַח יְדֵהּ לְהַשְׁנָיָה לְחַבָּלָה בֵּית־אֱלָהָא דֵךְ

דִּי בִירוּשְׁלֶם אֲנָה דָרְיָוֶשׁ שָׂמֵת טְעֵם אָסְפַּרְנָא יִתְעֲבִד

(6) עתה, תתני פחת   עבר הנהר, שתר בוזני ועמיתיהם
הפרסים אשר בעבר הנהר—רחוקים היו משם! (7) עזבו את
מלאכת בית האלהים הזה, פחת היהודים ולזקני היהודים
יבנו את בית האלהים הזה על מקומו. (8) וממני ניתן צו
למה שתעשו עם זקני היהודים האלה לבנות את בית אלהים
זה ומנכסי המלך של מנדת עבר הנהר, מהר ההוצאה—
תהיה ניתנת לאנשים האלה, אשר לא לבטל. (9) ומה
שצריכים, ובני בקר ואילים וכבשים לעולות לאלהי השמים
חטים, מלח, יין ושמן כמאמר הכהנים אשר בירושלים להיות

נִיתָּן לָהֶם יוֹם בְּיוֹמוֹ, לְלֹא הֲזָנָחָה. (10) אֲשֶׁר יִהְיוּ מַקְרִיבִים
נִיחוֹחִים לֵאלֹהֵי הַשָּׁמַיִם וּמִתְפַּלְּלִים לְחַיֵּי הַמֶּלֶךְ וּבָנָיו.
(11) וּמִמֶּנִּי נִיתָּן צַו כָּל אָדָם אֲשֶׁר יְשַׁנֶּה דָּבָר זֶה—יֵיעָקֵר עֵץ
מִבֵּיתוֹ וְזָקוּף יוּקַע עָלָיו וּבֵיתוֹ חֳרְבָּה יֵיעָשֶׂה עַל זֶה.

Ezra 6:6 ¶ "Now [therefore], Tattenai, governor of [the province] beyond the River, Shethar-bozenai and your colleagues, the officials of [the provinces] beyond the River, keep away from there.

Ezra 6:7 "Leave this work on the house of God alone; let the governor of the Jews and the elders of the Jews rebuild this house of God on its site.

Ezra 6:8 "Moreover, I issue a decree concerning what you are to do for these elders of Judah in the rebuilding of this house of God: the full cost is to be paid to these people from the royal treasury out of the taxes of [the provinces] beyond the River, and that without delay.

Ezra 6:9 "Whatever is needed, both young bulls, rams, and lambs for a burnt offering to the God of heaven, and wheat, salt, wine and anointing oil, as the priests in Jerusalem request, [it] is to be given to them daily without fail,

Ezra 6:10 that they may offer acceptable sacrifices to the God of heaven and pray for the life of the king and his sons.

Ezra 6:11 "And I issued a decree that any man who violates this edict, a timber shall be drawn from his house and he shall be impaled on it and his house shall be made a refuse heap on account of this.

Ezra 6:12 "May the God who has caused His name to dwell there overthrow any king or people who attempts to change [it], so as to destroy this house of God in Jerusalem. I, Darius, have issued [this] decree, let [it] be carried out with all diligence!"

Ezra 6:13 אֱדַיִן תַּתְּנַי פַּחַת עֲבַר־נַהֲרָה שְׁתַר בּוֹזְנַי וּכְנָוָתְהוֹן לָקֳבֵל
דִּי־שְׁלַח דָּרְיָוֶשׁ מַלְכָּא כְּנֵמָא אָסְפַּרְנָא עֲבַדוּ

Ezra 6:14 וְשָׂבֵי יְהוּדָיֵא בָּנַיִן וּמַצְלְחִין בִּנְבוּאַת חַגַּי נְבִיאָה [נְבִי־][אָ]
וּזְכַרְיָה בַּר־עִדּוֹא וּבְנוֹ וְשַׁכְלִלוּ מִן־טַעַם אֱלָהּ יִשְׂרָאֵל וּמִטְּעֵם כּוֹרֶשׁ
וְדָרְיָוֶשׁ וְאַרְתַּחְשַׁשְׂתְּא מֶלֶךְ פָּרָס

Ezra 6:15 וְשֵׁיצִיא בַּיְתָה דְנָה עַד יוֹם תְּלָתָה לִירַח

אֲדָר דִּי־הִיא שְׁנַת־שֵׁת לְמַלְכוּת דָּרְיָוֶשׁ מַלְכָּא

(13) אז תתני פחת עבר הנהר, שתר בוזני ועמיתיהם

לעומת אשר שלח דריוש המלך ככך מיד עשו. (14) וזקני

היהודים (היו) בונים ומצליחים, בנבואת חגי הנביא

וזכריה בן עדוא ובנו והשלימו לפי מצות אלהי ישראל,

ולפי צו כורש ודריוש וארתחחשתא מלך פרס. (15) ונגמר

הבית הזה עד יום שלושה עשר לחודש אדר, אשר היא שנת

למלכות דריוש המלך.

Ezra 6:13 ¶ Then Tattenai, the governor of [the province] beyond the River, Shethar-bozenai and their colleagues carried out [the decree] with all diligence, just as King Darius had sent.

Ezra 6:14 And the elders of the Jews were successful in building through the prophesying of Haggai the prophet and Zechariah the son of Iddo. And they finished building according to the command of the God of Israel and the decree of Cyrus, Darius, and Artaxerxes king of Persia.

Ezra 6:15 This temple was completed on the third day of the month Adar; it was the sixth year of the reign of King Darius.

    520 BCE — Egyptian satrap began to mint coins
    519 BCE — Darius passed through on way to Egypt
    515 BCE — 13 March (3rd of Adar) Temple finished:

Ezra 6:16 וַעֲבַדוּ בְנֵי־יִשְׂרָאֵל כָּהֲנַיָּא וְלֵוָיֵא וּשְׁאָר

בְּנֵי־גָלוּתָא חֲנֻכַּת בֵּית־אֱלָהָא דְנָה בְּחֶדְוָה

Ezra 6:17 וְהַקְרִבוּ לַחֲנֻכַּת בֵּית־אֱלָהָא דְנָה תּוֹרִין

מְאָה דִכְרִין מָאתַיִן אִמְּרִין אַרְבַּע מְאָה וּצְפִירֵי עִזִּין

לְחַטָּיָא [לְ][חַטָּאָה] עַל־כָּל־יִשְׂרָאֵל תְּרֵי־עֲשַׂר לְמִנְיָן שִׁבְטֵי יִשְׂרָאֵל

Ezra 6:18 וַהֲקִימוּ כָהֲנַיָּא בִּפְלֻגָּתְהוֹן וְלֵוָיֵא בְּמַחְלְקָתְהוֹן

עַל־עֲבִידַת אֱלָהָא דִּי בִירוּשְׁלֶם כִּכְתָב סְפַר מֹשֶׁה

Ezra 6:19 וַיַּעֲשׂוּ בְנֵי־הַגּוֹלָה אֶת־הַפָּסַח בְּאַרְבָּעָה עָשָׂר לַחֹדֶשׁ הָרִאשׁוֹן

Ezra 6:16 ¶ And the sons of Israel, the priests, the Levites and the rest of the exiles, celebrated the dedication of this house of God with joy.

Ezra 6:17 They offered for the dedication of this temple of God 100 bulls, 200 rams, 400 lambs, and as a sin offering for all Israel 12 male goats, corresponding to the number of the tribes of Israel.

Ezra 6:18 Then they appointed the priests to their divisions and the Levites in their orders for the service of God in Jerusalem, as it is written in the book of Moses.

Ezra 6:19 ¶ The exiles observed the Passover on the fourteenth of the first month.

> 512 BCE — Darius made first expedition to conquer
> Thrace
> 502 BCE — Tattenai mentioned on texts of this year.

B. FIFTH CENTURY

> 498 BCE — Ionic revolt
> 498 BCE — Sardis burned
> 497 BCE — Cyprus revolts from Persia
> 494 BCE — Battle of Lade, Persians conquer Miletus
> 492 BCE —Mardonius subdues Thrace and Macedonia
> 490 BCE — Battle of Marathon

> 486 BCE — Darius dies in Oct., followed by Aḥašwerosh
> (Xerxes)
> — **Revolt in Egypt!** (Herod. VII, 1, 4); had
> alreadybegun in same month that Darius died.
> Acusation against the Jews Ezra 4:6
> Bet. Dec., 486 and April, 485
> Ezra 4:6

וּבְמַלְכוּת אֲחַשְׁוֵרוֹשׁ בִּתְחִלַּת מַלְכוּתוֹ כָּתְבוּ
שִׂטְנָה עַל־יֹשְׁבֵי יְהוּדָה וִירוּשָׁלָם

Now in the reign of Ahasuerus, in the beginning of his reign, they wrote an accusation against the inhabitants of Judah and Jerusalem.

484/3 BCE — Persians regain control of Egypt (Jan., 484).

484 BCE — **Revolt in Babylon!** (June-July). Led by
　　　　　Bel-Shimanni.

482 BCE — **Revolt in Babylon!** In the summer, led by
　　　　　Shamash-eriba. The satrap Zopyrus slain
　　　　　(Ctesias, Pers. xiii, Epti. 52), Aug. to Oct. 428;
　　　　　Suppressed by Megabyzus, bro-in-law of the king.

481/479 BCE — War with Greece. Among peoples in the
　　　　　Persian fleet: (Herod. VII, 89)

The Phoenicians, with the Syrians of Palestine, contributed 300.
The crews wore helmets very like the Greek ones, and linen
corslets; they were armed with light rimless shields and javelins.
These people have a tradition that in ancient times they lived on
the Persian Gulf, but migrated to the Syrian coast, where they are
found today. This part of Syria, together with the country which
extends towards Egypt, is all known as Palestine.

480 BCE — Battle of Salamis (22.9.480) Xerxes returns home
　　　　　in his seventh year (Esth. 2:16)

479 BCE — Battle of Platea; Mardonius defeated; follow up
　　　　　victory at Mycale in Asia Minor.

464 BCE — Atraxerxes (Artaḥšasta) reigns till 424 BCE

462 BCE — Bēlšunu was gov. of Eber-nāri; he had an estate
　　　　　between Myriandos and Thapsacos (Tiphsah).

459 BCE — **Egypt revolts!** (Diod. XI, 71; Thuc. I, 104)

ABOUT THIS TIME ESHMUNAZER GETS GRANT OF DOR
AND JOPPE — Eshmunazer Insc. lines 18-20 —

(18) . . . . ועד יתן לן אדן מלכמ (19) אית דאר ויפי
ארצת דגן האדרת אש בשד שרן למדת עצמת אש פעלת
. . . . [מ]ויספננמ (20) עלת גבל ארץ לכננמ לצדנמ לעל

(18) . . . And further the lond of kings gave us (19) Dor and Yofē, mighty
grain lands in the territory of Sharon for the measure of the mighty deeds

which I did and we added them to the border of the land so that they would

belong to the Sidonians forev[er].

458 BCE — On August 4th, Ezra and his band arrive in Jerusalem: Ezra 7:7-9

Ezra 7:7 וַיַּעֲלוּ מִבְּנֵי־יִשְׂרָאֵל וּמִן־הַכֹּהֲנִים וְהַלְוִיִּם וְהַמְשֹׁרְרִים וְהַשֹּׁעֲרִים

וְהַנְּתִינִים אֶל־יְרוּשָׁלָם בִּשְׁנַת־שֶׁבַע לְאַרְתַּחְשַׁסְתְּא הַמֶּלֶךְ

Ezra 7:8 וַיָּבֹא יְרוּשָׁלַם בַּחֹדֶשׁ הַחֲמִישִׁי הִיא שְׁנַת הַשְּׁבִיעִית לַמֶּלֶךְ

Ezra 7:9 כִּי בְּאֶחָד לַחֹדֶשׁ הָרִאשׁוֹן הוּא יְסֻד הַמַּעֲלָה מִבָּבֶל וּבְאֶחָד

לַחֹדֶשׁ הַחֲמִישִׁי בָּא אֶל־יְרוּשָׁלַם כְּיַד־אֱלֹהָיו הַטּוֹבָה עָלָיו

Ezra 7:7 Some of the sons of Israel and some of the priests, the

Levites, the singers, the gatekeepers and the temple servants went

up to Jerusalem in the seventh year of King Artaxerxes.

Ezra 7:8 ¶ He came to Jerusalem in the fifth month, which was in

the seventh year of the king.

Ezra 7:9 For on the first of the first month he began to go up from

Babylon; and on the first of the fifth month he came to Jerusalem,

because the good hand of his God [was] upon him.

From Ezra 7:11-14

Ezra 7:11 וְזֶה פַּרְשֶׁגֶן הַנִּשְׁתְּוָן אֲשֶׁר נָתַן הַמֶּלֶךְ

אַרְתַּחְשַׁסְתְּא לְעֶזְרָא הַכֹּהֵן הַסֹּפֵר סֹפֵר דִּבְרֵי

מִצְוֹת־יְהוָה וְחֻקָּיו עַל־יִשְׂרָאֵל

Ezra 7:12 אַרְתַּחְשַׁסְתְּא מֶלֶךְ מַלְכַיָּא לְעֶזְרָא כָהֲנָא סָפַר

דָּתָא דִּי־אֱלָהּ שְׁמַיָּא גְּמִיר וּכְעֶנֶת

Ezra 7:13 מִנִּי שִׂים טְעֵם דִּי כָל־מִתְנַדַּב בְּמַלְכוּתִי

מִן־עַמָּה יִשְׂרָאֵל וְכָהֲנוֹהִי וְלֵוָיֵא לִמְהָךְ לִירוּשְׁלֶם עִמָּךְ יְהָךְ

Ezra 7:14 כָּל־קֳבֵל דִּי מִן־קֳדָם מַלְכָּא וְשִׁבְעַת יָעֲטֹהִי

שְׁלִיחַ לְבַקָּרָא עַל־יְהוּד וְלִירוּשְׁלֶם בְּדָת אֱלָהָךְ דִּי בִידָךְ

Ezra 7:11 ¶ Now this is the copy of the decree which King Artaxerxes gave to Ezra the priest, the scribe, learned in the words of the commandments of Yaahweh and His statutes to Israel:

Ezra 7:12 "Artaxerxes, king of kings, to Ezra the priest, the scribe of the law of the God of heaven, perfect [peace]. And now

Ezra 7:13 I have issued a decree that any of the people of Israel and their priests and the Levites in my kingdom who are willing to go to Jerusalem, may go with you.

Ezra 7:14 "Forasmuch as you are sent by the king and his seven counselors to inquire concerning Judah and Jerusalem according to the law of your God which is in your hand."

> 456 to 454 BCE — Megabyzus, now governor of *eber nāri*,
> reconquers Egypt (Diod. XI, 74; Thuc. I, 109)
> 454 BCE — Greek fleet captured in Egypt
> 450 BCE — Athenian admiral, Cimon, tried to capture Kition
> 448 BCE — "Peace of Callias" — Cyprus remains Persian
> 448 to 447 BCE — About now **Megabyzus rebelled!**
> (Ctesias, Pers. Epit. 68-70)

Accusation against the Jews about the walls
(Ezra 4:7-23)

Ezra 4:7 וּבִימֵי אַרְתַּחְשַׁשְׂתָּא כָּתַב בִּשְׁלָם מִתְרְדָת

טָבְאֵל וּשְׁאָר כְּנָוֹתוֹ [כְּנָוָתָיו] עַל־אַרְתַּחְשַׁשְׂתָּא

[אַרְתַּחְשַׁשְׂתְּ] מֶלֶךְ פָּרָס וּכְתָב הַנִּשְׁתְּוָן כָּתוּב אֲרָמִית

וּמְתֻרְגָּם אֲרָמִית

Ezra 4:8 רְחוּם בְּעֵל־טְעֵם וְשִׁמְשַׁי סָפְרָא כְּתַבוּ אִגְּרָה

חֲדָה עַל־יְרוּשְׁלֶם לְאַרְתַּחְשַׁשְׂתְּא מַלְכָּא כְּנֵמָא

Ezra 4:9 אֱדַיִן רְחוּם בְּעֵל־טְעֵם וְשִׁמְשַׁי סָפְרָא וּשְׁאָר

כְּנָוָתְהוֹן דִּינָיֵא וַאֲפַרְסַתְכָיֵא טַרְפְּלָיֵא אֲפָרְסָיֵא אַרְכְּוָי

[אַרְכְּוָי]א בָּבְלָיֵא שׁוּשַׁנְכָיֵא דְּהוּא [דֶּהָיֵא] עֵלְמָיֵא

Ezra 4:10 וּשְׁאָר אֻמַּיָּא דִּי הַגְלִי אָסְנַפַּר רַבָּא וְיַקִּירָא

וְהוֹתֵב הִמּוֹ בְּקִרְיָה דִּי שָׁמְרָיִן וּשְׁאָר עֲבַר־נַהֲרָה וּכְעֶנֶת

Ezra 4:11 דְּנָה פַּרְשֶׁגֶן אִגַּרְתָּא דִּי שְׁלַחוּ עֲלוֹהִי

עַל־אַרְתַּחְשַׁשְׂתְּא מַלְכָּא עַבְדָיִךְ [עַבְדָּךְ] אֱנָשׁ

עֲבַר־נַהֲרָה וּכְעֶנֶת

Ezra 4:12 יְדִיעַ לֶהֱוֵא לְמַלְכָּא דִּי יְהוּדָיֵא דִּי סְלִקוּ

מִן־לְוָתָךְ עֲלֶינָא אֲתוֹ לִירוּשְׁלֶם קִרְיְתָא מָרָדְתָּא

וּבִאִישְׁתָּא בָּנַיִן וְשׁוּרַיִ [וְ][שׁוּרַיָּ][א] אֶשְׁכְלִלוּ [שַׁכְלִלוּ]

וְאֻשַּׁיָּא יַחִיטוּ

Ezra 4:13 כְּעַן יְדִיעַ לֶהֱוֵא לְמַלְכָּא דִּי הֵן קִרְיְתָא דָךְ

תִּתְבְּנֵא וְשׁוּרַיָּה יִשְׁתַּכְלְלוּן מִנְדָּה־בְלוֹ וַהֲלָךְ לָא יִנְתְּנוּן

וְאַפְּתֹם מַלְכִים תְּהַנְזִק

Ezra 4:14 כְּעַן כָּל־קֳבֵל דִּי־מְלַח הֵיכְלָא מְלַחְנָא וְעַרְוַת

מַלְכָּא לָא אֲרִיךְ־לַנָא לְמֶחֱזֵא עַל־דְּנָה שְׁלַחְנָא

וְהוֹדַעְנָא לְמַלְכָּא

Ezra 4:15 דִּי יְבַקַּר בִּסְפַר־דָּכְרָנַיָּא דִּי אֲבָהָתָךְ וּתְהַשְׁכַּח

בִּסְפַר דָּכְרָנַיָּא וְתִנְדַּע דִּי קִרְיְתָא דָךְ קִרְיָא מָרָדָא

וּמְהַנְזְקַת מַלְכִין וּמְדִנָן וְאֶשְׁתַּדּוּר עָבְדִין בְּגַוַּהּ

מִן־יוֹמָת עָלְמָא עַל־דְּנָה קִרְיְתָא דָךְ הָחָרְבַת

Ezra 4:16 מְהוֹדְעִין אֲנַחְנָה לְמַלְכָּא דִּי הֵן קִרְיְתָא דָךְ

תִּתְבְּנֵא וְשׁוּרַיָּה יִשְׁתַּכְלְלוּן לָקֳבֵל דְּנָה חֲלָק בַּעֲבַר

נַהֲרָא לָא אִיתַי לָךְ

Ezra 4:17 פִּתְגָמָא שְׁלַח מַלְכָּא עַל־רְחוּם בְּעֵל־טְעֵם

וְשִׁמְשַׁי סָפְרָא וּשְׁאָר כְּנָוָתְהוֹן דִּי יָתְבִין בְּשָׁמְרָיִן וּשְׁאָר

עֲבַר־נַהֲרָה שְׁלָם וּכְעֶת

Ezra 4:18 נִשְׁתְּוָנָא דִּי שְׁלַחְתּוּן עֲלֶינָא מְפָרַשׁ קֱרִי קָדָמָי

Ezra 4:19 וּמִנִּי שִׂים טְעֵם וּבַקַּרוּ וְהַשְׁכַּחוּ דִּי קִרְיְתָא

דָךְ מִן־יוֹמָת עָלְמָא עַל־מַלְכִין מִתְנַשְּׂאָה וּמְרַד

וְאֶשְׁתַּדּוּר מִתְעֲבֶד־בַּהּ

Ezra 4:20 וּמַלְכִין תַּקִּיפִין הֲווֹ עַל־יְרוּשְׁלֶם וְשַׁלִּיטִין

בְּכֹל עֲבַר נַהֲרָה וּמִדָּה בְלוֹ וַהֲלָךְ מִתְיְהֵב לְהוֹן

Ezra 4:21 כְּעַן שִׂימוּ טְּעֵם לְבַטָּלָא גֻּבְרַיָּא אִלֵּךְ

וְקִרְיְתָא דָךְ לָא תִתְבְּנֵא עַד־מִנִּי טַעְמָא יִתְּשָׂם

Ezra 4:22 וּזְהִירִין הֱווֹ שָׁלוּ לְמֶעְבַּד עַל־דְּנָה לְמָה

יִשְׂגֵּא חֲבָלָא לְהַנְזָקַת מַלְכִין

Ezra 4:23 אֱדַיִן מִן־דִּי פַּרְשֶׁגֶן נִשְׁתְּוָנָא דִּי אַרְתַּחְשַׁשְׁתָּא

[אַרְתַּחְשַׁשְׂתְּ] מַלְכָּא קֱרִי קֳדָם־רְחוּם וְשִׁמְשַׁי סָפְרָא

וּכְנָוָתְהוֹן אֲזַלוּ בִבְהִילוּ לִירוּשְׁלֶם עַל־יְהוּדָיֵא וּבַטִּלוּ

הִמּוֹ בְּאֶדְרָע וְחָיִל

ועתה, (11) זו גסרת האגרת אשר שלחו אליו, אל ארתחששתא
המלך, עבדיך אנשי עבר הנהר—ועתה: (12) ידוע יהיה למלך,
שהיהודים אשר עלו ממך אלינו באו לירושלים; את העיר
המורדת והרעה הם בונים ואת החומות השלימו ועל היסודות
הרימו חומות. (13) עתה ידוע יהיה למלך, שאם העיר ההיא
תיבנה והחומות יושלמו, מנדה, בלו והלך לא יתנו ולכסא
המלכות תזיק. (14) ועתה, מאחר שאנחנו מולחים את מלח
ההיכל, וגנות המלך לא יאה לנו לראות, על כן שלחנו
והודענו למלך. (15) אשר יבדוק בספר הזכרונות של אבותיך,
ותמצא בספר הזכרונות ותדע כי העיר ההיא עיר מורדת
ומזיקה למלכים ולמדינות, ומרידות עושים בתוכה מימי
עולם. על זה העיר ההיא הוחרבה. (16) מודיעים אנחנו
למלך כי אם תיבנה העיר ההיא והחומות תושלמנה, לפי זה
חלק בעבר הנהר לא יהיה לך.

Ezra 4:15 so that a search may be made in the record books of your fathers. And you will discover in the record books and learn that that city is a rebellious city and damaging to kings and provinces, and that they have incited revolt within it in past days; therefore that city was laid waste.

Ezra 4:16 "We inform the king that if that city is rebuilt and the walls finished, as a result you will have no possession in [the province] beyond the River."

Ezra 4:17 ¶ [Then] the king sent an answer to Rehum the commander, to Shimshai the scribe, and to the rest of their colleagues who live in Samaria and in the rest of [the provinces] beyond the River: "Peace. And now

Ezra 4:18 the document which you sent to us has been translated and read before me.

Ezra 4:19 "A decree has been issued by me, and a search has been made and it has been discovered that that city has risen up against the kings in past days, that rebellion and revolt have been perpetrated in it,

Ezra 4:20 that mighty kings have ruled over Jerusalem, governing all [the provinces] beyond the River, and that tribute, custom and toll were paid to them.

Ezra 4:21 "So, now issue a decree to make these men stop [work], that this city may not be rebuilt until a decree is issued by me.

Ezra 4:22 "Beware of being negligent in carrying out this [matter]; why should damage increase to the detriment of the kings?"

Ezra 4:23 ¶ Then as soon as the copy of King Artaxerxes' document was read before Rehum and Shimshai the scribe and their colleagues, they went in haste to Jerusalem to the Jews and stopped them by force of arms.

Ezra 4:17-20

Ezra 4:17 פִּתְגָמָא שְׁלַח מַלְכָּא עַל־רְחוּם בְּעֵל־טְעֵם

וְשִׁמְשַׁי סָפְרָא וּשְׁאָר כְּנָוָתְהוֹן דִּי יָתְבִין בְּשָׁמְרָיִן וּשְׁאָר

עֲבַר־נַהֲרָה שְׁלָם וּכְעֶת

Ezra 4:18 נִשְׁתְּוָנָא דִּי שְׁלַחְתּוּן עֲלֶינָא מְפָרַשׁ קֱרִי קָדָמָי

Ezra 4:19 וּמִנִּי שִׂים טְעֵם וּבַקַּרוּ וְהַשְׁכַּחוּ דִּי קִרְיְתָא

דָךְ מִן־יוֹמָת עָלְמָא עַל־מַלְכִין מִתְנַשְּׂאָה וּמְרַד

וְאֶשְׁתַּדּוּר מִתְעֲבֶד־בַּהּ

Ezra 4:20 וּמַלְכִין תַּקִּיפִין הֲווֹ עַל־יְרוּשְׁלֶם וְשַׁלִּיטִין בְּכֹל עֲבַר נַהֲרָה וּמִדָּה בְלוֹ וַהֲלָךְ מִתְיְהֵב לְהוֹן

(17) דבר שלח המלך אל רחום המפקד ושמשי הסופר ושאר עמיתיהם אשר יושבים בשומרון ושאר עבר הנהר: שלום! ועתה, (18) המכתב אשר שלחתם אלינו נקרא לפני בפירוש. (19) וממני ניתן צו, ובקשו ומצאו, שהעיר ההיא מימי עולם מתנשאת נגד מלכים ומרד ומלחמה נעשו בה, (20) ומלכים חזקים היו על ירושלים ושליטים בכל עבר הנהר, מנדה, בלו והלך ניתן להם.

Ezra 4:17 ¶ [Then] the king sent an answer to Rehum the commander, to Shimshai the scribe, and to the rest of their colleagues who live in Samaria and in the rest of [the provinces] beyond the River: "Peace. And now

Ezra 4:18 the document which you sent to us has been translated and read before me.

Ezra 4:19 "A decree has been issued by me, and a search has been made and it has been discovered that that city has risen up against the kings in past days, that rebellion and revolt have been perpetrated in it,

Ezra 4:20 that mighty kings have ruled over Jerusalem, governing all [the provinces] beyond the River, and that tribute, custom and toll were paid to them.

Ezra 4:21 כְּעַן שִׂימוּ טְּעֵם לְבַטָּלָא גֻּבְרַיָּא אִלֵּךְ וְקִרְיְתָא דָךְ לָא תִתְבְּנֵא עַד־מִנִּי טַעְמָא יִתְּשָׂם

Ezra 4:22 וּזְהִירִין הֲווֹ שָׁלוּ לְמֶעְבַּד עַל־דְּנָה לְמָה יִשְׂגֵּא

(21) תנו צו לבטל את האנשים ההם, ושהעיר ההיא לאחבלא להנזקת מלכין עתה תיבנה עד שיינתן צו ממני. (22) והיו זהירים מעשות שגגה על זאת, פן יגדל הנזק להזקת המלך.

Ezra 4:21 "So, now issue a decree to make these men stop [work], that this city may not be rebuilt until a decree is issued by me.

<u>Ezra 4:22</u> "Beware of being negligent in carrying out this [matter]; why should damage increase to the detriment of the kings?"

<u>Ezra 4:23</u> אֱדַיִן מִן־דִּי פַּרְשֶׁגֶן נִשְׁתְּוָנָא דִּי אַרְתַּחְשַׁשְׂתָּא

[אַרְתַּחְשַׁשְׂתְּ] מַלְכָּא קֱרִי קֳדָם־רְחוּם וְשִׁמְשַׁי סָפְרָא

וּכְנָוָתְהוֹן אֲזַלוּ בִבְהִילוּ לִירוּשְׁלֶם עַל־יְהוּדָיֵא וּבַטִּלוּ

הִמּוֹ בְּאֶדְרָע וְחָיִל

(23) אז, מאחר שנקרא גירסת המכתב של ארתחששתא המלך לפני רחום ושמשי הסופר ועמיתיהם, הלכו בחפזון לירושלים אל היהודים וביטלו אותם בזרוע ובחיל.

<u>Ezra 4:23</u> ¶ Then as soon as the copy of King Artaxerxes' document was read before Rehum and Shimshai the scribe and their colleagues, they went in haste to Jerusalem to the Jews and stopped them by force of arms.

445 BCE — Word comes to Nehemiah (1:1) in December:
Neh. 1:1-3

<u>Neh. 1:1</u> דִּבְרֵי נְחֶמְיָה בֶּן־חֲכַלְיָה וַיְהִי בְחֹדֶשׁ־כִּסְלֵו

[כִּסְלֵיו] שְׁנַת עֶשְׂרִים וַאֲנִי הָיִיתִי בְּשׁוּשַׁן הַבִּירָה

<u>Neh. 1:2</u> וַיָּבֹא חֲנָנִי אֶחָד מֵאַחַי° הוּא וַאֲנָשִׁים מִיהוּדָה

וָאֶשְׁאָלֵם עַל־הַיְּהוּדִים הַפְּלֵיטָה אֲשֶׁר־נִשְׁאֲרוּ מִן־הַשֶּׁבִי

וְעַל־יְרוּשָׁלָ͏ִם

<u>Neh. 1:3</u> וַיֹּאמְרוּ לִי הַנִּשְׁאָרִים אֲשֶׁר־נִשְׁאֲרוּ מִן־הַשֶּׁבִי

שָׁם בַּמְּדִינָה בְּרָעָה גְדֹלָה וּבְחֶרְפָּה וְחוֹמַת יְרוּשָׁלַ͏ִם

מְפֹרָצֶת וּשְׁעָרֶיהָ נִצְּתוּ בָאֵשׁ

<u>Neh. 1:1</u> ¶ The words of Nehemiah the son of Hacaliah. ¶ Now it happened in the month Chislev, [in] the twentieth year, while I was in Susa the capitol,

<u>Neh. 1:2</u> that Hanani, one of my brothers, and some men from Judah came; and I asked them concerning the Jews who had escaped [and] had survived the captivity, and about Jerusalem.

<u>Neh. 1:3</u> They said to me, "The remnant there in the province who survived the captivity are in great distress and reproach,

and the wall of Jerusalem is broken down and its gates are burned with fire."

445 to 444 BCE — Nehemiah rebuilds the walls.

Neh. 4:6 (Eng. 4:12) "Those who live among them"

6 וַיְהִי֮ כַּאֲשֶׁר־בָּ֣אוּ הַיְּהוּדִים֮ הַיֹּשְׁבִ֣ים אֶצְלָם֒ וַיֹּאמְרוּ לָ֙נוּ֙ עֶ֣שֶׂר פְּעָמִ֔ים

מִכָּל־הַמְּקֹמ֖וֹת אֲשֶׁר־תָּשׁ֥וּבוּ עָלֵֽינוּ׃

Neh. 4:12 When the Jews who lived among them came and told us ten times, "They will come up against us from every place where you may turn,"

432 BCE — Nehemiah returns to Yehud (Neh. 13)

Neh. 13:6 וּבְכָל־זֶ֕ה לֹ֥א הָיִ֖יתִי בִּירוּשָׁלָ֑͏ִם כִּ֡י בִּשְׁנַת֩ שְׁלֹשִׁ֨ים וּשְׁתַּ֜יִם

לְאַרְתַּחְשַׁסְתְּא מֶֽלֶךְ־בָּבֶ֗ל בָּ֚אתִי אֶל־הַמֶּ֔לֶךְ וּלְקֵ֥ץ יָמִ֖ים נִשְׁאַ֥לְתִּי

מִן־הַמֶּֽלֶךְ Neh. 13:7 וָאָב֖וֹא לִירוּשָׁלָ֑͏ִם וָאָבִ֣ינָה בָרָעָ֗ה אֲשֶׁ֨ר עָשָׂ֤ה

אֶלְיָשִׁיב֙ לְט֣וֹבִיָּ֔ה לַעֲשׂ֤וֹת לוֹ֙ נִשְׁכָּ֔ה בְּחַצְרֵ֖י בֵּ֥ית הָאֱלֹהִֽים

Neh. 13:6 But during all this [time] I was not in Jerusalem, for in the thirty-second year of Artaxerxes king of Babylon I had gone to the king. After some time, however, I asked leave from the king,

Neh. 13:7 and I came to Jerusalem and learned about the evil that Eliashib had done for Tobiah, by preparing a room for him in the courts of the house of God.

423 to 405 BCE — Reign of Darius II

410 BCE — Temple destroyed at Yeb

408 BCE — Yeb letter to Bigvai (Bagoas) Cowley No. 1

407 BCE — Text refers to Bēlšunu gov. of BAL.RI ID

(= *eber nāri*) a certain tuition contract contains an allusion to a servant of Belshunu, governor of BAL: RI ID = eber nari. This would mean that in the 12th year of Darius II, i.e. 407 BCE, to which this text is dated, there was once again a ruler named Belshunu in charge of the Province Beyond the River. So the reference to Belysis in Xenophon's *Anabasis* might be to this second person rather than to the one known from the reign of Artaxerxes. But given the uncertainty in the reading of the signs, one cannot say for certain, this later Belshunu might have been governor of some other province.

404 BCE — Darius II died; Atraxerxes II Memnon to the throne (404-359)
Amytereus (404-398) led Egypt in a successful revolt.
XXVIII Dyn. at Sais (404-398).

The Egyptians managed to maintain their independence for the next 60 years in spite of repeated Persian attempts to reconquer them.

401 BCE —The Anabasis of Cyrus the Younger.

The accession of Artaxerxes II Memnon and the subsequent conflict between him and his brother, "Cyrus the Younger," not only saw an insurrectionist army marching across the province of "Beyond the River," it took the great Persian monolith to its very foundations and taught the Greeks that a well-disciplined force could easily penetrate to the heart of the empire.

Abrokomas governor of *eber nāri.*

He appears in Xenophon's account of the "ascent" by Cyrus the Younger. When Cyrus arrived in Cilicia he pretended that his aim was to attack this Abrokomas. The latter was thought to be waiting for him behind the Cilician Gates (Xenophon, *Anabasis* 1, 3:20). Diodorus (XIV, 20:5) only calls him "some Satrap of Syria." Although 400 Greeks transferred their allegiance from Abrokomas to Cyrus, it was still reported that he had a strong force at his command (Xenophon, *Anabasis* 1, 4:3, 5). Abrokomas was a field commander on a par with the other three senior officers supporting the king at Cunaxa (*Anabasis* 1, 7:12). Of these latter, Tissaphernos was the well known satrap of Asia Minor, Arbakes was satrap of Media, and Gobyas (Gubaru) was "governor of Akhad" according to a cuneiform text dating to the seventh year of Darius⁾ 11 (416 BCE).

C. FOURTH CENTURY

1. Dynasty XXIX

Nepherites (398-394) — scaraboid bearing his name at Gezer.
Achoris (393-380 BCE) — allied with Evagoras of Cyprus

2. Evagoras revolted from Persia in 391 (Diod. XV, 2:3)
with Athenian support until the "King's Peace" when the
Persian monarch dictated terms to the Greek cities (386 BCE)
3. Persians prepare to attack Egypt — Athenian general sent to Egypt
to help them prepare their defense.

Abrokomas joined Pharnabazos and Titthraustes in a
concerted drive to reconquer Egypt.

4. Evagoras captured Tyre and won over a large part of Phoenicia
and Cilicia. He had ample support from Hecatomnus, ruler of
Caria. If the suggested emendation of _barbaron_ to _Arabon_ in
Diodorus XV, 2:4, be accepted, then Evagoras⁾ forces included troops sent
by "the king of the Arabians."

5. The Persian forces, their supply lines cut, were beaten severely and
forced to retreat from Egypt.

6. Pharaoh Achoris has left some monuments in the province Beyond
the River, viz. an inscription at the Eshmunezzer Temple
north of Sidon and altar stand of polished grey granite
(from Syene) at Acco.

7. 381-379 — A renewed Persian force invaded Cyprus.
Finally forced Evagoras to surrender though the terms were

much lighter than those demanded earlier.

8. 380 BCE Nectanebes became the founder of the 30th Dynasty.

9. Pharnabazos, satrap of Cilicia —

Began mustering troops for a new assault on Egypt as early as 379 but it was only in 373 BCE that he finally brought his forces together at Acco. Though he had a large navy, 300 ships, and extensive land forces, 12,000 Greek mercenaries and many Orientals, he was unable to do more than to establish a bridgehead near the Mendesian mouth of the Nile. He was unable to enter via Pelusium and a strong Egyptian counterattack forced him to withdraw.

10. From about 368-360 BCE the "Satraps' Revolt" —

Nearly destroyed the Persian Empire altogether. Most of the rebel satraps governed districts in Asia Minor; but the Syrians and the Phoenicians also took part.

Although the Phoenicians had done their part in Pharnabazos' invasion by providing the naval support, they were not overly sympathetic. During the "Satraps' revolt," they leagued up with the Egyptians against the Persians.

11. 362 BCE — Tachos (Teos) became king of Egypt

a. Mobilised a great army including 10,000 Greek mercenaries (361). In collaboration with the rebel satraps, he executed an invasion of the province "Beyond the River" and gained control of the major seaports of Palestine and Phoenicia.

b. He was supposed to join another satrap, Aroandas, in Syria and march eastward in support of Datames who was crossing the Euphrates with an advanced guard.

c. Ochus, a younger son of Artaxerxes, was struggling to maintain control of Phoenicia in the face of the Egyptian attack, but the Greek mercenaries were steadily gaining ground against him.

d. However, Tachos' nephew, Nectanebos, rebelled against his uncle and this forced Tachos to surrender himself to Ochus at Sidon.

e. Disturbances in Egypt caused Nectanebos to withdraw from Phoenicia. Persian authority was gradually restored in the west as the rebel satraps were betrayed or captured, one by one.

12. 358 BCE — Ochus now succeeded his father, Artaxerxes II as Artaxerxes III

During the next several years he was engaged in quelling various disturbances throughout the empire, especially in Asia Minor.

By 351 he had gained firm control over his western provinces, including Phoenicia and was in position to launch a new invasion of Egypt.

The satrap of Syria at this time was another Belesys (Belshunu), possibly a grandson of the one who had governed the province in the fifth century (Diodorus XV1, 42:1). The province "Beyond the River" reached as far as Cilicia in the north and included Phoenicia and north Syria as far as the Euphrates. The satrapy evidently had remained unchanged in geographical extent.

13. Attempt to invade Egypt by Artaxerxes III.

He too was forced to retire after a year of hard fighting(c. 351-350).

14. An extensive revolt by the Phoenician cities.

Their representatives assembled at Tripolis and voted to throw off the Persian yoke. A large fleet of warships and a mighty mercenary army was financed by the vast wealth of Sidon. The Phoenicians were followed by nine Cypriote kings and parts of Cilicia also joined in the revolt.

The satrap of "Beyond the River," Belesys (Bēlshunu), had the job of quelling the rebellion. Accompanied by Mazaios, satrap of Cilicia, he made an unsuccessful assault on Phoenicia (Diodorus XV1, 12:1). The exact date of this attempt cannot be determined.

15. 345 BCE — Artaxerxes saw that his two satraps were ineffective so he decided to intervene personally. He assembled a huge force at Babylon and marched against Sidon.

The populace had made preparations for an extended siege but they were betrayed to the Persians by their leaders, including Tennes himself. They set fire to their ships and to their homes in order to escape capture. Artaxerxes sold the ruins to speculators who paid a handsome price for the right to search for melted gold and silver.

15. Mazaios, though retaining his satrapy in Cilicia, was also given charge of "Beyond the River."

Many of his known coins are of Phoenician, particularly Sidonian, style and are numbered from 16 to 21, representing the last five years of Ochus' reign (345-339 BCE). Another series of Mazaios' coins confirms his rule over Cilicia and Syria; they are inscribed: "Mazdai who is over 'Beyond the River' and Cilicia." Mazaios seems to have maintained his position as Satrap of "Beyond the River" throughout these final years. He has a series of Sidonian coins numbered 1 through 4. Experts believe that they date to the three years of Arses' reign (338-336) and the first four years of Darius III (336-333). Some have questioned whether he still held sway over Cilicia. It is probable that Mazaios was still governor of both Cilicia and Syria but that Arsames was his deputy in the northern province. But Mazaios does not appear at any stage in the Macedonian conquest of Cilicia, Phoenicia or the rest of Syria. Nevertheless, he was a field commander at the battle of Gaugamala (331 BCE). After the Persian defeat he withdrew to Babylon with a remnant of his forces and finally surrendered the city to Alexander (330 BCE). He was rewarded with the governorship of Babylonia, which he ruled until his death in 328.

16. 343 BCE — Artaxerxes finally did conquer Egypt.

He strengthened his position in the West that even the Cypriote kings had to fall back into line. But he himself was assassinated in 338 and followed by Arses; this brought an end to all hopes of a great Persian revival.

17. Egypt took advantage of the situation and revolted (c. 337 BCE).

18. 336 BCE —Arses was also murderedand replaced by Darius III.

This latter set about energetically to recoup the losses sustained since Ochus' demise and by 334 BCE he had even regained control over Egypt.

19. 333 BCE —Victory at Grannicus, then at Issus.

a. Alexander then marched southward from Issus and received the surrender of the Phoenician cities of Arwad (Arados), Byblos and Sidon. Tyre refused to grant him entrance and thus was forced to undergo the famous seven-month siege during which Alexander built a mole connecting the island with the mainland.

b. The next point of resistance was Gaza. Alexander found it strongly fortified and defended by a eunuch named Batis. Though he is thought by some to have been a Persian; however, the name *btšw*, probably a form like *Batisu*, "valiant," is well known in Nabataean inscriptions. The fact that he was supported by Nabataen troops also strengthens the assumption that he was one of them himself (Arrian 11, 25:4; Curtius IV, 6:7). This would indicate that by this time the control of the trade routes from Northern Arabia across the Negeb to Gaza was now in the hands of the Nabataeans who had supplanted the Kedarites in this role.

c. It required a two month siege to reduce Gaza; even Alexander sustained a personal injury (Arrian 11, 25-27). The slaughter of the population was greater than at Tyre; the women and children were sold into slavery. Henceforth, Gaza became a Macedonian garrison.

d. While Alexander was liberating Egypt from Persian rule, he entrusted the conquest of the remaining areas in Syria to his generals. The "Province Beyond the River", was henceforth known officially as Syria.

III.   GEOGRAPHY OF YEHUD:

1. Towns mentioned in Ezra 2:21-35

Ezra 2:21 בְּנֵי בֵית־לָחֶם מֵאָה עֶשְׂרִים וּשְׁלֹשָׁה

Ezra 2:22 אַנְשֵׁי נְטֹפָה חֲמִשִּׁים וְשִׁשָּׁה

Ezra 2:23 אַנְשֵׁי עֲנָתוֹת מֵאָה עֶשְׂרִים וּשְׁמֹנָה

Ezra 2:24 בְּנֵי עַזְמָוֶת אַרְבָּעִים וּשְׁנָיִם

Ezra 2:25 בְּנֵי קִרְיַת עָרִים כְּפִירָה וּבְאֵרוֹת שְׁבַע מֵאוֹת וְאַרְבָּעִים וּשְׁלֹשָׁה

Ezra 2:26 בְּנֵי הָרָמָה וָגָבַע שֵׁשׁ מֵאוֹת עֶשְׂרִים וְאֶחָד

Ezra 2:27 אַנְשֵׁי מִכְמָס מֵאָה עֶשְׂרִים וּשְׁנָיִם

Ezra 2:28 אַנְשֵׁי בֵית־אֵל וְהָעָי מָאתַיִם עֶשְׂרִים וּשְׁלֹשָׁה

Ezra 2:29 בְּנֵי נְבוֹ חֲמִשִּׁים וּשְׁנָיִם

Ezra 2:30 בְּנֵי מַגְבִּישׁ מֵאָה חֲמִשִּׁים וְשִׁשָּׁה

Ezra 2:31 בְּנֵי עֵילָם אַחֵר אֶלֶף מָאתַיִם חֲמִשִּׁים וְאַרְבָּעָה

Ezra 2:32 בְּנֵי חָרִם שְׁלֹשׁ מֵאוֹת וְעֶשְׂרִים

Ezra 2:33 בְּנֵי־לֹד חָדִיד וְאוֹנוֹ שְׁבַע מֵאוֹת עֶשְׂרִים וַחֲמִשָּׁה

Ezra 2:34 בְּנֵי יְרֵחוֹ שְׁלֹשׁ מֵאוֹת אַרְבָּעִים וַחֲמִשָּׁה

Ezra 2:35 בְּנֵי סְנָאָה שְׁלֹשֶׁת אֲלָפִים וְשֵׁשׁ מֵאוֹת וּשְׁלֹשִׁים

Ezra 2:21 the men of Bethlehem, 123;

Ezra 2:22 the men of Netophah, 56;

Ezra 2:23 the men of Anathoth, 128;

Ezra 2:24 the sons of Azmaveth, 42;

Ezra 2:25 the sons of Kiriath-‹je›arim, Chephirah and Beeroth, 743;

Ezra 2:26 the sons of Ramah and Geba, 621;

Ezra 2:27 the men of Michmas, 122;

Ezra 2:28 the men of Bethel and Ai, 223;

Ezra 2:29 the sons of Nebo, 52;

Ezra 2:30 the sons of Magbish, 156;

Ezra 2:31 the sons of the other Elam, 1,254;

Ezra 2:32 the sons of Harim, 320;

Ezra 2:33 the sons of Lod, Hadid and Ono, 725;

Ezra 2:34 the men of Jericho, 345;

Ezra 2:35 the sons of Senaah, 3,630.

2. Builders of the Wall Neh. 3:1-32

Neh. 3:1 וַיָּקָם אֶלְיָשִׁיב הַכֹּהֵן הַגָּדוֹל וְאֶחָיו הַכֹּהֲנִים

וַיִּבְנוּ אֶת־שַׁעַר הַצֹּאן הֵמָּה קִדְּשׁוּהוּ וַיַּעֲמִידוּ דַּלְתֹתָיו

וְעַד־מִגְדַּל הַמֵּאָה קִדְּשׁוּהוּ עַד מִגְדַּל חֲנַנְאֵל

Neh. 3:2 וְעַל־יָדוֹ בָנוּ אַנְשֵׁי יְרֵחוֹ וְעַל־יָדוֹ בָנָה זַכּוּר

בֶּן־אִמְרִי

Neh. 3:3 וְאֵת שַׁעַר הַדָּגִים בָּנוּ בְּנֵי הַסְּנָאָה הֵמָּה

קֵרוּהוּ וַיַּעֲמִידוּ דַּלְתֹתָיו מַנְעוּלָיו וּבְרִיחָיו

Neh. 3:4 וְעַל־יָדָם הֶחֱזִיק מְרֵמוֹת בֶּן־אוּרִיָּה בֶּן־הַקּוֹץ

ס וְעַל־יָדָם הֶחֱזִיק מְשֻׁלָּם בֶּן־בֶּרֶכְיָה בֶּן־מְשֵׁיזַבְאֵל

וְעַל־יָדָם הֶחֱזִיק צָדוֹק בֶּן־בַּעֲנָא

Neh. 3:5 וְעַל־יָדָם הֶחֱזִיקוּ הַתְּקוֹעִים וְאַדִּירֵיהֶם

לֹא־הֵבִיאוּ צַוָּרָם בַּעֲבֹדַת אֲדֹנֵיהֶם

Neh. 3:6 וְאֵת שַׁעַר הַיְשָׁנָה הֶחֱזִיקוּ יוֹיָדָע בֶּן־פָּסֵחַ

וּמְשֻׁלָּם בֶּן־בְּסוֹדְיָה הֵמָּה קֵרוּהוּ וַיַּעֲמִידוּ דַּלְתֹתָיו

וּמַנְעֻלָיו וּבְרִיחָיו

Neh. 3:7 וְעַל־יָדָם הֶחֱזִיק מְלַטְיָה הַגִּבְעֹנִי וְיָדוֹן
הַמֵּרֹנֹתִי אַנְשֵׁי גִבְעוֹן וְהַמִּצְפָּה לְכִסֵּא פַּחַת עֵבֶר הַנָּהָר

Neh. 3:8 עַל־יָדוֹ הֶחֱזִיק עֻזִּיאֵל בֶּן־חַרְהֲיָה צוֹרְפִים
וְעַל־יָדוֹ הֶחֱזִיק חֲנַנְיָה בֶּן־הָרַקָּחִים וַיַּעַזְבוּ יְרוּשָׁלַם
עַד הַחוֹמָה הָרְחָבָה

Neh. 3:9 וְעַל־יָדָם הֶחֱזִיק רְפָיָה בֶן־חוּר שַׂר חֲצִי פֶּלֶךְ
יְרוּשָׁלָם

Neh. 3:10 וְעַל־יָדָם הֶחֱזִיק יְדָיָה בֶן־חֲרוּמַף וְנֶגֶד
בֵּיתוֹ וְעַל־יָדוֹ הֶחֱזִיק חַטּוּשׁ בֶּן־חֲשַׁבְנְיָה

Neh. 3:11 מִדָּה שֵׁנִית הֶחֱזִיק מַלְכִּיָּה בֶן־חָרִם וְחַשּׁוּב
בֶּן־פַּחַת מוֹאָב וְאֵת מִגְדַּל הַתַּנּוּרִים

Neh. 3:12 וְעַל־יָדוֹ הֶחֱזִיק שַׁלּוּם בֶּן־הַלּוֹחֵשׁ שַׂר חֲצִי
פֶּלֶךְ יְרוּשָׁלָם הוּא וּבְנוֹתָיו

Neh. 3:13 אֵת שַׁעַר הַגַּיְא הֶחֱזִיק חָנוּן וְיֹשְׁבֵי זָנוֹחַ הֵמָּה
בָנוּהוּ וַיַּעֲמִידוּ דַּלְתֹתָיו מַנְעֻלָיו וּבְרִיחָיו וְאֶלֶף אַמָּה
בַחוֹמָה עַד שַׁעַר הָשֲׁפוֹת

Neh. 3:14 וְאֵת שַׁעַר הָאַשְׁפּוֹת הֶחֱזִיק מַלְכִּיָּה בֶן־רֵכָב
שַׂר פֶּלֶךְ בֵּית־הַכָּרֶם הוּא יִבְנֶנּוּ וְיַעֲמִיד דַּלְתֹתָיו
מַנְעֻלָיו וּבְרִיחָיו

Neh. 3:15 וְאֵת שַׁעַר הָעַיִן הֶחֱזִיק שַׁלּוּן בֶּן־כָּל־חֹזֶה שַׂר
פֶּלֶךְ הַמִּצְפָּה הוּא יִבְנֶנּוּ וִיטַלְלֶנּוּ וְיַעֲמִידוּ [וְ][יַעֲמִיד]
דַּלְתֹתָיו מַנְעֻלָיו וּבְרִיחָיו וְאֵת חוֹמַת בְּרֵכַת הַשֶּׁלַח
לְגַן־הַמֶּלֶךְ וְעַד־הַמַּעֲלוֹת הַיּוֹרְדוֹת מֵעִיר דָּוִיד

Neh. 3:16 אַחֲרָיו הֶחֱזִיק נְחֶמְיָה בֶן־עַזְבּוּק שַׂר חֲצִי
פֶּלֶךְ בֵּית־צוּר עַד־נֶגֶד קִבְרֵי דָוִיד וְעַד־הַבְּרֵכָה

הָעֲשׂוּיָה וְעַד בֵּית הַגִּבֹּרִים

<u>Neh. 3:17</u> אַחֲרָיו הֶחֱזִיקוּ הַלְוִיִּם רְחוּם בֶּן־בָּנִי עַל־יָדוֹ

הֶחֱזִיק חֲשַׁבְיָה שַׂר־חֲצִי־פֶלֶךְ קְעִילָה לְפִלְכּוֹ

<u>Neh. 3:18</u> אַחֲרָיו הֶחֱזִיקוּ אֲחֵיהֶם בַּוַּי בֶּן־חֵנָדָד שַׂר

חֲצִי פֶלֶךְ קְעִילָה

<u>Neh. 3:19</u> וַיְחַזֵּק עַל־יָדוֹ עֵזֶר בֶּן־יֵשׁוּעַ שַׂר הַמִּצְפָּה

מִדָּה שֵׁנִית מִנֶּגֶד עֲלֹת הַנֶּשֶׁק הַמִּקְצֹעַ

<u>Neh. 3:20</u> אַחֲרָיו הֶחֱרָה הֶחֱזִיק בָּרוּךְ בֶּן־זַבַּי [זַכַּי]

מִדָּה שֵׁנִית מִן־הַמִּקְצוֹעַ עַד־פֶּתַח בֵּית אֶלְיָשִׁיב הַכֹּהֵן

הַגָּדוֹל

<u>Neh. 3:21</u> אַחֲרָיו הֶחֱזִיק מְרֵמוֹת בֶּן־אוּרִיָּה בֶּן־הַקּוֹץ

מִדָּה שֵׁנִית מִפֶּתַח בֵּית אֶלְיָשִׁיב וְעַד־תַּכְלִית בֵּית

אֶלְיָשִׁיב

<u>Neh. 3:22</u> וְאַחֲרָיו הֶחֱזִיקוּ הַכֹּהֲנִים אַנְשֵׁי הַכִּכָּר

<u>Neh. 3:23</u> אַחֲרָיו הֶחֱזִיק בִּנְיָמִן וְחַשּׁוּב נֶגֶד בֵּיתָם

אַחֲרָיו הֶחֱזִיק עֲזַרְיָה בֶן־מַעֲשֵׂיָה בֶּן־עֲנָנְיָה אֵצֶל בֵּיתוֹ

<u>Neh. 3:24</u> אַחֲרָיו הֶחֱזִיק בִּנּוּי בֶּן־חֵנָדָד מִדָּה שֵׁנִית

מִבֵּית עֲזַרְיָה עַד־הַמִּקְצוֹעַ וְעַד־הַפִּנָּה

<u>Neh. 3:25</u> פָּלָל בֶּן־אוּזַי מִנֶּגֶד הַמִּקְצוֹעַ וְהַמִּגְדָּל הַיּוֹצֵא

מִבֵּית הַמֶּלֶךְ הָעֶלְיוֹן אֲשֶׁר לַחֲצַר הַמַּטָּרָה אַחֲרָיו

פְּדָיָה בֶן־פַּרְעֹשׁ

<u>Neh. 3:26</u> וְהַנְּתִינִים הָיוּ יֹשְׁבִים בָּעֹפֶל עַד נֶגֶד שַׁעַר

הַמַּיִם לַמִּזְרָח וְהַמִּגְדָּל הַיּוֹצֵא

<u>Neh. 3:27</u> אַחֲרָיו הֶחֱזִיקוּ הַתְּקֹעִים מִדָּה שֵׁנִית מִנֶּגֶד

הַמִּגְדָּל הַגָּדוֹל הַיּוֹצֵא וְעַד חוֹמַת הָעֹפֶל

<u>Neh. 3:28</u> מֵעַל שַׁעַר הַסּוּסִים הֶחֱזִיקוּ הַכֹּהֲנִים אִישׁ

לְנֶגֶד בֵּיתוֹ

Neh. 3:29 אַחֲרָיו הֶחֱזִיק צָדוֹק בֶּן־אִמֵּר נֶגֶד בֵּיתוֹ

וְאַחֲרָיו הֶחֱזִיק שְׁמַעְיָה בֶן־שְׁכַנְיָה שֹׁמֵר שַׁעַר הַמִּזְרָח

Neh. 3:30 אַחֲרֵי [אַחֲרָיו] הֶחֱזִיק חֲנַנְיָה בֶן־שֶׁלֶמְיָה

וְחָנוּן בֶּן־צָלָף הַשִּׁשִּׁי מִדָּה שֵׁנִי אַחֲרָיו הֶחֱזִיק מְשֻׁלָּם

בֶּן־בֶּרֶכְיָה נֶגֶד נִשְׁכָּתוֹ

Neh. 3:31 אַחֲרֵי [אַחֲרָיו] הֶחֱזִיק מַלְכִּיָּה בֶּן־הַצֹּרְפִי

עַד־בֵּית הַנְּתִינִים וְהָרֹכְלִים נֶגֶד שַׁעַר הַמִּפְקָד וְעַד

עֲלִיַּת הַפִּנָּה

Neh. 3:32 וּבֵין עֲלִיַּת הַפִּנָּה לְשַׁעַר הַצֹּאן הֶחֱזִיקוּ

הַצֹּרְפִים וְהָרֹכְלִים

Neh. 3:23 After them Benjamin and Hasshub carried out repairs in front of their house. After them Azariah the son of Maaseiah, son of Ananiah, carried out repairs beside his house.

Neh. 3:24 After him Binnui the son of Henadad repaired another section, from the house of Azariah as far as the Angle and as far as the corner.

Neh. 3:25 Palal the son of Uzai [made repairs] in front of the Angle and the tower projecting from the upper house of the king, which is by the court of the guard. After him Pedaiah the son of Parosh [made repairs].

Neh. 3:26 The temple servants living in Ophel [made repairs] as far as the front of the Water Gate toward the east and the projecting tower.

Neh. 3:27 After them the Tekoites repaired another section in front of the great projecting tower and as far as the wall of Ophel.

Neh. 3:28 ¶ Above the Horse Gate the priests carried out repairs, each in front of his house.

Neh. 3:29 After them Zadok the son of Immer carried out repairs in front of his house. And after him Shemaiah the son of Shecaniah, the keeper of the East Gate, carried out repairs.

Neh. 3:30 After him Hananiah the son of Shelemiah, and Hanun the sixth son of Zalaph, repaired another section. After him Meshullam the son of Berechiah carried out repairs in front of his own quarters.

Neh. 3:31 After him Malchijah, one of the goldsmiths, carried out repairs as far as the house of the temple servants and of the merchants, in front of the Inspection Gate and as far as the upper room of the corner.

Neh. 3:32 Between the upper room of the corner and the Sheep Gate the goldsmiths and the merchants carried out repairs.

List of settlements, Neh. 11:25-36

Neh. 11:25 וְאֶל־הַחֲצֵרִים בִּשְׂדֹתָם מִבְּנֵי יְהוּדָה יָשְׁבוּ
בְּקִרְיַת הָאַרְבַּע וּבְנֹתֶיהָ וּבְדִיבֹן וּבְנֹתֶיהָ וּבִיקַבְצְאֵל
וַחֲצֵרֶיהָ

Neh. 11:26 וּבְיֵשׁוּעַ וּבְמוֹלָדָה וּבְבֵית פָּלֶט

Neh. 11:27 וּבַחֲצַר שׁוּעָל וּבִבְאֵר שֶׁבַע וּבְנֹתֶיהָ

Neh. 11:28 וּבְצִקְלַג וּבִמְכֹנָה וּבִבְנֹתֶיהָ

Neh. 11:29 וּבְעֵין רִמּוֹן וּבְצָרְעָה וּבְיַרְמוּת

Neh. 11:30 זָנֹחַ עֲדֻלָּם וְחַצְרֵיהֶם לָכִישׁ וּשְׂדֹתֶיהָ עֲזֵקָה
וּבְנֹתֶיהָ וַיַּחֲנוּ מִבְּאֵר־שֶׁבַע עַד־גֵּיא־הִנֹּם

Neh. 11:31 וּבְנֵי בִנְיָמִן מִגָּבַע מִכְמָשׂ וְעַיָּה וּבֵית־אֵל
וּבְנֹתֶיהָ

Neh. 11:32 עֲנָתוֹת נֹב עֲנָנְיָה

Neh. 11:33 חָצוֹר רָמָה גִּתָּיִם

Neh. 11:34 חָדִיד צְבֹעִים נְבַלָּט

Neh. 11:35 לֹד וְאוֹנוֹ גֵּי הַחֲרָשִׁים

Neh. 11:36 וּמִן־הַלְוִיִּם מַחְלְקוֹת יְהוּדָה לְבִנְיָמִין

Social Structure:

Neh. 4:6 (Eng. 4:12) "Those who live among them"

וַיְהִי כַּאֲשֶׁר־בָּאוּ הַיְּהוּדִים הַיֹּשְׁבִים אֶצְלָם
וַיֹּאמְרוּ לָנוּ עֶשֶׂר פְּעָמִים מִכָּל־הַמְּקֹמוֹת
אֲשֶׁר־תָּשׁוּבוּ עָלֵינוּ׃

Neh. 4:12 When the Jews who lived near them came and told us ten times,
"They will come up against us from every place where you may turn,"

Neh. 11:1-4

Neh. 11:1 וַיֵּשְׁבוּ שָׂרֵי־הָעָם בִּירוּשָׁלָם וּשְׁאָר הָעָם
הִפִּילוּ גוֹרָלוֹת לְהָבִיא אֶחָד מִן־הָעֲשָׂרָה לָשֶׁבֶת
בִּירוּשָׁלַם עִיר הַקֹּדֶשׁ וְתֵשַׁע הַיָּדוֹת בֶּעָרִים
Neh. 11:2 וַיְבָרְכוּ הָעָם לְכֹל הָאֲנָשִׁים הַמִּתְנַדְּבִים
לָשֶׁבֶת בִּירוּשָׁלָם
Neh. 11:3 וְאֵלֶּה רָאשֵׁי הַמְּדִינָה אֲשֶׁר יָשְׁבוּ בִּירוּשָׁלָם
וּבְעָרֵי יְהוּדָה יָשְׁבוּ אִישׁ בַּאֲחֻזָּתוֹ בְּעָרֵיהֶם יִשְׂרָאֵל
הַכֹּהֲנִים וְהַלְוִיִּם וְהַנְּתִינִים וּבְנֵי עַבְדֵי שְׁלֹמֹה
Neh. 11:4 וּבִירוּשָׁלַם יָשְׁבוּ מִבְּנֵי יְהוּדָה וּמִבְּנֵי בִנְיָמִן
מִבְּנֵי יְהוּדָה עֲתָיָה בֶן־עֻזִּיָּה בֶּן־זְכַרְיָה בֶּן־אֲמַרְיָה
בֶן־שְׁפַטְיָה בֶן־מַהֲלַלְאֵל מִבְּנֵי־פָרֶץ

Neh. 11:1 ¶ Now the leaders of the people lived in Jerusalem, but
the rest of the people cast lots to bring one out of ten to live in
Jerusalem, the holy city, while nine-tenths [remained] in the
[other] cities.

Neh. 11:2 And the people blessed all the men who volunteered to
live in Jerusalem.

Neh. 11:3 ¶ Now these are the heads of the provinces who lived in
Jerusalem, but in the cities of Judah each lived on his own

property in their cities — the Israelites, the priests, the Levites, the temple servants and the descendants of Solomon's servants.

Neh. 11:4 Some of the sons of Judah and some of the sons of Benjamin lived in Jerusalem. From the sons of Judah: Athaiah the son of Uzziah, the son of Zechariah, the son of Amariah, the son of Shephatiah, the son of Mahalalel, of the sons of Perez;

Neh. 13

Neh. 13:1 בַּיּוֹם הַהוּא נִקְרָא בְּסֵפֶר מֹשֶׁה בְּאָזְנֵי הָעָם
וְנִמְצָא כָּתוּב בּוֹ אֲשֶׁר לֹא־יָבוֹא עַמֹּנִי וּמֹאָבִי בִּקְהַל
הָאֱלֹהִים עַד־עוֹלָם

Neh. 13:2 כִּי לֹא קִדְּמוּ אֶת־בְּנֵי יִשְׂרָאֵל בַּלֶּחֶם וּבַמָּיִם
וַיִּשְׂכֹּר עָלָיו אֶת־בִּלְעָם לְקַלְלוֹ וַיַּהֲפֹךְ אֱלֹהֵינוּ הַקְּלָלָה
לִבְרָכָה

Neh. 13:3 וַיְהִי כְּשָׁמְעָם אֶת־הַתּוֹרָה וַיַּבְדִּילוּ כָל־עֵרֶב
מִיִּשְׂרָאֵל

Neh. 13:4 וְלִפְנֵי מִזֶּה אֶלְיָשִׁיב הַכֹּהֵן נָתוּן בְּלִשְׁכַּת
בֵּית־אֱלֹהֵינוּ קָרוֹב לְטוֹבִיָּה

Neh. 13:5 וַיַּעַשׂ לוֹ לִשְׁכָּה גְדוֹלָה וְשָׁם הָיוּ לְפָנִים
נֹתְנִים אֶת־הַמִּנְחָה הַלְּבוֹנָה וְהַכֵּלִים וּמַעְשַׂר הַדָּגָן
הַתִּירוֹשׁ וְהַיִּצְהָר מִצְוַת הַלְוִיִּם וְהַמְשֹׁרְרִים וְהַשֹּׁעֲרִים
וּתְרוּמַת הַכֹּהֲנִים

Neh. 13:6 וּבְכָל־זֶה לֹא הָיִיתִי בִּירוּשָׁלָם כִּי בִּשְׁנַת
שְׁלֹשִׁים וּשְׁתַּיִם לְאַרְתַּחְשַׁסְתְּא מֶלֶךְ־בָּבֶל בָּאתִי
אֶל־הַמֶּלֶךְ וּלְקֵץ יָמִים נִשְׁאַלְתִּי מִן־הַמֶּלֶךְ

Neh. 13:7 וָאָבוֹא לִירוּשָׁלָם וָאָבִינָה בָרָעָה אֲשֶׁר עָשָׂה
אֶלְיָשִׁיב לְטוֹבִיָּה לַעֲשׂוֹת לוֹ נִשְׁכָּה בְּחַצְרֵי בֵּית
הָאֱלֹהִים

Neh. 13:8 וַיֵּרַע לִי מְאֹד וָאַשְׁלִיכָה אֶת־כָּל־כְּלֵי

בֵית־טוֹבִיָּה הַחוּץ מִן־הַלִּשְׁכָּה

Neh. 13:9 וָאֹמְרָה וַיְטַהֲרוּ הַלְּשָׁכוֹת וָאָשִׁיבָה שָּׁם כְּלֵי

בֵית הָאֱלֹהִים אֶת־הַמִּנְחָה וְהַלְּבוֹנָה פ

Neh. 13:10 וָאֵדְעָה כִּי־מְנָיוֹת הַלְוִיִּם לֹא נִתָּנָה וַיִּבְרְחוּ

אִישׁ־לְשָׂדֵהוּ הַלְוִיִּם וְהַמְשֹׁרְרִים עֹשֵׂי הַמְּלָאכָה

Neh. 13:11 וָאָרִיבָה אֶת־הַסְּגָנִים וָאֹמְרָה מַדּוּעַ נֶעֱזַב

בֵּית־הָאֱלֹהִים וָאֶקְבְּצֵם וָאַעֲמִדֵם עַל־עָמְדָם

Neh. 13:12 וְכָל־יְהוּדָה הֵבִיאוּ מַעְשַׂר הַדָּגָן וְהַתִּירוֹשׁ

וְהַיִּצְהָר לָאוֹצָרוֹת

Neh. 13:13 וָאוֹצְרָה עַל־אוֹצָרוֹת שֶׁלֶמְיָה הַכֹּהֵן וְצָדוֹק

הַסּוֹפֵר וּפְדָיָה מִן־הַלְוִיִּם וְעַל־יָדָם חָנָן בֶּן־זַכּוּר

בֶּן־מַתַּנְיָה כִּי נֶאֱמָנִים נֶחְשָׁבוּ וַעֲלֵיהֶם לַחֲלֹק לַאֲחֵיהֶם

פ

Neh. 13:14 זָכְרָה־לִּי אֱלֹהַי עַל־זֹאת וְאַל־תֶּמַח חֲסָדַי

אֲשֶׁר עָשִׂיתִי בְּבֵית אֱלֹהַי וּבְמִשְׁמָרָיו

Neh. 13:15 בַּיָּמִים הָהֵמָּה רָאִיתִי בִיהוּדָה דֹּרְכִים־גִּתּוֹת

בַּשַּׁבָּת וּמְבִיאִים הָעֲרֵמוֹת וְעֹמְסִים עַל־הַחֲמֹרִים

וְאַף־יַיִן עֲנָבִים וּתְאֵנִים וְכָל־מַשָּׂא וּמְבִיאִים יְרוּשָׁלַם

בְּיוֹם הַשַּׁבָּת וָאָעִיד בְּיוֹם מִכְרָם צָיִד

Neh. 13:16 וְהַצֹּרִים יָשְׁבוּ בָהּ מְבִיאִים דָּאג וְכָל־מֶכֶר

וּמֹכְרִים בַּשַּׁבָּת לִבְנֵי יְהוּדָה וּבִירוּשָׁלָם

Neh. 13:17 וָאָרִיבָה אֵת חֹרֵי יְהוּדָה וָאֹמְרָה לָהֶם

מָה־הַדָּבָר הָרָע הַזֶּה אֲשֶׁר אַתֶּם עֹשִׂים וּמְחַלְּלִים

אֶת־יוֹם הַשַּׁבָּת

Neh. 13:18 הֲלוֹא כֹה עָשׂוּ אֲבֹתֵיכֶם וַיָּבֵא אֱלֹהֵינוּ עָלֵינוּ

אֶת כָּל־הָרָעָה הַזֹּאת וְעַל הָעִיר הַזֹּאת וְאַתֶּם מוֹסִיפִים
חָרוֹן עַל־יִשְׂרָאֵל לְחַלֵּל אֶת־הַשַּׁבָּת פ

Neh. 13:19 וַיְהִי כַּאֲשֶׁר צָלֲלוּ שַׁעֲרֵי יְרוּשָׁלַם לִפְנֵי
הַשַּׁבָּת וָאֹמְרָה וַיִּסָּגְרוּ הַדְּלָתוֹת וָאֹמְרָה אֲשֶׁר לֹא
יִפְתָּחוּם עַד אַחַר הַשַּׁבָּת וּמִנְּעָרַי‏ הֶעֱמַדְתִּי
עַל־הַשְּׁעָרִים לֹא־יָבוֹא מַשָּׂא בְּיוֹם הַשַּׁבָּת

Neh. 13:20 וַיָּלִינוּ הָרֹכְלִים וּמֹכְרֵי כָל־מִמְכָּר מִחוּץ
לִירוּשָׁלָם פַּעַם וּשְׁתָּיִם

Neh. 13:21 וָאָעִידָה בָהֶם וָאֹמְרָה אֲלֵיהֶם מַדּוּעַ אַתֶּם
לֵנִים נֶגֶד הַחוֹמָה אִם־תִּשְׁנוּ יָד אֶשְׁלַח בָּכֶם מִן־הָעֵת
הַהִיא לֹא־בָאוּ בַּשַּׁבָּת

Neh. 13:22 וָאֹמְרָה לַלְוִיִּם אֲשֶׁר יִהְיוּ מִטַּהֲרִים וּבָאִים
שֹׁמְרִים הַשְּׁעָרִים לְקַדֵּשׁ אֶת־יוֹם הַשַּׁבָּת גַּם־זֹאת
זָכְרָה־לִּי אֱלֹהַי‏ וְחוּסָה עָלַי כְּרֹב חַסְדֶּךָ

Neh. 13:23 גַּם בַּיָּמִים הָהֵם רָאִיתִי אֶת־הַיְּהוּדִים הֹשִׁיבוּ
נָשִׁים אַשְׁדּוֹדִיּוֹת [אַשְׁדֳּדִיּוֹת] עַמּוֹנִיּוֹת [עַמֳּנִיּוֹת]
מוֹאֲבִיּוֹת

Neh. 13:24 וּבְנֵיהֶם חֲצִי מְדַבֵּר אַשְׁדּוֹדִית וְאֵינָם
מַכִּירִים לְדַבֵּר יְהוּדִית וְכִלְשׁוֹן עַם וָעָם

Neh. 13:25 וָאָרִיב עִמָּם וָאֲקַלְלֵם וָאַכֶּה מֵהֶם אֲנָשִׁים
וָאֶמְרְטֵם וָאַשְׁבִּיעֵם בֵּאלֹהִים אִם־תִּתְּנוּ בְנֹתֵיכֶם
לִבְנֵיהֶם וְאִם־תִּשְׂאוּ מִבְּנֹתֵיהֶם לִבְנֵיכֶם וְלָכֶם

Neh. 13:26 הֲלוֹא עַל־אֵלֶּה חָטָא־שְׁלֹמֹה מֶלֶךְ יִשְׂרָאֵל
וּבַגּוֹיִם הָרַבִּים לֹא־הָיָה מֶלֶךְ כָּמֹהוּ וְאָהוּב לֵאלֹהָיו
הָיָה וַיִּתְּנֵהוּ אֱלֹהִים מֶלֶךְ עַל־כָּל־יִשְׂרָאֵל גַּם־אוֹתוֹ
הֶחֱטִיאוּ הַנָּשִׁים הַנָּכְרִיּוֹת

וְלָכֶם הֲנִשְׁמַע לַעֲשֹׂת אֵת כָּל־הָרָעָה <u>Neh. 13:27</u>

הַגְּדוֹלָה הַזֹּאת לִמְעֹל בֵּאלֹהֵינוּ לְהֹשִׁיב נָשִׁים נָכְרִיּוֹת

וּמִבְּנֵי יוֹיָדָע בֶּן־אֶלְיָשִׁיב הַכֹּהֵן הַגָּדוֹל <u>Neh. 13:28</u>

חָתָן לְסַנְבַלַּט הַחֹרֹנִי וָאַבְרִיחֵהוּ מֵעָלָי

זָכְרָה לָהֶם אֱלֹהָי עַל גָּאֳלֵי הַכְּהֻנָּה וּבְרִית <u>Neh. 13:29</u>

הַכְּהֻנָּה וְהַלְוִיִּם

וְטִהַרְתִּים מִכָּל־נֵכָר וָאַעֲמִידָה מִשְׁמָרוֹת <u>Neh. 13:30</u>

לַכֹּהֲנִים וְלַלְוִיִּם אִישׁ בִּמְלַאכְתּוֹ

וּלְקֻרְבַּן הָעֵצִים בְּעִתִּים מְזֻמָּנוֹת וְלַבִּכּוּרִים <u>Neh. 13:31</u>

זָכְרָה־לִּי אֱלֹהַי לְטוֹבָה

<u>Neh. 13:1</u> ¶ On that day they read aloud from the book of Moses in the hearing of the people; and there was found written in it that no Ammonite or Moabite should ever enter the assembly of God,

<u>Neh. 13:2</u> because they did not meet the sons of Israel with bread and water, but hired Balaam against them to curse them. However, our God turned the curse into a blessing.

<u>Neh. 13:3</u> So when they heard the law, they excluded all foreigners from Israel.

<u>Neh. 13:4</u> ¶ Now prior to this, Eliashib the priest, who was appointed over the chambers of the house of our God, being related to Tobiah,

<u>Neh. 13:5</u> had prepared a large room for him, where formerly they put the grain offerings, the frankincense, the utensils and the tithes of grain, wine and oil prescribed for the Levites, the singers and the gatekeepers, and the contributions for the priests.

<u>Neh. 13:6</u> But during all this [time] I was not in Jerusalem, for in the thirty-second year of Artaxerxes king of Babylon I had gone to the king. After some time, however, I asked leave from the king,

<u>Neh. 13:7</u> and I came to Jerusalem and learned about the evil that Eliashib had done for Tobiah, by preparing a room for him in the courts of the house of God.

Neh. 13:8 It was very displeasing to me, so I threw all of Tobiah's household goods out of the room.

Neh. 13:9 Then I gave an order and they cleansed the rooms; and I returned there the utensils of the house of God with the grain offerings and the frankincense.

Neh. 13:10 ¶ I also discovered that the portions of the Levites had not been given [them], so that the Levites and the singers who performed the service had gone away, each to his own field.

Neh. 13:11 So I reprimanded the officials and said, "Why is the house of God forsaken?" Then I gathered them together and restored them to their posts.

Neh. 13:12 All Judah then brought the tithe of the grain, wine and oil into the storehouses.

Neh. 13:13 In charge of the storehouses I appointed Shelemiah the priest, Zadok the scribe, and Pedaiah of the Levites, and in addition to them was Hanan the son of Zaccur, the son of Mattaniah; for they were considered reliable, and it was their task to distribute to their kinsmen.

Neh. 13:14 Remember me for this, O my God, and do not blot out my loyal deeds which I have performed for the house of my God and its services.

Neh. 13:15 ¶ In those days I saw in Judah some who were treading wine presses on the sabbath, and bringing in sacks of grain and loading [them] on donkeys, as well as wine, grapes, figs and all kinds of loads, and they brought [them] into Jerusalem on the sabbath day. So I admonished [them] on the day they sold food.

Neh. 13:16 Also men of Tyre were living there [who] imported fish and all kinds of merchandise, and sold [them] to the sons of Judah on the sabbath, even in Jerusalem.

Neh. 13:17 Then I reprimanded the nobles of Judah and said to them, "What is this evil thing you are doing, by profaning the sabbath day?

Neh. 13:18 "Did not your fathers do the same, so that our God brought on us and on this city all this trouble? Yet you are adding to the wrath on Israel by profaning the sabbath."

Neh. 13:19 ¶ It came about that just as it grew dark at the gates of Jerusalem before the sabbath, I commanded that the doors should be shut and that they should not open them until after the sabbath. Then I stationed some of my servants at the gates [so that] no load would enter on the sabbath day.

Neh. 13:20 Once or twice the traders and merchants of every kind of merchandise spent the night outside Jerusalem.

Neh. 13:21 Then I warned them and said to them, "Why do you spend the night in front of the wall? If you do so again, I will use force against you." From that time on they did not come on the sabbath.

Neh. 13:22 And I commanded the Levites that they should purify themselves and come as gatekeepers to sanctify the sabbath day. [For] this also remember me, O my God, and have compassion on me according to the greatness of Your lovingkindness.

Neh. 13:23 ¶ In those days I also saw that the Jews had married women from Ashdod, Ammon [and] Moab.

Neh. 13:24 As for their children, half spoke in the language of Ashdod, and none of them was able to speak the language of Judah, but the language of his own people.

Neh. 13:25 So I contended with them and cursed them and struck some of them and pulled out their hair, and made them swear by God, "You shall not give your daughters to their sons, nor take of their daughters for your sons or for yourselves.

Neh. 13:26 "Did not Solomon king of Israel sin regarding these things? Yet among the many nations there was no king like him, and he was loved by his God, and God made him king over all Israel; nevertheless the foreign women caused even him to sin.

Neh. 13:27 "Do we then hear about you that you have committed all this great evil by acting unfaithfully against our God by marrying foreign women?"

Neh. 13:28 Even one of the sons of Joiada, the son of Eliashib the high priest, was a son-in-law of Sanballat the Horonite, so I drove him away from me.

Neh. 13:29 Remember them, O my God, because they have defiled the priesthood and the covenant of the priesthood and the Levites.

Neh. 13:30 ¶ Thus I purified them from everything foreign and appointed duties for the priests and the Levites, each in his task,

Neh. 13:31 and [I arranged] for the supply of wood at appointed times and for the first fruits. Remember me, O my God, for good.